Biological Psychology

Biological Psychology
A Cybernetic Science

F. J. McGuigan

United States International University

Prentice Hall
Englewood Cliffs, New Jersey 07632

Library of Congress Cataloging-in-Publication Data

McGuigan, F. J. (Frank J.) (date)
    Biological psychology : a cybernetic science / F. J. McGuigan.
      p.   cm.
    Includes bibliographical references and index.
    ISBN 0-13-146655-0
    1.   Psychobiology.   I.   Title.
QP360.M3534   1994
152—dc20   93-35572
                                                  CIP

Acquisitions editor: Pete Janzow
Editorial assistant: Marilyn Coco
Cover design: Anne Ricigliano
Production coordinators: Herb Klein and Tricia Kenny

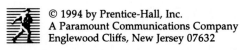

© 1994 by Prentice-Hall, Inc.
A Paramount Communications Company
Englewood Cliffs, New Jersey 07632

Printed in the United States of America
10 9 8 7 6 5 4 3 2 1

ISBN 0-13-146655-0

Prentice-Hall International (UK) Limited, *London*
Prentice-Hall of Australia Pty. Limited, *Sydney*
Prentice-Hall Canada Inc., *Toronto*
Prentice-Hall Hispanoamericana, S.A., *Mexico*
Prentice-Hall of India Private Limited, *New Delhi*
Prentice-Hall of Japan, Inc., *Tokyo*
Simon & Schuster Asia Pte. Ltd., *Singapore*
Editora Prentice-Hall do Brasil, Ltda., *Rio de Janeiro*

To Betty, Casius, and Tobias

Contents

CHAPTER 3
The Biology of Mental Processes   58

Part II
Systems of the Body
and How They Are Studied

CHAPTER 4
An Overview of How the Body Functions   81

CHAPTER 5
How We Gather and Interpret Information:
The Receptor Systems, Our Sense Modalities,
and Perceptual Processes   117

CHAPTER 6
Integrating and Processing Information:
Contributions of the Nervous Systems   153

CHAPTER 7
Behaving in Our External and Internal
Environments—The Effectors   190

Part III
Normal Biopsychological Functions

CHAPTER 13
**Cognitive Psychophysiology: The Biology
of Higher Mental Processes   404**

Part IV
Pathological Conditions
and Clinical Applications

CHAPTER 14
**Biology of Pathological Behavior
and Disease   439**

CHAPTER 15
Therapy and Control of Pathological and Normal Behavior   499

Part V
Confronting Society's Problems Through Science and Technology

CHAPTER 16
The Future of Humanity as It Relates to Biological Science   551

Preface

The original and enduring problem of psychology is that of understanding "the mind." Psychology's unique contribution has been to scientifically study mental processes as the components of mind. The first scientific approach was a physiological one espoused in 1879 by the father of psychology, Wilhelm Wundt — the title of his book, which has been called the most influential in the history of psychology, was *Principles of Physiological Psychology*. Biological approaches to psychology continued, as in Alexander Bain's influential work, into the twentieth century. Early American textbooks of psychology especially emphasized neuroanatomy and physiology. Notable among them were John Watson's (1919) *Psychology from the Standpoint of a Behaviorist* and John Dashiell's (1928) *Fundamentals of Objective Psychology*. More recently, with the contemporary development of highly sophisticated physiological and psychophysiological instrumentation, the study of biological psychology has been growing at an exponential rate. Interrelated, component fields of biological psychology include neuroscience, physiological psychology, neuropsychology, electropsychology, psychophysiology, neurobiology, and psychobiology.

As these fields have expanded, there has also emerged a growing recognition that we cannot understand behavior of the body if its components are studied only in isolation. Rather, to understand the body and how it functions to generate behavior in all of its complexities, we must study it in its entirety. As an illustration of contemporary recognition of the necessity for studying interactive systems, the following was a description written for an advanced work on behavioral states. It was edited by Richard Bandler and published by Alan R. Liss, Inc.:

> Research on brain–behavior relationships has been hampered by the shortcomings of studying specific brain regions as if they were anatomically and functionally discrete systems. These subsystems interact in ways that cannot be described solely in terms of their particular organization: to understand these higher-order functions it is necessary to elucidate the linkages interconnecting the brain's components. These linkages can be studied by careful correlation of the alterations in sensorimotor activity produced by changes in behavioral states.

Another recent indication of the growing biological and cybernetic *zeitgeist* is pointed out by John Naisbitt and Patricia Aburdene in their best seller *Megatrends 2000*. They hold that the 1990s are the age of biology and that "We are in the process of creating a society that is an elaborate array of information feedback systems, the very structure of the biological organism" (p. 241).

Cybernetics is an excellent model for understanding how the various systems of the body interact. Our effort is to present principles of biological psychology within a cybernetic framework. Cybernetics is a science of control and communication through circuits. As applied in biological psychology, we view numerous circuits functioning within the brain and between the brain and other systems throughout the body. The primary cybernetic principle by which systems of the body interact is that of negative feedback circuits. Additional control principles of feedforward and adaptive control are also applicable.

In this book, we focus on sensory, neural, and muscular systems as they interact to generate the extensive kinds of behavior that psychologists study. Our model is that cognitive (mental) processes are generated when those systems of the body intimately interact in a selective fashion. What follows is a biological explication of the nature of mind. Related phenomena within the province of biological psychology to which we attempt to apply a cybernetic model include those of motivated and emotional behavior, learning and memory, language and laterality of the body, aging, and pathological conditions with clinical applications. In the last chapters efforts are made to assess within a biopsychological framework major problems that society faces (Chapter 14), to present some potential solutions to those problems (Chapter 15), and finally to assess the future of humankind from a biological science point of view. There we consider both pessimistic and optimistic futures. A major hope for this book is that it might help us to more rationally pursue an optimistic future.

While we survey and present a number of data, our primary purpose is to develop an integrative system for incorporating those data into a framework that is both meaningful and interesting to the student. However, while this initial effort to apply cybernetic principles to the major areas of psychology regrettably is uneven, at least a start has been made. It is hoped that others will continue the effort. I would welcome suggestions from students and colleagues both for improving and for extending what is written here.

In order to facilitate the student's progress, I have cited only major references, eliminating a large number of detailed sources.

The main points throughout the book are presented in margin notes where they are discussed. Since these margin notes constitute a summary of the book, independent summaries would be redundant and thus are not presented at the end of the chapters.

Appreciation is given to the following reviewers who critically read earlier drafts of the manuscript: Douglas L. Grimsley, University of North Carolina at Charlotte; Yoshito Kawahara, Mesa College; William F. McDaniel, Georgia College; Matthew Olson, Hamline University; Ellen F. Rosen, College of William and Mary; Cheryl L. Sisk, Michigan State University; Jeffery J. Stern, University of Michigan-Dearborn; and Charlene Wages, Francis Marion College. Special appreciation is expressed to Sirichet Sangkamarn, Deanna Kahn, Ned I. Makaichy, Michelle Mullane, and Paula and Terry Tindall for their excellent help in preparing the manuscript. Thanks too to the students in my classes in Biological Psychology who offered many suggestions and critiques for improving earlier versions of the manuscript. Words are insufficient to indicate my thanks to and esteem for Maria Cristina Isolabella for her help in so many ways that it would be impossible to enumerate them.

FJM
San Diego, California

Biological Psychology

Part I
A Broad Perspective of Biological Psychology

CHAPTER 1

A Cybernetic Model
for Biological Psychology

MAJOR PURPOSE: To obtain an overview of biological psychology within a systematic cybernetic framework

WHAT YOU ARE GOING TO FIND:
1. What constitutes biological psychology
2. The major principles and concepts of cybernetics
3. Systems of the body viewed within the context of cybernetics
4. How cybernetic bodily circuits generate cognitive events

WHAT YOU SHOULD ACQUIRE: A broad perspective of how bodily systems interact to carry on the functions of organisms

CHAPTER OUTLINE

WHAT IS BIOLOGICAL PSYCHOLOGY?

Biology is the science that studies life processes. Since psychology is a study of behavioral processes, it is a subdivision of the broader field of biology. In psychology we seek to understand the behavior of humans and animals.

The dimensions of behavior are extensive and include **overt behaviors** such as running and talking as well as **covert** (hidden) **processes** such as thoughts, dreams, ideas, and images. Covert processes in the body are not readily observable, but they really exist. (Note that key terms are set in bold and are defined at the end of each chapter.)

Overt behavior is readily observable with the naked eye. Covert processes in the body are hidden from ordinary observation, but they do exist.

Biological psychologists study how interacting bodily systems and the environment influence behavior.

Biological Psychology Defined. Behavior, whether it be overt or covert, is best understood as a product of *interacting systems of the body.* The major systems of the body are the receptor, nervous, muscular, glandular, and circulatory systems. As we move through our world, our behavior is generated by intricate physiological interactions of these systems. **Biological psychology** *is that specialization within psychology for understanding behavior by studying how the systems of the body interact with each other and with the environment.*

Biological psychology is **interdisciplinary** in nature. Scientists from the disciplines of psychology, physiology, medicine, biological psychiatry, behavioral medicine, and biomedical engineering work in this interdisciplinary field. Biological psychology is a broad discipline that includes fields with related names such as physiological psychology, psychophysiology, and neuroscience.

A species is a group of organisms that have certain characteristics in common.

The scientist who studies the behavior of organisms from a biological point of view considers salient characteristics of all the various **species** of organisms in the world. The simple one-celled organisms named *amoeba* and *paramecium caudatum* are examples of species. Amoebae have in common the characteristic of being single-celled organisms that lack supporting structures. They thus look somewhat like small pieces of gelatin.

The Phylogenetic Scale. Species are classified by common characteristics along the **phylogenetic scale** (Fig. 1.1). The phylogenetic scale starts with the simplest single-celled organisms and progresses through frogs, dogs, and apes to the highest, most complex organisms, the species *Homo sapiens.*

COMPARATIVE PSYCHOLOGY

As a consequence of the effort to understand behavior throughout the phylogenetic scale, biological psychologists focus on the similarities and differences among species. A classic field of psychology devoted to such comparisons is known as **comparative psychology**. Comparative psychologists study abilities and behaviors of different species. For example, they have found that although the visual acuity of humans is excellent, their sense of smell is quite inferior to that of dogs.

The comparative study of organisms along the phylogenetic scale facilitates the development of general principles of behavior.

In this book we will concentrate on **vertebrates**—those organisms that, like humans, have a spinal cord. As species, they are high in the phylogenetic scale. However, it is important to emphasize the great value of the comparative study of all species. This value, in part, results from our being able to conduct research on lower animals to discover how simpler forms of behavior occur. On the basis of fundamental findings from animal research, we can often generalize more effectively to the complex behavior of humans. Throughout this book we will note the importance of information gained from research on lower animals.

THE NATURE OF SYSTEMS

Our task of understanding behavior in all its complexity throughout the phylogenetic scale is extensive indeed. To accomplish this task, we need to develop a theoretical framework or model with which to organize our thoughts and research findings. The major organizing principles that we will use center around the *interac-*

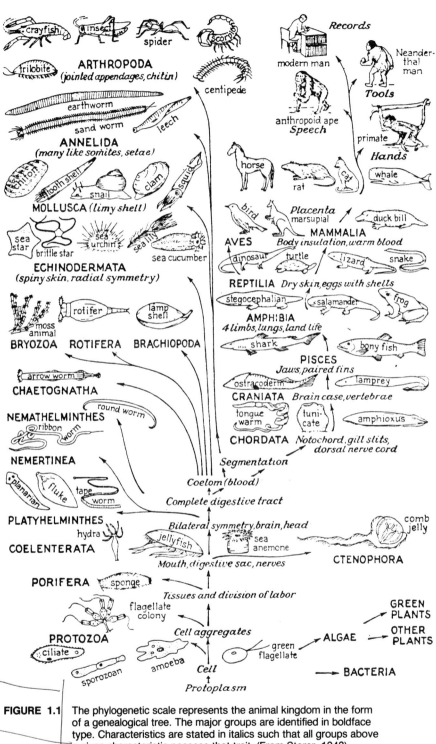

FIGURE 1.1 The phylogenetic scale represents the animal kingdom in the form of a genealogical tree. The major groups are identified in boldface type. Characteristics are stated in italics such that all groups above a given characteristic possess that trait. (From Storer, 1943)

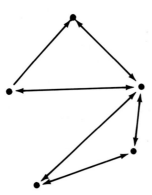

FIGURE 1.2
Representation of a system. The dots stand for elements and the arrows for their relations. A grand system of the body can be conceived as relationships of systems themselves, as in Figure 1.7. There the receptors would be one element, as in a dot, and the relation with the central nervous system (another dot) would be represented as an arrow.

tion of bodily systems. To understand how one system functions, it is necessary to study that system as it is influenced by other systems of the body. It is also important to understand how those bodily systems generate behavior that affects and is affected by the environment.

Systems Defined. A material object obviously consists of elements of matter that relate with each other to form the object. The formed object is a system. Thus, a **system** consists of material items (elements, components, parts) that interact with each other. The ways in which the elements of a system interact through connections are called relations (Fig. 1.2). A relation is the precise way in which elements of a system influence each other.

A system consists of elements (items, components) that are interdependent (related).

Examples of Systems. As an example of a system, consider that students, a teacher, and a location are elements of a school class. Those elements and the ways in which they relate with each other form a system. A teacher thus has a number of different kinds of relations with the students, just as students do with the teacher. Similarly, the central nervous *system* consists of elements contained within the brain and spinal cord and the relations among those elements. One part of the brain thus interacts with (is related to) its other parts. Systems themselves can also be elements that have relations to form more general systems. The body is such a general system that consists of elements (the elements are systems such as the nervous and muscle systems) that interact (are related). One prominent set of principles advanced to account for how the systems of the body interact is encompassed under the title **cybernetics.**

Historical Use of the Word Cybernetics. The word *cybernetics* was used over a century ago by Andre M. Ampere, a French physicist whose name is used to designate a unit of electrical current *(amp).* Ampere used the word *cybernetics* in a sociological context. However, it later appeared in other European writings in other contexts and has become applicable to a broad domain of human endeavors. Norbert Wiener (1894–1964) used *Cybernetics* as the title of his famous 1948 book. Wiener, a brilliant mathematician, selected the Greek word *cybernetica* from Plato's *Republic,* where it referred to the science of piloting ships. *Cybernetica* means steersman, and the steering system of a ship is one of the earliest and best examples of an application of cybernetics. In Plato's steering systems, the course of a ship was controlled. To understand how, let us look into the basic principles of cybernetics.

PRINCIPLES OF CYBERNETICS

The essential concepts in cybernetics are **communication** and **control**. The field of cybernetics originated in modern engineering as an effort to understand the nature of control mechanisms, such as how the cruise control on a car maintains a steady speed. Control is accomplished by transmitting *information contained in messages*. The messages can adjust a system to control it.

Communication of Information. In Figure 1.3 we see a source that yields information encoded in a message; the message is then transmitted along a communication channel to its destination where it is decoded so as to be understood. Then there is a return (a feedback) from the destination of other new or modified information to the original source. For example, when you speak into a telephone, you are the source of information. Your message is encoded and transmitted (communicated) along telephone wires to the listener whose telephone decodes the message at its destination for her understanding. There is, then, information sent back from the receiver to the original speaker.

Control of Systems with Information. We use a thermostat system to maintain (control) a constant room temperature. Information about room temperature (whether it is too hot or too cold) is transmitted in messages within the system to adjust the temperature to the reference value set on the thermostat. The fields of control engineering and communication engineering are thus inseparable because they both center around the fundamental concept of *information*.

Information is transmitted in the form of messages to control a system or merely for communication.

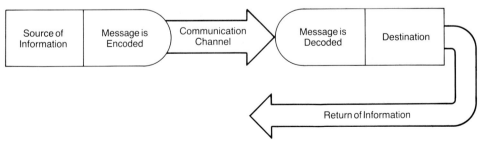

FIGURE 1.3
A communication system with feedback.

Communication and Control with Messages

A **message** *is a sequence of measurable events that contains information.* Messages may be used to actively control an engineering device, a bodily organ, and so on, or merely for communication. For example, you control the direction of your automobile by sending messages from the steering wheel to the rotating wheels. You also can communicate information when you talk with a friend.

Controlling Systems with Feedback.   In Plato's steering systems, messages from the rudder were communicated (fed back) to the steersman to inform him of the rudder's position. If the rudder was not in its proper position, the ship deviated from its intended course. That feedback informed the steersman that the position of the rudder needed to be corrected. Consequently, the steersman could return the ship to its course. The course was set as the **reference signal** or **target value** for the system —the value that is to be achieved and maintained (e.g., a course of due east for a ship). The target value for the temperature system of the human body is 98.6°F. Plato's excellent, classic example well illustrates the *control of a mechanism through feedback of information within circuits.*

Cybernetics is the study of communication and of control within feedback circuits.

Feedback Applications.   Today, **feedback** mechanisms are used within cybernetic circuits in numerous systems such as in factories with robots that build automobiles. Feedback mechanisms also abound elsewhere in our lives: A pilot puts an aircraft on automatic pilot; you set and maintain your oven at 300°F and your refrigerator at 50°F. The difference between how Plato's steersman and today's airplane pilot use feedback mechanisms is only one of technological details that have evolved in the last 2000 years.

To understand the basic notion of how systems are controlled through feedback, let us enlarge on the nature of messages that transmit information.

Kinds of Messages

One of the major questions in biological psychology involves the amount and kinds of information that a person receives from the environment. To study how organisms use such environmental data, we can consider information in terms of kinds of messages.

Information may be communicated by discrete or continuous messages.

Discrete Messages.   Messages may be *discrete* or *continuous.* By *discrete* we mean that messages can assume *numerical values* (integers) that differ by clearly defined steps with no intermediate values possible. **Discrete messages** are thus exact. For example, the integers 0 versus 1 specify a clearly defined difference with no intermediate value. Discrete messages may be communicated in series of zeros and ones that are precise values, as in digital computers. Whether a student is present or absent in a class is another example of a discrete value.

Modern computers typically use discrete messages that are transmitted in *binary* form (*bi* means "two"), as in the two values 0 and 1. For example, information is transmitted in sequences of 0 or 1, on or off, or yes or no messages. By rapid calculation in binary arithmetic using units of zero or one, computers perform the amazing mathematical feats that we daily witness. Another example of transmitting information by means of discrete messages is the International Morse Code—a sender communicates to a receiver with messages that consist of dots and dashes ("cat" is: $c = -.-., a = .-, t = -$).

Continuous Messages. A **continuous message** is one that may change by any amount and thus may assume any value along a continuum. For example, a scale constructed by means of a straight line contains an infinite number of points. By marking a point on the scale, you can communicate any of an infinite number of values of information about a person's weight or height. Continuous messages are thus inexact because their measurement is not limited to a finite value. For instance, the weight of an object may be measured as 124.123 lbs., but there will always be another more precise value possible (e.g., 124.1237 . . .). Speech, which continuously varies in intensity and frequency, is another example of a continuous message that often (but not always) carries information.

Continuous messages, because they are not discrete, transmit **analog signals**, such as in the continuous stream of the human voice or visual signals that flow to your TV set. Such analog signals may assume many values, including a tone that is sung in various frequencies.

The Amount of Information Received Depends on the Perceiver. Coded messages, such as the International Morse Code of dots and dashes that are transmitted from a sender, are not themselves meaningful. To become meaningful, messages must be interpreted by some perceptual system such as another telegrapher who understands Morse Code. The amount of meaning transmitted in a message thus depends in part on the amount of information that the perceiver is capable of understanding. An expert in a particular area would extract much more information from a message than a person with little background knowledge of the same subject matter. Consequently, the amount of information communicated from sender to receiver is determined not only by how much information is encoded in the message itself but also by the sophistication of the interpretive system — the perceiver. This general principle, incidentally, has important implications. For example, when a teacher is trying to educate a child, information is provided by the teacher. However, just the transmission of information does not guarantee that the child will receive it. Messages must be cogently interpreted in order for the information to be accurately transmitted from one person to another.

With this basic understanding of how information is transmitted from a sender to a receiver by messages, let us specify how such messages are used in control systems. This will also entail an understanding of the reverse process — of how messages are communicated (fed back) from the receiver to the original sender.

Discrete messages assume values that differ by clearly defined steps with no intermediate values possible, but continuous messages may assume any value along a continuum.

Two people can form a cybernetic system with information transmitted and fed back between them.

Control Through Feedback

The purpose of control is to develop a **controlled system**. In a controlled system, communication channels interconnect elements. Messages are sent along those communication channels to bring the controlled system to a reference (target) value; for example, through a thermostatic system, constant room temperature is maintained at the reference value of 65°F. Similarly, the cruise control system in an automobile maintains a rate of movement of 55 mph.

NEGATIVE FEEDBACK

The essence of feedback control is that *information is fed back within a circuit to affect a controlling mechanism.* To maintain a steady speed in your automobile (as James Watt did with the governor in his steam engine), a circuit can be designed to work as follows: If the speed exceeds the standard reference speed that you set, that information is fed back to your accelerator; as a result, the amount of gasoline delivered to the engine is automatically reduced. But if you start to go up a hill, the speed falls below the desired standard—whereupon *that* information causes the amount of gasoline flowing to the engine to be automatically increased. Deviations from the reference value are errors that are automatically corrected.

This type of feedback, known as **negative feedback**, functions to maintain a steady state by subtracting or adding energy as required (Table 1.1). The term

TABLE 1.1   Concepts and Principles of Cybernetics

Term	Definition	Example
Kinds of Feedback		
Negative Feedback	Information is fed back within a system to correct errors through addition or subtraction to achieve a stable value	A thermostatic system for controlling room temperature
Positive Feedback	Information is sent back in ever increasing amounts so that the system eventually goes out of control	A steam engine in which energy is continuously added
Anticipatory Feedback	The present location, speed, and direction of a target are fed back so that a future location of the target may be anticipated	A football player running out for a pass.
Kinds of Control Systems		
Negative Feedback Systems	These function as above.	
Feedforward Systems	Information is sent to directly control a variable without any feedback from the variable; however, there may still be a consistent error in the variable to be controlled	A core temperature of the body is specified as a target value of 98.6°F; skin thermoreceptors, which are feedforward sensors, sense changes in the environmental temperature and direct the body to rapidly compensate for any deviation from 98.6°F
Adaptive Control	Information is stored in a memory so that it is used for modifying the future status of the system; consequently there is no immediate or direct feedback	Learning how to serve a tennis ball; information is accumulated over trials
Disturbances	These are errors in a system that disturb the value of the variable to be controlled; disturbances may be eliminated by feedforward systems	Variables that change blood glucose concentration from its standard value

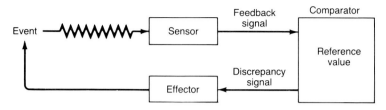

FIGURE 1.4a A negative feedback circuit in which a sensor monitors an event and transmits messages about it to a comparator. If the feedback signal is different from the reference value, a discrepancy signal causes the effector to modify the event to coincide with the reference value.

negative indicates that energy may be decreased, so that "negative feedback" does not carry an undesirable connotation.

Negative feedback is so named because it produces a change in the opposite direction from the input. Thus if the input is excessively high, the feedback subtracts from it. On the other hand, if the input is excessively low, the feedback adds to it. In either case the feedback produces a change in the direction opposite to the input. Mechanisms that function according to negative feedback are often called servo-mechanisms.

Achieving a Reference Value with Negative Feedback. To see more precisely how negative feedback functions, we can study the process in Figure 1.4a. Note that an event is monitored by means of a sensor that generates information about the event. That information is then transmitted as a feedback signal to a comparator that contains a standard reference signal. If the feedback signal is different from the reference value, a discrepancy (error) signal is discharged to the effector. The effector then modifies the event to bring its value more in line with that of the reference signal. Thus, if the value being monitored by the sensor is higher than the reference signal, the effector acts to lower it. However, if the value for the event is below the reference signal, the discrepancy signal informs the effector to raise the value of the event. Eventually, through the corrective action of the system, the discrepancy signal is reduced to zero whereupon the system maintains stability at the reference value inserted into the comparator. An example is presented in Figure 1.4b.

Examples of System Control Through Negative Feedback. The specific values of a negative feedback system for controlling room temperature could include setting the thermostat at a reference value of 70°F. A thermometer continuously monitors the temperature such that if it falls to 60°F, a discrepancy signal of −10°F is computed. This value is fed to the effector, which increases the heat sent to the room until the

Negative feedback is used within cybernetic circuits to subtract as well as to add values to achieve and maintain constant conditions.

FIGURE 1.4b An example of a negative feedback circuit in which the cruise control of an automobile maintains a steady speed.

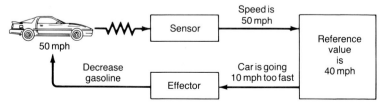

discrepancy signal is 0°F. Similarly, if the discrepancy signal is +10°F, the system can activate an air conditioner to maintain a reasonably constant temperature of 70°F.

Nyquist, who first used the term *feedback*, had a great influence in the field of electronics when he developed stable vacuum tube amplifiers by inserting a reference signal into the amplifier. The output signal of the amplifier was compared to the reference signal, and the difference was fed back into the amplifier at its input. The deviation between the input and the output values was then automatically corrected to achieve a discrepancy signal of zero. Negative feedback can thus be seen to be a method of controlling a system by reinserting into the system the results of its past performance and making corrections.

POSITIVE FEEDBACK

Positive feedback within a cybernetic circuit adds energy consistently so that the system eventually goes out of control (unless there is intervention).

In **positive feedback** *energy is only added* to the system—there is no subtraction of energy as in negative feedback, such as decreasing the amount of gasoline. Suppose, for example, that the controls are stuck so that each increase in the speed of a locomotive becomes a signal to add more fuel to the engine; the locomotive would then consistently increase its speed. Eventually the speed would become so great that the locomotive would go out of control and "jump the tracks." Loss of control is typical of positive feedback systems. Some systems of the human body that go out of control may well involve positive feedback mechanisms. In bulimia and drug addiction, each ingestion of a substance may cue an additional ingestion (a positive feedback system). Like the locomotive, the body may go out of control and malfunction.

ANTICIPATORY FEEDBACK

Anticipatory feedback is used by an organism to specify the present location of a moving target and then to predict the speed and direction of the target so that the organism can intercept the target at a future location.

Another type of feedback mechanism is the **anticipatory feedback** system that increases our response speed. Reflex reactions in humans and animals frequently involve anticipatory feedback. For example, in rapid volleying, a tennis player anticipates the future position of the ball and then quickly moves the racquet to where the opponent's ball is expected. The mechanism involves first specifying the present location of the ball, then making a prediction on the basis of the visual input and on the subjectively estimated speed and direction of the ball, and finally, placing the racquet in the advanced location so that it will be there by the time the ball arrives.

There are tremendous individual differences in anticipatory systems, which help to explain why professional athletes are superior to hackers; but even professionals make anticipatory errors—a fielder overruns a fly ball or a tennis player moves to the wrong spot on the court.

Other Control Strategies

The Body Has Several Control Systems. We have emphasized the importance of negative feedback, but the body also uses other systems for control. The concept that there are several automatic control systems of the body was put forth in the seventeenth century by the famous French philosopher René Descartes. Other relevant contributions by great physiologists include Claude Bernard's discovery that many internal variables are automatically regulated, Walter Cannon's analysis of homeo-

CLAUDE BERNARD (1813–1878)

Courtesy The American Physiological Society.

Claude Bernard has been recognized as France's greatest physiologist. Born the son of a vineyard worker in the small village of St.-Julien Rhone, he completed his M.D. degree under the famous François Magendie in 1843.

In his early life Bernard composed a vaudeville comedy and a drama that he took to Paris at the age of 21 to launch his career. Fortunately, the critics urged him to take up the study of medicine instead.

In 1852 Bernard inherited Ma-gendie's chair at the College de France. Eventually he completed a doctorate in science at the Sorbonne. He received so many honors that he was the first scientist in France to be given a state funeral. He sought general principles common to all animals, principally in the areas of digestion and neural activity. In part, his research on digestion guided Pavlov into his own research on digestion and then on conditional reflexes. Bernard's research established that organs may respond to both stimulation and inhibition in order to maintain a balance between the two, a conclusion that led to Cannon's concept of *homeostasis*. His research on the function of glycogen in the liver was important in establishing the cause of diabetes. A major strategy in science was established with this discovery, overthrowing the view that each organ has only one function. He established that not only did the liver secrete bile, but also that it was the seat of an "internal secretion" (insulin) that interacts with blood sugar.

static mechanisms, and Charles Sherrington's study of spinal reflexes. Sherrington's research formed a basis for Wiener to establish a relationship between physiological and engineering control theory, which was a principal development in cybernetics.

Feedforward and adaptive control are other control strategies used by the body, concepts discussed by James Houk (1988).

FEEDFORWARD CONTROL

We saw that a controlled system contains communication channels that interconnect elements by sending messages along these channels (Fig. 1.2). Information can also be fed forward in communication channels in a **feedforward control system** (see Table 1.1). First a goal or target value for the system is specified. Messages are fed forward from one element to influence or direct another element of the system so as

Other control systems are those of feedforward and adaptive control.

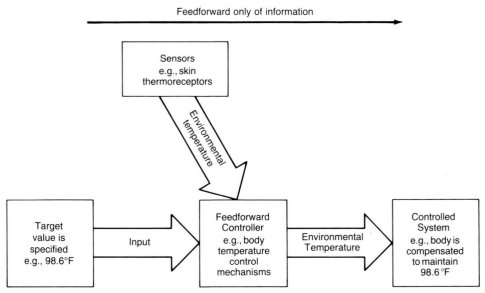

FIGURE 1.5   A feedforward control system in which information is transmitted in only one direction with no feedback.

to achieve a target value. For example, a core temperature of the body is specified as a target value of 98.6°F. Thermoreceptors in the skin, which are feedforward sensors, sense changes in environmental temperature. The body then rapidly compensates for any change sensed by the thermoreceptors to maintain the standard core body temperature at 98.6°F. There is no feedback from the core (internal organs) of the body to affect the thermoreceptors in the skin. Information is only fed forward from the skin to the body core.

In feedforward control, first a target value is specified. Then feedforward sensors communicate information to a feedforward controller. The feedforward controller then directs the controlled system to achieve the target value.

In Figure 1.5 we can see that a target value is set — maintaining a body temperature of 98.6°F. That target value is input into a feedforward controller — here the complex system within the body that maintains a constant body temperature. Feedforward sensors then sense information that is communicated to the feedforward controller — sensory skin thermoreceptors transmit the external temperature to the feedforward controller that directs the controlled system to achieve the target value. There is no feedback from the feedforward controller to the sensors, nor is there feedback anywhere else in the system.

ADAPTIVE CONTROL

An **adaptive control strategy** modifies the components of another control system. It may improve the properties of feedforward or feedback controllers. However, the modification of other systems by an adaptive controller is relatively slow.

Feedback and feedforward function to resolve immediate control problems. Adaptive control, on the other hand, is like long-range planning. An adaptive controller receives information about performance, stores it, and evaluates it over a

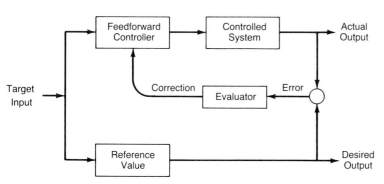

FIGURE 1.6 An adaptive control system that corrects a feedforward controller. Any discrepancy between desired and actual output (error) is ascertained by an evaluator and a correction is entered into the feedforward controller.

period of time. Eventually a decision is reached. Then adaptive actions are output to modify the way the system will respond to future inputs.

Adaptive controllers are especially valuable in conjunction with feedforward controllers because feedforward controllers by themselves typically make persistent errors; those errors may be adjusted by an adaptive controller. Consider the model for an adaptive control system in Figure 1.6. A target value is entered into a feedforward controller that inputs into a controlled system. The actual output of the controlled system is represented at the top of Figure 1.6. The target input also enters a reference model that computes the desired output. The desired output is then compared with the actual output, just as in negative feedback. Any error, which is a discrepancy between the desired output and the actual output, is then computed. If an error exists, it is entered into an *evaluator* that communicates the necessary correction to the feedforward controller. The feedforward controller then modifies its output to bring the controlled system to its desired (targeted) value. For example, saccadic eye movements, rapid responses that shift the gaze from one fixation point to another as when we read, use a controlled system that includes feedforward control. If the feedforward control system results in an error, blurred vision may result. In a normal person, adaptive controllers then adjust the output of the feedforward controller to prevent blurred vision in the future. Adaptive control systems thus do not directly and immediately produce changes in the output of feedback and feedforward systems. Rather, adaptive control systems modify the way other systems respond to future inputs.

Adaptive control can modify feedforward and feedback systems although it does not produce immediate responses. Adaptive systems store information so that in the long run the body can adjust to new situations and improve performance.

Disturbances

In controlled systems there are usually some inputs that disturb variables that the system seeks to control. Numerous such **disturbances** can be compensated for by computationally simple feedback. For example, we maintain a standard glucose (sugar) level in the blood. Glucose receptors serve as feedback sensors to monitor

Disturbances are unwanted influences that can be compensated for by feedback.

any change in blood glucose concentration from its target value. The nature of the disturbance that caused the change from the standard value is irrelevant—the feedback from the glucose receptors automatically corrects for the disturbance to return the concentration of glucose to its standard value.

Shortcomings of Feedforward and Feedback Regulation

We have been discussing the regulation of variables in order to maintain them in a constant state. Feedback and feedforward are both quite effective in doing so, although sometimes each has shortcomings. Feedback does not always completely compensate for errors, because it may not be sufficiently rapid in responding. Also, when there is excessive feedback, the effect is to produce an unstable system.

Feedforward and feedback systems both may have output errors that can be controlled by using the systems together, along with adaptive control systems.

Feedforward can overcome such disadvantages by rapidly bringing the system closer to the target value by detecting disturbances and immediately transmitting that information to a feedforward controller. The feedforward controller can then transmit that information to prevent the disturbance from affecting the variable to be controlled. In temperature regulation, there are systems within the body that are designed to maintain core body temperature at a target value of 98.6°F. However, external environmental temperature changes are disturbances that could cause the core temperature to deviate from its target value. To prevent that deviation, thermoreceptors in the skin function as feedforward sensors that can sense changes in environmental temperature. The thermoreceptors then feedforward information about the external temperature to the thermoregulatory mechanisms in the body. The internal thermoregulatory system then responds rapidly to compensate *before* there is any noticeable change in core body temperature.

Negative feedback control systems are probably the most extensively used, but they function intimately with feedforward and adaptive control systems in the complex regulation of the systems of the body.

Feedforward also has disadvantages; for example, the required computations may be complex and the errors in output may not actually be corrected. Thus if a feedforward controller calculates too large a feedforward command, the variable to be controlled would be excessively elevated. Such errors can eventually be corrected by special adaptive mechanisms that regularly adjust the feedforward controllers, as we saw in Figure 1.6.

CYBERNETICS—A HISTORICAL PERSPECTIVE

With this appreciation for the nature and importance of control systems, it is worth our while to spend a few moments on understanding the factors that led to the development of cybernetics.

Engineering Developments. As we have seen from Plato's work, the use of feedback principles has been in existence for over 2500 years. However, the first significant paper on feedback mechanisms was published by J. Clerk Maxwell in 1868. That paper dealt with the use of governors (elements of a system that control speed) as feedback devices. Earlier, James Watt (1736–1819) had invented a governor for the steam engine that could maintain a steady speed for locomotives. In contemporary engineering, we saw that in 1932 Nyquist applied negative feedback in vacuum tube amplifiers to correct for errors (the result was to maintain linearity and stability of the systems).

Societal Consequences of Cybernetics. The use of feedback mechanisms and communication processes in the Industrial Revolution of the nineteenth century greatly advanced science and technology and dramatically changed the nature of the world in which humans lived. The more recent revolutions in solid state electronics and computer technology have incorporated major principles of cybernetics — they threaten to change our world even more than did the Industrial Revolution. However, the social values of such revolutions are open to question. As with all advances in science and technology, whether or not changes benefit or harm humanity depends upon the wisdom with which society uses them.

Applications for Understanding How the Body Functions. Russian scientists Peter Anokhin and N. A. Bernstein were especially prominent in the development of physiological principles in the mid-1930s. Anokhin's thesis was that feedback from responses, which he called **reverse afferentation**, was of great importance in the functional systems of the body (see p. 315). Bernstein employed concepts similar to that of feedback and demonstrated the importance of sensory information fed back from a response in a reflex arc, somewhat like Sir Charles Bell did in 1842 (see p. 315).

Another important event was Norbert Wiener's application of cybernetic principles to the human body, which constituted his great contribution to biology and to biological psychology.

With precursors like these, cybernetics developed in the 1940s in the United States when scientists in various fields began thinking about some common matters. One was a philosophy centered about the mathematical use of symbols. To understand this, note that Wiener was a student of Bertrand Russell (1872 – 1970), who had collaborated with Alfred North Whitehead (1861 – 1947) to produce *Principia Mathematica,* one of the outstanding books of all time. The crowning feature of the *Principia* was the demonstration that the entire field of mathematics was reducible to symbolic logic. The advanced development of symbolic logic by Russell and Whitehead influenced Wiener in his use of mathematical symbols for a calculus of reasoning, which was important in cybernetics and information theory.

Another development that contributed to cybernetics was the new field of mathematical biophysics. In mathematical biophysics, hypothetical nerve nets (connections of neurons) are postulated, although not actually observed. The purpose of formulating hypothetical nerve nets is to try to account for how organisms behave. Warren McCulloch was one of the scientists in the forefront of the field. McCulloch astutely applied symbolic logic to represent hypothesized connections of neurons as models of how the nervous systems might function. For instance, certain circuits of neurons in the brain, when activated, may account for how we perceive moving objects. The neurons in these circuits and their interconnections were then symbolically represented in logical form.

In the 1940s, it was Wiener more than anyone else who applied cybernetics to understanding the human mind. It started more or less in this way: Wiener, who was involved in wartime planning and research, was influenced by colleagues to use a series of vacuum tubes as analogs of events in the nervous systems. (Vacuum tubes were precursors of transistors, which were precursors of chips.) As in McCulloch's hypothetical nerve nets, Wiener constructed the equivalent of neural circuits using vacuum tubes as "neurons," analogous to how they might function within organisms. This model suggested that the "ultra-rapid computing machine" (a computer that used vacuum tubes) was almost an ideal analogy of the human nervous system. Wiener's strategy was to interpret memory systems in animals as parallel with the artificial memories of computers. Groups of engineers, neurophysiologists, and psychologists were then formed to work on these and similar problems.

Although much progress was made in wartime efforts in research on cybernetics, you can imagine the difficulties that members of such different professions had in communicating with each other. Wiener (1948) made this point with the following observation about collaboration between physiologists and mathematicians:

> If the difficulty of a physiological problem is mathematical in essence, ten physiologists ignorant of mathematics will get precisely as far as one physiologist ignorant of mathematics, and no further. If a physiologist, who knows no mathematics, works together with a mathematician who knows no physiology, the one will be unable to state his problem in terms that the other can manipulate, and the second will be unable to put the answers in any form that the first can understand. (p. 9)

Difficulties in communication among members of the several professions that fall within the scope of biological psychology still continue. Nevertheless, considerable progress has been made since the early 1940s when the field of cybernetics was born. We now consider how the principles developed in this chapter apply to the human body.

CYBERNETICS OF THE BODY

The general strategy that we will follow in using a cybernetics model (Fig. 1.7) is to understand

1. The receptor processes by which we receive information from the environment
2. How, once that information enters the receptors, it is transmitted as messages to the brain where it is processed
3. How messages are then transmitted from the brain to and from the peripheral systems (the receptors, muscles, and glands)

It is critical to remember that feedback operates in each of these three phases. For instance, in phase 3, it is stated that information is transmitted from the brain back to the receptors. As illustrated in Figure 1.7, circuits operate between the receptors and the brain so that transmission of information is not a one-way street that runs only *to* the brain. Similarly, once information gets to the brain, it functions in circuits from the brain to the muscles and glands. *The major principle is that all bodily phenomena are influenced by messages that are transmitted within the numerous cybernetic circuits throughout the body.* It is our task to understand how these circuits function to integrate the various bodily systems. Successful integration of the bodily systems leads to the diverse kinds of behaviors that we seek to understand.

The bodily systems, including those for behavior, are regulated by messages transmitted within cybernetic circuits throughout the body; many of those circuits function with feedback characteristics.

One important application of cybernetics is to maintain the condition essential for life known as homeostasis. *Homeostasis* is the term used by the great physiologist Walter Cannon (1871–1945) in his studies of water balance and thirst. **Homeostasis** refers to the maintenance of certain consistent states of the body that are necessary for normal functioning. Cannon observed the continuous shifts of states of body

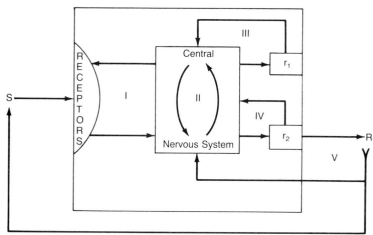

FIGURE 1.7 Several classes of interacting circuits within the body: I. Those between receptors and the central nervous system. II. Cortical and cortical–subcortical circuits. III. S-covert response (r_1) circuits that do not eventuate in overt behavior. IV. S-covert response (r_2) circuits that eventuate in overt behavior (R). V. Circuits involving overt behavior that feed back to the central nervous system as well as influence environmental events (S).

hydration and dehydration. If the level of water falls sufficiently, this information is fed back and the organism takes steps to restore the standard water balance by consuming liquids. Overconsumption of liquids leads to their elimination. A state of homeostasis (equilibrium) is thus achieved in either way.

Homeostasis is a very general concept and refers to more than the thirst drive. Organisms also maintain standard (homeostatic) conditions of body temperature, salt balance, blood pressure, and so on, and one can even think of homeostasis of the mind, a stability of mental processes. If for any reason a change in these balances or states of equilibrium occurs, negative feedback mechanisms may activate the organism to restore the original standard states. Although the goal of the body is to maintain various internal conditions at certain standard values, some variation from these standards is tolerable.

Homeostasis is a state of physiological equilibrium within an organism.

The normal body temperature on the average is 98.6°F. But when one is running, additional bodily heat is generated. Various mechanisms of the body then function to dissipate that heat: The blood vessels at the surface of the body dilate and allow heat to escape, and the sweat glands secrete sweat, which, on evaporation, produces a refrigeration effect. As a consequence, the body cools down to reach the standard of 98.6°F. If the body temperature falls below 98.6°F, other actions (such as shivering) function to increase heat and maintain the desired thermal homeostasis. Wiener (1948) summarized some of these homeostatic mechanisms as follows:

> A great group of cases in which some sort of feed-back is not only exemplified in physiological phenomena, but is absolutely essential for the continuation of life, is found in what is known as *homeostasis*. The conditions under which life, especially

WALTER B. CANNON (1871–1945)

Courtesy The American Physiological Society.

Walter Cannon was born in Wisconsin and studied and remained as a professor at Harvard University for forty-two years. As a physiologist and endocrinologist, he made a number of discoveries that were of great impor-tance for psychology. He criticized the James-Lange theory of emotions and advanced what is known as the Cannon-Bard theory of emotions (see p. 283). His theory holds that an emotion is an emergency reaction that causes the body to react with its resources in order to cope with an emergency. In his neurophysiological research, Cannon identified the hypothalamus as a control center for emotional behavior and the adrenal gland as a mobilizer of energy resources when the body is faced with stress. He formulated the concept of homeostasis as the tendency for the body to maintain a steady internal state, which is a constant bodily environment. If the constancy is disturbed, the body automatically attempts to restore equilibrium.

healthy life, can continue in the higher animals, are quite narrow. A variation of one half degree centigrade in the body temperature is generally a sign of illness, and a permanent variation of five degrees is scarcely consistent with life. The osmotic pressure of the blood and its hydrogen-ion concentration must be held within strict limits. The waste products of the body must be excreted before they rise to toxic concentrations. Besides all these, our leucocytes and our chemical defenses against infection must be kept at adequate levels; our heart rate and blood pressure must neither be too high nor too low; our sex cycle must conform to the racial needs of reproduction; our calcium metabolism must be such as neither to soften our bones nor to calcify our tissues; and so on. In short, our inner economy must contain an assembly of thermostats, automatic hydrogen-ion-concentration controls, governors, and the like, which would be adequate for a great chemical plant. These are what we know collectively as our homeostatic mechanism. (pp. 134–135)

Numerous homeostatic systems in the body function through negative feedback to maintain relatively constant conditions in the body (physiological equilibria).

Wiener also pointed out that feedback mechanisms differ depending on whether they function in automatic, homeostatic systems or in the voluntary systems of the body — the former tend to react more slowly. There are several reasons that reaction times are slower in homeostatic systems. For one, effectors of homeostasis are glands and smooth muscles, such as those used for digestion. Since digestion is not necessary for meeting an emergency situation, it can be a slow process.

However, if we need to jump out of the way of a car, the fast reaction time of the voluntary striated muscles in the legs is required.

The feedback circuit components for homeostatic systems use chemical messengers such as hormones and carbon dioxide, and these are distributed rather slowly throughout the body by the **circulatory** (blood) **system**. Furthermore, the nerve fibers for homeostasis (those of the autonomic nervous system centered in the gut) are often nonmyelinated. Nonmyelinated nerve fibers have a slow rate of transmission relative to myelinated nerve fibers (those that are surrounded with what is known as a myelin sheath). We will study these matters later.

Homeostatic systems function relatively slowly because of the flow of hormones in negative feedback circuits and the involvement of nonmyelinated nerve fibers that have a relatively slow rate of transmission.

In short, if you touch a hot stove, the voluntary striated musculature reacts very rapidly so as to prevent further bodily injury due to the heat, but such rapid reaction time is not necessary when adjusting the salt level of the body.

CYBERNETICS OF THE MIND

With a cybernetic approach we should be able to construct a symbolic representation of what people refer to as the human **mind**. Using the computer as a limited analogy is not terribly misleading in this particular respect. When messages are transmitted along circuits within a computer system, visual images are generated that can be readily viewed on the monitor. In like manner, a cybernetic model holds that visual imagery and other **mental (cognitive) processes** that constitute the content of mind are generated when circuits within the body selectively interact.

We understand the internal functions of the computer system, and it is our task to similarly understand how the circuits within organisms function. Someday perhaps we can attach something like a television monitor to the body and display the visual components of mental processes. Auditory and other components of thoughts could be similarly displayed. To understand this, Figure 1.7 illustrated how information is received from the environment and transmitted throughout the body. One particularly valuable characteristic of internally transmitted information throughout the receptor, nervous, muscular, and glandular systems is that when active, these systems generate electrical signals, such as brain waves. Consequently, electrical messages that are transmitted throughout the body along internal circuits composed of nerves, muscles, and so on can be studied by means of sensitive electronic equipment. In laboratories, we can actually record information as it is internally transmitted and processed within the body. In Chapters 8 and 13, we will more thoroughly study such electrical signals that could form the basis of a "thought-reading machine."

A thought-reading machine could be constructed by electronically monitoring and interpreting the messages transmitted among the various systems of the body.

Our long-term goal is a complete understanding of how mental processes are generated by the interaction of receptors, effectors, and the nervous systems. Such an accomplishment would solve the age-old problem of the nature of the human mind. This general strategy has already produced impressive results, but we still have a long way to go. Before we tackle the problem of mind, we should acquire a sound perspective for the development of biological psychology and for various views of mind and of systems of the body. For these purposes, we start in Chapter 2 with biological science.

EMPHASIS ON A CYBERNETIC PRINCIPLE— NEGATIVE FEEDBACK

At the end of each chapter we will summarize and extend a major principle in the chapter. Here we emphasize the importance of negative feedback.

To Summarize. Negative feedback control systems function as information is communicated within cybernetic circuits. The organism's body specifies standard target values to be achieved within a system. Sensors such as receptors then monitor the relevant event(s) for deviations (errors) from those standard values. Information is then fed back within the system's circuits to affect modifications. Those modifications correct the error(s) to achieve and maintain the various standard value(s).

A major use of negative feedback occurs with mental events, which, according to a cybernetic model, are generated as circuits reverberate between the brain and peripheral systems. However, sometimes the mental activity is excessive as when people complain of unwanted thoughts—when trying to sleep they may report that "my mind is racing." Many unwanted thoughts, such as obsessions and phobias, as well as those of depression, have clinical significance. Although in such cases the mind is overactive, at other times it is underactive, as when one is not sufficiently aroused to meet the demands of a situation. Thus, as in the famous Yerkes-Dodson law (modified in Fig. 1.8), there is an optimal target value for the *amount* of mental arousal so that behavior may proceed effectively. How might one behave to achieve the appropriate target value?

First, we need to objectively measure the amount of mental activity that, as we develop, can be accomplished by recording electrical measurements of circuits involving the brain and muscles. Then, by manipulating these neuromuscular circuits, we can increase or decrease the amount of mental activity. Tranquilizers can temporarily reduce excessive mental arousal. However, more effective, and more general, methods of control involve the striated (voluntary) muscles. By relaxing or tensing them, we can reduce or increase the amount of activity in the neuromuscular circuits and thus in the mind (see Chapter 15). For example, the best way to go to sleep when tormented by a racing mind is to relax the muscles. Similarly, clinical relaxation applications have eliminated obsessive, phobic, depressive, and other thoughts. On

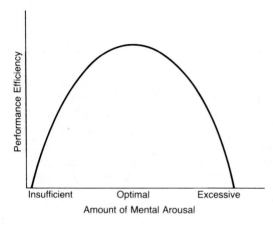

FIGURE 1.8
There is an amount of mental arousal that is optimal for performance. If arousal varies from that target value, performance deteriorates. (After the Yerkes-Dodson Law)

the other hand, we sometimes need to arouse ourselves mentally by exerting ourselves. The Australian tennis professional Evonne Goolagong found that she sometimes played poorly because of her "walk abouts" ("not thinking"), whereupon she would increase her efforts. Such control to achieve the target value for the amount of mental activity appropriate for any given situation is accomplished by the systematic tensing and/or relaxing of the voluntary musculature, as we develop in Chapter 15 and elsewhere (e.g., McGuigan, 1990, 1993b).

KEY TERMS

Adaptive control strategy—A control system that modifies such other control strategies as feedback and feedforward systems; it functions in a slow manner and stores information to help adjustment to new situations.

Analog signal—Information transmitted by continuous (not discrete) messages.

Anticipatory feedback—The present location, speed, and direction of a target is fed back so that a future location of the target may be anticipated.

Biological psychology—The specialization within psychology for understanding behavior by studying how the systems of the body interact with each other and with the environment.

Circulatory system—The complex system of vessels that transports blood and other vital fluids to and from the organs of the body.

Communication—The transmission of information along circuits, often for the purpose of controlling systems.

Comparative psychology—A subfield of psychology that attempts to describe and explain behavior by distinguishing and relating characteristics of species throughout the phylogenetic scale.

Continuous message—A message that may assume any value along a continuum, for example, the sounds emanating from a radio.

Control—The use of information transmitted as messages for the purpose of modifying the status of systems.

Controlled system—A system in which communication channels interconnect elements and messages are transmitted along those channels to bring the system to a target value.

Covert processes—Bodily events that are not readily observable without the use of apparatus to extend the scope of our senses. The process may be behavioral

(muscular or glandular) or neural (observable with electroencephalography).

Cybernetics—The science of communication and control in machines and organisms that function according to the same principles. The term is derived from the Greek word meaning "steersman."

Discrete messages—Messages that can assume integral numerical values. The values are whole numbers that differ by clearly defined steps with no intermediate values possible (e.g., zero versus one).

Disturbance—An unwanted influence in a control system that can cause errors (undesired changes) in the variables for which control is sought.

Feedback—A system or process in which information about the output is returned (fed back) to the input in order to control, or regulate, the operation.

Feedforward control system—A target is specified and information is directed within a system to achieve that target value with no feedback.

Homeostasis—The maintenance of equilibrium, or constant conditions, in biological systems by means of automatic mechanisms, for example, the maintenance of a standard salt level in the blood.

Interdisciplinary—Efforts to increase the quality of knowledge through the integration of the diverse data provided by various relevant fields of study.

Mental (cognitive) processes—Subjective experiences generated when systems of the body selectively interact, especially those of receptors, nervous tissue, and effectors.

Message—A sequence of measurable events that contains information. See discrete and continuous messages.

Mind—A commonsense term referring to the totality of mental processes. It is explicated here as follows: A self-programming operation of the body that consists of, and only of, the activation of complex cybernetic circuits.

Negative feedback—Arranging feedback signals to oppose an increasing or decreasing trend of a system; adding and/or subtracting from the input, feedback is employed to stabilize systems.

Overt behavior—Behavior readily observed with the naked eye, such as running and talking.

Phylogenetic scale—An ordering of species indicating their relative complexity in evolutionary development.

Positive feedback—Feedback that is only added to the trend of a system and thus does not decrease the trend, leading to instability.

Reference signal (target value)—An initially set value to be achieved by a control system.

Reverse afferentation—Russian scientist Peter Anokhin's thesis of the great importance of feedback from responses in functional systems of the body. Like negative feedback, it is a basic principle underlying the common elements in the functioning of machines and of the behavior of organisms.

Species—A group of organisms classified together because they have certain characteristics in common, for example, *amoebae* and *Homo sapiens* are different species.

System—A set of elements and their relations. The body is a general system that consists of elements such as the cardiovascular and nervous systems and the relations among them.

Vertebrates—Species that are high on the phylogenetic scale and have a spinal cord, as do humans.

STUDY QUESTIONS

1. Define biology, psychology, and biological psychology.
2. What is the phylogenetic scale?
3. Where was the word *cybernetics* originally used and what was the original context?
4. The essential concepts in cybernetics are *control* and *communication*. Explain them.
5. Define discrete and continuous messages.
6. Give examples of negative and positive feedback and feedforward control.
7. Briefly describe how Wiener first applied cybernetics for understanding the human mind.
8. Define homeostasis and relate it to cybernetics.

FURTHER READINGS

For the undergraduate student, there are numerous good books in the area of biological psychology that you can find in your library. You should browse through sections on biological psychology, physiological psychology, neuropsychology, and so on. This advice is especially appropriate also for Chapters 4, 5, 6, and 7. An excellent book in physiological psychology at a somewhat more advanced level is:

Carlson, N. R. (1991). *Physiology of behavior* (4th ed.). Newton, MA: Allyn & Bacon.

The following book is quite advanced but provides an appreciation of the field of cybernetics and of control strategies, particularly as applied to the human body. More generally, it is important for the serious student to at least get a "feel" for classical books such as this one by Wiener:

Wiener, N. (1948). *Cybernetics: Control and communication in the animal and the machine*. Cambridge, MA: M.I.T. Press.

Also see an advanced article:

Houk, J. C. (1988). Control strategies in physiological systems. *FASEB Journal*, 2, 97–107.

The following advanced work is a broad attempt to formulate principles to account for self-regulation across biological and nonliving systems such as computers:

Bertalanffy, L. von. (1968). *General systems theory*. New York: Braziller.

CHAPTER 2

Origin and Development
of Biological Science

MAJOR PURPOSES:	1. To trace what we know about the origin of life and how the minds of *Homo sapiens* evolved
	2. To develop how science, particularly biological science, came to flourish
WHAT YOU ARE GOING TO FIND:	1. How the advance to empiricism and inductive reasoning in our search for knowledge led to the flourishing of science
	2. That evolution theory was of paramount importance in the development of biological science
	3. That, in the long history of our evolution, there were two critical events: the origin of life and the origin of mind
WHAT YOU SHOULD ACQUIRE:	An understanding of the critical importance of historical perspective in understanding contemporary issues, of how science developed, and of the major principles of evolution theories and how these form the bases for contemporary biological psychology

CHAPTER OUTLINE

THE IMPORTANCE OF HISTORICAL
PERSPECTIVE

Understanding the history of a subject is critical for maintaining a realistic perspective of contemporary thought. Without the context of history, what we think we now know may be vacuous indeed. A knowledge of what has preceded us facilitates our proper evaluation of new thoughts. It also helps us avoid blind alleys that have already been explored by our predecessors as well as the errors that they made. As the philosopher George Santayana told us, those who do not study history are doomed to repeat it.

With an understanding of the historical roots of biological psychology, we can more effectively build on the accomplishments of the past and avoid "reinventing the wheel." Instances of duplication abound, for example, Sir Isaac Newton (1642–1727) is usually given credit for inventing the calculus (he called it "fluxions") because it was required in the development of his magnificent laws of motion. But his contemporary G. W. Leibnitz (1646–1716) independently invented the calculus because it was necessary for his account of physical and mental life based on the movement of monads ("atoms"). Had Newton and Leibnitz known about each other's work, they could have collaborated in true scientific fashion with much effort saved and perhaps even greater advances resulting.

Knowledge Is Systematically Accumulated.   Historical perspective also comes from the *cumulative character of science.* The building of structures of knowledge is well illustrated in Newton's work. "How is it," he was asked, "that you arrived at your magnificent laws of motion? How did you see so much further than anyone else?" "Because," Newton answered, recalling the work of Copernicus, Galileo, Brahe, and Kepler, "I stood on the shoulders of giants." Hedges (1987) has empirically demonstrated that knowledge is cumulative in psychology.

With appreciation of the great importance of understanding how we arrived at contemporary thought, let us consider the historical development of biological psychology. For this we first need to understand how the science of biological life processes developed.

An understanding of the history of your subject improves your perspective of contemporary knowledge, helps to avoid past errors and duplication of previous efforts, and facilitates the accumulation of knowledge.

Science is a process of systematically accumulating knowledge.

ANCIENT HISTORY OF BIOLOGY

The Start of Civilization.   Recent archaeological studies have indicated that the Cayonu people lived some 10,000 years ago in the southeastern portion of what is now Turkey (Fig. 2.1). The Cayonu people are historically important because they apparently represent a critical transitional period in human development. It was then that our ancestors were changing from vagabond hunters to farmers who lived in villages, a transition that may well have been the start of civilization as we now know it — the buildings of the Cayonu constitute the first instance of structures beyond simple domestic dwellings. They seemed to have had the concept of communal buildings that served special functions, although we can only speculate as to what those functions were. For example, one building had intricate mosaic floors with a human face carved in a slab of limestone. Another building contained the burned tops of about fifty skulls and leg bones cut off at the hip.

The Invention of Written Language.   Some 4000 years later, about 600 miles farther south in the region now known as Iraq, the Sumerian civilization developed. The Sumerians etched the world's first known written language on clay tablets. Writing symbols for speech sounds was of such significance that it ranks in importance well above the invention of the wheel. *With written language, civilization could accurately accumulate knowledge* over endless generations. Without writing, knowledge was transmitted orally with distortion from one generation to the next.

Another dramatic consequence of written language is that it allows us to efficiently manipulate the physical world with symbols, an ability that we needed to

Contemporary civilization seems to have originated with the Cayonu people some 10,000 years ago in southeastern Turkey.

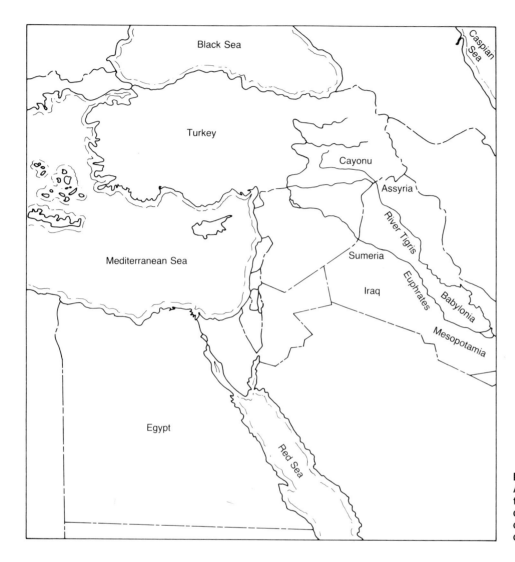

FIGURE 2.1
A map of important regions in the early development of civilization, indicating locations of Cayonu and Sumarian cultures.

construct great bridges and airplanes. Think, for instance, how much more effective it is to draw a set of plans for constructing a bridge using mathematical and other symbols than it is to create it by actually moving logs about in a trial-and-error fashion.

The Sumerians were prolific writers, but their language died out around 2000 B.C. despite efforts by the ancient Babylonians to translate and preserve it. Sumerian resembles no other language so it remains difficult to understand. Unfortunately, we know little of this culture's thoughts about biology because of these difficulties, but in a broad sense this civilization was a landmark development.

Other ancient records indicate that early civilizations of the river valleys of India and China in the Far East and of Mesopotamia and Egypt in the Near East were somewhat concerned with mental functions, but they are not very explicit. We do know, however, that the Indian and Chinese cultures speculated about the universal and abstract, with some indifference to the operation of the individual human mind.

Societal Restrictions Against Science.   In ancient Egypt and Assyria, medicine was not divorced from magic. Dissection of the body was forbidden so that acquisition of physiological and anatomical knowledge was retarded. Often in history, scientific biology was inhibited by cultural and religious restrictions against scientific observation and experimentation. Even today there are antiscientific movements such as those that oppose the study of animals; another example is the antievolutionary religious movement known as "Direct Creationism." In fact, it was only in relatively recent times that Florida repealed laws prohibiting dissection. Until then, Florida could not have a medical school.

The foundation of Western civilization and contemporary physiology was laid some 2500 years ago by Grecian culture and its philosophies.

Grecian Foundations for Western Civilization.   As the civilizations of the Near East declined, the Greek cultures developed. The Greeks were the first scholarly Europeans and their emergence was of dramatic suddenness. Within the space of two centuries (550–350 B.C.), the Greeks laid the foundation for the next 2500 years of Western thought.

Three important phases in the development of Greek philosophy were the

1. Platonic period (427–347 B.C.)
2. Aristotelian period (385–322 B.C.)
3. Alexandrian period (300–200 B.C.)

Empiricism, the strategy of answering questions by the observation of nature, is necessary for the acquisition of knowledge.

The first two periods were not favorable for developing a science of physiology because dissection of the body was forbidden. However, in the period named after Alexander the Great, science flourished because **empiricism,** including dissection of the human body, was encouraged. Herophilus and Erasistratus, for instance, discovered that nerves lead to the brain and spinal cord; they distinguished between sensory and motor nerve impulses; and they specified the anatomy of the eye and described the ventricles of the brain.

GREEK CONCEPTIONS OF SOUL–MIND

Psychology derives from psyche *(the "soul") and* ology *("the study of"). Consequently* psyche-ology *is the study of the psyche.*

The concept of the **psyche** was a central idea in Greek philosophy, but the word has no precise translation in English. It variously connotes "soul," "life," "spirit," and "self." Its essence was a vital characteristic of a person that was coextensive with, but independent of, the body. A popular Greek notion was that at death the psyche left the body and "floated" into the heavens. Throughout history the term has variously denoted the subject matter of psychology.

Contemporary psychology derived from the Greek concept of the psyche but evolved into the science of behavior.

The subject matter of psychology progressed from the nonphysical psyche, through an immaterial (nonphysical) mind, and finally to **materialism.** But **cultural lag,** the interval between acquisition and application of knowledge, often has delayed societal advances. In this instance, many basic characteristics of an immaterial mind hypothesized by the Greeks persist to this day — laypeople often still conceptualize the mind much as the Greeks did.

The tripartite Platonic soul consisted of three parts, the vegetative soul, the animal soul, and the immortal soul, each higher than the preceding both in function and physical location in the central nervous system.

Plato's Tripartite Soul.   Plato's notions are the starting point for contemporary Western conceptions of mind. Plato first proposed that the heart and the liver functioned for what he thought were lower level souls. However, he later considered them as seats for emotion and appetite, with the higher rational facilities focused in the brain. Eventually, he developed the tripartite **Platonic soul** that included (1) a *vegetative soul* that subserved the appetite and was placed in the lowest region of the spinal cord, the lumbar-sacral region (Fig. 2.2); (2) the *animal soul* for emotion was

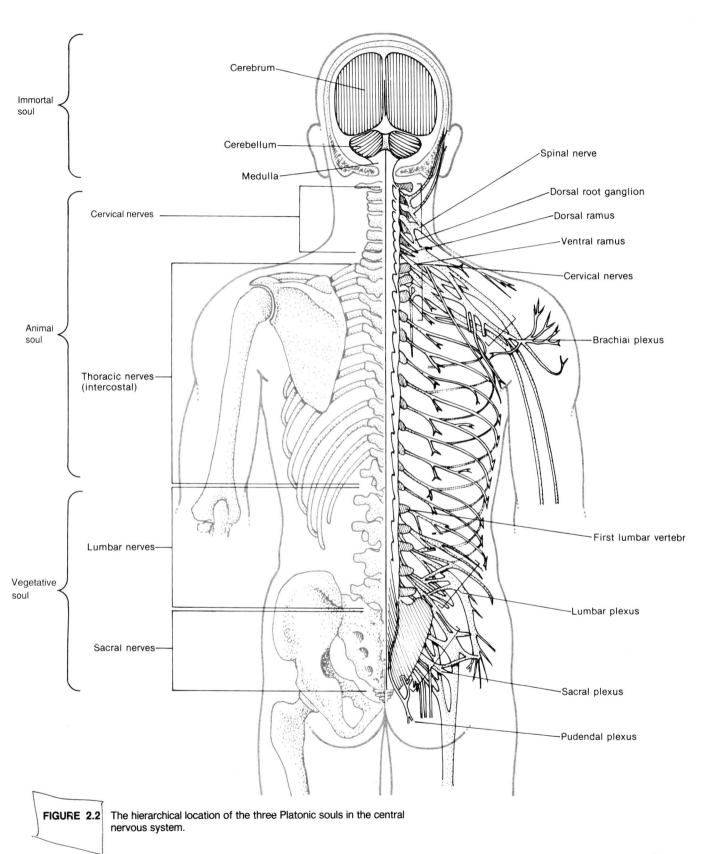

FIGURE 2.2 The hierarchical location of the three Platonic souls in the central nervous system.

27

next, being located in the cervical-thoracic region of the spinal cord; and (3) the *immortal soul,* subserving reason, occupied the highest seat, that of the brain.

In contrast to Plato, Aristotle located the soul in the heart. For Aristotle the brain was but a refrigerator for fluids of the body.

Memory Conceptions. The Greeks developed many important cognitive and physiological principles, including how memory functions. As great orators, they needed good memory skills, which caused them to place much emphasis on constant drill and repetition. A summary of one memory course, written about 400 B.C. by Hippias, reminds us of today's correspondence courses in memory training: First, closely attend; second, practice; and third, if you hear anything new, associate it with what you already know.

One Greek notion of memory is analogous to impressing the seal of a ring on a block of wax — the wax receives the impressions of the perceptions and stores them as memory. We thus remember what is imprinted on the wax as long as the image lasts. But when the image is effaced, we forget it.

Until several decades ago, our notions of memory remained essentially those of the Greeks. However, a tremendous amount of psychological and physiological research has contributed to a much greater understanding of how memory functions (see Chapter 10).

The Brain Ventricles. Cavities (ventricles) in the brain filled with cerebral-spinal fluid, as depicted in Figure 2.3, had special importance for the concept of the

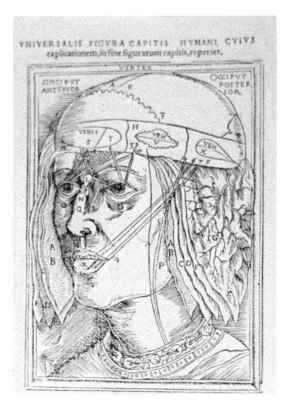

FIGURE 2.3
The brain ventricles after Vesalius. The Greeks developed an analogy between the three chambered plan of the early Greek law temples and the processing of information through the three depicted brain ventricles.

GALEN OF PERGAMON
(c. A.D. 129–199)

The Greek physician Galen is one of the greatest scientists in our history. He studied anatomy in Alexandria and returned to Greece to become a surgeon to the gladiators. Eventually he lived in Rome. His work is a landmark in our history because of his early insistence that experimental studies should form the basis for medical practice. Through empirical methods of conducting surgery in dissection of animals, he attempted to understand the functioning of the body, especially that of the brain.

An anecdote is told of an early cognitive physiological application in which Galen measured the pulse rate of a young woman on four successive days. On the first and fourth day he mentioned the name of a particular male dancer. On the second and third days, however, he mentioned the names of other male dancers. His finding that the pulse was faster on the first and fourth days led him to conclude that the young woman was in love with the dancer.

mind. Early Byzantine and later Arabic scholars developed an orderly system for localizing faculties within the ventricles. The great Greek physician Galen (c. A.D. 129–199) regarded them as reservoirs for the psychic *pneuma* (gaseous air) that passes through the pores of the brain and nerves. The flow of psychic pneuma was an early counterpart of what we now know as neural impulses being transmitted throughout the body.

An interesting psychological, information processing analogy was developed by the Greeks, based on the three-chambered plan used in their law temples: Information was collected in the first temple; the judgment was made in the second temple; and action (sentencing) was done in the third. Just so, they conceived of the brain as possessing three "chambers" (see Fig. 2.3). The sensory nerves passed into the first chamber (ventricle) where information from the environment was collected; associative functions were assigned to the middle ventricle; and motor actions were carried out in the posterior ventricle.

THE DARK AGES AND LOSS OF KNOWLEDGE

With the rise of the Roman Empire, the Greek states were subdued and their people enslaved. The Romans were good technologists, as shown by their marvelous road and plumbing systems. Although they added relatively little to scientific knowledge, they did respect knowledge and preserved what the Greeks had accumulated. However, with the fall of Rome in the fifth century A.D., barbarians from the north destroyed much of the Western world's knowledge. After that, the West entered the

Middle (Dark) Ages, wherein, once again, the individual human was regarded as too personal, too lofty for investigation. They had to be dethroned from that towering position in order to be studied. The lowering of humankind commenced with the acceptance of the **Copernican theory of planetary motion;** it continued when **Darwin's evolution theory** further lowered the status of humans, holding that they were but intelligent animals; then, this dethroning concluded for the present with the objective study of animals and human minds. Genetic engineering may unimaginably extend this dethroning process.

Knowledge that was developed through the Greek period was preserved by the Romans, but it was largely lost during the Middle Ages, a period that persisted from A.D. 500 until the scientific renaissance in the sixteenth century.

What knowledge remained after the fall of Rome was largely protected by the monasteries. Little new knowledge was acquired until about the sixteenth century because of theological restrictions against empiricism, the observation of nature. To study how we developed contemporary methods for acquiring knowledge, we need to trace the transition from the dark ages to the scientific renaissance.[1]

THE NATURE OF "TRUTH" AND THE "TRUTH" OF NATURE

The Method of Authority.   The story of how we arrived at today's methodology for seeking truth is a long, torturous one. Progress has been slowly and painfully achieved, but also retarded by such human-made disasters as the Hundred Years' War. Western civilization during the Middle Ages was dominated by the Catholic church. Accordingly, the "truth" about issues usually was "discovered" by asserting what was said in the Bible or by interpreters of the Bible such as St. Thomas Aquinas. An interesting story of how we shifted from this authoritative method of citing religious sources to contemporary scientific methods was related as follows by Gingerich (1982).

Geocentric vs. Heliocentric Theories of Planetary Motion.   As a product of his society, Galileo accepted the method of authority although he did not follow a literal interpretation of the Bible. His views about the Bible's teachings were well expressed by a saying that he borrowed from the librarian of the Vatican: Galileo believed "that the Bible told how to go to Heaven, not how the Heavens go." Consequently, in the fall of 1606, Galileo used his self-constructed telescope to study the phases of Venus. The prevailing theory of planetary motion, of how the "heavens go," was the **Ptolemaic theory,** which held that the earth was the center of the universe. According to the Ptolemaic theory, the sun and planets revolved about the earth.

The Ptolemaic (geocentric) theory holds that the earth is the center of the universe so that the sun and planets revolve about it. The Copernican (heliocentric) theory holds that the sun is the center of the universe so that the planets revolve about it.

Copernicus had published his magnum opus in 1533, putting forth the revolutionary thesis that the sun and not the earth was the center of the universe. However, there were no substantive data to support his theory. Copernicus merely had noted that if the planetary orbits were rearranged with the sun at the center, the planets could be described as moving in elliptical orbits about the sun. The Copernican theory thus provides a much simplified description of planetary motion. That is, according to Ptolemaic theory, the relative motion of the planets and sun is one of

---

[1] We are focusing on only the Western world. Civilizations elsewhere, such as in the Middle East, were prospering and during this period, scientific investigation, especially in medicine and biology, was encouraged.

GALILEO GALILEI (1564–1642)

Galileo was born in Pisa, Italy, where he became a lecturer in mathematics at the University of Pisa. His research into the theory of motion disproved the Aristotelian contention that bodies of different weights fall at different speeds. Later at the University of Padua, he proved theoretically that falling bodies obey the law of uniformly accelerated motion. Because of his pioneer work in gravitation and motion in the combining of mathematical analysis with experimentation, he is often referred to as the Father of Mechanics and Experimental Physics. He held that the book of nature is written in mathematical characters, which is taken as the foundation of the modern experimental method.

---

complex epicycles as illustrated in Figure 2.4. A planet moving about the sun has a much simpler relative movement.

However, the conflict between the Copernican and the Ptolemaic theories was itself not a critical issue for theologians. For them, and for us, the more important question has to do with the use of *inductive* versus *deductive* reasoning for ascertaining truth.[2]

Inductive Logic Is Necessary for Acquiring New Knowledge. The scholastic philosophers of Galileo's time knew, as we well recognize today, that inductive reasoning cannot lead to absolutely certain truth. Galileo, seeking to prove the truth of the Copernican theory, also realized that he could not accomplish this task with deductive logic. Instead of attempting to reach *absolutely certain* truth with deductive reasoning, he had to employ inductive reasoning whereby a conclusion could be reached that had *only a limited,* if high, degree of probability. His inductive process of inferring truth was as follows: First, Galileo made observations of the phases of Venus and they were compatible with the Copernican theory. He thus reasoned that the Copernican theory was probably true. In contrast, his observations were incompatible with the Ptolemaic theory. He thus also concluded that the Ptolemaic theory was not true.

We should emphasize the importance of the concept *probable,* since its use in inductive reasoning means that there could be other explanations than the one inferred. For instance, Galileo's observations of the phases of Venus could mean that some theory that was not then known, other than the Copernican theory, was true.

From a contemporary scientific point of view, Galileo's inductive methods of observation and reasoning are sound. However, the scholastic philosophers, who

Deductive logic uses only information that you already have. Galileo showed us that to acquire new knowledge we must replace deductive reasoning with inductive reasoning.

---

[2] Inductive logic is a process of reasoning whereby a probability inference is made from one set of statements (A), such as for a sample of observations, to another statement (B), such as a general conclusion. Thus we infer that if A is the case, then B is probable to the degree P, as specified by a specific value associated with the probability inference, that is symbolically, $A \underset{P}{\supset} B$. In deductive logic, a specific conclusion (B) *necessarily* (not just probably) follows from a set of premises (A) so that $A \supset B$. An inductive inference would be made if one observes five white pigeons in a park and infers that all of the pigeons in the park are probably white. A deductive inference would be made when one reasons that if all of the pigeons in the park are white, then the next pigeon observed will necessarily be white (For an elaboration, see Chapter 12 of McGuigan, 1993a).

Ptolemaic Epicycles

Sun

Copernican Elliptical Orbits

FIGURE 2.4
According to the Ptolemaic
theory, the relative motion of
the planets and sun is one of
complex epicycles. The
Copernican theory describes
the relative motion of planets
more simply as moving in
elliptical orbits about the sun.

reasoned only with deductive logic, concluded that Galileo had committed a logical fallacy (see the Enrichment Material at the end of this chapter for an elaboration). They consequently were greatly alarmed. Even the renowned astronomer Johannes Kepler criticized Galileo.

Although Galileo made a fallacious inference according to the rules of deductive logic, he made a sound (reasonable) inference within the framework of inductive logic. An inductive inference rests on a number of observations from which a certain conclusion is inferred. In walking through a park and observing one white pigeon after another, it is reasonable to inductively infer that the next pigeon will also be white. That conclusion is probably, but not necessarily, true. The next pigeon may be an exception and may turn out to be of another color.

Summary. We see this great issue in the history of Western civilization as follows: The dominant mode of thinking before Galileo was that one accepts the statement of authority as the basis of knowledge and may deductively reason from that. The Ptolemaic theory, for instance, which was compatible with statements in the Bible, served as the basis of knowledge from which deductions were made. Galileo, however, broke with tradition and questioned that knowledge base. He made his own observations that led to a conclusion different from the one handed down by the authority of the church. His observations and conclusions were incompatible with the Ptolemaic theory and with the teachings of authority, but he effectively used the method of inductive reasoning for finding truth.

We now recognize that the inductive method of discovering knowledge is the only one that has withstood the test of time — new knowledge can only be achieved by means of inductive reasoning, by making observations and inductively inferring conclusions from them. It was Galileo's method of scientific argument that formed the beginning of contemporary science with the shift from the use of deductive to inductive reasoning.

The Catholic church was inhospitable to empiricism and the use of inductive reasoning. By challenging the authority of the church, Galileo suffered great personal abuse, including imprisonment. Eventually, though, through great tribulation, the success of Galileo's method led to a change in the *Zeitgeist,* allowing Western culture to emerge from the Dark Ages (*Zeitgeist* is the German word for spirit of the time, wherein similar thoughts and beliefs are shared by many). The philosophy of science thus changed to one of asking about the truth of nature and the nature of truth through empirical and inductive methodology.

The Zeitgeist, the spirit of the times, gradually changed to discovering truth by inductively reasoning to new conclusions from a data base formed by the observation of nature (empiricism).

EMPIRICISM AND THE PROBABILISTIC NATURE OF KNOWLEDGE

The Rejection of Nativism.   Empiricism, the study of observable events in nature in an effort to solve problems, is in direct contrast with **nativism. Nativism is a philosophical position that holds that knowledge is inborn.** It is a doctrine of innate ideas. With the shift from the method of authority to the scientific method of inductive reasoning from observations, empiricism also replaced nativism as the supposed source of knowledge. Finally, it was increasingly recognized and accepted that inductive reasoning must be used in gaining knowledge about nature and that the deductive method, although valuable for other purposes, is not appropriate for discovering new knowledge.

Empiricism (the study of nature as the source of knowledge) has replaced nativism (the outmoded thesis that knowledge is inborn). Furthermore, only inductive, as against deductive, reasoning can lead to new knowledge.

Truth Is Held Only Until Further Notice.   But unfortunately, today we know that we can find no empirical statement that is absolutely true. In spite of our efforts to assert empirical statements that are precisely true with certainty, we must settle for probabilities. All knowledge comes in the form of statements that have a specifiable degree of probability. If the probability is high, then we believe that the statement is probably true (McGuigan, 1993a). However, the history of science has shown many times that what we thought to be true at one time has been revealed by later observations to be incomplete or even false. Prior to Isaac Newton, for instance, we believed that space was filled with ether and that "nature abhorred a vacuum." After Newton, however, we came to understand that space is simply vacant and does not abhor anything. Similarly, chemists used to believe that all matter contained phlogiston, but today's high school student never even hears of the phlogiston theory unless it is in a critical history of chemistry. "Truths" are only stated as sentences that are probable. As the philosopher Herbert Feigl has put it, "scientific truths are held only until further notice."

Strictly speaking, then, we should not even use the word *truth* in science since at best we must settle for statements with high degrees of probability. The word *true* is used only in the sense of an approximation — a true statement is one that has only a high degree of probability.

When reviewing this discussion, a student might think we have merely replaced the scholastic philosophers of the Catholic church with scientific authorities who hand down truth to us in a similar manner. The student who might thus reason, however, should think about an important difference: According to the method of authority, an authority is never to be questioned. On the other hand, *the essence of science is to constantly question authority, to ever be skeptical of what anyone (including oneself) says.* The scientist thus forms a probabilistic statement and, in a sense, challenges other scientists to either corroborate or disprove the statement. The longer the statement resists disconfirmation ("disproof"), the more likely it is to be true (in an approximate sense, of course).

Knowledge is expressed in the form of sentences that have specifiable degrees of probability such that the higher the probability, the more likely the statement is true. However, no empirical statement can ever be absolutely true.

Knowledge Defined. **Knowledge** is fundamentally a statement about nature that has been empirically confirmed. If the statement has been confirmed with a high degree of probability, we believe that it is likely to be true. It is with this general philosophy of science that we will approach all issues throughout this book.

These considerations also indicate that we have been given a probabilistic universe in which to live and the sooner we accept this fact, the better adjusted to reality we will be.

In Retrospect. It is interesting to note that the Copernican theory is preferred over the Ptolemaic theory because it is more parsimonious — it is simpler to describe planets moving about the sun in elliptical orbits than it is to describe the relative motion of planets according to complex epicycles (see Fig. 2.4). As Einstein cemented the point, the motion of two bodies in space is relative, there being no absolute motion such that one is stable and the other is moving. The Ptolemaic and Copernican theories are actually **equivalent descriptions** of the relative movements of planets, one being merely simpler than the other. As we have seen, however, the eventual discarding of the Ptolemaic theory had the impact of helping to dethrone humans by removing the earth (and humans) from the center of the universe. That, along with the later acceptance of evolution theory, shifted humankind to a more realistic, if more humble, place in the universe. Resolution of these issues was critical for the advancement of biological science.

GALILEAN VERSUS ARISTOTELIAN SCIENCE

It is difficult to overemphasize the importance of the shift to the inductive method for scientific reasoning. To understand this we contrast Galileo's method of thinking with that of the Aristotelians.

Aristotelian reasoning used dichotomies and held that causative agents were internal while Galilean reasoning used continua and held that causative agents were external.

Discrete vs. Continuous Variables. The **Aristotelian method** of scientific reasoning is characterized as one in which *classes* **(discrete variables)** rather than *dimensions* **(continuous variables)** dominate. Aristotelian logic, thus, emphasized dichotomies. Aristotelian physicists, for instance, formulated a dichotomy between heaven and earth with the laws of physics differing in each.

In contrast, Galilean physicists emphasized the continuous nature of variables, implying that the same laws of physics applied to both the heavens and the earth.[3]

Causality Resides in the Environment. Another important distinction between Aristotelian and **Galilean reasoning** concerns the nature of **causality.** In Aristotelian reasoning, causality is a characteristic of the object or organism being studied. For instance, to explain why humans are aggressive, an instinct for aggression would be postulated. In contrast, the Galilean view would seek to explain behavior by invoking causes from the environment — an organism is aggressive because of environmental influences. Contemporary psychology similarly holds that behavior is often caused by external stimuli to a large extent, although responses affect the environment too.

Incidently, this discussion is not meant in any way to disparage Aristotle; he was an amazingly accomplished empirical scientist and philosopher; for example,

[3] As you read on, think about whether we are using Aristotelian reasoning in contrasting that method with the Galilean method of reasoning. Why do we sometimes form dichotomies when in fact the underlying variable is a continuous one?

his system of classification of animals and plants was used for some 2000 years until that of Linnaeus finally superseded it in 1750.

Our views of nature have also changed in other respects, as scientists have moved from a mechanical model, based on the physics of Issac Newton, to an information processing model. A Newtonian model views nature as the movement of bodies when acted on by *external forces.* A modern information processing model considers nature as a source of information that is transmitted within cybernetic systems involving organisms.

SCIENCE AND TECHNOLOGY

To some, our discussion of the limits of science may be discouraging. We can only make statements about nature that have degrees of probability and our measurements cannot be specified as 100 percent precise. Such constraints force us to be realistic and accept that there are limitations in our abilities to discover knowledge. Because we cannot know how limited we are, we continue to seek knowledge through research until our current limits are reached.

In some positive sense, the great accomplishments of science speak for themselves. The impartial, objective principles of science are the most rational, demonstratively effective methods of solving problems that humankind has developed. By supporting science, society has benefited from many magnificent discoveries. To emphasize the point, we can look back at various "theories" that were advanced prior to the development of contemporary science. From folklore, for instance, we learn that smoke was blown into the ear for therapeutic purposes and that a warm chicken was held against the body to relieve pain. Such notions have been abandoned by reasonable people although cultural lag is sometimes long and many unsound practices persist. Today monkey heads are still sold in Japan to cure lunacy and the Japanese often make many decisions about their lives (such as when and if to marry) based on astrology. Similar primitive, nonscientific practices exist in the United States and elsewhere throughout the world.

We should, though, recognize that there has been some wisdom in folklore— some ancient practices have turned out to be beneficial and scientifically validated. For example, brewing the bark of plants to produce quinine is an effective therapy for malaria, and herbs such as digitalis are used for medications. Such prescientific practices have been crude hypotheses that were scientifically tested. Those that were validated have joined the body of knowledge, while those that were not, such as astrology, were abandoned by people guided by data.

Basic (Pure) Science. Many accomplishments were possible because **basic (pure) science** is a quest for knowledge for its own sake. Freed from the demands of solving practical problems that have immediate significance, scientists have been able to achieve important statements of knowledge that have impressively advanced our understanding of nature. Einstein's famous equation $E = mc^2$ is one such example; another would be the laws of thermodynamics.

Technology Defined. In contrast to science, **technology (applied science)** attempts to solve everyday, practical problems. The technologist typically applies the methods and findings of science for the purpose of improving our daily lives. The development of nuclear energy to make electricity is one instance of the application

Pure science, freed from immediate demands, has led to great understandings of nature which have benefited society in many ways. For one, it has distinguished between those aspects of folklore that are true and those that are false.

of Einstein's principle E = mc². Likewise, James Watt's invention of the steam engine was largely based on the scientific laws of thermodynamics. Other examples of the applications of scientific knowledge for technological purposes abound.

In basic science we seek knowledge for its own sake. Technology attempts to solve practical problems, often by applying the principles of science.

Among the more important technological fields are those of engineering, which applies the laws of the science of physics, and medicine, which is the technological application of principles of the science of physiology. In addition, scientific psychological learning theory is applied to education, clinical psychology, and other fields.

Science and Technology Are Mutually Facilitating.   Although the distinction between science and technology is important, it should be emphasized that both enterprises are mutually facilitating. Consequently, the fruits of pure (basic) science can often be applied to the solution of technological problems, just as research on technological (applied, practical) problems may provide foundations for scientific advances. The existence of practical problems may make gaps in our scientific knowledge apparent, and technological research can often lead to the development of new principles in science. We can thus replace the Aristotelian dichotomy of science versus technology with a more realistic, Galilean continuum wherein they overlap.

The uses of scientific knowledge have tremendous consequences for society, as, for example, when an invention or discovery enters into everyday cultural use. There were mass shifts in employment opportunities when automation began to perform tasks more efficiently than did humans. Major changes are occurring as the United States moves from being a heavy manufacturing society to one of "high technology" involving computers, chips, and so on and also to a society that is more service oriented.

THE SCIENTIFIC RENAISSANCE

The thoughts and work of Galileo were not his alone, but also products of his times, although he was at the forefront of that *zeitgeist*. The *Zeitgeist* is the period of reawakening from the Dark Ages that included the snowballing of many important scientific accomplishments that flowed from the questioning of authority: the refutation of nativism, the flourishing of empiricism, and the increased use of the inductive method.

Descartes's method of doubt typified the scientific renaissance and the rise of empiricism that led to the burgeoning of science.

Descartes and His Method of Doubt.   René Descartes (1596–1650), typifies the scientific renaissance, primarily because of his use of the **Method of Doubt.** The very act of doubting what authority handed down was indeed an act of great courage. Intellectually unique, it typified the Zeitgeist of the reawakening. Descartes found that he could doubt the existence of everything — of the world, of his body, and even of God, which was heretical in his day. There was only one thing that Descartes could not doubt and that, in essence, was that there was some doubting going on. Since someone was thinking, there must be even more to reality. His reasoning resulted in his famous conclusion *"Cogito Ergo Sum"* ("I think, therefore I am"). Since he was cogitating, he physically existed and on that basis reconstructed his belief in the existence of the world, leading to his proof of the existence of God.

Such an imaginative mind as Descartes's had many diverse thoughts about nature, which included philosophy and mathematics. Principal among Descartes's

FIGURE 2.5
Descartes's conception of
animal spirits flowing through
tubules. His conception of a
reflex arc is illustrated as a
stimulus causing the flow of
animal spirits to in turn cause
the child to withdraw from the
fire.

concepts of biology was that of the **reflex arc** (reflex). Following Greek conceptions, he held that animal spirits *(pneuma)* flowed throughout the tubules ("little nerves") of the body so that an external force (a stimulus) forced the animal spirits (neural activity) through the tubules to mechanically produce a movement (a response depicted in Fig. 2.5). Thus, in modern terminology, a stimulus excites a nerve impulse that is transmitted to the central nervous system and to muscle so that an organism mechanically reacts. Higher, rational mental processes emanated from the soul as it acted on the body through the pineal gland, a small body associated with the midbrain. The movement of the pineal gland directed animal spirits throughout the body to cause willed movements.

Today we know that the pineal gland (pineal body) secretes a hormone called melatonin that affects the estrus cycle. It also is thought to secrete serotonin, which is essential for normal brain functions.

Major Scientific Contributions. Some of the scientists who made biological advances that were especially important for biological psychology are schematized in Figure 2.6. The scientific reawakening from the Dark Ages began with such investigations as those of Vesalius in 1550, who provided the first comprehensive work on human anatomy. In 1660 Harvey experimentally demonstrated principles of blood circulation, showing that blood actually flowed throughout the body. Van Leeuwenhoek (1632–1723) was the first to use the microscope to describe such microorganisms as bacteria and spermatazoa. As happened with many scientific discoveries, the public was slow to intellectually accept them. You can imagine the social unrest that followed when people were told that "small animals" (microorganisms) inhabited their bodies.

In 1687 Newton published his monumental *Principia,* and Linnaeus (1707–1778) published his system of taxonomy, which, as we saw, finally replaced the magnificent system developed some 2000 years earlier by Aristotle. Another major event occurred in 1750 when von Haller demonstrated that tissue is irritable, indicating that muscles contain their own energy.

Other, technological contributions also facilitated the development of science, especially the invention of the printing press and the improvement in traveling conditions. The resulting increase in the ability to communicate replaced isolated

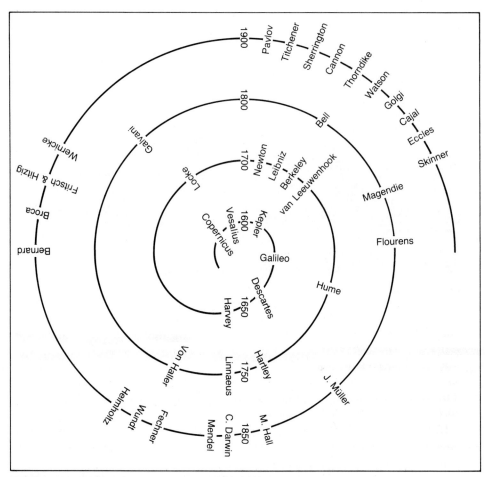

FIGURE 2.6   Scientists who made major accomplishments during and following the renaissance of science. (Adapted from Boring, 1942)

This brief sketch serves to illustrate how science began to flourish as it was freed from theological restrictions.

individual scientific research with a spirit of cooperation, as occurred in budding scientific societies. One of the major characteristics of successful science is cooperation among researchers throughout the world.

Scientific knowledge increased exponentially in the sixteenth, seventeenth, eighteenth, and nineteenth centuries with such landmark discoveries as those of Sir Charles Bell and François Magendie (Fig. 2.6). Among many other contributions, the great French physiologist Claude Bernard (1813–1878) sizably advanced our understanding of endocrinology. Broca in 1861 and Wernicke in 1874 located speech centers in the brain. In 1870 Fritsch and Hitzig demonstrated a localization function in the motor area of the brain by electrically stimulating the cortex. The concept of the reflex arc as developed by Descartes was considerably elaborated by Marshall Hall (1790–1857). Hall held that reflex behavior is unconscious and dependent on the spinal cord, while more complex behavior is dependent upon the brain itself.

The development of the neuron theory awaited a technological advance in staining nervous tissue known as the (Camillo) **Golgi stain technique.** With it

---

CAMILLO GOLGI (1843–1926)

Courtesy The American Physiological Society.

Camillo Golgi was born in Corteno, Italy, and eventually conducted research at the University of Padua where he studied neuroglia (see Chapter 6). In 1872 unfortunate circumstances led him to work in a small hospital for incurable patients where, in spite of the lack of laboratory facili-

ties, he developed his famous method for selective staining of nerve cells. His research in neurohistology, neuropathology, and malaria led him to a distinguished career. Golgi received the Nobel Prize in 1906 for his work on the structure of the nervous system; his Nobel lecture was entitled "The Neuron Doctrine, Theory and Facts." The neuron doctrine, which held that neurons were individual nerve cells that were not joined together, was very controversial at the time. Even though Golgi's staining technique had demonstrated that neurons looked as if they were separated, he held that they were not discrete. His reasoning was that anatomical data gained from dead structures (cadavers) "do not offer any basis firm enough to uphold this doctrine." His erroneous belief was that nerve cells *were* interconnected by continuous neural material.

Ramon Y. Cajal in 1889 anatomically studied neural synapses and described individual neurons. Johannes Müller's important **Law of Specific Energies of Nerves** was promulgated in 1838 in his influential *Handbook on the Physiology of Man.* His law stated, essentially, that we know the world through our nerves. Thus, regardless of how it is stimulated, each sensory nerve leads to one kind of sensation and no other. The sensation does not result because of the nature of the stimulus, but in the nerve connected to the sense organ and in the center where the nerve terminates. Using the eye as an example, no matter how the eye is stimulated (by light waves, by electricity, etc.), visual sensations will occur. We individually verify Müller's law in our own experiences when we see "stars" after we are hit in the head or, although not recommended, when we press on our eyeballs.

The Law of Specific Energies of Nerves holds that each sense organ has its own energy that determines the kind of sensation to which the sense organ will give rise.

Techniques for physiologically studying the brain were developed in the nineteenth century when, for example, in 1824 Pierre Flourens used brain extirpation and Rolando first electrically stimulated the brain to study its functions.

Finally, we must mention the work of the great physiologist Hermann Helmholtz (1821–1894) who, among many accomplishments, first measured the speed of neural impulses.

SANTIAGO RAMÓN Y CAJAL
(1852–1934)

Courtesy The American Physiological Society.

Santiago Ramón y Cajal was born in Petilla, a small village in the Spanish Pyrenees. Eventually he became a professor of normal histology and pathological anatomy at the University of Madrid, where he remained until his death. Cajal received the Nobel Prize in 1906 for his research on the structure of the nervous system. He used Golgi's staining technique, with his own refinements, to study the various cells and their interconnections throughout the nervous systems and sense organs. In his Nobel lecture, "The Structure and Connections of Neurons," he strongly supported the neuron doctrine that nerve cells are separate, independent biological units separated by space. He thus strongly opposed Golgi's view that the neuron doctrine was false. Cajal also conducted pioneering research in embryonic development and degeneration and regeneration in the nervous system.

Actual physical measurements of bodily events such as neural impulses led to the discarding of spiritualistic models of the body and the flourishing of physiological sciences.

The importance of these selected empirical research findings that typify the 1800s cannot be overemphasized. For one, they were critical in separating the science of how the body functions from spiritualistic explanations of the classical (often religiously oriented) philosophers. For instance, when Helmholtz actually measured the velocity of neural impulses, he helped to separate physiology as a materialistic science from the spiritual *pneuma*-type "explanations" of behavior. The argument was that if thought was a **metaphysical,** spiritualistic phenomenon, then it should occur instantaneously and be impossible to measure. When Helmholtz actually measured neural activity ("the flow of animal spirits"), metaphysical explanations of behavior became disfavored. Helmholtz thereby contributed mightily to the empirical scientific analysis of behavior that was rapidly developing in the 1800s.

This brief mentioning of some landmark accomplishments also provides a broad perspective for the beginnings of our contemporary knowledge explosion. Because they are so numerous, it would be impossible to briefly isolate similar important achievements for the twentieth century, yet throughout this book we will select and highlight some accomplishments that are critical for biological psychology. However, the magnificent development of **evolution theory** in the nineteenth century has had such staggering consequences for society at large, for science in general, and for biological psychology in particular that we will now enlarge on it.

This is particularly important as this text applies principles of evolution theories in numerous ways as we work our way through contemporary biological science.

THEORIES OF EVOLUTION

Much of biological psychology is dedicated to the study of the history of species of organisms, including *Homo sapiens.* Evolution theory helps us to understand how some special characteristics of animals and prehistoric humans have facilitated the survival of species. Human speech, for instance, had immeasurable survival value —we can imagine those early humans who were facile in a primitive sort of speech warning each other of specific dangers of the jungle. Those primitive people who were not able to effectively communicate probably failed to survive, and their hereditary characteristics are not present today. It was Charles Darwin who most assiduously developed evolution theory.

Charles Robert Darwin (1809–1882)

Darwin's powerful book *The Origin of Species* was published in November 1859. It precipitated an intellectual revolution with consequences that continue even to this day. (The complete title was *On the Origin of Species by Means of Natural Selection, or the Preservation of Favoured Races in the Struggle For Life.*) The entire printing of 1250 copies was sold out on the day of issue. Had he not published the book precisely then, he would not have received the scientific credit (or the abuse) that followed. Instead his fellow naturalist Alfred R. Wallace would have received those plaudits (and criticisms) because Wallace was ready to independently publish his own theory of evolution. There remains today, as there was then, some controversy as to whose theory, Darwin's or Wallace's, should receive priority. History has decided in Darwin's favor not only because of some small amount of temporal priority, but also because his data base was much more extensive. The fact remains, however, that the two contemporaneously developed similar theories, once again illustrating the power of the *Zeitgeist.*

Darwin was a student at Edinburgh ("Ed-in-burr-oh") University in Scotland, where for two years he suffered through what he described as "intolerably dull" medical lectures. He then studied for the clergy for three years at Cambridge University where his "time was sadly wasted," except for his field trips to study botany. In his observations of nature, he learned much that was later to be of value. The techniques acquired then contributed to his great effectiveness in collecting and organizing specimens on his famous voyage around the world on the HMS *Beagle* (he was not paid for that research; scholars of that time were usually self-supporting).

Darwin was chronically ill, suffering at different times in his life from nausea, stomach disorders, and sustained fatigue. He was thought by many to be a hypochondriac, which may or may not be true. In either case, it is ironic that such an enfeebled person developed the principle of the **survival of the fittest,** an irony that Darwin himself realized.

Darwin's publication of the *Origin of Species* was followed by six more books. Of most importance for evolution theory was his *Descent of Man and Selection in*

Relation to Sex, published a dozen years after the *Origin.* Another of his works formed a basis for contemporary gravitational physiology (the study of the effects of gravity on organisms)—his 1880 *The Power of Movement in Plants* was written with one of his four sons, Francis. Throughout all of his books Darwin employed a strategy of *combining empirical observations with interpretations and speculations as to their meaning* so that his method was not that of a mere empiricist. Rather, as is characteristic of scientific genius, he carefully observed and then developed a theory to account for his systematic data.

The Evolution of Evolution Theory

There are two essential components of classical evolution theory, those concerning variation and those concerning natural selection.

CAUSES OF VARIATION

Evolution theory involves variations (characteristics that result from unique combinations in the offspring of traits from two different parents) and natural selection *(individuals who survive life's difficulties pass their favorable characteristics onto their progeny).*

Individual differences (**variations**) among organisms include such characteristics as height, weight, and intelligence. Some of these individual differences are caused by environmental influences such as diet. Other variations, however, result because a male and a female produce offspring that are different from either parent. Darwin emphasized this source of variability, but he did not know about the genetic processes that are responsible for it. It was sufficient for him to establish that variations among organisms could be passed from one generation to the next and that some of those variations resulted in novel characteristics. It was up to nature to determine whether such novel characteristics had *survival value.*

NATURAL SELECTION AND THE SURVIVAL OF THE FITTEST

The dangers that organisms experience lead to the process of **natural selection.** Some cope with the threats to life and others succumb. In a sense, nature selects among members of a species such that there is survival of the fittest. The novel characteristics of those who fail are nonadaptive and die with them. In general, the least adapted succumb to the dangers of the "jungle." This is seen to apply to creatures of antiquity as well as to those of the modern cement jungle in which *we* seek to survive. It is as if "nature" proceeds in this trial-and-error process to see if the changes are improvements in the species. In the struggle for existence, those individuals who have the most adaptive characteristics have the greatest chance of surviving. The trials of nature thus help select for those traits that facilitate survival. The traits that are failures lead to death and are not passed on.

The successful process of artificial breeding (insemination) contributed to the formulation of Darwin's principle of natural selection. In artificial breeding, the semen of males selected for specific desirable characteristics is inserted into a female of the same species. The offspring can have superior qualities such as those achieved for the Arabian horse. Artificial insemination has resulted in increased variation among and within species. The artificial breeders then preserved the superior varieties. Darwin reasoned by analogy with artificial breeding that increased variation occurs naturally, resulting in new characteristics in a species.

In trying to understand the mechanisms by which natural selection occurred and what traits were selected for, Darwin was influenced by the reasoning of Thomas Malthus (1766–1834). Malthus, an economist, believed that the realization of a successful society will always be hindered by the miseries created by populations growing faster than the supply of food. **Malthus's Law** holds that food production increases arithmetically while populations grow geometrically. This means that there eventually would not be enough food for the faster growing population. At that point the poor would fail to survive and the population would be stabilized at a level commensurate with the amount of food available. Darwin again reasoned by analogy. His conclusion was that in the struggle for survival, only the fittest would survive. The weak would perish.

To Summarize. Darwin's principle of natural selection holds that in the struggle for existence, some variations among organisms of a given species facilitate successful adaptation, relative to organisms lacking those traits. Natural selection leads to survival of the fittest.

The principles of variation and of natural selection are important in biological psychology because they help us to understand why organisms behave as they do. A trial novel trait may be successful and be passed on for many generations, contributing to the effective behavior of a contemporary organism. Our attempts to understand contemporary behavior thus can be framed within the perspective of a long-term understanding of the evolution of species. The importance of evolution theory cannot be underestimated. As Sir John Eccles stated, "This theory stemming from Darwin must rank as one of the grandest conceptual achievements of man" (1967, p. 5).

But we must never forget that science, too, evolves! Darwin's formulation of a theory of evolution was an initial approximation offered many years ago, on which scientists seek to build. Shortly we will raise some questions about evolution theory as we attempt to be self-critical in the interest of improving the status of our knowledge.

Darwinian and Neo-Darwinian Theories Contrasted

Genetic Recombination Increases Variation. **Neo-Darwinian theories** were developed in the 1930s and 1940s by such scientists as T. H. Dobzhansky and Julian Huxley. Their modification of Darwin's theory of evolution incorporated Gregor **Mendel's** (1822–1884) **laws of genetics,** which, as we have noted, were not available to Darwin. Because of those principles of genetics, we now understand that new combinations of genes are produced in progeny by parents with different sets of genes. The resulting new genetic characteristics are heritable so that they are transmitted from one generation to the next. With recombination of genetic material from two different sources, unique individuals are created.

Mutations Increase Variation. Changes in the genetic code that are passed along to progeny also can occur by random **mutations.** A gene mutation is a modification in the genetic material of an individual. A mutation results in an individual with characteristics different from those of the parents. The process may be thought

Gene mutations, modifications in genetic material, are inheritable and are responsible for some changes in the characteristics of organisms.

of as nature's trial-and-error method, a blind groping, to provide possibilities for change that may be beneficial.

Mutations may occur naturally, as when one white-eyed fruitfly (Drosophila) suddenly appeared among normal red-eyed fruitflies. When the white-eyed fruitfly was bred, its progeny and their descendents had white eyes. Mutations may also be intentionally produced by doses of radiation (e.g., X-rays may increase two hundredfold the frequency of mutations). In either case, the changes occur in the genetic material in an individual's chromosomes. **Chromosomes,** contained in each cell of an organism's body, are complex molecules that contain codes for producing the protein required for cellular growth and functioning. The genetic material (DNA) in chromosomes contains the plans for the development of a species. When those plans are altered, as through mutations, there is variation in the organism's characteristics.

Few mutations are effective in helping the organism to survive. Those that do have survival value are passed in the genetic code to its progeny. An instance of a favorable mutation would be one in which a chromosome in a sperm cell is altered so that the offspring will be resistant to some disease. The surviving offspring may then continue to pass on the favorable mutation (e.g., one for resistance to bacteria) to future generations. Most mutations, though, are disadvantageous in that the individuals who possess them die and thus do not pass their genes along to the next generation.

Neo-Darwinian theory thus provides a biological explanation for how the favorable variations among species are passed on from parent to progeny, namely by the genetic transmission of hereditary information. Contemporary evolution theory is thus a two-step process in which there is first, the production of variation by means of mutations as well as by parental recombination of genes, both of which lead to genetic variability; and second, natural selection of those unique individuals who have genes that facilitate adaptation to the environment. Individuals with those favorable genes thus have an increased probability of surviving and procreating progeny who will survive and continue their particular variety of species.

Contemporary (Neo-Darwinian) evolution theory adds principles of genetics to Darwin's original theory, thus helping to explain how beneficial genetic variations are passed from generation to generation.

The major difference between Darwin's principles of evolution and contemporary principles is the incorporation of Mendel's laws of genetics.

TWO EVOLUTIONARY CRISES

The evolutionary process forms a continuum from the time at which life originated to the present status of humankind. As pointed out by Eccles (1967), two major events in this scenario, however, are not well understood. The first is how life originated in the first place, and the second is the origin of a human mind different from that of the lower animals. These two events were major turning points in our history and have been referred to as evolutionary crises.

The Origin of Life

There are two major theories as to the source of the organic materials necessary for constructing simple life cells from complex molecules: (1) They came from outer space on meteors and comets having originated in clouds of gas in stars; alternatively, (2) those complex molecules were formed when the earth itself was formed.

In either case, there are two leading theories as to where the organic materials generated simple life cells: the "primordial soup" and the "primordial clay" theories.

THE "PRIMORDIAL SOUP" THEORY

The long-favored notion is that life emerged from primitive oceans after millions of years of complex chemical reactions. The initial evolution was a transition from inorganic and crystalline matter to organic and molecular material. Any of a number of kinds of energy, such as lightning, shock waves, ultraviolet radiation, or hot volcanic ash could have converted the early surface materials into organic substances. A commonly accepted hypothesis is that the evolution to organic molecules occurred using photosynthesis (synthesis of chemical compounds with the aid of light). Eigen et al. (1981) have applied Darwin's principles to evolution far below the level of organisms to account for the creation of molecules. For instance, the principle of natural selection, they hold, applies to the complexity of large molecules. Primitive earth had a temperature and composition similar to those of today. These elements must have combined in numerous ways. Consequently, during early evolution an enormous number of chance combinations were tested; most were unsuccessful but some survived to form today's molecules.

One view is that life originated in or near hydrothermal vents on the ocean floor. Hydrothermal vent systems, through which all the world's oceans pass about every 10 million years, could have been favorable to life's beginnings because hydrogen, nitrogen, compounds of sulphur, carbon, and several metals are present in them. The heat from the earth's core could have provided the energy necessary to assemble and create the components of life from them. At that time, 4 billion years ago, the earth was relentlessly pounded by meteorites and lethal ultraviolet radiation that was not filtered by the atmosphere that exists today. The fragile compounds that might have led to the first life could have survived only on the ocean's floors, buttressing the theory that life originated there. Although the super-hot temperatures and pressures at the vents were far too great for the fragile building blocks of life to withstand (the vents can have a temperature as high as 700°C), the surrounding water may have been about 2°C. Consequently, if life was not formed at the vents, it could have been formed and/or maintained where the vent interfaces with the rest of the ocean.

All conceptions of the "primordial soup" from which life arose agree that it included not only certain amino acids, but also other substances that were molecules that do not exist naturally today. Regardless of just how, in some way chemical energy was extracted from the molecules in the "soup" to form early life forms. Fossil records suggest that primitive living cells existed in the oceans some 3.5 billion years ago and chemical evidence for life was some 3.77 billion years ago, both of which are within 1 billion years of the time when the earth was formed (Fig. 2.7). Within the earth's first billion years, there was thought to be a window of time when existing life forms first started. If life emerged before that time, which is a possibility, heavy bombardment by asteroids probably sterilized the planet by turning oceans into steam and destroying any earlier forms of life. The process by which life itself emerged from these organic molecules mixing around in a primordial soup is poorly

The favored theory for the first evolutionary crisis is that organic molecules were mixing in the oceans when some kind of energy source from the ocean or atmosphere created the first living cells.

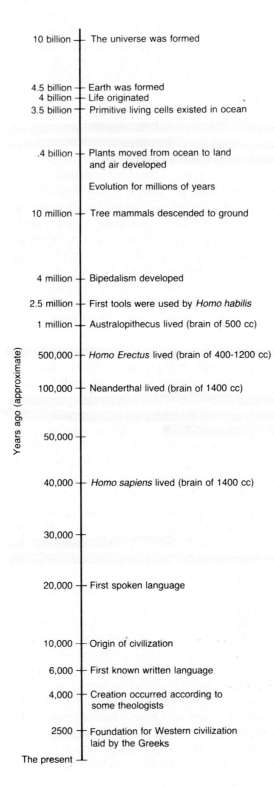

Years ago (approximate)

10 billion	The universe was formed
4.5 billion	Earth was formed
4 billion	Life originated
3.5 billion	Primitive living cells existed in ocean
.4 billion	Plants moved from ocean to land and air developed
	Evolution for millions of years
10 million	Tree mammals descended to ground
4 million	Bipedalism developed
2.5 million	First tools were used by *Homo habilis*
1 million	Australopithecus lived (brain of 500 cc)
500,000	*Homo Erectus* lived (brain of 400-1200 cc)
100,000	Neanderthal lived (brain of 1400 cc)
50,000	
40,000	*Homo sapiens* lived (brain of 1400 cc)
30,000	
20,000	First spoken language
10,000	Origin of civilization
6,000	First known written language
4,000	Creation occurred according to some theologists
2500	Foundation for Western civilization laid by the Greeks
The present	

FIGURE 2.7
A time scale indicating major evolutionary events in the development of life and civilization. Not drawn to scale.

understood. However, the steps in the process of chemical evolution are yielding to advances by biochemists.

However it did actually occur, and there is much research effort being directed to this critical question, the origin of life was an event that was amazingly improbable. It was so improbable, in fact, that it probably happened only once in the history of the earth. It is even thought by many knowledgeable on the subject that we are the only intelligent life in some 20,000 galaxies. How sobering it is to reflect on the tragedy that would befall the human race and indeed the entire galaxy if this life, this result of billions of years, were terminated.

Of all single-celled organisms, one is probably the last ancestor shared by all of today's life forms. That organism thus appears to be at the very base of the evolutionary tree. From it, apparently, all other organisms evolved. The likely candidate has been identified as having lived at least 3.5 billion years ago and resembled today's one-celled organisms called eocytes. Like contemporary eocytes, the organism probably lived in hot water and obtained its energy by processing sulphur (which releases hydrogen sulfide gas and is what makes sulphur springs smell like rotten eggs).

THE "PRIMORDIAL CLAY" THEORY

Another theory about the origin of life is that it evolved in clay rather than in the primordial seas. Recent evidence has indicated that clay can store and transfer energy. Storing and transfering energy are two essential properties for the generation of life. This theory holds that inorganic proto-organisms in clay were precursors of the building block molecules of life, such as amino acids. Such inorganic proto-organisms may also have provided a transitional evolutionary structure for life.

The clay theory holds that the first cells developed from molecules that existed in clay, but in either theory, those first organisms contained some kind of genes.

Regardless of the "primordial soup" vs. "primordial clay" controversy, there is good reason to believe that the first organisms in the seas and in clay had genes of some kind. Those genes passed on life to future organisms and were even capable of some kind of primitive mutation. It is thought also that the genes evolved on their own, leading to variations in the forms of future organisms.

Photosynthesis Was Critical. A number of critical steps in the evolution of these simple organisms were necessary for them to evolve. One was the development of aerobic **photosynthesis** by blue-green algae so that oxygen could be produced. Some 400 million years ago plant cells then moved from the oceans to land where air as we know it developed. Another critical event occurred when primitive plant life evolved into flowering plants that yielded seeds as food for animal life. Darwin referred to this evolutionary event as an "abominable mystery."

The chemical evolution of life seems to have been a random process whereby single cellular organisms that could gradually evolve were created.

Other Critical Developments. Multicellular organisms continuously evolved in the oceans to form animal life that could eventually invade the land. For this invasion to occur, there were two critical requirements: (1) The animals had to mechanically support themselves, and (2) they had to breathe oxygen. The requirement for mechanical support was satisfied with the development of back bones, which led to the vertebrates (those species with spines). One hypothesis is that organisms that developed back bones had an advantage in resisting the currents of streams as they sought food farther inland from the oceans.

Single-cell organisms gradually evolved into multicellular organisms that became, eventually, primitive animals that could invade the land and breathe oxygen.

There also was a change of the fin as in the ray fish to a single, stout leglike element, as in Crossopterygii; the limb of the land vertebrate may have derived from

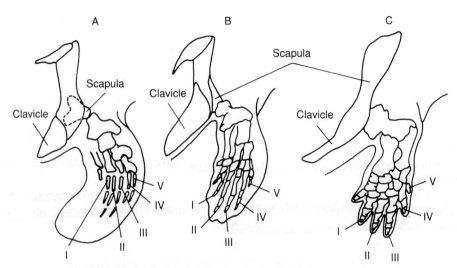

FIGURE 2.8   A representation of how the limb of a land amphibian (c) possibly derived through a hypothesized intermediate (b) from a Crossopterygian fish (a). Such a primitive amphibian is thought to have first invaded land from the oceans. The five digits are indicated by I–V. (Adapted from Storer, 1943)

that (Fig. 2.8). Some boney fishes had a swim bladder that was lunglike and some had nostrils and other structures that enabled them to breathe air in shallow, murky water. Those first **amphibians,** thought to be Crossopterygii, then developed a lung and associated structures so that they could directly consume oxygen on land. To escape the crowded oceans where the oxygen supply was limited, these primitive amphibians, nearly suffocating, began to crawl onto the beaches. Once on land, over an extended period of time, a great variety of complex animals developed. The animals that appeared came in huge numbers and some in bizarre forms. The variety of animals was much greater than today and many would look strange to us. For example the *Hallucigenia* had a heavy eyeless head and an elongated trunk supported by seven pairs of stiltlike spines. It was 1 centimeter long and had seven feeding tentacles on its upper side, each ending with a snapperlike structure perhaps used for feeding.

The cause of this evolutionary explosion is unknown, although one theory is that there were major shifts in the chemistry of the oceans and perhaps an increase in oxygen level to allow these complex animals to emerge. Prominent among these animals was the dinosaur that ruled its age. With the extinction of dinosaurs, other species roamed more freely and thus found various kinds of fruit. Mammals especially benefited by improved diet, which increased the rate of evolution.

Stereoscopic Vision and Prehensile Hands.   One form of mammal adapted to the tree environment, evolved stereoscopic vision and prehensile hands. Both of these abilities facilitated adaptation to tree life. **Stereoscopic vision** allowed perception of distance (depth perception) because the eyes were separated. **Prehensile hands** (*prehensile* means "ability to grasp") allowed the grasping of limbs of trees, and, with the ability for thumb and fingers to meet, were also critical for the later development of tools.

With the demise of the tree environment about 10 million years ago, the tree

Development of prehensile hands was critical in evolution, first by allowing mammals to live in tree environments, and later to develop and use tools.

mammals descended to the ground. Then about 4 million years ago it is thought that **bipedalism** (locomoting on two rather than four feet) developed along with a rapid increase in the size of the brain.

Bipedalism Was Important. Walking on two legs, one controversial hypothesis holds, increased the attraction between the sexes; more frequent mating thus produced more progeny. Bipedalism also freed the arms for more efficiently gathering food and carrying infants. This ability to use the hands while standing up was tremendously important for both the later use of tools and the development of culture in general.

Not only is it amazing that these developments occurred, but it is phenomenal that they occurred in the order that was necessary for our evolution, developments that have been described in our evolutionary history as "pure luck."

However life originated, we do have a fairly good understanding of how the human body evolved. The sequences in the evolutionary chain are rather well documented (although some hold that there are "missing links"); some of the important occurrences were represented in Figure 1.1. Let us now consider where in time the second evolutionary crisis occurred—that of the origin of mind.

Bipedalism in evolution allowed mammals to stand on two feet, facilitating the use of hands.

The Origin of Mind

From Homo habilis to Neanderthal. The oldest human artifacts ever found, important for providing clues to the evolution of humans, apparently are primitive cutting tools constructed in Central Africa about 2.5 million years ago. About 300 stone implements were thought to have been fashioned by *Homo habilis*, the first species of prehistoric humans to devise tools. The inhabitants of the region had been forced by a climate that had turned dry to supplement their vegetarian diet by hunting. The tools were generally smaller than a thumb and have near-random shapes because they were produced by flaking away pieces of quartz to form sharp edges.

Right handedness is almost certainly universally human, indicating that it is a biological endowment. Corballis (1989) holds that cerebral asymmetry (linked to handedness, see Chapter 11) is more marked and extensive in humans than in other animals. Consequently, brain laterality provides a criterion for assessing human uniqueness. Both right handedness and left cerebral representation of language may go back to *Homo habilis*, 2 to 3 million years ago, but a distinctively human mode of cognitive representation may have emerged perhaps 1.5 million years ago.

The second evolutionary crisis was the origin of what we think of as contemporary mind, which perhaps first occurred in the Neanderthals.

Australopithecus, who lived in Africa about 3 million years ago, was the earliest ancestor of humankind that was completely distinguishable from the apes. They walked erect and used primitive pebble tools, although their brains were still the size of those of apes (about 500 cubic centimeters [cc]) (see Fig. 2.9). About half a million years ago, *Homo erectus*, with a brain capacity of about 900 to 2000 cc, lived in Java, China, Africa, and Europe, where they domesticated fire. The Neanderthal race lived about 100,000 years ago in Europe and Asia, used primitive stone tools and fire, and may well have used animal skins to clothe themselves. Their brain capacity is estimated at about 1400 cc, which is about the same as that of modern humans.

In considering the second evolutionary crisis, Eccles (1967) speculates that Neanderthals may have possessed a human mind. He reasoned that they had a rudimentary spirituality because they buried their dead using a ceremonial burial

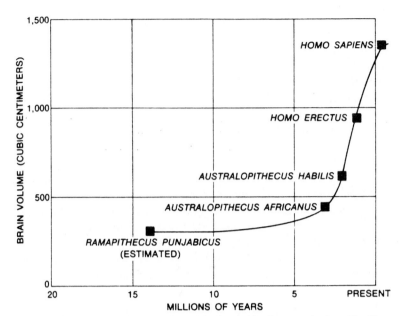

FIGURE 2.9   The human brain almost quadrupled in size over the last 15 million years, most increases being within the last 2 million years. (From Miller, 1981)

custom that may be the first evidence of the evolutionary process of self-consciousness. They could have been aware of their own mortality since only one who knows that he or she will die is likely to be concerned about the death of others. Neanderthals thus may have conceived of the living person as more than just a body, as also having a conscious or spiritual existence. This implies that Neanderthals had a self-awareness similar to what we experience today — they thought others were like themselves.

However, other motives for burying the dead were possible. Perhaps they feared the spirits, were asking the spirits to protect them, or buried bodies to keep them from being devoured by animals.

Wherever and however it occurred, in our long history there was a break of some sort and humans became cognitively different from lower animals. It is not that the other animals are unintelligent; rather, it is that humankind seems to be the only species that is aware of itself and of the future and the past: As has been said, although animals may know, only humans know that they know.

Neanderthals were superseded by *Homo sapiens* (modern humans), probably about 35,000 to 40,000 years ago, but questions about their relationships continue. One view is that Neanderthals became extinct by evolving into modern humans. One reason for this view is that there is a continuity in characteristics suggesting that Neanderthals are direct ancestors of *Homo sapiens*. Another view is that the two coexisted, which, if true, raises questions about whether they fought with each other and competed for the limited resources available, or whether they lived peacefully together and even interbred. In any case, we still do not know just how Neanderthals died out. The question as to where modern humans arose, therefore, is far from settled, but a prominent conclusion is Africa. The inference is that there was an

African "founder" population that migrated and then gave rise to all non-African populations.

As a wandering race, *Homo sapiens* traveled over Europe, Asia, Africa, America, and Australia. Early humans seem to have been confined to the tropical regions but later migrated to the north, developed fire, and clothed themselves to protect their bodies from the elements. In order to hunt large animals, they learned to cooperate. All of these advances required intelligence. Those who survived the environmental changes may well have had larger, more highly developed brains and muscular coordination leading to advanced intelligence and cognitive processes.

Use of Language. Our earliest evidence of a spoken language is from southern France and northern Spain about 20,000 years ago. A highly civilized people capable of symbolic thought lived there, as evidenced by paintings and carvings that have been preserved in their caves. However, theirs was not a written language. As we have seen, that magnificent achievement awaited the Sumerians some 6000 years ago.

Development of spoken and then written language ranks as the highest achievement in human evolutionary development.

The Uniqueness of Humans. Looking back at this evolutionary chain, there seems to have been no central line leading steadily from one-celled organisms to humankind. Instead, evolution has been a process of intricate branching (see Fig. 1.1). Being so intricate and branched, it is likely that our evolutionary process is unique and not repeatable. Apparently, no species has ever evolved twice.

What does this imply about our previous question concerning life elsewhere in the universe? Many consider life elsewhere that is humanlike or even superhuman-like as highly improbable. As Eccles has stated, "There are certainly no humanoids [human-like creatures] elsewhere in our solar system, but the possibility of some extremely lowly life is not wholly excluded as regards Mars" (1967, p. 20). One would think that humanoids could only evolve elsewhere if there is an environment like earth's.

Commonality of DNA. One quite remarkable feature of life is that the same **DNA** code seems to be shared by all living things. (DNA as we discuss later stands for "deoxyribonucleic acid" and is the hereditary material located on chromosomes contained in the nucleus of cells.) One interpretation is that in the evolution of species over a period of some 2 billion years, no new aspects of the code have been added or lost. This interpretation is compatible with the hypothesis that life arose only once and that all living things stem from this one highly improbable event. An alternative possibility, though, is that existing genetic codes are the most efficient. Other forms of life that had codes other than DNA died out so that the present one is the only one that survived.

SCIENTIFIC CONTROVERSIES
ABOUT EVOLUTION THEORIES

Falsification of Religious Creation. As you can well imagine, the *Origin of Species* created considerable controversy when it was first published. One reason was that it contradicted the consensual belief that God had created all species, including humans, in six days. Estimates were offered by some theologians that the creation occurred at specific times, such as in October of 4004 B.C. This controversy was soon settled in the nineteenth century when science established that organisms had a history of hundreds of millions, rather than only thousands of years. Slow evolution rather than instantaneous creation thus became tenable.

Scientific theories, including those of evolution, are subject to continuous modification in the light of new data. Consequently, although there is unanimity about the basic principles, scientists continually debate aspects of evolutionary theory.

Gradual vs. Sporadic Evolution.   It should be noted, however, that scientists even today disagree about various aspects of any evolution theory. For instance, there are two opposing views about the pace and character of evolution, a theory of gradualism versus one of sporadic "jumps." The former holds that the evolution of species was by small changes at a smooth, consistent rate. Some evidence consonant with the gradualism theory is that the fossil tooth structure of small tree-dwelling North American primates indicates a slow change. Over a 1-million-year period, the jaw gradually shortened, front teeth gradually enlarged, and all teeth moved closer together. These fossil records are sufficiently complete and there are no major gaps.

The contrasting theory holds that changes were greater, that they occurred sporadically and quickly, and then were followed by long periods of no change. Perhaps, though, this theory exists because of missing fossil data that, if found, would show the continuum assumed by the theory of gradualism. In either case, however, a theory of instantaneous creationism of species is disconfirmed by the data.

Further Dethroning of Humankind.   The consequences of Darwin's theory that humans were animals continuous with other animals created a Copernican-scale controversy. We were not merely a descendent of apes but, worse, just a part of the whole conglomerate of organisms that fought for survival with tooth, fang, and claw. We were descendents of single-celled organisms from the primordial slime. Perhaps anticipating this controversy, in *The Origin* Darwin did not include humans in the evolutionary struggle. However, a dozen years later in *The Descent of Man*, he did include humans in the evolutionary chain. The social impact was to continue the dethroning of humankind from the unique status that started with the acceptance of Copernicus's heliocentric theory.

Why Are Species of Animals So Well Matched with Their Environments?   Darwin's theory of natural selection held that as environments change, some animals survive better than others. For example, long-necked giraffes survived better than short-necked giraffes, for instance, because they could reach higher to eat the leaves off trees. Natural variation among organisms thus led to the survival of some species.

Darwin's theory held, for instance, that only giraffes with long necks could survive. In contrast, the theory of random genetic mutations held that only those giraffes survived that, through mutations, developed long necks.

In contrast, a theory that incorporated mutations offered a different explanation. A random genetic mutation theory held that there were first changes in the animal population, regardless of changes in the environment. Once the giraffes changed (developing longer necks through mutations), they sought a new environment to take advantage of that change. According to this theory, then, species are so well matched to their environments because mutations caused changes that then led to their seeking better environments in order to survive.

Darwin's explanation is further weakened because it does not answer the question of why other species without long necks survived in the same region with the giraffes. How, for instance, did antelopes, deer, and other foragers survive without long necks?

Do Organisms Inherit Acquired Characteristics?   Yet another controversy has been between Darwin's theory of evolution and the theory of the inheritance of **acquired characteristics.** The essence of this latter theory is that environmentally acquired characteristics taken on during the lifetime of one generation of species are inherited by the next. For instance, the progeny of fish that live in a dark cave should acquire the characteristic of having nonfunctional eyes. However, this theory of the inheritance of acquired characteristics has been thoroughly disconfirmed. In this example, fish that have lived in darkness for a number of generations still have functional eyes when restored to light. Their genetic material for developing eyes remained constant and the acquired characteristic of blindness was not passed on from generation to generation.

The theory of heritable acquired characteristics has had serious advocates, sometimes with disastrous consequences, as when the theory was applied to the Soviet Union's agricultural program by Trofim Lysenko. Since the theory of inheritance of acquired characteristics emphasizes the importance of environmental influences, it was quite compatible with the materialism of communist philosophy. Lysenko attempted to improve agricultural production by concentrating on environmental influences instead of hereditary ones. Lysenko believed that each generation of successful crops would pass on its favorable characteristics, regardless of its genetic material. Dramatic failures in the agricultural production of the former Soviet Union followed.

The disconfirmation of the theory was critical in our understanding of genetics and of why organisms possess the characteristics that they do. It also facilitated the development of contemporary evolution theory.

WHO IS OUR CLOSEST RELATIVE?

Leading to this interesting question, Darwin concluded that "the difference in mind between man and the higher animals, great as it is, certainly is one of degree and not of kind" (1874, p. 193). A common answer is that our closest relative is the gorilla or orangutan. An early argument in favor of the orangutan was that it has anatomical features resembling those of the human, but this is hardly a sound datum for such an inference. More serious studies of relationships among humans, chimpanzees, and gorillas indicate that humankind's ancestors probably walked on their five knuckles just as present-day chimps and gorillas do.

Modern biochemical analysis tells us that at the molecular level, humans and chimpanzees are at least 98 percent identical, possibly close enough to make a hybrid species possible (Lovejoy, 1981; Miyamoto, Slightom, & Goodman, 1987). Research comparing chemicals (albumin and transferase) in the blood of humans and other primates suggests the gorilla or orangutan as our closest relative. Sensitive comparisons using radioactive tracers yield data that indicate that it is perhaps the chimpanzee. Genetic research indicates that there is a gene that is present in both people and in chimpanzees and gorillas, suggesting that the chimpanzee and the gorilla are our closest cousins. Humans and chimpanzees apparently had a common ancestor who lived some 4.5 million years ago.[4]

Various biological research indicates that the chimpanzee and perhaps the gorilla have a common ancestor with humans. This would make them our closest relatives, but not our ancestors.

With this understanding of how contemporary science, and biological science in particular, developed, we will now turn to how a science developed that focused on mental processes. That development led to biological psychology.

[4] Yet other criteria can be used to answer this question, such as the species that produces the most similar milk. In this case one would apparently conclude that it is the donkey. As interesting as this issue is, we are not going to settle it here.

EMPHASIS ON A MAJOR CYBERNETIC PRINCIPLE—THE BIOLOGICAL AND SCIENTIFIC VALUES OF FEEDBACK

Feedback, in a very general sense, is at the base of all kinds of progress. Without knowledge of the consequences of an act or event, there is no guidance for improvement. One can envision the evolutionary process as having successfully followed this principle such that the consequences of nature's trials resulted in some successes and some failures. The successes, those organisms who survived in the struggle for existence, fed back their genetic material for prolongation of the species while the nonadaptive genes were discarded.

In an analogous manner, we can think of scientific successes as having fed back reinforcing results that sustained them. On the other hand, scientific failures, lacking rewarding consequences, became extinguished. Scientists receive feedback in the form of knowledge of results that may confirm or disconfirm their acts. We have studied many examples of discovery, formulation of new principles, and invention of instruments that have been reinforcing and thus advanced science (see Fig. 2.6). Feedback from scientific research may also indicate blind alleys or the need for improvement. The disconfirmation of the theory of the inheritance of acquired characteristics, for instance, provided feedback that led away from a false evolutionary path and toward a true one. In these ways, we accumulate scientific knowledge in which we have confidence and discard false statements.

ENRICHMENT MATERIAL

Viewed within deductive logic, the fallacy that Galileo committed is known as the fallacy of affirming the consequent. In this instance, in the form of a logical syllogism, it goes as follows:

Premise 1:	If a is true, then b is true
Premise 2:	b is true
Conclusion (invalid):	Therefore a is true

Thus his fallacy was:

Premise 1:	If the Copernican theory is true (a), then Galileo's observations of the phases of Venus are true (b).
Premise 2:	Galileo's observations of the phases of Venus are true (b).
Conclusion (invalid):	Therefore the Copernican theory (a) is true.

That was the invalid conclusion reached by Galileo. His was a fallacy in deductive logic because, in deductive reasoning, inferences must conform to the rules of deductive logic. A valid inference that follows those rules yields a conclusion that is necessarily true, assuming the premises (such as 1 and 2) are themselves true. The valid inference would be as follows:

Premise 1:	If *a* is true, then *b* is true
Premise 2:	*a* is true
Conclusion (valid):	Therefore *b* is true

That is, the scholastics thought Galileo should have reasoned:

Premise 1:	If the Copernican theory is true *(a)*, then Galileo's observation of the phases of Venus are true *(b)*.
Premise 2:	The Copernican theory is true *(a)*.
Conclusion (valid):	Therefore Galileo's observation of the phases of Venus are true *(b)*.

Obviously the inference according to deductive logic was not the truth that Galileo sought. Rather, he sought to make the inference represented in the first paradigm that meant that he simply could not use deductive logic. His revolutionary reasoning required the use of inductive, probability logic, which is what caused all of the fuss. But he showed that new knowledge can only be acquired through the inductive (not the deductive) method.

KEY TERMS

Acquired characteristics—A disconfirmed theory that environmentally acquired characteristics taken on during the lifetime of one generation of species are inherited by the next.

Amphibians—Organisms that are characterized by glands in the skin without external scales, gills during development, and eggs that have no membranes around the embryos (members of the class amphibia, subphylum vertebrata, phylum chordata).

Aristotelian method—Scientific reasoning in which classes (discrete variables) rather than dimensions (continuous variables) dominate.

Bipedalism—Standing and locomoting on two rather than four feet. Tree mammals supposedly descended to the ground 4 million years ago and became bipedalic.

Causality—The relation between one event, a cause, and another event, its effect. Regularly correlated events may or may not be causally related.

Chromosomes—Structures occurring in pairs in the nucleus of cells carrying genes. The number of chromosomes varies from species to species, from two to several hundred. In humans, each cell has 46 chromosomes in 23 pairs.

Continuous variables—Those that contain an infinite number of values between adjacent units on a scale (e.g., speech).

Copernican theory of planetary motion—Copernicus placed the sun, not the earth, at the center of the universe in his *De revolutionibus orbium caelestium* (*On one revolution of heavenly spheres*, 1543).

Cultural lag—The failure to rapidly apply knowledge that we possess. Thus past aspects of a culture are preserved even though they are ineffective for contemporary life.

Darwin's evolution theory—Evolution occurred through natural selection with survival of the fittest. Darwin realized that principles similar to those in Malthus's essay on population applied to environmental selection and all living species. His triumph was in seeing the relationship between natural selection and heritable variations in populations.

Deductive reasoning—A specific conclusion necessarily follows from a set of premises. However, the conclusion is only true if the premises are true.

Discrete variables—Those for which there are no possible values between adjacent units of the scale (e.g., number of baseball pitches).

DNA (deoxyribonucleic acid)—Hereditary material located on chromosomes in the nucleus of cells.

Empiricism—A broad tradition in Western philosophy. The term comes from the Greek *emperia*, meaning "experience." The basic thesis is that knowledge arises from information provided by the senses through experience.

Equivalent descriptions—Different but equally valid ways of understanding phenomena.

Evolution theory—Present animal and plant species have evolved or developed by descent, with modification, from other preexisting species. It holds that some special characteristics of animals and prehistoric humans have facilitated the survival of species. See Darwin's evolution theory.

Galilean reasoning—Method of inductive logic emphasizing the continuous nature of variables.

Golgi stain technique—The staining of nervous system tissue which confirmed the neuron theory.

Inductive reasoning—A probability inference is made from premises to conclusions that are less than certain.

Knowledge—A statement about nature that has been empirically confirmed.

Law of Specific Energies of Nerves—Promulgated by Johannes Müller in 1838 and stating, essentially, that we know the world by our nerves, each sense organ having its own energy that determines the kind of sensation to which the sense organ will give rise.

Materialism—The position that (physical) matter is the only fundamental reality and that all being and processes and phenomena can be explained as manifestations or results of matter.

Mathus's Law—Food production increases arithmetically while populations grow geometrically.

Mendel's laws of genetics—An Austrian monk, Gregor Mendel, conducted garden pea experiments (1865) that provided the basis for principles of genetics.

Metaphysical—Refers to explanations of phenomena that are transcendent or supersensible and thus are not testable.

Method of Doubt—The act of doubting used by René Descartes to establish truth—the suspension of judgment in regard to possible truths until they have been demonstrated to be either true or false.

Mutation—An inheritable change in the character of a gene. Most often mutations occur spontaneously but they can be induced by some external stimulus such as irradiation or certain chemicals.

Nativism—An outmoded philosophical position that knowledge is inborn.

Natural selection—A principle of evolution theory that over a period of time selection results in changes in the gene pool that can facilitate survival.

Neo-Darwinian theory—A biological explanation for how the favorable variations among species are passed on from parent to progeny by the genetic transmission of hereditary information. It incorporates the concept of mutations, which was not in Darwin's theory.

Photosynthesis—The biological process by which the energy of sunlight is absorbed and used to power the formation of organic compounds from carbon and hydrogen.

Platonic soul—Plato's tripartite soul includes a vegetative soul that subserves the appetite (located in the lumbo-sacral region), an animal soul for emotion (in the cervico-thoracic region), and the immortal soul subserving reason (in the brain).

Prehensile hands—Ability of thumb and fingers to meet, allowing grasping, which led to the development of tools.

Psyche—The Greek concept of *psyche* is approximately translated as "soul," "life," or "self." Its essence was a vital characteristic of a person that coexisted with, but was independent of, the body.

Ptolemaic theory—Claudius Ptolemy (ca A.D. 150) propounded the geocentric world system theory that prevailed for fourteen centuries. It held that the earth is the center of the universe. His two major works, *The Almages* and *The Geography*, deal with the mathematical theory of the motions of the sun, moon, and planets and the earliest known map of the world, respectively.

Reflex arc—A circuit whereby a stimulus excites a receptor which transmits a nerve impulse to the central nervous system and then to muscle so that an organism automatically reacts.

Science—(Basic, Pure)—The search and systematic accumulation of knowledge without regard to practical applications.

Stereoscopic vision—Depth perception

produced by the slightly dissimilar but overlapping images that each eye sends to and receives from the brain.

Survival of the fittest — Evolution principle that species evolve by a natural process through which the most fit members survive and pass their genes to their progeny.

Technology (applied science) — An enter-

prise for solving practical problems for society, often applying the principles of pure (basic) science.

Variations — Changes of characteristics in species caused by sexual reproduction and by mutations.

Zeitgeist — The spirit of the time, general trend of thought characteristic of a particular period of time.

STUDY QUESTIONS

1. The philosopher George Santayana told us that those who do not study history are condemned to repeat it. In what ways do you think the history of biological psychology can help us to understand contemporary problems?
2. Why are the Cayonu people so meaningful in the history of humans?
3. What were the three important phases in the development of Greek philosophy?
4. What is the etymology of the word *psychology?*
5. Explain a Greek conception of soul and mind.
6. Explain the difference between the Ptolemaic (geocentric) and the Copernican (heliocentric) theories.
7. Explain this statement: Galileo showed us that we must replace deductive reasoning with inductive reasoning in order to acquire new knowledge.
8. What was the "scientific renaissance"? Name some of its most important scientists and philosophers.
9. Discuss Darwin's publication of the *Origin of Species* and the importance of his evolution theory.
10. Define DNA.

FURTHER READINGS

In your library you can find a number of good books on the history of psychology. The classic one is

Boring, E. G. (1942). *A history of experimental psychology.* New York: Appleton-Century.

For an elementary presentation of the nature of science, especially psychological science, see

McGuigan, F. J. (1993). *Experimental psychology: Methods of research* (6th ed.). Englewood Cliffs, NJ: Prentice Hall.

Other recommendations:

Denny, M. R. (1980). *Comparative psychology: An evolution analysis of animal behavior.* New York: Wiley.

Darwin, C. (1859). *On the origin of species by means of natural selection.* London: Murray. (Also published in New York in 1860 by Appleton).

Darwin, C. (1871). *The descent of man and selection in relation to sex.* London: Murray.

Gingerich, O. (1982). The Galileo affair. *Scientific American, 247,* 132–143.

CHAPTER 3

The Biology
of Mental Processes

MAJOR PURPOSE:	To understand the origin of psychology and the problem of mind
WHAT YOU ARE GOING TO FIND:	1. How the mind–body problem developed and four historically proposed solutions to it 2. How a scientific approach to the study of mind and behavior evolved 3. The evolution of a circuit model of the brain and of the brain and body for the generation of mental processes
WHAT YOU SHOULD ACQUIRE:	A historical perspective of biological psychology, of the concept of mind, and further understanding of a cybernetic circuit model of bodily/mental processes

CHAPTER OUTLINE

THE ORIGIN OF THE CONCEPT OF MIND
PROPOSED SOLUTIONS TO THE MIND–BODY PROBLEM
  Two Dualistic Proposals About Mind and Body
    Psychophysical parallelism
    Psychophysical interactionism
  Two Monistic Proposals About Mind and Body
    Subjective idealism ("mentalism")
    Materialistic monism
A BRIEF HISTORY OF A NATURAL SCIENCE APPROACH TO MENTAL PROCESSES

The Direct Antecedents of Psychology
The Transition to Monism in Psychology
The Natural Science Approach of Early Behaviorism
WHERE IN THE BODY IS THE MIND?
  Two Hypotheses About the Location of Mind
  What Do the Relevant Data Tell Us?
  Science Moves from a Brain Center Model Toward an Extensive Circuit Model of Cognition

EMPHASIS ON A CYBERNETIC PRINCIPLE—ORGANISMS FUNCTION AS WHOLE INTEGRATED UNITS BY CIRCUITS WITHIN THE BRAIN AND THROUGHOUT THE BODY
KEY TERMS
STUDY QUESTIONS
FURTHER READINGS

THE ORIGIN OF THE CONCEPT OF MIND

As you look at the world about you, you note solid objects such as chairs and tables. The bodies of your friends, as well as those of dogs and cats, have a similar *physical,* material existence. But there is much more in your world than that. You know people have minds, and you suspect your dog also has some kind of consciousness. Just how do mental processes of people and animals fit into the physical world of the objects about us? More than this, we can wonder how people ever developed the notion that there *are* mental processes in addition to the readily apparent physical phenomena.

Certainly we have no records of how the concept of **mind** arose in the first place, although we can speculate. Suppose you were a prehistoric person struggling to survive in a hostile world. What kind of sense would you make of your dreams about the dead? When awakening from such a dream, perhaps you would postulate that your body was inhabited by spirits that did not have a physical existence. Another "nonphysical" event would have been your personal experience of silently talking to yourself when awake. Such awareness would have no apparent physical location. Primitive people could well have reasoned from such sleeping and self-conscious waking experiences that they had psychic entities (minds) that were different and separate from their bodies.

We can speculate too about how the ancients explained devastating storms and earthquakes that were inflicted on them. Perhaps they believed there were powerful immaterial gods whom they had displeased. Maybe such religious and personal mental experiences led to the belief in another kind of world, a nonmaterial one that was independent of the hard, materialistic world of physical objects. From the belief in a spiritual world, words such as *consciousness, mind, thoughts,* and *ideas* eventually evolved to refer to *mental* experiences as separate from physical ones (those that are concrete and able to be seen). After becoming commonplace in our experiences and languages, such mentalistic concepts became part of our accepted "reality" and were eventually incorporated into the systems of mental philosophers. Elite academicians as far back in time as the early Greeks pondered the nature of mind. Just as we do today, they asked if mental and physical (bodily) events are related. To better understand this enduring "mind–body problem," we will briefly examine the major historical philosophical solutions that have been proposed.

PROPOSED SOLUTIONS TO THE MIND–BODY PROBLEM

The number of philosophers who have wrestled with the question of how the mental and physical worlds relate to each other cannot be easily counted. Realizing, though, that humankind has struggled with this basic question for well over 2000 years, the number of proposed solutions is staggering. There are a great number of positions on this question because it is the most complex problem in the history of philosophy and psychology. A summary of the proposed solutions to the mind–body problem starts with two basic categories known as **dualism** and **monism**.

Monism holds that there is one kind of world while dualism holds that there are two kinds.

Two Dualistic Proposals About Mind and Body

The *dualistic* approach holds that reality has a *dual* existence, that there are *two* kinds of "energies" in the universe, or as philosophers have referred to them, two kinds of "stuff." The dualist point of view postulates that there *is* a *mental* world that has a different kind of existence from that of a *physical* world. This leads to the question, "How are they related?" Two suggested answers are that (1) they are independent and do not interact, and (2) they are different but *do* interact.

PSYCHOPHYSICAL PARALLELISM

Psychophysical parallelism is a prominent form of dualism that holds that the mental world (denoted by the use of the term *psyche*) and the physical world (including the body) are independent. The psychic and the physical universes flow

Psychophysical parallelism holds that mental and physical events are independent but occur simultaneously.

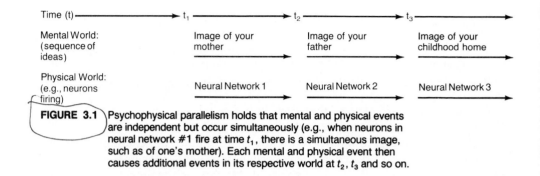

FIGURE 3.1 Psychophysical parallelism holds that mental and physical events are independent but occur simultaneously (e.g., when neurons in neural network #1 fire at time t_1, there is a simultaneous image, such as of one's mother). Each mental and physical event then causes additional events in its respective world at t_2, t_3 and so on.

along in parallel fashion, neither influencing the other. Here we may think of two streams of events, two kinds of energy that flow endlessly on, without contacting the other, as in Figure 3.1.

The outstanding exponent of psychophysical parallelism was the famous philosopher G. W. Leibnitz (1646–1716) who held that activities of the mind and of the body are predetermined and simply run their courses in parallel fashion. A psychophysical parallelist might describe a situation in which certain neurons fire in the brain (a physical event) while there is a *simultaneous* mental event (an idea). The key word here is *simultaneous* for it indicates that the physical event did not cause the mental event, or vice versa—they simply occurred together at the same time. An event in the mental world may cause a later mental event, but a mental event does not cause a material event in the physical world. Analogously, physical phenomena cannot cause mental events.

PSYCHOPHYSICAL INTERACTIONISM

Psychophysical interactionism is an alternative form of dualism. It maintains that the two worlds *do* interact so that an event in the physical world may influence an event in the mental world, and vice versa, as in Figure 3.2.

The renowned philosopher-mathematician-scientist René Descartes (1596–1650) exemplified psychophysical interactionism when he asserted that the soul, an instrument of the mental world, controls the body. After a complex set of inferences, Descartes located the region of soul ("mind")–body interaction at the pineal gland (see Figs. 2.5 and 6.5). As we saw in Chapter 2, Descartes held that the soul could move the body mechanistically through space.

FIGURE 3.2 Psychophysical interactionism holds that mental and physical events interact to cause each other; t_1, worrying about the house rent, may produce deleterious effects on the body at time t_2 and vice versa, continuing in kind of a cybernetic circuit.

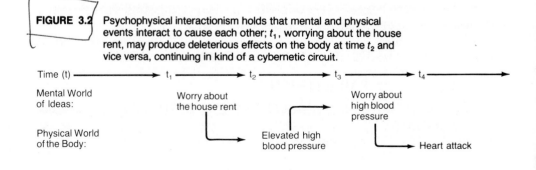

Many people today believe in psychophysical interactionism, exemplified in belief systems that include the principle of "mind over matter." Some believe, for instance, that illnesses of the body are really illnesses of a spiritualistic mind, which precludes the necessity for physical medicine. Another example of interactionism would be in psychosomatic medicine wherein it is held that mental anguish (a psychic event) has disruptive effects on the body (the soma), as when excessive worry produces a stomach ulcer.

Psychophysical interactionism holds that mental and physical events are causally related.

TWO MONISTIC PROPOSALS ABOUT MIND AND BODY

Monism, the major alternative to dualism, denies that we have a dualistic universe. Instead, there is only one kind of energy in the world, which may be mental *or* physical. Accordingly, two basic varieties of monism are known as subjective idealism and materialistic monism.

SUBJECTIVE IDEALISM ("MENTALISM")

Subjective idealism, sometimes referred to as **mentalism,** holds that the only kind of stuff in the world is mental. There is no physical reality; tables and chairs are simply ideas in our minds. The outstanding exponent of subjective idealism was the Irish bishop, George Berkeley (1685–1753). Berkeley's basic principle was *"esse est percipi,"* which is Latin for "to be is to be perceived." His basic concept is that what appear to be physical objects, such as tables, exist only when they are in the presence of a perceiver—*the essence of existence is to be perceived.* If no one is perceiving the table, it does not exist!

Subjective idealism (mentalism) holds that there is only a mental world and denies that there is any physical, material existence.

Although subjective idealism may seem like a strange philosophical position, it is actually quite compatible with a materialistic one. If you think about it, it makes no difference whether or not we assume that a table (or whatever) exists if there is no one to perceive it. Here we can recall the classic problem of whether or not a falling tree produces a noise in a forest devoid of perceivers—you can just as well assume that there *is* or *is not* a noise, for it makes no difference which position you take. If there were noise, it would not affect anybody anyway. If there were no noise, we would not know that. Berkeley would say that it is the same with the table. It is only an idea in your mind that exists when you perceive it. More generally, all components of our world are but ideas in our minds and those ideas lack physical reality.

MATERIALISTIC MONISM

The second major variety of monism, **materialistic monism,** holds that there is only one kind of energy in the world, and it is all *physical* material. Materialism thus denies the existence of a unique kind of nonphysical energy that constitutes "mental events or ideas." In fact, the term *nonphysical energy* is itself a contradiction—*energy is by definition physical* and to try to detect a kind of nonphysical energy through physical methods is obviously impossible.

Materialistic monism is the dominant position among biological scientists. Scientific psychologists, for instance, typically believe that the assertion of a nonphysical world of mental ideas is a doctrine of despair—if we cannot study it with our physiological senses, how do we know it is there? If you believe there *are* mental

Materialistic monism holds that there is only a material world so that ideas and thoughts are physical events within the body.

events that are impossible to observe, you can just as well assume that they do or do not exist. Like the question of whether or not the falling tree in the forest creates a noise, it makes no difference which position you take. Consequently we should get along with the task of learning what we can with our ordinary sensory apparatus and not posit worlds that, by definition, are and always will be impossible to study.[1]

This text will adhere to the position of materialistic monism. It is important to understand that materialistic monism does not deny the existence of mental events! Rather, what we call "mental events" are seen as observable aspects of the physical world. Therefore, mental phenomena do not have an existence independent of the physical world. From a biological point of view, it is important to clearly understand this position as a philosophical underpinning. Thus *there is no unique kind of mental energy that can be differentiated from physical energy.* Thoughts and ideas are generated by the world within our skin. It is the aim of biological psychology to understand how the brain functions in concert with the body to generate the physical phenomena that we refer to as mental events.

As developed in Chapter 1, cybernetic circuits reverberate between the brain and other systems of the body to produce subjective mentalistic experiences. The analogy of how circuits within a TV set interact to generate the visual images that we perceive remains quite appropriate. Materialistic monism is quite consistent with the development of a cybernetic model of how the body functions, which includes how we generate mental events.

Materialistic monism is a foundation in the development of the cybernetic model used to understand human behavior.

With this perspective, let us now continue our scientific study of mental (cognitive) phenomena within a biological framework. We will review how historical biological science, as examined in the last chapter, and materialistic philosophy developed into biological psychology.

A BRIEF HISTORY OF A NATURAL SCIENCE APPROACH TO MENTAL PROCESSES

The continuous development of empirically inclined philosophers throughout the recent history of Western civilization has led to our current materialistic conception of mind. These mental philosophers were strongly influenced by the great productivity of science in the seventeenth and eighteenth centuries. For instance, in the early seventeenth century, the British philosopher John Locke (1632–1704) developed a model of mind based on the successful models of atoms that were prominent in chemistry. His reasoning was that the mind consisted of "atoms" that he called ideas. The mind could thus be analyzed into its components (ideas) just as the chemist could analyze physical matter. Water, for instance, was analyzed into two atoms of hydrogen and one atom of oxygen (H_2O). Mind, Locke thought, could be similarly understood by analysis into its units of ideas. This process of understanding something by analyzing it into its parts is known as **atomism** or **reductionism.** Atomism holds that the specification of the basic units (elements) of a phenomenon (water, mind, etc.) and of how those units are connected together (related) consti-

---

[1]These matters are far more complex than this summary treatment allows us to indicate. For instance, materialism does not deny that there are *processes* as in information processing. Images on a TV screen, for instance, are processes that are strictly the result of physical events. This example illustrates how a visual image (which some regard as a mentalistic event) can be generated by the strictly physicalistic processing of information within circuits.

tutes an understanding of that phenomenon. Today, we call the results of such an analysis a *system* consisting of *elements* and their *relations,* as developed in Chapter 1. Atomism has led to many powerful successes in science as in the analysis of matter into atoms and all that has followed from that.

Atomism is an approach to understanding a phenomenon by specifying its components and the laws of their connections.

The Direct Antecedents of Psychology

Contributions of British Empiricism.   The philosophical movement of which John Locke was a part was known as **British empiricism or associationism,** a movement that held that mental events were to be understood through empirical means. British empiricism started in the early 1600s with Thomas Hobbes and John Locke and later included such eminent thinkers as John Stuart Mill and David Hume. British empiricism and associated movements throughout the world made a radical contribution to psychology, for according to empiricism, questions about mind were to be answered by *observation* of natural phenomena—attempts to answer questions on the basis of inborn knowledge (nativism) or through mystical (spiritualistic) means were thus rejected.

British empiricism contributed mightily to the position that knowledge is derived only through experience gained with our sensory systems and led to a materialistic conception of mind.

Contributions of Physicists.   While British empiricism contributed significantly to a *natural science* approach to mind through philosophy, a second major contribution was one generated by scientists themselves. Physicists, for instance, found it necessary to understand sense receptor organs such as the eyes and ears because sense organs were part of their own observational equipment necessary to study the nonliving world. For example, different astronomers reported slightly different time values in their astronomical observations. Those time differences were first considered to be errors. However, they later were attributed to differences in the sensory capacities of different astronomers—one astronomer, for instance, simply had a faster **reaction time** than another. To correct for such "errors," physicists had to study the contribution of the visual sense receptors to their observations. Consequently, physicists studied the psychological topic of sensation within the field of physics.

Scientists recognized the need to study and understand human sensory systems that can influence the accuracy of their "observations."

Contributions of Physiologists.   At about this same time physiologists also were asking questions about sensation, perception, and the mind itself. In particular, they, too, sought to understand the functioning of the receptor and nervous systems. Extensive research by giants such as Helmholtz was conducted on vision, audition, kinesthesis, and so on. There was considerable effort to understand how we perceive

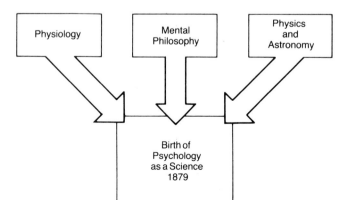

FIGURE 3.3
The common interests of physiology, mental philosophy, and physics/astronomy evolved into the new science of psychology fathered by Wilhelm Wundt in 1879.

WILHELM WUNDT (1832–1920)

research, structuralists analyzed conscious processes into basic elements and sought to discover how these elements may be associated according to laws of their connections. Wundt introduced the concept of *apperception*, which is that the creative synthesis of the elements of immediate experience is an active process out of which comes something new. He wrote what was said to be the most important book in the history of psychology, *Principles of Physiological Psychology.*

Later, Wundt became interested in levels of mental development expressed through language, myths, art forms, social customs, laws, and morals. The results were ten volumes of *Folk Psychology,* wherein psychology was divided into realms of experimental and social (nonexperimental) approaches of sociology and anthropology.

Wilhelm Wundt, the father of psychology, developed the first school of psychological thought, structuralism. In his laboratory for experimental

color, depth, time, and movement (see Boring, 1942, for a thorough development of physiological contributions to psychology).

Psychology Is Born. We can thus see that the diverse endeavors of three intellectual disciplines, those of the mental philosophers, natural scientists (physicists and astronomers), and physiologists had a common interest: All sought to understand such cognitive phenomena as sensations, perceptions, and ideas (Fig. 3.3). Inevitably, a unique science was born that specialized in the study of mental phenomena. At Leipzig, Germany, in 1879, the great Wilhelm Wundt founded **psychology** as the first science devoted exclusively to the study of mind, and it was a physiological (but "dualistic") approach.

The Transition to Monism in Psychology

The original task of psychology was to understand the mind, and many early psychologists followed Wundt in taking a dualistic approach. They attempted to scientifically study mental processes that had no physical (physiological) existence. Gradually within psychology a physicalistic approach arose, with the battle between dualism and materialistic monism continuing for many decades. The transition within psychology from dualism to monism was slow and often painful as materialistic conceptions of mind were initially quite unpopular. For instance, the renowned anatomist F. J. Gall (1758–1828) advocated a science that was a precursor to psychology known as **phrenology** (described today as identifying personality characteristics by feeling bumps on the head). One underlying thesis of phrenology was that the brain was the organ of mind (Fig. 3.4). Gall was thus a materialistic monist who denied that there were mental processes independent of the brain—ideas could only be physiologically generated by the brain. This radical materialistic conception caused Gall great personal abuse—he was even denied a religious burial.

Phrenology was an empirical attempt to identify characteristics of individuals by means of depressions and protrusions on the surface of the skull.

FIGURE 3.4 The location of Gall's organ of mind in his system of phrenology.

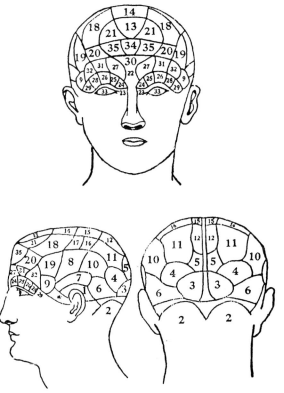

AFFECTIVE FACULTIES		INTELLECTUAL FACULTIES	
PROPENSITIES	SENTIMENTS	PERCEPTIVE	REFLECTIVE
? Desire to live	10 Cautiousness	22 Individuality	34 Comparison
* Alimentiveness	11 Approbativeness	23 Configuration	35 Causality
1 Destructiveness	12 Self-Esteem	24 Size	
2 Amativeness	13 Benevolence	25 Weight and	
3 Philoprogenitiveness	14 Reverence	Resistance	
4 Adhesiveness	15 Firmness	26 Coloring	
5 Inhabitiveness	16 Conscientiousness	27 Locality	
6 Combativeness	17 Hope	28 Order	
7 Secretiveness	18 Marvelousness	29 Calculation	
8 Acquisitiveness	19 Ideality	30 Eventuality	
9 Constructiveness	20 Mirthfulness	31 Time	
	21 Imitation	32 Tune	
		33 Language	

In the early part of this century, Charles S. Sherrington (1857–1952), one of the greatest physiologists of all time, sought in vain for a special nonmaterial energy of mind. And even the Nobel laureate Sir John Eccles today holds to a special kind of dualism. So it is clear that not all scientists agree on the issue of mind; nor should they, for science is the epitome of democratic controversy. The basic fact is that decades of scientific investigations by dualistic psychologists and physiologists led to the accumulation of considerable evidence of what now seems so very obvious — that is, it is not possible to *scientifically* study nonphysical phenomena. One merely needs to trace the demise of Wundt's structuralism and its decades of introspection on an immaterial consciousness to reinforce this summary statement (cf. Boring, 1929). Consequently, the concept of an immaterial consciousness had to be dismissed from psychology.

Beginning with John B. Watson and his colleagues, psychology increasingly became the study of behavior.

Behaviorism Is Materialistic.   **Behaviorism** in America, led by John Broadus Watson (1878–1958), dealt the death blow to dualistic psychology. Psychology became the study of behavior because behavioral responses are materialistic events that can be objectively observed. *The essence of science is that the phenomena studied must be publicly observable.* Behavior can be observed by more than one person. Thus, observers should be able to agree that a certain response did or did not occur. In contrast, it is not possible to publicly observe another person's immaterial consciousness, at least when it is defined as something nonphysical in nature.

Responses that compose behavior can be studied by anyone, but an immaterial consciousness cannot.

A response is a contraction of muscle or secretion of a gland.

In the redefinition of psychology, "behavior" was very broadly defined to include not only readily observable *overt* actions of the body but also small-scale, minute, *covert* muscular responses that could not be observed with the naked eye. Covert behavior also includes responses of the glandular systems such as when one sweats, salivates, or secretes hormones. A **response** is thus defined as a contraction of muscle or secretion of a gland. In short, the behaviorist's program was to study both overt and covert behavior.

The Natural Science Approach of Early Behaviorism

Behaviorists sought scientific stimulus–response (S–R) laws that could also be technologically used to predict behavior and control it for the benefit of society.

Predicting and Controlling Behavior.   The broad program of the early behaviorists was to predict and control behavior. To accomplish this they sought to establish behavioral laws (relationships) in which certain stimuli (S) had been found to evoke certain responses (R). The basic form of their laws was typically diagrammed as S–R. Once a psychologist had established a specific **stimulus–response relationship,** it was possible to predict that a given response would occur when a specific stimulus was presented. For a simple example, if the stimulus of a bright light is presented, the prediction is that the pupils of the subject's eyes will contract (a response evoked by the stimulus). In a similar way if one wants to control a given response, one can make it occur by presenting the stimulus specified in the S–R law that evokes that response. If, for instance, one wants an automobile driver to stop at a given street corner, one places the stimulus of a stop sign there. Based on a well-established S–R relationship, the stop sign stimulus will evoke a driver's foot-pedal response, stopping the automobile.

The strategy of the early behaviorists was to accumulate enough basic S–R laws that society could effectively use them. Their goal of controlling behavior to reduce crime, mental illness, and starvation has seen some success, as in token

JOHN BROADUS WATSON (1878–1958)

John B. Watson is best known as the major force in the founding of behaviorism, a movement that replaced the structuralism of Wundt and his influential student Edward Bradford Titchener. Watson's influence is felt in many ways today, particularly in the contemporary definition of psychology as the science of behavior. His early studies of animal behavior led him to develop a psychology following the strategy of the science of physics. For this he advocated that psychology become deterministic, mechanistic, materialistic, and objective. He applied the methodology gained from the study of animals to humans and developed a strong interest in infant behavior. In his laboratory at the Johns Hopkins University, he concluded that human infants have innate emotions of fear, love, and rage. Based on these response patterns and through conditioning, the human personality develops. Watson was a major influence in the acknowledgment of the importance of early childhood experiences for later personality development. He was thus a strong believer in environmentalism — that learning influences human behavior to a greater extent than do innate factors.

Watson contributed heavily to applied problems particularly during World War I after which he concentrated in the ways in which psychology could be used as an instrument of social control. These included psychology as a management tool, as a pedagogical method, and as an advertising technique. The influence of behaviorism in the business world emphasizes the notion of efficiency. More broadly, Watson envisioned a scientifically managed society based on psychological principles. B. F. Skinner followed many of the paths laid out by Watson, including their common strong interest in developing a scientifically managed society that would maximize productive and enjoyable behaviors and eliminate destructive and maladaptive ones.

Eventually Watson became successful as an advertising executive and as a popularizer of self-help psychology.

economies for controlling schizophrenia. However, success in such behavioral engineering has been limited because society has not applied existing S–R laws to a sufficient extent (a matter we take up in Chapter 15). An optimistic view of cultural lag is that eventually we will apply what we already know to solve some of our problems. Success has also been limited because some of society's problems are so tremendously complex that we do not know how to solve them, nor have we devoted enough research energy to them.

"Mental" Events Materialistically Defined. Although the young science of psychology was defined as the study of behavior, it still inherited many mentalistic terms. It was also strongly influenced by physiology to become a biological science. By the early part of this century, physiologists had accumulated considerable knowledge about receptor systems for vision, for audition, and so on. Physiologists had also learned much about response mechanisms, principally the muscles of the body. Borrowing what they could from physiology, the behaviorists dealt with classical mentalistic terms but redefined them as physiological, bodily phenomena. The behaviorists thus continued the study of mental phenomena, although the approach was modified to materialistic monism. For instance, the principles of natural science led Watson to redefine "emotion" in terms of visceral responses. Instead of being some unknowable, nonphysical phenomenon, emotion could now be objectively studied by measuring activity of the **viscera** (the internal organs of the body). Accordingly, emotion has been successfully measured by recording events in the digestive, respiratory, endocrine, cardiovascular, sexual, and other systems.

Thinking and Other Mental Processes Are Behaviors. John Watson was especially interested in the phenomenon of thought and developed an extensive theory of thinking. Thinking for him was, once again, a material process—a complex of psychophysiological events that included extensive, *minute* (covert) reactions throughout the body, especially those in the speech region. Similarly, he defined **consciousness** in terms of objectively observable behavior; one's consciousness is one's description of events within the body (the internal environment) as well as those in the outside world (the external environment). Consciousness, defined in this way, is a publicly (objectively) observable phenomenon. When you are conscious, therefore, you can indicate your awareness of your world by reporting on it (verbal reports). You can, for instance, report your conscious awareness of a stomach pain by describing it to your physician (or any other observer). The later behaviorist Professor B. F. Skinner (1904–1990) extensively analyzed such subjective experiences behaviorally, referring to them as "private" (yet physical) events.

It is worth our while to reflect a moment on what we have just said because there is a common misconception about behaviorism. The misconception is perpetuated because many authors do not study the original writings of the early behaviorists as previously cited. Rather, modern authors often rely only on secondary sources. For instance, one prominent scientist has written that "Behavioral psychologists tend to avoid serious discussion of the mind and of 'mental' processes" (Schmitt, 1972, p. 113). Had this author read Watson carefully (and the example could be multiplied), he would have seen that Watson was *extremely* interested in mental processes. Watson, for instance, developed an extensive theory wherein one thinks with the entire body, including the brain. Similarly, the renowned early behaviorist Walter Hunter in 1924 and 1934 wrote articles on "The Problem of Consciousness," "The Symbolic Process," and "Voluntary Activity from the Standpoint of Behaviorism" (an analysis of the will). Another early behaviorist, Herbert

Mental processes were redefined by behaviorists as bodily events so that they were measurable.

Langfeld, in 1931 wrote a classic article entitled "A Response Interpretation of Consciousness." Skinner held that "the simplest and most satisfactory view is that thought is simply behavior — verbal or nonverbal, covert or overt. It is not some mysterious process responsible for behavior but the very behavior itself" (Skinner, 1957, in McGuigan, 1966, p. 17).

A Meaningless Concept of Mind Discarded. What these early behaviorists discarded from psychology, then, was the meaningless concept of an immaterial ("spiritual") mind. Being immaterial means that such mental processes lack spatial–temporal coordinates — mental processes as dualists conceived them could not be located on either a spatial or a temporal physical dimension. But since a human body does have material existence, it therefore can be located in a spatial–temporal system; consequently, events of the body, including mental ones, occur in specifiable (spatial) locations at specifiable (chronological) times. In a sense, then, efforts of the dualists were self-contradictory. That is, they attempted to study a nonmaterial phenomenon that lacked spatial–temporal coordinates, which cannot be done. Although these mental events are typically private (we do sometimes think aloud), they still have physicalistic reality within a spatial–temporal body.

We will have more to say about the bodily aspects of mental (cognitive) events in Chapter 13. For now we want to emphasize that the transition from dualism to materialistic monism was accomplished with the dominance of behaviorism. As a result, psychology was redefined — psychology was no longer a study of an immaterial consciousness that was unobservable by others. Instead psychology became the study of "the other one."

In order to understand mental events, to understand mind itself, covert processes (which we study in the psychophysiology laboratory, see Chapter 8) were emphasized. With this change from psychology as the study of an immaterial subjective consciousness to the study of behavior, we are now studying mental phenomena that can be publicly (objectively) observed. No longer were mental events mystical and unobservable. We thus can see how interested the early behaviorists such as Watson and Hunter were in cognitive (mental) events. Similarly, the famous behaviorists Clark Hull and Edward Tolman sought to understand the nature of mind as cognition (see McGuigan, 1978). Unfortunately, however, some psychologists who accept Watson's basic prescription for studying behavior still conceive of mental processes dualistically. They are cognitive psychologists who attempt to infer mental processes from behavior, often conceiving of immaterial cognitions as controlling behavior. Although cognitive psychology incorporates advances in computers, information processing, linguistics, brain research, and the like, it sometimes resembles the dualism of Wundt.

Given, then, that mental processes exist in an extensive spatial–temporal system that exists within the body, the location of the mind can be empirically ascertained.

Behaviorists rejected a dualistic concept of mental events that lacked spatial–temporal characteristics, but they accepted materialistic mental concepts that did have spatial–temporal coordinates.

With the ascendence of behaviorism, the transition from dualism to materialistic monism was accomplished.

WHERE IN THE BODY IS THE MIND?

Notions about the location of the mind and of the historically related religious concept of the soul are numerous and varied. The mind–soul as a nonmaterial phenomenon has been "placed" variously in the heart, in the head, as coextensive throughout the body, and as Descartes believed, external to the body but acting on the pineal gland. Many interesting philosophical issues about these matters have been debated over the centuries, such as the "coextensive-throughout-the-body theory." Questions include, "What happens to the part of the mind–soul in an arm if the limb is severed from the body? Does one simply discard that part of the mind–soul when the arm is lost?" One answer has been, "Well, no—that portion of the mind–soul located in the severed arm instantaneously leaps from the arm to maintain integrity with the rest of the mind–soul in the remainder of the body." Throughout history, the nature and location of the mind have been elusive indeed!

Is the Mind in the Brain? Mind usually refers to the composite of mental events, so to locate the mind we could ask where mental events occur. One commonsense notion is that an idea "starts in the brain" which then gives commands to the body to carry it out (Fig. 3.5). But, how does the idea occur in the first place?

Many consider these issues by saying, "Everyone knows that the mind is in the brain," and that settles that! It has been demonstrated that when one thinks, the brain generates events such as electrical brain waves and identifiable chemical processes. Does this mean that cognition occurs in and only in the brain—that mental phenomena are confined to processes within the skull? Is it reasonable to imagine a brain thinking by itself, isolated from the body? A famous science fiction story called "Donovan's Brain" was about this possibility—that a brain *could* be

FIGURE 3.5   A commonsense notion is that an idea starts in the mind located in the head and causes actions of the body. But what was the antecedent of the idea?

An idea starts in the mind

and causes the body to respond.

But what causes the idea in the first place??

preserved in a sort of fishbowl so that Donovan could continue thinking after his normal life ceased. One obvious difficulty with a "Donovan's Brain" theory is that if such an isolated preparation *could* think, without input from the environment, it probably could not think very well, and most assuredly it would not have much to think about. Nor, without external attachments to motor nerves and muscles would it be able to do anything about what it might have thought. Is it possible that other systems of the body contribute to the generation of thought? Let us reason as logically as we can about this issue.

Two Hypotheses About the Location of Mind

Consider two positions: (1) The mind is located solely within the brain and (2) the brain, as well as other systems of the body, cooperates in the generation of mental processes; consequently, the mind is located extensively throughout the body and not just within the skull.

Now, suppose that we proceed with position number 1, assuming that "everyone knows" mental processes are generated strictly (only) within and by the brain. If this hypothesis is false and position number 2 is true, "we miss the boat." Or more precisely, our myopia has caused us to miss an understanding of some of the bodily systems that are critical for generating mental processes. To be excessively crude, we would have missed a good part of the mind.

On the other hand, suppose that we proceed with position number 2 and that position turns out to be true. In that case, we could arrive at a satisfactory understanding of the mind. Even if position number 1 turns out to be true such that the mind is only in the brain, we still would discover this fact by following position number 2. We simply would determine that the body outside of the brain was not part of mind. The reverse would not occur.

In Short. If we follow position number 1 and position number 2 turns out to be true, we would reach an erroneous conclusion and be unlikely to discover our error. But if we follow position number 2 and position number 1 turns out to be true, we will still find that out and avoid reaching an erroneous conclusion.

Therefore, the optimal and most flexible approach is to not have any predispositions as to the location of the mind. We should follow the data wherever they might lead and include the possibility that any bodily system might be at least a partial component of mind. To exclude the second strategy without even looking at the data would be myopic indeed.

The Brain–Body Theory Espoused Throughout History. Actually, position number 2 has been espoused by some of our greatest thinkers and has a venerable and respected history. Alexander Bain (1818–1903), who ended the long line of British empiricists in the late nineteenth century and evolved into one of the earlier psychologists, had this to say about the location of mind:

> The organ of mind is not the brain by itself; it is the brain, nerves, muscles and organs of sense. . . . We must . . . discard forever the notion of the sensorium commune, the cerebral closed, as a central seat of mind, or receptacle of sensation and imagery. (Bain, 1855)

The great Russian physiologist I. M. Sechenov (1829–1905), who began the tradition of contemporary physiology in the former Soviet Union that was followed

Mind *is a term that stands for the composite of mental processes that, by a cybernetic model, are generated as circuits selectively interact throughout the body.*

ALEXANDER BAIN (1818–1903)

Alexander Bain has been considered by many to be the first physiological psychologist, basing his work on nineteenth-century physiology. His primary goal was to relate mental events with physiological phenomena of sense organs, reflexes, and the brain.

Bain wrote on learning and memory and collated the psychological knowledge of his time. He relied upon similarity and contiguity as the two basic laws of association.

Bain's most important works were *The Senses and the Intellect* and *The Emotions and the Will,* books perceived by many as the first true books of psychology.

---

by Ivan Pavlov, V. M. Becchterev, and others until contemporary times, held that "All the endless diversity of the external manifestations of the activity of the brain can be finally regarded as one phenomenon—that of muscular movement" (Sechenov, 1863, cited in Herrnstein & Boring, 1965, p. 309).

Hughlings Jackson, the great physiologist of the last century said that "a motor element is involved in every conscious activity" and that "In the anatomical substratum in which the feeble discharge corresponds to that which we call thinking of an object, there is a motor as well as a sensory element" (cited by Jacobson, 1938b, p. 165).

In 1895, Oswald Külpe said that

> *Movements are everywhere important.* It is perhaps not too much to say that voluntary recollection never takes place without their assistance. When we think of intense cold, our body is thrown into tremulous movement as in shivering; when we imagine an extent of space, our eyes move as they would in surveying it; when we recall a rhyme, we mark its rise and fall with hand or foot. Most important of all, however, are the movements of speech, which stand in unequivocal relation to the perception of every department. (cited by Jacobson, 1938b, p. 165, italics in original)

Wilhelm Wundt in 1907 recalled that Gustav Fechner (the father of psychophysics) observed a slight tenseness *(eine leise Spannung)* in the sense organs during attention to an outer stimulus, for example, in the ears during hearing, or about the eyes during vision (cited by Jacobson, 1938b, p. 166).

Alfred Binet in 1886 said that

> It is enough to remember that all our perceptions, and in particular the important ones, those of sight and touch, contain as integral elements the movement of our eyes and limbs; and that, if movement is ever an essential factor in our really seeing an object, it must be an equally essential factor when we see the same object in [our] imaginations. (quoted by Ribot, cited by Jacobson, 1938b, pp. 166–167)

A more contemporary illustration is a conclusion from the work of the psychophysiological pioneer Edmund Jacobson: "It might be naive to say that we think with our muscles, but it would be inaccurate to say that we think without them" (Jacobson, 1967), and as Nobel laureate Ralph Lilly stated, Jacobson's studies "proved that the brain had no closed circuits when it came to mental activity" (McGuigan, 1978, p. iii).

Evans (1983) points out that neural tracts extend from the cortex to the hypothalamus, that the hypothalamus influences the pituitary gland which in turn influences the other endocrine glands. In this way he holds that mental processes influence physiological "processes throughout the body, which in turn influence brain activity. This cyclic pattern between brain and body processes is known as the *circular theory of mind and body relations, or somatopsychosomatic theory*" (p. 230, italics in original).

To conclude with a cybernetic principle, Norbert Wiener considered how feedback circuits within a body generate mental processes. Wiener emphasized that in order to understand the brain, we have to study it within the context of the entire body, and he expressed the principle this way:

> The central nervous system no longer appears as a self-contained organ, receiving inputs from the senses and discharging into the muscles. On the contrary, some of its most characteristic activities are explicable only as circular processes, emerging from the system into the muscles, and re-entering the nervous system through the sense organs, whether they be proprioceptors or organs of the special senses" (Wiener, 1948, p. 15).

What Do the Relevant Data Tell Us?

The study of behavior in all of its complexity throughout the body is a formidable task indeed, requiring the extensive use of sensitive laboratory equipment. Much of that apparatus has been borrowed from the older biological sciences, especially physiology. We need, for instance, specialized psychophysiological equipment to study activities of the brain such as the well-known electroencephalograph (EEG) for studying brain waves during thought. The study of other events throughout the body when one thinks also requires specialized equipment, as we develop in Chapter 8. But the following discussion from extensive research summarized by McGuigan (1978) briefly illustrates such procedures. An electrocardiograph (EKG) is required for indicating that the heart responds uniquely during cognition (e.g., when we fear, it beats faster). Measurement of eye responses with an electro-oculograph (EOG) has shown the eyes to be especially active during thought, such as when we visualize. Visceral activity is *intricately* involved in cognitive processes. For instance, the esophagus always contracts during fear and we have emotional feelings in the "pit of our stomach" due to activity there and in our intestines. Electrodermal responding, as in the galvanic skin response (GSR) and autonomic nervous system in general, is very active during a variety of cognitive activities, such as emotional experiences. Typically, people who are engaged in thought increase their pulse rate, breathe faster, and make a wide variety of small-scale covert muscular responses throughout the body (as studied through electromyography, EMG). Most important, the muscles in the speech region have been shown to be active when one engages in any of a variety of cognitive activities, as when we subvocalize during reading.

The theory that one thinks with the whole body, including the brain (position number 2), accords well with scientific findings. Not only are there unique brain waves observed during thought, but researchers have also recorded numerous other events throughout the body when one thinks, including those previously mentioned. Indeed, research has documented that the entire body is covertly active during many cognitive acts. In Chapter 13 we will examine some of these data in

The theory that cognitive events are generated throughout the brain and body, in contrast to being solely within the brain, has a long and respectable history continuing into contemporary science.

A variety of specialized equipment, such as the electroencephalograph for studying brain waves, is used in the psychophysiological laboratory for directly measuring mental processes.

Numerous psychophysiological data confirm the theory that as we think, there is a tremendous amount of brain–body interaction.

detail. But first we need to study how the systems of the body that generate widespread reactions might *interact* during cognition.

Science Moves from a Brain Center Model Toward an Extensive Circuit Model of Cognition

We have seen that early conceptions of mind typically embodied the limited notion that mind is strictly a brain phenomenon. Due to cultural lag, this continues to be the typical notion of laypersons. Furthermore, brain functioning is depicted by a "center" model that holds, for example, that there are specialized regions in the brain that, when activated, cause a person to behave in a special way.

Phrenology and Its Disconfirmation. Perhaps the most extreme example of a center model was that of cerebral localization advocated by the anatomist F. J. Gall (1758–1828) in his phrenology (see Fig. 3.4). Gall was actually a respected anatomist who put forth a well–thought out, empirically based model of the relationship between cerebral characteristics and mental activities. Through painstaking research, he attempted to establish correlations between mental powers and regions of the brain that were depressed or elevated. Powers or faculties of the mind could thus be directly measured, since a protrusion would be an index of a large amount of the faculty centered in that region of the brain. On the other hand, if there was a recession of the skull in that particular region, the individual should have a lack of the corresponding faculty. According to phrenology (see Fig. 3.4), a person with an enlarged region directly above the ear would be judged to be quite destructive.

Phrenology was disconfirmed because Gall overgeneralized from his sample of people and because the surface of the skull did not conform to the surface of the brain.

The major hypothesis of phrenology was eventually disconfirmed for a variety of reasons. For one, Gall studied a highly selected (nonrandom) sample of people and overgeneralized from them to larger populations. We can understand now that over a century ago Gall had only a superficial and erroneous knowledge of brain anatomy and physiology, leading to erroneous predictions from phrenology. Even if a certain location in the brain actually is a center for a particular psychological characteristic, the skull above that brain center would not be particularly depressed or heightened. A brain center that is relatively large or small simply does not affect the skull. This is because the brain is engulfed in cerebral-spinal fluids and separated from the skull further by the meninges (the dura mater, arachnoid, and pia mater), thin layers that surround the brain (Fig. 3.6). Any variation in brain size thus merely displaces cerebral-spinal fluids and the meninges, with no effect on the skull.

Where is phrenology today? With a long cultural lag, it still persists in carnivals, along with such other pseudosciences as astrology. You can pay good money to have your personality "told" by someone who will read the "bumps" on your head, even though phrenology has been thoroughly discredited by science.

Research Gradually Confirmed Circuit Models. It was the Frenchman Pierre Flourens (1794–1867) who made the most influential early attack on Gall's concept of localization in the brain. Although Flourens did conceive of brain functioning in terms of cerebral localization, he had a wider and more generalized concept of localization than did Gall. Flourens based his conclusions on the earliest precise use of brain **extirpation** (or **ablation,** removal of neural tissue). He found that the amount of neural tissue removed from the brain was more important than its location (anticipating Karl Lashley's Law of Mass Action). Flourens concluded that although there were some localized regions in the brain, the cerebrum functioned as

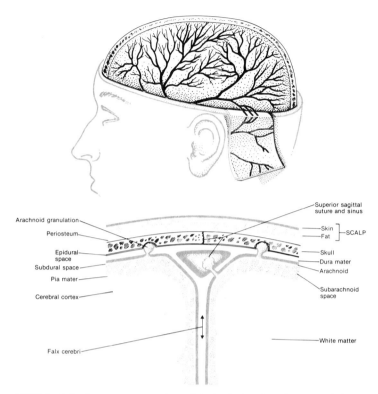

Arachnoid granulation

Periosteum

Epidural
space

Subdural space

Pia mater

Cerebral cortex

Falx cerebri

Superior sagittal
suture and sinus

Skin
Fat
SCALP

Skull

Dura mater

Arachnoid

Subarachnoid
space

White matter

FIGURE 3.6   A contemporary view of the brain (cerebrum) surrounded by the
dura mater and its blood vessels (top). The other meninges and
space between the cortex and skull are represented below.

a whole unit to generate willing, judging, remembering, and perceiving. He similarly
concluded that the cerebellum (the "little brain," see Fig. 6.14) functioned as a whole
organ to coordinate movement.

That work served as a basis for Karl Lashley's (1890–1958) research in the
1930s in which he attacked the strict localized brain model. Lashley's extensive
research, and that of his associate Shephard Ivory Franz, led him to formulate the
laws of equipotentiality and mass action, which indicate that the brain functions as
an entire, integrated system in many respects. The **Law of Mass Action** states
essentially that the efficiency of an organism's performance is determined by the
amount (not location) of brain tissue that remains intact. Consequently, the cortex
functions as an entire integrated unit such that the more of the brain that remains,
the better the performance. The **Law of Equipotentiality** holds that the various
cortical regions contribute to the efficiency of any complex behavior in an equal
fashion. Given that various regions of the cortex are of equal potential, this law
denies much specialization of centers within the cortex.

Although Lashley's principles were important in the development of biological
psychology, we note that they apply more to simpler brains such as the rat's, on
which Lashley conducted much of his research, than to human brains.

*The work of Flourens and
Lashley led to a discarding of
a strict center model of the
brain in favor of a principle
that the brain functions more
as an entire integrated system, particularly as formulated in Lashley's Laws of
Equipotentiality and Mass
Action.*

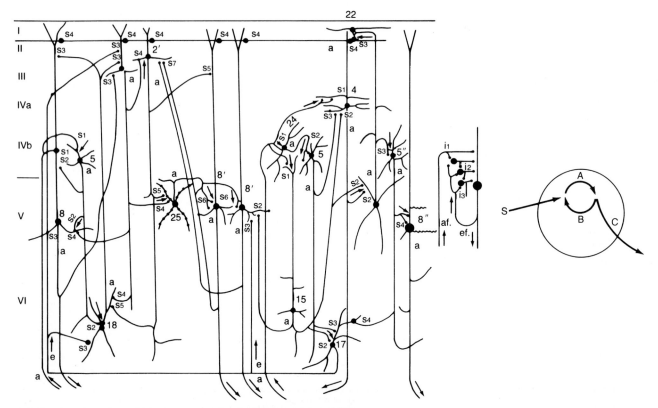

FIGURE 3.7 Lorente de No's description of closed neural circuits within the brain (from Fulton, 1943); an example of Hebb's concept of cell assemblies based on de No's research is represented to the right (adapted from Hebb, 1966), wherein an incoming stimulus (S) evokes a reverberating circuit (A ⊃ B) that has peripheral consequences (C).

Donald Hebb (1904–1985) employed the anatomical findings of Lorente de No that suggested that there were closed circuits of neurons in the brain (Fig. 3.7). Reasoning from the anatomical specification of neural circuits, Hebb developed the concept that neurons form **cell assemblies** that, when activated by reverberating neural impulses, generate conscious thoughts. Although highly conceptual and unrealistic, Hebb did in this way advance further the notion of brain circuits that by our model have cybernetic characteristics. Hebb, furthermore, implicated peripheral events (outside of the brain) that interact with cell assemblies. He thus extended the concept of circuits to brain–body interactions that have cybernetic characteristics.

Hebb implicated peripheral events that interact with central cell assemblies, which are concepts of cybernetics for brain–body and brain circuits.

This brief review shows how theorists moved from a localized brain center model of the mind toward a loop or circuit conception. The next issue became one of specifying the nature of these circuits.

Neurological science from the time of Flourens advanced from a localized brain center model to a circuit model.

Through much research, physiologists and anatomists have succeeded in tracing intricate pathways throughout the brain, suggesting that there are complex circuits that connect various important localized cerebral regions. Although, in gen-

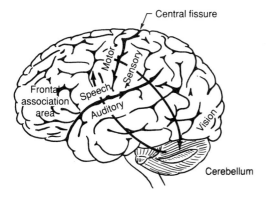

FIGURE 3.8
A representation of brain circuits relating various brain regions such as the motor areas and cerebellum.

eral, the brain does not function in a manner depicted by a strict center model of localization, we *have* discovered a number of highly localized brain centers such as that of the motor area located in each cerebral hemisphere (Fig. 3.8). By systematically stimulating along the motor area, movements of the body can be elicited from the top of the head down through the toes. Other localized regions in the brain are those for speech, vision, hearing, and so on. These centers are components of circuits that integrate them with other regions of the brain. Furthermore, the brain itself is a component of another class of circuit, one that integrates the brain with the rest of the body. We can, for instance, trace neural pathways between various parts of the body to and from the brain. Such a class of circuits was advocated by the early behaviorists when they sought to understand mental processes as a function of total reflex arcs that functioned from receptors to the brain then to effectors and back to the brain, and continuing on. Early electrical measurement of muscle activity led Edmund Jacobson to postulate and eventually confirm that **neuromuscular circuits** function throughout the body during mental activities.

Brain centers are themselves components of complex cerebral circuits.

EMPHASIS ON A CYBERNETIC PRINCIPLE— ORGANISMS FUNCTION AS WHOLE INTEGRATED UNITS BY CIRCUITS WITHIN THE BRAIN AND THROUGHOUT THE BODY

We have emphasized that there are numerous circuits to and from the receptors and the brain, and between the brain and effectors throughout the body (Fig. 3.9). These complex circuits interact and function according to feedback as well as adaptive control and feedforward principles (see Chapter 1). The various systems of the body are integrated by means of these circuits, with the brain serving as the major coordinating region. Furthermore, it is during the complex, highly intricate, and selective interaction of these circuits that, by our conception, mental processes are generated. The major empirical problem is to determine more specifically the nature and conditions of these interactions when they do generate mental processes.

By a cybernetic conception, mental processes are generated through the selective interaction of complex circuits within the brain and between the brain and the body.

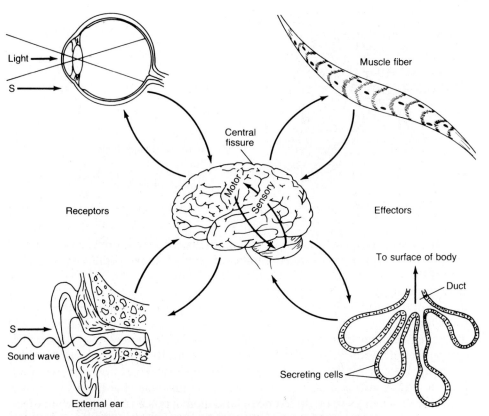

FIGURE 3.9 A general overview of how information is received and transmitted in circuits that integrate the brain with the body. When stimuli (S) activate receptor organs such as the eyes and ears, neural impulses are conducted along nerves between the brain and receptor systems in reverberating circuits (⟨⟩). The neural impulses also set off brain circuits (⟨⟩) and circuits to and from effectors (muscles and glands) to produce responses. Organisms are constantly activated by numerous stimuli so that numerous receptors–brain–effector circuits are simultaneously conducting information in parallel channels resulting in continuous waves of covert and overt responses. Complex feedback interactions of each event back to earlier systems are indicated by the reverse arrows.

In Chapter 13, we enlarge on these cybernetic principles of cognition and present a number of specific applications to better understand mental phenomena. For now, though, let us develop in the next chapter a foundation by obtaining an overview of how these systems of the body function.

KEY TERMS

Atomism/reductionism—An approach to understanding a phenomenon by specifying its components and laws of their connection. Atomism has been tre-

mendously successful in the history of science.

Behaviorism—The approach of those who define psychology as the study of behavior. Direct observable activity of organisms expressed in operational/physicalistic terms is used to explicate mental events.

British empiricism/associationism—A philosophical movement extending from Thomas Hobbes and John Locke in the early 1600s to Alexander Bain into the twentieth century. It held that the mind is to be understood through empiricism and the association of ideas.

Cell assembly—Hebb's concept of a hypothetical circuit of brain neurons formed by repeated stimulation.

Consciousness (behaviorism)—John B. Watson's definition involved objectively observable behavior, as in one's verbal description of events within and outside the body (internal and external environments).

Dualism—Holds that there are two fundamentally different kinds of worlds, one of the immaterial mind and one of matter.

Extirpation (ablation)—A method of studying functions of brain regions by removing nervous tissue.

Law of Equipotentiality—The various cortical regions contribute to the efficiency of any complex behavior in an equal fashion.

Law of Mass Action—The efficiency of an organism's performance is determined by the amount of brain tissue that remains intact.

Materialistic monism—"Mental events" are physical phenomena and are part of the material world.

Mind—For the purpose of this text, self-programming operations of the body that consist of, and only of, the selective activation of complex receptor-neuromuscular circuits that have cybernetic characteristics.

Monism—There is only one kind of reality, either mental *or* physical.

Neuromuscular circuits—Circuits consisting of central neural components, muscular components, and neural pathways between them. In these circuits, the musculature and brain interact by way of the afferent and efferent nervous pathways. Reverberation of neuromuscular circuits with cybernetic characteristics is the essential operation in internal information processing. The processing of external and internally stored information can explicate commonsense terms such as thinking and creativity. Consequently, mental events are not just central phenomena, but processes that involve the entire body.

Phrenology—The study of contours of the skull as indicative of character traits and location of mental faculties; from a disproven hypothesis of F. J. Gall.

Psychology—Science of behavior which includes physical cognitive phenomena. The first science devoted exclusively to the study of mind was founded in 1879 in Leipzig, Germany, by the father of psychology, Wilhelm Wundt.

Psychophysical interactionism—Dualistic position on the mind–body problem that mental and physical events are causally related.

Psychophysical parallelism—Dualistic position that mental and physical events are independent but occur simultaneously.

Reaction time—The time between the *onset* of a stimulus and *onset* of a response.

Response—A contraction of muscle or secretion of a gland, which constitutes behavior.

Stimulus–response relationship (law)—An empirically confirmed law with which we can control and predict a given response if a specific stimulus is presented.

Subjective idealism (mentalism)—The monistic mind–body position that holds that the only kind of energy in the world is immaterialistically mental.

Viscera—Internal organs of the body.

STUDY QUESTIONS

1. Discuss dualistic approaches to the mind–body problem.
2. What is the difference between psychophysical parallelism and psychophysical interactionism?
3. Explain monism.
4. Outline the differences between subjective idealism and materialistic monism.
5. Discuss the origins and birth of psychology and its transition to materialistic monism.

6. "Through behaviorism, the transition from dualism to monism was complete." Briefly explain this statement.
7. Illustrate the two hypotheses regarding the location of the mind.
8. "It might be naive to say that we think with our muscles, but it would be inaccurate to say that we think without them." What do you think about this statement?
9. What is phrenology?
10. How are mental processes generated in the perspective of the principles of cybernetics?

FURTHER READINGS

As you browse through your library you can select a good book in basic philosophy that elaborates on the various positions of the mind–body problem.

For a broad understanding of the evolution of psychology defined as the science of behavior, see the biography by

Buckley, K. W. (1989). *Mechanical man—John Broadus Watson and the beginning of behaviorism.* New York: Guilford.

For an elaboration of the transition to a circuit model of the brain and a relevant, extensive summary of psychophysiological measurements of mental activity see

McGuigan, F. J. (1978). *Cognitive Psychophysiology.* Englewood Cliffs, NJ: Prentice Hall.

Part II
Systems of the Body and How They Are Studied

A note to the student: The strategy for Part II is to present in Chapter 4 an overview of the important information processing systems, first the *receptor systems,* then the *nervous systems,* and finally the *effector systems.* In Chapter 4 we also focus on cells of the systems to help us better understand how they interact with each other. Then, we focus in greater detail on each system so that in Chapter 5 we emphasize the receptor systems, in Chapter 6 the nervous systems, and in Chapter 7 the effector systems. Although we are presenting these systems in the sequence of input, throughput, and output, we should not forget that in each of these stages there are important feedback mechanisms through which later events affect earlier stages of processing.

CHAPTER 4

An Overview of How the Body Functions

MAJOR PURPOSE:

To acquire a surface understanding of the major information processing systems of the body and how they interact through circuits

WHAT YOU ARE GOING TO FIND:

1. Structures and functions of systems of the body and how they relate among themselves and with the external environment
2. A discussion of the cells of the body, especially those specialized for receptor, nervous, and effector systems
3. How cells are depolarized, particularly when they transmit neural impulses throughout the body
4. Topographical terms that will help you refer to different structures and regions of the body

WHAT YOU SHOULD ACQUIRE:

A basic vocabulary for systems of the body, their components, and how those systems are integrated with each other

CHAPTER OUTLINE

DETERMINANTS OF BEHAVIOR THROUGH CYBERNETIC CIRCUITS
STIMULUS RECEPTION FROM THE EXTERNAL ENVIRONMENT
NEURAL TRANSMISSION AND RESPONDING

THE INTERNAL ENVIRONMENT
CELLS—THE BUILDING BLOCKS OF THE BODY AND CYBERNETIC SYSTEMS
Receptor Systems
Audition
Vision

The Nervous Systems and the Neuron
Parts of a neuron and neural activity
Kinds of neurons
Glial cells
Nerves contain axons
The reflex arc

DETERMINANTS OF BEHAVIOR
THROUGH CYBERNETIC CIRCUITS

When you examine how animals and humans behave when they move through life, you recognize the great complexity of environmental influences. These influences are often both subtle and quite intricate. So many stimuli affect the behavior of organisms that even if we knew them all, it would take a good-sized library to discuss them in detail. Generally, though, we can divide the factors that determine behavior patterns into **environmental** and **genetic** (inherited) influences. The environmental factors may be further divided into those of the **external environment** and those of the environment within us, the **internal environment.** All of these factors result in *patterns of behavior* that themselves are extremely complex, subtle, and constantly changing.

Behavior is influenced by the external and internal environments as well as genetic factors.

Internal Information Processing and Feedback. To understand behavior patterns, we first consider influences from the external environment. Later we turn to internal environmental factors. Our purpose is to develop a broad perspective of (1) *how we receive stimuli from the world about us;* (2) *how the information contained in those stimuli is processed throughout the body to influence our behavior;* and (3) *how the resulting behavior, in turn, feeds back to influence the internal and external environments.* As we saw in Figure 3.9, all of these stages are instances of the general principle of how cybernetic circuits function. In each case, the external environment sets off internal circuits that result in covert and overt behaviors. Those behaviors in turn influence the internal and external environments in continuous, complex interactions.

Stimuli from the external environment are internally processed within circuits and are covertly and overtly responded to; our overt and covert behaviors, in turn, affect our external and internal worlds through continuing feedback circuits.

We must emphasize how rapidly information is processed within the human body so that these internal receptors cause the neural and neuromuscular circuits to continuously reverberate with great rapidity. Some may ask, "Which part of a circuit starts first?" As we will see later in the book, the receptor, neural, and muscular events are the components of a fantastic number of receptor-neuromuscular circuits simultaneously reverberating; since those circuit components occur with such brief duration and so close together in time, it is almost impossible to specify that one starts before another. It is like asking when you view many pictures of interacting circles, "Where does one particular circle start?"

STIMULUS RECEPTION FROM THE EXTERNAL ENVIRONMENT

Stimulus *and* Environment *Defined.*   When energy from the external environment strikes (impinges on) an organism, it *may* influence the organism's behavior. If the energy impinges on an appropriate receptor organ, such as an eye or ear, and if it is intense enough to excite the receptor cells in the organ, we call that bit of energy a stimulus. A **stimulus** *is energy that impinges strongly enough upon an appropriate receptor organ to activate it with ongoing consequences.* Stimuli carry information that is then processed within the receptor organ and passed throughout the rest of the body. As a result, responses are fed back to the environment to further affect future environmental stimuli, as we saw for circuit class V in Figure 1.7.

Light is a specific type of energy in our environment. If a light ray of sufficient intensity impinges on an organism's eye, the eye is excited because the eye is the *appropriate* receptor organ for light (i.e., a light ray has little effect on an ear!). Other examples of stimuli that activate their appropriate receptor organs are odors that excite receptors in the nose and heat that may impinge on the skin. At any specific time an incredible number of different stimuli are impinging on any organism that is moving through its world. *The sum total of all those stimuli outside the body that could impinge on an organism constitutes that organism's external environment.* A critical function of those stimuli is to inform the organism about its world—stimuli thus carry information that can be used for effective living and even for bare survival.

The external environment consists of numerous stimuli that carry messages and that can potentially excite receptor organs to generate neural impulses that transmit those messages.

NEURAL TRANSMISSION AND RESPONDING

Neural Impulses Are Electrochemical Phenomena.   When a stimulus excites a receptor organ such as the eye, **nerve (neural) impulses** are generated that are conducted within nerves to the brain. Complex networks of these nerves, along with the brain and the spinal cord, constitute the *nervous systems,* which widely distribute neural impulses throughout the body, as we can study in Figure 4.1. For the moment, we may think of neural impulses as analogous to the flow of electricity. The analogy is not too misleading because neural impulses do have important electrical components. Electricity is conducted along wires and analogously neural impulses are conducted along nerves. Because neural impulses also have chemical components, another analogy, a chemical one, is with a trail of gunpowder. If you ignite one end of the trail, the gunpowder will burn continuously to the other end. But remember that analogies are never perfect.

From Receptors to Effectors.   At any given time the numerous **receptor organs** being excited generate a myriad of neural impulses that are simultaneously conducted to the brain. For example, think about yourself walking along a busy street at night—lights impinge on your eyes, sounds on your ears, odors on your nose, wind pressure on your skin, and on and on. Certainly such environmental energies keep your receptor systems active as they generate complex patterns of neural impulses that are received by your brain.

When neural impulses enter the brain, exceedingly complex events occur. They are so complex, in fact, that we understand only some of them. One conse-

Neural impulses have both electrical and chemical components and carry information along numerous neural circuits to and from the brain.

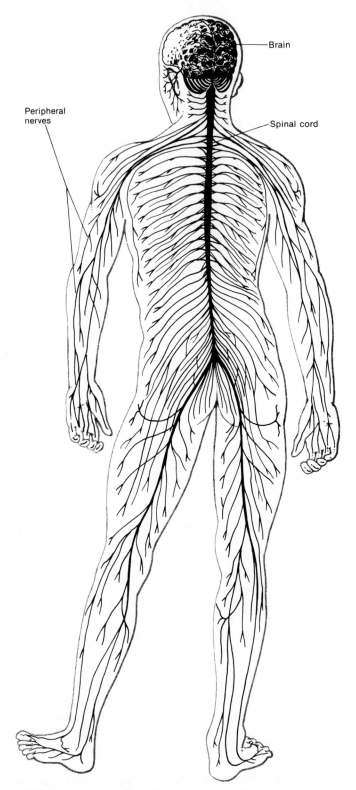

Brain

Peripheral
nerves

Spinal cord

FIGURE 4.1 An overview of the nervous systems.

quence of stimulus reception that we do know about, however, is that the neural impulses are transmitted back out of the brain to the receptor organs as well as to and from the muscular and glandular systems of the body. When the muscular and glandular systems receive neural impulses from the brain, **responses** occur. The activation of muscles and glands (e.g., when we raise an arm or secrete sweat), collectively called **effector systems,** constitutes these responses.

Thus when any specific stimulus that is part of an organism's external environment excites a receptor organ, it produces a response of some kind. The response may be an obvious *overt* one, such as when a baby touches a hot stove. On the other hand, responses may be quite subtle *covert* ones such as a slight wink of an eye, an extremely small twitch of a finger, or other even more subtle behaviors that cannot be readily observed without special instrumentation (e.g., galvanic skin responses, blood/sugar changes, etc.). We thus classify behavior according to whether responses are *overt* or *covert,* but more of this later.

In Review. We will concentrate on the following systems of the body because their primary use is for information processing: (1) *receptor systems* that generate neural impulses activated by energy from the external environment; (2) *nervous systems* that transmit and process neural impulses that carry information received by the receptor systems; and (3) *effector systems* that receive that information and, when activated, produce overt and covert responses. We also emphasize the important feature that transmission and processing of information from receptor to effector systems is not a one-way street. For example, when information from a receptor organ enters the brain, there is return stimulation from the brain back to modulate the receptor organ. We will continue enlarging on this critical cybernetic principle as we attempt to understand how the body functions.

External stimuli generate neural impulses that can evoke overt and covert responses; feedback from these responses affects the brain and often the external environment that provided the original external stimuli.

Each time an event occurs in receptor, neural, and effector systems, that event feeds back onto another system to affect it.

THE INTERNAL ENVIRONMENT

Circuits Activated by Internal Stimuli. This brief glimpse of how the body functions in relation to the external environment also provides us with an overview of how information is received and transmitted from the internal environment. Circuits that are directly set off by internal stimuli fit our cybernetic model well. The internal environment consists of energies that (like those for the external environment) can affect numerous internal receptors of the body. For instance, a pressure on the bladder or a noxious substance in the stomach can stimulate internal receptors in those regions. They, in turn, can generate neural impulses that are conducted to and from the brain to affect behavior in many ways. The resulting responses can also be obvious to an observer (these are overt responses) or they may be less obvious or hidden (covert responses) within the body. We may marvel at the richness and complexity of our internal environment, which is at least on a par with that of our external world. Consider the internal organs of the body — the liver, the kidneys, the stomach, the intestines, the heart. All of these contain receptors that are constantly being stimulated. We now may begin to realize the massive size and complexity of the internal communication system of the human body. Think of the numerous internal channels of information constantly running from those internal organs to and from the brain; then think of those channels carrying information from the external world. The combination of these networks in each person is a communica-

An extremely large number of internal receptors generate neural impulses that are transmitted to and from the brain within the internal environment.

The internal environment, composed of information processing circuits between the brain and numerous other systems within the skin, is a world probably at least as complex as that of the external environment.

tion system that is more intricate and complex than all of the computers of the world put together. As Emerson Pugh put it, if the brain were so simple that we could understand it, we would be so simple that we couldn't. What a mystery! And the brain is only one part of the complex human body. We certainly are going to have to settle here for less than a thoroughly detailed understanding of the body's systems. Our general purpose in this chapter is limited to developing a sufficient understanding of those systems to provide a broad perspective that can be developed later.

With this introduction using a cybernetic model to understand the functioning of the body, we now turn to how the basic units of these bodily systems, the **cells** of the body, are constructed. By momentarily focusing on the parts, we will enhance our understanding of how bodily systems all interact to carry out the body's purposes.

CELLS—THE BUILDING BLOCKS
OF THE BODY AND CYBERNETIC SYSTEMS

Cells, the basic units of the body's systems, contain cytoplasm and various structures within a membrane.

The Anatomy of Cells. The body consists of cells and various materials that connect them. Cells differ widely in their structures, sizes, appearances, and functions. Yet there is some commonality in this diversity. Figure 4.2 represents common features of an idealized cell.

Components of a Cell. A cell is essentially composed of **cytoplasm** and a number of structures contained within a **membrane.** Cytoplasm is a jellylike material that contains a nucleus and various small structures. Membranes are metabolically very active, quite labile, and dynamic. Membranes are mainly composed of lipids (fats), proteins, and a small amount of carbohydrates. The nucleus, the heart of the cell, contains **chromosomes** that carry genetic material. More specifically, genetic information (plans) for the development of the organism is contained in the **DNA (deoxyribonucleic acid)** of the chromosome. The DNA can be translated into **messenger ribonucleic acid (mRNA),** which leaves the nucleus and carries information (a "message"). The message initiates and controls the functioning of events in the surrounding cytoplasm. In particular, messenger RNA provides the blueprint for making protein; enzymes, the most important proteins, are called "the chemicals of life." Protein synthesis sustains the life of the cell (in a more complex process than we need to elaborate here). There are also intricate feedbacklike circuits functioning in these processes that are critical for the maintenance of cellular life.

The various other structures contained in the cytoplasm also carry out important functions for the cell. For instance, **mitochondria** are small structures that are loci for oxidative reactions—reactions that use oxygen to generate energy for the metabolism of the cell. Other components of the cell in Figure 4.2 are also identified to give a further hint as to the cell's complexity and for your further study in biological science. We now elaborate on the principle that cells of the body are specialized for different functions.

Specialized cells include receptor cells for receiving energy, neurons for transmitting information, neurosecretory cells for secreting chemical substances, and effector cells for responding.

Specialized Cells. Cells that are highly specialized in receptor organs, known as *receptor cells,* detect *very* subtle environmental changes. For example (assuming there is no atmospheric interference such as smog), the receptor cells in a human eye can detect a lighted match miles away. **Neurons** are nerve cells that are highly specialized for transmitting information throughout the body by means of coded

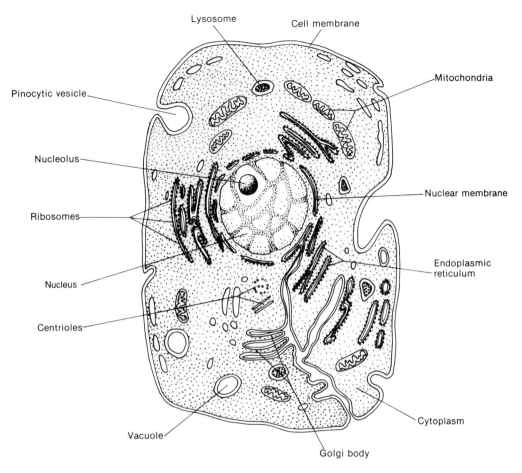

Lysosome

Cell membrane

Pinocytic vesicle

Mitochondria

Nucleolus

Nuclear membrane

Ribosomes

Nucleus

Endoplasmic reticulum

Centrioles

Cytoplasm

Vacuole

Golgi body

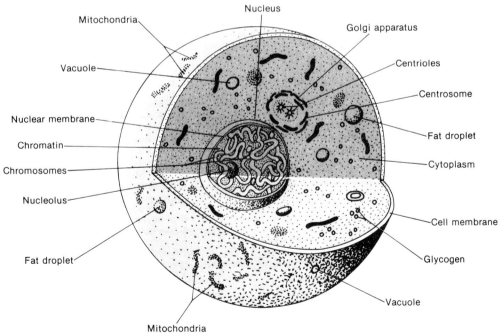

Mitochondria

Nucleus

Golgi apparatus

Vacuole

Centrioles

Centrosome

Nuclear membrane

Fat droplet

Chromatin

Cytoplasm

Chromosomes

Nucleolus

Cell membrane

Fat droplet

Glycogen

Mitochondria

Vacuole

FIGURE 4.2 An idealized cell emphasizing the cell membrane, the nucleus, and the cytoplasm. The top is a cross section. Not all cells contain all of the components specified.

neural impulses. *Neurosecretory cells* secrete hormones and other chemical substances that are distributed throughout the body in the circulatory (blood) system. *Muscular* and *glandular* cells uniquely respond to and influence our environments.

Let us now focus on some of these specialized cells that function in the receptor, nervous, and effector systems. This discussion enlarges on some of the components of cybernetic circuits that function among these three systems.

Receptor Systems

It is commonly, but erroneously, thought that humans possess "five senses." In addition, to "explain" certain mystical phenomena, people sometimes postulate a "sixth sense" and develop interesting stories about "twilight zones." Actually, though, we possess *many* more than six senses with a unique type of receptor system for each sense. Various receptor cells are especially sensitive to particular types of (internal or external) environmental energies. Just to start, we can list receptor cells for pain, cold, sweet, sour, direction, and pressure, in addition to vision and audition. This brief list could be extended considerably.

AUDITION

Auditory stimuli are sound waves that excite tiny hair receptor cells in the inner ear to send neural impulses to and from the brain.

Receptor cells in the ears are constantly activated by energy in the form of sound waves. Sound waves are sent through the air by vibrating molecules, as shown in Figure 4.3. Unfortunately, in our increasingly noise-polluted world, *many* vibrating objects, such as auto horns, school bells, lawn mowers, and compulsive talkers, generate more sound waves than we wish to or perhaps can handle. Sound vibrations are transmitted into the ear along the auditory canal. Eventually, tiny hair receptor cells in the cochlea generate nerve impulses that are conducted along the auditory nerve to and from the brain. Of course, there is *much* more to the auditory receptor system than this, but it gives us a general picture — we will fill in many of the details in Chapter 5.

FIGURE 4.3 Sound waves are the stimuli that carry information through the external and middle ears to activate hair cells within the inner ear. When activated, the hair cells generate neural impulses that are carried along the auditory nerve to and back from the brain.

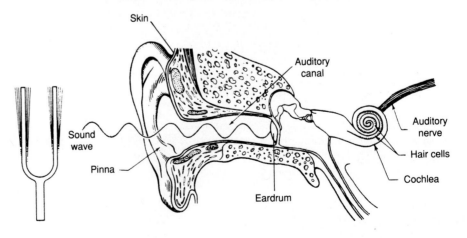

VISION

Radiant energy is the type of environmental energy that constitutes a visual stimulus. Some objects, such as light bulbs, emit radiant energy while other objects merely reflect it from other sources. In either case, it is radiant energy that enters the eye and is transmitted to the **retina** at the back of the eye. The retina contains a number of layers of cells, among which are ganglion cells, bipolar cells, rods, and cones. As can be seen in Figure 4.4, when light strikes the back of the eye, it can pass through the ganglion and bipolar cells to the rods and cones, which generate neural impulses when stimulated by light. The rods and cones are shielded from direct exposure to light by the ganglion and bipolar cells. The neural impulses generated by the rods and cones are then transmitted to bipolar cells, which act as links in a chain, conducting the neural impulses further to ganglion cells. The ends of the ganglion cells depicted in Figure 4.4 are tiny nerve fibers that join together to make up the major **optic nerve** that transmits neural impulses to and from the brain. All of these events (and more) are critical for the sense modality of vision.

Visual stimuli are radiant energies that excite rods and cones in the retina to generate neural impulses transmitted along bipolar and ganglion cells to the optic nerve and eventually to the brain.

Audition and vision constitute two of our most important senses and, in fact, they are the ones on which we humans primarily rely as we interact with our environments. Other animals are more dependent on other senses. Dogs, of course, rely more on smell than we do. Even so, this brief illustration of two sense modalities should suffice as an introduction to the receptor systems of the body. We will consider these and other receptor systems in greater detail in Chapter 5, but for now we continue our overview of how information generated by receptors is received and processed by neurons within the nervous systems and then by the effectors.

The Nervous Systems and the Neuron

It will not be in our lifetimes that we reach a really advanced understanding of the some 10 billion or so neurons in the human brain. We even have difficulty understanding the brains of the ant with but 250 neurons or of the bee with 900 neurons. But research does move on.

PARTS OF A NEURON AND NEURAL ACTIVITY

Figure 4.5 illustrates a representative neuron (and its four major parts): (1) the **dendrite,** (2) the **cell body,** (3) the **axon,** and (4) the **collaterals,** which branch and contain **terminal buttons** (often referred to in French as *les boutons*).

Dendrites and Cell Bodies May Transmit Graded Reactions. Dendrites look somewhat like bushes or trees (the term actually comes from the Greek *dendron* for "tree"). Dendrites may be excited by impulses that carry information from a receptor cell or from another neuron. An excitation that occurs at the dendrite is called a **graded reaction** because it varies (is graded) in intensity. Thus, an intense or lengthy stimulus that excites a dendrite generates an intense graded reaction. But if a stimulus is weak or brief, the graded potential would be of low intensity.[1]

A neural excitation transmitted from a dendrite is a graded reaction with an intensity that varies according to the intensity and/or duration of the stimulating excitation.

---

[1]The All-or-None Law, which will be discussed later, is a phenomenon of the axon and not of the dendrite and cell body. It also applies to striated muscle fibers and to the heart as a whole.

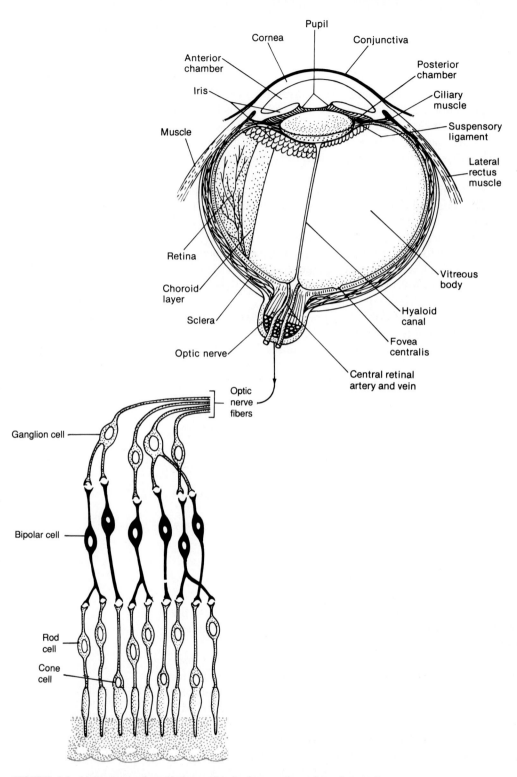

FIGURE 4.4 Light passes through the pupil to impinge on the rods and cones in the retina at the back of the eye (top). The resulting neural impulses are transmitted along bipolar and ganglion cells and then along the optic nerve to the brain as illustrated in the enlargement at the bottom.

90

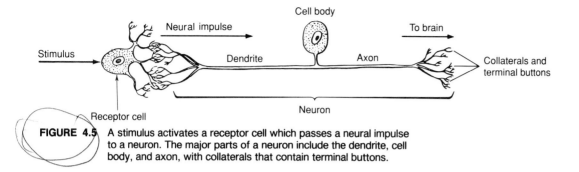

FIGURE 4.5 A stimulus activates a receptor cell which passes a neural impulse to a neuron. The major parts of a neuron include the dendrite, cell body, and axon, with collaterals that contain terminal buttons.

Axons Transmit Nerve Impulses. The cell body of the neuron, like a typical cell of the body, nourishes the cell. Cell bodies can also be directly excited by neural impulses from other neurons. Regardless of whether excited at the dendrite or the cell body, the graded reaction is transmitted toward the axon. If the graded reaction is sufficiently intense when it reaches the axon, a nerve impulse is generated that is transmitted along the axon to the terminal buttons. The axon always transmits neural impulses *from* the cell body toward another neuron, or some other type of cell such as a muscle cell. Axons in the body are typically very long so that they can rapidly conduct messages in the form of neural impulses to and from various systems. Neurons whose axons project for relatively long distances are called projection neurons.

Dendrites and cell bodies transmit neural impulses to axons, activating terminal buttons in the collaterals, which typically liberate chemical **transmitter substances.** These chemicals may then transmit information that is carried in neural impulses to adjoining cells. We will have more to say about these chemical transmitter substances, which are called neurotransmitters.

Neural excitations are transmitted along a neuron from the dendrite and/or cell body through the axon to terminal buttons at the collaterals, which may transmit information to the adjoining cells.

KINDS OF NEURONS

Remember that we are offering typical generalizations that, by definition, have exceptions. It is, for instance, typical that neurons have one axon with branches like those depicted in Figure 4.5, but some neurons have no axons at all because their cell bodies themselves make a junction with another cell. Yet other atypical cells may have two axons. The great variety of neurons, especially regarding their dendrites and axons, makes it impossible to offer hard and fast rules for anatomical classification. The least confusing classification is made according to their functions as **sensory (afferent), association (connective),** and **motor (efferent)** neurons (Fig. 4.6).

When a sensory (afferent) neuron is activated, it transmits neural impulses to the brain (*afferent* is derived from the Latin word *afferre,* meaning "to bring to"; hence, *a*fferent neurons conduct impulses toward the brain). Motor or *e*fferent neurons conduct neural impulses out of the brain to effectors (*ef* is derived from the Latin word *efferre,* meaning "to carry outward"). The association (connective) neuron found inside the brain and spinal cord associates or connects the two.

The sizes of neurons vary greatly; some are as small as 4 microns in diameter with short axons and dendrites (one micron is one-millionth of a meter). Such small

Neurons serve sensory, association, and motor functions.

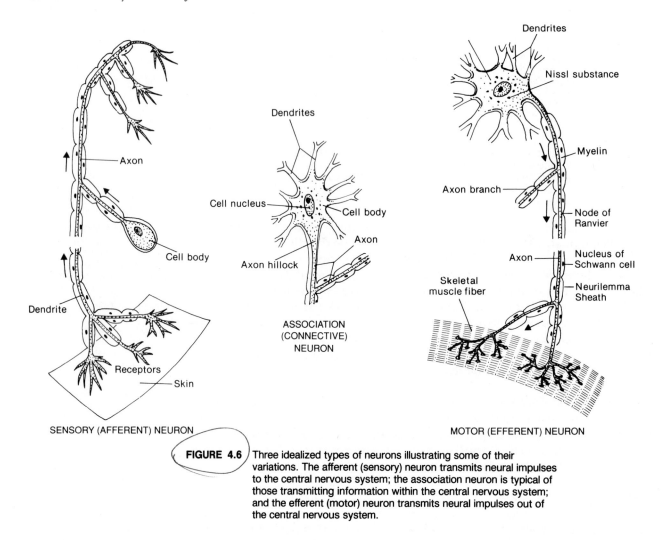

ASSOCIATION
(CONNECTIVE)
NEURON

MOTOR (EFFERENT) NEURON

FIGURE 4.6 Three idealized types of neurons illustrating some of their variations. The afferent (sensory) neuron transmits neural impulses to the central nervous system; the association neuron is typical of those transmitting information within the central nervous system; and the efferent (motor) neuron transmits neural impulses out of the central nervous system.

neurons occur frequently in the brain. Larger neurons are 100 microns or more in diameter and can be seen with the naked eye.

GLIAL CELLS

Glial cells serve many important functions.

The brain also contains **glial cells,** which constitute approximately 50 percent of the volume of the central nervous system (CNS). The term derives from the Greek word *glia* meaning glue, and the cells are so-called because it was previously thought that glial cells merely "glued" neurons together. However, now we know they are more complex in their function: Glial cells generate chemicals that are transmitted to neurons; they insulate some neurons from each other so as to prevent cross talk among those particular neurons; they function as "housekeepers" by removing neurons that die as a result of either old age or some kind of insult; and they contribute to a phenomenon known as neural induction (which is more complex than we need to consider here). Clearly glial cells are not just for "glue."

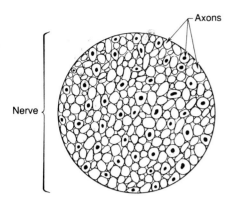

FIGURE 4.7
A cross section of a nerve composed of numerous axons. Within a nerve, some axons conduct impulse in one direction while other axons conduct in the opposite direction. Consequently, neural impulses are conducted along neurons in both directions simultaneously within a nerve as cybernetic circuits reverberate.

NERVES CONTAIN AXONS

Figure 4.7 represents a cross section of a nerve that is composed of numerous (hundreds or even thousands) of axons. Some axons within a nerve are oriented in one direction while others within the same nerve are oriented in the opposite direction. Consequently, neural impulses are simultaneously conducted in both directions within the same nerve. This phenomenon of two-way conduction within a nerve is quite important, as we will develop at various points throughout the book. It means, for instance, that while neural impulses are conducted from one bodily system to another, that same nerve may function to return the effects from the second to the first system—the flow of neural impulses between two systems is a "two-way (cybernetic) street." As the axon conducts the neural impulses, there are also active processes within the nerve that influence the coding of messages.

Myelination and Nodes. Most axons are covered by fatty myelin sheaths that insulate the axons within a nerve from each other. The myelin sheaths in such **myelinated fibers** become very thin or absent about every two millimeters in regions called nodes. Neural impulses are conducted along myelinated axons by "jumping" from one node to the next, a feature that increases the rate of neural transmission. Nonmyelinated fibers, lacking nodes, conduct neural impulses more slowly. Myelination seems to have developed relatively late in the nervous system of animals higher on the phylogenetic scale. The myelin sheath in many nerve fibers in the brain is not completed until sometime after birth. Perhaps slower transmission of neural impulses in the brain is important for the development of some behavioral characteristics during maturation.

THE REFLEX ARC

The functional classification of neurons as sensory, association, and motor is represented in a **reflex arc** (Fig. 4.8). The reflex arc is the simplest possible arrangement of neurons functioning together to affect behavior. The three different types of neurons thus act together in an integrated fashion.

Reflexes Are Numerous, Rapid, and Have Survival Value. In some reflex arcs there is more than one single association neuron. However, in others, there is no association neuron at all so that the afferent neuron simply makes junction with the efferent neuron. In any case, the activation of a series of neurons that form a reflex

Many neural impulses can be conducted simultaneously and in opposite directions along different axons within a given nerve.

In a reflex arc, an afferent neuron transmits neural impulses from a receptor to an association neuron which in turn transmits impulses to an efferent neuron and then to an effector.

Reflex arcs function to make rapid responses, usually of a protective variety.

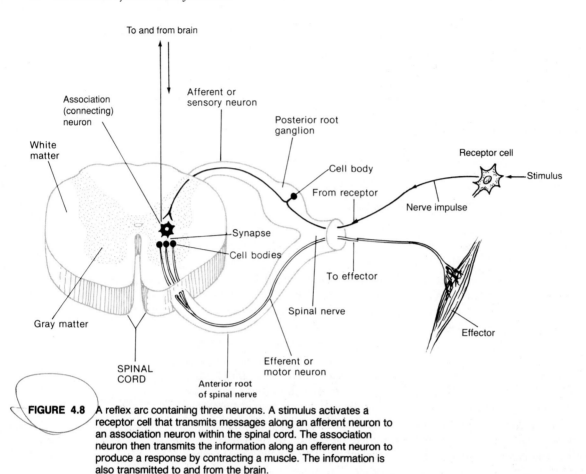

FIGURE 4.8 A reflex arc containing three neurons. A stimulus activates a receptor cell that transmits messages along an afferent neuron to an association neuron within the spinal cord. The association neuron then transmits the information along an efferent neuron to produce a response by contracting a muscle. The information is also transmitted to and from the brain.

arc requires but a fraction of a second. Think how fast you can reflexively react to danger—neural impulses are *very* quickly conducted into, through, and back out of the spinal cord to the muscles. The largest neural fibers in humans conduct at perhaps 60 meters per second and total reflexes occur in perhaps 200 milliseconds (ms; 1 ms is one one-thousandth of a second).

Nor do we have to learn reflex reactions because reflex arcs are "wired in," born within us or genetically programmed to eventually appear. In any case, reflexes have considerable survival value. Numerous reflexes, such as the contraction of the pupil of the eye to light, help us automatically adjust to the demands of our environments.

Reflex Information Is Also Transmitted to and from the Brain. As neural impulses enter the spinal cord for the afferent part of the reflex arc, they simultaneously ascend the spinal cord to the brain (see Fig. 4.8). As they enter the brain, additional complex events occur, some of which produce neural impulses that descend the spinal cord to affect further behaviors. Those additional behaviors (e.g., muscle contractions) in turn produce neural impulses that enter the spinal cord and brain in continuing reverberating cybernetic circuits. Let us now focus on how the transmission of neural impulses from the central nervous system acts on effectors to produce responses.

The Effectors

Behavior is composed of responses and a response is the activation of effectors (the muscles and glands).

Responses are behaviors that occur when muscles contract or glands secrete their products.

MUSCLES

There are three kinds of muscle cells: (1) **striated (skeletal, striped, voluntary),** (2) **smooth (involuntary)** and (3) **cardiac** muscle fibers (Fig. 4.9). A muscle is similar to a nerve in that both are collections of tiny fibers. Figure 4.9a depicts a number of skeletal muscle fibers bound together to form a muscle. A single efferent nerve fiber joins several of the muscle fibers so that when a neural impulse arrives along it, a number of muscle fibers contract. Since a number of efferent neurons connect with each muscle, a number of neural impulses can arrive simultaneously at a muscle to cause a large number of muscle fibers to contract.

FIGURE 4.9   There are three kinds of muscle tissue.

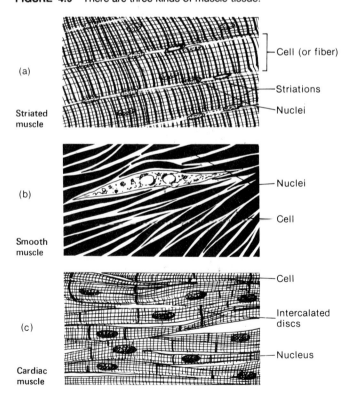

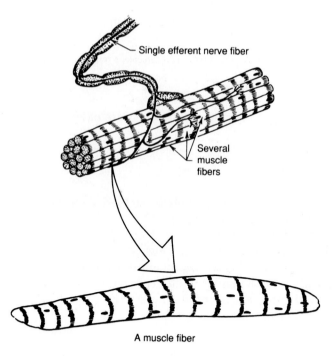

— Single efferent nerve fiber

Several
muscle
fibers

A muscle fiber

FIGURE 4.10
Striated muscle fibers are
activated by neural impulses
delivered along efferent neural
fibers (top). The striations
(stripes) are shown in a single
muscle fiber (bottom).

Striated Muscle

Note in Figure 4.10 that striated muscle has small stripes or striations (threadlike lines), so that it also is called striped muscle. Another name is skeletal muscle, derived from the fact that the muscle (with several exceptions) is attached by tendons to the bones or skeleton of the body.

The muscle cell is the structural unit of striated muscle. To the naked eye it appears much like a fine piece of thread or a hair from the head. Like all cells, striated muscle fibers contain cytoplasm which, in this case, is called *sarcoplasm*. Similarly, the cell membrane in muscle fibers is referred to as *sarcolemma*.

To understand how striated muscles function we note in Figure 4.11 the well-known biceps and triceps muscles of the upper arm. When neural impulses are conducted along nerve fibers (a), the biceps muscle contracts whereupon the biceps pulls on the upper bone of the lower arm, causing the arm to move up. When neural

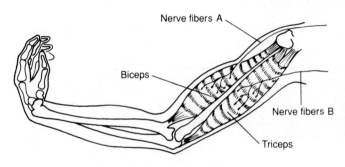

Nerve fibers A

Biceps

Nerve fibers B

Triceps

FIGURE 4.11
Example of how we move
parts of our body—
contraction of the biceps
muscle pulls the arm up while
contraction of the triceps
muscle extends the arm.

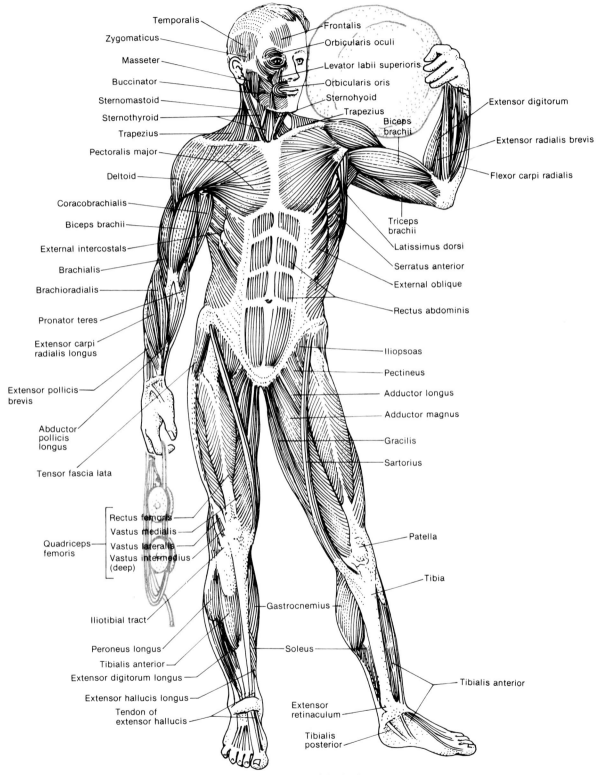

FIGURE 4.12 Some of the approximately 1030 striated muscles of the body.

impulses arrive at the triceps muscle along nerve fibers (b), the triceps muscle contracts, thereupon straightening the arm out by pulling the lower bone in the forearm.

We behave in our environments by voluntarily contracting our striated muscles.

A number of other striated muscles are illustrated in Figure 4.12. By the systematic contraction of these muscles throughout the body, we perform such activities as sitting, running, and talking, which are **voluntary responses**—you ''decide'' to raise your hand above your head and, in fact, you can say whether or not you are going to do so prior to your actual response. Hence striated muscles are synonymously called voluntary muscles. In fact, the term *voluntary muscles* has a long and rich history that we will develop in Chapter 15 when we talk about self-management/self-control.

Smooth Muscle

Internal visceral functions are mainly carried out by the contraction of smooth muscles, such as those of the gastrointestinal and cardiovascular systems.

Smooth muscle cells lack striations and are smooth in appearance to the naked eye (Fig. 4.13). Smooth muscles are located more in the internal **(visceral)** parts of the body while striated muscles are distributed just underneath the skin. The stomach and intestines are examples of internal organs that contain smooth muscles. Smooth muscle fibers are also smaller and function differently from striated muscle fibers. Skeletal muscle fibers contract almost immediately after receiving a nerve impulse (known as a short latency period), while it takes much longer for smooth muscles to contract (long latency). The short response latency for rapid responding with striated muscles has obvious survival value. For example, we have to be fast in jumping out of the way of an oncoming car (by means of our striated muscles), but we do not need to respond so rapidly when moving food along our gastrointestinal tract (with our smooth muscles). On the other hand, smooth muscles have the ability to sustain contractions for longer periods of time, which is necessary for visceral functions.

Smooth muscle also surrounds the blood vessels so widely distributed throughout the body, thus influencing the flow of blood throughout the cardiovascular (circulatory) system. A continual supply of fresh blood, needed in various regions of the body, is furnished by the automatic functioning of the cardiovascular system. Quite fortunately, you do not have to decide that you will contract or relax smooth muscle as you distribute blood throughout your body to meet emergency requirements or to digest your food. It is because their activities are automatic that the smooth muscles are also referred to as *involuntary muscles.*

Cardiac Muscle

This third type of muscle cell, the cardiac cell, appears somewhat striated and the fibers form quite an irregular meshwork (see Fig. 4.9). Cardiac muscle fibers are intimately interwoven with numerous complex connections to form the walls of the

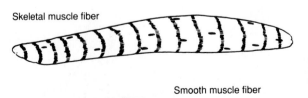

Skeletal muscle fiber

Smooth muscle fiber

FIGURE 4.13
A smooth muscle fiber contrasted with a striated muscle fiber. Note that the smooth muscle lacks striations and is smaller than the striated muscle fiber.

heart. The primary function of the heart, of course, is to pump blood throughout the cardiovascular system. In this way, blood is involuntarily, and in the appropriate amounts, distributed throughout the body wherever and whenever it is required.

THE GLANDS

There are two general classes of glands: exocrine and endocrine glands.

Exocrine Glands

Exocrine glands are so named because they secrete their products through *ducts* to a surface of the body (*ex* derives from the Greek *exo* meaning "out of" or "outside"). They thus secrete into the *ex*ternal environment. A synonym for exocrine gland is *duct gland.* An example is the sweat gland—it secretes sweat through an attached duct to the skin (Fig. 4.14). Similarly, salivary glands manufacture saliva and secrete it through attached ducts into the mouth. Because the inside of the mouth is continuous with the outer skin of the body, it too is a bodily surface. In a similar manner, the gastrointestinal tract may also be considered an external surface of the body because it is exposed to the external world through the mouth at the top and through the anal orifice at the bottom.

Endocrine Glands

Endocrine glands (derived from the Greek *endo* meaning "within") secrete their products within the body directly into the bloodstream. Lacking ducts, they are synonymously referred to as *ductless glands.* The products they secrete are the chemical compounds called **hormones.** Once hormones enter the bloodstream, they are widely distributed throughout the body to produce an amazing variety of consequences. For example, note in Figure 4.15 the suprarenal glands that secrete the hormone adrenalin directly into the bloodstream. Adrenalin is then carried to the liver where it triggers an increased amount of blood sugar to flow into the bloodstream. This extra blood sugar provides additional energy to respond in an emergency situation.

Exocrine glands secrete their substances into the external environment while endocrine glands secrete their products into the internal environment.

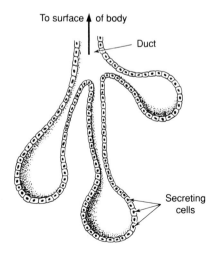

FIGURE 4.14
This sweat gland is an example of an exocrine gland that secretes its substance directly to the surface of the body through ducts.

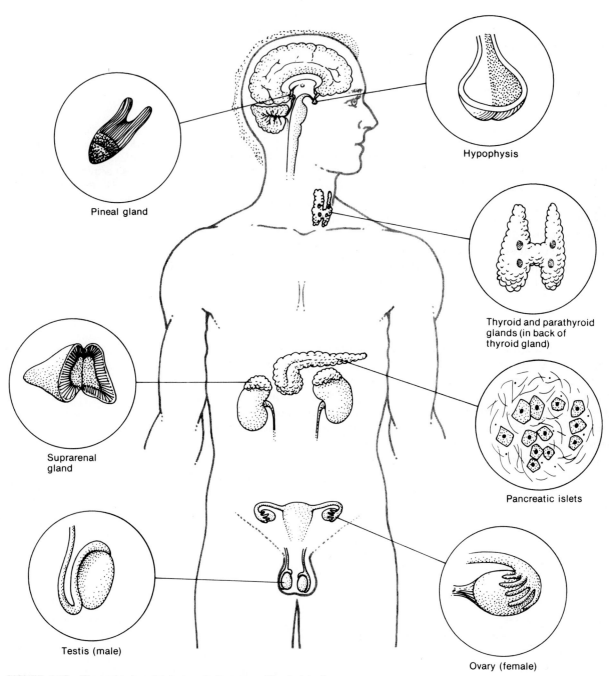

Pineal gland

Hypophysis

Thyroid and parathyroid glands (in back of thyroid gland)

Suprarenal gland

Pancreatic islets

Testis (male)

Ovary (female)

FIGURE 4.15 The endocrine glands secrete hormones directly into the circulatory system and thus have far-reaching effects throughout the body.

FIGURE 4.16
A goiter as produced by
enlargement of the thyroid
gland.

Another example is the thyroid gland in the neck region (see Fig. 4.15) that secretes the hormone called thyroxin. Excesses and shortages of thyroxin in the bloodstream have a number of interesting effects. A shortage of thyroxin may result in a goiter, an enlargement of the thyroid gland (Fig. 4.16). What happens is this: When the thyroid gland is deficient, it does not produce enough thyroxin. Because the body demands more thyroxin, the thyroid gland compensates by growing larger. The enlarged gland thus produces an increased supply of thyroxin so as to achieve a homeostatic level of thyroxin.

This completes our overview of the systems of the body and how they function as we go through our everyday lives. We now need to understand these functions in greater detail. For this purpose, we need to study how the cells of the body conduct and process information.

CELLS — THEIR EXCITABILITY IN TRANSMITTING AND PROCESSING INFORMATION

Cell excitability is the ability of a cell to react to some stimulus: A muscle cell may contract; a glandular cell may secrete its product; and a nerve cell may conduct a graded reaction. Reactions of cells may also be *inhibitory*. **Inhibitory reactions** slow or prevent cells from contracting, secreting, or conducting.

In nerve and muscle cells, excitability reactions are chemical *and* electrical in nature. The electrochemical reaction in these cells involves reactions of the cell's *membrane*. The reaction in a membrane is a localized disturbance of the resting state of the cell. In nonliving systems such as computers, we usually transmit messages electrically and mechanically. Within the human body messages are most frequently transmitted by localized disturbances that are propagated within the nervous sys-

When a cell is excited there is a localized disturbance of the resting state that is propagated along the neuron.

tems. Let us see how excitability as a localized disturbance becomes a **propagated disturbance** in nerve cells, noting that much of what we have to say is applicable as well to other living cells of the body. First, consider the status of a cell (neuron) that is not excited.

The Resting Nerve Cell

A potential difference exists between the inside and outside of the membrane of a neuron (and other cells) that constitutes an electrical potential in the resting state.

A magnified portion of a neuron is represented in its resting state in Figure 4.17. Note that the neuron, like all body cells, is enveloped by a membrane and that there is a difference in **electrical potential** between the inside and the outside of the cell's membrane. The inside is electrically *negative* relative to the outside. The negative status of the inside relative to the outside constitutes a **potential difference** — the difference in electrical potential between two points. The potential difference represents the amount of energy that may (potentially) be transferred between those two points. The resting membrane potential thus represents the potential amplitude of (amount of energy in) a propagated disturbance. The amount of membrane potential difference varies with many conditions and in a variety of mammalian cells. They have been measured as low as about 45 **millivolts (mv)** in the giant axon of the squid to about 100 millivolts in skeletal muscle fibers of the rat (*milli* means "thousandths" so that 1 millivolt is one one-thousandth of a volt).

This potential difference in the resting neuron is the way that the neuron stores electrical energy. That energy can then be released when a neural impulse from another neuron creates a localized disturbance in a resting neuron. The resting neuron (muscle cell, etc.) is thus like a bullet waiting to be fired. Like many components of the body, it is advantageous to have the neuron ("bullet") ready to fire when needed, rather than having to generate energy starting from zero. In this way we can more quickly react in an emergency situation.

FIGURE 4.17   Representation of a resting neuron with positive charges outside and negative charges inside the membrane.

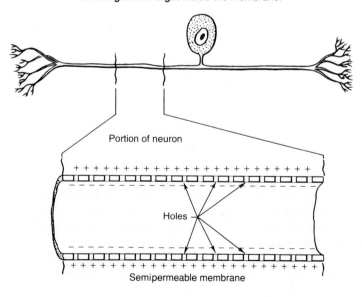

Portion of neuron

Holes

Semipermeable membrane

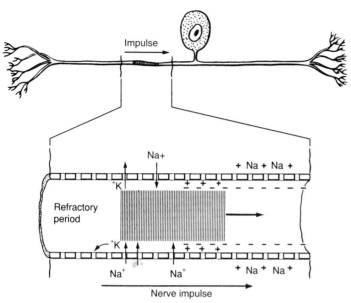

FIGURE 4.18 A propagated disturbance being conducted along a neuron wherein positive sodium (Na^+) ions pass through the minute holes in the semipermeable membrane.

The Propagated Disturbance

When there is a disturbance of the balance between the positive ions on the outside of the membrane and the negative ions on the inside of the membrane, the neuron starts to transmit a propagated disturbance. To understand how this happens, note that in Figure 4.18 the shaded portion of the neuron indicates a graded reaction/nerve impulse traveling along it. *The passage of a graded reaction and nerve impulse is a localized disturbance that is propagated along the neuron.* During the propagated disturbance, the balance between positive and negative ions that exists during the resting state is disturbed. The disturbance of this balance occurs as the positive ions move to the inside of the membrane. As the disturbance moves along the neuron, positive ions *continue* to move inside so that the balance in each succeeding section of the neuron is disturbed. Let us see in more detail how the propagated disturbance occurs.

The graded reaction and nerve impulse are propagated disturbances wherein the balance between positive and negative ions is modified.

Electrical and Chemical Reactions in the Nerve Cell

SEMIPERMEABLE MEMBRANES

First note that electrically charged ions float in the protoplasm of cells and in the liquids surrounding the cells. Some of these ions are maintained *within* the resting nerve cell by the membrane. The membrane is **semipermeable,** which means that some ions can pass through it but others cannot. The semipermeable membrane is analogous to a strainer or colander that lets small particles pass through the holes but retains larger materials. In the neuron, some ions can thus move through the small

A semipermeable membrane allows the passage of some small ions through the openings but not of larger ions during the propagated disturbance.

holes in the membrane while others cannot. More particularly, note that the small openings in the membrane in Figures 4.17 and 4.18 are sufficiently large to allow the passage of small ions from the inside of the membrane to the outside (and vice versa); however, the openings are too small to allow the similar passage of larger ions. Because of this construction, *the membrane controls the passage of ions into and out of the cell.* The concept of a semipermeable membrane is important for an understanding of the biochemical and electrical components of the propagated disturbance.

Potassium and Sodium Ions Pass Through the Semipermeable Membrane. The positive ions depicted in Figure 4.18 existing on the outside of the semipermeable membrane are chemical particles called sodium ions (symbolized as Na^+). Potassium ions (K^+) that are also positively charged are concentrated on the inside of the semipermeable membrane. There are also various other ions present (e.g., chloride, Cl^-) that contribute to the potential difference, but these other ions are not germane to this limited discussion.

The inside of a resting cell is negative relative to the positive outside because of the movement of some ions (mainly K^+) but not others (mainly Na^+) through the holes in the membrane.

We can thus see that the potential difference in the resting state occurs in large part because the membrane is semipermeable to ions and thus does not allow much movement of sodium ions—the cell's membrane keeps the larger sodium ions concentrated on the outside. On the other hand the smaller potassium ions *can* flow to the inside where they are concentrated within the resting neuron. The flow of Na^+ and K^+ ions through the semipermeable membranes is governed by a sodium–potassium "pump"; this pump is a complex phenomenon that we need not go into except to say that it is a set of molecules inside the membrane that functions to transport sodium ions out of the cell and potassium ions into the cell.

Depolarization and the Action Potential

The Start of a Neuron's Excitation. Consider that a stimulus, such as a neural impulse from a neighboring nerve cell, is applied to a resting cell. The resting state where the stimulus is applied is thereby disturbed, creating a localized disturbance, which, as we see in Figure 4.18, is then propagated along the entire membrane. The region of the cell from which the localized disturbance is transmitted is then **depolarized.** As a consequence, the polarization of that region is changed so that the outside of that part of the cell is no longer positive relative to the negatively charged inside. That is, when depolarization of a region occurs, there is a change in the electrical potential and chemical status of that region of the resting neuron. During this change, the flow of electricity (electrical current) constitutes the *electrical* component of the propagated disturbance. If the change in the electrical potential (the flow of electrical current) across the membrane is sufficiently great, *the permeability of the cell membrane increases* (the openings get larger). As a consequence, there is increased permeability to sodium ions. They can now pour into the inside of the semipermeable membrane (see Fig. 4.18). As the depolarization continues, the membrane's permeability to sodium further increases, whereupon the holes open even wider for sodium inflow.

Depolarization of regions of a cell occurs as ions are exchanged through the small openings in the cell's membrane and a disturbance is propagated.

The Excitation Is Conducted Along the Neuron. When the flow of sodium ions becomes greatest, the change in the electrical potential reaches its maximum. The outside of the depolarized portion of the cell membrane now becomes negative with respect to the inside. The disturbance in the localized region is then propagated along the membrane to continuously permit the flow of sodium ions to the inside. This process, being repeated all along the neuron, generates the (electrical) action potential. Eventually then, some positive ions all along the nerve cell move to the inside of the semipermeable membrane. In this manner, an excitation that enters a neuron at the dendrite is conducted along the dendrite and through the cell to the axon as a graded reaction. If the graded reaction is sufficiently intense, it generates a nerve impulse that is conducted along the axon to the terminal buttons.

When the change in the electrical potential reaches its maximum in a given region of a nerve cell, the permeability of the membrane suddenly changes again — it becomes highly *impermeable* to sodium ions and somewhat more permeable to potassium ions. The sodium ions remaining on the outside no longer enter the cell (actually the large majority of them never do pass to the inside). Then, potassium ions rapidly move from the inside to the outside of the semipermeable membrane, as illustrated in Figure 4.18. *The electrical aspects of a nerve impulse are thus largely produced by the passage of sodium ions to the inside and the later passage of potassium ions to the outside of the semipermeable membrane.*

In Brief. As a propagated disturbance moves along a neuron, electrical depolarization occurs as the permeability of the membrane increases to allow the inflow of sodium ions. As the flow of sodium ions becomes maximized, the change in electrical potential reaches its maximum, whereupon the permeability decreases so that sodium ions no longer flow in and potassium ions rapidly move to the outside.

Other phenomena that occur (such as those affecting other ions and electrostatic and osmotic pressures) are beyond the scope of this limited discussion of the basic principles of the propagated disturbance.

The propagated depolarization due to selective ionic movement through the openings in the semipermeable membrane may be electrically sensed in a single cell by means of cellular electrodes. Let us now see how this sensing is accomplished.

Studying the Electrical Aspects of the Propagated Disturbance

Figure 4.19 shows one electrode inserted into a neuron and a second electrode placed immediately on its outside. To study the electrical aspects of a nerve impulse, the electrodes are connected to a sensing instrument such as a cathode ray oscilloscope (CRO, as on a TV set), which allows us to measure the amount of change in electrical potential. Thus, when a nerve impulse is conducted along a neuron, electrical current will flow along the attached electrodes, whereupon the sensing instrument is activated. By observing the activity on the CRO, we can measure the change from the resting potential to the excitation, which is the electrical aspect of a nerve impulse that is conducted along a neuron. This change is called the **action potential.**

Graphing Electrical Changes of Neural Excitations. Figure 4.20 shows the action potential as the disturbance passes through any given region in a neuron. Note that the vertical axis is labeled "membrane potential in millivolts (mv)" and that the horizontal axis is labeled time in milliseconds. The resting potential is about −80mv. By studying Figure 4.20 we can tell the amount of change in the electrical potential (the amplitude or the intensity of the action potential) generated at any given time during depolarization. Note that a small "bump" occurs just before the large **spike potential.** This small rise indicates that before the spike potential occurs, the change

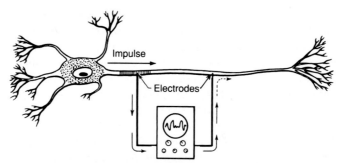

FIGURE 4.19   The electrical components of a propagated disturbance is measured by inserting a microelectrode inside the neuron and placing another one on the outside; each is connected to a sensing instrument such as a cathode ray oscilloscope completing the circuit.

A neuron's (electrical) action potential is primarily the spike potential. Following that is an absolute refractory period when the neuron cannot conduct a nerve impulse. Then there is a relative refractory period when the neuron can conduct an impulse of greater than normal intensity.

in membrane potential (the flow of electrical current) is quite small. After that, the spike potential is a large change in membrane potential (it is from about −80mv to about 40mv), after which there is a prolonged decrease in amplitude. Although these characteristics are typical, the actual form of the recorded action potential varies with a large number of factors, including the character of the particular cell with its special parameters for depolarization and recovery, the speed with which the propagated depolarization is transmitted along the cell membrane (fast in neural tissue, slow in muscle cells), and the orientation of the electrodes with regard to the source of the action potential.

Refractory Periods

Immediately after a neuron fires, it is in an "exhausted" state. Hence, the neuron needs to recharge before it can fire again. This period immediately following the spike potential of the nerve impulse is known as the **refractory period,** which consists of an *absolute* followed by a *relative* phase. It is during the **absolute refractory period** that the neuron is completely unable to conduct a nerve impulse. During

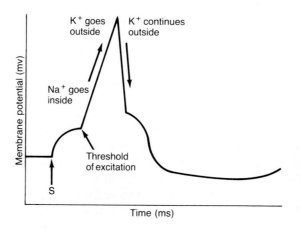

FIGURE 4.20
The electrical record of a typical propagated disturbance (top). The flow of Na^+ and K^+ ions following the stimulus (S) and the exceeding of the threshold of excitation are indicated (bottom).

the **relative refractory period,** the neuron *can* conduct another nerve impulse, provided that the new impulse reaching the neuron is quite intense. To further understand transmission of neural impulses throughout the nervous systems, we should turn to the concept of the synapse.

From One Cell to the Next—Synapses

Synapse Defined. How are messages that are coded in neural impulses transmitted from one cell to another? The axonal branches of a neuron make junction with other cells, with a small space between the transmitting and receiving cells. A neural impulse may be transmitted across that space, the **synapse,** to these next cells. A synapse is a region between an axon (specifically a terminal button on the axon, see later discussion) and the membrane of an adjoining cell.

Kinds of Synapses. Each axonal branch may have a synapse with various kinds of structures. If it comes in contact with a dendrite, it is known as an axodendritic synapse. If it makes junction with a cell body of another neuron, it is referred to as an axosomatic synapse (*soma* means "body"). It is an axoaxonal synapse if the part of the next cell is an axon, and it is a neuroeffector synapse if that adjacent cell is an effector cell. When the effector cell is muscle, the synapse is a neuromuscular (or myoneural because *myo* means "muscle") junction. There are also instances in the brain when dendrites actually synapse with each other as well as with the axons and cell bodies of other neurons. There may be thousands of synapses on the surface of a single neuron and its axons and dendrites. They form numerous circuits in the brain, as we later depict in Figures 6.8 and 6.9.

Anatomy of a Synapse. Actually, terminal buttons at the end of axonal branches synapse with membranes of adjoining cells (Fig. 4.21). At the end of a terminal button is a presynaptic membrane, which is a specialized thickening. In *chemical synapses,* a *chemical transmitter substance* (a neurotransmitter) is released when a neural impulse reaches the terminal buttons. The substance passes through the

Information in neural impulses is transmitted across synapses to other cells.

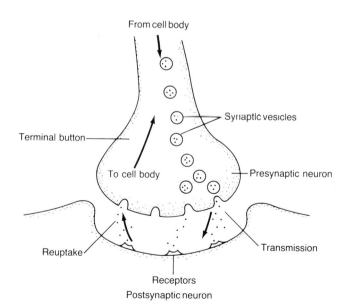

FIGURE 4.21
A synapse with some major components.

presynaptic membrane and crosses the **synaptic cleft,** the space between two cells that constitutes the synapse. It reaches the postsynaptic membrane, which is thicker than the rest of the membrane on the neighboring cell.

The synaptic cleft is about 200 to 300 Å wide and contains a fluid that transmits the transmitter substance (Å stands for angstrom units; one Å is one ten-billionth of a meter). The synaptic cleft also contains the synaptic web, which is a weblike substance thought to hold the pre- and postsynaptic membranes together.

The transmitter substance is produced in the cisterna depicted in Figure 4.21. **Synaptic vesicles** store the transmitter substance (*vesicle* means "little bladder"). The synaptic vesicles, located only on the presynaptic side of the synapse, liberate the transmitter substance into the synapse so that information from a neural impulse can only be transmitted in one direction. For this reason, synapses are *unidirectional.*

Given that a neuron may have thousands of synapses with other cells, and that there are some 10 billion neurons in the brain with some billions outside the brain, each with its own great number of synapses, we can well understand why the number of cybernetic circuits that simultaneously interact in the body can be mind- (i.e., body) boggling.

Synaptic Transmission

Chemical synapses transmit neural impulses across synaptic clefts by liberating chemical transmitter substances (neurotransmitters) that can link up with receptor sites in adjacent cells.

Neurotransmitters. As an axon conducts a neural impulse to its many terminal buttons, synaptic vesicles in those terminal buttons actually move to the presynaptic membrane to liberate their contents into the synaptic cleft (Fig. 4.22). The chemical nature of synaptic transmission is understood to some degree. Principally, synaptic transmission is mediated by **neurotransmitters** such as acetylcholine (ACh) and norepinephrine (NE). We will discuss neurotransmitters (which include endorphins and neuropeptides) in Chapter 6.

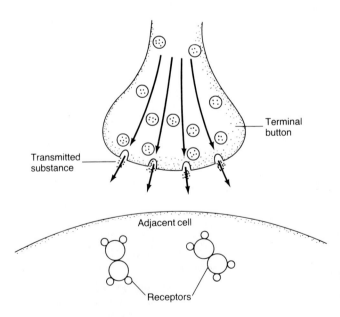

Transmitted substance

Terminal button

Adjacent cell

Receptors

FIGURE 4.22
The process of liberating transmitter substances (neurotransmitters) that conduct information from the neural impulse across a synapse.

The process of releasing the transmitter substance is very rapid, amounting to only a few milliseconds. The neurotransmitter moves across the synaptic cleft to link up with receptor sites in the neighboring cell and possibly to activate it. Although the intensity of a neural impulse in a given axon is always the same, some neurons generate larger intensity impulses than do others. The intensity of the neural impulse conducted along the axon of a neuron is one factor in determining whether or not the neighboring cell *will* be activated by the transmitter substance that it receives — a neuron that generates an intense neural impulse will liberate more chemicals to cross a synapse than will a neuron that generates a less intense neural impulse. The larger the amplitude (intensity) of the neural impulse, the greater the change in electrical potential and the greater the amount of transmitter substance liberated.

Neural impulses are of different intensities in specific neurons and their intensity in part determines whether they excite the neighboring cell.

The Threshold of Excitation of Neurons

Many neurons may share a single synapse so that one neuron may not liberate enough transmitter substance to pass an impulse at a common synapse while another neuron may. Whether or not a neighboring cell, such as another neuron, will be activated is determined by the **threshold of excitation** for that neighboring neuron. The threshold of excitation is the intensity of a stimulus necessary to generate an action potential; the intensity of a stimulus must exceed the threshold value of the resting potential at the membrane of the cell in order to depolarize it. If the intensity of the neural impulse from the first neuron is sufficient to exceed the threshold of excitation of the neighboring neuron, then the neighboring neuron will be excited. If the neural impulse is relatively weak, however, the neighboring neuron will not be activated, because it was below the threshold of excitation. The threshold of excitation is determined by the potential difference that exists in a neuron or other cell. If a neural impulse is of sufficient intensity that it will disturb that existing potential difference in the neighboring neuron causing it to depolarize, then that neural impulse exceeds the threshold of excitation of that neighboring neuron.

The threshold of excitation is that value of a membrane potential difference that must be exceeded for a neuron to be activated (depolarized) so that it can conduct a neural impulse.

The All-or-None Law

The axon of a neuron that is conducting a neural impulse to its synapses has a certain amount of energy that can be released. That amount of energy, which is constant all along the axon, yields an action potential that, itself, is constant. This characteristic of axons is stated in the **All-or-None Law of Neural Conduction** — that is, *if an action potential of a neural impulse is triggered in an axon by a graded reaction, the neural impulse is propagated with a constant intensity to the end of the axon.*

Consider the intensity of the neural impulse being conducted along the axon of one neuron. Now suppose that the amplitude of that nerve impulse releases sufficient transmitter substance across the synaptic cleft to cause a neighboring neuron to depolarize. The neighboring neuron will then conduct a graded reaction along its dendrite and cell body. If the threshold of excitability of that neighboring neuron's axon is exceeded, the axon "fires" with all of its energy — it thus generates its maximum action potential. But if the intensity of the graded reaction is below the threshold of excitation of the axon, the axon will *not* depolarize.

The All-or-None Law applies to the axon of a neuron such that if an axon "fires" it does so with all of its energy; otherwise, it will not fire at all.

Coding of Information in Neural Activity

There are probably several mechanisms for coding neural information. For one, discrete (vs. analog) messages are carried by the spikes of neural impulses. When they arrive at a synapse, the information is transformed to analog signals by the release of synaptic transmitters. That information is then transmitted to the next neurons in the circuit. Another set of coding mechanisms is the relationships between neural spikes. Thus, the average frequency of neural spikes is one code; others are the number of spikes following a stimulus, latency of a spike following an event, and whether or not a neuron does fire.

To a large extent we will expand on these complex matters in Chapter 6 when we explore relationships among neurons. Their relations are complex indeed as numerous impulses are spread among many neurons in extensive networks. Our present purpose is accomplished with this general understanding of how information is transmitted by chemical substances from one neuron to another or from one neuron to some kind of effector cell. But there is also the electrical synapse.

Electrical Synapses

Electrical synapses have low electrical resistance so as to transmit neural impulses by passing electrical currents between cells.

These synapses are quite common in the embryonic brain, in many invertebrate nervous systems, and in certain parts of the adult nervous systems. In electrical synapses, the membranes of the neighboring cells are extremely close together (about 20 Å as compared to 300 Å for chemical synapses) and they contain few, if any, synaptic vesicles. With the presynaptic and postsynaptic membranes so close together, there is extremely low electrical resistance between the two cells. For this reason, currents may flow across the synaptic cleft without the necessity of chemical transmission.

Some years ago there was a controversy between those who held electrical theories of synaptic transmission and those who held chemical theories. Largely through the research of Eccles we now know that *both* chemical and electrical synapses exist and we need not choose between these two apparently conflicting theories. Another scientific controversy was thus resolved with the empirical finding that the electrical theory applies to one type of synapse and the chemical theory to another. In a sense, though, the chemical theory "won" because more synapses throughout the human body are chemical than electrical.

In Chapter 5 we will consider in greater detail the receptor systems, in Chapter 6 the nervous systems, and in Chapter 7 the effector systems. As we approach these topics, it is important to acquire some topographical terms that will guide us in describing various anatomical regions and physiological functions of the brain and body.

SOME TOPOGRAPHICAL TERMS FOR ORIENTATION OF THE BODY

A standard nomenclature for bodily anatomical–spatial relations starts with the axis of the spinal cord, the **neuraxis.** The neuraxis is vertical in bipeds such as humans and horizontal in quadrupeds (four-footed animals).

SIR JOHN CAREW ECCLES (1903–)

Courtesy The American Physiological Society.

Sir John Eccles was born in Melbourne, Australia, and continued his research in Sherrington's department of physiology at Oxford. He became a professor of physiology at the National University in Canberra, but he eventually moved to the United States and then to his retirement retreat in Switzerland. His Nobel lecture in 1963 was entitled "The Ionic Mechanisms of Postsynaptic Inhibition." While at Oxford he was a strong defender of the electrical theory of transmission in central synapses. However, through his own microelectrode study of spinal reflexes, he provided sound evidence for the chemical nature of central synaptic transmission.

The front of the neuraxis of the human is the **anterior (ventral)** surface of the body while the rear is the **posterior (dorsal)** surface (Fig. 4.23). The top of the head (and thus the brain) of the biped is referred to as the **superior (rostral)** surface just as the bottom of the head and brain that faces the ground is the **inferior (caudal)** surface. The applications of these terms to the quadruped may also be studied in Figure 4.23.

The term **lateral** refers to the side of the body, whereas **medial** denotes the midline, the center of the body.

As we progress we will have occasion to use these terms.

In humans, ventral *and* anterior *refer to the front of the body, as in the stomach region, while* posterior *and* dorsal *refer to the back surface.*

The top of the head of a biped is the superior (rostral) *surface while the bottom is the* inferior (caudal) *surface.*

EMPHASIS ON A CYBERNETIC PRINCIPLE— SYSTEMS OF THE BODY AND THEIR INTERACTION

First, we need to briefly specify various systems of the body. Then, recognizing that none of them exists in isolation, we will attempt to represent some of the extremely complex interactions among them.

Cardiovascular (Circulatory) System: This circulatory system is comprised of the heart and blood vessels. As the heart pumps blood, blood circulates and transports such substances as food, water, hormones, antibodies, and oxygen to nourish cells throughout the body.

Digestive (Gastrointestinal) System: The mouth, teeth, esophagus, stomach, intestines, liver, and pancreas make up this system. It breaks down food particles so that they can

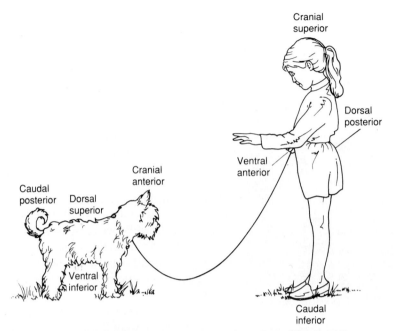

FIGURE 4.23 Terms denoting anatomical directions. They differ depending upon whether the organism is a quadruped such as the dog or a biped such as the human.

be absorbed into the blood system for energy, growth, and tissue repair. Waste products are discharged as feces.

Endocrine System: This system is composed of the glands that secrete hormones directly into the circulatory system. The endocrine glands include the thyroid, parathyroid, pituitary, adrenal, and some components of the pancreas, testes, and ovaries, as we saw in Figure 4.15.

Integumentary System: This system consists of the skin, hair, nails, and so on. It is supplied with blood vessels, nerves, receptors, and sweat and oil glands, and it protects the body, helps maintain a constant temperature, and senses environmental changes.

Nervous Systems: The brain, spinal cord, and nerves that run throughout the body comprise these systems. They transmit information among other systems and serve integrative functions (see Fig. 4.1).

Reproductive Systems: Including the sex organs, the male system produces sperm cells and hormones (principally testosterone) while the female reproductive system produces ova (eggs) together with hormones (principally estrogen).

A critical feedback circuit exists between animals and plant life whereby animal organisms provide carbon dioxide necessary for the survival of plant life, and plant life in turn provides oxygen for animal breathing.

Respiratory System: All cells of the body require oxygen which is turned into carbon dioxide that must be removed. In breathing, oxygen is taken from the air by the lungs where it is transferred to the cardiovascular system. Carbon dioxide is excreted from the system to the atmosphere by the lungs. The diaphragm, a muscular sheet that separates the chest from the abdomen, contracts to help force fresh air into the lungs.

Receptor Systems: Various receptor organs are located throughout the organism to receive information from the external and internal environments. They include the ears, eyes, and kinesthetic receptors, as well as other receptor cells in essentially every organ and system of the body.

Striated (Skeletal) Muscular System: This system consists of striated muscles and their tendons. Cardiac (heart) muscles and blood vessels are included in the cardiovascular

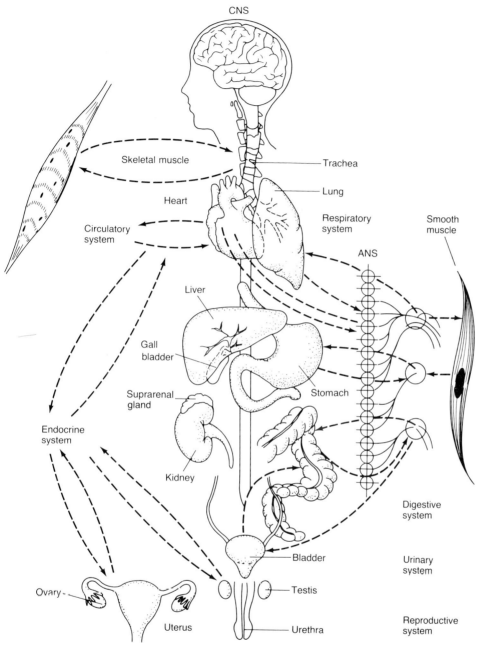

FIGURE 4.24 A representation of some of the interactions among various systems of the body. New information received by the organism is processed in extremely complex ways in circuits throughout the body, some of which are represented here.

system while smooth muscles of the stomach and intestines are included in the digestive system.

Skeletal System: This system of bones, cartilage, and ligaments that hold the bones together at joints supports the body.

Urinary System: Waste products of the body are filtered as the blood passes through the two kidneys after which the waste products enter the urine. The kidneys are connected to the bladder by long tubes called ureters. The bladder passes urine to the outside by another tube, the urethra. Urine is surprisingly "clean"; the saliva of the mouth contains more potentially harmful bacteria.

Some Relationships Among Bodily Systems.   Although these arbitrarily defined systems are listed separately, they all interact in ways far too complex for us to specify within the limitations of this text. Yet, to continue emphasizing the holistic nature of the organism, we will describe some of the relationships shown in Figure 4.24. Some of these interactions are rapid, carried out by feedforward and negative feedback circuit controls, while others function more slowly according to adaptive control systems. The foremost region for integration of these complex interactions, however, is the central nervous system. The central nervous system is constantly bombarded by information from external and internal stimuli, integrates that information in ways far too complex for us to understand at present, and transmits and retransmits that information to various other systems of the body. The various systems that receive information from the CNS return information to the brain. At each stage of transmission of information from receptors through afferent pathways, central integration, efferent pathways, and return afferentation, there is complex processing and transformation of the information. New information received is also integrated with memories stored in the brain, adding to the integration of the information processing function.

It is our task to apply the model of Figure 4.24 to understand the phenomena that constitute the domain of biological psychology.

KEY TERMS

Absolute refractory period—A recuperative period following an action potential during which a neuron is completely unable to conduct a nerve impulse.

Action potential—The change from the resting membrane potential that constitutes the firing of a neuron (the nerve impulse) or the contraction of muscle.

All-or-None Law of Neural Conduction—If an axon "fires," it does so with all of its energy; otherwise it will not fire at all.

Anterior (ventral)—In humans, the front of the body.

Association (connective) neuron—Transmits information in a reflex arc from a sensory to a motor neuron.

Axon—The relatively elongated part of a neuron that conducts impulses away from the cell body.

Cardiac (heart) muscle—Somewhat striated muscle whose fibers form quite an irregular meshwork.

Caudal (inferior)—The bottom of the head that faces the ground.

Cell—Basic unit of the body's systems; contains protoplasm within a membrane.

Cell body—The central part of the cell that governs the life process of the entire cell.

Cell excitability—The ability of a cell to react to some stimulus.

Chromosome—A unit that contains genes that transmit hereditary characteristics.

Collaterals—Branches of a nerve cell axon containing terminal buttons.

Cytoplasm—The substance contained within the membrane of every living cell.

Dendrite—Part of a neuron that may be excited by information from a receptor cell or from another neuron; conducts a graded impulse to the cell body.

DNA (deoxyribonucleic acid)—The genetic material, contained in the nucleus of all living cells, that controls the synthesis of proteins in cells.

Depolarization—Change in the potential difference in regions of cells because of the exchange of ions through the minute openings in the cell's semipermeable membrane.

Dorsal (posterior)—In humans, refers to the back of the body.

Effector systems—Muscles and glands that generate responses when neural impulses arrive over efferent neurons.

Electrical potential—A potential difference that exists between the inside and outside of the membrane of a neuron (and other cells) in the resting state.

Endocrine (ductless) glands—Glands that secrete their products directly into the bloodstream (e.g., the pituitary and thyroid glands).

Environment—The sum total of stimuli that may affect an organism's receptors. The stimuli may be in the external environment such as light that excites the eye and/or in the internal environment such as muscle contractions that excite muscle spindle receptors for the kinesthetic modality.

Exocrine (duct) glands—Glands that secrete their products through ducts to a surface of the body (e.g., sweat glands).

External environment—Sum total of all of those stimuli outside the body that could impinge on an organism.

Genetic—Refers to the genes that constitute the plans for the development of an organism. Genes are subunits of the chromosomes that determine the particular structure and function of the cells.

Glial cell—Supportive brain cell that generates chemicals transmitted to neurons; insulates some neurons from each other to prevent cross talk among them; also serves "housekeeping" functions by absorbing unneeded materials in the brain.

Graded reaction—A neural excitation transmitted from a dendrite with an intensity that varies according to the intensity and duration of the stimulating excitation.

Hormones—Chemical compounds secreted by endocrine glands.

Inferior (caudal)—The bottom part of the head that faces the ground.

Inhibitory reactions—Reactions that slow or prevent cells from contracting, secreting, or conducting.

Internal environment—Includes systems and organs beneath the skin, particularly energies that can affect numerous internal receptors of the body.

Lateral—The sides of the body.

Medial—The midline, the center of the body.

Membrane—Thin layer surrounding a cell that is composed of lipids, proteins, and a small amount of carbohydrates. It contains the cytoplasm and structures within the cell.

Messenger ribonucleic acid (mRNA)—A substance in a cell that exits from the nucleus to carry information that affects events in the cytoplasm.

Millivolt (mv)—One-thousandths of a volt.

Mitochondria—Small structures within a cell where oxidative reactions occur.

Motor (efferent) neurons—From the Latin for "to carry outward," they conduct neural impulses out of the brain and toward effectors.

Myelinated fibers—Those axons covered by fatty myelin sheaths that thus insulate them from other neurons within the same nerves.

Nerve impulses—Propagated electrical/chemical disturbances that result from above threshold stimulation of the axon of a neuron.

Neuraxis—The axis of the spinal cord. It is vertical in bipeds such as humans and horizontal in quadrupeds (four-footed animals).

Neurons—Nerve cells highly specialized for transmitting information throughout the body by means of coded neural impulses.

Neurotransmitter—A chemical substance such as norepinephrine that makes it possible for one neuron to communicate with another at the synapse. It is liberated at terminal buttons and locks into receptors of adjacent cells.

Optic nerve—Nerve fibers that join together to transmit neural impulses to and from the brain.

Posterior (dorsal)—In humans, the back of the body.

Potential difference—Electrical potential representing the amount of energy that may (potentially) be transferred between two points.

Propagated disturbance—Localized disturbance of the resting state that is transmitted along a neuron when it is excited.

Radiant energy—A type of environmental energy that may constitute a visual stimulus.

Receptor organs—Those that generate neural impulses when activated by energy from the external and internal environments.

Reflex arc—Typically an afferent neuron transmits nerve impulses from a receptor through association and efferent neurons that then activate an effector.

Refractory period—See absolute and relative refractory periods.

Relative refractory period—A period following an absolute refractory period when a neuron can only conduct an impulse of greater than normal intensity.

Response—The activation of muscles and glands, collectively called effectors.

Retina—A layer of cells within the eye, including ganglion cells, bipolar cells, rods, and cones.

Rostral (superior)—The top of the head of the biped.

Semipermeable membrane—A membrane surrounding neurons and other cells containing openings that allow smaller but not larger ions to pass through.

Sensory (afferent) neurons—Transmit neural impulses toward the brain.

Smooth (involuntary) muscles—Muscles that lack striations, are not under voluntary control, and are found in the viscera (intestines, blood vessels, etc.).

Spike potential—The maximum electrical/chemical action potential when a neuron is excited.

Stimulus—Energy that impinges upon and activates receptor cells.

Striated, voluntary, striped, or skeletal muscles—Muscles that are almost always attached (with tendons) to the bones (skeleton) of the body.

Superior (rostral)—The top of the head of the biped.

Synapses—A (synaptic) cleft between a neuron and another cell across which neural impulses may be transmitted.

Synaptic cleft—Space between two cells constituting the synapse.

Synaptic vesicles—*Vesicle* means "little bladder." They store transmitter substances, are located only on the presynaptic side of the synapse, and liberate transmitter substances into the synapse so that information from a neural impulse is transmitted.

Terminal buttons—Chemical-releasing structures at the end of axonal terminal branches for generating reactions across synapses.

Threshold of excitation—The intensity of a stimulus necessary to generate an action potential; the stimulus intensity must exceed the value of the resting potential at the membrane of the cell in order to depolarize it.

Transmitter substances—Chemicals (neurotransmitters) that carry information across the synaptic cleft to possibly activate neighboring cells.

Ventral (anterior)—In humans, "ventral" and "anterior" refer to the front of the body.

Visceral—Pertaining to the viscera, organs enclosed in the abdominal and thoracic cavities.

Voluntary response—A response that can be reported prior to its being made.

STUDY QUESTIONS

1. "A stimulus is energy that impinges upon and activates receptor cells." Comment and give examples.
2. Define the nervous systems.
3. How is information received and transmitted from the external and internal environments?
4. Which part of the cell contains chromosomes, and what do chromosomes carry?
5. Draw and label the parts of a neuron.
6. Outline the differences among sensory, association, and motor neurons.
7. Describe the three kinds of muscle cells.
8. What is the difference between exocrine and endocrine glands?
9. Explain polarization and depolarization of cells.
10. Explain how neural impulses are transmitted from one cell to another.
11. List the various systems of the body.

FURTHER READINGS

You can browse through a library in the area of physiological psychology to find such books as:

Carlson, N. R. (1991). *Physiology of Behavior.* Boston: Allyn & Bacon.

CHAPTER 5

How We Gather
and Interpret Information
The Receptor Systems,
Our Sense Modalities,
and Perceptual Processes

MAJOR PURPOSE: To learn in some detail the anatomy of our sensory systems and their physiological functioning

WHAT YOU ARE GOING TO FIND: How the sensory systems are structured and how they receive and process information from the environments

WHAT YOU SHOULD ACQUIRE: An understanding of how the receptor systems interact in cybernetic feedback circuits with the brain, the rest of the body, and the external environment

CHAPTER OUTLINE

HOW DO WE PERCEIVE OUR WORLD?

Sensory Information Is Continuously Received and Integrated. When we perceive an object or event in our external environment, we are activating a number of our **sense modalities.** The sensory systems are specialized for processing information received by the various receptors. When we watch TV, for instance, we process information with our visual and auditory sense modalities. But we also activate other modalities, only more subtly. If we see a pie thrown in a comic's face, we empathize with the recipient by having similar feelings in our own faces. These subtle feelings of empathy occur when we activate numerous cutaneous and kinesthetic receptors. If we view a person attacking another with knife in hand, we subtly recoil and twitch with our entire body in empathy for the victim. The combined activity of all of our sense modalities leads us to a continuous perceptual experience of the TV show that we are watching. It is a rich bodily phenomenon indeed.

Perceptions Are Generated Through Receptor–CNS–Effector Circuits. An ancient question that continues to receive considerable scientific attention is, "How do we internally represent features of the external environment that we perceive?" For instance, what happens within us that allows us to perceive a dog, a tree, or a friend? A general answer is by a combination of our many sensory modalities. That is, we perceive the visual aspects of a friend (such as height, build, and hair color) by means of our visual modality, the friend's auditory characteristics (such as quality and tone of voice or cadence and strength of footsteps) through our auditory modality, and so on.

We perceive stimuli when information activates receptor–neuromuscular circuits that reverberate between the brain and peripheral regions of the body.

To be more specific, we must consider just how the receptor systems are structured and how they function. But the entire perceptual experience depends on much more than the receptor systems. Consequently, we must understand how the sensory messages from the outside world are transmitted to and from the central nervous system, and how that processed information is then directed to and from other systems throughout the body.

The brain, acting in concert with the rest of the body, adds memories and based on memory interprets these numerous combinations of sensory messages that continuously bombard us.

In this chapter we focus on how the receptor systems function as we receive information from the environment. Later we will integrate their functioning within complex cybernetic circuits throughout the body. According to the cybernetic model, perceptual experiences are generated when receptor–brain–effector circuits reverberate and interact by numerous feedbacks.

DO NERVES HAVE SPECIFIC UNIQUE ENERGIES?

The Law of Specific Nerve Energies holds that the nature of a sensory message is determined by the specific sensory pathways that are activated, no matter what stimulus activated those pathways.

The cornerstone of our contemporary reasoning about sensations is the **Law of Specific Energies of Nerves** formulated by the renowned German physiologist Johannes Müller (1801–1858). As we saw in Chapter 2, this famous doctrine holds that *the nature of a sensory message is determined by the specific sensory pathways that are activated.* Each sensory nerve, no matter how it is activated, leads to only one kind of sensation. We saw, for instance, that if the optic nerve is activated, there is a visual experience *and it does not matter how the optic nerve is activated!*

One important consequence of Müller's Law of the Specific Energies of Nerves is that the particular nature of a sensation (seeing light, hearing sound, etc.) is *not* determined only by the kind of stimulus that a person receives (a flash of light, a noise, etc.). Rather, any way in which the circuits from a receptor organ to the brain are stimulated results in the sensations appropriate for that sense modality. Thus, if you apply an electrical stimulus at the eye or at any place along the optic nerve, even at a visual region of the brain, there will be visual sensations.

THE PRINCIPLE OF LABELED LINES

Neurons in Receptor Nerves Serve Varied Functions. Although Müller's principle has a hallowed place in the history of our science, it has been refined. All scientific laws are subject to revision, modification, or refinement. We used to believe that all of the neurons in a nerve were homogeneous (uniform), but we now know that neurons within a given receptor nerve, such as the optic nerve, are actually constructed differently. Because of these anatomic differences, the neurons within a nerve have varied, unique functions. Consequently, Müller's law has been refined according to the **Principle of Labeled Lines,** which forms the basis of contemporary theories of vision and hearing and also applies to other modalities.

According to the Principle of Labeled Lines, individual sensory neurons are labeled (constructed) so that each labeled neuron has a unique function in the perceptual experience. For instance, the axons of the ganglion cells in the retina that combine to form the optic nerve are structurally quite different among themselves. These differences among cells form several different subclasses that function physiologically in different ways as they uniquely contribute to perceptual experience. Thus, not only is the sense of vision dependent upon general stimulation of the optic nerve, but the characteristics of any given visual experience depend on the highly specific nature of the particular neurons stimulated. As the sensory message is transmitted higher and higher into the nervous system, the neurons become increasingly specific in their contributions to the visual perception. For example, within the visual system there are well-defined subpathways that transmit different kinds of information about our external environment, although they are all still within the visual modality. These subpathways typically project to six or so regions in the cortex. There probably is some kind of central integration among the messages from those subpathways at those regions of the cortex. After the incoming messages are so integrated, there is further transmission to various regions outside the brain. In the case of vision, we know that incoming information is fed back from the brain to the eyes whereupon the status of the eyes is modified. As this eye–brain–eye–brain . . . circuit reverberates, events in the eyes, in their controlling muscles, and in the brain occur whereupon visual perceptions are generated. As we will see, visual images (which occur in the absence of external stimuli) are also generated in the same way.

Labeled lines have also been identified for the auditory and the somatosensory systems. As a consequence, the general principles that we have presented for the visual modality also apply to the other sensory modalities. They too have labeled lines within the major nerves and tracts that transmit information from receptor organs to the cortex. Furthermore, there are similar multiple representations in the cortex for the other sensory modalities. We do not have, for instance, only one auditory area in the brain.

It now remains for us to integrate these concepts of labeled lines into a broader framework to account for perceptual experiences. To accomplish this, our first task is

Although the specific sensory pathways that are stimulated determine the nature of the sensation in general, neurons within those pathways differ and have different functions.

The Principle of Labeled Lines refers to different tracts of neurons within a nerve that serve different functions within a sensory system.

Different neural tracts within a sensory system simultaneously carry different kinds of information to and from a number of different regions of the brain.

Reverberating cybernetic circuits between the eyes and the brain generate visual perceptions and visual images.

The Principle of Labeled Lines is generally applicable for the various sensory system.

to individually consider the sensory processes in greater detail. The first sensory modality we take up, because it is primary for that distinctively human characteristic of speech, is that of audition. We will see how acoustic information is received and processed through the ears to and from central neural mechanisms.

THE RECEPTOR SYSTEMS

A stimulus is a change in energy from the environment that excites receptor cells. The energy is then transduced to neural impulses that go to and from the brain.

Changes in Environmental Energies Are Transduced by Receptors.   The essential characteristic of any **stimulus** is that it is a *change* in energy. The receptors adapt and stop firing in response to any stimulus that remains constant. After information is received, it is **transduced** (changed from one form of energy into another) by receptors in the eyes, ears, and so on. For example, electrical energy may be transduced into mechanical energy so as to drive a machine with electrical signals from the body. For example, the electrical signals generated by the eye muscles can control the direction of a wheelchair just as those from an upper arm can control a prosthetic lower arm. Environmental stimuli are transduced by the receptor organs so as to change, for instance, sound waves that strike the ear into mechanical and then neural signals.

Audition

If auditory stimuli (sound waves) are of sufficient intensity to excite the receptor cells of the ear, they will generate neural activity that reverberates in circuits to and from the brain wherein there is perception of the sounds.

Any solid body that is struck vibrates, causing air molecules to collide with each other. Those collisions transmit air pressure variations that constitute the sound waves that may activate the ears. If the sound wave stimuli are sufficiently intense to excite the auditory (ear) receptors, then neural messages will be processed in circuits to and from the brain. In this way, the external **auditory stimulus** is perceived ("heard").

Amplitude and Frequency of Sound Wave Stimuli.   The intensity (amplitude) of a sound wave is determined by the amount of energy that it carries. Thus if an object is struck very hard, the resulting sound waves will be of large amplitude and will be perceived as loud. However, the ear is not capable of responding to all sound waves. To understand this, let us note that in Figure 5.1 a sound wave may be subdivided into cycles such that the region between lines A and B indicates one cycle. The number of cycles of a sound wave that occur during any given period of time is the frequency of a sound wave; that is, if 20 cycles occur in one second, the frequency is 20 cycles per second (cps). However, it is conventional to use the unit **Hertz (Hz)**, named for the German physicist Heinrich Hertz (1857–1894). One Hz equals one cycle per second so that 20,000 cps is 20,000 Hz.

To be perceived, an auditory stimulus (a sound wave) must be sufficiently intense. It must also be of a frequency to which the ear is sensitive, which in humans is about 20–20,000 Hz and in other species as high as 100,000 Hz.

The human ear is generally capable of responding to sound waves of frequencies between about 20 Hz and 20,000 Hz. Thus, the human ear is not capable of responding to a low frequency, such as 3 Hz, or to a high frequency such as 40,000 Hz. Furthermore, it is not equally sensitive at all frequencies. Stimuli at the lower (around 20 Hz) and upper (around 20,000 Hz) regions need to be of relatively greater intensity to be perceived. The human ear is most sensitive around 2000 Hz.

Species Differences.   The range of frequencies to which the ear is capable of responding differs among species. The ear of the dog, for instance, is capable of being excited by auditory stimuli of greater frequency than is the ear of humans. The

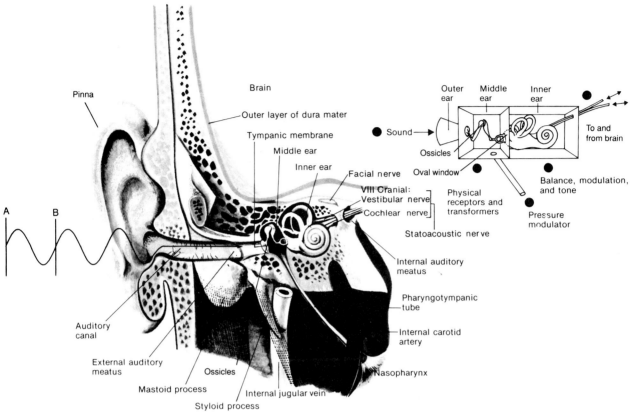

FIGURE 5.1   Components of the ear involved when sound waves enter it. The human ear is sensitive to frequencies of about 20–20,000 Hz (cycles per second). One Hz is indicated from A to B.

dog whistle, based on this fact, emits sound waves with frequencies greater than 20,000 Hz, which humans cannot hear, so that dogs can be trained to approach us at what *is* sound for them. Bats and whales can detect frequencies up to 100,000 Hz. Small animals such as rodents can also hear extremely high frequencies, sometimes as high as 100,000 Hz. In general, the smaller the head, the higher the frequency that can be perceived.

STRUCTURE AND FUNCTION OF THE AUDITORY SYSTEM

Anatomy of the Ear.   As we saw in Figure 5.1, sound waves enter the external ear **(pinna)** that collects sounds from the environment. They then travel through the **auditory canal (external auditory meatus)** and strike the eardrum **(tympanic membrane),** which is a thin, soft sheet of tissue.[1] The varying pressure of the sound

---

[1]We have noted that the external ear is called the pinna, that the auditory canal is the external auditory meatus, and the eardrum is the tympanic membrane. Although such duplication may be thought inefficient, it is well to learn such synonyms because sometimes one term is used and at other times its synonym is used. If you do not know both terms, you may not realize what is being discussed.

wave causes the eardrum to vibrate (it literally moves back and forth). As the tympanic membrane vibrates, those vibrations are carried through the three small bones of the middle ear, collectively referred to as the **ossicles.** The first ossicle, the **malleus (hammer)** is directly attached to the eardrum so that it receives the vibrations produced by the external stimulus. The malleus is connected to the **incus (anvil)** and the **stapes (stirrup)** by means of ligaments. These three bones vibrate almost together carrying the information in the sound wave into the **oval window** and thence to the **inner ear.** To prevent the ossicles from being overdriven by loud sounds, two muscles are attached to them and modulate their activity: The **tensor tympani** muscle restrains the malleus and the **stapedius** muscle restrains the stapes. Without the action of these important middle ear muscles, we would suffer even more injury than we do from loud sounds.

The **eustachian (pharyngotympanic) tube** enters the middle ear from the back of the mouth, allowing air to enter and equalize any pressure differences between the inner ear and the external auditory meatus. Thus, if you go up a high mountain, the outside pressure decreases. When you swallow you equalize the pressure within the middle ear by bringing air through the eustachian tube.

Transmission of Auditory Information Through the Ear. As the ossicles conduct vibrations to the oval window, those vibrations are transmitted to the fluid within the inner ear. Pressure waves in the fluid then affect the **cochlea** (Fig. 5.2), so named from the Greek word meaning "snail shell" because it is spiraled like the shell of a snail. The cochlea contains the **basilar membrane** (Fig. 5.2), which vibrates when

FIGURE 5.2 The cochlea. (a) External appearance; (b) internal appearance, specifying the basilar membrane, the organ of Corti, and the tectorial membrane.

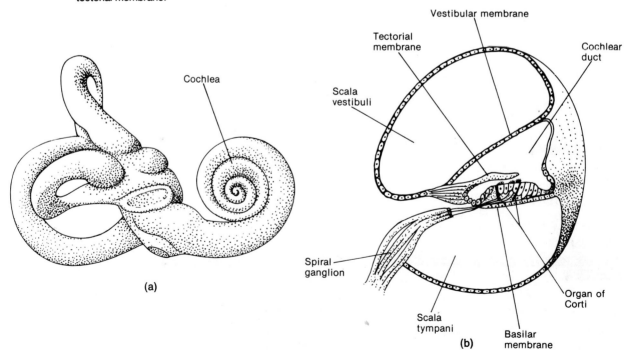

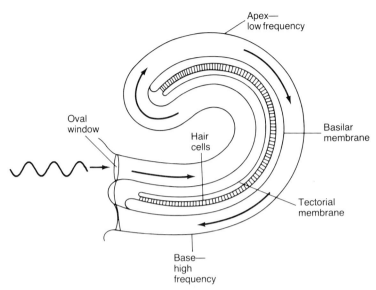

FIGURE 5.3 The organ of Corti showing the relationship between the basilar and the tectorial membranes within the cochlea.

there are pressure waves in the fluid of the inner ear. Those vibrations of the basilar membrane are called **traveling waves.** A traveling wave is one in which the vibration travels along the basilar membrane or some other medium, such as in the ocean. When the basilar membrane conducts traveling waves, it activates **hair cells** that are anchored on the basilar membrane (Fig. 5.3). The hair cells touch the **tectorial membrane,** a membrane that is located along the basilar membrane, somewhat like one shelf is above another. The hair cells are actually bent when the basilar membrane vibrates because the hairs are thrust into the overlying tectorial membrane. When they are moved sufficiently, electrical signals are generated and the axons of the hair cells, which form the auditory nerve, conduct afferent neural impulses to the brain. The basilar and tectorial membranes, together with the hair cells, compose the **organ of Corti.**

Sound waves vibrate the tympanic membrane and are carried through the ossicles to activate hair cells on the basilar membrane within the organ of Corti. Neural impulses are then carried along the auditory nerve to and from the brain.

PERCEPTION OF FREQUENCIES

We will consider two theories, the **place theory,** which accounts for the perception of all frequencies, and the **volley theory,** which applies to frequencies below about 4000 Hz.

The Place Theory

The organization of the basilar membrane is of great importance. In particular, hair cells near the base of the basilar membrane respond more to sounds of high frequencies, while hair cells near the apex are relatively more sensitive to sounds of low frequencies (Fig. 5.3). That is, the traveling waves that begin at the oval window travel along the basilar membrane toward the apex. The distance that they travel depends upon the frequency of the sound wave. High frequencies generate traveling waves that activate the region near the oval window (the base) and then cease (die).

High-frequency sounds activate hair cells near the base of the basilar membrane; medium frequencies activate hair cells in the middle; and low-frequency sounds activate those near the apex. The higher the frequency, the higher is the perceived pitch.

On the other hand, low frequencies generate traveling waves that are transmitted along the basilar membrane toward the more distant end (the apex) to activate hair cells there. Sounds of medium frequency activate the middle region of the basilar membrane. We thus discriminate the frequency of sounds depending on the region of the basilar membrane that is most active. The higher the frequency and thus the higher the perceived pitch, the closer is the region of maximum displacement of the basilar membrane to its base, that region nearest the oval window.

Young animals typically do not hear all frequencies that they will be able to perceive as adults. They first hear the low or mid-low frequencies. The ability to perceive the higher frequencies develops later. Thus, one might think that the apical (near the apex) or mid-apical regions of the cochlea should be the first to mature and the basal regions last. However, just the opposite is actually the case, presenting another riddle for science.

In Summary. The place theory is the most fundamental principle in understanding how the auditory system functions for perceiving frequencies. Essentially, the place theory states that there are positions along the basilar membrane that are relatively more sensitive to given frequencies with successively lower frequencies perceived progressively from the base to the apex.

History of the Place Theory. Hermann von Helmholtz made the first adequate formulation of a place theory in 1863 when he indicated that pitch (perceived frequency) of sounds is determined by the part of the organ of Corti that is stimulated by a given frequency. More particularly Helmholtz's theory was that the fibers of the basilar membrane vibrate in a specific region depending upon the frequency of the sound. Furthermore, he held that the hair cells and connected nerve fibers inform the brain of what part of the basilar membrane is vibrating and hence of the pitch of the sound.

The contemporary place theory was substantially formulated by Georg von Békésy (1899–1972), for which he received the Nobel Prize. He worked in the

The place theory states that there is a progression of positions along the basilar membrane that are increasingly sensitive to successively lower frequencies.

GEORG VON BÉKÉSY (1899–1972)

Georg von Békésy, a physicist, was born in Budapest, Hungary. His father was a diplomat, and he obtained his primary education in many countries. His main research was performed in the Hungarian Telephone Research Laboratory where he developed an ingenious method for discovering defects in the network of telephone lines by the resonant responses to click stimuli. He later used the technique to analyze the properties of the cochlea of the inner ear, which led to his place theory of audi-

tion. Eventually he conducted research in the psychology department at Harvard University, much of which contributed to his being awarded the Nobel Prize in 1961. His Nobel lecture was entitled "Concerning the Pleasures of Observing and the Mechanics of the Inner Ear." He was the first physicist to receive the Nobel Prize in physiology or medicine for his application of physical principles to sensory physiology. His research was summarized in his book *Experiments in Hearing* (1960).

psychology department at Harvard University, although Békésy, himself, was not a psychologist. His work is known as **cochlear mechanics,** and it started in 1928 when he was given the job of improving the Hungarian telephone system. Békésy's strategy was to reason, by analogy, from how the ear functions so as to construct a more effective telephone system. He focused his attention on the basilar membrane. In order to enhance his chances of direct observation, he studied the inside of elephants' ears (for enlarged structures) and among many other preparations including human cadavers. His model indicated, as we have previously summarized, that pressure changes in the fluid of the inner ear cause the basilar membrane to vibrate at different frequencies. His important empirical conclusion was that traveling waves move systematically along the basilar membrane from the basal end toward the apex depending on the frequency of the sound.

Questioning the Place Theory.   Recently, some problems have led to the questioning of some of Békésy's findings. For instance, his observations were made on dead cochlear preparations that have been found to function differently from live preparations. Furthermore, to observe the mechanical vibrations of the cochlea, he used intense sound stimulation, up to a 150 db (decibels, a unit of sound intensity) sound pressure level, which is well above the natural range of stimulus intensity appropriate for the human ear. As a result of these and other methodological problems, some of his conclusions have been modified. For instance, Rhode (1984) compared measurements of the basilar membrane vibrations in live *and* dead cochleas. He found that there are both amplitude and phase changes when an animal dies, including a rapid and progressive decrease in amplitude with a shift to the lower frequencies. The place theory in general, though, remains intact. Scientific advances have merely brought us closer to the "truth" through successive approximation.

The Volley Theory

Although Békésy concluded that the mechanical properties of the basilar membrane were primarily responsible for hearing, other studies have shown that this is not the entire story. Newer techniques in cochlear mechanics include recording from within a single hair cell and within single fibers of the auditory nerve. Acoustic emissions were found in the external ear, indicating that there are other ways in which acoustic energy is transduced within the inner ear. Mechanical properties are thus not the single all-important element of the basilar membrane for hearing. Instead, sound-induced vibrations of the middle ear are also encoded by the cochlea into sequences of action potentials in the cochlear nerve fibers. These nerve fibers then conduct encoded sound messages to the brain (Rhode, 1984). This constitutes what is known as the volley theory, which holds that at low frequencies (below about 4000 Hz), volleys of neural impulses are encoded according to the frequency of sounds. That is, information from the sound waves is implanted into groups of neural impulses that are carried along afferent neurons to the brain. Thus, sound waves produce a number of neural impulses in various auditory neurons depending on their frequency. For instance, one neuron in the auditory nerve would fire now, then it would fire somewhat later, and then again still later. In the meantime, another neuron would carry similar volleys of neural impulses at slightly different times and yet another neuron at still different times. In this way the nerve fibers in the auditory

The volley theory states that sounds of frequencies below about 4000 Hz drive volleys of neural impulses in different neurons at different times along the auditory nerve.

nerve could conduct impulses in synchronized volleys to code external sounds with firing rates as high as 4000 neural impulses per second.

Robert Woodworth offered the following analogy: Imagine a group of soldiers each of whom loads and fires his rifle at different frequencies. The commander has his men fire only at his command and he gives his commands at short intervals. At the first command, a quarter of the men are commanded to fire. At the second command another quarter fire. At the third command yet another quarter fire and at the fourth command the slowest loaders are ready and are commanded to fire. At the fifth command the first quarter is ready again and in this way the soldiers fire volleys at a rapid rate, more rapid than any individual soldier could manage. Analogously, volleys of neural impulses in the auditory nerve can be coded so that frequencies of sound up to about 4000 Hz can be coded by different neurons firing at different times. No single neuron could fire anywhere near as rapidly as 4000 Hz due to the refractory period of each neuron. The reason that the volley theory is limited to low frequencies is that auditory nerve cells apparently cannot fire in volleys above about 4000 Hz.

In Summary. We apparently sense the frequency of sounds below about 4000 Hz according to both the place and the volley theories and above that frequency only according to the place theory. However, the controversy continues with some scientists not accepting the volley theory at all.

PERCEPTION OF LOUDNESS

We have spent so much time on how frequency information of sounds is perceived because the topic is relatively complicated and not yet completely settled. Amplitude perception of sounds is another matter. Simply put, we perceive the loudness of sounds depending only on the number of hair cells that are activated. That is, the more intense the sound, the more active is the motion of the basilar membrane, and the greater the number of hair cells stimulated.

The greater the amplitude of a sound wave, the larger the number of hair cells that are activated and thus the louder the perception of the sound.

LOCALIZATION OF SOUNDS

It is of great importance for organisms to be able to locate other organisms and threatening events in their vicinity. For many species the auditory system is of prime value in this regard. In the jungle where an organism cannot see an adversary, subtle sound cues as to where danger might lie can literally determine survival or death. Similarly, for humans localization of cues is especially important anywhere at night when we cannot see well.

The direction of sound waves below about 1500 Hz is perceived according to the difference in time that sound waves enter the two ears; above about 3000 Hz, the cue is that the more intense sound enters the ear that is closer to the source of stimulation.

Important Localization Cues Are Differences in Perceived Time and Intensity of Sound Waves. First, organisms orient toward novel stimuli whether or not they are threatening. Much research has documented this **orienting response (OR),** as when an organism briefly orients to a novel stimulus asking, "What is it?" At least six relatively independent cues are used to localize sounds (Masterson & Imig, 1984). The two main cues are a temporal difference and an intensity difference when organisms compare information separately received by the two ears. Sound waves travel farther to reach one ear than the other, so they reach the two ears at different times. Receptors in the ear that is closer to the sound are thus activated temporally ahead of those in the farther ear. This temporal cue allows accurate localization for sounds below about 1500 Hz, but it is not very accurate for higher pitches.

The intensity cue for localizing sound is that a sound is more intense and thus perceived as louder in the ear that is closer to the stimulation. However, this loudness cue seems to be accurate only for frequencies above about 3000 Hz and is considerably less accurate for sounds of lower frequencies.

But what about intermediate frequencies? The human ear is relatively inaccurate for localizing sounds with frequencies between about 1500 Hz and 3000 Hz, which poses an interesting evolutionary question, "Could it be that there were not important dangers for our ancestors in 'the jungle' that generated sounds with frequencies between 1500 Hz and 3000 Hz?" We can only speculate about such a vexing question, but that is part of the fun of science.

Another cue comes from muscle movements resulting from neck and pinna (external ear) reflexes as the ears move within the sound field. That is, such muscle movements generate neural impulses that carry sound intensity information within circuits interacting with selected regions of the brain.

AUDITORY PATHWAYS
TO AND FROM THE CORTEX

In Figure 5.4 we can trace the route by which auditory information is transmitted from the cochlea as it ascends to the higher regions of the brain. To start, information from the left and right ears goes to the cochlear nuclei of the left and right sides of the medulla respectively. Using methods of the field of cochlear microphonics, actual sounds can be recorded from the cochlea and cochlear nerve. For instance, in a classical experiment, Wever and Bray (1930) amplified the signals from a cat's cochlear nerve and transmitted them to a loud speaker. They found that by talking into the cat's ear, the voice could be heard over the loud speaker.

After the cochlear nuclei (see Fig. 5.4), the majority of the fibers then cross over the brain stem at the level of the pons to the other side of the brain. From there the fibers go to the **superior olive** in the medulla. The superior olive is the earliest stage in the neural tract of the auditory system to receive information from both ears. It seems to be the most important neural region for contrasting the two sounds and thus for helping us to localize the origin of sound. Following the pathways shown in Figure 5.4, that information then goes through structures called the lateral lemniscus, to the inferior colliculus, to the medial geniculate nucleus, and finally to regions in the cortex for audition. There are many synapses along the way from the cochlea to the cortex.

Information from the ears is transmitted to the cochlear nuclei. It then crosses to the other side of the brain to the superior olive; then it is transmitted through other structures to and from the auditory cortex.

Tonotopic Representation.   When auditory information *does* reach the cortex, it is registered systematically at a specific point, depending on where it came from in the basilar membrane. There is thus a point-to-point relationship between regions in the basilar membrane and the auditory cortex, a relationship that is referred to as **tonotopic representation** (*tonos* means "tone" and *topos* means "place"). Thus tonotopic representation means that afferent fibers that serve successive points along the basilar membrane are successively represented in the surface of the auditory cortex. More specifically, the region of the basilar membrane that is near the base is represented higher in the auditory cortex. Systematically, regions of the basilar membrane from there toward the apex are represented in the auditory cortex in a descending (lateral) fashion.

There is a systematic relationship between points along the basilar membrane and the surface of the auditory cortex—the base of the basilar membrane is tonotopically represented high in the auditory cortex and the apex at the lower regions.

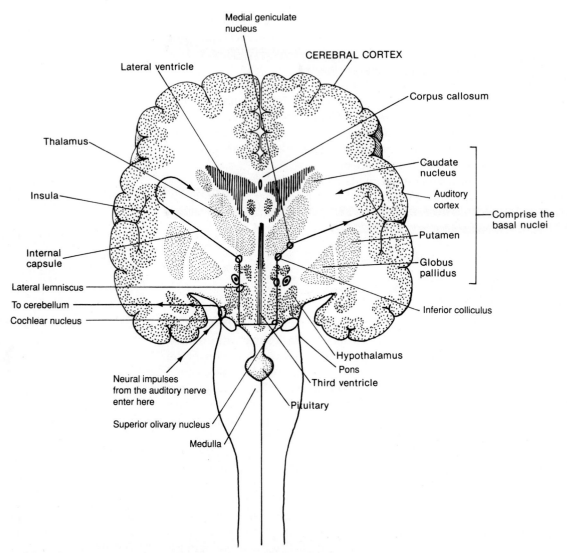

FIGURE 5.4   Routes through the auditory system in the brain after sound waves are transduced to neural signals. Entrance into only one hemisphere is indicated at left.

From the auditory cortex, information is relayed to the cerebellum and to the reticular formation. But more of this in Chapter 6 when we discuss the brain in greater detail.

Complex cybernetic circuits return information from the brain to components of the ear, including the hair cells.

CYBERNETIC FEEDBACK WITHIN THE AUDITORY SYSTEM

Research is increasingly leading to an understanding of feedback characteristics from the brain to the periphery. Among relevant phenomena is the discovery of "echoes" that influence cochlear mechanics. That is, healthy human ears typically emit narrow band noises that can be audible, as in weak **tonal tinnitus**—the perception of sounds such as hissing or roaring when there is no appropriate external stimulation. These echoes are due to feedback from the **crossed olivocochlear bundle,** which is the primary *efferent* input to the cochlea from the higher auditory pathways. When the crossed olivocochlear bundle is electrically stimulated, the sensitivity and selectivity of auditory nerve fibers change. These efferents from the crossed olivocochlear bundle primarily innervate the outer hair cells of the cochlea, thus implicating these outer hair cells in altering cochlear mechanics.

Nerve fibers at the base of hair cells carry incoming information to the brain. Information also comes back to these hair cells along the efferent fibers of the cochlear nerve. Those efferent fibers synapse directly upon hair cells. Efferent neural transmission along them seems to inhibit sensory neural impulses from the hair cells, causing the hair cells to decrease their sensitivity to incoming sounds. Why, we are not sure. Perhaps the desensitization causes momentary resting of the hair cells after they have just processed incoming information. The cell bodies of these efferent fibers are in the superior olivary nuclei of the medulla (see Fig. 5.4). They leave the superior olivary nuclei on both sides of the brain and travel to both cochlea.

We emphasize again that there are few "one-way streets" in the body that function according to feedforward principles. There are numerous efferent circuits from the brain to receptors so that the cybernetic model of negative feedback fits most bodily processes.

HOW HAIR CELLS FUNCTION

The hair cell is quite a remarkable receptor cell. It functions in the vestibular system (as in the sense of balance) as well as for hearing. It is a **mechano-electrotransducer,** which means that it senses mechanical force and transduces it into electrochemical signals; those signals are then conducted to the brain as components of neural impulses. We are not quite sure how the mechanical vibration is transduced into an electrical signal. There is some evidence that there is a change in permeability of the cell's membrane and an exchange of ions. Consequently, positively charged ions may pass through a membrane not unlike the way in which neural impulses are generated.

Hair cells are extremely sensitive and rapidly transduce mechanical vibrations into electrochemical signals.

As Hudspeth (1983) discusses, any given hair cell is sensitive to only a limited range of stimuli. Consequently, many of them must function systematically together to provide various kinds of information about the external world. As we have seen, depending on which hair cells are activated at which region of the basilar membrane, the individual may or may not perceive sounds of a given frequency.

There are about 15,000 hair cells in the human ear. The sensitivity of the tip of the hair cell is so great that it can respond when moved by a mere 100 picometers (one picometer equals one-trillionth of a meter), a distance about the diameter of an atom. Hair cells also respond very rapidly. Now let's study the hair cells in the vestibular system.

The Vestibular Sense

One Component of a Multimodal System. The **vestibular sense** informs us of the general orientation, location, position, and movement of the entire body in space. For example, the vestibular sense informs us that we are right side up instead

The vestibular sense functions with visual and somatic inputs as a multimodal system that informs an organism of the general orientation, location, position, and movement of its entire body in space.

of upside down. However, the vestibular apparatus is only one source of information in a more complex multimodel system of balance and orientation. The several modes of the multimodal system are vestibular, visual, and somatic in nature. That is, to balance and orient ourselves, the vestibular system also receives input from the eyes and somatic receptors in the skin and joints. In addition, the kinesthetic sense adds to this information about the position of our limbs in space. The interaction of the vestibular with the visual and somatic systems can compensate for a disturbance in balance or orientation. For example, a cat dropped upside down will compensate and land on all four feet, just as a newborn infant tilted backward will roll its eyes forward so that its gaze remains fixed. Similarly, if you shake your head rapidly from side to side as you read this text, the print is perceived as standing still. The multimodal system of balance and orientation is also adaptable so that if the vestibular apparatus itself is damaged, the remaining systems may learn to function without it.

In addition to the cochlea, the organ of hearing, the inner ear also contains structures that function for the vestibular sense. These structures are the (1) semicircular canals, (2) utricle, and (3) saccule (Fig. 5.5).

Anatomy of the Vestibular Sense—The Semicircular Canals.   There are three
The three semicircular canals correspond to the three planes that meet in the corner of a room.
semicircular canals located directly above the cochlea, each in one of three planes. Each plane is perpendicular to the other as in a room—the floor is in the horizontal plane while the two walls that meet at a corner are in the vertical planes. The semicircular canal for each plane furnishes us with information about our movement in that plane. We simultaneously receive information for each of the three planes.

FIGURE 5.5   The semicircular canals, the utricle, and saccule, structures that function for the vestibular sense.

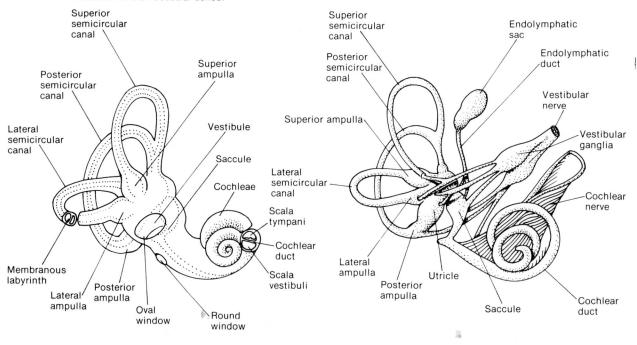

(a)

(b)

Each semicircular canal is filled with a fluid called **endolymph.** Immersed in the endolymph of each semicircular canal is a set of hair cells very much like the hair cells in the cochlea. When you move your head in rotation, the endolymph also moves. But due to inertia, it does not start to move as fast as do the semicircular canals. When the endolymph does start to move, it exerts pressure on the vestibular hair cells. As in the cochlea, when the hair cells are bent, the force is transduced, generating an electrochemical potential in the small afferent nerve fibers that are at the end of the hair cells. These small nerve fibers connect with the auditory nerve that leads to the brain. Information is transmitted resulting in the sensation that the head is accelerating in some particular direction within the three planes monitored by the three semicircular canals.

Information about changes in head movement direction comes from the semicircular canals of the vestibular sense. The lag between movement of the semicircular canals and that of the endolymph causes the endolymph to put pressure on the vestibular hair cells, generating information.

Note that it is not the movement or the rotation of the head itself that produces the stimulus for the vestibular sense. To understand this, observe that when the head is rotated it increases and decreases speed. It is the decreasing or increasing of speed that produces the stimulus for the vestibular sense. When you change the speed with which you move your head, you change the pressure of the fluid (endolymph) within the semicircular canals. If you are standing still and start to walk, the vestibular sense will be activated. But if the head is moving at a constant speed in a constant direction, you are neither increasing nor decreasing your speed and the vestibular sense will not be activated.

The Utricle and Saccule. The second set of organs in the inner ear having to do with the vestibular sense, the **utricle** and **saccule,** contains a gelatin-like substance within which hair cells are embedded. The gelatin-like substance also contains small crystals of calcium carbonate known as **otoconia** (sometimes called **otoliths**). The otoconia are close to the tiny hair cells and those hair cells terminate in small nerve fibers that join the auditory nerve that runs to the brain. Thus when there are changes in pressure, as when the head is tilted, the gelatinous substance within the saccule and the utricle causes the otoconia to exert pressure against the hair cells. Consequently, neural impulses are generated that transmit information to the brain for further processing. Because the hair cells in the utricle and saccule are oriented in all directions we know when the head is tilted in any direction.

Changes in the angle of the head are sensed by the utricle and saccule of the vestibular sense.

In Summary. The semicircular canals contain receptors that respond to changes in *motion,* but the utricle and saccule contain receptors that respond to changes in *angles* of head tilt. When you tilt your head, you change the pressure of the fluid within the utricle and saccule. This change of pressure causes the otoconia to exert pressure on the hair cells and to generate neural impulses. When you lie down to go to sleep, the events that we have just described tell you that your body is in a horizontal position. In an old experiment, the vestibular mechanism, including the utricle and saccule, was removed from a frog. It was then observed that the frog swam upside down about as frequently as it swam right side up. Without the mechanisms within the utricle and saccule, an organism does not appropriately control its position in space (unless, of course, it uses other senses such as vision). The combined functioning of the semicircular canals and the utricle and saccule constitute the vestibular sense.

Similarities of the Semicircular Canals and the Utricle and the Saccule. The semicircular canals and the utricle and saccule all contain a gelatinous fluid. They each contain hair receptor cells that are immersed in fluid and the pressure of the fluid inside them changes with the activity of the head. In both the semicircular canals and the utricle and saccule, the hair cells are activated as the pressure of the fluid changes, whereupon information is transmitted along tiny nerve fibers to and from the brain along the auditory nerve.

Information about increases and decreases of speed is furnished by the semicircular canals while information about the position of the head in space is furnished by the utricle and the saccule.

Differences.   Among the differences, the utricle and saccule contain otoconia, whereas the semicircular canals do not. The semicircular canals respond to increases and decreases in the *speed* with which the head moves. Changes in the *position* of the head, however, activate the utricle and the saccule.

Vision

VISUAL STIMULI

Wave and Photon Conceptions.   Although their frequency is much greater than that of sound waves, visual stimuli can still be conceived of as light waves that carry energy. Light waves travel much faster (about 186,000 miles per second) than do sound waves (about 1100 feet per second).

We have seen that some objects (light bulbs, lighted matches, etc.) *emit* radiant energy in the form of light waves, while other objects (books and pictures) merely *reflect* light from other sources. Visual stimuli can also be conceived of as particles of energy called **photons.** The photon model suggests that the rods and cones are so sensitive that a single photon that enters the eye can excite a rod. However, light as a wave phenomenon is the more widely accepted model.

Light stimuli can be conceived of as either waves or particles of energy (photons).

The Visible Spectrum.   The frequencies for visual stimuli are presented in Figure 5.6. Like the human ear, all wave frequencies cannot be sensed by the human eye. Infrared rays, as well as radar and radio waves, are at frequencies that are too slow to activate the human eye. On the other hand, ultraviolet rays, X-rays, and gamma rays are frequencies that are too high to activate the human eye.

The frequencies that can excite the eye make up the **visible spectrum.** For example, in Figure 5.6, the frequencies for blue and red light both fall within the visible spectrum, with blue light having a higher frequency than red.

THE HUMAN EYE

Adjusting Pupil Size.   The amount of light that can enter the human eye is regulated by the size of the **pupil,** the dark center that we see when we look in a person's eye. This opening changes in size to admit smaller or larger amounts of light. The size is regulated by the muscles of the iris that contract and relax to

As the pupil dilates and constricts, the amount of light that falls upon the retina increases and decreases.

FIGURE 5.6   Electromagnetic frequencies including the visible spectrum.

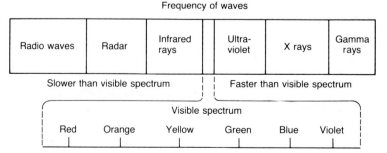

constrict and enlarge the pupil, constituting a defensive reflex. This defensive reflex is carried out by a cybernetic circuit that is set off by a summation of activity in the rods and cones. If the sum of the reaction of the rods and cones to incoming light exceeds the standard (reference) value for most efficient performance of the retina, this information is fed to the pupillary muscles to produce a constriction. When the pupil then constricts, the amount of light striking the retina is reduced, lowering the intensity of the reaction of the rods and cones. Then, when the intensity of the summed neural information in the rods and cones approximately equals the standard value, no further information is directed to the pupillary muscles so that they cease their constriction. By means of this cybernetic circuit – reverberating feedback loop, optimal functioning of the processing of information by the rods and cones is assured.

The size of the pupil also depends upon the degree of arousal of the organism such that as one becomes more aroused, the pupil dilates. Presumably this also has survival value in that it allows a better visual assessment of threatening events in the environment.

Focusing Images. The **lens** of the eye is similar in function to the lens of a camera—it focuses the image of a stimulus object onto the retina. The fovea (Fig. 5.7) is the region of sharpest focus. When the eyes converge (move together), there is further accommodation of the lens to help us focus on objects. Just as you adjust binoculars, your eyes move together so that you can focus on objects at different distances.

FIGURE 5.7 The human eye.

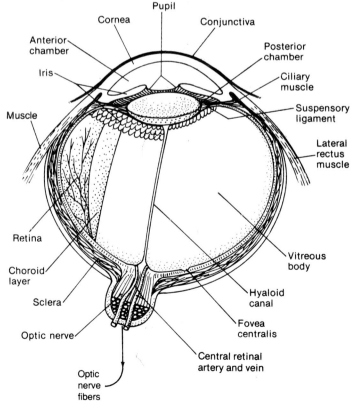

Movement of the Eyes. Eye position is controlled by six small muscles surrounding the eyeballs, known collectively as the **extraocular muscles** (see Fig. 5.7). Contraction of these muscles activates sensory organs within the eye muscles that send information about muscle length to and from the brain.

The Retina. As the muscles that regulate the lens contract and relax, the lens changes its shape to assure that a sharp image of a stimulus object falls on the **retina.** If the lens did not focus the stimulus object, the image on the retina would be fuzzy rather than sharp and clear. We can actually look inside a person's eye with instrumentation and see the image of a stimulus object on the retina.

Rods are distributed around the periphery of the retina and are used for black–white vision while cones are distributed mainly at the center of the retina and function for color vision.

The retina of the human eye contains about 120 million rods, so-called because of their cylindrical shape, and 6.5 million cones which are rather tapered (see Fig. 4.4). Rods are distributed around the outer regions of the retina and are used in "black–white vision." Cones, on the other hand, are distributed mainly in the posterior (back) regions of the retina where light is primarily directed and are used in "color vision." (An aid to remembering this difference is that the first two letters of "cones" and "color" are the same.) Thus, if you perceive a colored object, the cones at the back of the retina are the cells that are excited. Because they are used in black–white vision, rods are the cells that function at night. The old saying "at night all cats are gray" illustrates the point—at night even a yellow cat looks gray, but in daylight signals from its color can excite the cones.

In Chapter 4 we discussed how the rods and cones at the bottom of the retina are connected to bipolar cells and ganglion cells. Actually, the retina is much more complicated than that. The retinal circuitry in Figure 5.8 indicates that there are also horizontal cells that synapse with a number of **photoreceptors (rods and cones)** and with **bipolar cells.** The distal ends of the bipolar cells are interconnected by way of amacrine cells, and ganglion cells send axons toward the optic disk within the retina. These axons of the ganglion cells comprise the optic nerve (which contains about 1 million neurons).

Visual perception occurs when light waves enter the pupil and lens to project an image on the surface of the retina; in turn, information is transmitted along the bipolar cells to ganglion cells and along the optic nerve to and from the brain as the eyes move.

The Blind Spot. The blind spot is a region in the retina where the tiny nerve fibers of the ganglion cells converge to form the optic nerve. Because this area consists exclusively of nerve fibers, it does not contain cones and rods. Consequently, an image of a stimulus object falling at this blind spot cannot set off nerve impulses. The story is told of kings who used the fact that we cannot see the part of a stimulus object that falls on the blind spot for their enjoyment; they would close one eye and look at the court jester in such a way that the jester's head would fall on the blind spot. If the king liked the way the jester looked without a head, he would have the jester beheaded. With a little practice, you can cause a part of an object to not be seen if you close one eye and allow its image to fall on the blind spot of the other eye.

Components of cybernetic circuits send information along efferent fibers from the brain to the eyes. Other circuits serve for intermodal interactions among visual, auditory, and somatic systems.

Cybernetic Circuits Involve the Visual, Central, Auditory, and Somatic Systems. Efferent fibers from the brain send information to direct eye movement, pupil size, accommodation of the lens, and some control of retinal information. In addition to cybernetic circuits between the eyes and brain, there are also complex intermodal circuits such as those for interaction between the auditory and visual modalities. For instance, clicks in the ear can produce electrical activity in the optic nerve. Movements of the eyes and arms are also closely integrated by complex cybernetic circuits between visual and kinesthetic systems. In visual processing, there also seems to be an interaction with a speech processing stage such that we subvocalize much of what we see (McGuigan & Dollins, 1989).

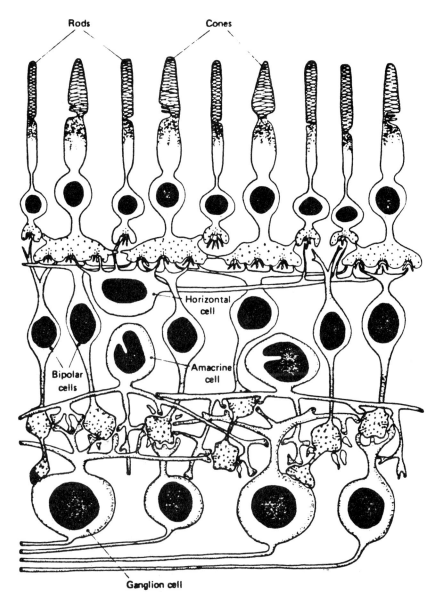

FIGURE 5.8 Representation of the complicated circuitry within the retina of the human eye. However, it is now known that the axon of the horizontal cells does *not* contact cones, only rods. (By permission of the Royal Society and the authors from Dowling, S. E. and Boycott, B. B., *Proceedings of the Royal Society [London],* 1966, Series B; *166,* 80–111.)

In Summary. Consider that light waves from an object pass through the pupil and lens to project an image of the object on the surface of the retina. The radiant energy of the light waves that form the image is transmitted to the bottom or back of the retina where it stimulates rods and cones. When the radiant energy from a stimulus object reaches the back of the retina, a chemical reaction occurs, where-

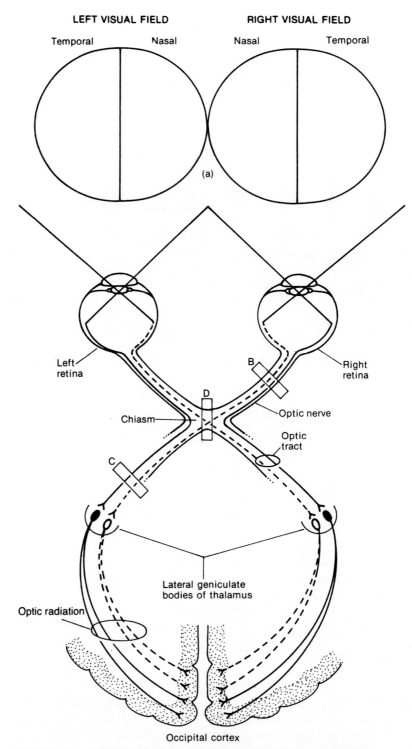

LEFT VISUAL FIELD   **RIGHT VISUAL FIELD**

Temporal   Nasal   Nasal   Temporal

(a)

Left retina

B

Right retina

D

Chiasm

Optic nerve

Optic tract

C

Lateral geniculate bodies of thalamus

Optic radiation

Occipital cortex

FIGURE 5.9   The optic nerve goes from half of each retina to each half of the brain. Signals pass through the optic chiasm (cross) along the optic tract and the lateral geniculate nuclei to the visual (occipital) cortex.

upon graded reactions are transmitted to the bipolar cells, to the ganglion cells (circuiting with other cells as in Fig. 5.8), and then to nerve fibers of the ganglion cells that make up the optic nerve. In this way nerve impulses are transmitted along the optic nerve to the brain.

ASCENDING VISUAL PATHWAYS TO THE CORTEX

We have just seen that neurons in the retina form complex circuits that reverberate, emphasizing that the retina is an extension of the brain. As represented in Figure 5.9, the optic nerve ascends toward the brain itself until it reaches the optic chiasma at which there is a half-crossing (this is known as semidecussation). These pathways for transmission of information to the two sides of the brain will assume special importance when we discuss the split brain experiments in Chapter 11.

The **optic tract** (the visual pathways are referred to as a *tract*, rather than a nerve, after the optic chiasma) of each side enters the **lateral geniculate nucleus (LGN).** There they synapse with thalamic neurons. To be more specific, neurons that form the left half of each retina enter the LGN in the left hemisphere. On the other hand, axons from the right half of each retina enter the LGN in the right hemisphere. In either case, information then reaches the **visual cortex.** That is, the medial fibers (those toward the nose) in the ganglion axons cross to the opposite lobe of the brain. The lateral fibers, those toward the sides of the head, do not cross to opposite lobes. Rather, they go to hemispheres on the same side of the head. Thus, visual information from the medial half of the retina of each eye goes to the opposite cerebral hemisphere (the **contralateral** side). However, visual information that strikes the lateral half of each retina does not cross over so that information received there goes to the hemisphere on the same (**ipsilateral**) side. Visual perception such as of depth and recognition of patterns then results from processing the information received on the retina.

The left half of each retina projects to the left cerebral hemisphere while the right half of each retina projects to the right hemisphere.

Olfaction

Overview. **Olfaction** is the technical term for the sense of smell, which concerns how the receptor cells in the nose receive and process odors. Olfactory stimuli are odors that are in a gaseous state — a mixture of air and molecules that comes from numerous stimulus objects. A cup of coffee, for instance, emits its unique molecules that mix with the air to create the odor enjoyed in the morning by many. In Figure 5.10, we see a diagram of an odor entering the nasal cavity of a human nose where it may activate olfactory receptors. If the number of molecules per unit of air (the intensity of an odor) is above the threshold of excitability of the olfactory receptors, the receptors will be activated and the odor is perceived.

The first part of the olfactory receptor cell is a fine filament (Fig. 5.11), which is actually a nerve ending that projects into the nasal cavity. The middle part of the olfactory receptor cell is the cell body that nourishes it, while the third part is a tiny nerve fiber that conducts nerve impulses toward the brain.

In Figure 5.10, we can see that the olfactory receptors connect to the **olfactory bulb (nerve).** The olfactory bulb then receives nerve impulses coded for smells and transmits them along the olfactory tract to and from the brain.

Olfactory stimuli are odors made up of air and an object's molecules. They excite filaments of olfactory receptors to transmit information through cell bodies and along nerve fibers of the olfactory receptors to the olfactory bulb, then along the olfactory tract to the brain.

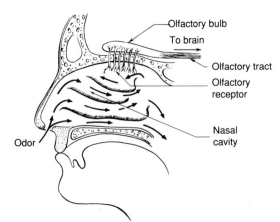

FIGURE 5.10
Olfactory stimuli enter the
human nose to activate
pathways to the brain.

One Theory of Smell.   We do not know with any great precision just how
molecules in gases excite olfactory receptors. One theory is that chemicals in the
gases that are homogeneous in size and shape produce one kind of odor, while a
different set of molecules homogeneous in size and shape produce another kind of
odor. The contention is that one class of molecule fits into certain receptor sites to
activate one set of neurons. The pattern of afferent neural impulses would then lead
to the perception of that particular kind of odor. Another set of homogeneous
molecules would then activate a different set of olfactory receptors leading to the
perception of a different kind of odor.

Species Differences.   There are considerable differences in olfactory systems
among species, depending on how much they rely on the sense of smell. For instance, subhuman mammals typically have more extensive nasal passages that are
richer in olfactory receptors and have larger olfactory bulbs than do humans. No
doubt such characteristics are responsible for their relatively enhanced sensitivity to
odors. Smells must have greater survival value for nonhuman animals.

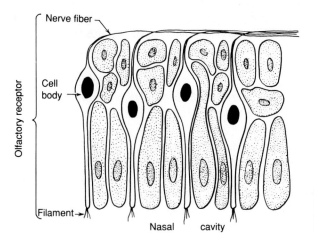

FIGURE 5.11
Olfactory receptors,
emphasizing the filaments, cell
bodies, and nerve fibers.

Somaesthesis

Somaesthesis derives from *soma,* meaning "body," and *esthesis* meaning "sensations," so that the term refers to sensations generated throughout the body. Somaesthesis concerns sensations generated by cutaneous receptors in the skin and those from kinesthetic receptors in the muscles and joints. We first consider the senses within the skin, the cutaneous senses.

The receptors for somaesthesis consist of cutaneous and kinesthetic receptors that generate sensations throughout the body.

THE CUTANEOUS SENSES

It is common to classify the **cutaneous (skin) senses** as those for pressure, pain, and temperature (cold and heat).

The cutaneous (skin) senses are those for pressure, pain, and temperature (heat and cold).

Pressure

A pressure stimulus such as a light touch can mechanically deform (indent) the skin **(dermis).** If the intensity of the pressure is above the threshold of excitability, it excites receptors embedded in the lower layers of the skin (Fig. 5.12). Since pressure receptors are widely distributed throughout the skin, their nerve fibers connect to quite a large and complex network of nerves to conduct nerve impulses to the brain.

FIGURE 5.12 Representation of layers of the skin that include various structures.

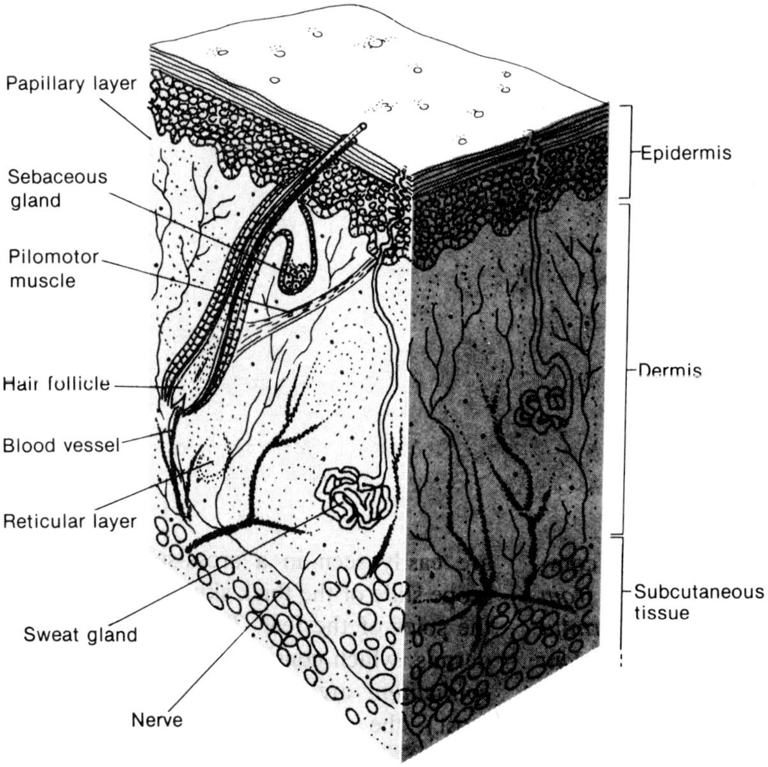

Three classes of pressure receptors in the skin are basket nerve endings, Meissner corpuscles, and free nerve endings. Pacinian corpuscles in subcutaneous tissue also respond to pressure.

Pressure Receptors.   There are three classes of receptors in the skin that may respond to pressure stimuli and one other kind that is located below the skin (the subcutaneous tissue in Fig. 5.12). The first class, **basket nerve endings,** are portions of tiny nerves that wrap around the roots of hairs. In Figure 5.13a, you can see that a small nerve ending runs from the end of the basket nerve ending to a series of larger nerves. If the surface of the skin near a hair is bent or depressed, then the basket nerve ending may be activated whereupon neural impulses are generated. Basket nerve endings may be excited by either touching the skin or moving a hair with sufficient intensity.

A second kind of pressure receptor is the **Meissner corpuscle,** which is embedded in the skin in hairless regions of the body. Meissner corpuscles are especially sensitive to very light pressures such as a touch of the finger tips. In Figure 5.13b, we can note that a tiny nerve fiber, attached to the end of a Meissner corpuscle, joins larger nerves that conduct neural impulses to the brain.

The third type of pressure receptor is the **free nerve ending** (Fig. 5.13c), which consists of a large number of nerve branches. Like the basket nerve ending and the Meissner corpuscle, free nerve endings are activated when the skin is bent or depressed, transmitting neural impulses to the brain.

The Pacinian Corpuscle.   This is another type of pressure receptor located deep *below* the skin to sense "deep pressure" stimuli. Even though it is below the dermis, we include the **Pacinian corpuscle** (Fig. 5.13d) here as a cutaneous receptor because it does respond to skin surface deformations. Pacinian corpuscles are also found in the viscera where they sense movements of the gastrointestinal tract and cue the need for urination and defecation.

The cutaneous and the kinesthetic senses receive information from other people and process it through circuits from stimulated skin and muscle receptor cells to the brain.

Communicating Through the Sense of Touch.   Touch is a very important method of communicating because we transmit messages to others according to how and where we touch them—the message given depends on the part of the body touched, on the relationship between the individuals involved, and on the culture; for example, in the United States, we do not touch strangers, startle others with a touch, or interrupt ongoing activity by touching.

We naturally communicate through sight and sound, but efforts to communicate with others by the systematic use of language through touch has a long history. Various tactile devices for individuals who are blind produce patterns of vibrations on the skin in accordance with certain rules for communication. For instance, one can type letters on a typewriter (a system called the Optohapt) that activates systems of vibrators on another person's skin to communicate with that person. Research continues as we seek a truly effective system for communicating through the skin.

Pain

Receptor Cells.   Pain can be generated by a large variety of stimuli such as pinching the skin, being hit by a hard object, excessive heat, cuts, and pricks. Such pain stimuli have in common that they can all damage body tissues. Pain stimuli thus have survival value in that we are warned of potential damage. Some people lack receptors for pain and can be injured without reacting to shut off the pain stimuli. Consequently, they usually do not live beyond their late twenties.

The receptors for pain are free nerve endings located throughout the skin and internal organs.

In Figure 5.13c, you can see that free nerve endings are embedded in the skin. They are widely distributed so that we feel pain throughout the skin and internal parts of the body. However, some organs such as the lungs lack free nerve endings so pain is not experienced there.

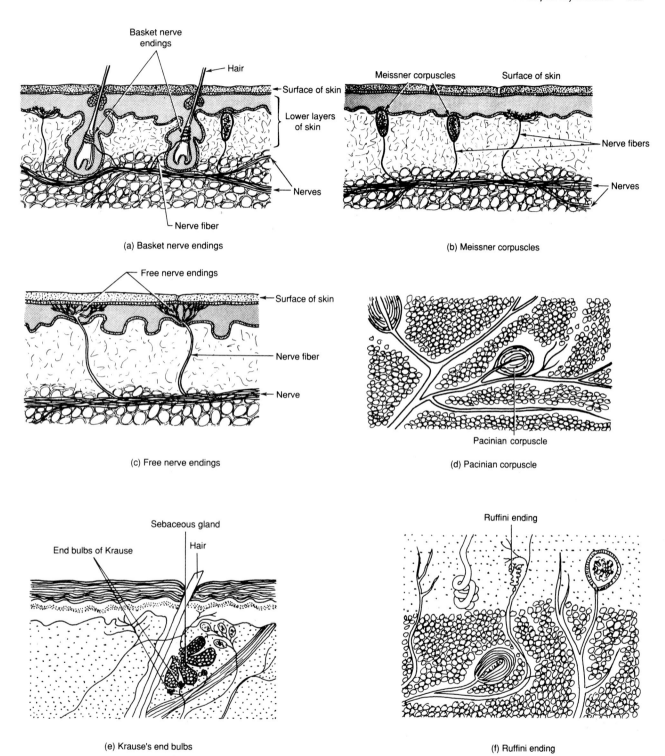

(a) Basket nerve endings

(b) Meissner corpuscles

(c) Free nerve endings

(d) Pacinian corpuscle

(e) Krause's end bulbs

(f) Ruffini ending

FIGURE 5.13 Receptor cells in the skin. Not all receptors are found in any given area of skin.

Pain stimuli seem to activate free nerve endings by causing them to stretch in a lengthwise ("up and down") direction. When free nerve endings are stretched, it is thought that nerve impulses result and are conducted along the tiny nerve fibers to large nerves and thence to the brain. Another theory is that the tissue surrounding the free nerve endings release chemicals (possibly potassium, histamines, and/or substance P) when traumatized and indirectly stimulate the nerve endings.

Pain is an extremely complex phenomenon and is of tremendous importance in everyday life, in medicine, and in psychology. Consequently, we will devote special sections to the topic in Chapters 9, 14, and 15.

Temperature

We are not sure what the receptors for cold and heat are, although they may be Krause's end bulbs and Ruffini's endings respectively.

There are distinctively different receptor spots in the skin for warm and cold, but we are not sure where their receptors are. Some believe that the receptors for cold lie near the surface of the skin, whereas the receptors for heat are embedded in the lower layers of the skin. Regions of the body have been sampled to determine sensitivity to cold and warm stimuli. Then small amounts of tissue have been removed from some of these regions for detailed analysis. It has been found that **Krause's end bulbs** (see Fig. 5.13e) are concentrated in areas that are particularly sensitive to cold stimuli, suggesting that they might be cold receptors. Similarly, **Ruffini's endings** (Fig. 5.13f) are concentrated in regions of the body that are especially sensitive to warm stimuli. Yet, research has indicated that areas of the body that lack these receptors still yield the perception of warmth and cold. There are only free nerve endings in those regions, suggesting that they may, in some cases, function to receive warm and cold stimuli.

Specific skin regions have constant temperatures, but different regions have different constant temperatures.

The temperature of a given skin region remains rather constant; yet, there is considerable variation among different regions throughout the body. For example, the normal temperature of the face and hands is about 90°F, but other regions are higher or lower. Any stimulus object that reduces the temperature of a cutaneous region by about 2°F would activate the cold receptors that generate neural impulses leading to the perception of cold. Similarly, any stimulus object that is about 2°F warmer than the region about it will activate receptors for heat that generate neural impulses that lead to the perception of warmth.

THE KINESTHETIC SENSE

The kinesthetic sense provides information about the body's movements and location in space for coordinating complex behaviors.

Its Functions. The **kinesthetic sense** provides perceptions of body movements and helps to coordinate activities. It typically functions automatically in that we do not normally pay attention to it. It is, though, of extremely great importance to us. For one thing, the kinesthetic sense informs us about the location of our limbs in space—if you place your left arm behind you, you know its location perfectly well. It is also of critical importance in the coordination and integration of such complex behaviors as walking, driving a car, writing a letter, and talking. Behavior that is not well coordinated or integrated is erratic and jerky, making even such a seemingly simple activity as walking extremely difficult. This point is well illustrated in some clinical cases involving forms of syphilis, such as *tabes dorsalis* in which the nervous systems are attacked and the victim walks with jerky, uncoordinated movements.

The Kinesthetic Receptors.   There are three locations for kinesthetic receptors: (1) muscles, (2) tendons, and (3) linings of the joints.

Muscle spindles (intrafusal muscle fibers) function as kinesthetic receptors in muscles. As you will note in Figure 7.4, the muscle spindle is within the muscle fiber. When you move your arm, you naturally contract and lengthen various muscles in it. As a consequence, numerous muscle spindles are activated that generate neural impulses that are transmitted to the brain. As you can well imagine, an enormous number of muscle spindles are constantly being activated as we move our bodies. An amazing number of neuromuscular circuits reverberate to carry out the body's functions.

The type of kinesthetic receptor embedded in the tendons is called the **Golgi tendon organ.** Tendons are groups of fibers that do not stretch to any appreciable extent, somewhat analogous to strong pieces of rope. Tendons are connected to muscles at one end and to bones at the other. If a muscle such as the biceps in the upper arm contracts, the forearm below the elbow moves up. This is because the muscles of the upper arm pull on the tendons that are attached to the bone of the forearm. Consequently, when Golgi tendon organs are activated, nerve impulses are generated and conducted along tiny nerve fibers to larger nerves and thence to and from the brain. The activation of Golgi tendon organs also helps us to manifest smooth, integrated, well-coordinated movements.

The third location of kinesthetic receptors is in the linings of the joints. Pacinian corpuscles there apparently tell us something about the relative location of the two bones that meet in the joint. (There is a joint at every point in the body where two bones come together, as at the knee, the ankle, and the shoulder.) When a limb moves, the Pacinian corpuscles located in the joints are activated; they then generate neural impulses that are conducted by a series of neurons to and from the brain.

Free nerve endings are widely distributed throughout the body to serve a variety of functions, one of which may be as a fourth class of kinesthetic receptor. To understand this, let us first note that all muscles contain a number of free nerve endings that connect to the blood vessels contained within the muscles. Blood vessels contain very small smooth muscles so that when those muscles contract, they probably activate the free nerve endings that are attached to them. Consequently, those free nerve endings may also furnish information about the location of our limbs. In this way they apparently sense continued vigorous use of muscles and muscle cramps. In the joints, free nerve endings produce pain, as in arthritis.

Pacinian corpuscles are also in the membrane surrounding muscles to apparently sense lower (deeper) regions of muscles when those muscles are acted upon by substantial pressure.

The sense of kinesthesis is in many ways of great importance to us. Consequently, we will enlarge on this topic at various points throughout the book.

Taste Circuits

Gustation, the sense of taste, is activated when food dissolves in the saliva of the mouth. Once dissolved, the food is chemically "broken down" and chemicals, the stimuli for gustation, are "released" to activate **taste buds** (Fig. 5.14). Unfortunately, we know relatively little about these numerous chemical reactions, and indeed about

Kinesthetic receptors include muscle spindles, Golgi tendon organs, Pacinian corpuscles in the linings of joints, and probably free nerve endings in muscles and joints.

Gustation, the sense of taste, is activated when chemicals from food dissolve in saliva to stimulate taste receptors in taste buds located throughout the mouth. Neural impulses are then transmitted along three cranial nerves to the brain.

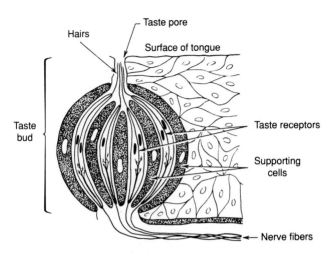

Hairs

Taste pore

Surface of tongue

Taste bud

Taste receptors

Supporting cells

Nerve fibers

FIGURE 5.14
A taste bud containing taste receptors.

the physiology of gustation in general. For instance, while there are numerous stimuli that have a bitter taste to us, we know of no common chemical or physiological property among them; we do know that they are potentially harmful.

Receptors for Taste. Although taste buds are located throughout the mouth, and to some extent in the larynx, their density is greatest on the top (dorsal) surface of the tongue. Hence, the upper surface of the tongue is more important for taste than is any other section of the mouth.

A taste bud is made up of supporting cells and a number of taste receptors embedded within it. Taste receptors are continually replaced, perhaps about once a week, not unlike the cells in your skin. In Figure 5.14 we can see that several hairs toward the top of the taste bud project into a small opening called the taste pore. When food goes into solution in the saliva of the mouth, the chemicals contained in the saliva enter the taste pore and come into contact with taste receptors. If the combined intensity of the gustatory stimuli in the mouth is above the threshold of excitability, taste receptors will generate messages that are transmitted along nerve fibers that join three cranial nerves to the brain. This contrasts with audition, vision, and olfaction, for which nerve impulses are transmitted to the brain by means of a single nerve. Taste buds (like the cutaneous receptors) are widely distributed throughout the mouth, so that it would be inefficient for a single nerve to receive nerve impulses from all of them.

The four primary qualities of taste in descending order of sensitivity are sour, bitter, salt, and sweet. These combine to produce more complex and subtle taste perceptions.

Primary Taste Qualities. In determining that the four primary qualities of taste are sour, bitter, salt, and sweet, researchers have devised methods for ruling out other sense modalities, especially smell, but also temperature and somaesthesis. In tests for taste qualities, we are most sensitive to hydrochloric acid (sour), then to quinine (bitter) (these characteristics have obvious survival value as in facilitating our spitting out poisonous foods); next in sensitivity are salty substances, and we are least sensitive to sweet substances. These four primary qualities combine to yield more complex tastes. One can only marvel at how the stimuli sour, bitter, salt, and sweet combine in subtle ways to generate the delicate tastes of the wide variety of foods that we enjoy.

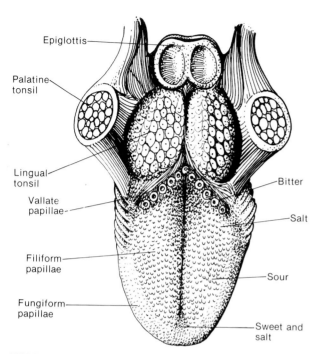

Epiglottis

Palatine tonsil

Lingual tonsil

Vallate papillae

Filiform papillae

Fungiform papillae

Bitter

Salt

Sour

Sweet and salt

FIGURE 5.15 The tongue, illustrating relative sensitivity in its various regions to the four primary qualities of taste.

The human tongue is most sensitive to bitter at its posterior and to other stimuli as shown in Figure 5.15. Sensitivity to sweet is greatest at the anterior (tip) of the tongue while the entire tongue is generally sensitive to salt.

SOME UNUSUAL SENSORY SYSTEMS

With this overview of mammalian sense modalities, let us consider some rare sense modalities. Sampling unusual senses provides us with a perspective that has value in a number of ways. It tells us something about how some organisms evolved and survived in unique environments in the struggle for existence, and maybe even something that can be extrapolated to extraterrestrial life.

A variety of sensory systems used by nonhuman organisms are important for a broader understanding of terrestrial behavior as well as possibly for extraterrestrial life.

Magnetic Sensory Systems

Magnetic Characteristics of the Earth. To understand how the magnetic field of the earth is useful to many species of animals, let us summarize some of its characteristics. From one point of view, the earth is a large magnet with the field primarily in the earth's core. The magnetic pull of the earth, however, is not stable. Every 10,000 to 100,000 years the field reverses itself.

In addition to the large magnetic field generated inside the earth, a smaller and more dynamic field is present in the ionosphere produced by electrically charged particles in the jet streams high above the earth. Because the jet streams move from north to south every day as the earth is heated and cooled by the sun, they generate a regular **circadian** (24-hour) **rhythm** of magnetic signals. Those signals can be useful to species that can sense them. However, when there are disturbances on the sun, such as sun spots, numerous charged electrical particles from the sun arrive after a day or so in the jet streams. These particles often cause magnetic storms that radically modify standard circadian patterns and thus can alter the extent to which signals from them can be effectively used.

Kinds of Information in the Earth's Magnetic Fields. Organisms might use (1) the *direction* in the magnetic field, (2) magnetic latitudes in order to ascertain their *location,* and (3) the circadian rhythm of the field to estimate *time.* What is the behavioral evidence that organisms do, in fact, use these three kinds of information?

Honey bees and homing pigeons have high-precision magnetic sensitivity and there is evidence of a "compass sense" in other species.

The Evidence That Organisms Are Sensitive to Magnetic Fields Is Abundant. As discussed by Gould (1984), bacteria and honey bees sense and use the direction of magnetic fields. Many species of reptiles, birds, and fishes navigate over long distances apparently using magnetic fields as a kind of compass sense; particularly impressive here are the data on the homing skill of pigeons. Sharks and rays are able to detect the strength of the earth's magnetic field, and tuna have been experimentally conditioned to respond to the presence or absence of the earth's magnetic field. Apparently salmon can orient themselves magnetically. Some data indicate that humans can sense magnetic direction, but efforts to confirm this conclusion have not been successful.

What kind of receptor systems might exist for sensing magnetic fields? One relevant finding is that there are localized concentrations of magnetite crystals in animals that are sensitive to magnetic signals. Perhaps they are the basis of magnetic receptor systems, but we need to know more about the relevant anatomy and physiology.

The Sonar System of Bats

Bats employ a kind of sonar system that includes feedback to locate other organisms and objects.

Bats generate sound impulses and analyze the echoes from them to infer the location of a possible prey to capture. They also avoid objects by these sound impulses, which is a kind of sonar system with a highly sensitive feedback process.

The Sensing and Generation of Electrical Fields

Some fishes have electrical senses while others generate electrical fields that help in their survival.

In Fishes. In lieu of hearing, some fishes have an electrical sense (see Heiligenberg & Bastian, 1984). Sharks have special organs on the snout to sense electrical fields generated by ion currents in the muscles of their prey. These fields are so weak, however, that this sensing system is of value only at short range, just before the prey is ready for capture.

Some fishes produce electric fields that can be synchronized and oriented by their own muscles. When there are disturbances of these electrical fields, the disturbing organism (the prey) can be sensed by the emitter (the hunter).

There are anatomic and physiologic similarities between electroreceptors and the hair cells in acoustic and vestibular systems. These electroreceptors are tuned to the dominant frequency of the animal's electric organ discharge. When communicating with others, the electroreceptors of the African electric fish are activated by electric organ discharges from its neighbors—the fish does not perceive its own signals. However, when seeking to locate others, using what is called electrolocation, the African electric fish selectively receives feedback from its own discharged electrical signals. There is thus an analogy with the "sonar" feedback system of the bat.

An Electrical Sense in the Duck-billed Platypus. The platypus is unusual and unique. In the eighteenth century stuffed platypuses were sent to Europe for study, but they were dismissed as a joke, thought to be but combined pieces of parts of various animals. Eventually, though, scientists did take the platypus seriously and discovered that it did lay eggs.

Since the platypus swims with its eyes and ears closed, the question arose as to how it finds its food. In a series of experiments by Chris Tidemann, it has been shown that it detects electrical signals generated by its prey—mainly shrimp and frogs in streams along Australia's east coast. For example, in laboratory water tanks platypuses head for flashlight batteries but ignore dead shrimp.

Under an electron microscope it has been found that the platypus's head contains receptors for electric signals, which is unique in mammals. The only other animals that have electroreceptors are fishes and a few amphibian larvae. The electrical signal given off by prey that is detected is that generated by muscle movements. Electrical impulses from rotting vegetation and some rocks also serve to help the platypus navigate.

The platypus possibly dates back 22 million years. The discovery of the electrical sensors indicates that the platypus is still evolving into an even more unique organism. An electric sense provides information much more valuable than that from the sense of touch. How advantageous it would be if humans had this sense.

The duck-billed platypus is the only mammal that has receptors for the electrical signals generated by its prey, thus helping it to obtain food.

Infrared Sensors of Snakes

Pit vipers, which include the rattlesnake, the cottonmouth (water moccasin), and the copperhead, have pit organs that are sensitive to infrared radiation emitted by warm-blooded organisms. As discussed by Newman and Hartline (1982), when stimulated, the pit organs send information to the brain along heat-sensitive nerve fibers. The snakes have specialized nuclei in the brain to receive and process information from the pit organs. These nuclei relay information to the midbrain where it is combined and integrated with visual signals from the eyes. Consequently, they can strike accurately in light but also at night. Pythons, distant relatives of the pit vipers, have heat-sensitive pits on scales bordering the mouth.

The cavity of a pit organ, 1 to 5 millimeters (mm) in diameter, is located in the head bone. The cavity is filled with air and bounded by a thin membrane containing some 7000 thermosensitive neural endings.

In one experiment that demonstrated the existence of infrared sensors, it was found that rattlesnakes could differentiate between warm and cold light bulbs that were covered with opaque cloth. The snakes attacked the warm bulbs as long as their pits remained functional. But if their pits were blocked, they ignored both bulbs.

Pit vipers have infrared sensors to detect radiation emitted by warm-blooded organisms.

In Conclusion

These unusual senses for magnetic, sonar, infrared, and electrical stimuli well illustrate how, through natural selection, such organisms won their struggle for survival. One can imagine them added to the normal sensory systems of humans to create a "super person." If there is life on other planets, might such superior sensory systems have evolved?

Is There Subliminal Perception?

The term *subliminal* derives from the Latin meaning "below" *(sub)* and the hallowed psychophysical concept of **limen,** which means "the threshold of consciousness." Consequently, **subliminal perception** refers to a hypothesized process of being influenced by stimuli with intensities or durations below the limen (threshold of conscious awareness). For example, one would be influenced if a picture were flashed with such a short duration or low intensity that it was not possible to report being aware of it.

Commercially, there have been efforts to deliver subliminal messages to us in a variety of ways. They have been inserted into music played in retail stores to get us to buy certain items, and they were visually presented in the movies to encourage us to buy cokes and popcorn. In magazines and other media, advertisements for "subconscious subliminal stimulation" is rampant. We are offered many easy pathways to read faster, to improve our memory, to do better on examinations, to lose weight, to stop smoking, to creatively dream, to relieve stress, to improve self-esteem, and to improve enjoyment of sex. All we have to do is to send $9.99 with a no-risk order form. Is subliminal perception really effective in motivating us to unconsciously buy a product that we had no intention of purchasing?

Although subliminal stimuli do not affect overt behavior, through the process of subception they can influence some psychophysiological reactions of which we are not consciously aware.

In the 1950s, experimentation thoroughly discredited the subliminal perception hypothesis. More recently, though, the phenomenon has come to the fore again. The data still indicate that subliminal stimuli cannot affect overt behavior. We certainly have no sound basis for asserting that they can be successfully used by advertisers to direct individuals toward specific actions such as buying popcorn in a theater. Results of studies also indicate that we cannot extract meaning from information subliminally presented to us. Thus meaningful communication does not occur through stimuli below sensory thresholds. As the National Academy of Sciences reported in *In the Mind's Eye: Enhancing Human Performance,* the unambiguous conclusion is that "there is neither theoretical foundation nor experimental evidence to support claims that subliminal self-help audiotapes enhance human performance" (p. 116).

However, some data do indicate that there are *some* covert, but not overt subliminal effects. These effects are of an emotional nature and are manifested in perceptual defenses. For instance, emotional stimuli that have negative connotations are less readily recognized than are neutral stimuli. Although the recipient of subliminal stimulation cannot verbalize the nature of the impinging negative stimuli, psychophysiological measures such as the galvanic skin response indicate that the observer's body does respond to them. Perceptual defense seems to protect us from the conscious recall of painful memories, although our body does respond to them. For this reason we may have unpleasant feelings generated by distasteful memories or thoughts, although we are unaware of the processes involved. **Subception** is the term denoting the body's psychophysiological response to subliminal stimuli that cannot be verbally reported.

EMPHASIS ON A CYBERNETIC PRINCIPLE—CENTRIFUGAL INFLUENCES FROM THE BRAIN DURING SENSORY TRANSMISSION

We have noted that central brain mechanisms influence sensory transmission at early stages in the major sensory systems. These **centrifugal influences** feed back information within cybernetic circuits from the highest brain regions to lower neural peripheral regions. In the visual system, there is considerable evidence of efferent fibers (neurons that carry information *from* the brain) in both the optic nerve and retina of vertebrates, including humans. The estimate of the number of efferents relative to afferents in nerves ranges from 1 percent in birds to 10 percent in humans and other primates. The centrifugal activity carried by these neurons is considered to alter the flow of incoming information as far down as the spinal cord for the somatic sensory system and the olivocochlear bundle (see Fig. 5.4) for the auditory system. Some data indicate that irrelevant auditory information may be filtered at the level of the olivocochlear bundle in humans, although there are other conflicting (negative) results for this conclusion. There *are* considerable data from animal studies that support the existence of such filters well below the cortex. It is clear that information is processed in stages from receptors to the brain as well as in the brain. It is also processed in circuits between the brain and effectors.

Although information comes from the receptors to the brain, there is much evidence of cybernetic circuits being completed by reverse (centrifugal) information going from the brain to the periphery.

These considerations emphasize again that cognitive and other processing is not limited to the brain. Much of it goes on in the periphery and in peripheral–central interactions.

To carry on our continuing analogy with the computer, much of the incoming information is in the form of a special language. We enter information into the "brain" of a computer in various computer languages (e.g., Basic and Fortran). Consequently, the computer can process that information more efficiently than if it were in "raw" form. Similarly, incoming sensory information that reaches the brain has already been processed to some extent in the receptor systems of the body. These peripheral systems include those in the muscles and in the afferent nerves that perform specialized processing functions (recall the Principle of Labeled Lines). Thus, coding of information received by receptors occurs as messages are transmitted along these sensory pathways. The feedback of information from the brain to these sensory pathways is important in such peripheral processing. The brain, in receiving sensory information as messages in special languages, can thus process it with increased efficiency because of its continuous interaction with receptor and effector systems and their connecting neural pathways.

KEY TERMS

Auditory canal (external auditory meatus)—The canal that leads from the external ear (pinna) into the middle ear to conduct sound waves.

Auditory stimulus—Changes in amount of energy in sound waves that activate the receptor cells of the ear.

Basilar membrane—The membrane in the cochlea upon which the organ of Corti rests; responds with traveling waves to stimuli.

Basket nerve endings—Tiny nerves that wrap around the roots of hairs and function as receptor cells for pressure.

Bipolar cells — Cells having branches arising from both ends of a cell body, such as bipolar neurons.

Centrifugal influences — Signals sent from higher brain regions to lower and peripheral regions to modulate incoming signals in circuits.

Circadian rhythms — Rhythmic biological cycles occurring at approximately 24-hour intervals.

Cochlea — Spiral portion of the inner ear that contains the receptor cells for hearing.

Cochlear mechanics — The study of how the ear functions, advanced in 1928 when Georg von Békésy attempted to construct a more effective telephone system.

Contralateral — The side of the body opposite to where one is referring (e.g., the left cerebral hemisphere is contralateral to the right hand).

Crossed olivocochlear bundle — Neural pathways that transmit primary efferent inputs to the cochlea from higher auditory pathways.

Cutaneous (skin) senses — The skin senses of pressure, pain, cold, and heat.

Dermis — The skin containing various cutaneous receptors.

Endolymph — Gelatinous substance within each semicircular canal.

Eustachian tube — A tube that conducts air between the middle ear and mouth.

Extraocular muscles — Six muscles surrounding the eye and controlling its movements.

Free nerve endings — Small nerve branches activated when the skin is bent or depressed. They are also present throughout the body and function as pain receptors.

Golgi tendon organs — Receptors activated when tendons are stretched whereupon nerve impulses are generated and conducted along nerve fibers to the brain.

Gustation — The sense of taste.

Hair cells — Receptor cells that transduce mechanical vibrations into electrical signals.

Hertz (Hz) — One cycle per second, a measure of frequency for sound, EEG waves, visual stimuli, and so on.

Incus (anvil) — One of the three auditory ossicles (bones) in the middle ear.

Inner ear — The portion of the auditory apparatus containing the cochlea; it is related to the utricle and saccule and the semicircular canals.

Ipsilateral — The same side of the body (see Contralateral).

Kinesthetic sense — Informs us about the location of our body and limbs in space by activating receptors in the muscles, joints, and tendons.

Krause's end bulbs — Receptors concentrated in skin areas that are particularly sensitive to cold stimuli.

Lateral geniculate nucleus — A nucleus relay station in the thalamus that functions for vision, audition, and so on.

Law of Specific Nerve Energies — The nature of a sensory message is determined by the specific sensory pathways that are activated no matter what stimulus activated those pathways.

Lens — A transparent structure attached to the front of the eyes and controlled by muscle.

Limen — The minimal level of a stimulus that can be sensed by an organism.

Malleus (hammer) — One of the auditory ossicles in the middle ear attached to the eardrum that articulates with the incus.

Mechano-electrotransducer — Transduces (changes) mechanical into electrical energy.

Meissner corpuscle — A skin receptor especially sensitive to very light pressures such as a touch of the finger tips.

Muscle spindle (intrafusal muscle fiber) — A muscle fiber that detects length (see Chapter 7).

Olfaction — Technical term for the sense of smell.

Olfactory bulb (nerve) — Olfactory receptors connect to the olfactory bulb, which receives nerve impulses and transmits them to the cerebral cortex along the olfactory nerve.

Optic nerve and tract — Transmit neural impulses from the eyes to the occipital lobes of the brain.

Organ of Corti — Located in the inner ear and composed of basilar and tectorial membranes, together with hair cells.

Orientating response (OR) — The tendency of an organism to orient toward novel stimuli.

Ossicles — Middle ear bones (see incus, malleus, stapes).

Otoconia (otoliths)—Small crystals in the gelatin-like substance contained in the utricle and saccule.

Oval window—Connects the middle with the inner ear.

Pacinian corpuscle—A type of pressure receptor, located deep below the skin, responding to skin surface deformations.

Photons—Particles of visual energy.

Photoreceptors (rods and cones)—Receptors for which the adequate or normal stimulus is light.

Pinna (external ear)—Collects sounds from the environment that then travel through the auditory canal.

Place theory—There is a progression of positions along the basilar membrane that are most sensitive to successively lower frequencies of sounds.

Principle of Labeled Lines—Holds that there are subpathways within sensory nerves that have specialized functions so that, for instance, the neurons within the optic nerve are not homogeneous.

Pupil—The aperture in the eye that admits light, its size is controlled by pupillary muscles.

Retina—The innermost layer of the eye that contains light sensitive cells (rods and cones).

Ruffini's endings—Receptors concentrated in regions of the body especially sensitive to warm stimuli.

Saccule—An organ in the inner ear, which, together with the utricle and the semicircular canals, has to do with the vestibular sense.

Semicircular canal—Located directly above the cochlea, it functions as a portion of the vestibular sense.

Sense modalities—Sensory systems, such as for warm, cold, pain, taste, audition, and vision.

Somaesthesis—Sensations generated throughout the body.

Stapedius—A small muscle in the middle ear that restrains the stapes.

Stapes (stirrup)—Ossicle (small bone) in the middle ear that conducts auditory information to the cochlea. It is attached to the oval window of the cochlea.

Stimulus—A change in environmental energy that excites a receptor.

Subception—The process by which subliminal stimuli influence covert behavior.

Subliminal perception—Disconfirmed hypothesis of overt behavior being influenced by stimuli with intensities below the "limen" (threshold) for a stimulus.

Superior olive—Earliest stage in the neural tract of the auditory system to receive information from both ears.

Taste buds—Activated by the chemicals that serve as gustatory stimuli.

Tectorial membrane—Located along the basilar membrane, it functions for audition.

Tensor tympani—A small muscle in the middle ear that restrains the malleus.

Tonal tinnitus—False perception of sounds such as hissing or roaring when there is no external stimulation.

Tonotopic representation—A point-to-point relationship between regions in the basilar membrane and the auditory cortex.

Transduction—The change of one form of energy into another.

Traveling waves—In audition, vibrations of the basilar membrane activated by auditory stimuli.

Tympanic membrane—The eardrum.

Utricle—An organ in the inner ear near the semicircular canals which, together with the saccule, contributes to the vestibular sense.

Vestibular sense—Informs us of the general orientation, location, and position of the body in space.

Visible spectrum—The frequencies of light that are sensed by the human eye.

Visual cortex—The primary receiving area in the cortex for visual information, located in the occipital lobes.

Volley theory—Holds that at low frequencies (below about 4000 Hz), sounds are coded according to volleys of neural impulses carried along afferent neurons to the brain.

STUDY QUESTIONS

1. Discuss the role of the receptors in the reception of information from the external and internal environments.
2. What is the importance of the Law of Specific Energies of Nerves and who formulated it? What is its relationship to the Principle of Labeled Lines?
3. Specify the nature of the major receptor organs of the human body, how they are activated, and the ways in which information from them is transmitted to the brain.
4. T or F: The apex is the end of the basilar membrane farthest from a point at which the stirrup meets the cochlea.
5. T or F: The base of the basilar membrane is the region adjacent to the stirrup.
6. T or F: The higher frequencies of sound produce relatively more displacement at the basal end of the basilar membrane.
7. Why is Georg von Békésy important for science?
8. Discuss reception of external information in terms of internal processing within cybernetic circuits, with special reference to audition.
9. Distinguish between subliminal perception and subception.
10. Summarize some unusual sense modalities and evaluate their importance.

FURTHER READINGS

You can browse through a library in the area of physiological psychology to find such books as Carlson's *Physiology of Behavior* (1991). Also, there are more advanced presentations available that include the following:

Rhode, W. S. (1984). Cochlear mechanics. *Annual Review of Physiology, 46,* 231–246.

Hudspeth, A. J. (1983). The hair cells of the inner ear. *Scientific American, 248,* 42–52.

CHAPTER 6

Integrating and Processing Information
Contributions of the
Nervous Systems

MAJOR PURPOSES:	1. To understand how the several nervous systems are structured
	2. To understand how they function together and with other systems of the body to transmit, process, and integrate information sensed by the receptors
WHAT YOU ARE GOING TO FIND:	1. Anatomical definitions of the nervous systems
	2. How the brain functions with other components of the nervous systems
	3. Some examples of the intricate, complex interactions among the neural and muscular systems
	4. An introduction to biochemical phenomena in the brain
WHAT YOU SHOULD ACQUIRE:	An understanding of the critical roles of the nervous systems when they reverberate as components of cybernetic circuits both within themselves and with other systems throughout the body

CHAPTER OUTLINE

DEFINING THE SEVERAL NERVOUS SYSTEMS

More than in any other aspect of an organism, complex cybernetic circuits function throughout nervous tissue. Consequently it deserves our special attention. For convenience, nervous tissue is separated into several nervous systems, but that does not imply that any nervous system functions independently. An event in one system has consequences in others, which in turn feed back to the first.

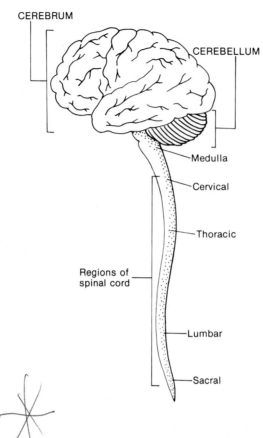

CEREBRUM

CEREBELLUM

Medulla

Cervical

Thoracic

Regions of
spinal cord

Lumbar

Sacral

FIGURE 6.1
A side view of the brain
depicting the relationship of
the cerebrum with the
cerebellum, the spinal cord,
and the brain stem. Nerves
exit from the brain and spinal
cord to form divisions of the
peripheral nervous system.

*Nervous material throughout
the body is used for the extensive transmission and processing of messages, but for
convenience we arbitrarily
categorize it into central and
peripheral nervous systems
and their subdivisions.*

I. The **central nervous system (CNS)** consists of the brain and spinal cord (Fig. 6.1).
II. The **peripheral nervous system** consists of all the nerves outside the central nervous system.
  A. The **somatic nervous system** is that subdivision of the peripheral nervous system that sends nerve fibers to and from the striated musculature.
  B. The **autonomic nervous system (ANS)** innervates smooth and cardiac muscle and glands. The ANS has two divisions:
    1. The **sympathetic nervous system** consists of the **spinal nerves** in the thoracic and lumbar regions of the spinal cord.
    2. The **parasympathetic nervous system** consists of some **cranial nerves** and the sacral spinal nerves.

THE CENTRAL NERVOUS SYSTEM (CNS)

The Brain—An Overview

MODELS OF THE BRAIN IN HISTORICAL PERSPECTIVE

Hydraulic Models.   The dominant machine used in society during a particular era emerged as that era's model of how the brain functions. Long ago, when hydraulic systems were dominant, we held somewhat of a "plumbing" model of the central nervous system. According to Galen, nutritive substances in the liver formed spirits (gases) that combined with air in the lungs to create vital spirits. When the vital spirits were conducted ("flowed") to the brain, they entered the ventricles (reservoirs) where they formed a new "gas." That gas was called "animal spirits" and it had a characteristic related to the soul. These gases flowed throughout the nervous systems by means of tubules (what we now call nerves). When the gases reached the effectors, they activated the body to move. Descartes followed Galen in holding that pneuma (the animal spirits) flow throughout the body by tubules to the effectors. The soul acting at the pineal gland (shown in Fig. 6.5) could influence pneuma to direct behavior for reasoning and other acts (see Fig. 2.5).

Outmoded Mechanical and Telephone Models. With the rise of the Industrial Revolution, the human brain was thought of as a magnificent *mechanical* machine. Many models employing gears and levers were developed. Then in the 1920s, with the rise of effective telephone systems, a telephone model of the brain and body was prominent: Information comes in through receptors (you talk into your telephone), information is put through the brain (it goes to the central part of the telephone exchange system), and the output of the brain activates effectors (you activate the listener with your speech). By this model, the brain functions as a complex switchboard to coordinate vast amounts of incoming and outgoing information (Fig. 6.2). Although we have abandoned hydraulic and mechanical models, this telephone model of the nervous systems often persists today. The weakness of this model is that it completely neglects feedback stages.

The Brain Is Always Active. One common misconception of the telephone model that persisted well into this century was that the brain was an inactive system when it was not being stimulated. When no telephone calls come into "central" (the brain), the CNS did not operate. Even the great physiologist Sir Charles Sherrington offered the analogy of the brain as a sleeping city whose lights fade and disappear at night.

Hans Berger's 1929 discovery of spontaneous brain waves in humans not only established the field of electroencephalography but also made it clear that the brain is constantly active, rather than sometimes being in a state of quiescence. Much research since then, especially that on sleep and dreams, has established that the brain remains active 24 hours a day. As we will develop when we discuss the topic of sleep, the brain, along with the body, is often even *more* active at night than during wakefulness, although the patterns of the firing of the neurons during sleep and wakefulness are quite different.

Contemporary Computer Models. Today it is natural for us to think of the brain in terms of computer models. The brain stores information in memory and coordinates complex input–output functions. As with analogies to earlier models, though, the brain is a much more complex system than that depicted by any computer. Nevertheless, there is some validity to a computer model: In spite of obvious differences, some similarities are striking. For instance, like an advanced computer, the brain engages simultaneously in many processes through multichannel systems that function in parallel fashion. This analogy breaks down, however, because brain function on some tasks is quite slow, relative to a computer. For instance, we normally take seconds to perform simple mathematical operations that an average computer does in milliseconds.

Some Anatomical Features of Cybernetic Circuits. Since the brain is the most complex structure of which we are aware, we will have to try to understand it through stages. To begin to appreciate the complexity of cybernetic circuits, some estimates of anatomical features follow.

Historical models to understand the brain have included hydraulic "plumbing" systems in which gases flowed through the nervous systems; mechanical models of gears and levers; telephone systems of linear input, throughput, and output; and computer models that incorporate feedbacks and feedforwards.

Contemporary psychophysiological research has disconfirmed the belief that the brain and mind shut off during sleep. Instead, cognitive activities of the brain and body persist throughout sleep.

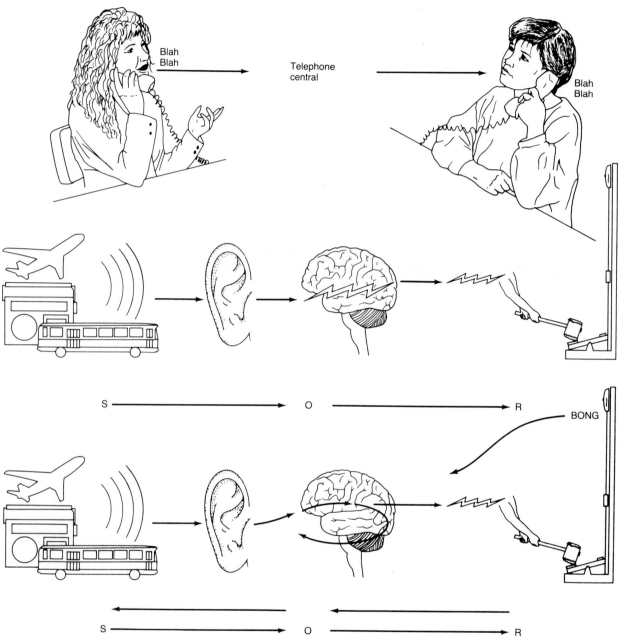

FIGURE 6.2 An analogy between the telephone system and the functioning of the body (top two figures). Information (S) enters the organism (O) and goes directly through it to evoke a response (R). In contrast, a more realistic model is diagrammed at the bottom to include feedbacks at each stage.

There are 130 million rods and cones in the human eye that make junction with 1 million nerve fibers in the optic nerve (see Fig. 4.4). This ratio of 130 to 1 indicates that exceedingly complex events must occur in the transfer of information from the receptor cells to the optic nerve even before information reaches the brain. How might information be transferred from 130 fibers to one (on the average) and then transformed again to a different number of fibers? On the motor side, the oculomotor nerve (a cranial nerve) contains 25,000 fibers, and the muscles that produce eye movements have approximately three muscle fibers for each nerve fiber. This ratio of one neural fiber to three muscle fibers invites thought about the transfer of information back from the brain to the eye musculature. For comparison with the optic and oculomotor nerves, other cranial nerves contain about 70,000 fibers, and motor roots of spinal nerves contain about 100,000 fibers.

Some ten billion cerebral neurons, held together by 90 billion glial cells, make perhaps 500 trillion synapses in the cortex.

There are approximately 1030 muscles with numerous muscle fibers in each, constituting almost half of the weight of the human body. The brain and its interactions with the periphery involve complex transformations of sensory input. The Principle of Labeled Lines tells us that we abstract some features from coded stimuli and neglect other information. Then, that coded information is stored as internal representations of the external world. Information about bodily movements also is coded and retained as internal representations of those physical movements.

As information is processed and stored, amazingly complex transformations occur in interactions among a multitude of sensory, synaptic, and effector cells.

To start on our journey of understanding these matters, we will consider the gross anatomy of the central nervous system. Then we will study the various specific CNS regions and discuss their functions in greater detail.

GROSS ANATOMY OF THE BRAIN

Note in Figure 6.3 that the **cerebrum** constitutes the major part of the brain. The cerebrum is divided by the **longitudinal fissure** into the *left* and *right* **cerebral hemispheres.** The smaller **cerebellum** projects below (inferior) to it and the upper part of the **spinal cord** extends into the **brain stem.**

FIGURE 6.3 A frontal view of the brain showing the longitudinal fissure separating the two hemispheres.

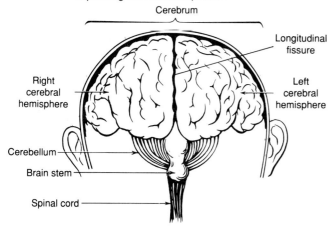

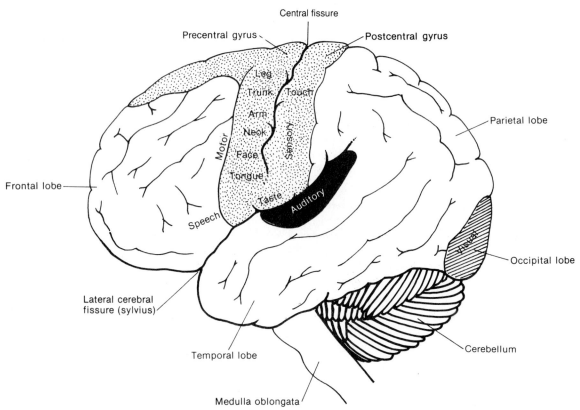

FIGURE 6.4 The four lobes and other features of the brain. Included is a region for speech (known as Broca's area) and the motor, sensory, and visual areas.

The brain is surrounded with meninges that protect it. The cortex beneath the meninges has numerous convolutions with major anatomic landmarks of the longitudinal, central, and lateral fissures.

The brain and spinal cord are covered with tough connective tissue called **meninges.** Three layers of the meninges surround the brain. The outermost layer, the *dura mater,* is especially protective. The middle layer is the *arachnoid,* while the innermost layer is the *pia mater.* The wavy lines indicate folds (convolutions) of the **cerebral cortex.** These convolutions allow the oversized human brain to "fold" in order to fit into the cranium (skull). Figure 6.4 shows two of the major identifying features of the cerebral cortex. One is a vertical groove or fissure, the **central fissure,** so-called because of its central location in each hemisphere. The second major identifying mark of the cortex is the **lateral fissure,** which runs in a somewhat lateral or sidewise fashion. The lateral and central fissures help to mark off the four major regions (lobes) of each cerebral hemisphere:

Each cerebral hemisphere consists of a frontal lobe anterior to the central fissure, a parietal lobe posterior to it, a temporal lobe inferior to the lateral fissure, and an occipital lobe at its extreme posterior.

1. The **frontal lobe** in each hemisphere is anterior (forward) of the central fissure; note in Figure 6.4 the speech and motor areas which we will soon discuss.
2. The two **parietal lobes** are posterior to (in back of) the central fissures and they contain the sensory areas.
3. The **temporal lobes** are inferior to (below) the lateral fissure and anterior to (in front of) the occipital lobe.
4. The **occipital lobes** are at the posterior (far rear) of each cerebral hemisphere.

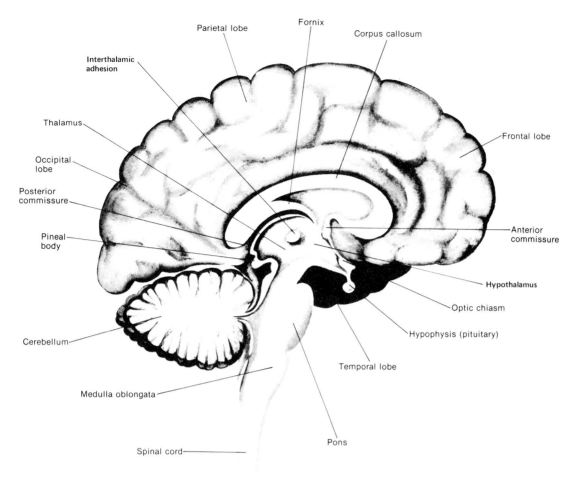

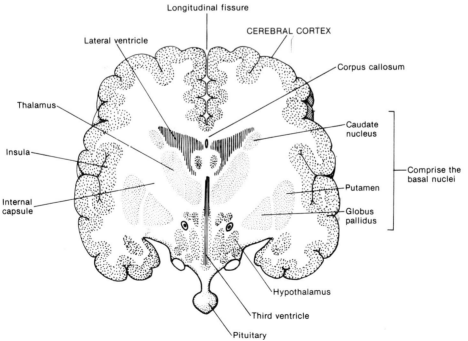

FIGURE 6.5 A side view of the brain specifying its four lobes and including a portion of its interior (top) and a frontal section (bottom).

The cerebral cortex, the outer layer of the cerebrum, is composed largely of the cell bodies of neurons. Cell bodies are gray in color, leading to the cortex's being referred to as our "gray matter." Humans have the most highly developed cerebral cortex; it is about one-fourth inch in thickness.

A side view of the interior of the brain reveals several important structures, especially the **thalamus** and the **hypothalamus** (Fig. 6.5). The hypothalamus is directly below the thalamus (*hypo* means "below"). Also note that the brain stem includes the **medulla** (medulla oblongata) and the **pons,** so that ascending nerve impulses from the spinal cord are transmitted first through the medulla and then through the pons.

We will return to these structures after we develop a similar overview of the spinal cord.

Important subcortical regions of the brain include the thalamus and the hypothalamus.

The brain stem descends from the brain and includes the medulla oblongata and the pons. The brain stem descends into the spinal cord, which has dorsal roots at the back and ventral roots at the front.

The Spinal Cord

The brain and spinal cord interact to carry out the functions of the central nervous system. In Figure 6.6, we can observe a cross section of the spinal cord as if it were severed and bent forward toward you. The inner part of the spinal cord, in the shape of a butterfly, is gray since it contains primarily cell bodies of neurons. The matter on the outer parts consists of white axons and dendrites.

The top of Figure 6.6 is at one's back, the dorsal surface of the spinal cord. The bottom part is the ventral surface, toward the front surface (stomach) of the body. Sensory nerve fibers generally enter the spinal cord through left and right dorsal roots (roots are also called "horns") and motor nerve fibers exit from left and right ventral roots as shown in Figure 6.6. Association neurons and the cell bodies of efferent neurons are primarily within the gray matter.

The Bell-Magendie Law. According to the **Bell-Magendie Law,** afferent neural impulses enter the spinal cord through the dorsal roots and efferent neural impulses leave the spinal cord by means of the ventral roots. However, more recent research indicates that the Bell-Magendie Law is not 100 percent accurate. That is, there are some relatively few efferent neurons that exit the spinal cord through the dorsal roots and some afferent neurons enter the spinal cord by means of the ventral roots. Indeed, remember that there are both afferent and efferent neurons within any given nerve, so that neural impulses pass in both directions. Given the fact that there are perhaps 25,000 to 100,000 neurons within a typical nerve, it is not surprising that any given nerve serves both afferent and efferent functions. This characteristic

The Bell-Magendie Law holds that afferent neural impulses enter the spinal cord through the dorsal roots, and efferent neural impulses exit through the ventral roots. However, some efferent neurons also exit through the dorsal roots and some afferent neurons also enter through the ventral roots.

FIGURE 6.6   A cross section of the spinal cord illustrating the Bell-Magendie Law.

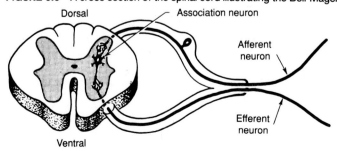

emphasizes the cybernetic nature of interacting systems wherein information feeds back between those systems.

If the dorsal roots of the spinal cord were destroyed, one could receive few afferent neural impulses for the regions affected — the brain could not receive sensory information from stimuli normally transmitted along those nerves. A person who does not feel pain in a certain part of the body, for instance, might have a lesion in the relevant dorsal roots. In like manner, a lesion in the ventral roots would not allow one to make a response for the region affected. With polio, for instance, a person may be partially paralyzed because nerve cells in the ventral roots are destroyed.

Major Components of the Brain

THE LOWER BRAIN STEM

The medulla and the pons in the brain stem have critical life-sustaining functions. The medulla, for instance, has a nervous center that functions in a circuit for breathing and another for heart rate. The brain stem is also important for the kinesthetic sense, as it receives nerve impulses from the kinesthetic receptors in muscles. Recall that when a muscle lengthens, it stimulates the muscle spindles embedded in it to generate nerve impulses that are transmitted to the brain stem. The brain stem, in turn, transmits nerve impulses down the spinal cord to the muscles. This rapid and frequent interchange between the muscles and the brain stem contributes to some of our well-coordinated, integrated behavior, such as walking. When we take a step, the contraction of muscles in our legs sends afferent neural impulses to the brain stem. Immediately on receipt of these afferent neural impulses, the brain stem sends neural impulses back down to the muscles, causing them to contract again so that the next step may be taken. And so on, in continuing cybernetic circuits involving the 1030 or so muscles of the body.

The brain stem contains centers for circuits interacting with the lungs for breathing and with the heart. It also functions with the kinesthetic sense with a continual exchange of neural impulses between the muscles and the brain stem.

RETICULAR FORMATION

The term *reticulum* literally means "little net"; the **reticular formation** is so named because of its netlike appearance. In Figure 6.7 we see a representation of the reticular formation located in the brain stem. Afferent neural impulses may be conducted directly to the brain stem by means of cranial nerves, or they may ascend the spinal cord to enter the brain stem and the reticular formation.

When afferent neural impulses enter the reticular formation, they are transmitted by direct axonal connections and also through the thalamus to the cerebral

The reticular formation is a network of neurons in the brain stem that, when activated, increases behavioral arousal by means of cybernetic circuits to and from the cortex.

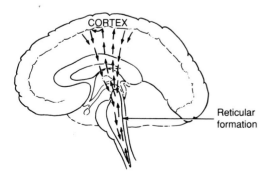

Reticular formation

FIGURE 6.7
Representation of circuits involving the reticular formation and the cortex.

cortex. The cerebral cortex is thereby excited over its previous state of activity, presumably so that it is better prepared for the receipt of additional neural impulses; it also then sends nerve impulses back down into the reticular formation. As the arousal of the cerebral cortex is increased, it in turn further excites the reticular formation, creating a positive feedback circuit. The existence of these circuits has been experimentally demonstrated by electrically stimulating the cerebral cortex (this is not painful) whereupon the reticular formation is also excited. Similarly, by electrically stimulating the reticular formation, an increase in the activity of the cerebral cortex follows.

Early research suggested that the reticular formation served a general arousal function. However, later research found that it functions to arouse specific regions in the head and body, such as for limb movements.

The early research on the reticular formation demonstrated that destruction of the midbrain reticular formation in cats produced a comatose state, while electrical stimulation of that area led to behavioral and cerebral arousal. The conclusion was that the reticular formation serves to arouse neural and behavioral events generally. However, later research using microelectrodes that measured single unit activity in freely moving cats found that the activity of individual neurons performed more specific arousal functions. In particular it was found that the activity of individual neurons was connected to the occurrence of specific movements within the head (of the eyes, ears, face) and of specific bodily and limb movements. Thus, the early conclusions that the reticular formation functioned for general arousal and for general sleep–waking cycles was disconfirmed. To better understand this, note that there are over 90 nuclei in the reticular formation (a **nucleus** is a group of homogeneous neurons). One important nucleus is the **locus coeruleus** that projects throughout the forebrain and cerebellum; the locus coeruleus is involved in rapid eye movement sleep. Other nuclei of the reticular formation function in respiration, sneezing, coughing, and vomiting and play a role in the control of posture and locomotion. The activity of individual neurons is closely related to specific movements of the eyes, ears, face, head, body, and limbs. Another group of nuclei, the raphe nuclei, is involved in slow-wave sleep (see Chapter 9). Projections down the spinal cord from the raphe nuclei apparently block transmission of pain impulses to the brain and have an effect on autonomic functioning. The reticular formation is thus an important component of diverse circuits involving the motor system — specifically those that influence muscular tonus and muscular movements. Instead of serving a general cortical-behavioral arousal function, as first concluded, it became clear that the reticular formation functions to more specifically arouse localized behavioral events.

The reticular formation plays a role in arousal, muscle tonus and movement, and autonomic functions. Axons from ascending sensory pathways activate it to arouse specific regions of the cerebral cortex by direct connections and connections relayed through the thalamus.

THE THALAMUS

The thalamus is a major subcortical center that functions as a switching station to direct incoming information to and from various higher regions of the brain.

On their way to the cortex from the reticular formation, neural impulses go through the thalamus (see Fig. 6.5). Like the brain stem, the thalamus contains several specific nervous centers that consist of nuclei. Some of these nuclei receive incoming sensory information from lower in the brain stem and direct it to various parts of the cortex. The thalamus thus serves as a switching or relay station.

The cortical areas that receive impulses from sensory relay nuclei in the thalamus are known as **sensory projection areas.** For example, neural impulses from the eyes arrive by means of the optic nerve at the sensory relay nuclei for vision in the thalamus. They are then directed to and from appropriate sensory projection areas, in this case to the visual areas in the occipital lobes of the cerebral cortex (see Fig. 6.4).

Other nuclei in the thalamus that project to other cortical regions include those for auditory stimuli and for the motor cortex. Yet, other projections are widely distributed throughout the cortex so that the entire cortex may be diffusely activated. So extensive are these projections that a large part of the cortex can be mapped according to neural impulses received from the thalamus.

THE HYPOTHALAMUS

The hypothalamus is a structure at the base of the brain below the thalamus (see Fig. 6.5). Although relatively small, it is of considerable importance in a variety of ways. It functions in cybernetic circuits with the autonomic nervous system and the endocrine system, and it is important in circuits for feeding, drinking, mating, and so on. Involvement of the autonomic nervous system and the hypothalamus in motivated and emotional behavior will be discussed in Chapter 9 and again in this chapter when we relate it to the limbic system.

Subcortical regions that function in the two-way transmission of information between the cortex and peripheral regions of the body are the brain stem, the reticular formation, the thalamus, and the hypothalamus.

THE CORTEX

Discovery of Cortical Circuits. One major anatomical characteristic that makes the human unique and superior among all species is the highly developed, complex cerebral cortex. An understanding of its anatomical structure has been advanced considerably through the use of staining techniques. With them, by the middle of the nineteenth century, we had learned that the cortex was a multilayered structure made up of different cells and fibers. By the end of the nineteenth century, with the development of the Golgi technique of staining, the concept of cortical circuits was advanced (see pp. 74–77). When the electron microscope was developed in the middle of this century, we could identify synapses between neurons. With yet more advanced staining techniques, we have actually traced miniature (micro) neural circuits. Earlier we diagrammed some of the complex microcircuitry in the retina, which is actually an extension of the brain. Much more complex microcircuits have been specified in the cortex. Advanced techniques in anatomy, physiology, and chemistry facilitated success in studying how cortical circuits interact.

One Illustrative Cortical Circuit Model. A prominent model of cortical architecture developed by John Szentagothai consists of a complex network of cortical neurons. Indeed, his model is much more complex than we need to consider here (it is discussed in some detail in McGuigan, 1978, p. 322). Figure 6.8 provides some notion of his conception of how multilayered cortical neurons interact. Following Vernon Mountcastle, Szentagothai (1984) described cortical neural tissue as having "massive re-entrant circuitry" (see Figures 6.8 and 6.9). These classes of cortical circuits were represented at a more global level as class II in Figure 1.7). Thus, when information enters the cortex, it goes through an amazing amount of processing within these re-entrant circuits. That is, cybernetic characteristics of re-entrant circuits depicted in Figure 6.8 decode coded messages sent to and from receptors as well as add stored information to those messages. Szentagothai estimated that 80 to 90 percent of all connections of components of the cerebral cortex are strictly cortical (within the cortex). He proposes that only about 10 to 20 percent of the connections in the cortex are extrinsic in that they exit from the brain.

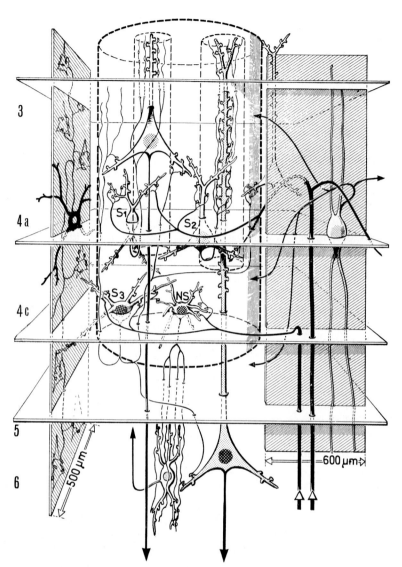

FIGURE 6.8 Hypothesized circuits within the cortex as represented by
Szentagothai.

Complex microcircuits with cybernetic characteristics function throughout the cortex in layers for processing and integrating incoming information from throughout the body.

Closed Circuits in the Cortex.   Another representation of brain circuits is based on findings in the cat visual cortex as seen in Figure 6.9. It is also similar to that found in the monkey. Layers of the cortex are different in appearance. Any cortical layer can receive input from the thalamus as well as from other cortical layers, but the strongest input from the thalamus is to layer 4. Cells in layer 4 project to the superficial layers. From layers 2 and 3 there is a substantial projection to layer 5 and from 5 to 6. The layer 6 cells then form a closed loop by projecting back to layer 4.

Important research continues in understanding the microcircuitry of the cortex. Just how these complex circuits interact to process important information and to interact with other systems of the body continues to remain a major research puzzle.

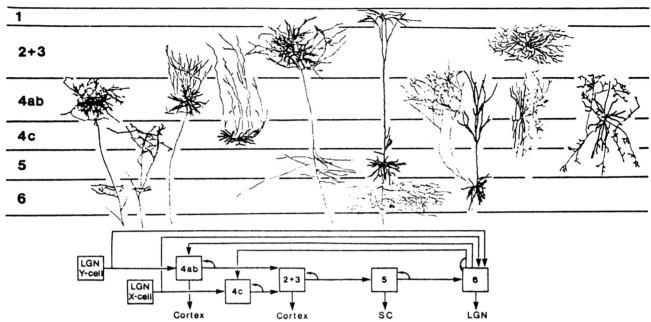

FIGURE 6.9   Intracortical connections of a portion of the cat's cortex representing several different kinds of neurons. The microcircuitry is indicated in the block diagram at the bottom. The main point of this figure is to indicate how complex these neural circuits are in the cortex. (Reproduced, with permission, from the *Annual Review of Neuroscience*, Volume 6, ©1983 by Annual Reviews Inc.)

However, with small steps we can expect a continued gradual accumulation of knowledge. Eventually, we should acquire a more precise understanding of the cybernetic characteristics of these circuits as they reverberate throughout the brain and in integration with other bodily systems.

Leaving this microscopic view of the cortex, we return to considering a more gross view of cortical anatomy. The frontal lobes, the parietal lobes, and the temporal lobes are areas of the human cerebral cortex that are relatively larger than those of other animals. These lobes are assumed to be especially important for unique human abilities.

The Frontal Lobes

Because human frontal lobes are so large relative to other primates, they have traditionally been implicated in special human abilities. Over the years it has been hypothesized that they are the seat of higher mental processes, of intelligence, and of the "will." They have even been considered to be responsible for the entire period of human evolutionary existence. Although some data provide support for such claims, those data have typically been only clinical in nature and therefore must be cautiously evaluated (Chapter 8). However, one principal role of the frontal lobes persists in various findings, and that is that they permit us to monitor, and thereby to anticipate, our own movements. This monitoring ability allows us to assimilate feedback from peripheral responses after we execute particular motor acts. With

The ability to anticipate future actions has long been thought to be a major function of the frontal lobes, especially of the prefrontal cortex.

Broca's area, located in the left frontal lobe in most people, is critical in circuits for speech production.

such feedback information, we can anticipate and thus predict consequences of our actions. Our capacity to think about the future and to develop plans sharply distinguishes us from the other species. This ability for foresight is related to the presence of **Broca's area,** typically located in the *left* frontal lobe.[1] Broca's area (the speech area in Fig. 6.4) is necessary for speech production and verbalizing about the future; certainly it is important for developing plans. Try as you can, you can never succeed in getting the family dog to think about tomorrow or reflect on yesterday. Its frontal lobes and lack of Broca's area are simply not sufficient for the task, not to mention anatomical shortcomings in the speech mechanism.

The Prefrontal Cortex.   Previous to recent research, it was thought that primates alone were endowed with a prefrontal cortex. Now we know that projections from the thalamus (specifically the thalamic mediodorsal nucleus) indicate that all mammals have a prefrontal cortex. Further evidence for this view is that humans and other mammals have in common a strong dopaminergic innervation in the prefrontal cortex, relative to other areas of the cortex. (Dopaminergic innervation means that there are tracts that release the neurotransmitter dopamine.)

The intellectual superiority of humans has been thought to be due to their relatively large prefrontal cortex—it covers as much as 30 percent of the total cortical surface. However, a prefrontal cortex is not even unique in mammals, again showing some continuity along the phylogenetic scale. Further research has now shown that nonmammalian species have an equivalent of a prefrontal cortex. In fact, the Australian spiny anteater (echidna) has an estimated cortex area that receives thalamic afferents from the mediodorsal nucleus that is about 50 percent of its entire cortex. Birds also have been found to have the equivalent of a prefrontal cortex (see for instance Divac & Mogensen, 1985).

Frontal Lobe Lesions

Clinical research on cerebral insults has confirmed that the frontal lobes, which are most highly developed in humans, contribute sizably to unique human abilities.

Frontal lobe damage can lead to **stimulus-bound behavior;** for example, human patients are unable to accurately predict the path of objects visually monitored. Instead, they are "bound" to perceive the moving object itself instead of being able to extrapolate its future position. They are unable to employ anticipatory feedback such as that used by duck hunters and baseball fielders (see p. 10).

After a review of studies concerning damage to the prefrontal areas (the frontal lobes anterior to the motor area of the cortex), Stuss and Benson (1984) reached some tentative conclusions about their functions. Patients

1. Are unable to separate action from knowledge. Such patients understand what action is expected of them but cannot carry out the behavior that corresponds to that knowledge. For instance, they may know how to perform a simple sorting task but cannot carry it out.
2. Have impaired ability to carry out sequential behaviors such as putting items together in an organized sequence.
3. Have impaired ability to establish or change a psychological set. Without the ability to plan or modify behavior, the patient's behavior appears random or highly perseverative (rigidly persistent) and thus nonadaptive.
4. Have impaired ability to correct behavioral errors so that the errors continue to be made.

[1] A small minority of people have their Broca's area in the right frontal lobe. People who have lesions in Broca's area often have speech aphasia, which is the inability to properly express one's self in oral language, sometimes even being totally incapable of speech. However, typically such aphasics can understand spoken language (see Chapter 11).

5. Often appear unconcerned, unaware, and apathethic, such that they ignore or actively deny many of their difficulties.

After reviewing these conclusions, the traditional interpretations about the functions of the frontal lobes do not greatly miss the mark. For instance, it has long been thought that they help to facilitate attention. When the frontal association areas of monkeys are extirpated, the monkeys do not maintain their attention while trying to perform a task. Humans who have had their frontal association areas damaged have similarly displayed difficulty in maintaining attention. Such people also appear to not worry and have lost much of their concern for future events, so that the frontal lobes do appear important for judgment, planning, and taking responsibility.

Cerebral Circuits Involving the Frontal Lobes. Anatomically, the importance of the frontal lobes derives from the fact that they contain a large amount of frontal *association* areas. These association areas are especially well developed in humans and have rich connections, both afferent and efferent, with almost all other parts of the central nervous system. Information comes in from the external environments to the **cortical projection areas** (vision, olfaction, etc.), which have direct connections with the frontal lobes. Sensory information is also sent directly to the frontal lobes by way of the thalamus. The frontal lobes have well-developed connections with the limbic system (as we will later develop) and with subcortical areas that function in monitoring the internal environment.

Frontal Lobe – Muscle Circuits. Neurons in the **motor area** (directly anterior to the central fissure in Fig. 6.4) extend downward to neurons in the brain stem and the spinal cord. Those neurons eventually make junction with muscles. Thus, if a particular place in a person's motor area (as represented by the motor *homunculus*, meaning "little man," in Fig. 6.10) is electrically stimulated, there results a contraction of muscles at that specific location in the body (e.g., if the region for the hand is stimulated, the hand moves). Stimulation applied in the top extreme part of the motor area would cause movement of the toes, whereas stimulation in the bottom part of the motor area would activate the speech musculature. Since neurons from the left hemisphere cross over (decussate) to the right side of the body as they descend the brain and spinal cord, stimulation of the motor area in the left cerebral hemisphere produces movement in the right side of the body. If a person has a lesion in the motor area of the left cerebral hemisphere, a paralysis develops in the right side of the body.

Although the representation of specific regions of the head and body in the motor homunculus remains accurate, more recent research indicates that the cortical organization in the motor area is not as rigid as originally thought. That is, although there are regions devoted specifically to the face, arm, and leg movements arranged topographically as in Figure 6.10, we now know that there is overlapping representations within those regions. Neuronal discharges to forelimb muscles, for example, go to several different muscles located there. Thus the organization of the motor area is labile and provides flexibility in associations between sensory input to neurons there and their association with muscles.

The Parietal Lobes

The Sensory Homunculus. One sensory relay nucleus in the thalamus receives nerve impulses from all over the body and directs them to the sensory (somatosensory) areas of the cerebral cortex. The somatosensory area is immediately posterior to

Complex neural circuits function between the frontal lobes, other regions of the brain, and peripheral organs to carry out important visual, olfactory, muscular, and other activities.

The motor and sensory areas of the cortex have systematic topographic representations as indicated by the sensory and motor homunculi.

SENSORY   MOTOR

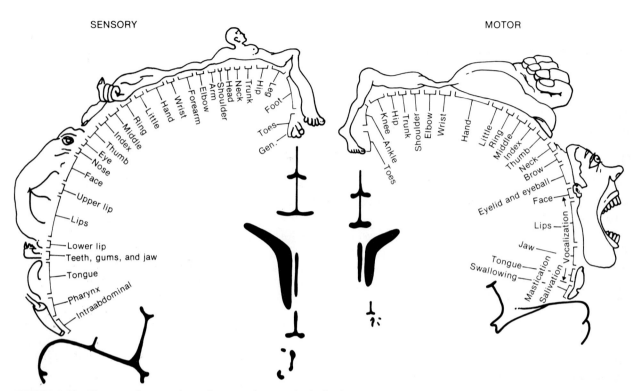

FIGURE 6.10   The motor homunculus and sensory homunculus indicating some sensory and motor functions in the cortex.

The prime functions of the parietal lobes are for sensory processing.

(behind) the central fissure, lying within the parietal lobe (see Fig. 6.4). When a slight electrical stimulus is applied to the sensory area (Fig. 6.10), the patient reports various kinds of body "feelings," depending on the specific region stimulated. Analogous to the motor homunculus, stimulation would evoke statements such as "My leg feels warm," or "I have a funny tingly sensation in my arm," or "I feel like my hand is moving" (even though it really is not). Descending neural impulses typically decussate to the opposite side of the body, at some level. If the sensory area in a person's right cerebral hemisphere is stimulated, nerve impulses descend the spinal cord and decussate to produce feelings in the left side of the body. Ascending nerve impulses also typically decussate in the spinal cord to the opposite side. Thus, if a person is stuck with a pin in the left arm, neural impulses would arrive in the sensory area of the right cerebral hemisphere. The resulting descending neural impulses back to the muscles in the left arm constitute a cybernetic circuit, activation of which would result in the conscious sensation of the pinprick.

Sensory Integration.   Afferent inputs from many sensory systems are integrated in the parietal lobe. These include the visual and vestibular systems as well as sensations from the skin and deeper regions of the body. The parietal lobe is thus presumed to be important for interpreting the meaning of stimuli wherein association is made among different modalities. The meaning of the word *apple,* for instance, results from the intermodal association of its visual, taste, kinesthetic, and other cues.

The Temporal Lobes

The temporal lobes contain projection areas. Neural input is by way of the thalamus, from the ears (for hearing) and from the vestibular organs (for balance and equilibrium). The left temporal lobe contains **Wernicke's area,** which is important for understanding language. The inability to comprehend language may be due to a lesion in Wernicke's area. We will enlarge on Wernicke's aphasia and its relationship to Broca's aphasia in Chapter 11.

Wernicke's area, typically located in the left temporal lobe, is important for the comprehension of language.

The Occipital Lobes

Located at the posterior end of the brain (see Fig. 6.4), the occipital lobes contain projection areas for vision, with neural input from the retinas of the eyes through the thalamus to the occipital cortex. Specific regions of the retina project to specific regions in the visual cortex. Visual information is then processed through extensive and complex cortical circuits. It has been estimated that there are over 1 billion neurons in the visual cortex that function in intricate interrelations for visual perception. These cells are anatomically in various layers as illustrated in Figures 6.8 and 6.9.

When light falls on the retina, neural impulses are transmitted along the optical tract to project, by way of the thalamus, onto the visual cortex in the occipital lobes.

Visual Feature Detector Neurons. David Hubel and Torsten Wiesel identified three types of cells in the visual cortex, each having different information processing functions. Hubel and Wiesel's model holds that various geometric figures are perceived according to how they affect those three types of cells. The three types of neurons are simple, complex, and hypercomplex. The simple cortical cell is particularly sensitive to stimuli that are elongated and angular, such as a straight line at a 45° angle. The complex cortical cell reacts to any kind of straight line stimulus, such as the edge of the table. The stimulus may move and still affect the complex cortical cell, providing that the movement is continuous. Finally, the hypercomplex cortical cell functions similarly to the complex cortical cell except that for the complex cortical cell to function, the stimulus must be of a prescribed length. If the length of the stimulus (e.g., a straight line) varies, the complex cortical cell would not be affected but the hypercomplex cell *would* respond to the varying length. We only need to add that there must be feedback from these events in the visual cortex. Such feedback would function with other parts of the brain; it would also interact with the skeletal muscles, particularly those that control movement of the eyes for the complete perceptual experience.

Hubel and Wiesel's model for visual perception holds that specific features in stimuli activate three types of cells in the visual cortex: simple, complex, and hypercomplex cells that have specific feature detectors that function in the perception of various stimuli.

THE CEREBELLUM

Brain–Muscle Circuits for Coordination of Behavior. A number of regions of the brain contribute to the integrated contraction of our muscles that constitutes complex motor behavior. These regions are connected together, either directly or indirectly, by complex networks of neurons. In studying the kinesthetic sense, we saw that nerve impulses go in circuits from muscles to the brain stem, and from the brain stem back to the muscles. We have also seen how the muscles on the right and left sides of the body are activated by stimulation of the left and right motor areas of the cerebral cortex, respectively. In addition to the motor area of the cortex and the brain stem, the cerebellum is another part of the brain that is intimately concerned with motor functioning (see Figs. 6.4 and 6.5).

The cerebellum ("little brain") functions in circuits with muscles and other regions for highly skilled and integrated behavior.

DAVID HUNTER HUBEL (1926–)
TORSTEN NILS WIESEL (1924–)

Hubel

Wiesel

David Hubel and Torsten Wiesel received the Nobel Prize in 1981 for discovering how sight stimulation in infancy is tied to future vision and how the brain interprets signals from the eye. Hubel was born in Windsor, Canada, and eventually became a professor at Harvard University. Wiesel was born in Uppsala, Sweden, and collaborated with Hubel at Harvard. With microelectrodes they recorded the firing of single cells in the visual cortex and lateral geniculate body in response to different visual patterns, movements, color and so on. They demonstrated how synaptic organization can even be permanently deformed by lack of appropriate visual experience early in life. For example, when one eye was sutured during the first few weeks of life of the cat and monkey, the visual cortex permanently changed. Consequently, "feature detectors" in the visual system are dependent upon visual experience during an early critical period of development in infancy.

In appearance, the cerebellum is a spongelike structure that is inferior (below) and posterior to the cerebrum. It has widespread neural connections with the brain stem and the motor areas of the cortex. Thus, nerve impulses from the kinesthetic receptors are received by the brain stem, the motor area of the cortex, and the cerebellum. The cerebellum functions to integrate these afferent neural impulses so that a series of smooth, coordinated responses results. A lesion in the cerebellum could result in jerky responses, rather than in a series of smooth, integrated movements. Highly skilled and integrated responses depend, in large part, on the cerebellum. The highly refined movements of a bird in flight are possible because a bird has a relatively large and well-developed cerebellum.

THE LIMBIC SYSTEM — A HYPOTHESIS

Its Anatomy. The concept of a **limbic system** was first formulated by J. W. Papez in 1937 when he related a diverse group of brain structures to the emotions. The term *limbic system* was applied to a reformulated concept in 1949 by Paul MacLean. The hypothesized limbic system structures comprise the older cortices that form the medial-most (inner) edge of the cerebral hemispheres as well as subcortical areas near the deep gray matter masses of the basal ganglia, the amygdala, thalamus, and so on. One representation of the limbic system is shown in Figure 6.11. However, there continue to be anatomical arguments over the validity and the heuristic value of relating these components to a concept of emotions and over just what structures do comprise a limbic system.

The limbic system hypothesis holds that certain subcortical structures function importantly for the generation of emotions.

Central and Peripheral Circuits Involving the Limbic System. The reasoning that these structures comprise a common limbic system is based on the connections among them as well as with the hypothalamus. The hypothalamus has long been implicated in various characteristics of emotions, and validly so. The limbic system thus internally interacts with the hypothalamus which functions with the endocrine and the autonomic nervous systems, both especially involved in emotional behavior. There are, for instance, specific nuclei in the hypothalamus that project to sympathetic and parasympathetic centers in both the brain stem and spinal cord. Research has also found that there are extensive two-way connections that unite portions of the limbic system which function for generating emotional behavior. For this, many parts of the limbic systems connect with key parts of the motor system; for example, the cortices of the limbic system project to the motor area of the cortex and to subcortical motor structures such as the caudate nucleus and pons. Consequently, the limbic system and hypothalamus interact with major effector activities of the brain and body. In addition, there are limbic projections throughout the cerebral cortex, so that all parts of the brain are influenced by the limbic system.

The hypothalamus and the limbic system interact with activities of the endocrine system, the autonomic nervous system, motor areas of the cerebral cortex, and skeletal muscles, all of which are involved in circuits for generating and maintaining emotional behavior.

In Review. When the limbic system is activated, the entire brain and body are affected. Neuromuscular and hormonal circuits, functioning according to principles of cybernetics, activate distant peripheral components which in turn influence the limbic (and other central) systems through feedback. We thus must study all these

Neuromuscular and hormonal circuits with cybernetic characteristics include components that influence the limbic system, motor cortex, skeletal muscles, and so on.

FIGURE 6.11 One representation of components that form the hypothesized limbic system.

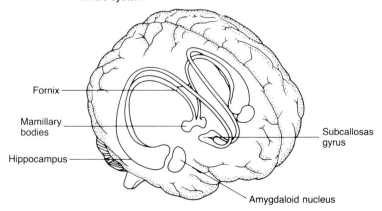

components that influence each other in rapidly reverberating circuits for a proper understanding of how the body generates emotional behavior (Chapter 9).

THE BASAL GANGLIA

The basal ganglia function in circuits with the cortex, the cerebellum, and other cerebral regions for coordinating motor behavior.

The **basal ganglia** are inferior and lateral to the thalamus and include groups of nuclei known as putamen, globus pallidus, and caudate nucleus (see Fig. 7.6). These basal ganglia nuclei are critical components of circuits for motor behavior. The basal ganglia receive inputs from the cortex, the cerebellum, and numerous other cerebral regions, including the reticular formation. Apparently, coordination of body movements depends to a large extent upon integration of impulses within these cerebral regions. For example, in Parkinson's disease, there is degeneration of dopaminergic cells that send axons to the caudate nucleus.

CONCLUSION

In this section, we have discussed historical models of the brain, concluding with a contemporary computer model. Then we presented the gross anatomy of the brain and spinal cord, emphasizing major anatomic and physiologic characteristics of the more important brain structures. The highly developed cortex of *Homo sapiens* made enormous contributions to the relatively advanced behaviors of our species. We turn now to the integration of the central nervous system with the rest of the body, which involves the peripheral nervous systems.

THE PERIPHERAL NERVOUS SYSTEMS

The central nervous system is composed of the brain and the spinal cord while the neural material that lies outside of the CNS composes the peripheral nervous systems.

Afferent and efferent neural impulses are conducted to and from the central nervous system by means of spinal and cranial nerves that compose the peripheral nervous system.

The peripheral nervous systems conduct neural impulses into and out of the central nervous system by transmitting messages along the spinal and cranial nerves that compose it.

The Spinal and Cranial Nerves

Thirty-one pairs of spinal nerves and 12 pairs of cranial nerves of the peripheral nervous system connect with the spinal cord and brain respectively.

Neural impulses that enter the spinal cord typically decussate to the opposite hemisphere just as descending neural impulses typically decussate to the opposite side of the body. Those impulses that do not decussate ascend to the brain and descend on the ipsilateral (same) side.

There are 31 pairs of spinal nerves that conduct afferent and efferent impulses into and out of the spinal cord (Fig. 6.12). Once neural impulses arrive in the spinal cord, they are also transmitted up to the brain and, of course, impulses also leave the brain and move back down the spinal cord. Nerve impulses typically ascend to the brain along the dorsal part of the spinal cord and descend from the brain along the ventral part of the spinal cord. As they ascend to the brain, the large majority of neural impulses from the body cross over (decussate) to the opposite side of the brain. Therefore, neural impulses from the right side of the body mainly go to the left cerebral hemisphere while the large majority of neural impulses from the left side of the body decussate to the right cerebral hemisphere. A relatively small proportion of neural impulses from the left side of the body stay on the *ipsilateral* (same) side and go to the left hemisphere. Similarly, some neural impulses from the right side of the body stay on the ipsilateral side and go to the right hemisphere.

In Figure 6.13 we see a representation of the 12 cranial nerves that go directly to and from the brain without going through the spinal cord. These nerves are ex-

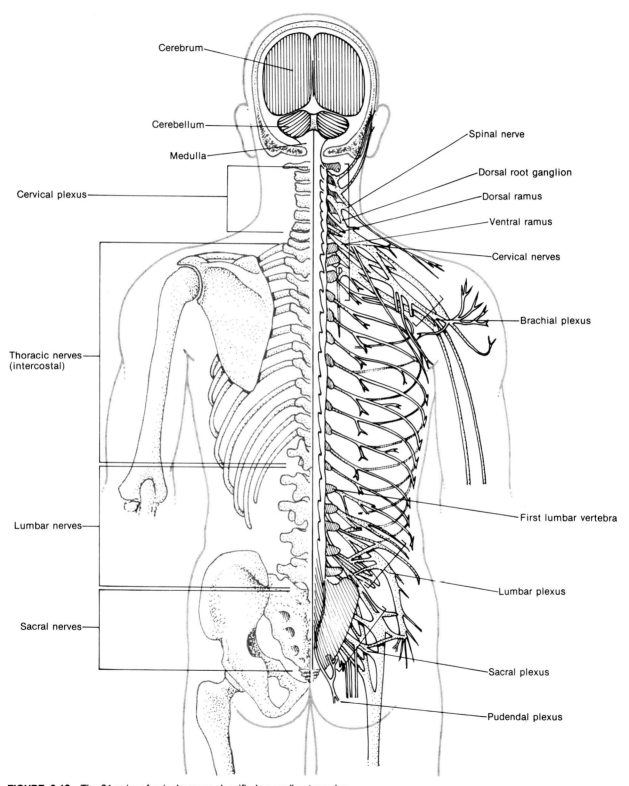

FIGURE 6.12 The 31 pairs of spinal nerves classified according to region.

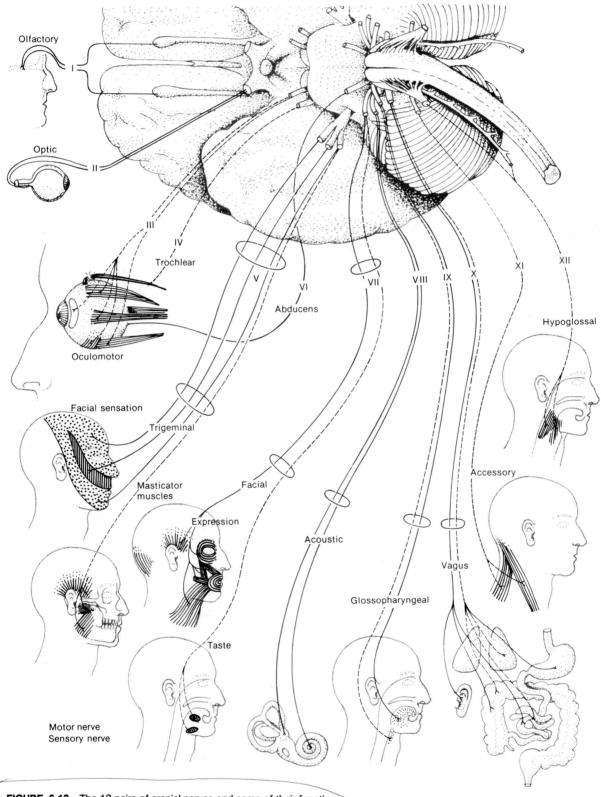

FIGURE 6.13 The 12 pairs of cranial nerves and some of their functions.

tremely important for transmitting sensory information to the brain and efferent information from the brain to the regions depicted.

The Somatic Nervous System

Circuits Reverberate Among Receptors, Muscles, and the Brain. The somatic nervous system receives neural impulses from receptors and transmits them to and from the CNS. In so doing, the skeletal muscles are activated for walking, talking, writing, and so on. The somatic nervous system, being both afferent and efferent in nature, feeds back information (1) from the brain to the receptors and (2) from the muscles back to the brain. Always keep in mind, though, that these reverberating circuits do not stop their functioning when feedback from the muscles arrives at the brain or when feedback from the brain arrives at the muscles. Rather, the neuromuscular circuits continually reverberate to activate muscle, then brain, then muscle, then brain, in an ongoing circular fashion.

The Somatic Nervous System Functions for Voluntary Behavior. Whereas the autonomic nervous system functions automatically, the somatic nervous system functions in a more "voluntary" fashion. For example, you do not directly decide that you are going to secrete adrenalin (it is automatic), but you could decide that you will raise your right hand. A **voluntary act,** such as raising your right hand, results from the neural transmission along cybernetic circuits between the central nervous system and muscles in the right arm. A voluntary act is one that you can describe before it is performed—you can say to yourself (or to others) that you have just "decided" to raise your right hand. Then you do it. You contract those muscles and your right arm is raised.

The Autonomic Nervous System (ANS)

As the cranial and spinal nerves of the peripheral nervous system extend farther away from the central nervous system, they branch and divide into numerous smaller nerves. These smaller nerves receive neural impulses that are generated by receptors distributed throughout the body and deliver efferent neural impulses to effectors. Those components of the cranial and spinal nerves that make junction with the skeletal muscle system comprise the somatic nervous system. The remainder, those that go to and from cardiac and smooth muscles and to and from glands comprise the autonomic nervous system (*autonomic* means "self-governing").

We noted in Figure 6.12 the various regions of the brain and spinal cord. At the top is the *cranial* region (the skull and head), next is the *thoracic* (chest), then the *lumbar* (middle-lower back), and finally the *sacral* region and the coccyx. The coccyx, incidentally, is a vestigial organ in humans; it is what remains of the tail so prominent in subhuman primates such as monkeys. The cranial and spinal nerves differentially innervate the two divisions of the ANS.

The Sympathetic Nervous System and Emergency Reactions. As we can note in Figure 6.14, thoracic spinal nerves (numbers T1–T12) and lumbar spinal nerves (L1, L2, and L3) compose the sympathetic (or thoracolumbar) division of the autonomic nervous system. The general function of the sympathetic nervous system is to

Twelve pairs of crainal nerves attach to the ventral surface of the brain and innervate the head and neck regions.

The peripheral nervous system has two divisions: the autonomic nervous system and the somatic nervous system.

The somatic nervous system consists of nerves that make junction with skeletal muscles while nerves of the autonomic nervous system go to and from smooth and cardiac muscles and glands.

A voluntary response is one on which you can report and control prior to its performance. An involuntary response is one that you cannot talk about before it is made and therefore you cannot control its appearance.

The ANS has two divisions, the sympathetic and the parasympathetic nervous systems.

The sympathetic nervous system functions to mobilize and expend energy in order to effectively react to a danger.

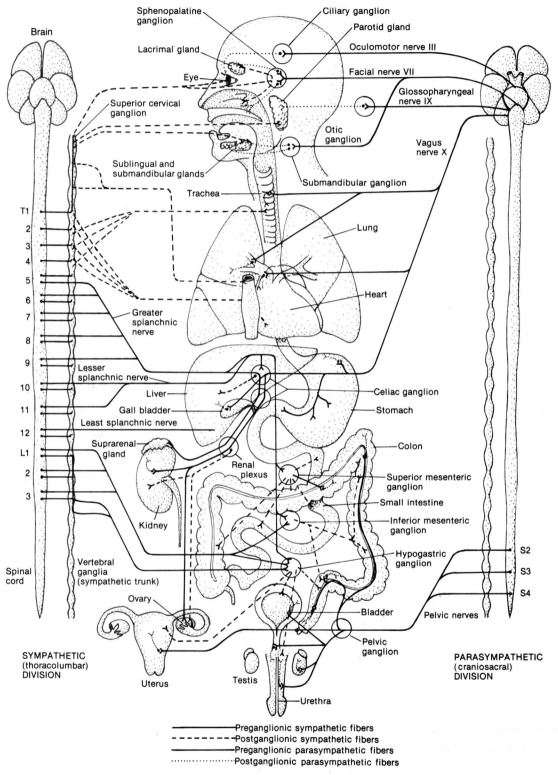

Brain

Sphenopalatine ganglion
Ciliary ganglion
Parotid gland
Lacrimal gland
Oculomotor nerve III
Eye
Facial nerve VII
Glossopharyngeal nerve IX
Superior cervical ganglion
Otic ganglion
Vagus nerve X
Sublingual and submandibular glands
Submandibular ganglion
Trachea
Lung
T1
2
3
4
5
6
Heart
7
Greater splanchnic nerve
8
9
Lesser splanchnic nerve
Celiac ganglion
10
Liver
11
Gall bladder
Stomach
Least splanchnic nerve
12
Colon
L1
Suprarenal gland
2
Superior mesenteric ganglion
Renal plexus
3
Small intestine
Inferior mesenteric ganglion
Kidney
Hypogastric ganglion
S2
Vertebral ganglia (sympathetic trunk)
S3
Spinal cord
S4
Ovary
Bladder
Pelvic nerves
SYMPATHETIC (thoracolumbar) DIVISION
Pelvic ganglion
PARASYMPATHETIC (craniosacral) DIVISION
Uterus
Testis
Urethra

———— Preganglionic sympathetic fibers
– – – – Postganglionic sympathetic fibers
━━━━ Preganglionic parasympathetic fibers
·········· Postganglionic parasympathetic fibers

FIGURE 6.14   The autonomic nervous system, distinguishing its sympathetic and parasympathetic divisions with some of their functions.

mobilize and expend energy stored in reserves to meet emergencies. Thus, if a primitive man faced the proverbial tiger in the jungle, his immediate action would be the **startle response,** whereupon he would rise upon the balls of his feet ready to spring into action for fight or flight. No doubt in the event of meeting a tiger, flight would be the mode of action that would have the greater survival value. We can speculate that our predecessors who chose to fight in such a case failed to survive so that their genes were not passed on.

To meet an emergency, blood is shunted to the skeletal muscles which are required to react rapidly. The sympathetic system functions in circuits that dilate the pupils, decrease the flow of saliva, increase sweat, dilate cerebral and skeletal muscle blood vessels, and release adrenalin. The sympathetic nervous system also inhibits activities of the stomach and colon and urinary/fecal excretion. Such digestive and excretory organs are not needed in an emergency, for at that time it is not helpful to continue digesting and eliminating.

Inhibition of the Salivary Glands. Saliva is not needed in an emergency because it is used principally to facilitate ingestion of food. A dry mouth occurs when one is emotional or nervous, a fact that has served as the basis for detecting liars. In ancient lands such as China and Turkey, a person accused of a crime would be interrogated with rice or cotton in his or her mouth. If the rice or cotton were found to be dry after the interrogation, a guilty verdict was reached. For obvious reasons such a lie-detecting method is not very valid, which can be said of the typical lie detector test even today—if you are to be interrogated for a crime, you may well be nervous regardless of your guilt or innocence (see Chapter 13).

Adrenalin Is Secreted. Humans have two adrenal glands (the suprarenal gland in Fig. 6.14) located on each side of the body at about the waistline and above the kidneys (*renal* means "kidney"). When a person is in an emotional state, the sympathetic nervous system delivers neural impulses to the internal part of the adrenal glands. They are thereby stimulated to secrete *adrenalin* into the circulatory system, where it is distributed throughout the body to help prepare a person to meet an emergency. For example, when the liver receives adrenalin by means of the blood-stream, it releases more blood sugar into the bloodstream to provide the muscles with increased energy for fight or flight.

Consider someone who sees an oncoming truck. The eyes generate afferent neural impulses that are conducted through the central nervous system. The skeletal musculature tenses in the startle reaction whereupon the person presumably does not attack but runs. Neural impulses are then received by the autonomic nervous system which conducts them to various internal organs of the body. The increased activation of these internal organs of the body helps the person to meet the emergency situation. Furthermore, these functions of the autonomic nervous system are "automatic." For example, a woman does not "decide" that her heart will beat, that she will sweat, or that she will stop digesting her food.

The Parasympathetic Nervous System. The parasympathetic nervous system is also called the craniosacral system because it is composed of the cranial and the sacral nerves. These are the oculomotor, facial, glossopharyngeal, and other cranial nerves shown in Figure 6.13 and the sacral nerves S2, S3, and S4 shown in Figure 6.14. The parasympathetic system helps to store energy and functions to maintain the integrity of the body for digestion, sleep, and relaxation. The parasympathetic system contracts the pupillary openings, decreases heart rate, increases peristalsis

The parasympathetic nervous system functions for digestion, metabolism of foods, excretion, etc. in circuits with relevant organs.

and gastric juice flow, and facilitates urinary and defecation responses, all in circuits with the relevant organs.

Recall that there is a center in the medulla that functions in a circuit for regulating heart rate. Neural impulses from the heart rate center in the medulla are conducted to and from the heart by means of the autonomic nervous system. The heart beats continually in an automatic fashion as impulses flow between the heart and the medulla.

ANS–CNS: Two-Way Circuits. We used to think that the autonomic nervous system was entirely motor in function in that it only received efferent neural impulses from the central nervous system. However, we now know that it also directs afferent neural impulses to the central nervous system. This afferent characteristic of the autonomic system is very important for cybernetic functions. More particularly, afferent neurons from the ANS help us to detect visceral pain, amount of stretch in the walls of organs such as the bladder and blood vessels, the acidity of the contents of the digestive tract, and the amount of dissolved oxygen in the blood. These afferents transmit such information to the CNS through the spinal cord and through the vagus nerve (a cranial nerve that is distributed throughout the body). Although we usually are not consciously aware of such afferently carried information, it probably affects us in vague ways, including generalized feelings such as nervousness ("free-floating anxiety"), nausea, and hunger. Neither can we precisely localize visceral pains. Rather, they often are referred to *as if* they were located in areas of the skin, which probably sends somatic afferents to the same segment of the spinal cord as the affected visceral organ. Thus, rather than our detecting activity in a specific visceral organ, we falsely have sensations in the area of the skin that also has neural connections with the organ.

The two anatomically and functionally distinct divisions of the ANS, the sympathetic and the parasympathetic nervous systems, have structures within the hypothalamus that serve important functions in ANS–CNS circuits. Afferent fibers from various internal organs and those that carry information about the external environment converge at the hypothalamus. Signals are then sent along autonomic efferent fibers to various internal organs of the body, such as the heart, the glands, and blood vessels. The contraction of the muscles in the stomach when we digest food is an example of an internal organ that receives such efferent neural impulses and returns information to the CNS.

Independent Organ Functioning. In spite of carrying out many functions of the body, much of the ANS is not really essential for life. Large portions of the ANS have been removed from both animals and humans with relatively little functional impairment because glands and smooth muscles that are innervated by the ANS usually also have their own intrinsic innervation. Consequently, they can function without ANS connections. For instance, the intestines can function even though they have been isolated from the nervous systems.

Both divisions of the ANS are slow and diffuse relative to the somatic nervous system which is fast and highly specific to certain muscles. Responses last several seconds when innervated by the autonomic nervous system. The smooth muscle fibers of the viscera are much smaller than striated muscle fibers and are so compact that when one region of visceral smooth muscle is stimulated, the action potential generated stimulates the next sections of smooth muscle fibers. In this way, activity of smooth muscle spreads along the intestines, pushing the internal contents along,

Much information is transmitted between the CNS and the ANS. ANS information comes from many areas in the body, and it is difficult to localize specific sources. Since we often cannot verbalize about that information, we have vague general feelings that we cannot understand.

Some internal organs have neural connections with specific areas of the skin; consequently, we sometimes falsely experience sensations in skin locations when they actually come from a specific visceral organ.

Action potentials are distributed slowly over entire organs that are composed of smooth musculature.

whereupon additional action potentials are generated and may be recorded as electrogastrograms.

In Conclusion.   The autonomic nervous system innervates the viscera, which includes the digestive, reproductive, urogenital, and cardiovascular (heart and blood vessels) systems. It serves to regulate such functions as body temperature and pupillary dilation and to contribute to emotional behavior. When we are emotional, the various internal organs of the body become "hyperactive" due to increased activity of the autonomic nervous system (Chapter 9).

BRAIN-MUSCLE RELATIONS

We have sketched out the major characteristics of the nervous systems and have developed a good perspective for how intricately they interact and transmit and process information throughout all regions of the body. We now illustrate with greater specificity some of the interactions between the brain and the striated musculature. Numerous important cybernetic neuromuscular circuits constantly reverberate to carry out the myriad of cognitive and noncognitive functions of the human body. To illustrate how complex and intricate these brain–peripheral systems really are, we will discuss central relationships with the cerebellum (which we saw is specialized for motor functions) and central relationships with eye movements. In all of these interactions, there are special *monitoring* functions carried out by the brain.

Central Systems and Motor Activity

We know that intricate reactions of the brain are subtly influenced by afferent bombardment set off by muscles, as well as by other sources throughout the body. In return, there are many complex ways in which the brain influences and monitors important activities of the muscles. In addition to the cerebellar, limbic system, and other motor interactions, the following important circuits illustrate this general principle.

CEREBRO-CEREBELLAR CIRCUITS

How Do We Plan and Execute Movements?.   Eccles (1967) advanced a hypothesis for planning responses and for knowing whether or not responses have been correctly executed. It is a model of dynamic circuit control whereby the cerebellum has a large store of information. A motor discharge (A in Fig. 6.15) from the cerebrum (set off by unspecified antecedents, indicated by the question mark) includes information that can institute a plan for movement. The discharge can be monitored by nuclei in the cerebellum that contain some of that information (B). The correctness of the motor discharge is computed by the cerebellum and any modification required is returned to the cerebrum for the further action. The accuracy of the movement plan from the cerebrum is thus monitored prior to making the movement; that is, the efferent messages are checked to see if the movement is going to be

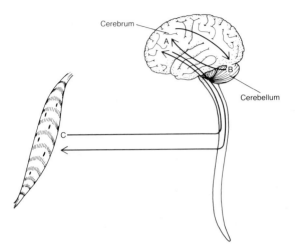

Cerebrum

A

B

Cerebellum

C

FIGURE 6.15
A model for planning and executing accurate previously learned movements. A plan initiated by a motor discharge (A, which may be set off by muscular movements) is rapidly checked by a circuit with the cerebellum (B). The movement may be later modified by feedback from the muscles (C) if correction is necessary for future responding.

Eccle's model includes a circuit that can rapidly check the accuracy of a planned motor act before it is executed. Feedback from the response can then confirm its accuracy or modify the plan or the next response.

accurate. This checking occurs prior to the arrival of peripheral feedback from actual muscular movement as it later occurs. This internal loop time from the cerebrum to and from the cerebellum has been estimated by Eccles (1973) to be 20 milliseconds. Then when the act is actually made, sensory feedback from the muscles in the periphery relays the consequences of the act (C in Fig. 6.15). That feedback informs higher centers as to whether the planned movement was in fact executed properly. If it was incorrect, the central plan can be modified for the next trial.

Neural and Muscle Feedback Can Function Together.   Note that Eccles's model emphasizes the importance of both peripheral feedback from muscular responses and central neural feedback from the cerebellum to the cerebrum. Both feedback circuits provide important information for carrying out precise responses. Originally, we must make responses in order to learn them. But when they become habitized, a neural representation (engram) for them may be activated to represent the response in a plan "as if" it actually occurred. Then, the response must be made (rather than merely having the engram activated) in order for the feedback from it to assure that the response *was* accurate. Eccles's model is reminiscent of Dunlap's (1927) conjecture that learned responses may find a neural representation in the cerebellum (Fig. 6.16).

CENTRAL SYSTEMS AND EYE MOVEMENTS

Plans for responding are developed in the brain in coordination with other systems of the body. Some are executed with feedforward control (e.g., pursuit eye movements) while others use feedback.

The Eyes Make Saccadic and Pursuit Movements.   Two kinds of eye movements are saccadic responses and pursuit movements. **Saccadic eye movements,** very rapid movements of the eyes, are directly controlled by the eye muscles. But **pursuit eye movements** (slower, more continuous movements made when tracking a target) are themselves controlled by a unique kind of central feedforward pathway, a feedforward brain system that monitors outgoing motor commands to the eye muscles. The system obtains knowledge from those commands of what the specific eye positions are going to be. When saccadic responses are preprogrammed, those monitored efferent commands apparently contain the information in that feedforward

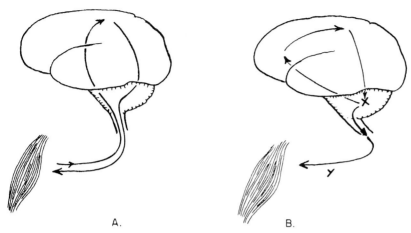

FIGURE 6.16   Possible centralization of a response. Although in the early history of the response, overt and then covert responding were necessary components of the circuit (A) eventually cerebellar representation (X) of the response would allow more rapid activation of the circuit (B). There still could also be consequent motor activity (Y). (Concept from Dunlap, 1927)

program. That is, there is a set of central cybernetic circuits that plan the extent and direction of saccadic eye responses. Furthermore, those circuits tap (monitor) the efferent neural impulses that descend to the eye muscles; they thus determine very rapidly whether or not the eye movements are going to where they are supposed to be. Apparently, then, proprioceptive feedback from the muscles that move the eyes does not inform us as to whether or not the desired saccadic eye movements were actually made. This is indeed a unique kind of central feedforward circuit.

On the other hand, in pursuit eye movements, a person follows a target but does not know its final location. Consequently, the efferent signals from the central monitoring system used for saccadic eye movements provide imprecise information about eye movements when we track a moving object in the pursuit mode. For pursuit movements, peripheral information in the form of feedback from muscles is of great importance in carrying out smooth, well-coordinated tracking responses.

In General.   There is potency in the notion that we preselect certain acts among many possible ones. This occurs when unspecified antecedents produce one of a number of efferent discharges such as A in Figure 6.15. After it is determined which kind of behavior is going to occur, cerebro-cerebellar circuits can monitor the discharge to determine its accuracy. Then, peripheral feedback from muscles can help to make corrections so that in the future we emit more accurate responses. To adequately understand behavior, then, we must analyze it in terms of the organization of motor output from the brain, as well as the relationship of the sensory input from the muscles to the brain. To carry out accurate responses, we use peripheral feedback from the muscles to the brain as well as the efferent feedforward control of muscular systems.

SYNAPSES, NEURONS, AND THE BIOCHEMISTRY OF THE BRAIN

The Development of the Synapse and Neuron Concepts

History. Our understanding of brain chemistry began in 1897 when Charles Sherrington hypothesized that gaps exist between nerve cells. He named them *synapses.* It was Ramon y Cajal (p. 40) who, in 1889, developed histological methods to study the brain in detail. He disconfirmed the prevailing theory that nervous material is continuous. Instead, Cajal determined that there are gaps in it. Between the gaps was the neuron, the structural and functional unit of the nervous systems. Networks of neurons were then identified whereupon it was hypothesized that *sensations* were transmitted along them to, from, and within the brain. The metabolic (chemical and electrical) properties of neurons were discovered later.

Numerous synapses are active during any given millisecond as they integrate information through spatial and temporal summation.

Spatial and Temporal Summation at the Synapse. Sherrington hypothesized that the neuron integrates information, but we now know that the neuron is a much more extensive integrator than he ever imagined—more than 20,000 synapses impinge on some cortical neurons to integrate information. The integration occurs when two kinds of summation exert their effects at a neuron: (1) **spatial summation** occurs

SIR CHARLES SCOTT SHERRINGTON (1857–1952)

Courtesy The American Physiological Society.

Sir Charles Sherrington, born in Islington, London, conducted research on the function of neurons when he was at Cambridge University. He ended his career as a professor of physiology at Oxford University. His Nobel lecture in 1932 was entitled "Inhibition as a Coordinative Factor," in which he described the nature of spinal reflexes as based upon a balance of central inhibitory and excitatory states. He emphasized the importance of inhibition for posture and in the control of the reciprocal action of antagonistic muscles in movement and locomotion. In 1904 he delivered the Silliman Memorial Lectures at Yale University, which resulted in his classic book *The Integrative Action of the Nervous System.* Sherrington was one of the physiologists whom Lashley attacked for his dualism, which Sherrington developed in his classic book *Man on His Nature* (1940).

when neural impulses simultaneously arrive at a synapse from different spatially located neurons and (2) **temporal summation** occurs when information is integrated as neural impulses arrive at a synapse at slightly different times. Spatial and temporal summation of impulses arriving almost simultaneously at a synapse increases the probability of exceeding the threshold of excitability for graded reactions to be generated at neurons that share the synapse.

Neurotransmitters

Once synapses were specified, a major riddle was how information was transmitted from one neuron across synapses to other adjacent neurons. In 1921 Otto Loewi discovered that when neurons are stimulated, chemicals are released into the synapse. (He also established that electrical activity was associated with this chemical activity.) Later it was found that those chemicals cross the synapse to the connecting neurons. Thus they are known as **neurotransmitters.** If the axon of a neuron transmits an impulse to the synapse with sufficient intensity, it will liberate sufficient neurotransmitter substance to generate graded reactions on adjoining neurons.

Neural transmitters are chemicals that are liberated by the terminal buttons of an axon and transmit information across synapses to adjoining neurons.

In the 1950s it was generally thought that acetylcholine (ACh), the most common neurotransmitter, was the only important neurotransmitter in the brain. ACh is found widely in synapses throughout the brain and spinal cord, particularly in the hippocampus, which is important for the formation of new memories. ACh is also present in every neuromuscular junction and thus is important for muscular contraction. By the 1960s it was well recognized that norepinephrine and serotonin were also important neurotransmitters. By now more than 50 neurotransmitters have been specified, including dopamine (DA), norepinephrine (NE), serotonin (5-HT), gamma aminobutyric acid (GABA), glutamic acid, substance P, and glycine. The important neurotransmitter norepinephrine is particularly prominent in the brain stem, although axons from which it is secreted project to wide areas throughout the brain. NE thus exerts effects (either excitatory or inhibitory) on target organs in the sympathetic nervous system. The major neurotransmitters in the peripheral nervous system are acetylcholine and epinephrine.

There are various kinds of neurotransmitters that serve different functions. There are **catecholamines** which include norepinephrine and dopamine. Another subclass of neurotransmitter consists of **neuropeptides,** or simply **peptides,** which consist of two or more amino acids (see later discussion).

Discovering Neurotransmitters.   How is it determined that a substance actually is a neurotransmitter? First, it must be present in neural terminals and released when a neuron is stimulated. Second, enzymes must be present in the vicinity of the terminal ending that can synthesize and metabolize the substance. Third, we should be able to mimic the effects of the candidate neurotransmitter by using other substances. Fourth, drugs that potentiate (augment) or block synaptic reactions should simulate or antagonize the effects of other materials that are administered. It is expected that numerous additional neurotransmitters remain to be identified according to these criteria.

How Do Neurotransmitters Function at Synapses?.   We have seen that synaptic vesicles are embedded in the buttons at the terminal portion of axons and that these vesicles liberate chemical transmitters into the synapse when an action potential arrives at the axonal terminal (see Fig. 4.22). Usually each neuron produces one

When nerve impulses arrive at axon terminals, synaptic vesicles discharge neurotransmitters that diffuse across the synapse to receptors in the cell membrane of adjacent neurons or other cells.

transmitter substance. When it is released, about 1000 molecules of the neurotransmitter diffuse across the synaptic cleft to stimulate receptors in membranes on the dendrites or cell bodies of the adjoining neurons or other cells. The postsynaptic region of neurons contain many different kinds of receptors that are sensitive to various kinds of neurotransmitters.

Some neurotransmitters generate excitatory postsynaptic potentials (EPSPs) that may depolarize neighboring cells while others generte inhibitory postsynaptic potentials (IPSPs) that tend to retard depolarization. Other single neurotransmitters may generate inhibitory potentials in some cells and excitatory responses in others.

When molecules of the transmitter substance enter receptors in the receiving neuron, they change the permeability of the membranes of the receiving cells. Some neurotransmitters are excitatory and thus increase the permeability of membranes. Excitatory neurotransmitters may then produce excitatory postsynaptic potentials (EPSPs) which may be transmitted along the adjacent cells. Inhibitory neurotransmitters decrease the permeability and thus tend to retard depolarization. Inhibitory neurotransmitters thus generate inhibitory postsynaptic potentials (IPSPs). If the net effect of the excitatory molecules is sufficiently greater than the inhibitory ones at a synapse, the excitation will be transmitted to the adjacent cells.

A single neurotransmitter substance can also have opposite effects on different target organs; for example, epinephrine can relax bronchial muscles but constrict some pulmonary muscles because the effects of chemical substances on an organ depend also on the kind of receptors embedded therein. This flexibility of differential responding provides greater control of bodily functions.

After neurotransmitters act on neighboring cells, their molecules are cleared from the synapse by the process of reuptake (see Fig. 14.2). In reuptake, the neurotransmitter is reabsorbed by the axon terminals that released them. Enzymes, contained in the cytoplasm of each button, are involved in the synthesis and the degradation of transmitters. The action of neurotransmitters is terminated with the action of enzymes in the reuptake of the transmitter into the axon terminal.

Neuropeptides

A variety of neuroactive peptides function as neurotransmitters in the brain.

Neuropeptides, a subgroup of neurotransmitters, consist of strings of amino acids. Major research efforts have identified a large number of peptides that are secreted by both central and peripheral neurons. Although some peptides play a primary role in chemically transmitting information in the nervous system, they are also active in numerous other processes. Neuropeptides are unique transmitters in that they have their own specialized receptors in the nervous systems. They affect various systems and chemicals throughout the body such as when they stimulate growth of smooth muscle cells or the production of interleukin. They are especially prominent in the hypothalamus. Peptides coexist and often function together with classical neurotransmitters such as dopamine, noradrenaline, and serotonin. Some prominent peptides are enkephalins, endorphins, Angiotensin II, oxytocin, vasopressin, neurotensin, and somatostatin. There may be hundreds of peptides yet to be discovered.

The Discovery of Endorphins and Other Neuropeptides. Important research on neuropeptides during the 1970s led to the discovery of opiate receptors in the brain. Most neurotransmitters were discovered first, and later their receptors were sought and found. In contrast, opiate *receptors* were discovered before the endorphins that fit into them. The identification of opiate receptors and endogenous (originating within the body) opiate-like substances is certainly one of the landmarks in our understanding of the body, especially how these substances relate to mood. It is their complex interactions with hormones that make them so important in understanding variations in mood behavior.[2] By 1975 it was found that opiate or morphine-like chemicals occur naturally in the body (morphine is derived from opium; the euphoric powers of the wild poppy from which opium is made were understood by the Greeks as early as 380 B.C.). The peptides called **endorphins** (short for "endogenous morphines") are chemicals that are made in the brain (these are enkephalins); others are found in the intestine, stomach, adrenal glands, spinal cord, and elsewhere in the body. There are at least three different types, all of which act like drugs such as heroin or morphine. These chemicals are manufactured by the human body for its own use and are many times more powerful than heroin. They have been found in other species too. Endorphins are inhibitory neurotransmitters in that they act to slow down the transmission of information, as when they regulate (slow down) pain in cancer patients.

Endorphins has become a household term. Their secretion has been held responsible for pleasurable experiences such as "runner's high," laughing, gambling, aerobics, and eating. Of great importance, it was found that endorphins have analgesic (pain-killing) properties. As neurotransmitters, endorphins function at most synaptic relay points in the major pain pathways, as in the dorsal roots of the spinal cord, in the thalamus, and in the cortex.

It has been established that there are antagonists for endorphins such as the drugs naloxone and naltrexone. These antagonists counter the analgesic actions of endorphins. They also antagonize exogenously (made outside of the body) administered opioid peptides. For instance, beta endorphins have been shown to increase after running a marathon. But the analgesia produced in long-distance running has been shown to be blocked by naloxone.

Biochemicals called "opioid peptides" (natural opiates called endorphins and enkephalins) that fit into opiate receptors in postsynaptic neurons were first discovered in various areas of the brain.

The Influence of Neurotransmitters on Behavior

Methods of Varying Neurotransmitters. Considerable research has been conducted on the influence of neurotransmitters on behavior and to establish neurochemical concomitants of deviant behavior. To study changes in behavior, the activity of certain neurotransmitters has been increased by administering compounds that directly stimulate receptors, that increase the release of neurotransmitters, or that block reuptake. By injecting compounds into the brain, efforts are made to determine whether a particular neurochemical has an important function in a specific brain region and thence on behavior. Yet another approach has been to reduce neurotransmitter effects by inhibiting the synthesis of the neurotransmitter, by blocking the receptors for a particular neurotransmitter, or by destroying nerve endings by using neurotoxins (poisons). Results have indicated that some neurotransmitters have been related to a number of psychological disorders.

Various methods have been used to determine that at least some neurotransmitters influence different kinds of behavior.

[2] Specific subclasses of endorphins have been identified as follows: beta-lipotroprin containing beta endorphins, gamma endorphins, and alpha endorphins; enkephalins containing met-enkephalin and leu-enkephalins; and dynorphin. Among these, beta endorphins and gamma endorphins especially have analgesic properties.

Possible Influences on Depression and Schizophrenia. Endogenous depression has been related to a decrease of brain norepinephrine and serotonin as well as changes in the amounts of dopamine and acetylcholine. Excessive dopamine activity has, in limited studies, been related to schizophrenia. The number and sensitivity of norepinephrine and dopamine receptors have been related to depression and schizophrenia respectively.

The goal of this kind of research is to develop chemical agents that may be useful in biological psychiatry for treating or managing such disorders, as we develop in Chapter 15.

We noted that the identification of opiate receptors and of endogenous opiate-like substances is a landmark in neuroscience. Understanding the effects of these substances on mood, cognition, perception, and so on and how they interact with other neurotransmitters and hormones has considerably advanced our understanding of the biology of normal and abnormal behavior. The discovery of endorphins and their apparent distribution in the nervous system makes it seem likely that these substances do have a role in schizophrenia and the affective disorders. Some experimental and clinical studies indicate this possibility and it has even been suggested that reports of "near death experiences" may be related to a sudden release of beta endorphins.

More General Roles of Endorphins. Animal experiments have attributed a role to endorphins in the control of blood pressure, food and water intake, sexual activity and the estral cycle, and pain perception, as well as learning and immune responses. Human conditioning research indicates that endorphins may be responsible for some of the reinforcing aspects of rewards and that norepinephrine may help strengthen the memory of the response that caused the reinforcement. The amazing accomplishments to date in understanding the biochemistry of nervous tissue will no doubt be dwarfed by the accomplishments yet to be seen.

EMPHASIS ON A CYBERNETIC PRINCIPLE— NEUROTRANSMITTERS MAY FUNCTION IN POSITIVE FEEDBACK CIRCUITS

The discovery of and research on neurotransmitters has led to a revolution in our understanding of systems of the body. Various kinds of behavior influence the flow of neurotransmitters, and neurotransmitters in turn influence behavior in many ways. Endorphins may produce reinforcing "experiences" to increase the strength of contingent responses. One interpretation of the analgesic function of endorphins is that they are components of positive feedback systems that affect the experience of pain. That is, the more we experience pain, the greater the secretion of endorphins; consequently, the act that produced the pain is reinforced, creating a vicious cycle. This can lead to an abnormal masochistic-like behavior pattern; for example, animals have been shown to boost their endorphin levels by inflicting pain on themselves—they get caught in a self-reinforcing positive feedback circuit such that the more they inflict pain the greater the endorphin levels, and the greater the endorphin levels (an increase in reinforcement) the more they inflict pain. Such a positive feedback cybernetic model could help to account for self-inflicted injuries of various sorts such as in self-mutilation and autistic children injuring themselves by banging their heads against walls. As Akil et al. (1984) summarized research in this area, the advances in our study of endogenous opioids have changed our way of looking at biochemical phenomena: "Suddenly, *we can think in terms of circuits* rather than in 'humors' or in black boxes. In our study of function, we can no longer ignore . . . multiple systems," which in this case includes neurotransmitters, neural activity, and behavior (p. 223, italics added).

KEY TERMS

Autonomic nervous system (ANS)—A division of nervous tissue that consists of peripheral fibers that function with visceral and glandular responses. The system consists of two divisions, the sympathetic and parasympathetic nervous systems.

Basal ganglia—Include the caudate nucleus, globus pallidus, putamen, and amygdala. The first three are important parts of the extrapyramidal motor system.

Bell-Magendie Law—Holds that afferent neural impulses enter the spinal cord through its dorsal roots, and efferent neural impulses exit through the ventral roots, although there are typically exceptions as when some relatively few efferent neurons also leave the dorsal root and afferent neurons enter the ventral root.

Brain stem—The portion of the brain excluding the cerebrum and cerebellum.

Broca's area—A region in the left hemisphere that is important for speech production. A lesion there may cause Broca's aphasia, an inability to properly express one's self in oral language.

Catecholamines—A group of neurotransmitters that exerts effects (either excitatory or inhibitory) on target organs in the sympathetic nervous system. This group includes norepinephrine and dopamine.

Central fissure—A deep groove that begins in the middle of the cortex of each cerebral hemisphere and runs downward and slightly forward.

Central nervous system (CNS)—The tissue in the brain and spinal cord.

Cerebellum—The "little brain" posterior and inferior to the cerebrum functioning for motor coordination.

Cerebral cortex—The surface layer of the cerebrum consisting of cell bodies, about one-fourth inch thick.

Cerebral hemispheres—The two halves (left and right) of the cerebrum divided by the longitudinal fissure.

Cerebrum—The largest and most important division of the brain consisting of two hemispheres.

Cortical projection areas—Entry stations in the cortex for visual, auditory, and tactile-somatosensory input.

Cranial nerves—The 12 pairs of nerves that have points of origin or termination within the cranium (skull).

Endorphins—General term used for all endogenous peptides that act as opiates.

Frontal lobe—The anterior of a hemisphere, anterior to the central fissure; the left lobe contains Broca's speech area.

Hypothalamus—A body at the lower part of the thalamus consisting of a group of nuclei believed to function in circuits for the regulation of hunger, temperature, and emotional behavior.

Lateral fissure—A deep fissure in the cortex that separates the temporal lobe from the parietal and frontal lobes.

Limbic system—A hypothetical system to serve emotional functions. It is composed of structures comprising the older cortices that form the medial-most inner edge of the cerebral hemispheres. It also includes subcortical areas near the deep gray matter masses of the basal ganglia, the amygdala, thalamus, and so on.

Locus coeruleus—A group of neurons in the pons.

Longitudinal fissure—The fissure that divides the cerebrum into the left and right hemispheres.

Medulla—A region in the brain stem that contains nervous centers that function in the control of breathing and beating of the heart.

Meninges—The three membranes that cover the brain and spinal cord: dura mater, arachnoid, pia mater.

Motor area — Neurons in the cortex that lie directly anterior to the central fissure and serve motor functions.

Neuropeptides — An important subgroup of neurotransmitters which consists of strings of amino acids, for example, enkephalins and endorphins that affect various systems and chemicals throughout the body.

Neurotransmitters — Chemical substances that make it possible for one neuron to communicate with another at synapses.

Nucleus — A group of homogeneous neurons.

Occipital lobe — The lobe in each hemisphere posterior to the parietal lobe; it serves visual functions.

Parasympathetic nervous system — A division of the autonomic nervous system.

Parietal lobe — The cerebral lobe posterior to the central fissure, containing sensory areas.

Peptides — See neuropeptides.

Peripheral nervous system — Consists of cranial and spinal nerves. It has two divisions, the somatic nervous system and the autonomic nervous system. The somatic nervous system connects receptors and effectors with the central nervous system while the autonomic nervous system functions together with visceral organs and glands.

Pons — A swelling at the base of the brain on the underside of the medulla formed by a transverse band of fibers connecting the cerebrum with the opposite side of the cerebellum.

Pursuit eye movements — Slow, continuous movements of the eyes while tracking a target.

Reticular formation — A loosely defined network of cells extending from the upper part of the spinal cord through the medulla and pons to the upper brain stem.

Saccadic eye movements — Rapid movements of the eyes controlled by the eye muscles.

Sensory projection areas — Specific areas of the cerebral cortex where the afferent fibers originating in receptors terminate.

Somatic nervous system — The nervous system enervating the striated (voluntary) muscles.

Spatial summation — The joint action when neural impulses simultaneously arrive at a synapse from different spatially located neurons.

Spinal cord — The large bundle of neurons that runs through the spinal column.

Spinal nerves — The pairs of nerves that leave the spinal cord at each vertebral level. They are the cervical, thoracic, lumbar, sacral, and coccygeal pairs of nerves.

Startle response pattern — The involuntary response pattern to a surprising stimulus that prepares one for fight or flight.

Stimulus-bound behavior — Behavior that is controlled by an immediate stimulus such that the behavior is not flexible.

Sympathetic nervous system — A division of the autonomic nervous system associated with responses to emergencies.

Temporal lobe — The cortical lobe inferior to the lateral fissure and anterior to (in front of) the occipital lobe, containing Wernicke's speech area.

Temporal summation — Information integrated as neural impulses arrive at a synapse at slightly different times.

Thalamus — A mass of gray matter near the base of the cerebrum projecting onto the cortex, functioning as a relay station for neural impulses.

Voluntary act — An act that a person "decides" to do and can describe before it is performed.

Wernicke's area — A region in the left temporal lobe that is important for understanding language. A lesion in Wernicke's area precludes the adequate understanding of language.

STUDY QUESTIONS

1. Summarize some of the ways the human brain has historically been compared to dominant machines of the respective eras.
2. List the four major lobes of each cerebral hemisphere and state their recognized functions.
3. Identify regions where spinal nerves exit the spinal cord.
4. Discuss the reticular formation.

5. Enumerate activities related to the frontal lobes.
6. List some activities of the sympathetic and parasympathetic nervous systems.
7. Are various internal organs affected by emotional states? Explain.
8. Define voluntary and involuntary responses.
9. What is the importance of endorphins?
10. Compare information input to the brain with information input to a computer.
11. Discuss the importance of cybernetic circuits involving brain and muscle interactions.

FURTHER READINGS

You can browse through a library in the area of physiological psychology to find such books as Carlson's *Physiology of Behavior* (1991). The following are also advanced presentations that you could consider:

Akil, H., Watson, S. J., Young, E., Lewis, M. E., Khachaturian, H., & Walker, J. M. (1984). Endogenous opioids: Biology and function. *Annual Reviews of Neuroscience, 7*, 223–255.

Bloom, F. E. (1988). Neurotransmitters: Past, present, and the future directions. *FASEB Journal, 2*, 32–41.

The following is a recommended general textbook relevant to this chapter as well as to Chapters 4, 5, and 7:

Kolb, B., & Whishaw, I. Q. (1990). *Fundamentals of human neuropsychology* (3rd ed.). New York: Freeman.

CHAPTER 7

Behaving in Our External and Internal Environments— The Effectors

MAJOR PURPOSE:	To specify the anatomical structures, processes, and principles by which we respond to our environments
WHAT YOU ARE GOING TO FIND:	1. A review and extension of the two major classes of effectors: muscles and glands 2. A discussion of how we perform well-coordinated complex movements and high-speed tasks
WHAT YOU SHOULD ACQUIRE:	An advanced understanding of the nature of the effectors and of feedback and feedforward principles that guide our behavior

CHAPTER OUTLINE

MUSCLES—MECHANISMS FOR REACTING
  Striated Muscles
    Muscular contraction
    The motor unit
    Joint and tendon receptors activated by movements
    The neuromuscular (myoneural) junction
    Mechanics of contraction
    How muscles generate internal stimuli
  Coordination, Timing, and Muscle Integration
    Interactions between the brain and the skeletal muscles

Kinds of bodily movements
Kinds of information for learning and performing
How might central control systems originate?
The problem of high-speed serial order behavior
How do we know where our limbs are in space?
Some data and theories relevant to closed and open circuit conceptions of how we function
  Smooth Muscle
  Cardiac Muscle
GLANDS AND HORMONES
  Endocrine and Exocrine Glands

  Information Processing in the Endocrine System
EMPHASIS ON A CYBERNETIC PRINCIPLE—THE INTEGRATED USE OF FEEDBACK AND FEEDFORWARD IN THE CONTROL OF BEHAVIOR
ENRICHMENT MATERIAL—THE ENERGY FOR MUSCULAR CONTRACTION
KEY TERMS
STUDY QUESTIONS
FURTHER READINGS

MUSCLES—MECHANISMS FOR REACTING

When we take in information and internally process it, we do so primarily to produce some effect. That effect is carried out by the effectors of the body. Without effectors, we can do nothing.

We have seen that there are two major classes of effector cells: muscle fibers and glandular cells. Those muscle cells that can affect the external environment by moving parts of the body constitute the striated (skeletal, striped, or voluntary) musculature.

Striated Muscles

We saw in Chapter 4 that striated (skeletal) muscle fibers are generally attached to the ends of bones of the skeleton by tendons (strong bands of connective tissue). There are a few exceptions, such as the eye, tongue, and lip muscles. When skeletal muscles contract, they pull on tendons to move the bones and thus move the body.

Striated muscle fibers generally vary in length from about 1 mm to 10 cm (centimeters); although some rare muscle fibers may exceed 34 cm in length. They are about as wide as a human hair — 10 to 100 microns (a micron is one-thousandth of a millimeter). Striated muscle fibers are aligned alongside each other in parallel fashion within a muscle.

The information that we receive from the environment is for the purpose of doing something with our striated muscles.

MUSCULAR CONTRACTION

When an efferent neural impulse arrives at a muscle, it arrives at the central regions of muscle fibers. Each stimulated fiber then rapidly contracts with a **latency** of about 10 milliseconds (*latency* is the time between the *onset* of a stimulus to the onset of a response); contraction occurs, of course, only if the intensity of the neural impulse is above the threshold of excitability of the fiber's membrane. Since muscle fibers, like neurons, obey the all-or-none law, they either contract to their maximum extent or they do not contract at all. A striated muscle fiber contraction lasts for approximately 2 milliseconds, after which the fiber relaxes. Generally, the muscle continues to contract if efferent neural impulses repeatedly arrive in rapid succession, or until the muscle becomes exhausted. When efferent neural impulses cease, the muscles cease their contraction.

Striated muscle fibers are innervated and contract when neural impulses arrive at their central regions from efferent neurons.

Muscle fiber contraction occurs according to the general principles of propagated depolarization that we developed for neurons; that is, the efferent neural impulse produces a localized depolarization that is transmitted along the membrane surrounding the fiber. The velocity of the propagated depolarization varies between 3.5 and 5.0 meters per second, depending on the size of the muscle fiber.

The muscle fiber, the structural unit of striated muscle, obeys the all-or-none law in that it maximally contracts or it does not contract at all.

THE MOTOR UNIT

The **motor unit** is the *functional* unit of striated muscle (Fig. 7.1). *Functional unit* refers to the way in which striated muscle fibers contract together in conjunction with neural impulses from efferent neurons.

Components of a Motor Unit. A motor unit consists of (1) a nerve cell body that is located in the ventral root of the gray matter of the spinal cord; (2) an axon that descends from the motor neuron; (3) the terminal branches of the axon; (4) the **myoneural (neuromuscular) junction;** and (5) the muscle fibers that are neurally supplied by these branches of the axon.

Motor Unit Contraction. We can see in Figure 7.1 that neural impulses do not arrive simultaneously at the muscle fibers of a motor unit. Hence, although the contraction time for each fiber is approximately 2 milliseconds, the fibers of a single motor unit contract at slightly different times. Consequently, the time that it takes for the entire motor unit to contract from one impulse is longer than 2 milliseconds. By adding together the times that each muscle fiber contracts, a single motor unit of the size depicted in Figure 7.1 is active for perhaps 5 to 10 milliseconds (Fig. 7.2).

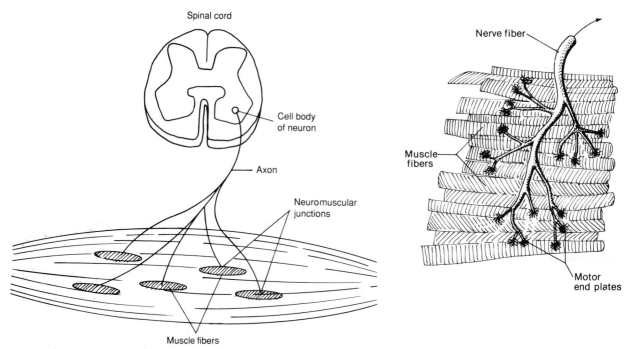

FIGURE 7.1 The components of a motor unit (left). Because the muscle fibers are at different distances from the axon, neural impulses arrive at them at different times so they cannot simultaneously contract. A closer view of the fibers and axon endings is to the right.

The motor unit is the functional unit of striated musculature because all of the muscle fibers innervated by a single motor neuron contract as an integrated unit.

Anatomical and Functional Characteristics of Motor Units. The anatomical and functional characteristics of motor units vary according to the location of the motor unit in the body. The smallest number of fibers per motor unit is about two or three for muscles that perform very fine movements, as do the muscles of the larynx and the ossicles of the ear, as well as those that control movement of the eyeballs. The largest number is 2000 or so for muscles that perform gross functions, such as those of the thigh. Such large muscles have overlapping, intermingled motor units within a given area. However, the precise control of movements of the eyes, for instance,

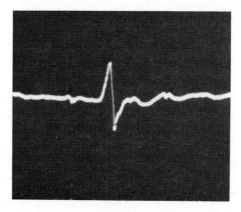

FIGURE 7.2
The electrical record of a small motor unit contracting.

dictates that there be relatively little overlap of motor units there. Also, any given muscle fiber may be activated by more than one efferent neuron coming from different CNS locations. This anatomical arrangement of a muscle fiber being supplied by different neurons serves different control functions. That is, since muscle fibers may contract due to varied neural impulses that carry different messages ("instructions"), our ability to differentially control our muscles is enhanced. We can thus make more precise, highly differentiated, coordinated, and integrated responses. More on this later.

Firing Rate Increases with Strength of Contraction. As a person increases the strength of a muscular contraction, the number of motor units activated and the rate of their contraction also increase. When one makes weak contractions, few motor units fire and the rate of contraction is approximately 5 to 10 per second. Strong contractions may produce rates much higher, such as 50 per second.

> *Muscles that perform precise movements have few muscle fibers per motor unit, while those that perform grosser functions have numerous muscle fibers in each motor unit.*

JOINT AND TENDON RECEPTORS ACTIVATED BY MOVEMENTS

Bones move at their joints because muscles contract, whereupon receptors in the joints and tendons are activated. The three major types of receptors in the joints and the ways in which they function are

1. The Golgi tendon organ (which obviously resides in tendons) is affected indirectly as the attached muscles contract. The Golgi tendon organ is thought to signal the exact joint position as well as the direction in which the related body part is moving.
2. Ruffini's endings are not affected by muscle tension at the joints, so they may signal resistance to movement and perhaps help us discriminate active from passive movement.
3. Pacinian corpuscles are believed to detect extremely small movements as well as acceleration in movements.

THE NEUROMUSCULAR (MYONEURAL) JUNCTION

The region between an axon terminal and an effector cell is a neuroeffector junction. One subclass is the striated muscle fiber junction, called a neuromuscular or myoneural junction (see Fig. 7.1). Branches of axons from motor neurons in the spinal cord and in the brain stem form synaptic endings at the synaptic cleft between the **sarcolemma** (muscle membrane) of muscle fibers. The neuromuscular synapse is large, relative to other synapses throughout the body. Neuromuscular synapses are approximately 1200 Å as compared to 200 Å for synapses in the nervous system (an **angstrom unit,** Å, is one ten-thousandth of a micron and one micron is one one-millionth of a meter).

> *Receptors in the joints and tendons generate* afferent *neural impulses that transmit information about joint position, speed, direction, acceleration, and nature of movements.*

When an efferent neural impulse reaches the end of the axon, acetylcholine (ACh) is liberated as a neurotransmitter at the terminal button whereupon the ACh crosses the synaptic cleft. When sufficient ACh reaches the motor end plates along the surface of the muscle fibers (see Fig. 7.1), it depolarizes the sarcolemma. That depolarization is referred to as an **end plate potential (EPP).** The EPP is of quite large amplitude relative to depolarizations of neurons in the central nervous system. Once the depolarization occurs, the muscle fiber always contracts.

> *When efferent neural impulses arrive at muscles, they liberate acetylcholine as a neurotransmitter; when sufficient ACh crosses the neuromuscular junction, muscle fibers are depolarized and end plate potentials (EPPs) are generated.*

MECHANICS OF CONTRACTION

How a Muscle Fiber Contracts. As the muscle fiber contracts, an action potential is generated. Just as for neural impulses, the permeability of the sarcolemma also increases for sodium (Na^+) and potassium (K^+) ions. The action potential is then propagated along the sarcolemma. Note in Figure 7.3 that the internal part of a muscle fiber has a **myosin** filament with cross bridges and an actin filament. Calcium ions that are present with the Na^+ and K^+ ions can enter into the **sarcoplasm** of the muscle fiber. When they do, the cross bridges become temporarily attached to the actin filaments. The cross bridges then bend and release repeatedly as they move against the actin filaments. That is, the myosin cross bridges bend back and forth so that a single bridge hooks onto an actin site; it then pulls the thin actin filament a short distance and releases it, whereupon it hooks onto the next actin site. The movement of the cross bridges along the actin filaments causes a shortening (contraction) of the muscle fiber. The entire muscle thus changes length when the myosin and actin filaments throughout the muscle slide past each other. When the muscle shortens sufficiently, the ends of the myosin and actin filaments within it meet. In this way muscles contract by shortening their muscle fibers. If a sufficient number of muscle fibers shorten, an overt movement occurs. Otherwise, the response is covert.

Muscle fibers contract when cross bridges of myosin filaments move against actin filaments in repeated rowing-like movements.

Adenosine Triphosphate Provides Muscular Energy. About 20 percent of the weight of a muscle is protein; the remainder is water plus a small amount of salts and other matter. The contractile structure of a muscle consists almost entirely of proteins. About 90 percent of the proteins are myosin, actin, and tropomyosin. About half of that is myosin, which is significant because myosin is also the enzyme that acts on **adenosine triphosphate (ATP).** In particular, myosin removes a phosphate group from ATP which thereby liberates energy. *The liberation of ATP provides the energy for muscles to contract.* ATP is the energy that is used to slide actin filaments toward each other. When nerve impulses arrive at a muscle cell, the myosin triggers the ATP breakdown, which starts the shortening process (see Enrichment Material

The release of adenosine triphosphate provides the energy for muscle contraction.

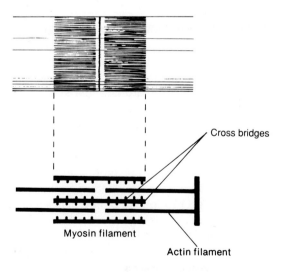

Cross bridges

Myosin filament

Actin filament

FIGURE 7.3
The internal part of a muscle fiber (top). An enlargement below shows the actin and myosin filaments in the fiber. The myosin cross bridges "row" like oars to cause the actin and myosin filaments to move relative to each other, causing the fibers to contract.

A, p. 214). To relax a muscle, the muscle fibers lengthen, which saves energy (ATP). In Chapter 15 we will discuss further how to relax muscles.

HOW MUSCLES GENERATE INTERNAL STIMULI

Information Is Generated by Intrafusal Muscle Fibers. There are two kinds of striated muscle fibers, **extrafusal** and **intrafusal muscle fibers** (Fig. 7.4). These fibers are aligned side by side in striated muscles. It is the extrafusal muscle fiber that does the work, whose contractions accomplish movements. The intrafusal muscle fiber, also called a **muscle spindle,** monitors the length of the extrafusal fibers. The intrafusal fiber contains a spiral-like ending wrapped around it that is called an **annulo spiral ending,** or a muscle sensory receptor. When the extrafusal muscle fibers lengthen, neurons from them send impulses to the intrafusal muscle fiber. Thereupon the intrafusal fiber also lengthens so that its annulo spiral ending stretches and sends the information that the extrafusal fiber is lengthening to the spinal cord (and brain) (Fig. 7.5).

Cessation of Messages from Intrafusal Muscle Fibers. On the other hand, when the extrafusal muscle fiber shortens (contracts), no neural impulses are generated so that no messages are conducted along its efferent neuron to the intrafusal fiber. Consequently, the intrafusal fiber stops sending sensory neural impulses to the spinal cord (Fig. 7.5). There is a complex interaction between the extrafusal and intrafusal fibers that, through the spinal cord, constitutes a negative feedback circuit as explained on pages 7–10.

Muscle Contraction Information from Golgi Tendon Organs. Golgi tendon organs are stretch receptors that detect the strength of the pull of muscles on the tendons and bones: the greater the muscle tension, the greater the pull on the tendons, and the greater the activity of the Golgi tendon organs. Consequently, the degree of muscle contraction is indicated by the rate of firing of afferent neural impulses from the Golgi tendon organs to the CNS.

Extrafusal and intrafusal muscle fibers (muscle spindles) exist alongside each other such that annulo spiral endings wrapped around intrafusal muscle fibers detect the length of extrafusal fibers.

Extrafusal fibers do the work and intrafusal fibers send information about extrafusal length to the spinal cord (and then to the brain).

Efferent neural impulses from extrafusal muscle fibers stimulate the intrafusal fibers to signal changes in extrafusal muscle fiber length; the intrafusal fibers generate neural impulses when the extrafusal fiber lengthens and stop the neural impulses when it shortens.

Golgi tendon organs indicate the strength of a muscle contraction by firing in proportion to the tension of the muscle.

Information contained in volleys of neural impulses fed to the central nervous system from intrafusal fibers and Golgi tendon organs functions in negative feedback control systems that continuously regulate muscle length and tension.

FIGURE 7.4 The annulo spiral ending, a sensory ending, is wrapped around the intrafusal muscle fiber (muscle spindle). Efferent neurons from the extrafusal fiber innervate intrafusal fibers.

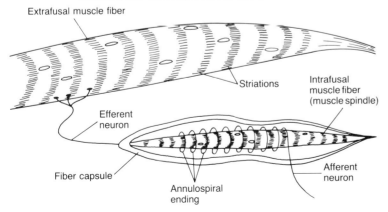

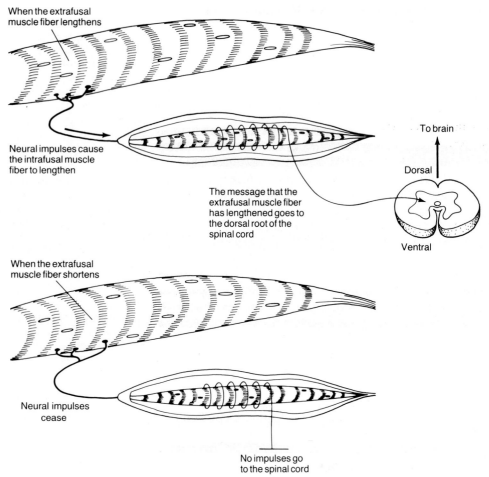

When the extrafusal
muscle fiber lengthens

Neural impulses cause
the intrafusal muscle
fiber to lengthen

The message that the
extrafusal muscle fiber
has lengthened goes to
the dorsal root of the
spinal cord

To brain

Dorsal

Ventral

When the extrafusal
muscle fiber shortens

Neural impulses
cease

No impulses go
to the spinal cord

FIGURE 7.5   When extrafusal muscle fibers lengthen, neural impulses to the
intrafusal muscle fibers cause the annulo spiral ending to lengthen;
neural impulses are then generated which send that information to
the spinal cord and to the brain (top). When the extrafusal muscle
fiber shortens, neural impulses are no longer generated so that the
intrafusal muscle fiber stops sending information to the spinal cord.
The cessation of information constitutes a message that the
extrafusal muscle fiber has shortened (bottom).

*Complex movements require
highly coordinated inter-
changes of information
carried by neural impulses in
circuits between the brain,
striated muscles, and Golgi
tendon organs.*

The importance of sensory feedback from intrafusal fibers and Golgi tendon
organs cannot be underestimated. This sensory feedback provides important information about the activity of the muscles in covert and overt movements, sending
critical information for processing to the brain. When we recognize the tremendous
number of muscle spindles and Golgi tendon organs throughout the body, the
numerous afferent neural impulses that bombard the brain when we make responses can well be appreciated. As we will elaborate in the next section, the brain
and body, acting in concert, constitute an amazingly effective central–peripheral
system for performing highly complex, integrated, precise movements.

Coordination, Timing, and Muscle Integration

INTERACTIONS BETWEEN THE BRAIN AND THE STRIATED MUSCLES

Efferent Neural Impulses and the Pyramidal System

When central cybernetic circuits are activated, efferent impulses produce numerous overt and covert muscular responses. One efferent component of brain activity comes from the motor cortex through the **pyramidal system** (so-called because the cells are shaped like pyramids). Cybernetic circuits also carry out efferent interactions with other descending components, such as the basal ganglia (nuclei) (Fig. 7.6). The pyramidal system includes axons of cells from the motor area of the cortex, the premotor cortex, and the parietal lobes, as well as the lateral and ventral corticospinal tracts (Fig. 7.6). These regions are activated when we make a response involv-

An important component of a cybernetic circuit for carrying information to the muscles is the pyramidal system, which goes principally from motor areas of the cortex to motor neurons in the spinal cord.

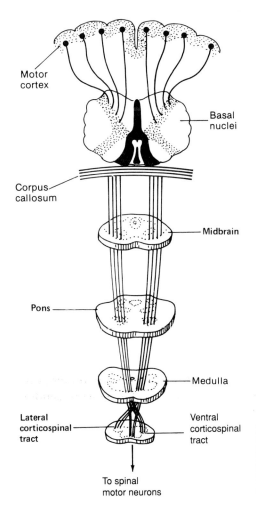

FIGURE 7.6
Motor regions of the brain interact with muscles through the pyramidal system along the lateral and ventral corticospinal tracts.

ing the striated musculature. In particular, neural fibers pass from the motor and parietal areas of the cortex down the spinal cord, without any synapses, until they reach spinal motor neurons. Since these axons have direct synapses with the spinal motor neurons, information from the cortex can be transmitted extremely rapidly along long neurons to the muscles. Once information gets to the spinal motor neuron, it goes directly to the muscle.

About 15 percent of the pyramidal system fibers continue down the ipsilateral half of the spinal cord. The large majority thus decussate to the contralateral side of the body.

Afferent Neural Impulses and the Lemniscal System

A sensory component of circuits that may activate motor circuits like those previously described includes afferent neurons from intrafusal fibers that send information to the brain via the **lemniscal system.** The lemniscal system is composed of large neural fibers that ascend the dorsal region of the spinal cord to reach the medulla. From the medulla, the tract ascends to the thalamus and finally to the sensory area just posterior to the central fissure.

The lemniscal system carries proprioceptive input to the brain as the pyramidal system carries messages from the brain to muscles.

The lemniscal system includes neural fibers that can rapidly conduct information to the sensory area about touch, pressure, vibration, and movement. The information that the lemniscal system transmits to the higher regions of the brain triggers mechanisms that in turn start motor responses, such as when we manipulate external objects. Reverberation of circuits including the lemniscal and pyramidal systems constantly functions to carry out the numerous activities of the body.

Intracerebral Circuits and Muscular Responding

Intracerebral (within the brain) circuits are critical for relating sensory input such as from the lemniscal system with striated muscle responding through the pyramidal system. Thach (1978) concluded that three components of the motor system of the central nervous system—the motor cortex, the cerebellum, and the basal ganglia—are activated prior to overt movements. Observations in monkeys and human patients are consistent with this conclusion. A brain circuit that may function for activating muscle activity involves the ventral lateral nucleus (VL) of the thalamic way station. The VL nucleus is a major point of convergence between the cerebellum and the basal ganglia. However, just how each of these components of the brain's motor system carry out their functions is not entirely clear. One clue comes from research that indicates that the entire output of the cerebellar cortex is inhibitory—it inhibits and disinhibits rather than excites and not excites. But more pieces of the jigsaw puzzle are required for a completely adequate understanding of what happens in these motor components of brain cybernetic circuits.

Thalamic VL neurons relay and integrate cerebellar and basal ganglia motor activity in relationship to the motor cortex.

KINDS OF BODILY MOVEMENTS

In homeostasis we maintain a variable such as salt level at an approximately constant value. In contrast, when we make movements, we systematically vary responses. Two types of overt and covert movements made by the striated muscles are **ballistic** (rapid) **movements** and **continuously controlled** (pursuit) **movements.**

Ballistic Movements Do Not Require Feedback. An example of a ballistic movement is pitching a baseball. It starts with a burst of energy and continues until the movement is completed, usually without being modified. The outcome of the response is determined by the initial burst of energy. Thus, once the movement has started, it continues its course until the ball leaves the pitcher's hand. Since ballistic movements are relatively rapid, they usually need not be modified by feedback in order to be successful. The few instances in which we do modify ballistic movements to some extent occur with input from other systems of the body. Saccadic eye movements are examples of ballistic movements that can be somewhat changed by input from other systems of the body.

Continuously Controlled Movements Are Modified During Their Course. Feedback from peripheral receptors (intrafusal muscle fibers and Golgi tendon organs) modifies continuously controlled movements in order to bring them closer and closer to the desired standards or goals. An example of a continuously controlled movement would be a hunter who uses anticipatory feedback to shoot a flying duck (see Chapter 1). The hunter continuously modifies the movement of the gun in accordance with feedback from muscles and tendons, as the arms, shoulders, and eyes track the duck.

Ballistic movements are rapid, start with bursts of energy, and are usually not modified by feedback from muscles. Continuously controlled movements are longer in duration and rely on feedback from peripheral receptors.

KINDS OF INFORMATION FOR LEARNING AND PERFORMING MOVEMENTS

Three possible kinds of information are important in modulating movements of the body, eyes, and head: (1) *sensory feedback* from peripheral muscular contractions within feedback systems; (2) *feedforward information,* which is generated in a **central control system** prior to making a response; and (3) **knowledge of results (KR)**, information from the external environment that results from overt muscular contractions made in an attempt to reach a goal.

Sensory feedback from muscles and knowledge of results from the external environment serve to guide learning of motor behavior, while feedforward information directs responses yet to be made.

Sensory Feedback in Closed-Circuit Systems

Closed-circuit systems function with negative feedback such as in learning a motor skill.

Sensory Feedback in Learning a Continuously Controlled Movement. In the early stages of learning a continuously controlled movement, there is feedback from muscles. Responses may also be guided by covert speech behavior. For example, we covertly tell ourselves how we should make specific movements, such as tossing the tennis ball into the air and visually tracking it as we serve. Then, we plan the next movement in a sequence of movements on the basis of information fed back from the previous movement.

Developing a Motor Image. As learning progresses, we develop some kind of internal representation of the response. Presumably the representation has a major component in the brain. One descriptive name for the representation is **motor image** (Adams, 1976). The motor image is a reference criterion of a good response. The motor image is quite like a visual image that develops from visual experience. A stored visual image allows us to recognize (perceive) a certain visual stimulus such as a table when it reappears. By comparing an ongoing response with the motor image, we have knowledge of how correct our movements are at any given time. If the

As we practice a response, feedback from the ongoing movement is compared with an internal representation of the desired movement, which is a motor image.

match between the feedback from an ongoing response and the motor image is good, the error signal in a negative feedback circuit is zero and we proceed confidently in making the movement. If there is a mismatch between the motor image and feedback from the movement, an error signal is registered. We then make a correction to eliminate the error. There is thus an ongoing correction of errors throughout the course of the continuously controlled movement. In the example of a tennis player, she or he has a motor image of the correct movements necessary to hit the tennis ball on the serve. As the movement is started, feedback from the muscles is compared with the motor image of a good serve. If there is an error as the arm is being raised, the player can correct the movement and improve the quality of the serve. This might happen if there is an error in the toss of the tennis ball and compensatory movements of the arm and body are necessary to register a correction.

Knowledge of Results (KR) Improves the Motor Image. Feedback in the form of knowledge of results is received from the external environment. We determine the adequacy of the most recent response and incorporate that information in our motor image. The motor image thus contains stored information about past movements. For example, the server may double-fault and lose the point. Seeing the balls hit the net is knowledge of results. That information then may improve the quality of the motor image, thereby improving the quality of the next movement. As practice continues, there is a gradual improvement in performance that we call *learning*. It is apparent that the motor image develops according to the principles of adaptive control, as we developed in Chapter 1.

Although verbal guidance, usually in the form of covert speech, is used in the early phases of learning, performance becomes automatic as learning progresses. Consequently, verbal guidance is no longer needed for adequate response.

In Review. Peripheral feedback from small discrete movements yields information that guides the learning of coordinated muscular activity and the development of a motor image. That feedback sequence continues to guide subsequent performance of responses. The learning of continuously controlled movements is also guided by external knowledge of results.

Feedforward Information in Open-Circuit Systems

Open-circuit systems function through feedforward information. Consequently their channels do not return feedback, and there is no closed circuit for returning information to its source. An example of such a circuit offered by Adams (1976) is a traffic light system that has a fixed timing sequence of red, amber, and green. It does not have the capability of correcting the timing, depending on the flow of traffic. Thus, when the traffic load is great, a traffic jam will result, but when the traffic load is light, traffic flow is unnecessarily impeded. If we build feedback into the traffic light system so that the duration of red and green is determined by how much traffic there is in each direction, that feedback would lead to a smoother flow of traffic. Traffic jams and excessive impeding of the flow of traffic would then decrease.

The alternative to the peripheral feedback model for explaining complex motor behaviors is a central control theory that employs an open- (vs. closed-) circuit system. A central control system hypothesizes that feedback from a movement is not necessary for running off coordinated muscular activity. Rather, high centers of the brain have stored information (such as a motor image) that can command (direct) the patterning of movement. Consequently, these high brain centers need not be in-

As learning of a motor skill proceeds, the skill can be automatically performed without step-by-step verbal guidance in the form of covert speech behavior.

An open-circuit system, in contrast to a closed-circuit negative feedback system, does not use feedback to correct errors.

A central control system employs an open-circuit system which directs a movement without relying on peripheral feedback.

Feedforward information is transmitted in open-circuit control systems—the circuit is not closed so that information cannot be returned back to the brain.

formed about the particular phase of a movement that has been completed in order to initiate the next component of the movement, as a peripheral theory would hold. The central control system is a motor program in which there is a stored plan for a movement sequence. The plan controls the movement by feedforward during its entire course, such as in ballistic movements, making feedback from the periphery unnecessary.

The vestibulo-ocular reflex is one example of an open-circuit control system in which there is feedforward of information. To understand this, let us review and extend what we learned about eye movements. We previously saw that there are two kinds of eye movements carried out by the striated muscles that surround the eyes. Both are products of the oculomotor system (*oculo* refers to eyes and *motor* to muscles). As we discussed in Chapter 6, these movements are (1) saccadic eye movements (saccades) that function to search for targets and (2) smooth pursuit tracking movements that we use to track objects such as the flight of a bird. The saccadic eye movements are quick, jerky movements that we make as we continuously monitor stimuli in our environment. Smooth pursuit tracking movements, however, are slow, continuous eye movements. Saccades are apparently too fast to be continuously controlled by visual feedback. However, smooth eye movements are continuously regulated depending on information returned from observing a moving stimulus—information from numerous sources, including the cortex, retina, and peripheral receptors (cutaneous, in tendons, muscles, and joints) is monitored and analyzed by the cerebellum. In both kinds of eye movements, it is important that the retinal image of the object that we are perceiving be stabilized as we move our heads. There are two reflexes that help us to stabilize the image: (1) the vestibulo-ocular reflex and (2) the vestibulo-spinal reflex.

The Vestibulo-Ocular Reflex as an Example of a Feedforward Control System. The vestibulo-ocular reflex is influenced by the semicircular canals and helps us stabilize a retinal image as the head moves. More particularly, the oculomotor system functions to bring the fovea of the retina into alignment with a visual target and to maintain that alignment during tracking. The **fovea** is the region in the back of the retina where vision is sharpest (see Fig. 5.7). Individuals with particular damage to the vestibular mechanism cannot maintain a consistent image on the retina when they walk; consequently their visual world is like a "jumping blur."

A change in position of the head is signaled by the vestibular component of the vestibulo-ocular reflex. Feedforward information from the vestibular apparatus evokes compensatory movements of the eyes to maintain a constancy of input to the retina. Information about the retinal position of the image apparently is not returned to the vestibular mechanism. Because the circuit is not closed, information about retinal position is not returned to the brain as it would be in a closed-circuit in which negative feedback functions.

Another Example of Feedforward Theorizing. Consider again the phenomenon of anticipatory timing, by means of which an accurate movement can be initiated *before* the actual occurrence of an environmental stimulus. A response can be timed to occur simultaneously with a stimulus that is *going* to appear. Examples of anticipatory timing are numerous—one is a tennis player who anticipates where his or her opponent is going to hit the ball.

If we have a well-functioning central control system, that is, if we know just where and when we want to make a response in the future, according to this notion, no sensory information from the muscles would be necessary; we would not need to

The central control system transmits feedforward information from the brain to produce responses, but there is no return information about the status of the response.

Feedback guides the relatively slow pursuit movements, but the more rapid saccadic eye movements are controlled only by feedforward information.

The vestibulo-ocular reflex is influenced by the semicircular canals and helps stabilize a retinal image as the head moves by means of an open-circuit control system.

The vestibulo-ocular reflex, an open-circuit control system, provides some support for a central control plan since such a system can function without peripheral feedback.

know when we have obtained the desired position. The outflow of information from the central control system would be sufficient to inform us about the spatial location of the part of the body that is making the anticipated movement. On the other hand, if as happened early in the learning process, we do not have a well-functioning central control system, sensory information from muscles would be of especially great importance in informing the higher centers of the status of the ongoing movement and of its outcome.

The vestibulo-spinal reflex is a closed-circuit system that helps maintain a stable retinal image.

The Vestibulo-Spinal Reflex and Negative Feedback. The **vestibulo-spinal reflex** also helps us to maintain the head in a stable orientation when we are moving. When the head moves, the vestibular mechanism in the inner ear is activated. That activation generates neural impulses that are transmitted to neurons in the vestibular nuclei located in the brain stem near the neck. The vestibular nuclei then connect with motor neurons in the neck muscles. The vestibular mechanism and the neck muscles thus form a part of a negative feedback system that helps maintain stability of the head in space and thus also of the retinal image.

Two Notions About Why Some Movements Are Controlled by Feedback and Others by Feedforward Information. Why are we in some ways designed for strictly feedforward control, as in the vestibulo-ocular reflex for stabilizing a retinal image, and in other systems we use proprioceptive feedback circuits, as in the control of limb movements. Why is feedback not used for saccadic eye movements? One notion is that feedback from the limbs is necessary because of the different loads that the limbs must function against. For instance, an arm can carry a load of a weighted object and its muscles must adjust with feedback in accordance with that load. In contrast the load for the eyes is slight—only the slight load of the eyeballs must move for vision.

A similar notion is that muscles cushion the impact of mechanical interactions between the body and the environment, much like shock absorbers do on automobiles. Therefore, proprioceptive feedback compensates for the variations in the mechanical (tension) interactions of limb muscles. Eye muscles are faster and less variable than limb muscles and they do not have mechanical interactions with the world. Consequently, by this line of thinking, eye muscles do not cushion the eyes and thus do not need peripheral feedback.

HOW MIGHT CENTRAL CONTROL SYSTEMS ORIGINATE?

It is almost universally accepted that early in the learning of a movement, such as hitting a tennis ball, the learner's progress depends on peripheral feedback from tendons, muscles, and joints. That peripheral feedback keeps the higher nervous system continuously aware of the progress of movements. Consequently, through negative feedback circuits to and from the brain, correction of a movement can be made. As learning progresses, changes in the brain come to represent the sequences of muscular responses required to properly execute that movement. Such a representation is the motor image we have discussed. According to the feedforward–central control model, when that representation of the movement is once established in the brain through learning, the slower feedback systems from the periphery are no longer necessary—the higher brain structures can then take over control of the movement. More specifically, internal negative feedback circuits in the brain may

Brain representations of well-learned movements may substitute for actual feedback from positions in the muscles.

substitute for normal peripheral feedback. These cerebral circuits would be stable and would run off rapidly. That is, when an internal model of the desired perform- ance is established within the brain as an adaptive control mechanism, feedforward information alone can control the movement. However, as we discussed previously, the central control system that controls a feedforward system could still be quite flexible — it could be adjusted for later responses by feedback from the periphery, if necessary. It is also possible that other central nervous system sources could influ- ence the particular ongoing central program. But when such a central control system is properly running automatically from a preprogrammed routine, input from other central sources or feedback from the periphery is unnecessary and, in fact, would be redundant. Many years ago, the famous psychologist Knight Dunlap (1927) sug- gested that a representation of motor responses could be established in the cerebel- lum (see Fig. 6.16).

These issues about feedback and feedforward systems are intimately tied to a major question with a long history in psychology, "How do we coordinate and time intricate movements of our muscles to produce high-speed serial behavior, such as speaking?"

THE PROBLEM OF HIGH-SPEED SERIAL ORDER BEHAVIOR

omit

Many muscle fibers must contract and relax in precise temporal orders to coordinate the movements for the specific acts in serving a tennis ball. The integration of contracting and relaxing muscles in precise temporal orders is complex. Speaking and sentence construction are significantly *more* complex.

Karl Lashley's (1951) classic paper entitled "The Problem of Serial Order in Behavior" was an attempt to account for the logical and orderly arrangement of thought and action, which he regarded as the most complex type of behavior. The integrative functions of the cerebral cortex reach their highest development in human thought processes. Language behavior, so important in thought, requires such integration.

The Associative Chain Theory. Prior to Lashley the existing theory for speech was an associative chain theory in which one response provides a stimulus for the next response (Fig. 7.7). Speech, according to that theory, is a succession of vocal responses wherein kinesthetic impulses (sensory feedback) from each speech move- ment evoke the next in the series.

Lashley Held That Feedback from One Movement Cannot Evoke the Next. Lashley attacked the associative chain theory by holding that extremely quick movements are not caused by the preceding response. Instead, he held, they are independent of

FIGURE 7.7
A classical associative chain theory for complex behavior. An external stimulus (S_1) evokes an overt response (R_1). The feedback from R_1 is s_1 and s_1 evokes the next response in the chain (R_2). Feedback from $R_2 \cdot s_2$ continues the chain.

them. He thought (erroneously, as we will see) that an entire movement from initiation to completion is made in less time than the reaction time for tactile or kinesthetic stimulation of the arm. Lashley counted the finger strokes of a musician and determined that they must be as fast as 16 per second. Such a succession of movements, he argued, is too quick for even **simple reaction time** (compared to **complex reaction time**) such as the feedback from one response leading to the next. Consequently, sensory control of movements as in the associative chain theory would be ruled out. Donald Hebb (1958) agreed with Lashley. Hebb argued that if as many as 16 responses can occur in one second, at most there are about 60 milliseconds for feedback from the immediately preceding movement to produce the next (1000 ms divided by 16 = 62.5 ms). Since simple reaction time to tactile or kinesthetic stimulation of the arm is around 125 milliseconds, the feedback from one response is not sufficiently rapid to produce the next response. For the same reason, speech could not function as a succession of vocal acts in which kinesthetic impulses from each movement serve as a stimulus for the next. Consequently, Lashley and Hebb reasoned that a response must be made independently of sensory control from previous responses. Instead, both Lashley and Hebb postulated some central nervous mechanism (a central control system) that fires with a predetermined plan to activate different muscles in a predetermined order.

Lashley and Hebb argued that because the feedback from one response must activate a second response within about 60 ms, and since tactile and kinesthetic reaction time is about 125 ms, the associative chain theory of temporal integration cannot account for high-speed serial order behavior.

Errors in Lashley's Theory. There are two major difficulties with Lashley's argument. First, it is not legitimate to use reaction time data based on an overt response to an external stimulus for the purpose of understanding internal feedback phenomena and attendant responses. Second, and of greater importance, is the physiological fact that the feedback from one response *can* produce a second response well within the 60 milliseconds that Lashley and Hebb thought was required. The numerous data about internal transmission time indicate how very rapidly information is transmitted from one region of the body to another. For example, Bowman and Combs (1969) stimulated the deep radial nerve of the monkey's elbow and obtained a response in the cerebellum in 4 milliseconds. In other research, stretching the extraocular muscle of the cat produced a response in the cerebellum in 4 milliseconds and in the brain stem in 3 to 4 milliseconds. The time from the cerebellum back to the eye muscle has been measured as 5.5 milliseconds, indicating that the complete trip from the eye muscle receptors to the brain and back to the eye muscles takes about 10 milliseconds. (See McGuigan, 1978, p. 56.)

In view of his criticism of a feedback model for high-speed serial behavior, it is interesting that Lashley *did* recognize the importance of kinesthetic feedback from the musculature in another context. He explained the moon illusion — that the moon appears larger at the horizon than at its zenith — by saying that this illusion is solely a function of the position of the eyes in their orbits. The kinesthetic impulses from the eyes, he said, determine the immediate perception (illusion) of size.

A Multichannel Processing Model. Considerations throughout this chapter, and indeed throughout the book, make it clear that feedback from muscular responses *is* important for guiding complex, ongoing, high-speed serial order behavior. Lashley's physiological arguments were simply incorrect. On the other hand, the early associative chain theory was excessively simplistic. A more appropriate model than either the associative chain theory or central control system by themselves is a composite one involving numerous (perhaps thousands) of parallel information processing channels. These channels must simultaneously transmit information

High-speed serial order behavior is probably carried out by both a central control system directing feedforward information from the brain to the muscles and feedback from the muscles that modifies and guides the further development of the central control system.

between the brain, muscles, and viscera along neuromuscular cybernetic circuits as we carry out complex behaviors. The reasoning that many systems function in generating the numerous behaviors of which humans are capable is consonant with the position expressed by the Nobel Laureate Edelman (1987). As he pointed out, the motor system was considered by Head, Sherrington, and Sperry to be especially important for such higher brain functions as perception and memory and the means by which the sensory system operates. As he stated, "the motor and sensory structures can be understood only as a coordinated selective system . . . selection by early signals in both motor and sensory systems acting *together* in a global mapping is considered to be crucial in solving the problem of adaptive perceptual categorization" (Edelman, 1987, p. 210, italics in original). He adds that because the analysis of motion is so complex, no single generalized explanation of motion is likely to be general enough to account for all motor responses. Rather, all components of the motor ensemble (muscles, joints, proprioceptive and kinesthetic functions, and appropriate portions of the brain) must all evolve and function as a unit. Ongoing research by psychologists, psychophysiologists, psycholinguists, and those in related professions may eventually allow us to specify more precisely the psychophysiological processes that constitute our complex linguistic behaviors. In the next sections, we discuss a topic related to high-speed serial behavior.

HOW DO WE KNOW WHERE OUR LIMBS ARE IN SPACE?

A Bit of History. How do we become aware of our body and limbs, of where they are in space, and how do we perceive their movement? Scientists have debated these issues for some two centuries. Sir Charles Bell (1842) held that the muscles play the primary role. Duchenne (1855) rejected Bell's theory in favor of one involving the joints. Thinking along the lines of Bell's theory, Sherrington (1906) developed the concept of a muscle sense (proprioception) as being primarily responsible for how we perceive limb movement and position. According to Sherrington, sensory proprioceptive information arises from the kinesthetic and vestibular receptors. Force and extent of movements, muscular tension, physical pressures, and the position of the body and its components in space are sensed through **proprioceptors.**

Muscle and Joint Feedback. Kelso and Wallace (1978) reviewed extensive data relevant to Sherrington's concept of a muscle sense. Some of the findings were counter to Sherrington's theory, but Kelso pointed out that they were derived from early experiments that were methodologically faulty. For instance, some researchers had concluded that intrafusal fiber receptors and Golgi tendon organs were incapable of indicating the absolute length and tension of a muscle. Consequently, muscle receptors were thought to be incapable of supplying information about learned movements. The Golgi tendon organs and intrafusal muscle fiber also were considered incapable of accessing central mechanisms. But methodologically improved experiments performed since then indicate that muscle receptors do contribute to conscious proprioception. These most recent data clearly establish the importance of the role of muscle receptors in providing conscious information about position and movement.

Feedback from muscles and joints tells us where our limbs are in space.

When the biceps muscle is vibrated, muscle spindles are activated.

By artificially inducing abnormal afferent discharge from muscle receptors, there is an illusory perception of movement.

Apparently, afferent muscle information in the higher levels of the central nervous system is dominant over joint information.

In deafferentation, nerve fibers from the muscles and joints to the motor centers of the brain are severed. The behavior of the organism is then studied to determine whether or not it can carry out complex behaviors.

Joint Receptors Also Contribute. Evidence also supports the importance of joint receptors for sensory movement and for a concept of cortical encoding (representation) for those movements.

One line of research that indicates that information from the muscles leads to the conscious experience of movement is derived from vibrations studies. If a person's arm is vibrated, and the arm is prevented from flexing, the subject reports experiencing the feeling of flexing, although flexing does not actually occur. Furthermore, vibrating the arm alone activates intrafusal muscle fibers, leading to afferent feedback to the brain and the illusion of movement.

Neural projections to the brain for afferent neurons from muscles are quite defuse throughout the cortex. Afferent information from muscles activates widespread transcortical circuits, part of which are known projections of afferent neurons from intrafusal muscle fibers to the sensory motor cortex (Kelso and Wallace, 1978, p. 16). Given that there are representations for movements in the cortex that are encoded through information from joint receptors and also representations for information from muscles, how might those two central representations interact? Kelso and Wallace indicate that under some conditions joint information is overridden by muscle information during processing by higher centers in the central nervous system. The receptors in muscles are thus not just limited sources of proprioceptive feedback, but they are important elements in control of movement.

SOME DATA AND THEORIES RELEVANT TO CLOSED- AND OPEN-CIRCUIT CONCEPTIONS OF HOW WE FUNCTION

How the Two Theories Were Developed

Origin of a Closed-Circuit Theory. It was in 1895 that Mott and Sherrington's data formed for the first time the basis for a peripheral closed-circuit system. It was then that they demonstrated in monkeys the importance of muscular and cutaneous sensation for purposive movement of a limb. They attempted to **deafferent** a limb (a limb left intact but with afferent neural pathways to the brain removed). The monkey's ability to grasp an object was abolished. Thus, it appeared that feedback from the periphery (which normally "closes the circuit" from muscles to brain to muscles) was necessary for movement. Later research, such as that cited by Kelso and Stelmach (1976, p. 2), confirmed that afferent impulses from the skin, muscles, and joints are necessary for the execution of high-level movements. However, the deafferentation studies are not that simple, as we will soon see.

Origin of a Central Control Hypothesis. It was Lashley who first developed and empirically supported an open-circuit system. His data and conclusions conflicted with those of Mott and Sherrington and thus argued for a central control theory and against a closed-circuit theory. After studying a patient who had a gunshot injury to the spinal cord that produced an accidental deafferentation, in 1917 Lashley advanced the concept of a central control theory for motor behavior. When blindfolded, the patient could always correct a voluntary movement so that the movement was quite competent. Since he appeared to lack peripheral feedback, that feedback was thought to be unnecessary to guide the movement.

Lashley, influenced by John Watson, had been a peripheralist. However, from that point on he became a centralist who denied muscle feedback a role in the regulation of movements. For instance, in 1926 Lashley placed lesions in the cerebellum of rats; in 1929 he severed proprioceptive afferents in rats. In neither study was there a reduction in the accuracy of maze running, although there were considerable motor disturbances. Lashley's conclusion from such research was that a central plan in the brain determines motor sequences. His conclusion was widely (and uncritically) accepted. However, as pointed out by Kelso and by Adams, these particular findings were refuted many times. Among those who effectively criticized Lashley were the accomplished scientists Walter Hunter, Ivan Pavlov, and M. D. Honzik. One of their criticisms was that Lashley denied the animals only one sense modality. The loss of only one modality should not detract from accuracy of performance because the animals could still substitute feedback from other senses. Lashley's efforts have been referred to as merely being a "crusade" against the function of peripheral feedback.

Lashley originally developed the concept of central control for motor behavior, a theory that continued to be held because of Lashley's prestige in spite of wide criticisms of his theories and conclusions.

Data Supporting an Open-Circuit Theory

Several kinds of research have been cited as supporting an open-circuit theory, including deafferentation studies and findings of cerebral reactions prior to the occurrence of muscular responses.

Contemporary Deafferentation Studies. Edward Taub and his colleagues (cf. Taub, 1980) attempted to eliminate all such modalities in order to answer the criticisms leveled at Lashley's work. They conducted an impressive series of studies. For instance, they placed opaque collars about the necks of monkeys that had been deafferented. The effort here was to eliminate visual feedback in addition to the deafferentation. In general, the conclusion was that the animals could still perform motor tasks adequately, suggesting that sensory feedback from the muscles was not necessary for the performance of a learned act. These studies thus have been cited in favor of a central control theory. Yet, Taub's conclusions have also been criticized. One criticism was that vision of the surrounding room was not actually eliminated by the opaque collar. Movements of the head or eyes could still provide visual feedback to the animals that could be informative of the progress of movements as learning continued. That is, although they could not see everything in the room, the mere movement of their heads and eyes could provide information about their progress. Similar attempts to eliminate auditory feedback have been criticized. For instance, animals were trained to make a conditional response that terminated a buzzer. The fact that the buzzer was terminated when the animals made the desired response itself provided informative feedback for the movement of making the response. An anatomic difficulty also remained.

The Bell-Magendie Law Revisited. The problem is complicated even further by noting the anatomical characteristics of the nerves through the dorsal and ventral roots of the spinal cord. We used to believe, in accordance with the Bell-Magendie Law, that all nerve fibers entering the dorsal root are sensory (afferent) in function, and similarly that all fibers exiting from the ventral root are motor (efferent) in function. We now know that this is not completely true. There actually are some efferent fibers entering the dorsal root and some afferent fibers exiting the ventral root. Consequently, deafferenting an animal by severing nerves into the dorsal root still allows sensory information from the muscles to enter the central nervous system by means of the ventral root. Other investigators have reported that deafferented animals can have lost coordination restored when emotionally aroused.

Further, extensive criticism of the deafferentation studies has been summarized by Adams (1976). One point made by Adams is that **ataxia** (the inability to coordinate voluntary muscular movements) is greatly accentuated in blindfolded, deafferented animals, but ataxia can be absent without the blindfold. In 1932, Pavlov made similar observations on ataxic humans with *tabes dorsalis.* That is, he observed that the ataxic individuals could stand on one leg when their eyes were open but they fell when their eyes were shut. These observations indicate that motor activity such as standing can be facilitated by relying on the visual modality. A precise deafferentation test of a central control theory is thus extremely difficult, if not impossible. What is required is that all other sources of feedback that can possibly provide information for movement must be eliminated. It may be that these other channels are normally not used, but they can be backup channels if required. Even the autonomic nervous system can provide clues for movement (as when Mowrer, 1947, used fear stimuli as the cues for motor avoidance responses). Thus, any of many sources of peripheral feedback can be informative for movement. We are truly magnificently constructed organisms in the sense that there is a great deal of redundancy built into our bodies—if we are deprived of one sense modality, we often can still function quite well by relying on others. These studies also conform with numerous others by indicating how bodily systems intricately interact, as examined here in the case of the visual and motor systems.

In Conclusion: On Deafferentation Studies.   It is critical to note that in these experiments, sensory feedback was not completely eliminated, nor perhaps can it ever be and still maintain a living organism. Consequently, like Lashley, what Taub has shown is that skilled responding is still possible when proprioceptive (sensory) feedback is *reduced.* (When Charles Osgood and McGuigan were planning some research to eliminate *all* sensory feedback by pharmacologically paralyzing muscles in humans, Edmund Jacobson advised obtaining a coffin and a coroner for the subject; see Osgood and McGuigan, 1973.)

Antecedent Brain Reactions to Responses.   Some research that has been cited in favor of the existence of central control systems has been based on brain reactions in advance of overt movements. In particular, Evarts (1973) reported that the precentral motor cortex, basal ganglia, and cerebellum all discharge prior to overt movement. The suggestion is that these three structures function together in some kind of internal feedback system. Thach (1978) found that cerebellar and thalamic neurons changed frequency both before and after a response by monkeys to visual input. Brain events occurred 80 to 100 milliseconds before any observed change in arm or trunk EMG, indicating to Thach that feedback from the movement did not influence the monkeys' responses.

In evaluating these conclusions, we must recognize that we do not really know whether these central discharges that occur prior to overt movement result from other brain structures, or whether they are evoked by sensory feedback from covert or overt muscle responses. Considering the mass of muscle throughout the body and the tremendous complexity of the brain, it would be a staggering project to establish a causal connection between two specific, naturally occurring brain reactions; it would be even more difficult to establish a causal relationship between the brain event and a particular covert or overt response in some of that mass of muscle. In order to establish a causal relationship between a unitary brain reaction and a specific antecedent behavioral event, we would have to at least determine that there is a high correlation between the two. The brain reaction would have to be *very* tightly coupled to the response as when we stimulate the motor area of the cortex and causally evoke a localized bodily response. Considering that a particular motor response must involve many neuronal circuits, establishing such a correlation is unlikely in the forseeable future. In studies such as those by Evarts and Thach, it is not clear exactly which of the body's considerable muscle activities should be recorded. Consequently, in the interval between the onset of the change in the brain activity and the first muscular response observed, we do not know how many other muscular responses might have preceded that one.

Data Relevant to a Closed-Circuit Theory

Anticipatory Timing of Movements. We do not know whether anticipatory timing is based on a central control system, on sensory feedback from the muscles and tendons as one is in the process of anticipation, or on some combination of these two possibilities. Major research efforts are required to understand how anticipatory timing occurs.

Speech Muscle Feedback. One line of evidence supporting a closed-circuit hypothesis for high-speed movements comes from the anatomy and physiology of the tongue. Intrafusal muscle fibers, so important for providing feedback during speech, are absent in the tongues of lower animals such as the cat. However, they are present in primates. The monkey and human tongues have muscles richly laced with intrafusal fibers and they are arranged in transverse, vertical, and longitudinal dimensions to indicate the position of the tongue in three-dimensional space. These sensors of the tongue are well structured to function in a highly discriminative feedback system as certainly occurs during speech. Of all the speech muscles, the tongue is the one that generates the most information. (See McGuigan, 1978, Chapter 9, for an elaboration on the topic of "what the tongue tells the brain"; see also Sussman, 1972.)

Having now surveyed the anatomy and functions of the striated musculature, we turn to the remaining two kinds of muscle, smooth and cardiac. These will be only briefly discussed to elaborate on the overview given in Chapter 4.

Smooth Muscle

Most organs of the body contain smooth (involuntary) muscle, as do the walls of blood vessels. Smooth muscle is also located around the hair follicles so that when they contract there is an involuntary erection or bristling of the hairs. Smooth muscle is innervated by the sympathetic division of the autonomic nervous system (ANS). When we are frightened or shocked, the ANS is diffusely activated; one reaction then evoked is having our "hair stand on end" (technically known as piloerection).

Smooth muscle is primarily in the visceral organs of the body and blood vessels, being innervated by the autonomic nervous system (ANS).

Smooth muscle fibers are typically arranged in bundles with gap (electrical) junctions between them. When the motor nerve fibers of the autonomic nervous system approach a bundle of smooth muscle cells, they divide into thin neural filaments. Those filaments interweave among the smooth muscle cells and eventually synapse with the muscle cells. The number of synapses and the number of neural filaments in any given region vary considerably. In most visceral organs of the body, such as the arteries, the colon, and the uterus, the amount of nerve supply is relatively small. In these cases, when a bundle of smooth muscle cells is activated by means of their chemical synapses, the excitation spreads to other muscle cells across gap junctions. Slow electrical action potentials result in waves of smooth muscle contraction. These contractions carry out a variety of functions, such as passing feces along the intestinal tract.

Cardiac Muscle

The heart is composed of cardiac muscle that rhythmically contracts to pump blood to lungs and into the cardiovascular system.

Cardiac muscle, so named from the Greek word for "heart," appears somewhat like striated muscle in that it has striations of its own. In spite of that appearance, cardiac muscle functions more like smooth muscle. It is well adapted for relatively long-continued rhythmic contractions to pump blood for oxygenation of the lungs. It also directs blood into the vascular system to supply oxygen and various nutrients to the cells throughout the body.

One of the major discoveries in the history of physiology was that of William Harvey in 1628 when he published his *Essay on the Motion of the Heart and the Blood of Animals.* It was the first clear demonstration that blood circulates throughout the body and that the heart functions to circulate blood.

Note in Figure 7.8 the sinus node of the human heart. The sinus node receives neural impulses that help regulate contractions of the cardiac muscle. Thus, when contractions start at the sinus node, those contractions spread to the intimately interconnected muscle fibers in the rest of the heart. When the muscle fibers of the heart contract, blood inside the heart is forced out into the blood vessels. Blood is then carried along the blood vessels as smooth muscles in the vessels contract and relax.

Complex circuits among the medulla, the autonomic nervous system, and the heart influence the automatic heart beat. Hormonal and striated muscle activity also can influence heart rate.

Circuits Influencing Heart Rate.   A center in the medulla in the brain stem is part of a circuit running to and from the sinus node. On their way from the medulla, nerve impulses are transmitted through the autonomic nervous system so that their regular arrival at the sinus node influences the heart to beat in a regular fashion. Although the immediate supply of neural impulses for the heart comes directly from the autonomic nervous system, if that nerve supply is removed, the heart will still continue to beat regularly. The circuits involving the medulla, the autonomic nervous system, and the heart thus merely influence the heart's activity. They do not completely control it. In short, the heart controls its own rhythmic activity, but heart rate can be modified by autonomic nervous system activity, by certain hormones that function through the endocrine system, and of course, by activity in other systems, such as the striated muscle (as during exercise).

A gap junction in the heart is an electrical synapse of low electrical resistance. Excitation spreads from one cardiac muscle fiber to another across gap junctions to produce the automatic beating of the heart.

Current flows across gap junctions between cardiac muscle fibers (gap junctions also occur between smooth muscle fibers). The gap junctions that connect fibers of cardiac muscle are **intercalated discs** that have low electrical resistance. Consequently, there can be current flow across the synapse rather than activation from one cell to the next by chemical means as in chemical synapses. Apparently, then, there is a spread of electrical excitation from one cardiac muscle fiber to another across these intercalated discs, producing the automatic beating of the heart. In this way, the heart obeys the all-or-none law as an entity such that it contracts maximally or not at all.

Communication and Blood Pressure.   There is a subtle interaction between the act of communicating and the level of blood pressure (see McGuigan & Ban, 1987). Gantt studied the "effect of person," what Pavlov called the "social reflex," and its

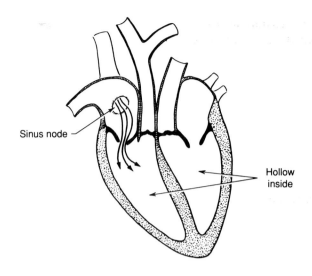

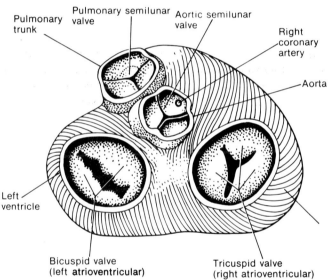

FIGURE 7.8   Two representations of the heart. The sinus node that receives
neural impulses for regulating contractions of the cardiac muscle is
shown in the top diagram. The bottom diagram illustrates an
external view of the heart emphasizing its valves.

relation to the cardiovascular system. Gantt confirmed that the mere approach of a
person influences the heart rate in the dog, as does actual petting. Other research
shows that when we speak to someone and when deaf people sign to communicate
with each other, blood pressure also rises. Apparently psychophysiological systems
used for communication interact with the heart to produce changes in blood pressure.

   The Heart as an Endocrine Gland.   Recent research has indicated that in addition
to being a pump, the heart also functions as an endocrine gland. It secretes a peptide
hormone called **atrial natriuretic factor (ANF).** Once ANF enters the bloodstream,

it is distributed widely throughout the body where it contributes to the regulation of blood pressure and blood volume. ANF also functions in the excretion of water, sodium, and potassium.

In addition, ANF affects various brain regions, including the hypothalamus, as well as the pituitary gland, lungs, liver, small intestine, adrenal glands, kidneys, and the vascular system. Of special interest is the finding that ANF relaxes the smooth muscle cells of blood vessels and inhibits the secretion of aldosterone. (Aldosterone is a hormone secreted by the adrenal glands that tends to raise blood pressure.) We are just on the verge of better understanding how ANF interacts with other systems throughout the body. Perhaps future research will establish ANF as an effective agent for lowering blood pressure in individuals who are hypertensive.

We are now ready to enlarge on our previous presentation of the endocrine system in Chapter 4.

GLANDS AND HORMONES

We have seen how striated muscle effectors affect the external environment through the manipulation of limbs as well as in other ways. Also, we have noted how contraction of smooth muscle affects internal organs of the body, such as regulating the size of such openings as the anal sphincter. Glands are effectors that affect the body by secreting various chemicals that affect overt and covert behavior in their own ways.

Endocrine and Exocrine Glands

To review, endocrine glands discharge their chemical secretions (hormones) into the bloodstream, while exocrine glands secrete their substances to the surface or into a cavity of the body. There are hundreds of hormones in the human body. Examples of exocrine glands are the liver which secretes bile, sweat (sebaceous) glands which secrete sweat and oil to the surface of the body, and lachrymal glands which secrete tears to the inside of the eyelids to lubricate the eyes.

The dermatologist Babba Nicholson has implicated the sebaceous glands as important contributors to the human emotion of "love." They secrete a substance, he said, called sebum in particularly large quantities on the scalp, face, neck, female nipples, and breasts—apparently, sebum is a chemical that lovers seek in each other by kissing. The passion of courtship, he holds, generates heat that releases torrents of sebum. By generating in each other an increase in sebum secretion rate, individuals develop feelings of love. This would be an instance of a positive feedback system wherein the more sebum one lover generates the more is developed in the other and vice versa. One could hypothesize that the eventual loss of control typical of positive feedback systems could help explain some of the bizarre behaviors of lovers.

Information Processing in the Endocrine System

We have seen how neurons function for communication and integration of various systems of the body. For instance, information is encoded at a source, such as a nucleus in the brain, then dispatched and transmitted along neural communication channels to destinations for decoding (see Fig. 1.3). Similarly, numerous secreted substances also serve for communication in both the nervous and endocrine systems; for example, the **neuroendocrine cell** secretes chemical signals that are distributed widely throughout the body. When the secreted substances function on glands, they are called hormones. But when the same substances function with neurons, they are called neurotransmitters. For example, epinephrine is a neurotransmitter substance secreted by the adrenal glands into the bloodstream where it activates (excites or inhibits) many sympathetic nervous system target organs. But epinephrine also functions as a hormone to increase blood flow to the striated muscles, brain, and liver for meeting emergency situations.

Hormones are chemicals that are excreted by a gland and transmitted through the circulatory (including lymphatic) systems to influence organs of the body.

When an endocrine signal reaches a target cell, specific receptor molecules there recognize the signal, decode it, and act on it. When a message encoded as a neural signal reaches a neuroendocrine cell, it is re-coded into chemical signals by means of the release of neurotransmitters. The neurotransmitters are then decoded by postsynaptic cells.

The neuroendocrine systems also function according to cybernetic circuit principles. For example, the hypothalamus secretes the hormone TRF (thyrotropin releasing factor) that regulates the secretion of the hormone thyrotropin from the anterior pituitary gland. When the anterior pituitary gland releases thyrotropin, it causes the thyroid gland to release thyroid hormones into the bloodstream. When the thyroid hormone level rises to a sufficient level, there is feedback to decrease the production of thyrotropin. Hence the amount of thyroid hormone is regulated within definite limits, an example of homeostasis.

Neuroendocrine cells secrete hormones that are transmitted by the circulatory system to influence glands and neural tissue. They have slow, diffuse, and long-lasting effects throughout the body.

Hormones, the chemicals excreted by ductless glands, are transmitted through the circulatory and lymphatic systems in complex feedback circuits whereby many organs of the body are influenced. Some hormones mainly influence peripheral mechanisms, while others mainly influence the central nervous system. When carried by the circulatory system throughout the body, the effects are diffuse with slow onset compared to those of neural conduction. The effects of hormones last longer too, in that they are not turned off immediately.

The secretion of TRF by the hypothalamus and its interactions are examples of how the endocrine system functions according to cybernetic circuit principles.

Although negative feedback circuits function for both neural and endocrine systems, the regulation of hormones is much slower.

EMPHASIS ON A CYBERNETIC PRINCIPLE— THE INTEGRATED USE OF FEEDBACK AND FEEDFORWARD IN THE CONTROL OF BEHAVIOR

A compromise theory incorporating both peripheral closed-circuit feedback and central open-circuit control systems uses both sensory feedback and feedforward information. The feedforward control system includes downward discharges of neural impulses from the central (CNS) to the periphery of the body that would direct certain responses such as saccadic eye movements. The feedforward control system could include central circuits within the brain that monitor sensory feedback. The central system could also alter later feedforward information to modify it in accordance with sensory feedback. For instance, anticipatory timing of responses could be controlled by a central system wherein the feedforward information would be modified if necessary. Later sensory feedback from muscles could indicate that even such a corrected movement is in error. The central system would then be

A compromise position between peripheral and central theories is that feedback from the periphery may be used intermittently to report on the progress of a movement and possibly to adjust an ongoing motor program.

activated to correct the error by modifying feedforward information. Consider the following example.

In visuomotor coordination, we project an arm toward a visually perceived object to handle it. The trajectory of the limb is the variable to be controlled. Visual input to a central visuomotor control system perceives the target whereupon it generates motor commands. These central motor commands are translated by a motoneuronal network (one that involves motor areas of the brain, the cerebellum, etc.) into patterns of efferent discharges. These efferent discharges then activate muscles to move the limb. There follows continuous proprioceptive feedback from movements of the muscles to the spinal cord that contains motoneuronal networks. Those motoneuronal networks located in the spinal cord function to receive that feedback and send information to the brain. Further limb movements may then be modified if necessary so that the limb grasps the target object. In such a way both feedforward and feedback may work together.

We have seen that theories of motor control have been based on central and peripheral mechanisms. In an extensive review of the relevant data, Gentner (1987) concludes that the data do support a composite model of motor control in which performance is determined by both central and peripheral mechanisms. Motor performance, he concludes, is inseparable from perceptual and cognitive processes, the physical properties of the body, and the environmental context of the task. As he put it, "it is now generally recognized . . . that normal motor behavior is based on a collaboration of perceptual, cognitive, and memory processes in the brain, reflexes and pattern generators in the spinal cord, and sensory input" (p. 255). This conclusion fits well with a biopsychological cybernetic model.

ENRICHMENT MATERIAL

The Energy for Muscular Contraction

Muscle tissue is about 75 percent water, 20 percent protein (actin, myosin, etc.), and 5 percent nonprotein organics and minerals. Some of the nonprotein organics, such as adenosine triphosphate (ATP), phosphocreatine, creatine, and urea contain nitrogen.

How chemical energy is converted to cause the mechanical contraction of muscles is extremely complex, and not completely understood. Some of what we do know follows.

The ultimate source of energy for metabolism in any cell is oxidation of a carbohydrate such as glycogen to produce carbon dioxide and water. But the immediate source of energy for muscular contraction is the high-energy phosphate compound ATP. The breakdown of ATP provides the energy for actin and myosin to interact.

When an efferent neural impulse leads to the release of acetylcholine (ACh) at the neuromuscular junction, the ACh increases the permeability of the sarcolemma to calcium ions. The calcium ions catalyze the breakdown of ATP to ADP (adenosine diphosphate) whereupon energy is released. The release of energy seems to activate the bridges between the actin and myosin filaments leading to contraction.

ATP is constantly being used when muscles contract. It is replaced by phosphocreatine through normal metabolism. Phosphocreatine is a compound that occurs only in muscle tissue. It consists of creatine attached to a phosphate group and gives up its phosphate to ADP whereupon ATP is formed.

ATP is stored in muscle cells and supplies the energy for reformation of phosphocreatine. ATP is synthesized from adenosine and phosphate that comes from foods that enter the cell. The energy for synthesizing ATP in muscle cells comes from the breakdown of carbohydrates such as glucose, which comes from glycogen, which is stored in muscle tissue and the liver.

The metabolic source for ATP is glucose along with carbon dioxide and water.

During relaxation of muscle, the events that led to contraction are reversed. Calcium ions return to the sarcolemma and the interaction between myosin and actin is inhibited by troponin. During contraction, calcium ions interact with the muscle protein troponin whereupon troponin loses its inhibiting power. But when a muscle fiber is not contracting, troponin prevents the myosin and actin from interacting.

Striated Muscle Fibers and Cybernetic Circuits

The annulo sensory endings in the intrafusal muscle fibers actually detect the *difference* between the length of intrafusal and extrafusal muscle spindles. That output constitutes the error signal in a negative feedback circuit. But since a negative feedback system lacks the capability of accumulating errors over time, feedback from intrafusal muscle fibers has only immediate effects within the muscle system. Still, when such error signals are transmitted to and from the brain, they may also function for adaptive control. Adaptive control adjustments do not produce immediate output, but they can change the way the control system responds on its next response. Thus, adaptive controllers may use negative feedback in a slow, cumulative fashion. In such a way, negative feedback circuits involving intrafusal and extrafusal muscle fibers may also function with adaptive control systems. They may do this by furnishing information to a central adaptive controller that may accumulate error information. That information could then affect future responding. This is but one of many complex interactions among different kinds of cybernetic control systems.

KEY TERMS

Adenosine triphosphate (ATP)—A high-energy phosphate compound that provides energy for muscular contraction and neural impulses.

Angstrom unit—A unit equal to one ten-thousandth of a micron, a micron being one one-millionth of a meter. It is employed in specifying the wavelength of light and is symbolized as Å.

Annulo spiral ending—A muscle sensory receptor wrapped about an intrafusal muscle fiber that sends information to the CNS.

Ataxia—Inability to coordinate voluntary muscular movements.

Atrial natriuretic factor (ANF)—A peptide hormone secreted by the heart that relaxes the smooth muscle cells of blood vessels and inhibits the secretion of aldosterone.

Ballistic movements—Rapid overt and covert movements made by the striated muscles that start with an initial burst of energy and continue without feedback.

Central control system—Transmits feedforward information from the brain to produce a response with no return information about the status of the response being necessary.

Closed-circuit system—A negative feedback, self-regulating system that compensates by making changes according to the amount of deviation from the reference criterion. Sensory feedback from muscles to the brain functions to guide ongoing behaviors, according to this theory.

Continuously controlled (pursuit) movements—Continuously controlled overt and covert movements made by the striated muscles that rely on feedback from peripheral receptors.

Deafferentation—The process of attempting to sever all nerve fibers from the muscles and joints to the motor centers of the brain. The purpose is to study the behavior of an organism and its subsequent competence in carrying out complex behaviors.

End plate potential (EPP)—Electrical potential that develops on membranes of muscle fibers when acetylcholine is released from terminal buttons at the myoneural junction.

Extrafusal muscle fibers—Exist in striated muscles; their lengthening is monitored by intrafusal muscle fibers that send sensory feedback information to the spinal cord and then to the brain.

Fovea—The region in the back of the retina where vision is sharpest.

Intrafusal muscle fibers (muscle spindles)—Highly specialized sensory receptors that monitor the extrafusal muscle fiber length and send that information to the CNS.

Intercalated disc—Material in the gap junctions connecting fibers of cardiac muscle.

Knowledge of results (KR)—Information from the environment (as in reinforcement) that results from muscular contractions when one is striving to reach a goal.

Latency—The time between the onset of a stimulus to the onset of a response.

Lemniscal system—Composed of large neural fibers that ascend the dorsal region of the spinal cord to reach the medulla.

Motor image—A reference criterion of a good response. By comparing an ongoing response with the motor image, a person is provided with knowledge of results informing how correct movements are at any given time.

Motor unit—The functional unit of skeletal musculature. It consists of a cell body in the spinal cord, its axon, and the muscle fibers. All of the muscle fibers innervated by a single motor neuron contract as an integrated unit.

Myoneural (neuromuscular) junction—The synapse between a motor neuron and the sarcolemma of a muscle.

Myosin—An enzyme that acts on adenosine triphosphate (ATP) to liberate energy for muscle and neural activity.

Neuroendocrine cell—A cell that secretes chemical signals that are distributed widely throughout the body.

Open-circuit system—A system in which control is by feedforward and not feedback.

Proprioceptors—Those receptors that are sensitive to and signal changes in positions of the body.

Pyramidal system—The large group of motor neurons that originates in the cerebral cortex, passes down through the medulla, where about 85 percent decussate, and continues downward to terminate in the ventral horns of the spinal cord.

Reaction time (complex)—The time required to respond to one of two stimuli wherein a decision is required.

Reaction time (simple)—The time required to respond to a single stimulus (without a requirement to "decide" whether or when to react).

Sarcolemma—The surrounding membrane of a muscle cell.

Sarcoplasm—The cytoplasm of a muscle cell.

Vestibulo-ocular reflex—A reflex that uses feedforward control to help stabilize a retinal image as the head moves.

Vestibulo-spinal reflex—A reflex that helps to maintain a person's head in a stable orientation when in motion so as to maintain a stable retinal image. It employs a closed-circuit system with feedback.

STUDY QUESTIONS

1. Explain how muscle fiber contraction occurs.
2. Describe what is meant by "functional unit of striated muscle" and of what the motor unit consists.
3. How does the body move and how are joint receptors activated when muscles contract?
4. T or F. Relaxation can be produced by active neural impulses.
5. Discuss interactions between the brain and the skeletal muscles.
6. Give an example of a ballistic movement.
7. T or F. An open-circuit system does not use feedback to correct errors.
8. What is a motor image?
9. T or F. In fast ballistic movements, feedforward control is usually considered the dominant mode of control.
10. Discuss Lashley's point of view about the classical associative chain theory.
11. Name the three principal ways in which we communicate verbal information.
12. Summarize some data relevant to closed vs. open loop systems.
13. T or F. The heart cannot continue to beat regularly if the nerve supply from the autonomic nervous system is removed.
14. Discuss an interaction in the body between the act of communicating and the level of blood pressure; that is, discuss how blood pressure is affected by the act of expressive communication.

FURTHER READINGS

You can browse through a library in the area of physiological psychology to find such books as Carlson's *Physiology of Behavior* (1991).

The following are two excellent advanced treatments of muscular contraction:

Merton, P. A. (1972). How we control the contraction of our muscles. *Scientific American, 226,* 30–37.

Hibberd, M. G., & Trentham, D. R. (1986). Relationships between chemical and mechanical events during muscular contraction. *Annual Review of Biophysics and Biophysical Chemistry, 15,* 119–161.

CHAPTER 8

Methods of Studying Systems
of the Body and Brain

MAJOR PURPOSE:	To survey the techniques and methods used in biological psychology and related fields.
WHAT YOU ARE GOING TO FIND:	1. The major methods used in psychophysiology to study covert and overt processes. 2. Methods of studying the brain.
WHAT YOU SHOULD ACQUIRE:	1. An understanding of how we sense, amplify, record, and quantify events generated by systems of the body. 2. An understanding of the major methods for acquiring knowledge about how the brain functions. 3. An appreciation for the importance of the development of apparatus and research methods for the advancement of knowledge.

CHAPTER OUTLINE

OVERVIEW OF BIOBEHAVIORAL PHENOMENA
AND RESEARCH TECHNIQUES

The essence of our approach is to understand how the systems of the body and brain function and how they interact to generate behavior. When the receptors, brain, muscles, visceral organs, and so on interact by means of cybernetic circuits, a wide variety of psychological phenomena are generated, as elaborated throughout this book. These psychological phenomena include overt behavior that interacts with the external environment, as well as cognitive events such as dreams, thoughts, hallucinations, and images. When some system of the body becomes aberrant, we can develop two general categories of psychopathological phenomena: psychiatric disorders (phobias, depression, anxiety states, etc.) and somatoform (psychosomatic) disorders (headaches, ulcers, high blood pressure, etc.). In order to advance our understanding of how the body generates such phenomena, we must focus on the ways in which we acquire knowledge of these various systems.

As bodily systems interact through cybernetic circuits, overt behavior and cognitive events are generated. These include normal and abnormal (psychiatric and psychosomatic) phenomena.

New Research Techniques Can Lead to Great Advances in Knowledge. The effective use and advancement of our research methods will always be one of our top priorities. Many times in the history of science gigantic leaps forward in the acquisition of knowledge have come with the development of new kinds of apparatus and/or methods of research. With the invention of the microscope by Antoni van Leeuwenhoek in 1673, new worlds were opened up. When we were able to observe the microorganisms that live within us, the consequences for physiology (and therefore for medicine) were immeasurable. Yet those advances were dwarfed in comparison with the later development of the electron microscope, revealing even more miniscule events in the microcosm. The atom used to be viewed as but a mathematical concept lacking physical reality, but we now have pictures of it. What would van Leeuwenhoek think of the advances made since his invention of the primitive microscope? What would Galileo think of the magnificent astronomical observation instruments of today, relative to his crude use of the early telescope to "spy on God's heavens"? The possibilities for new methodological advances yet to come may well stagger our own imaginations.

Major advances in the acquisition of knowledge often come with the invention of new kinds of apparatus and scientific techniques.

There have been a host of technological breakthroughs in the last few decades that have impacted the area of biological psychology. We now have computerized axial tomography (CAT) scanners that provide intimate pictures of the brain and other regions of the body. There is magnetic resonance imaging (MRI spectroscopy), which uses magnetic field and radio frequency energy to determine the chemical structure of an object and provides a three-dimensional image of it; with this technique we can study minute structures and the metabolism of the brain. Laser beams now allow us to look into (and affect) internal regions of the body with amazing precision and detail. Such important methodological advances will no doubt help us to learn much, much more about how we are structured and how we function. Before taking up some of these advanced techniques, however, let us first consider some more traditional measures used in biological psychology. To do this we need to enlarge on our distinction between overt and covert behavior.

OVERT AND COVERT BEHAVIOR CONTRASTED

The goal of psychology is to understand all behavior (Fig. 8.1). Psychologists, in placing primary emphasis on overt behavior (e.g., waving the hand, speaking aloud), have been impressive in their ability to develop relationships (laws) between overt response patterns (R) and external environmental events (S, stimuli). These are

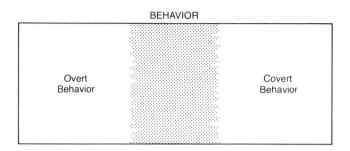

FIGURE 8.1
The realm of behavior as a continuous dimension delineating overt (large) and covert (small) responses with a "twilight zone" between them.

the familiar S–R laws. Some theories about covert behavior (e.g., a slight thumb twitch, the brief contraction of a small muscle in the tongue, an increase in cardiac rate) were developed in the early part of the century, but the technology for studying small-scale responses was simply not available.

Psychology Turns to an Emphasis on Covert Behavior. With the development of the vacuum tube (a predecessor of today's computer chips) in the 1920s, more sensitive psychophysiological measurement techniques became possible. In particular it became possible to electrically study muscles and the brain. This has led to impressive progress in the understanding of covert reactions. As psychology has vigorously turned to the study of covert reactions, we can expect much greater understanding of the internal world of the body.

Behavior may be overt, readily observable without apparatus, or covert, not readily observable with the naked eye, and thus requires specialized apparatus for its observation.

Some events, such as a slight whisper (subvocalization), a partial blink of the eyes, or an arrested nod of the head fall within a "twilight zone" between overt and covert behaviors (see Fig. 8.1). However, the fact that specialized apparatus is required for the observation of such behaviors does not mean that they differ in kind from large-scale, overt behaviors. Overt and covert behaviors are the same in that they both involve activation of effectors, which are usually muscular contractions. The task of psychology is to understand behavior—all behavior—regardless of whether the response is a large or a small muscular contraction. To accomplish this task, we must concentrate a great deal of our energy on that subrealm of behavior that is covert. The frequent reference in the psychological literature to covert behavior and to similar terms such as *implicit response, subvocalization, silent speech,* and *inner speech* attests to the historical and contemporary importance of these covert events. Our long-term goal is to more thoroughly develop the concepts and principles that will constitute a mature science of covert processes and, hence, a more complete science than one built merely on overt behavior.

The use of numerous terms for covert behavior by many different psychologists attests to the importance of this behavioral subrealm.

The Study of Covert Processes Requires Laboratory Equipment. There is no problem, of course, in observing overt responses—difficulties arise only insofar as recording and measurement techniques are concerned. Covert events, on the other hand, can be observed only through the use of equipment that extends the scope of our senses. That magnification is required in order to observe phenomena is, of course, not unusual. We have developed numerous kinds of apparatus that allow us to detect events that could not otherwise be studied. The microscope and the telescope are obvious examples. They serve to emphasize that covert processes are in no sense mystical simply because they must be amplified for study. We first review how we measure overt behavior, then turn to covert events.

OVERT RESPONSE MEASURES

Overt response measures are an extremely broad class that includes such diverse phenomena as the number of errors a rat makes in a maze, the time it takes a person to solve a problem, the number of words spoken in a given period of time, the accuracy of throwing a baseball, and judgments on scales about personality traits. Whatever the response, it is best to measure it as precisely as possible. In some research great precision can be achieved, while in other research the characteristics of the events studied dictate cruder measures. Here are some standard ways of measuring overt responses:

Overt response measures include those of response accuracy, latency, duration, frequency (rate) and amplitude.

    1. *Accuracy.* One measure of response accuracy uses a numerical system. For example, when we throw darts at a target, a hit in the bull's-eye might be scored a five, in the next outer circle a three, and in the outer circle a one. Frequency of successes or errors is another response measure of accuracy, as in the number of baskets that one makes from the free throw line on a basketball court or the number of blind alleys a rat enters while running a maze.

    2. *Latency.* **Latency** is the time that it takes from the introduction of a stimulus to the *beginning* (the actual start) of a response. **Reaction time,** like latency, is the time interval between the *onset* of a stimulus and the *onset* of a response. One difference is that reaction time is measured as an intentional overt response; while latency may be measured as a tissue reaction, such as in a brain event produced by a flash of light.

    3. *Duration.* This is a measure of how long it takes to complete a response once it has started. The time measure would be quite short for pressing a telegraph key. But for solving a difficult problem, the time measure would be longer. To emphasize the distinction between latency and duration measures: Latency is the time between the onset of the stimulus and the onset of the response, while duration is the time between the onset of the response and its termination.

    4. *Frequency and rate.* Frequency is a measure of the number of times a response occurs (e.g., the number of responses an organism makes before a response is extinguished). If the number (frequency) of responses made within a given period of time is divided by that time unit, the rate of responding is computed. If ten responses are made in one minute, the rate of responding is ten responses per minute. The rate gives an indication of the probability of the response—the higher the rate, the greater the probability that it will occur in a similar situation at some future time. Response rate is often used in experiments in operant conditioning. For example, an organism is placed in an operant conditioning chamber (a "Skinner box") and each depression of a lever is automatically recorded on a moving strip of paper. B. F. Skinner thought that the use of response rate as a dependent variable was one of his most important achievements.

    5. *Response amplitude.* The force (intensity) of an act can be measured as an index of amplitude (magnitude). For instance, the intensity with which a rat presses a bar in a Skinner box, the number of drops (and thus amount) of saliva a dog secretes at the sight of food, and the amplitude of the galvanic skin response in a conditioning study are measures of response amplitude.

    Additional Overt Response Measures. Sometimes it is difficult to adequately measure the dependent variable with any of these techniques. In this event one might devise a rating scale, such as one for anxiety that contains five gradations: 5 = extremely anxious, 4 = moderately anxious, and so on. Competent judges would then mark the appropriate position on the scale for each participant. The participants could even rate themselves. Another response measure could be level of ability that a person manifests (e.g., how many problems of increasing difficulty are solved with an unlimited amount of time).

Objective tests can also serve as overt response measures. For example, if you want to know whether psychotherapy decreases a person's neurotic tendencies, you might administer a standardized test of neuroticism. If a suitable standardized test is not available, you might construct your own, as one student did in developing a "Happiness Scale." In Chapter 10 we further discuss overt response measures when we study learning and memory.

COVERT PROCESSES

Covert processes are divided into effector and central nervous system reactions. This separation of response and central nervous system reactions emphasizes that these two classes of events are quite different phenomena.

We have emphasized that major information processing systems of the body include the receptor, nervous, and effector systems. We have further emphasized the interaction of components of these systems such as the brain, the striated muscles, the cardiovascular system, the gastrointestinal system, and various glandular phenomena. All of these systems yield electrical signals when they are active. In Table 8.1, we specify the covert processes electrically generated by these systems, which we now discuss in greater detail.

Responses Differ from Brain Reactions. The primary division in Table 8.1 is between I. responses (muscular and glandular events) and II. neurophysiological processes. Striated muscle responses are best measured electrically through **electromyography (EMG)** (*myo* means "muscle" and *graph* means "to record"). Brain

TABLE 8.1 Psychophysiologically Measured Covert Processes in Humans

---

I. Covert responses (consist of, and only of, muscular and glandular events)
    A. Covert speech (oral) responses
        1. Skeletal muscle electromyographic measures, principally from the tongue, lips, chin, laryngeal region, and jaw
        2. Pneumograms
        3. Audio measures of subvocalization ("slight whispering")
    B. Covert nonoral responses
        1. Skeletal muscle electromyographic measures from the fingers, arm, leg, etc.
        2. Visceral muscle activity (electrogastrogram)
        3. Eye responses, principally the electrooculogram
        4. Cardiovascular measures
            a. Heart rate
            b. Electrocardiogram
            c. Finger pulse volume
            d. Blood pressure
        5. Electrodermal measures (galvanic skin response, skin conductance, etc.)
II. Neurophysiological Processes
    In the normal human, electrical activity is studied and recorded through electroencephalography and often further processed to yield evoked potentials and the contingent negative variation (see p. 236).

---

events are often studied through **electroencephalography (EEG)** (*enceph* means "brain"). Although we use similar electrical methods for studying them, responses obey different laws than do neural events. For an obvious example, muscle fibers move, but neurons do not. Moving muscle fibers and stationary neurons that fire are two different kinds of events. They do, however, interact within neuromuscular circuits according to cybernetic principles. How they interact constitutes a major question that repeatedly comes up throughout this book.

A Taxonomy of Covert Events. The speech (oral) responses, the first major classification of responses (I.A. in Table 8.1), are distinguished from the nonoral bodily areas (I.B.). Most data on covert speech behavior have been gathered through electromyographic recording (I.A. 1). When we process language, for example, when we subvocalize during silent reading, the tongue is the most active region; the lips appear to be next in terms of activity, and although they still respond during subvocalization, the jaw, chin, and laryngeal regions are relatively insensitive. We briefly mention these covert processes here and will enlarge on most of them later.

Pneumograms B (I.A. 2), recorded with a **pneumograph,** are important measures of covert speech behavior (e.g., breathing rate increases when voices are heard during auditory hallucinations). Examples of audio measures of subvocalization (I.A. 3), including highly amplified sounds from the mouth, allow us to understand portions of the text that children silently read and the verbal content of a paranoid schizophrenic's auditory hallucinations (see Chapter 13).

Measures of covert, nonoral responses (I.B. in Table 8.1) during cognition yield such information as covert electromyographic finger activity in deaf individuals that tells us something about their thought processes (see Chapter 13).

Various neurophysiological measures (II) help advance our understanding of the function of the brain during thought. One major advance within the last several decades has been the development of signal averaging—a number of electroencephalograms during an experimental treatment are averaged so that it has been possible to "tease out" very interesting neural phenomena. We will shortly discuss two methods of signal averaging, the contingent negative variation and the evoked potential ("expectancy wave").

LABORATORY TECHNIQUES FOR MEASURING COVERT PROCESSES

Four Components of a Laboratory. There are four essential features of an electropsychology laboratory for the study of covert processes: (1) **sensors,** devices that detect the electrical signals generated by the body; (2) **amplifiers,** which increase the amplitude of the signals sensed; (3) **readout devices,** (e.g., computers) which display and record the signals; and (4) **quantification systems,** which render the signals into numerical values.

Figure 8.2 shows these four major components of a psychophysiological laboratory. Sensors are placed on a subject in a room that contains special metallic shielding in the walls to shield out stray electrical signals. Such unwanted signals come from sources such as electric lights and the local radio station—the body acts like an antenna to pick up such stray externally generated signals that interfere with the accurate recording of the sensitive electrical signals generated by the body.

The laboratory for the study of covert components of cybernetic circuits includes sensors, powerful amplifiers, readout systems, and quantification systems.

Electrically studied covert processes are sensed, amplified, displayed, and quantified.

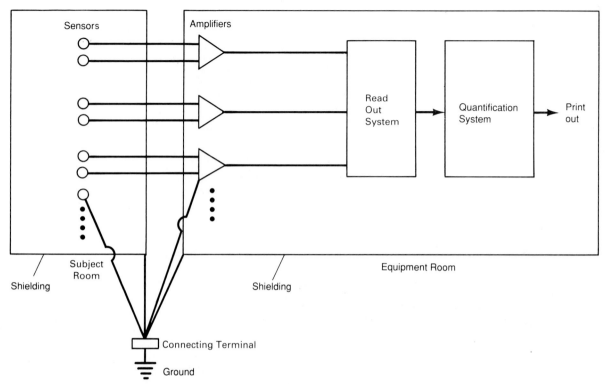

FIGURE 8.2 A laboratory for studying covert processes, emphasizing its four major features: sensors, amplifiers, readout devices (CRO, recorders, etc.), and quantification systems. The shielded rooms, the shielded equipment, and the subject are all connected to a common ground.

Sensors

Electrodes Sense Muscle and Brain Events. Sensors detect the signals listed in Table 8.1 just as a receptor organ such as the eye detects visual stimuli. Both are specialized to be sensitive to a given kind of energy. Consequently, sensors are designed so that each type of receptor detects only certain kinds of events while others are rejected. For instance, the eye will detect visual stimuli but is not sensitive to auditory stimuli. Most sensors in psychophysiology are **electrodes** that sense electrical signals. A pair of electrodes may be fixed on the appropriate location of the body, and a difference in electrical potential between the two electrodes may be detected (Fig. 8.3). (One electrode by itself cannot sense a difference between two locations).

Surface electrodes, attached *on* the skin, are more widely used in normal human psychophysiology than are inserted (wire or needle) electrodes.

A Number of Simultaneous Measurements Should Be Made. More than one pair of electrodes should be attached to the subject, so that measurements may be made simultaneously from a number of bodily locations. Since the entire body is active during thought, single-response recording with only one pair of electrodes is of

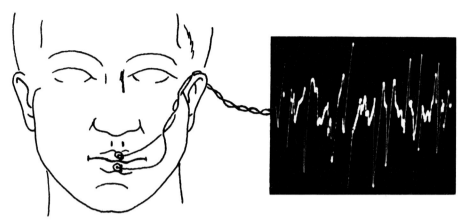

FIGURE 8.3 Two electrodes are required to detect differences in the electrical potential in a region. An electromyographic signal generated by contracting muscles in the lips is illustrated.

limited scientific value. A number of simultaneous measures tell us something about the cybernetic circuits that are active during cognition. Another advantage of multiple electrode placement is that suggestion to the subject is prevented or reduced; that is, if only one set of electrodes is attached in a certain bodily location, the subject would expect that something special should occur there, resulting in biased behavior. Consider, for instance, how you would feel if electrodes were attached only on your lips—there might be excessive "forced" responding or even inhibition of lip behavior. Hence, leg or nonpreferred arm placements are often used as control measures because these areas are not so active during cognition (unless you are doing something like imagining you are running).

It is important to measure the patterns of an individual's reactions throughout the body, rather than a response in only one region.

Amplifiers

Once electrical signals are sensed, they are carried from the subject to a second room to be amplified (see Fig. 8.2). The amplification stage is extremely important because of the small amplitude of covert processes. Important striated muscle responses in the tongue, for instance, may be but 1 microvolt (one one-millionth of a volt) in amplitude, which is infinitesimal compared to the 110 volts (110 million microvolts) in the light circuits of your room (Table 8.2). Extremely sensitive amplifiers, indeed, are required for such measurement—although a covert response may be slight and fleeting, it may be very important in contributing to the generation of a thought.

Readout Systems

Note that the amplified signals are recorded on a direct recorder so that they can be studied as they are "written out" (the readout). An ink-writing polygraph (electroencephalograph) is a frequently used recording system. The signals are simultaneously monitored on a **cathode-ray oscilloscope (CRO),** which is somewhat like your television set (Fig. 8.4). The signals from the amplifiers can also be recorded on a computer disk or on a data tape recorder. The recorded data may then be played

TABLE 8.2 Some Units in Psychophysiology and Their Abbreviations

Unit	Interpretation
Millisecond (ms)	One-thousandth of a second
(e.g., 10 ms)	10 one-thousandths of a second
Microvolt (μv)	One-millionth of a volt
(e.g., 10 μv)	10 one-millionths of a volt
Millivolt (mv)	One-thousandth of a volt
(e.g., 20 mv)	20 one-thousands of a volt

into a readout device such as a computer monitor or an ink-writing polygraph or they may be "frozen" for study on a storage CRO and photographed. Typically these data are analyzed in detail in a computer. The ability to store data adds flexibility in that the experimenter can try a variety of techniques of data analysis, some of which may be suggested only after extended study of the tracings that were recorded on-line. It is important that the readout system allows for the simultaneous recording of a number of different reactions so that their relationships can be studied as components of cybernetic circuits.

FIGURE 8.4 A cathode-ray oscilloscope (CRO) for monitoring transitory psychophysiological signals. (Courtesy of Tektronix Inc., Beaverton, Oregon)

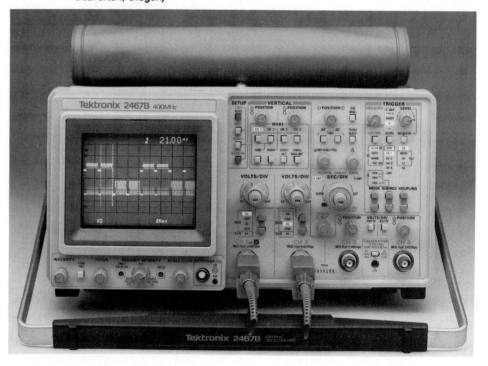

Quantification Systems

Investigations of covert processes may be divided into two general classes: (1) those studying a brief, momentary phenomenon, and (2) those studying sustained, long-term processes. The investigator studying a momentary event is probably most interested in amplitude measures, although other parameters, such as duration and latency, may also be important.

Establishing That a Response Was Caused by a Treatment. The amplitude of the measured event should be compared to some control or baseline value to ascertain whether or not the event occurred reliably; that is, did it consistently occur or was it just an unusual chance occurrence that is not systematically related to the treatment condition (Fig. 8.5). That is, a continuous recording is made during an experimental treatment, such as presenting a flash of light to the subject. We would then expect heightened response values following the presentation of the treatment. But all bodily systems are already continuously changing, regardless of whether or not the treatment is presented. Hence, the experimenter might measure the maximum height of the tracing within a short interval immediately after presentation of the treatment and then compare that amplitude with the maximum value in a temporally equated control (baseline) interval sampled some seconds prior to stimulus presentation. A positive effect would be indicated if values following the treatment were reliably higher (statistically significant, considering a number of trials) than those during the control (baseline) interval. But to establish that a particular treatment caused a particular response, we need to show that the control responses did not change, emphasizing the importance of simultaneous recording of a number of responses. For instance, a flash of light should cause an eye response but would not be expected to affect covert responding in a leg, as illustrated in Figure 8.5.

In the study of longer-term records, signals may be quantified by either amplitude and/or frequency measures, depending on their characteristics. If the signal is cyclical and repetitive, frequency measures are typically used. For example, the pneumogram and electroencephalogram are usually quantified by counting the number of cycles per unit of time; then they are converted to a rate, such as number

Transitory covert responses may be measured by changes in amplitude while long-term events such as cyclical responses are measured in frequencies such as Hz (cycles per second).

FIGURE 8.5 A change of amplitude from baseline in a particular covert response (r_1) following administration of an experimental treatment. The failure of a change to occur in a control measure substantiates that the treatment caused r_2.

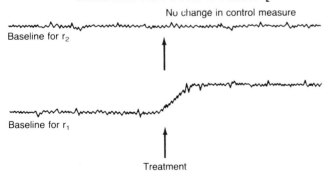

No change in control measure

Baseline for r_2

Baseline for r_1

Treatment

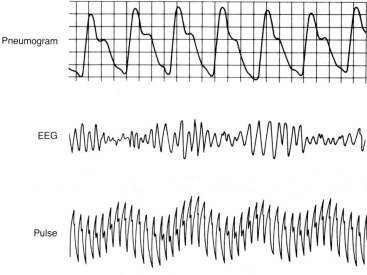

FIGURE 8.6   Records of cyclical signals such as for breathing, brain wave, and pulse can be measured as frequencies and converted to rates.

of respirations per minute or Hz (Fig. 8.6). For instance, frequency of respiration rate for adults is generally 15–19 respirations per minute, but in a well-relaxed individual it may drop much lower.

Simplicity Is Preferable

Everything else being equal, the simpler the laboratory system, the more efficiently the research can be conducted.

Although complex laboratory equipment is necessary for the study of covert processes, the laboratory system should still be kept as simple as possible. Each additional device increases the chance of both instrument and human error. In all research one should use as little apparatus as is reasonable and should never develop equipment that is more complicated than necessary to get the job done. The Law of the Hammer applies well in the laboratory. Like the little boy with a hammer who finds many things that "need" hammering, the scientist with a computer may find many things that needlessly "need" computing. The flip side, though, is that we should not be excessively simple. As Einstein indicated, everything should be made as simple as possible, but not simpler.

ELECTROPSYCHOLOGY— PSYCHOPHYSIOLOGICAL MEASURES OF COVERT (AND OVERT) PROCESSES

This completes our taxonomic overview of some of the principal covert processes that are psychophysiologically measured during cognitive functions. Since electrical components of these covert processes are most prominently sensed, the term *electrophysiology* is frequently used to denote this area of study. However, because we are primarily interested in psychological processes, the term **electropsychology,** used by Ralph Hefferline is more appropriate.

Electropsychology is the electrical study of small-scale covert bodily events.

Electrical measurement of covert processes with these systems has yielded many important findings. Electrical measurement and analysis systems have become increasingly sensitive and versatile for recording of signals generated by the body. As a consequence, the psychophysiological study of covert processes has been progressing exponentially. We now study several of these methods in greater detail.

Electromyography

The record of an action potential given off by contracting muscle fibers (an electromyogram) is the result of changing voltage differences between two electrodes (see Fig. 8.3). The amplitude of a recorded muscle signal is much greater with inserted (needle electrodes or hair-fine insulated wires) than with surface electrodes. A signal of 100 millivolts from within a muscle may be as low as 10 microvolts when sensed by surface electrodes on the skin, due largely to the resistance of the skin.

Electrogastrography

Complex interactions occur in circuits between the viscera and central nervous system for cognitive and other purposes. Visceral activity, such as contractions of the esophagus, intestines, and stomach, is of considerable cognitive importance, adding "emotional tone" to our thoughts. For instance, when we have certain disturbing thoughts we may have an uneasy feeling in the pit of our stomach. Electrical records of smooth muscle activity in the abdomen provide **electrogastrograms (EGG)** (Fig. 8.7). Typically, either a surface or an inserted electrode is affixed to the abdomen and a second electrode is placed at a remote location, such as the forearm. The frequency of smooth muscle activity, such as that in the intestines, is low—less than 1 cycle per second (1 Hz). The amplitude is large, between 0.5 and 80 millivolts at the surface.

A variety of techniques like swallowing a balloon or a magnet have been used for the study of visceral events, although electrical recording techniques are preferable.

A technique for electrical recording from the esophagus uses surface electrodes attached to a "swallowed" balloon. As we develop in Chapter 14, the esophagus contains striated as well as smooth muscle and is clinically important for fear and chronic anxiety.

Covert responses in the striated musculature are recorded by means of electromyography and in visceral smooth muscle by means of electrogastrography.

FIGURE 8.7 An electrogastrogram recorded from surface electrodes over the abdomen.

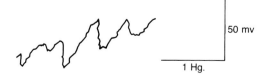

50 mv

1 Hg.

Electrooculography

Historically, techniques such as the "peep-hole" method were used to observe the eyes through a small hole in a screen that separated the subject from the experimenter. Another historical method was to directly attach a small rod to the cornea. The rod was then attached to a readout device to record movements of the eye. Today an optical method is sometimes used such that reflections of a light source onto the cornea are photographically recorded. Another contemporary method mounts small television cameras on each side of spectacles and processes the information by computer. The most sophisticated system is a scanning laser ophthalmoscope, whereby a laser spot scans the eye and produces an image on a monitor. However, electrical methods of registering eye movements are generally used.

Contemporary **electrooculography (EOG)** (*oculo* means eyes) was launched by measuring changes in the electrical potential about the eyes during mental activity (Jacobson, 1930). The relationship between rapid eye movements and dream content has long been recognized (e.g., by George Trumbul Ladd in 1892 and Jacobson, 1938a). But it was electrical measurement of covert processes during dreaming using Jacobson's techniques that has made dream research a major field. This growth was largely brought about by Nathaniel Kleitman and his students, who employed Jacobson's observations and methods. For an extensive summary of the use of electrooculography during waking and sleeping cognitions see McGuigan (1978).

The Source of the EOG. EOG measurements are obtained from electrodes placed just posterior to both eyes so that they are equidistant from the cornea and the central region of the retina (Fig. 8.8). The electrodes sense a signal of approximately 1 mv that originates from a difference in potential between the cornea and the retina. The cornea is relatively positive because the retina has a higher metabolic rate that generates a negative potential. The positive cornea and negative retina constitute an electrical potential difference referred to as the "standing potential," first reported in 1849 by E. Bois-Reymond. When the eyes are active, the eyeballs move between the electrodes. As the standing potential approaches one electrode, that electrical potential changes. Continuous eye movement thus produces changing

Horizontal and vertical electrooculograms (EOGs) may be recorded by placing electrodes posterior to both eyes and superior and inferior to one eye, respectively.

FIGURE 8.8 Placements for electrodes to record eye movements in the horizontal (left) and vertical (right) dimensions.

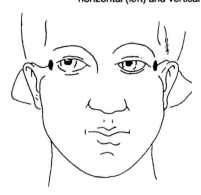
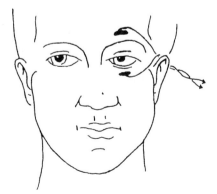

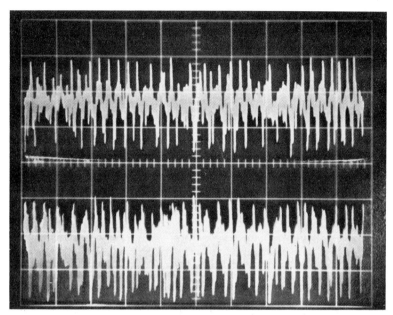

FIGURE 8.9 An electrooculogram recorded from a horizontal eye placement when the subject was reading. Each cycle indicates reading of a line. When finished with one line, the eyes move to the next as indicated by the start of a new cycle. The top trace was for a child before a reading rate improvement course; the lower trace was taken at the course's conclusion.

potential differences between the two electrodes. Measurements of these variations in electrical potential constitute signals that may be led into amplifiers and recorded (Fig. 8.9).

Electrical signals result not only from changes in the EOG standing potential between the cornea and the retina, but also from numerous small saccadic movements and grosser movements that can be directly observed. Eye movements may be very small and fast (30 to 70 times each second), large oscillatory movements, slow drifts, or rapid jerks. But whatever their characteristic, they represent important visual information, especially for cognition (see Chapter 13).

Pneumography

Sensitive respiration measures can yield valuable covert speech data because of the intimate participation of the breathing mechanism in speech activity. The source of the respiratory signal is the change in lung capacity that is produced by contraction and relaxation of the intercostal (chest) and abdominal muscles.

A pneumograph measures amplitude and frequency of breathing.

A simple pneumograph involves the placement of a rubber bellows ("tube") about the chest. On inhaling air, the bellows stretches so that air pressure in it increases. On exhaling, the bellows expands and pressure decreases. The variations in air pressure act on a sensitive rubber diaphragm that can direct an attached ink pen on a recorder. The pressure variations may also be transduced (changed) to electrical signals that can be entered into an amplifier and recorded (see Fig. 8.6).

There are various other pneumographic arrangements, such as positioning a heat sensor (a thermistor) below the nose to sense the temperature of the air exhaled. As the heat status of the thermistor changes according to whether air is being inhaled or exhaled, a signal from the thermistor may be transduced to an electrical signal and recorded.

Electrocardiography

Early electrode procedures developed for recording **electrocardiograms (ECGs or EKGs)** required subjects to sit with their hands and feet in saline- (salt) filled buckets. An early improvement over this cumbersome bucket procedure was to wrap large metal electrodes in saline-soaked bandages that were applied to the skin. Modern equipment for recording ECGs uses standard electrodes and the nature of the substance between them and the skin seems irrelevant: Mayonnaise, mustard, tomato paste, hand creams, and tooth pastes have been used to produce electrocardiograms that are indistinguishable from those made with regular electrode jelly (McGuigan, 1979).

The electrocardiograph measures the complex activity of the heart, which includes P-waves, Q-waves, R-waves, S-waves, and T-waves.

Changes in the electrical potential associated with heartbeat provide the signal for ECGs. This electrical activity is transmitted over the entire body so that the signal may be sensed at distant locations. A standard placement for electrodes to sense the signal is illustrated in Figure 8.10. The signal is transmitted by leads (wires) to the electrocardiograph, which records and analyzes the electrical activity. Five waves are distinguishable in the typical electrocardiogram: a P-wave, Q-wave, R-wave, S-wave, T-wave (Fig. 8.11). Variations in the parameters of these waves constitute dependent variable measures in scientific studies and they also have clinical significance for diagnosing cardiac abnormalities.

FIGURE 8.10   One placement of electrodes for leads to record an electrocardiogram.

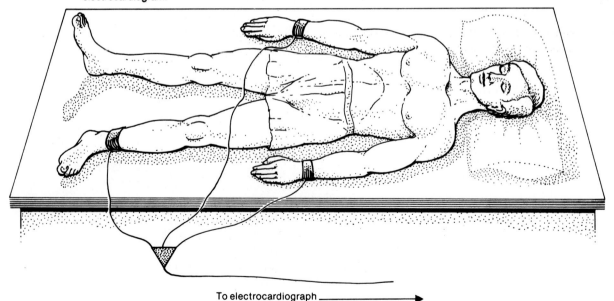

To electrocardiograph ⟶

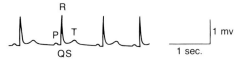

FIGURE 8.11 A typical electrocardiogram illustrating five component waves: P, Q, R, S, T.

Clinical Applications. The ECG is clinically useful in the diagnosis of various kinds of heart disease. For instance, coronary thrombosis, which is a clot in a coronary artery, may produce damage to the muscle of the heart. It may be diagnosed by an S–T interval that is longer or shorter than normal. Abnormal rhythms of the heart (arrhythmias) include tachycardia, wherein the heart beats too rapidly; bradycardia, slow heart rate; and fibrillation, which is characterized by small regions of the heart beating weakly and independently of each other. No blood is pumped by the heart during fibrillation, so that death usually follows. There are some preliminary data that suggest that the amplitude of the T-wave is somewhat predictive of coronary heart disease.

Blood pressure is a clinically useful measure for heart and other diseases. Since blood pressure is often taken by individuals at home, it may be instructive to specify the correct procedure, which often is not followed (see Enrichment Material, p. 250).

Electrodermal Methods

Electrodermal activity (EDA) refers to the electrical activity of the skin sensed by electrodes placed on the palms of the hands and on the fingers. The electrical activity is generated by a particular kind of sweat gland, an *eccrine* gland, located in those regions. Eccrine sweat glands are innervated by the sympathetic branch of the autonomic nervous system. Consequently, the amount of activity of the sympathetic nervous system determines the number of sweat glands activated and the degree to which sweat rises in them toward the surface of the skin. Regardless of whether or not sweat actually reaches the surface, when the eccrine glands are activated, there is a measurable change in EDA. As a consequence of sympathetic nervous system activity, the eccrine sweat glands provide a measure of emotional states and other psychological conditions. In contrast, other kinds of sweat glands in the body respond more to temperature increases.

The term **galvanic skin response (GSR)** was used in the past to refer to various aspects of electrical skin activity, but EDA has now replaced the term for several technical reasons that need not detain us. Another measure is that of skin resistance, sometimes made and reported as skin conductance (SC).

Electroencephalography

A Bit of History. Our major source of information about neurophysiological activity in the normal human derives from electrical reactions recorded from the surface of the skull. The first tracings of electrical activity from the human skull were published by Hans Berger (1929), although he had difficulty in finding acceptance by the scientific community for his conclusions. Neurophysiologists of the day were reluctant to think that any events other than the well-known spike potentials occurred in the nervous systems. Acceptance of the slow alpha potentials (see the electroencephalogram in Fig. 8.6) occurred only when confirmed in 1934 by Adrian and Matthews, no doubt also aided by the prestige that Lord Adrian added to the cause. Even then those who did accept that the signals were generated by the brain regarded them as rather dull because the alpha frequencies were so constant that they could not be indicative of momentary thoughts.

Classifications of EEGs.   Brain waves have been classified primarily by their frequency range, in large part because the amplitude values are so variable. (The amplitude of EEG signals is usually within 1–100 microvolts at the surface of the scalp, although it may reach as high as 500 microvolts.) Frequency ranges for various brain wave classes are presented in Table 8.3. Theta rhythms apparently appear earliest in humans and are recordable during the first year of life. Basic alpha rhythms emerge during the second or third year, but the faster components of alpha frequencies usually do not appear until about the seventh or eighth year of life.

What Generates Brain Waves?   The principles by which some 12–15 billion cerebral neurons generate the various brain waves are still not adequately understood, although we are making good progress in studying them. Because brain events are so complex, we still have a long way to go to understand them.

It is commonly (although not universally) accepted that the electrical signals originate in cerebral tissue. As with electromyograms, the skin is the main source of resistance when using surface electrodes to sense potential difference. In both, skin resistance may be reduced by applying a special jelly and removing the dead cells of the skin. Inserting electrodes just below the skin, a common and not painful procedure, obviously avoids the problem of skin resistance.

Changes in electrical potential tend to concentrate in specific regions of the brain (e.g., alpha frequencies are greatest in the occipital lobe); consequently, alpha amplitudes decrease with distance from the occipital region. Since electrical potentials differ according to brain region, it is common to place a number of electrodes on

We do not understand exactly how brain waves are generated, but the consensus is that they originate in cerebral tissue and are concentrated in specific brain regions.

TABLE 8.3   Classes of Electroencephalograms Defined by Their Frequency Ranges

Brain Wave Class	Frequency
Sub-Delta	0–0.5 Hz
Delta	0.5–4 Hz
Theta	4–8 Hz
Alpha	8–13 Hz
Sigma	13–15 Hz
Beta	15–30 Hz
Gamma	30–50 Hz

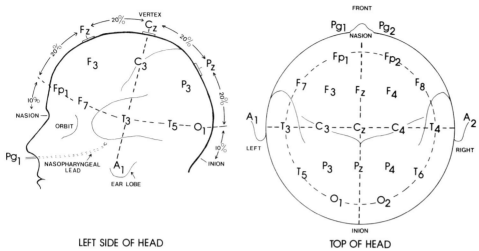

FIGURE 8.12 Standard EEG placements for electrodes coded for the brain region monitored (e.g., 0 is over an occipital lobe).

the scalp and simultaneously record a number of signals. Standard electrode placements are indicated in Figure 8.12.

Averaging EEG Signals. Efforts to develop "lawful" relationships involving the everchanging patterns of electrical gradients generated by the brain have resulted in a wide variety of methods of analysis. One popular method for studying the electrical activity of the brain is that of averaging evoked potentials from the human scalp, yielding an event that is not apparent in the spontaneous EEG (Fig. 8.13). In 1947, a signal averaging method was developed by Herbert Dawson, who superimposed a number of synchronized EEG traces (evoked by a common stimulus) on a cathoderay oscilloscope. He then recorded the traces on a single photographic record. In this way, a consistent time-locked relationship appeared as a consequence of the commonality of the individual traces in the group of traces, revealing the average **evoked potential.** The importance of Dawson's work was that it led to improved methods for recording evoked potentials (viz., signal averaging with the use of small commercial computers that calculated average transients such as those in Fig. 8.13). A veritable flood of research on the evoked potential followed.

The Evoked Potential. Average evoked reactions have been extracted from the scalp from as many as sixty-four separate electrodes, yielding valuable information, for example, separating individuals according to the type of drug that they had ingested along with estimates of the dosage (John, 1972).

The computer can average EEG signals that are repetitively evoked by specific stimuli to yield the average evoked potential, resulting in numerous research studies.

FIGURE 8.13
An averaged evoked potential to a stimulus (S) recorded from the human scalp made apparent by signal averaging. Note the peaks indicated as P 100, P 200, P 300, and P 400.

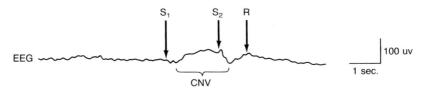

FIGURE 8.14   An example of the contingent negative variation (CNV). The CNV is a slow negative shift that results when two stimuli (S₁ and S₂) are presented and a response is made to the second.

The contingent negative variation results from a response that is made to the second of two successive stimuli that are separated by a constant time interval.

The Contingent Negative Variation.   Another major advance in the electrical measurement of brain activity was the recording of the **contingent negative variation (CNV),** also known as the *expectancy wave.* The CNV also is not readily observable in the raw EEG trace so that the computer-averaging technique is required. The CNV is a slow, negative shift in the EEG baseline that is recordable when there is a contingent response to the second of two successive stimuli (Fig. 8.14). One stimulus (S₁) is followed after a constant time interval by a second stimulus (S₂). The subject must make a response contingent on the second stimulus. The slow negative potential (CNV) can be observed within the S₁–S₂ interval. The subject's response terminated S₂ and also the negativity of the CNV.

Widespread Interest in EEG.   Electrical brain potentials are studied in such disparate fields as psychiatry, neurology, physiology, electroencephalography, psychology, ophthalmology, audiology, computer science, and medical engineering. The early promise of advancing our understanding of brain functioning through these electrical techniques has been realized to some extent, but we should recognize that the field is still in its infancy.

With this introduction to the electrical study of some of the important systems of the body, let us now concentrate on the central nervous system, particularly the brain.

METHODS OF STUDYING THE BRAIN

Gross Methods and Ordinary Inspection

The most obvious (and primitive) method for understanding the nervous systems is looking at them. Through ordinary inspection, early studies were able to describe the shape, size, location, and landmarks of the brain. In the second century A.D. Galen dissected portions of the nervous system and observed structures below the surface of the cortex. Among them, he described the cerebral aqueduct and several cranial and spinal nerves.

Gross Observation in Utero.   Studies have plotted the schedule of development of various organs in the body with attempts to specify temporally when certain physiological and behavioral characteristics occur. The study of morphological development has led to the famous principle that "**ontogeny** [the biological development of the individual] recapitulates **phylogeny** [that of the species]." According to this classic principle, the morphological development in the embryonic and fetal stages resembles the evolutionary development from lower organisms to *Homo sapiens.* For instance, the gradual enlargement of the brain as a human is developing in utero resembles the gradual enlargement of the brain as humans evolved from lower stages. Although there are some interesting analogies, the principle of "ontogeny recapitulates phylogeny" is limited by so many exceptions that it remains just that—merely an interesting, limited analogy.

The morphologic (structural) development of organisms in embryonic, fetal, and postnatal phases has been observed in efforts to determine when certain physiological and behavioral functions develop.

Microscopic Methods—Staining Techniques and Histological Sections

With the invention of the microscope, the minute anatomy of the nervous system could be studied. Living cells were directly observed, although their thickness prevented learning about them in detail. Consequently, various staining techniques were developed and tissues of cells were cut into thin slices called *histological sections.* Histological sections of tissues, when stained with the appropriate dye, show particular characteristics of cells. The cells can then be studied on microscopic slides with the light microscope. However, truly fantastic details of tissues have been revealed with the development of the electron microscope in 1933. This instrument enlarges the image by focusing beams of electrons on items of interest producing enormous magnification and high resolution. Our understanding of the fine structure of the nervous systems, the nature of synapses, and the structure of cell membranes has been greatly advanced with this marvelous instrument.

Contemporary knowledge about the anatomy of the nervous systems is based on the development of techniques for staining histological sections. The light and the electron microscopes also contributed sizably.

Electrical Stimulation

By stimulating a portion of the brain and observing the consequences, some advance in our understanding of the function of the structure stimulated has been obtained. In 1870 Fritsch and Hitzig, in their classic research with this method, electrically stimulated the motor area of the cortex and elicited muscular movements.

Evoking Cognitive Experiences. In contemporary research, electrical stimulation has elicited hunger behavior, aggressive behavior, general arousal, reports of feeling happiness and unhappiness, and sleep. In the course of therapy for Parkinsonism and epilepsy, electrical stimulation almost anywhere in the limbic system has produced changes in mood, temporarily relieving anxiety and depression—patients seem slightly euphoric, relating such reports as, "I feel very good on the right side of my head."

Professor Wilder Penfield (1958) conducted classic research using stimulation techniques in the course of operating on the cortex of epileptics. He found that electrical stimulation of certain regions evoked experiences of déjà vu, reports of fear, and reproductions of previous experiences. He referred to these as illusions, emotions, and hallucinations, respectively. Some of the reports following stimulation were "It is winter and the wind is blowing outside and I am waiting for a train" (the patient was at the time on the operating table); "feeling as though I have lived through all this before," accompanied by fear; another patient reported that he was listening to music from "Guys and Dolls." Figure 8.15 indicates points of stimulation that produced positive responses.

Is the Mind Really Only in the Brain? Some scientists have argued that because reports of feelings and cognitions can be elicited through artificial stimulation, the

Electrically stimulating various regions of the brain results in a variety of reactions including reports of cognitive experiences.

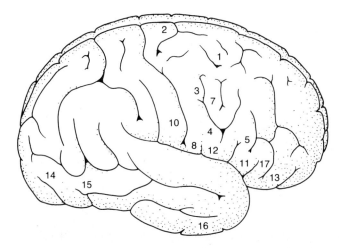

FIGURE 8.15
An exposed right cerebral cortex showing points of electrical stimulation that produced reports of various mental experiences while the patient was on the operating table. (Adapted from Wilder Penfield, *The Excitable Cortex in Conscious Man*, 1958. Courtesy of Charles C Thomas, Publisher, Springfield, Illinois.)

brain is *the* organ of the mind. The assumption is that the reports of feelings and cognitions are produced because, and only because, of brain stimulation; as it was with phrenology, mental qualities are thereby assumed to be located in the stimulated regions of the brain. Consequently it is assumed that is where the mind is located!

An error in this interpretation is that it assumes that the effects of stimulation are confined to the stimulated region of the brain. The cybernetic model postulates that artificial stimulation results in *numerous* neural impulses that are distributed widely throughout the brain and body. In addition to the area in the immediate vicinity of stimulation, important regions throughout the person, including the viscera, are activated.

The brain-centered argument also assumes that electrical stimulation is the same as when the brain is stimulated naturally in the generation of feelings and behaviors, such as reports of pleasurable experiences. However, in the normal human, we really do not know how a pleasure center in the brain is naturally stimulated.

Activation of important brain regions functioning within cybernetic circuits through-out the body can generate a variety of cognitive experiences.

Using a cybernetic model, one can trace the cybernetic circuits that function within the brain as well as to and from it throughout the body. Natural stimulation of brain regions often comes from afferent neural impulses that arise in the numerous receptors throughout the body, especially those within the muscles. Consequently, a conclusion that the brain is *the* organ of mind because stimulation of it evokes mental experiences is inappropriate. The more proper conclusion is that both artificial and natural brain stimulation activate numerous neural and neuromuscular circuits that have cybernetic characteristics. If one seeks to answer the question of where the mind is located, then the appropriate answer is that it is located throughout the entire person, including within the head (Chapter 3). As Pythagoras believed in ancient Greece, the brain is the chief (and therefore not the only) organ of mind.

Example of Erroneous Reasoning. We dwell on this problem because misinterpretation of research findings is so rampant. Two anecdotes from Yoshito Kawahara help to illustrate the problem.

A scientist, Dr. Pseudo, was trying to discover the function of the wings of a fly.

He placed a fly on a table, released it, and shouted "fly!" The fly took off and flew (pretest). Next he lesioned the wings with scissors and repeated the procedure. After shouting "fly!" several times, the scientist discovered that the fly did not take off and fly (posttest). He concluded that the function of the wings of a fly was to . . . hear! Obviously, the fly was now deaf and could not hear the command to fly.

Frank Beach had studied sexual behavior, primarily in beagle dogs, for years at the University of California. When asked if he had finally discovered where the center for sex was, he answered that if he cut off the hind legs of a male dog, the dog could not perform sex anymore. Did that mean that the hind legs of the dog were the center of sex because they were crucial for the performance of the sex act? Since the entire organism is involved in the sex act, it is too simplistic to ask for the location of a "center" for sex. A localized lesion by itself is too simplistic a procedure to use in such a study. If we cut out a person's tongue and observe that the person could no longer speak, does that mean that the tongue is the center for speech?

In all complex phenomena like sexual and cognitive behaviors, there are numerous necessary and sufficient systems, mechanisms, and regions of the body that contribute. To say that any one, such as a particular brain region, is *the* controlling center regresses psychology to the last century when phrenology was popular. It also regresses us from a circuit to a center model. The combination of such techniques as the following has had some value in understanding systems of the brain and body.

> *Loss of a particular kind of behavior following removal of part of the body or brain means only that that region probably functioned as a component of an important circuit involved in producing that behavior.*

Ablation (Extirpation) Techniques

The Logic of Ablation Research. A researcher may study portions of the brain by using the **ablation,** or **extirpation,** technique. Ablation is a technique of surgically removing a portion of the brain, thereby producing a lesion. (A lesion is some kind of damage to the brain.) In experimentation with animals or in clinical surgery on humans, an effort is made to determine whether behavior differs after the operation compared to what it was before. The reasoning is that if an animal or human reacts differently to certain stimuli after a lesion is produced in a given region (relative to behavior before the surgery), the change in the behavior is ascribed to damage in that region. The purpose is to understand the function of the portion of the brain that was excised (removed).

> *Ablation (extirpation) has been used to produce a lesion (destruction of a part) to see if some behavior changes, thus ascribing a function to that region.*

KINDS OF ABLATION METHODS

The brain ablation paradigm is one of the oldest and most widely used methods. A wide variety of techniques have been developed for the purpose of experimentally producing brain lesions.

The experimental animal is anesthetized and treated so as to prevent pain or discomfort. The simplest and most straightforward method is to remove a portion of the cortex by means of a scalpel or vacuum pump. The vacuum pump technique has been highly developed to produce very precise lesions.

Another technique, not as widely used because the lesion cannot be so precisely localized, is cauterizing. With this method, the region is destroyed with an instrument that can be made very hot at its point (e.g., an inserted electrode that delivers electrical current to its end). Yet another technique is to insert certain chemicals (drugs) through a hypodermic-type needle into specific regions of the

Ablation techniques include destroying cerebral areas with a scalpel or vacuum pump, by cauterizing or inserting chemicals, and the preferred method, using high-frequency alternating current introduced by an inserted electrode.

The stereotaxic instrument is used to guide the insertion of microelectrodes to specific target regions in the brain.

brain to destroy specific kinds of neurons. The preferred method is to insert an electrode and transmit high-frequency alternating current to produce a localized radio frequency lesion.

The Stereotaxic Instrument and Its Limitations. In both animal and human studies, **stereotaxic apparatus** is used to guide the researcher to insert the electrode into the desired region. This calibrated instrument holds the head stationary and allows one to insert the electrode to the target locus along the three dimensions so that there can be a precise destruction of a highly localized brain region. As reported in Chapter 15, the stereotaxic instrument is also very effective for inserting stimulating electrodes for pain reduction in humans.

Whatever the technique used, the precise locus of the brain lesion in animals should later be ascertained through histological means. Although the stereotaxic apparatus usually allows the researcher to precisely place the lesion in the appropriate place, sometimes the later histological examination reveals that the mark was missed. If so, the results from the animal may well have to be discarded or used as control data or for other purposes.

The stereotaxic instrument and inserted microelectrode were used especially in the 1950s and 1960s. They have led to much research in which characteristics of the brain were related to phenomena of sleep, eating, sexual motivation, emotion, learning, memory, and so on. More recent advances in the techniques of neuroanatomy and neurochemistry, however, have indicated that the brain is much more complicated than the typical model used in research during that period. For example, recent work in learning and memory (Chapter 10) has revealed extremely important synaptic and cellular changes that in no way could be studied except through a more microscopic brain model than that implied by the use of the stereotaxic instrument.

EVALUATION OF ABLATION TECHNIQUES

Assume that an animal has established the ability to successfully respond to a certain visual stimulus. A highly localized subcortical region of the brain, such as in the thalamus, is then extirpated. After recovery from the operation, the animal can no longer successfully respond to that particular visual stimulus. What do we now conclude?

The basic logic of the ablation paradigm has traditionally been to assert that the specific brain region extirpated had the function of *controlling!* the particular behavior that is now missing. The reasoning is straightforward: The animal could perform well with the brain region present; but when it was removed, the behavioral deficit appeared. Hence, that brain region had the specific function of controlling the behavior in question.

Diaschisis Defined. We have already considered what is wrong with this reasoning. But in the last century the great Hughlings Jackson made a different point. He noted that postoperative behavior is not necessarily a result of a lesion per se. Rather, the behavioral deficit may be the result of how the rest of the brain functions in the absence of the removed tissue. Lesions cause **diaschisis** and other nonspecific effects. Diaschisis is the phenomenon of a specific brain lesion's disrupting the broad pattern of functioning of the brain. Thus the behavioral deficit may not have been

A lesion in the brain may affect neighboring tissue which itself is responsible for a behavioral change, a phenomenon called diaschisis.

caused by the specific region extirpated. Instead, the lesion may have interrupted a critical system elsewhere in the brain. Since the various regions of the brain are intimately interconnected through cybernetic circuits, a lesion in one region certainly affects others. Consequently we cannot assert that any one of numerous regions is responsible for a specific change in behavior.

Other Limitations of the Ablation Technique. One limitation is that there are effects of the mere insertion of electrodes that damage neural tissue above the lesion. For another, there are changes in synapses near the brain lesion that themselves may be responsible for the change in behavior — brain cells can reorganize themselves following a lesion. For instance, axons develop new sprouts and innervate synaptic regions that were destroyed by a brain lesion. Finally, suppose there is no change in an animal's behavior. The region extirpated still could have served some important function, but because of the great redundancy in the brain, other brain regions and circuits could well have compensated for the missing tissue.

Yet, in spite of the shortcomings of the ablation technique, with it we have learned some very important things about how the central nervous system functions. Data gained on animal studies have been most valuable for generalizing to the human, for whom, of course, experimental techniques on normal people are not possible. Sometimes, too, findings in lower animals are actually species-specific, which is informative in another sense. They tell us something about *differences* between the brain of the lower species being studied and the human brain.

Because we do not conduct experimental surgery research on the normal human, for direct information on humans we must rely on clinical studies of lesions that occur in everyday life. Such insults result from strokes, injuries, and tumors. But we must realize that the conclusions from clinical studies, as with all nonexperimental studies, are relatively weak compared to those resulting from experimental research. To emphasize this point, as it is important throughout the book, we devote the following section to it.

A Methodological Note on the Relative Validity of Conclusions from Experimental Compared to Nonexperimental Research

The Importance of Randomization. In experiments, participants (subjects) are *randomly* assigned to two or more groups and experimental conditions (treatments) are *randomly* assigned to those groups. In nonexperimental research, participants are *not* randomly assigned nor are treatments randomly assigned to groups. In correlational research, for instance, all we can know is that one variable is related with another. We cannot assert a causal relationship between those variables. Possible conclusions from correlational research are that one variable may cause the second, the second may cause the first, or both may be caused by a third. The reliability and validity of causal conclusions from clinical research is lower yet. However, in sound experimental research, it can be concluded that there is a causal relationship between the experimental treatment and the resulting behavioral variable (the independent–dependent variable relationship). This difference is of tremendous importance so that studies cited throughout this book should be critically evaluated according to whether they used experimental or nonexperimental methods. For

Random assignments of subjects and treatments to groups define the experimental method that can yield causal relationships; nonexperimental methods do not allow sound inferences about cause-effect relationships.

instance, if, in an experiment, it was found that the brighter the light, the smaller the pupil of the eye, then it could be concluded that the light *caused* changes in pupil diameter. On the other hand, if this relationship were found in a nonexperimental study, it could only be concluded that the two variables were correlated so that we do not know if one caused the other. For elaboration, see McGuigan (Chapter 4, 1993) on why nonexperimental research is always **confounded**.

Clinical Methods

When the brain is injured or diseased, the patient typically develops some functional deficiency. Symptoms that are manifested may later be related to some structural pathology that may be found during an autopsy. Numerous clinical studies such as these have yielded considerable information about functions of regions of the brain. For instance, two landmark discoveries were made by the physicians Pierre-Paul Broca (1824–1880) and Carl Wernicke (1848–1905).

The clinical method used in autopsies related brain lesions with speech disorders. A result was the discovery of Broca's and Wernicke's areas in the left cerebral hemisphere.

 The Discovery of Broca's Speech Area. Pierre-Paul Broca, a French professor of medicine in Paris, is considered to be the founder of French brain surgery. He developed a theory of localized brain function and attempted to test it as follows: Through a trephine operation (drilling a hole in the skull), he searched for a cerebral abscess in order to relate a particular brain structure deficiency to the patient's symptom. In 1861 he postulated that the posterior portion of the left hemisphere (specifically, the inferior frontal gyrus) was involved in speech mechanisms. His research with his famous patient Tan led to the discovery of the speech center known as Broca's area.

 Wernicke's Speech Area. Carl Wernicke was a German physician whose classic case was published when he was 26 years of age. Also interested in language, he established that aphasias resulting from lesions in Broca's area in the left frontal lobe were quite different from aphasias due to lesions in the left temporal lobe. The temporal lobe speech region has come to be known as Wernicke's area. He incorporated observations on both Wernicke's area and Broca's area, thus developing a theory of aphasia that has had considerable influence on our understanding of linguistic brain functioning.

 These two classic cases illustrate one use of the clinical method. In Chapter 11 more recent clinical cases will be considered. However, the need to assess brain damage without waiting for an autopsy has led to other methods such as the development of neuropsychological tests.

Neuropsychological test batteries seem to be sensitive techniques for establishing the presence, laterality, and localization of cerebral dysfunction.

Neuropsychological Testing

 The Halstead Battery. Contemporary neuropsychological testing developed from the work of Ward Halstead at the University of Chicago. Halstead's patients had massive frontal lobe lesions, but they were quite normal according to conventional neurological examinations. Futhermore, results of psychometric measures of their intelligence were also quite normal. There was clearly a discrepancy that had to be resolved. Halstead constructed a battery of seven tests over a period of years and by 1947, he was able to successfully discriminate between patients with frontal lesions and those with nonfrontal lobe lesions. His test battery included measures of critical flicker frequency, tactual performance, Seashore rhythm, perception of speech sounds, finger oscillation, time sense, and ability to categorize.

The Halstead-Reitan Neuropsychological Test Batteries. Through continued use and refinement, Halstead's battery of tests was modified by his first graduate student, Ralph Reitan. The instrument now includes the Wechsler Intelligence Scale, an Aphasia and Sensory Perceptual Battery, the Trailmaking Test, and a dynamometric measure of hand strength. The Halstead-Reitan Battery has been successfully used to predict lateralization, localization, and the neuropathological nature of independently verified cerebral lesions.

The Luria Neuropsychological Investigation Battery. This related battery consists of 282 items that have been formed to discriminate between brain-damaged and comparison populations. Data indicate that it is quite accurate.

Neuropsychological measures also provide independent criteria for some clinical psychiatric syndromes. But as useful as neuropsychological tests have been, they have been replaced to some extent with more direct methods of observing the brain. We speak, of course, of the use of computers and magnetic imagery techniques. Another stage in direct observation of the brain was the use of **pneumoencephalography** (*pneumo* means "air"; *encephalo* means "brain"; *graph* means "record").

Pneumoencephalography

With this technique, air is injected into the skull to enhance our ability to observe structures highlighted by the contrast of air with neural tissue. The technique originated through one of those strange events in which a patient's skull was damaged in a traffic accident. Air accidentally entered the skull, highlighting particular features of the brain when the patient was X-rayed. One example of a pneumoencephalographic study indicated an organic brain basis for chronic schizophrenia. In particular, there was atrophy and enlargement of the brain ventricles (dilitation) in 80 percent of the deteriorating schizophrenic patients who were studied. Later studies using computer tomography confirmed these conclusions.

Brain Scans (Neuroimaging)

Overview of Scanning Devices. To produce images of the brain and other structures of the body, computerized axial tomography (CAT scans), positron emission tomography (PET scans), and nuclear magnetic resonance imaging (MRI) are used. All these methods scan and feed information into a sophisticated computer. The information is sensed from electrical signals, radioactive compounds, or magnetic ions and is decoded and displayed in the form of images, often color-coded.

X-rays of the brain structures had been quite indistinct, although they were improved by pneumoencephalography. The CAT scan was the first sensitive method for studying the soft tissues of the body. Next came the PET scan, which combined the computerized analysis of CAT with the technique of glucose mapping. MRI followed, providing the capability of viewing the brain, chest, abdomen, spine, and other areas of the body hidden by bone, without the need for radiation or surgical operations. Let us discuss these three techniques in greater detail.

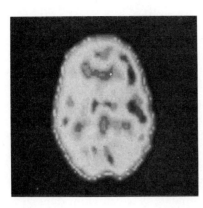

FIGURE 8.16
A CAT scan showing a lesion
in the left cerebral hemisphere.

COMPUTERIZED AXIAL TOMOGRAPHY (CAT SCANS)

Computerized axial tomography (CAT scan) uses a computer to collate and process numerous X-rays passed in different angles through an organ or structure to provide an image of the region.

Computerized axial tomography (CAT scan) is a radiological technique which typically is used to scan the brain, but it is also used to study other portions of the body. The technique was introduced by the European Musical Instruments Laboratory in Great Britain. In using the technique, a dye is inserted to develop contrast in the brain structures; X-rays are then passed through sections of the head from hundreds of different angles. The combined information provides pictures of the interior. Cross sections of the brain can be examined to study systematically all of its regions.

Some Applications. Small differences in the density of cerebral structures can be measured so that anomalies such as tumors or hemorrhages can be diagnosed (Fig. 8.16). These data can be stored to study changes in the brain morphology across time. The system has been used to study structural changes associated with aging, dementia, alcoholism, various neurological diseases and so on. Through CAT scans, some functions of the brain have been related to various anatomical structures. Not only does a CAT scan provide detailed information, but it is relatively noninvasive. Consequently, the risks inherent in invasive techniques such as angiography (where the heart is entered) and pneumoencephalography (where air is pumped in) are avoided.

A related development in neurodiagnostics is SPECT (single-photon emission computed tomography, see later discussion) scanning. While regular CAT scans provide static views of tissue, SPECT scans reveal the perfusion of blood flow to any given area of brain tissue. SPECT scanning has been useful in diagnosing seizure disorders and differentiating between stroke and Alzheimer's symptoms.

POSITRON EMISSION TOMOGRAPHY (PET SCANS)

Positron emission tomography (PET scan) employs radioactive substances that indicate the rate of use of glucose by cells of the brain. Continuous energy "explosions" are transformed by a computer into images of brain activity.

The Method. With **positron emission tomography (PET scan),** the patient is injected with a short-lived radioactive substance that circulates through the bloodstream. That substance is a radioisotope that attaches to circulating glucose (blood sugar) or oxygen. The brain's activity may then be mapped by tracing the path of

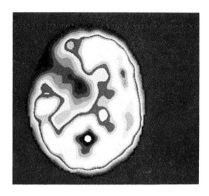

FIGURE 8.17
A PET scan of a normal brain.

glucose with the radioactive substance. (Glucose is the chief fuel used by the brain. In fact, 80 percent of the body's glucose is consumed by the brain.)

About half an hour after injection, the radioactive glucose enters the brain and is used by the individual cells. In that use, high-energy particles are released, providing a signal that may be detected. In effect, there are many tiny "explosions" that are sensed by a PET scanner positioned around the head. The rate of use of glucose is calculated and then averaged to provide an image density. The PET scanner records the radiation activity in a series of thin cross sections of the brain. The information sensed is then transformed into shadings that provide a brain image in color that is displayed on a computer screen (Fig. 8.17). The PET scan thus allows us to view the brain as it continuously functions.

Clinical Applications.   One can observe what is occurring in the brain by studying the absorption of radioactive glucose in individual cells or regions of interest. In one clinical study, obsessive-compulsive individuals had significantly increased glucose metabolism in a region of the left frontal lobe. The right hemisphere showed no substantial increase in metabolic activity.

The PET scan has also been used for the study of tumors, various kinds of mental disorders, epilepsy, and stroke. For instance, the PET scan can identify where an epileptic seizure starts, as well as which part of the brain is underactive or overactive during mood disorders such as severe depression and mania. Other findings include a diminution of cerebral energy metabolism in the frontal and temporal cortices associated with a chronic stage of schizophrenia.

Applications have also been possible in the study of normal subjects; for example, a story read into either ear activated metabolism in the right temporal lobe, suggesting that the meaning of spoken information from both ears may, in part, be processed there. But when *memory* for the story was requested, there was increased metabolism in the hippocampus, indicating a memory function for that region (which other research has also shown).

Evaluation of PET Scans.   Unfortunately, PET scans have finer resolution when used on animals than when used for humans. This relatively poor resolution for humans thus limits our ability to study fine structures and function, such as neurotransmitter activity. Another limitation of findings with the PET scan is that the scanning procedure itself could alter the mental state of patients more than for healthy, control subjects, leading to biased information. On the positive side, as with the CAT scan, clinical applications have allowed us to obtain information without resorting to invasive techniques.

MAGNETIC RESONANCE IMAGING (MRI)

Active nervous tissue generates a slight magnetic field that may be sensed by placing a small doughnut-shaped coil around living nerves and amplifying the signal. Basic research in the field has been conducted since the mid-1940s. Early recordings were made from the sciatic nerves of rats and frogs. Later, similar techniques were constructed for the human brain.

Magnetic resonance imaging (MRI) senses the frequency of signals when magnetic fields stimulate the nuclei in hydrogen atoms and project a computerized image of specific tissue structures.

The Method. The first contemporary **magnetic resonance imaging (MRI)** system was introduced in 1983. The equipment creates magnetic fields by passing current through supercooled coils of wire that weigh about six tons. A radio transmitting and receiving system is in circuit with a computer that records and analyzes the data. The system also contains a ten-ton magnetic scanner that has a magnetic pull 40,000 times greater than that of the earth's gravity. Only a fraction of that power, however, is used on humans.

Nuclei in the proteins of hydrogen atoms are stimulated by highly charged magnetic fields. For instance, a magnetic field directed at the human body causes the nuclei of hydrogen protons to align in its direction. Then a radio signal is beamed at the body so that the nuclei absorb some of the radio energy. The nuclei then change direction until the radio signal is terminated. The nuclei then return to their original position, thereby releasing the energy absorbed from the radio signal. The signal

FIGURE 8.18 Images of the head using MRI. No pathology is indicated. (Courtesy Chris Hayman)

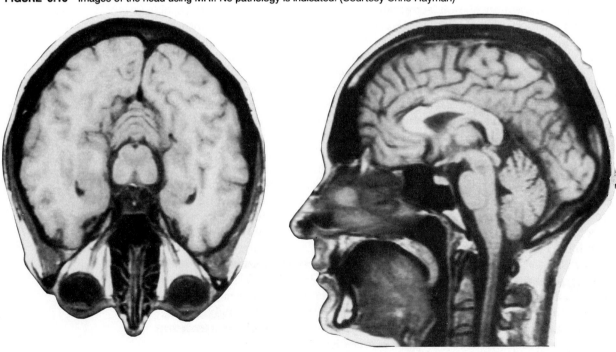

generated by that release is sensed by an antenna, processed by the computer and displayed on a monitor as the image of bone and tissue structure. (Fig. 8.18).

Some Applications. Active tumors or blockages appear in varying shades of gray. A cerebral hemorrhage or benign tumor may appear as bright white.

Brain lesions such as those in epilepsy and multiple sclerosis, various kinds of cancer, and skeletal problems can be diagnosed with great accuracy.

Evaluation of MRI. This magnetic measurement system has several advantages over classical EEG and other techniques. The EEG signal must pass through the scalp, fluid, meninges, and skull, all of which distort the signal. In contrast, the magnetic field signal passes through these layers undistorted. Consequently, the MRI system has a much greater degree of accuracy than do EEG measures. Also, the magnetic signal is not interfered with by other sources as is the EEG by eye movements. Finally, the signal does not cause damage to genes or normal tissues as do some forms of radiation treatment.

Yet, there are some difficulties. First, the signal of the magnetic fields in the brain is so small that the sensor used is kept at an extremely low temperature (approximately 4 degrees Kelvin), which requires complex equipment. Also, the high cost of the system limits application (e.g., there are few studies on cognition, although the potential is great).

SINGLE-PHOTON EMISSION COMPUTED TOMOGRAPHY (SPECT)

Other advanced scanning methods include SPECT, MSI, and TES.

The **single-photon emission computed tomography (SPECT)** scan of the brain provides an image based on hypometabolism in some areas. Radioactive tracers are introduced into the bloodstream whereupon they cross the blood–brain barrier. They then highlight certain areas depending on the amount of blood flow in them. Those areas that receive relatively little blood (they are hypometabolic) may indicate injury through photography. However the tracers remain fixed for but a brief period of time so that ongoing events cannot be studied as they can with PET scans. On the other hand, SPECT is several times less expensive than PET and may become more frequently used for diagnosing epilepsy, tumors, and other conditions. It has been used to confirm diagnoses of head injury that were indicated by neuropsychological tests, yet were not diagnosed by MRI.

MAGNETIC SOURCE IMAGING (MSI)

Magnetic source imaging (MSI) is a newer method for sensing electrical activity associated with the functioning of the brain and heart. The technique displays information based on the physical relationship between moving electrical charges and magnetic fields. Electrically charged ions associated with the firing neurons and the contraction of muscles generates a magnetic field that can be displayed for study. An example of an application is that MSI can detect and locate brain tissues that have been damaged as in a heart attack or stroke, even though there is no anatomical lesion. Thus, other methods of imaging anatomical characteristics may be incapable of detecting the kinds of functional abnormalities that MSI may provide.

It is likely that MSI will be widely applied clinically particularly because it is a completely noninvasive technique.

THERMOENCEPHALOGRAPHY (TES)

The heat generated by the brain is conducted through the cranium where it may be sensed at the scalp. The sensed radiated heat is in the infrared frequency range and can be amplified, digitized, and processed by apparatus placed at distances from centimeters to meters from the head. Since there is no contact with the head, **thermoencephalography (TES)** is completely noninvasive. Through a thermomap of the brain, small regions can be studied in detail as a function of an experimental or clinical condition; for example, a flash of light to the retina produces a small heated zone in the striated cortex of a rat that then expands up to about 3 mm and then disappears. TES should have scientific as well as clinical applications.

Cerebral Laterality Paradigms

Cerebral laterality paradigms constitute another valuable method of studying the brain. In cerebral laterality and dichotic listening studies, information may be sent by the eyes and ears to either the left or right hemisphere of the brain. With such studies we can better understand how the two hemispheres differentially process various kinds of information. Since we develop this topic in Chapter 11, we merely note it here for completeness.

Neuropharmacological and Psychopharmacological Methods

Drugs may be administered to determine whether or not certain functions of the nervous system are altered. One method is to implant cannulae (tiny hypodermic needles) to inject chemical solutions or crystalline chemicals into a selected part of the brain. A technique for continuous sampling and measurement of those chemicals in a part of the brain is called a "push-pull system" whereby two or more cannulae are implanted side by side in the brain. A solution can be slowly pushed in one cannulum, while the solution plus chemicals from neural structures around the cannulae tips are pulled out of the other cannulum by a suction system. This technique is now being used rather frequently in contemporary research.

In Conclusion

Electrical Methods of Recording.   Living tissue generates electromagnetic signals that may be detected with specialized electronic equipment and studied in many ways. Computer methods of processing electroencephalographic recordings include the average evoked potential and the contingent negative variation. Electrocorticograms may be recorded from electrodes placed directly on the exposed cortex. Single-cell activity is studied by means of microelectrodes. By inserting microelectrodes we have been able to trace out central nervous system pathways that form cybernetic circuits within the brain. Eccles, using what was then a new technique, implanted microelectrodes inside neuron cell bodies to record their bioelectric responses. With these neuroelectrodes, he was able to specify neuronal circuits in the brain and to enlarge our information about the physiology of the synapse. One of his more important findings was that many synaptic inputs, particularly in the cerebellum, are inhibitory rather than excitatory. In the 1950s and 1960s, microelectrodes

Breakthroughs using microelectrodes were made in the 1950s and 1960s, generating an explosive expansion of our knowledge of membranes, synapses, and neurons.

also allowed us to analyze signals of central brain neurons when animals were awake and to learn more about ways in which individual neurons function and communicate with each other. During the 1970s, the focus was on how different groups of neurons acted together in neuronal systems. During the 1980s, studies were largely of how neuronal networks are assembled to function for cognition, motor control, emotion, memory, and so on. In Chapter 10 we will discuss some valuable studies wherein electrical recording from single neurons implicated them as critical during learning.

Biochemical Methods. Biochemical methods have told us much about membrane functions, the chemical constituents of neurons, and the general metabolism of neural cells. Our understanding of neurochemistry and the characteristics of neurotransmitters is consistently advancing. Radioisotopic techniques as in assessing glucose uptake radioactively in cerebral blood flow are of special importance.

Less Soundly Established Techniques. Some approaches are candidates for either providing valuable information or dismissal from science. One fringe technique is Kirlian photography, used to study hypothesized electromagnetic auras that surround living tissue. Photographs of auras about a hand or plant have been offered. Another is the study of possible extrasensory perception. As scientists, we need to remain flexible about such possible phenomena and not prejudge their validity with insufficient data. It is entirely possible, although not many contemporary psychologists would bet on it, that we will find extrasensory perception receptors and transmitters in the brain that have the characteristic of sending messages with the speed of light. This characteristic of ESP seems to be demanded when "thoughts" are reported to be instantaneously sent and received halfway around the globe. Who knows what future scientific investigations may yield? On the other hand, we need to be highly skeptical of *all* matters scientific and demand sound replicable data for any technique and finding that is admitted into science.

With microelectrodes, powerful methods have been developed for studying the characteristics of individual neurons and relationships among them, as in mapping axon projections and connections to specific brain cybernetic circuits.

EMPHASIS ON A CYBERNETIC PRINCIPLE— STRATEGY FOR MEASURING RECEPTOR– NEURAL–MUSCULAR CIRCUITS

Given that there may be thousands of cybernetic circuits simultaneously reverberating in parallel and in interacting fashion throughout the body, we face an almost overwhelming task when attempting to measure them. Even if we were to use all of the techniques and methods discussed in this chapter, we still would not be able to adequately carry out the task. The phenomena are just too complex for contemporary technology. Yet, our strategy is clear. We need to make as many simultaneous measures of bodily activities as is reasonable, including behavioral phenomena, cognitive or otherwise, that we desire to study. Thus, the following strategy is now possible.

To study a cognitive phenomenon such as auditory hallucinations, it obviously would be inadequate to take a measure only on the brain. Rather, we should employ a number of measures in various locations, the more the better. Based on the findings of previous research, a priority region for study would be the speech musculature. Thus we might place electrodes on the tongue and lips to record electromyograms while a patient experiences auditory hallucinations. We might wish to obtain measures from the auditory and speech regions of the brain and would thus place electrodes over the left temporal and frontal lobes. Since we know that individuals typically visualize what they are cognitively processing, eye movements during the hallucinations could be recorded through electrooculography. Involvement of the breathing apparatus would be measured through pneumograms. Records of slight changes in breathing patterns would provide information about subvocalization during hallucinations. Because the preferred arm is generally active during cognitive processing, relevant covert responses could be recorded there through electromyography. Finally, we would want a control measure to assure us that any activity is not merely a component of general bodily arousal. For this we might electromyographically record from the nonpreferred leg and arm. By recording such psychophysiological events through these methods, we can make strong inferences as to which circuits are reverberating as the hallucinations are generated. If we could add scanning and other recently developed methods, additional valuable data could be brought to bear.

The precise temporal occurrences of relevant responses could provide hints as to which components of the cybernetic circuits occurred first, providing useful information as to which bodily system has priority in controlling others. We can also thereby better distinguish among negative feedback, feedforward, and adaptive control systems during various bodily functions.

In short, to adequately understand information processing systems within the body, multiple simultaneous measures need to be taken. The study of any system or organ in isolation will never provide sufficient information to understand how it functions within the context of the whole, integrated bodily system(s).

ENRICHMENT MATERIAL
How to Measure Blood Pressure

Blood pressure measurements result in such values as 140/86 where 140 is the systolic pressure and 86 is the diastolic pressure. (See Figure 8.19 for elaboration.) The usual technique is to place a strap somewhat tightly about the upper arm. The sensor for listening is then placed on the inner surface of the arm just *below* the strap. *It should not be placed underneath the strap* as is often done because that location of the sensor may artificially elevate **systolic pressure** (highest arterial blood pressure of a cardiac cycle) by as much as ten points. With one hand, pressure is increased while the pulse is monitored at the wrist with the other hand. **Diastolic pressure** (lowest arterial blood pressure of a cardiac cycle) is taken *on the way up* as the pressure within the strap is increased by pumping. Next note the systolic pressure. *An accurate reading of systolic pressure can only be taken on the way up.* The other hand monitoring the pulse can note that the pulse is eliminated when the value for systolic pressure is exceeded on the visual monitor. The procedure frequently employed of pumping pressure in the strap well above systolic and then getting the two readings on the way down also artificially elevates both readings. By increasing pressure with the excessive inflation, one increases arterial pressure itself above what it actually is. Often the act of measuring a phenomenon disturbs the phenomenon itself and to a greater extent if improperly taken.

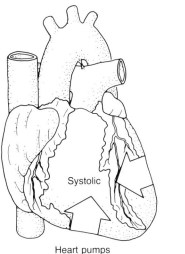 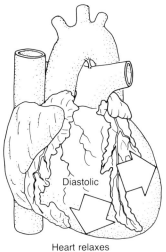

Systolic

Diastolic

Heart pumps

Heart relaxes

FIGURE 8.19   Blood pressure is measured in terms of systolic pressure relative to diastolic pressure. Systolic pressure is the value measured during the heart's pump or squeeze phase that expels blood (top). Diastolic pressure is the value when the heart relaxes (bottom). The conventional maxima for normal blood pressure values are 140 millimeters of mercury (mm Hg) systolic and 90 mm Hg diastolic.

Individuals who take their own pressure with a "drugstore" sphygmomanometer should also note that the process of taking their own blood pressure can artificially increase it. One should continuously practice and, perhaps after a week or so, a relatively stable set of readings that are of greater accuracy can be obtained. A tendency toward hypochondriasis should be avoided by not worrying about one's self-taken blood pressure. Variations in pressure can be expected and should not be alarming. In fact, huge variations due to circadian rhythms (see Chapter 9) can be expected, perhaps varying blood pressure as much as 25 percent depending upon time of day. Accurate readings taken at home *can* be obtained and provide valuable information; for example, someone on medication can take his or her blood pressure at sample periods several times during the day, keeping records that can be reported to the physician. Dosage and time of dosage might thereby be systematically altered for greater effectiveness.

KEY TERMS

Ablation (extirpation)—Technique of surgically removing a portion of the brain to produce a lesion; the purpose is to determine if some aspect of behavior changes. If so, a behavioral function might be ascribed to the region lesioned.

Amplifiers—Instruments that increase the amplitude of the sensed signals.

Cathode-ray oscilloscope (CRO)—An instrument (like a TV set) for displaying a changing electrical or other signal.

Computerized axial tomography (CAT scan)—A radiological technique used to scan the brain and other portions of the body.

Confounding—Occurs when an extraneous variable is systematically related to the independent variable; it might differentially affect the dependent variable values of the two or more groups in the investigation.

Contingent negative variation (CNV)—

Slow, negative shift in the EEG baseline that is recordable when there is a contingent response to the second of two successive stimuli.

Diastolic pressure — Measured as the lowest arterial blood pressure of a cardiac cycle.

Diaschisis — General disruption of brain functioning due to a specific lesion.

Electrocardiogram — An electrical measure of heart activity consisting of a complex of signals monitored by an electrocardiograph.

Electrode — A metallic device used to sense a signal or to apply electrical current to tissue.

Electrodermal activity (EDA) — The electrical activity of the skin sensed by electrodes placed on the palms or fingers of the hands (term replaces GSR — galvanic skin response).

Electroencephalography (EEG) — The method of recording unprocessed electrical activity of the brain taken from electrodes placed on the scalp.

Electrogastrograms (EGG) — Electrical records of smooth muscle activity in the abdomen.

Electromyography (EMG) — A method of recording action currents in muscle.

Electrooculogram (EOG) — An electrical recording of activity of the eyes.

Electropsychology — The study of small-scale bodily events, especially those that occur during cognition.

Evoked potential — (also called average evoked potential, AEP, or event-related potentials, ERP) — A time-locked signal (most commonly from the brain) that is revealed as a consequence of the commonality of the individual traces in a group of traces. The evoked potential is obtained by averaging a number of signals such that those events not in common are "randomized" or "averaged out."

Galvanic skin response (GSR) — A change in the resistance of the skin to the flow of electrical current that results from changes in sweat gland activity.

Latency — Time between the presentation of a stimulus and the onset of response.

Magnetic resonance imaging (MRI) — Imaging technique sensing the frequency of signals when magnetic fields stimulate the nuclei in hydrogen atoms and project a computerized image of specific tissue structures.

Magnetic source imaging (MSI) — Method for sensing electrical activity associated with the functioning of the brain and heart based on the physical relationship between moving electrical charges and magnetic fields. It is completely noninvasive.

Ontogeny — The development of the individual as distinguished from phylogenesis or the evolutionary development of the species.

Phylogeny — The evolutionary development of any plant or animal species; ancestral history of the species, as opposed to ontogenesis, the development of the individual.

Pneumoencephalography — A technique in which air is injected into the skull to enhance the ability to observe structures with X-rays highlighted by the contrast of air with neural tissue.

Pneumograph — An instrument for recording the force, form, and rapidity of the respiratory movements resulting in a pneumogram.

Positron emission tomography (PET scan) — A technique to map the brain's activity by tracing the path of glucose with a radioactive substance and projecting an image.

Quantification system — Renders signals into numerical values.

Reaction time — The time interval between the onset of a stimulus and the onset of a response.

Readout devices — Instruments for displaying signals (e.g., a cathode-ray oscilloscope).

Sensors — Devices to detect signals, mainly electrical, generated by the body.

Single-photon emission computed tomography (SPECT) — Brain scan based on hypometabolism in some areas. Radioactive tracers are introduced through the bloodstream highlighting areas that are receiving little blood, indicating possible injury.

Stereotaxic instrument — An apparatus for positioning accurately the tip of an electrode in three dimensions in the brain.

Systolic pressure — The highest arterial blood pressure reached during any given ventricular cycle.

Thermoencephalography (TES) — Brain scan based on the heat generated by the brain. It is completely noninvasive.

STUDY QUESTIONS

1. Define overt and covert behavior and give examples of each.
2. List the four essential features of an electropsychology laboratory for the study of covert processes and explain their purposes.
3. Summarize the principal covert processes that are psychophysiologically measured during cognitive functions.
4. How did the invention of microscopes advance the study of nervous systems?
5. Criticize the basic logic of the ablation paradigm.
6. Discuss the principle: "Ontogeny recapitulates phylogeny."
7. What did Broca and Wernicke discover?
8. Discuss the differences and advantages of CAT, PET, and MRI scans.

FURTHER READINGS

This book, for a broad range of readers, presents brain-imaging techniques with each technique's limitations:

Andreasen, N. D. (Ed.). (1989). *Brain imaging: Applications in psychiatry.* Washington, DC: American Psychiatric Press.

This book covers information processing, psychophysiology, motivation, and emotion together with psychophysiological measures:

Jennings, J. R., & Coles, M. G. H. (Eds.). (1991). *Handbook of cognitive psychophysiology: Central and autonomic nervous system approaches.* New York: John Wiley.

Part III
Normal Biopsychological Functions

CHAPTER 9

Motivated and Emotional Behaviors

MAJOR PURPOSES:

1. To learn major behavioral principles of motivated and emotional behaviors
2. To relate various motivated and emotional behaviors to physiological conditions that participate in their generation
3. To view those behaviors within a cybernetic framework

WHAT YOU ARE GOING TO FIND:

1. Motivated behavior consists of approach and avoidance behaviors
2. There are complex physiological and biochemical components of motivated and emotional behaviors
3. Subjective emotional experiences may be studied psychophysiologically and by means of verbal reports
4. The studies of biological rhythms, behavior genetics, and species-specific behavior are also relevant to motivated behaviors

WHAT YOU SHOULD ACQUIRE:

An understanding that motivated and emotional behaviors are generated as circuits among receptors, the nervous systems, and effectors reverberate, well fitting a cybernetic model.

CHAPTER OUTLINE

BIOLOGICALLY MOTIVATED
  BEHAVIOR
  Instincts and Drives
  Classification of Motivated Behaviors
    Approach behaviors and physiological needs
    Cerebral functions in motivated behaviors
    Avoidance behaviors
  Chronobiology and Rhythms of the Body
    Circadian rhythms
    Biological clocks
    Infradian and ultradian rhythms
    Sleep and wakefulness cycles
    Do moon cycles affect behavior?

EMOTIONAL BEHAVIOR
  Some Traditional Theories of
  Emotion
    Evolutionary theory
    Cognitive arousal theory
    Neurophysiological theories
  Some Behavioral, Physiological and Anatomical Data
    Origin of emotional behavior
    The hypothalamus and emotions
    Laterality and processing of emotional stimuli
    Facial feedback findings
  BEHAVIOR GENETICS
    Genes and DNA
    Genotype and Phenotype

SPECIES-SPECIFIC BEHAVIORS
A SUMMARY OF SOME IMPORTANT ADVANCES IN THE
STUDY OF MOTIVATED BEHAVIOR
EMPHASIS ON A CYBERNETIC
PRINCIPLE—EVOLUTION OF
A CENTRAL-PERIPHERAL
MODEL OF MOTIVATED BEHAVIOR
ENRICHMENT MATERIAL—
PURPOSIVE BEHAVIOR AND
HOMEOSTASIS
KEY TERMS
STUDY QUESTIONS
FURTHER READINGS

BIOLOGICALLY MOTIVATED BEHAVIOR

Why Do We Have a Concept of Motivation? One reason for a concept of motivation has been to explain why an organism responds to a particular stimulus at one

Motivation has been developed as a concept to explain variability in behavior— why an organism will respond to a particular stimulus at one time, but not at another.

time but does not respond to the same stimulus at a different time. For instance, an organism will now respond to a piece of food by eating it but at a later time will ignore that stimulus. Psychologists have hypothesized an internal state of **motivation** (e.g., a hunger drive) to explain such variability. In general, the notion is that we behave in one way at one time when there is a motivational (drive) condition and behave in another way at another time when our level of motivation is different.

Instincts and Drives

Hypothesized Internal Motivational States Have Been Replaced by Observable Behavior.   Another concept related to motivation is **instinct,** which has been used to attempt to explain why organisms sometimes behave as they do. Like motivation, instinct has many different definitions, but they all hold that instincts are inherited (innate) and not learned. Also like motivation, the instinct doctrine has been advanced to account for changes in responding even though environmental stimulation is relatively constant.

Historically, a motivational concept of **drive** replaced that of instinct. Drives, such as that for aggression, were thought to be states of arousal that could be reduced by actions. Currently neither instinct nor drive notions are commonly held because neither contributes to the understanding or control of behavior.

A main reason that instinct and drive theories of motivation were discarded was that they were viciously circular.

Vicious Circularity.   One criticism of drive and instinct theories is that they are viciously circular. **Vicious circularity** means that the antecedent condition of a statement is used to explain the consequent condition, while the consequent condition is also used to explain the antecedent condition. For example, the famous frustration–aggression hypothesis states that if an organism is frustrated (antecedent condition), then aggression results (consequent condition). Thus, to explain why an organism is aggressive, one says "because it was frustrated." But how do we know that it really was frustrated? "because it was aggressive," a viciously circular answer! Instinct theories, which were prominent in the early part of the century, met their downfall when it was realized that they were viciously circular. New instincts were being advanced endlessly to explain a wide variety of behaviors. For example, why are humans *sociable*? Because they have a *gregarious* instinct. How do we know that they have a *gregarious* instinct? Because they behave *sociably*. The ultimate logic of this reasoning could be to postulate a thumb-twiddling instinct (or drive)—why do people twiddle their thumbs? Because they have a thumb-twiddling instinct. How do we know they have a thumb-twiddling instinct? Because they twiddle their thumbs.

To prevent viciously circular reasoning, the antecedent and consequent conditions of a hypothesis must be independently defined. For instance, in the frustration–aggression hypothesis, a state of frustration should be defined independently of any consequent aggressive behavior. Thus, if we have an independent definition of frustration and if we note that aggression does follow, then we can confirm the frustration–aggression hypothesis, as was done by Berkowitz (1989).

The concept of hypothesized, unobserved internal states of motivation has been largely replaced by the more objective phenomena of motivated behaviors.

Contemporary Status of Motivation.   We simply do not have widely accepted, sound definitions and principles for drives and instincts. To be more objective, investigators now speak of observable **motivated behavior** rather than of unobserved internal states of motivational drives. For example, scientists now refer to **ingestion** (eating behavior) rather than **hunger drive, mating behavior** rather than

sex drive and **flight behavior** rather than fear. The result is that we seek causes of such behavior in terms of objective, observable, external stimulation and internal physiological conditions rather than in hypothetical internal states such as drives, motives, and instincts. In thus specifying actual *observed* influences on behavior, it became possible to formulate laws about learned stimulus–response– reinforcement contingencies. Much motivated behavior is understandable as merely learned behavior (see Chapter 10).

Classification of Motivated Behaviors

Motivated behaviors may be classified as approach or avoidance behaviors. Examples of **approach behaviors** include ingestion of food and water, sex and mating, thermal regulation, and maternal caring. **Avoidance behaviors** are those in which the organism removes itself from stimuli and conditions (we subjectively report experiencing such conditions as painful, noxious, or as producing fear).

Motivated behaviors are classified as approach behaviors whereby an organism advances toward stimuli or as avoidance behaviors in which an organism moves away from stimuli.

APPROACH BEHAVIORS AND PHYSIOLOGICAL NEEDS

Several criteria for establishing **physiological needs** include their presence throughout the phylogenetic scale, their presence in all human cultures, and a physiologic basis for them. According to these criteria, mammalian physiological needs include oxygen, water, and food. These needs are essential, that for oxygen being the most urgent. Thirst is the next most demanding need because without fluid, humans can expect to die of dehydration within about five days. We can survive for weeks or months without food, particularly with a large amount of body fat. Organisms purposively behave to satisfy such physiological needs by consuming the appropriate substance.

Criteria for establishing essential physiological needs: They are present along the phylogenetic scale, occur among different human cultures, and have a physiological basis. Needs for water, food, oxygen, and perhaps sleep meet these criteria.

Whether or not sleep is a physiological need is argued among researchers. Regardless, sleep is among physiological variables that influence behavior and will be considered under the topic of biological rhythms.

Drinking Behavior and the Need for Water

Processing Water.   Consumed water enters the bloodstream where it, along with essential nutrients and electrolytes, is transmitted into cells throughout the body. Excretions from the cells are then carried by the bloodstream to the kidneys where blood is filtered and waste products are concentrated in urine. The filtered, clean blood is then returned to the circulatory system. The adult human uses about 2½ quarts of water a day in this way. About 1½ quarts are discharged as urine while the remainder is excreted as sweat, as moisture in fecal matter, and by evaporation through the lungs.

Physiological Basis of Thirst.   We become aware of a need for fluids because of dryness of the mouth and throat. However, when the mouth and throat are wetted, the need still continues. The sensation generated by the dryness is thus probably a conditional stimulus which warns us that we should consume liquid. The actual physiological basis of the need involves other systems of the body. For one, when the body is deprived of water for a brief period of time, blood pressure falls. With further

Sensory feedback from the mouth and throat indicates that the body needs water, but the physiological condition of need is more general, involving lowered blood pressure, osmoreceptors in the brain, and other events in the lateral hypothalamus.

Approach behaviors of eating and drinking involve circuits that include the lateral hypothalamus.

Carbohydrates, proteins and fats provide the principal fuels for the body. Carbohydrates are converted into glucose which is the main fuel for most of our cells and is stored as glycogen in the liver or as fat if not immediately needed.

Insulin, secreted by the pancreas, is essential for the use of glucose.

deprivation, water is drawn out of the cells of the body so as to increase the volume in the circulatory system. The movement of water across cell membranes is sensed by **osmoreceptors,** which are located deep in two regions of the brain (known as the preoptic area and zona incerta). If either of these brain areas is damaged, the organism does not exhibit drinking behavior, even if the organism's homeostatic condition is below its standard set level. On the other hand, if excessive salt is injected into these brain regions when they are undamaged, drinking behavior occurs. Apparently, the salt draws water out of the cells in the affected area and thus produces a local state of cellular dehydration. Complex circuits are then activated whereby the organism seeks and consumes fluid to reestablish a condition of homeostasis.

Most research investigating neurological mechanisms that are involved in motivated behaviors has been conducted for water, food, and sex needs. It has been determined that the lateral hypothalamus (see Fig. 6.5) is involved in both drinking and eating. By electrically stimulating this region, a satiated animal will either drink or eat, depending on the precise location of the electrode. Similarly, injection there of a small amount of salty solution will cause excessive drinking in a satiated animal while injection of pure water causes a thirsty animal to stop drinking. Habits can be acquired by electrically stimulating the lateral hypothalamus and then rewarding specific responses with food or water, even though the animal has no need for either substance. However, the neural, chemical, and other events involved in drinking behavior are so complex that we must not conclude that there are specific centers in the hypothalamus that control ingestive behaviors (see pp. 240–241).

Food Ingestion

Processing Food.   Carbohydrates, proteins, and fats provide our principal fuels. The body converts carbohydrates into glucose, which is the main fuel for most of our cells. When glucose is not immediately needed, it is stored as glycogen in the liver or in the body as fat. When we fast, fat and liver glycogen are reconverted into glucose to provide energy for us to function.

If we have excess protein, it, too, is converted into fat and stored. When we fast and use up our fat, muscle protein is broken down into amino acids and converted by the liver into glucose for energy.

Fats are stored as free fatty acids or as glycerol. When fasting, the liver converts fatty acids into ketone bodies, which serve as a major source of energy for all tissues except the liver itself.

Insulin, a hormone produced by the pancreas, is essential for the body's use of glucose. Considerable insulin is released shortly after eating. When fasting, insulin secretion decreases and only the brain uses glucose—the remainder of the body mainly uses fatty acids and ketone bodies.

Physiological Basis of Hunger.   It was once thought that stomach contractions provided the subjective experience of hunger, but this notion has been discarded for a number of reasons. For one, people who have had their stomach and major portions of their intestines removed, as in treatment for ulcers or cancer, still experience hunger. Similarly, when the sensory feedback from the stomach is blocked by transection of nerves that supply the gastrointestinal tract, individuals still experience hunger. Furthermore, by injecting sugar into the bloodstream, stomach contractions can be prevented, yet the person still reports hunger. Thus, even though stomach contractions do occur when we experience hunger, they are not essential for producing hunger sensations. Apparently, like dry mouth sensations for thirst, they are merely conditional responses that become associated with more direct physiological conditions of the need for food.

The Hypothalamus Is Important for Hunger Behavior. We do not have a good theory of why organisms eat as they do or of subjective hunger and satiety experiences in humans, but it is clear that the hypothalamus plays a key role. Two regions of the hypothalamus that have been implicated are the ventromedial hypothalamus and the lateral hypothalamus. The ventromedial nucleus of the hypothalamus (which is located in the middle and lower region of the hypothalamus) apparently functions to produce the ventromedial hypothalamus (VMH) syndrome. The VMH syndrome consists of various behaviors resulting from a lesion in the VMH. For instance, an experimentally produced lesion of the VMH causes the animal to overeat and become obese and apparently hyperphagic (heightened need for food). Electrical stimulation of the VMH leads to a cessation of eating. Formerly, these findings led to the conclusion that the ventromedial hypothalamus was a satiety center, but the concept of a satiety center has been replaced by that of a VMH syndrome. In particular the lesioned animal does not merely ingest food, but is particular about its eating behavior; for example, its overeating is mostly limited to carbohydrates, quinine injected in the food inhibits the overeating behavior, and there are complex effects in the autonomic nervous system such as the secretion of insulin.

The ventromedial hypothalamus serves a function in eating and in cessation of eating, but the anatomy and physiology involved are quite complex.

The Lateral Hypothalamus. When lesions were made in the lateral hypothalamus on both sides, the animals did not eat and eventually starved to death. Research also showed that stimulation of the lateral hypothalamus elicits eating behavior. Similar to the conclusion that the VMH functions as a satiety center, these research findings led to the conclusion that the lateral hypothalamus is an eating center. However, while the lateral hypothalamus serves a function in eating behavior, later research disclosed that rats also suppressed behavior in general.

The lateral hypothalamus serves a function in generating eating behavior.

Although the hypothalamus is clearly implicated in eating behavior, we must never forget that it functions cybernetically with other parts of the body. For instance, the liver is an important part of the eating circuits in that it apparently signals the brain as to when the organism should stop eating. The ventromedial hypothalamus seems to receive these signals and to return them to the liver.

In General. Circuits apparently function between specific regions of the hypothalamus and the body for food ingestion and cessation of eating.

Such neurological research seeking the mechanisms that generate the need for food has led to the hypothalamic theory for the origin of hunger and satiety. This theory holds that information is collected about the body's needs for energy through neural and hormonal channels and is directed to a center in the lateral hypothalamus. The amount of hunger is thought to be proportional to the amount of neural (including chemical) activity in this center. We have often seen this type of reasoning to be excessively simplistic.

Circuits among the lateral hypothalamus, the ventromedial nucleus, and other parts of the body including the liver function cybernetically to signal when the organism should start and stop eating.

A Circuit Conception for Hunger Behavior. There is little doubt that the hypothalamus is intimately involved in ingestive behavior, as well as in thirst. Yet, one trouble with the hypothalamic-center theory is that the hypothalamus may not at all contain centers for hunger and satiety. That damage and/or stimulation to the hypothalamus lead to changes in eating behavior do not, by themselves, establish that such centers exist. This is particularly true since lesions and stimulation in the

According to the hypothalamic theory, a hunger center is located in the lateral hypothalamus and a satiety center is located in the ventromedial nucleus of the hypothalamus, but these notions are excessively simplistic.

hypothalamus do not just start and stop eating behavior. Likely, those operations may simply have activated or disrupted circuits involving other areas of the brain and body that are also important for hunger. That is, although circuits in the brain for hunger may well run through the hypothalamus, stimulation or disruption any place along those circuits including in the hypothalamus may modify ingestive behavior.

Researchers are increasingly employing this circuit-based line of reasoning. Consequently, efforts to establish limited neural centers that organize response patterns are decreasing. Current studies concentrate on how the brain interacts with the rest of the body. As the liver does for eating behavior, peripheral systems and organs play important roles in regulating motivated behavior. Similarly, while obesity can be induced by hypothalamic lesions, vagotomy (severing of the vagus nerve that runs throughout the body) can prevent obesity. Hence, peripheral mechanisms are also important in the control of obesity. Hunger control is thus not simply in a center in the hypothalamus; rather, various components of cybernetic circuits throughout the body influence each other to exercise the control. Indeed, extensive research has indicated that ingestive behavior involves an amazing number of brain and body regions, neurotransmitters, specialized neurons, and receptors such as glucose receptors.

Motivated behavior is generated by complex central-peripheral circuits whereby regions of the body neurally and chemically interact with the brain.

Sexual and Mating Behavior

WHAT CAUSES SEXUAL BEHAVIOR?

In spite of the fact that scientists from many fields have long been studying human sexual behavior, it is still difficult to say what makes people engage in sex or experience "sexual feelings." People differ considerably in the need that they feel for sex and there is variability within the same person from one time to another. Sexual behavior and sexual feelings are no doubt due to many different causes. For one, it is clear that the ebb and flow of hormones influence the strength of sexually motivated behavior. But it is also clear that we learn how to experience and express sex from our cultural experiences.

Sexual behavior is influenced to a large degree by several kinds of hormones secreted by the endocrine glands as well as by learning experiences.

Hormones—Testosterone and Estrogen. The **androgens,** the male **hormones,** include especially **testosterone,** which is produced in the male **gonads,** the testes. The female hormones, the **estrogens,** are released by the female ovaries and include especially **estradiol.** Both males and females produce androgens and estrogens, but males produce more androgens and females produce more estrogens.

The primary male and female hormones are testosterone and estradiol respectively.

A Hormonal Negative Feedback Circuit. The pituitary hormones play a major role in the manufacture and release of male and female hormones. The female cycle is the more complex and involves several negative feedback circuits, such as that involving the hypothalamus, the pituitary gland, and the ovaries (Fig. 9.1). When the pituitary gland releases FSH (folical-stimulating hormone), the ovaries react by releasing estrogen. The secretion of estrogen then activates the hypothalamus to release LRF (luteinizing hormone-releasing factor), which acts on the pituitary gland to reduce FSH secretion and thus also estrogen secretion. In this way a homeostatic level of estrogen is maintained in the bloodstream. Negative feedback circuits involving the release of ova (egg cells that may be fertilized) are much more complex than this, and if pregnancy follows, it has its own complex of hormonal phenomena.

Negative feedback circuits maintain hormones such as estrogen at standard values within the bloodstream.

Much research has been devoted to the study of possible effects of testosterone and estrogen on sexual behavior.

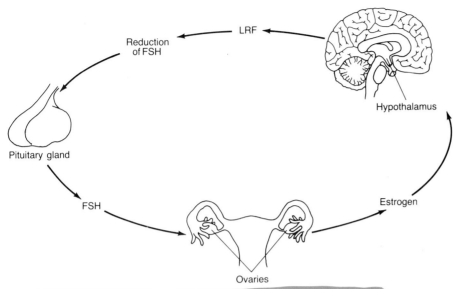

FIGURE 9.1 Components of a negative feedback circuit for controlling the level of estrogen in the female circulatory system.

Testosterone. Some results obtained from the study of animals have enlarged our understanding of how these hormones function. For instance, the Stanford physiologist Julian Davidson concludes that testosterone administered to animals of either sex increases the intensity of their sexual behavior as well as their aggressiveness. Female rats administered testosterone begin behaving like males by mounting other females.

In a review of hormones and sexual behavior, Feder (1984) reported that pregnant guinea pigs who were (prenatally) injected with high levels of testosterone had both male and female progeny that exhibited increased frequency of mounting behavior.

However, hormonal effects in humans are much more complex than in animals and research is methodologically more difficult. Variations in intensity of sexual behavior are often unsystematic and quite subtle. Consequently, we cannot assert any causal relationships between levels of testosterone or estrogen and sexual behavior, although some correlations are suggestive. Some illustrative findings follow.

As the eroticism in pornographic movies increased, penile erection and level of testosterone in human males increased. Feder (1984) concludes that there is a relationship between the onset of androgens in boys during adolescence and the onset of sexual activity (nocturnal emission, masturbation, and dating behaviors), a relationship that is not so evident in girls.

Estrogen. As summarized by Feder (1984) there are some controversial data that indicate that there is a slight rise in women's sexual desire in the middle of their menstrual cycle when the amount of estrogen is highest. However, the effect is also present in women on birth control pills, whose hormone levels are nearly constant

Studies on animals and humans indicate that as testosterone level increases, the intensity of sexual behavior increases, although a causal connection is unclear.

throughout the month. The administration of estrogen in menopausal women results in an increase in sexual activity, and in interest in and frequency of orgasm. On the other hand, the removal of ovaries in adult females is not generally associated with a decrease in sexual activity or interest. There is some evidence that estrogen may act as an antidepressive in humans.

In Conclusion.   As we have noted, research on the relationship between hormones and behavior in humans is methodologically difficult to conduct. Many findings seem contradictory and the relationships are only correlational. Nevertheless, the consensus seems to be that subtle variations in sexual behavior are probably more influenced by learning (cultural, social, and psychological) factors than by hormonal variations.

Some data indicate that as estrogen levels in the female increase, sexual behavior also increases, although learning variables are probably more influential.

These considerations about the effects of testosterone and estrogen on sexual behavior lead to the ancient question of whether or not there is a substance that can be used to increase sexual behavior in humans.

Is There an Aphrodisiac?.   Traditional folklore tells of efforts to increase sexual behavior, including the consumption of bees' wings, fat in a camel's hump, rhinoceros horns, "Spanish fly" and yohimbine. **Yohimbine** is in the bark of the tropical tree corynanthe yohimbine, but it is now available as a synthetically manufactured prescription drug sometimes used for heart problems. As reported by Julian Davidson, yohimbine injected into male rats caused them to mount females about twice as often as control males that were administered an inert placebo. Yohimbine is thought to increase the activity of norepinephrine and related chemicals such as monoamine neurotransmitters, which may be involved in influencing sexual behavior. Even though yohimbine may be an aphrodisiac for rats, it has not been so established for the vastly different sexual systems of humans.

Other suggestive research has shown that changing the level of serotonin in the brains of rats also increases sexual behavior. It has also been noted that L-Dopa arouses sexual desires of those who take it for Parkinson's disease.

Results of one study suggest the possibility that eating fresh fruit and vegetables could improve the sex life of humans. The reasoning is that vitamin A, found in spinach, carrots, melons, mangos, and apricots, helps to convert cholesterol into active sex hormones and that vitamin B, abundant in potatoes and bananas, is also involved in the manufacture of sex hormones.

There is no sound evidence of an effective aphrodisiac for humans.

In humankind's long search for an aphrodisiac, the best bet is testosterone, which would be impractical to use given our present state of technology. The best aphrodisiac continues to be romance.

The Biochemistry of Love.   Levels of various endogenous (naturally occurring within the body) chemicals such as neurotransmitters vary with emotional behavior. **Catecholamines** such as tyrosine, L-Dopa, dopamine, norepinephrine, and epinephrine contain phenylethylamine, which stimulates the brain and is associated with emotional behavior. Perhaps the sight of a loved one is a conditional stimulus that releases catecholamines in the brain, producing subjective feelings of love. Reports of the feelings of romantic love do resemble those following the ingestion of such drugs as alcohol and cocaine. In fact, love has been likened to drug addiction. The reasoning is that in the beginning partners see each other rather casually, but similar to drug addiction, tolerance builds up so that the "dosage" must be increased. Finally, as with the addict, withdrawal symptoms of unhappiness may develop if the lover is away. The agony may be so great that lovers commit suicide if they cannot be

Romantic feelings may have a biochemical basis such as the release of catecholamines.

together, as happens in *Romeo and Juliet.* Indeed, it is appropriate that we celebrate love on the day of St. Valentine. He was a Christian physician who was beaten and beheaded by the Romans in the year 269 and has become a symbol of pain.

Another biochemical interpretation of romantic love was advanced by Dean Delis. His notion is that one who is in love is experiencing danger because of the fear of being rejected by the loved one. When experiencing such danger, the brain secretes endorphins and amphetamine-like chemicals as in any fight or flight situation. The blissful state of falling in love is a natural high subjectively experienced as love.

Further evidence for the traditional belief that people who are in love have the "right chemistry" comes from the hormone oxytocin, a chemical that is used to hasten childbirth and promote lactation. Oxytocin has been associated with certain brain regions during emotional behavior. For instance, levels of oxytocin rise dramatically during sexual behavior and seem to influence how animals relate to one another. Oxytocin was given to prairie wolves; they immediately formed a monogamous bond, as reported by Sue Carter. In the wild these small animals pair up only after they have sex, at which time oxytocin levels are high.

In contrast, a behavioral (nonbiochemical) interpretation has been that what we identify as romantic love is the result of maladaptive learning, an emotional habit that is resistant to reasoning. Viewed as maladaptive behavior, romantic love could, through relearning, be modified into a more reasonable, mature love.

Love's Survival Value

For the survival of our species, males and females need to be attracted to each other to mate. Their progeny are helpless and must be protected by loving parents so they can survive. We can speculate that the progeny of parents who were not emotionally attached to them were not protected and failed in the struggle for survival.

Survival Value of Homosexuality

Although sexual behavior is critical for the survival of a species, most sexual behavior is not performed for that evolutionary purpose; rather, its reinforcing value maintains it so that it *can* be used for procreation. But homosexuality has no survival value for the species at all. Why, then, do some people engage in homosexual practices?

Research on this topic is extremely difficult methodologically, particularly in efforts to generalize to all humans. Furthermore, it is a heated issue so that political pressures often preclude sound conclusions. For instance, Simon LeDay published a study in 1991 in which he found that a section of the hypothalamus was smaller in homosexual men compared to heterosexual men. However, the fact that all of his subjects had died of AIDS leaves open the possibility that the brain difference was caused by AIDS and was not constitutionally determined. Similarly, a study of twins reported by J. Michael Bailey concluded that there was frequently a genetic reason for homosexuality. However, researchers in these areas questioned whether findings from such twin studies can be applied to the general population. Surveying the broad research in this area, it is apparent that efforts have changed from seeking a single cause of homosexuality to finding various factors that may influence individuals to be homosexual. In a broad review, L. J. Hatterer (1984) concludes, "currently there is no scientific proof that homosexuality is caused by inborn constitutional, genetic, or hormonal factors. . . . The consensus of this work is that all forms of homosexuality . . . are learned" (p. 136). The research of Shelton Hendricks and John Money in particular has shown that homosexuals and heterosexuals do not differ in circulating hormones, a conclusion consonant with that of Feder (1984). Physique, genital development, glandular and reproductive functions, and chromosomal constitution are all quite normal in both male and female homosexuals, according to West (1967). His comprehensive review led him to conclude that it is individual learning that influences sexual preferences, that psychological factors channel sexual urges in either heterosexual or homosexual directions.

The consensus in the literature is that genetic and endocrinological research does not substantiate a theory that there is a constitutional endowment for homosexuality; rather, homosexuality is considered to be learned.

CAN GENDER BE CHANGED BY HORMONES?

Studies in the infant rat, by Roger Gorski, Gary Arandish, and Roger Hammer, concluded that gender has been changed by altering hormone balance affecting a part of the brain known as the medial preoptic area (MPOA). By administering hormones (especially testosterone) during a critical period in the early development of the infant rat, the pattern of neural receptors for endorphins and enkephalins in the MPOA is changed. This change seems to cause sexual behavior that is typical of the opposite sex. Also, transplanting male rat brain tissue from the MPOA into a female infant rat during the critical period creates malelike receptor patterns that cause male gender behavior and decrease female gender behavior. These behavioral changes and changes in the number and patterns of endorphin and enkephalin receptors indicate that gender and gender behavior are in part regulated by the MPOA through its opiate system (as for endorphins).

Administration of sex hormones and brain transplants in the rat have altered the structure of endorphin and enkephalin receptors in the opiate system of the MPOA; apparently gender in embryos can thereby be influenced.

Roger Hammer concludes that for female animals of every mammalian species that has been investigated, treatment with testosterone has increased masculinity. It is quite possible that the gender of humans could also be controlled prenatally with testosterone and other substances. Whether or not that would be wise is another question. Even so, we may influence the fetus through opiate drug use or extensive exercise. For instance, Hammer believes that pregnant women who engage in strenuous jogging may increase their beta endorphin levels, thereby possibly affecting the fetus.

CONTRACEPTION AND ALLEVIATING SEXUAL NEEDS

Survival Value of Sexual Behavior. When we have a physiological need for food, we ingest it and report that we experience pleasure. It is reinforcing ("pleasurable") when we ingest water to reduce a thirst need. Such needs have survival value in that they maintain the health of the organism. Similarly, sexual behavior that reduces sexual needs is reinforcing and subjectively pleasurable. However, sexual behavior also has a unique purpose in maintaining the species. In fact, one can surmise that sexual behavior evolved with reinforcing effects and thus enhanced the likelihood that progeny will be produced for survival of the species. But a major

When motivated behavior is terminated by consuming an incentive (such as food), humans report that the reinforcement is pleasurable.

All of our motivated behaviors with physiological bases have survival value and are maintained through reinforcement, as in sexual behavior.

concern of society is that the pleasure of sexual behavior threatens catastrophe for the world through overpopulation (see Chapter 16). Consequently, to prevent pregnancy, contraceptive practices have considerable social relevance.

Limiting Population Growth. Studies of methods of birth control in the United States indicate that the birth control pill is the most frequently used (by almost one-third of women), followed in descending order by female sterilization, condoms, male sterilization, diaphragms, the intrauterine device (IUD), and the rhythm method. Research on birth control, however, indicates that people dislike all contraceptives. Women report a dislike of condoms and diaphragms more than do men. Older people prefer male or female sterilization to other methods, while younger people (under 35 years), prefer the pill, diaphragm, and condom, in descending order.

Greater use of birth control methods could help to curb the population explosion.

The birth control pill was approved for sale in the United States in 1960. Within two years, 1.2 million American women were using it, and by 1973 10 million were using it. It had a profound effect on society, including increasing sexual freedom of women and changing male – female relationships. For one, the proportion of women who delayed sexual intercourse until marriage declined from about one in two among women marrying during the period 1960–1964 to about one in five among women marrying in the years 1975–1979, as found in a survey of 7,969 women conducted in 1982 by the National Center for Health Statistics. White women have been more likely than black women to delay intercourse until marriage by an average of 35 percent to 9 percent. Premarital sexual activity among teenagers has steadily increased; even with the increased availability of birth control, the percentage of unmarried females who had children increased from 5 percent in 1960 to 19 percent in 1980. It seems that in the 1980s many unmarried high school girls actively sought to have babies, further increasing these figures.

The consequences of the birth control pill for society have been enormous.

As with any medication, there are side effects of the pill, including blood clots, heart attacks, and strokes. It is particularly risky for those women who smoke; are over 35; or have high blood pressure, diabetes, or high cholesterol levels. A beneficial side effect is that the female hormones contained in birth control pills appear to have lowered women's risk of cancer of the ovaries and the endometrium (the lining of the uterus). It also appears to decrease the risk of some forms of pelvic inflammatory disease and infection in the uterus and the Fallopian tubes that can, in serious cases, cause infertility.

The effectiveness of birth control techniques is less than perfect largely because they are not always properly used. Birth control pills apparently are most effective, but sometimes not taken; the condom sometimes breaks or slips off, but provides some protection against sexually transmitted diseases. Sterilization is more than 99 percent effective in men and women. In male sterilization, called vasectomy, cutting or clamping the tubes causes the sperm to stop traveling through. Female sterilization, called tubal ligation, is accomplished by cutting or clamping the tubes that carry eggs from the ovaries to the uterus.

Abstention has increased in part due to the herpes and AIDS epidemics and increased frequencies of contraction of syphillis and gonorrhea; however, this is partly because people have often become immune to the antibiotics that control these diseases. For some, there is a new morality wherein partners discuss sexual histories and negotiate about establishing relationships. We can expect fidelity in

Sexual fidelity seems to be greater now than during the sexual revolution because of the herpes and AIDS epidemics.

sexual behavior to increase since a vaccine for the control of AIDS is unlikely before the year 2000, if then.

In Conclusion. Population growth could be limited by more extensive use of birth control methods and by increased abstinence.

Addictive Behavior

Addiction, the most powerful of motivated approach behaviors, is discussed more fully in Chapters 14 and 15. We mention it here because of its theoretical as well as its practical relevance for motivated behavior in society.

Addictive behavior is extremely powerful motivated behavior that is maintained by the reinforcing effects of drugs; being learned, it can be controlled by the judicious application of conditioning principles.

Addictive behavior is classically defined as repeated self-administration of drugs. It is a unit of a complex feedback circuit that is maintained by the powerful reinforcing effects of drugs. Rats have been conditioned to self-inject a variety of drugs by means of venus catheters; the drugs include alcohol, heroin, cocaine, methadone, and nicotine. Since they are learned, conditioning principles are applicable in controlling addictive behavior. We will have a better understanding of the learning characteristics of addictive behavior after we study principles of learning in Chapter 10.

Aggressive Behavior

There are many notions as to why humans are aggressive. One is that aggression is an instinct, a view that has long been held by the general public. This unsophisticated notion is that a unique kind of aggressive energy is generated within a person and may be released by an appropriate stimulus. As the amount of aggressive energy accumulates within a person, increasingly weak stimuli become sufficient to release the energy into overt aggressive behavior. Finally, if a sufficiently large amount of aggressive energy accumulates, it will be released regardless of the stimulus presented, similar to the explosion of steam in a boiler. One simplistic view is that we can relieve aggression by "letting it out."

Instinct and drive theories have been abandoned by many scientists as explanations of why we are aggressive. They hold that there is an accumulation of aggressive energy that can be harmlessly released.

Another commonsense notion is that to prevent aggressive explosions, aggressive energy should be channeled into nondestructive activities. For instance, one can displace aggressive energies through sexual activities or exercise. Such myths derive in large part from Freud's psychoanalytic notion of **catharsis.** More realistically, instead of safely letting out aggressive energies; there is counter aggression. If I am aggressive toward you, either verbally or physically, you probably will then be hostile toward me. There may well follow an increasing spiral of aggression as in a positive feedback circuit, making matters worse rather than better.

Aggressive Behavior Is Learned. Aggressive behavior is an approach behavior that is aversive to other organisms in that it is hostile and potentially destructive. In humans it is usually irrational and often occurs when one is under the influence of drugs. Considerable research has indicated that aggressive behavior is evoked by a variety of aversive events such as verbal insults or physical assaults. Threats to one's reputation or public humiliation have been shown to be major evokers of aggressive behavior. Research has also shown that it is maintained by reinforcing events such as achieving material rewards or improving social status. As with other motivated behaviors, researchers have dismissed instinct and drive theories of aggression. Clearly the maintenance of aggressive behavior through reinforcement implies that it is a learned behavior. Yet, there may also be contributing factors such as genetic predisposition for aggression. Indeed, behavior as complex as aggression must have multiple causation factors. As Eron (1990) has summarized, the causes of human aggression and violence range from genetics, neural anatomy, endocrinology, and physiology, as well as environmental influences. When there is a convergence of a number of these variables, aggressive or violent behavior may occur in "one who has been programmed to respond in this way through previous experience and learning. Aggressive behavior must somehow have been learned in the past (although not necessarily [overtly] performed)" (p. 6).

Albert Bandura has developed a social learning theory to explain how specific forms of aggressive behavior are learned. To start, the organism must have the capacity to be aggressive, which may be based on genetic, hormonal, and other physiological characteristics. Given the capacity to be aggressive, Bandura holds that specific forms of aggression are learned vicariously. **Vicarious learning** is observational learning, similar to learning by imitation—one learns an act by observing it in others. Children who observe aggressive behavior in their parents acquire similar behavior merely be experiencing (observing, etc.) that behavior. More precisely, what happens when one learns by imitation is that one covertly mimics the behavior that is observed. Thus in vicarious (observational or imitational) learning, the observer makes covert responses similar to those made overtly by the people being observed. For instance, if you view one person striking another with a fist, you covertly make such striking responses throughout your arm. Electromyographical measures have confirmed that the observer does make such covert responses (Berger & Hadley, 1975; Irwin & Frommer, 1970). Once the observer makes specified, physical muscular events (those "copied" covert responses made in empathy), those responses may be reinforced, resulting in the learning of the particular aggressive behavior that was observed.

Social learning theory holds that children learn to be aggressive by observing aggressive behavior in their parents and others; probably they covertly mimic the aggressive behavior that can be learned.

A major question for society is whether or not there is a genetic basis that predisposes organisms to be aggressive. If there is, will we always have wars?

Organized warfare is a relatively new phenomenon which started with the spread of agriculture that led to permanent settlements about 10,000 years ago. Villages began to fight over farmland. As populations increased, cities developed and armies were organized. Apparently the first major war was in Jericho about 7500 B.C. The psychologist John Paul Scott argues that it was not possible for aggressive genetic change to develop in such a short period of time. Rather, the reason for the change from peaceful to warring societies must have been accomplished through learned cultural phenomena.

Defining Human War. Scott advances several distinctive characteristics of human warfare: It is fought with tools; it is between groups that use language to direct coordinated behavior as in marching; each group has a different appearance or language; its goals are to kill or injure the opposition to acquire land, for religious conversion, and so on.

War is defined as being fought with tools and directed by language to coordinate behavior, with major differences between the groups. The goal is to acquire land and other valuables by destroying the opposition.

Other animal species have been reported to have some of these behaviors. Examples include ant armies, conflicts between packs of wolves and troops of rhesus monkeys, and attacks by groups of chimpanzees on individual chimps. However, Scott holds that most of these reports are based on less than completely sound observation. And in any event, no other species includes all of the human characteristics previously noted, which is taken as further evidence that warfare is not a

Some evidence indicates that human aggression is probably culturally learned and not genetically determined; if so, aggressive behavior could be controlled through learning principles and possibly through the administration of chemicals.

genetic phenomenon. Consequently, we learn to be warlike or to be peaceable. For instance, the Vikings were very aggressive people, but now the people in Scandinavia are among the most peaceful in the world. Similarly, Indians in the southwestern United States have developed cultures that are either peaceful (the Hopi Indians) or warlike (the Comanches).

In one behavioral learning study to modify aggressive behavior, gerbils were raised with barriers separating them from other gerbils. When the barriers were removed, the two groups fought each other violently. Other gerbils were raised with no barriers so that the young could mingle. This group did not fight. Scott generalizes these findings to humans: Communication and trust between opposing groups are important. We should continue forming strong international organizations to facilitate communication among peoples throughout the world.

Physiological Variables in Aggression. Biological research on a number of different species has found that anticholinergic drugs decreased attack behavior. Some other findings are that higher levels of catecholamines are associated with higher levels of aggressive behavior among male animals; higher levels of serotonin are associated with lowered levels of aggressiveness, while cholinergic antagonists facilitate aggressive behavior; endocrinological research on animals has yielded the conclusion that gonadal hormones activate aggressive behavior.

Anthropological Research. It has been established that in every culture studied, boys are physically more aggressive than are girls. Apparently this is due to both cultural learning factors and to biological factors, perhaps hormone differences.

Males are more physically aggressive than are females because of cultural learning differences and perhaps biological differences in hormones.

CEREBRAL FUNCTIONS IN MOTIVATED BEHAVIOR

Brain Components of Circuits for Motivated Behavior. We noted that one of the criteria for defining a physiological need is that it has a demonstrated physiological basis. To find such bases, researchers have searched for centers in the brain for "controlling" behavior; for example, ablation or stimulation of a specific brain area has been found to modify drinking behavior. However, that does not mean that a controlling center for drinking has been found. Such a brain region may be an important part of complex circuits that, when activated, result in the specified kind of behavior. An alternative is that the stimulated or extirpated region is not part of such a circuit at all but merely sets off, or results from the activation of, another region that *is* itself important for the behavior.

A number of regions in the hypothalamus have been related to a variety of motivated behaviors, such as for food and water ingestion, sexual behavior, aggressive behavior, and temperature regulation.

The Hypothalamus as a "Motivation Center." The hypothalamus is an example of a brain region that has been related to food and water ingestion, sexual behavior, aggressive behavior, and temperature regulation. For example, some ablations in some parts of the hypothalamus eliminate sexual behavior, whereas ablations elsewhere in the hypothalamus exaggerate sexual behavior. Exaggerated sexual activity (persistent mounting by a male of a female rat for intercourse and an unusually large number of ejaculations) also results when the rats' hypothalamus (specifically its anterior dorsolateral region) is electrically stimulated.

One reason that the hypothalamus has been thought of as a motivation center of the brain is that it is part of the old brain, that beneath the cortex (the cortex is "new brain"); the hypothalamus thus is thought of as serving a primitive function in motivated behavior for higher organisms along the phylogenetic scale.

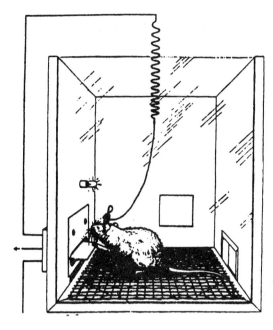

FIGURE 9.2
A rat in a Skinner box with an electrode painlessly inserted into its septal region will continuously press the bar to deliver brief reinforcing shocks to that region.

Reward and Punishment Areas. Regions in the brain important for reward and punishment have attracted considerable amounts of attention. In 1954 James Olds and Peter Milner made the first discovery of a reward function of the septal region, which is considered by some as part of the limbic system. As illustrated in Figure 9.2, Olds found that rats would press a lever that delivered electrical stimulation (which was reinforcing to them) to their own septal regions. The finding was later confirmed in other organisms, including humans. Other reward areas were later found widely scattered throughout the subcortex of the rat's brain. However, stimulation of a specific reward area that continues for a few seconds or more may become aversive. Perhaps there are "punishment" (negative) cells in the vicinity of "reward" cells so that when stimulation lasts for a few seconds, the stimulation spreads out to activate those negative cells. Another possibility is that as stimulation continues, the stimulated region adapts and becomes neutral or aversive.

The existence of areas in the brain related to punishment sets the stage for us to consider aversive behavior, behavior that is motivated to avoid noxious conditions. To a large extent, avoidance behavior is accompanied by the **subjective experience** that we report as pain or the threat of pain.[1]

Regions in the brain have been related to approach and avoidance behaviors ("reward" and "punishment" areas). Their discovery represents a great advance in pinpointing critical components of cerebral and neuromuscular circuits.

AVOIDANCE BEHAVIORS

The Motivating Effect of Pain

Efforts to avoid or discontinue **pain** are probably the most powerful motivated behaviors. They take precedence over all our other needs and wants. When pain is acute, it *demands* immediate response. Intense pain comes across strongly to insist that we control its cause. *Pain signals the organism to stop what it is doing!*

[1]When we use such subjective terms as *pain,* they are but shorthand for more lengthy objective concepts. In the case of pain, for instance, we more objectively refer to avoidance or escape behavior evoked by noxious stimuli.

Pain Helps Us to Survive. Pain is a necessary part of living. It is a warning signal that we are being harmed. By learning that something can produce pain, we also learn to avoid (and in some ways to fear) it. Humans have learned to avoid oncoming trucks, but dogs stand fearlessly in front of them. Some people have been born without the ability to feel pain and are not warned of dangers. As a consequence, such individuals suffer many injuries that might have been avoided if they *were* sensitive to pain and could experience the caution that pain provides. They have, for instance, died of ruptured appendices. The child with congenital insensitivity to pain does not learn what fear is, cannot connect pain to punishment, and rarely lives long. However, sometimes pain has no value — for example, that experienced by a terminally ill person whose body has already suffered destruction and additional pain cannot prevent further damage. If such pain has some kind of function, it certainly is not the usual one.

Avoidance behaviors evoked by noxious stimuli and accompanied by reports of subjective experiences of pain, have top priority among all behaviors and have considerable survival value.

We now consider some psychological and physiological characteristics of pain, some kinds of clinical pain, and theories of pain. Controlling pain is discussed in Chapter 15.

THE PSYCHOLOGY OF PAIN

Traditionally, researchers have thought of pain strictly in physiological–medical terms, but now we also seek to determine the behavioral variables that control it. Recent research has indicated that psychological and cultural variables are quite relevant for our perception of pain. As a consequence, therapy has moved from a strict medical–surgical model to one that also includes psychological aspects. Pain can often be alleviated or eliminated entirely by relaxing and ignoring it, as we will discuss in Chapter 15. Pain can also often be studied as an interesting sensation.

Pain is thought to be determined by physiological, cultural, and psychological variables such as suggestion.

The Suggestion of Pain Enhances It. To understand psychological influences on pain, picture yourself about to receive an injection or a drilling from a dentist. If you anticipate pain, especially if you fight it, you intensify it. Your thoughts about what you expect can become a self-fulfilling prophecy. The effectiveness of suggestion to experience pain is illustrated in a study in which dummy (nonfunctional) shocking electrodes were attached to the subjects' heads. They were then told that they were going to receive mild electrical shocks through the electrodes that might induce headaches. Two-thirds of the subjects reported some degree of headache during the experiment even though no current was actually used. Just the word *pain* in the instructions influenced some subjects to rate a nonpainful stimulus as painful. Suggestion of pain has clinical importance. About one-third of patients who go to general medical practitioners report some kind of pain, principally in the abdomen, head, and back, although examinations reveal no apparent organic cause. Behavior therapy, rather than medical treatment, is typically indicated for such psychologically induced or enhanced pain experiences.

THE PHYSIOLOGY AND BIOCHEMISTRY OF PAIN

Pain Receptors and Ascending Pathways. Scientists have studied the sensory characteristics of pain much more than they have its motivational properties. We have learned that pain receptors (free nerve endings) are extensively located throughout the body, in the skin, in various organs and joints, in the sarcolemma that encapsulates muscles, in the membrane about the bones of the body, in the

Free nerve endings located in most tissues throughout the body function as pain receptors.

cornea of the eye, in the pulp of the teeth (causing toothaches), and so on. In fact, pain receptors are in all tissues except bone, brain, lung tissue, and nonliving parts of the teeth, hair, and nails.

A pain message begins when harmful stimuli release chemicals that activate free nerve endings to warn the body of danger. The number of nerve endings stimulated determines the intensity of the pain. These chemicals are the peptide bradykinin, which is one of the most painful substances; histamine, which is characteristic of allergic reactions; and prostaglandin, which is among the body's most transitory yet most powerful chemicals. These chemicals sensitize free nerve endings to assist in the generation and transmission of afferent neural impulses. Those neural impulses from free nerve endings are conducted along unmyelinated afferent axons which are pain fibers.

Harmful stimuli release the chemicals prostaglandin, bradykinin, and histamine, which activate free nerve endings to carry afferent messages that conditions threaten the body.

Pain receptors, known as **nociceptors,** throughout the body transmit impulses to the spinal cord. The primary sensory pain fibers terminate in a region in the dorsal horns of the spinal cord. When information about pain enters a dorsal horn of the spinal cord, various neuropeptides (such as substance P, somatostatin, and calcitonin) may then be liberated. These peptides no doubt serve important functions at this point, although we do not yet adequately understand them. It is possible that noxious mechanical information liberates substance P, and that thermal (heat) information liberates somatostatin.

Two Afferent Pathways for Pain. In any event, the pain information is transmitted from the dorsal horns of the spinal cord and ascends to the brain. There are several major afferent pathways for transmitting and processing information to the brain. In one for pain (Fig. 9.3), fibers transmit information across the spinal cord and ascend to the brain along the lateral spinothalamic tract, fibers of which terminate primarily in the thalamus. Perception of pain occurs when information reaches the thalamus. The thalamus receives information about the location, character, quality, and duration of the pain stimulus. These messages also pass to and from other areas of the brain, including the limbic system, the reticular formation, the somatosensory and parietal cortices, and the frontal cortex where sensory information is further processed. As messages from throughout the body enter the thalamus, neural circuits within the cerebral cortex are activated for the specific bodily region involved.

Other pathways that carry pain information to the brain go through the reticular formation. The information that ascends through the reticular pathways is slower and more diffuse than that carried along the lateral spinothalamic tract.

Information that a stimulus is painful and destructive enters the dorsal horns of the spinal cord and can ascend to the thalamus at which time pain perception occurs.

Analgesic Events in the Brain. Once pain information gets into the brain, complex phenomena occur. The net result is that if the person does not react to interrupt the stimulation, tissue damage may occur. Among the complex events are biochemical phenomena, such as the action of serotonin to inhibit pain pathways. Other chemicals that naturally occur in the brain and spinal cord to block pain are opioid substances (endorphins and enkephalins) which activate descending inhibitory neurons. Electrical stimulation of specific areas of the brain has indicated that these chemicals are released to decrease pain. In fact, there are several sites in the brain which produce analgesia (relief from pain) when electrically stimulated (see Chapter 15).

Endorphins are neural secretions that, like morphine, block pain. Morphine and endorphins share similar sites of brain action and minute amounts of endorphins injected into the brain produce the same pain-reducing effects at those sites as

The brain produces analgesia, blocking incoming pain messages through the actions of serotonin, endorphins, and enkephalins.

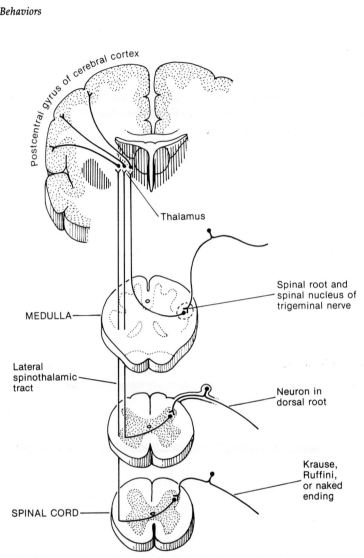

FIGURE 9.3 The lateral spinothalamic tract is one of several ascending pathways that transmits pain messages to the brain.

does morphine. Animals become analgesically tolerant to electrical stimulation such that repeated stimulation comes to have a lesser analgesic effect, just as morphine addicts develop tolerance and require larger doses to produce the same effect. An animal that has developed tolerance to electrically elicited pain relief is also found to be tolerant to morphine injection. The suggestion is that electrically produced analgesia acts by the same medium as does morphine and other opiates, which is the release of endorphins.

The general conclusion is that the brain has developed its own pain-relieving system through the release of endorphins. Morphine simply mimics the body's own means of pain relief. Both morphine and endorphins create a euphoria, apparently like the "jogger's high." Yet, when we control pain through the injection of opioids such as morphine, patients still report pain but say that they just do not care about it.

Opioids are the most efficacious chemical agents available for relieving pain. They activate several descending regions to inhibit pain at supraspinal and spinal sites. However, one can develop a dependence as well as a tolerance for the substance. To allay that dependence, the amount of morphine necessary to be effective can be reduced by simultaneously administering amphetamines, which enhance the analgesic relief of the morphine. **Enkephalins** are released from the brain and endorphins from the pituitary gland and hypothalamus. The number of endorphins released to inhibit pain signals depends on the intensity of the pain. The production of endorphins may be responsible for our becoming oblivious to pain—note a marathon runner's tolerance for pain. These internal pain-killing systems are also closely linked to other hormonal systems, such as the adrenal glands, which prepare the body for danger and pain. These chemicals may block the transmission of pain signals by acting along pathways descending from the brain to the spinal cord.

DESCENDING PATHWAYS AND PAIN KILLERS IN THE CNS

Analgesia in the Descending Pathways. Events in the brain that reduce pain generate messages carried by complex descending pathways. Animal research has traced some of these pathways as follows:

Hypothalamus ⟶ Midbrain ⟶ Rostal Medulla ⟶ Spinal Cord

After the brain processes pain information, it may reduce or eliminate the pain by inhibiting ascending pain messages and by liberating endorphins and serotonin.

By electrically stimulating these pathways, pain relief that lasts for hours can be produced. Stimulation in the periaqueductal gray and the locus coeruleus also has analgesic effects. Injecting morphine in the periaqueductal gray results in reduction of pain as well. Apparently, the stimulation can inhibit the upward transmission of pain signals through the spinothalamic tract. Since electrical stimulation in the pathways relieves pain for hours, it is likely that hormones that have an enduring effect are released. These hormones probably relieve pain through the action of opioids (endorphins, meaning "internally made morphine").

Electrical stimulation of specific sites in the descending pathways produces analgesia probably by releasing endorphins.

THEORIES OF PAIN

The Specificity Theory. The **specificity theory** asserts that specific noxious stimuli act on specific pain receptors, principally those embedded in the skin. When these pain receptors generate afferent neural impulses, information is coded for the specific type of pain stimulus. When that information is transmitted to the brain, perception of that particular kind of pain occurs.

The Pattern Theory. While the specificity theory holds that specific pain receptors and specific neural patterns carry messages for pain, the **pattern theory** emphasizes that patterns of pain receptors and neural pathways are coded for carrying pain messages to the brain.

The Gate-Control Theory. Neither of these theories is sufficient to handle the facts of pain perception. The dominant theory is the **gate-control theory,** proposed by Ronald Melzack and Patrick Wall in 1965 that reconciles and integrates both the specificity and the pattern theories. It agrees that specialized receptors and specialized neural fibers are activated by noxious stimuli, and that patterns of stimuli and ensuing neural impulses are important too. More important, there are "gates" in the CNS that when open allow pain messages through to the thalamus, but can also block them when closed (Fig. 9.4). For example, the **substantia gelatinosa** in the

Theories of pain include the specificity theory, the pattern theory, and the currently dominant gate-control theory.

The specificity theory holds that specific pain receptors and stimulated nerve fibers lead to the perception of pain. The pattern theory holds that certain combinations of stimuli evoke coded patterns of neural impulses that lead to pain experiences.

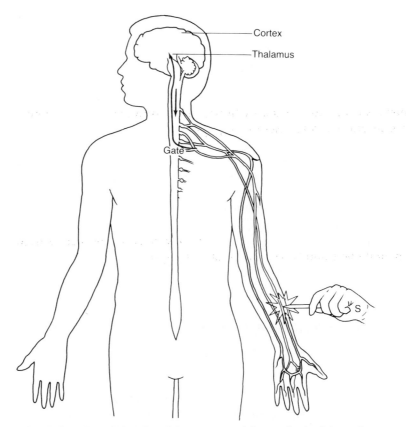

FIGURE 9.4   A representation of the gate-control theory of pain. Cybernetic circuits between the brain and the spinal cord function to influence each other for opening and closing the gate.

dorsal horns of the spinal cord receives incoming afferent impulses coded for pain. Gates in the substantia gelatinosa control the entrance of pain information (there are other gates elsewhere). If the gates are open, incoming signals from the periphery are sent to the thalamus whereupon there is perception of pain. Specific information about the pain, such as the body region where it originates, may be retrieved and processed by thalamic–cortical circuits. But if the gates are closed, pain impulses will not proceed to the brain.

The gate-control theory holds that when gates throughout the body, such as at the substantia gelatinosa, are closed, coded incoming pain sensations are inhibited, preventing the perception of pain; when the gates are open, perception of pain occurs when those afferent impulses reach the thalamus.

Opening and Closing Gates.   The gates are normally open, but how do they close? One way is that signals from other sensory fibers inhibit incoming injury information. Another possibility is that central modulating systems send neural impulses down from the brain; as we noted in our discussion of descending pain tracts, those messages can inhibit signals from incoming injury-sensitive fibers. Gates may then be blocked at the substantia gelatinosa; if enkephalins and endorphins are present there, they may stimulate relevant synapses to close the gates. The closing of gates may occur by raising the threshold of excitability at the synapses so that the impulses coded for pain do not cross.

Factors that may close a gate include inhibitory neural impulses from the brain and other sources and reduction of neural impulses when muscles relax.

For example, an athlete may not perceive pain until after the game is over because one such system has closed the gates. On the other hand, a person in a dentist's chair may be anxious (over-tense) in anticipating and exaggerating pain, thereby opening gates so that pain is perceived. We know that muscular tension exacerbates pain and that we can often relax pain away (see Chapter 15). Apparently by relaxing, the cessation of afferent neural impulses from the muscles can allow the gate to close. So, if one relaxes in a dentist's chair, gates can close and the perception of pain is prevented.

A cybernetic system thus functions when injury-sensitive fibers send afferent neural impulses to affect central modulating systems; those central modulating systems, in turn, influence the pattern of injury-sensitive fibers by sending descending neural impulses. A nonpainful state may then result by temporarily closing gates.

In Review. The gate-control theory includes the following elements: (1) There are specialized receptors that are activated by injurious stimuli; (2) if gates are open, injury-sensitive neural fibers conduct afferent signals that lead to pain perception when they reach the thalamus; (3) gates may be closed thereby blocking incoming signals from those injury-sensitive fibers; (4) gates may be closed by signals from other sensory neural fibers and by central modulating systems.

Gates Are Components of Circuits. Gates at the substantia gelatinosa in the spinal cord and elsewhere in the CNS are influenced by patterns of events throughout the body to determine whether an injurious stimulus is perceived as painful. No doubt endorphins and enkephalins, which are widespread throughout the CNS, stimulate certain synapses to close gates, thereby reducing or eliminating pain. Thus, the complex interaction of diverse influences, according to this theory, generates the basic phenomenon of pain perception or lack thereof, all of which fits our cybernetic model.

A pattern of diverse events determines whether or not a stimulus is perceived as painful by closing gates or leaving them open.

Implications for Research and for Clinical Practice. The gate-control theory has had an extensive and important impact on neurophysiological pain research, such as specifying pathways that carry pain messages to and from the brain. Neurochemical research has advanced our understanding of pain by specifying the roles of endogenous opioid substances and the functioning of gates. For instance, there can be a balance (homeostatic state) of enkephalins and endorphins within the central nervous system that may be disturbed. If sufficiently disturbed, the subjective experience of pain may be enhanced. Such an imbalance could cause the descending impulses from the brain to close gates and effectively inhibit incoming pain messages. The gate-control theory also has important implications for the clinical control of pain by psychologists. For instance, the fact that you can stimulate or relax selective regions in the body and that relaxation of the body reduces pain conforms with the essential features of the gate-control theory.

Fear, Anxiety, and Conditional Avoidance Behavior

Fear Has Survival Value. Noxious stimuli can lead to the motivated behaviors referred to as fear and anxiety that energize us for flight or fight. We learn to fear things because they are associated with pain or the prospect of pain. Fear has survival value—when we fear a painful stimulus, we can anticipate it in order to avoid it. If we have too little fear, we might not behave effectively to avoid a painful and harmful stimulus. The average student who has too little fear of an examination might not study sufficiently well for it. There is an optimal amount of fear for efficient behavior.

Fear and anxiety of stimuli are conditional responses that have been associated with pain.

Pathological Fears.   However, excessive fear can generate behaviors that interfere with effectiveness. If we are fearful to the point of anxiety, we may not perform well at certain tasks, or in solving problems. Anxiety is an extreme condition of fear which is pathological (i.e., it has clinical significance).

Many fears and anxieties are of symbolic stimuli and are not useful (e.g., the color yellow may evoke the anxiety that an aversive event might occur, yet the color itself is harmless). Avoidance behavior of symbolic stimuli such as yellow is unrealistically maintained because the organism never verifies whether or not the aversive event will occur — when one always avoids yellow, one never finds out that nothing bad would happen should the color be approached. Consequently, such conditional avoidance behavior is extremely difficult to extinguish.

Fear is motivated avoidance behavior which can have a useful energizing function with survival value.

Excessive fear becomes anxiety which can cause one to freeze or otherwise behave ineffectively.

When unreasonable fears become extreme, they can be classified as phobias. Having been conditioned, they are best controlled with conditioning principles (see Chapter 10) as applied in behavior therapy (see Chapter 14.)

Chronobiology and Rhythms of the Body

The physiological functioning of the body follows a number of cyclic patterns through which behaviors are rhythmically influenced. These bodily events motivate us to behave in a number of specific ways, such as seeking sleep at night. It is within the field of **chronobiology** (*chrono* refers to "time") that scientists study lawful temporal phenomena within the body. Although biologists have long studied cyclic physiological events, chronobiology has recently been expanding as psychologists and psychiatrists have contributed to the field. Circadian rhythms are among the most common cyclic events studied.

Chronobiology is the study of regular temporal phenomena within the body, such as sleep–waking cycles.

CIRCADIAN RHYTHMS

All organisms, from humans to vegetables, follow circadian rhythms. **Circadian rhythms** are daily rhythms of 24-hour duration. *Circadian* derives from the Latin *circa diem*, meaning "about a day."

Humans and animals maintain many circadian activity cycles that last approximately 24 hours.

One circadian rhythm is body temperature, which is highest at noon and lowest in the early morning. Other 24-hour cycles include those for blood sugar level, urine excretion, pulse rate, plasma cortisol concentration, and hormonal secretions such as that of adrenaline. Cognitive experiences of being hungry and tired are often related to certain times of the day.

What Drives Circadian Rhythms?   It used to be thought that circadian rhythms were learned, but this notion was disconfirmed in several ways. One was by raising fruit flies in constant environmental conditions. When the flies were not exposed to a 24-hour light–dark cycle, they still exhibited 24-hour behavioral rhythms. Other research in which humans lived in underground caverns for months at a time yielded conclusions that humans have spontaneous periods of activity and rest each day. Even if individuals are isolated from external environmental cues, they generally continue to sleep about eight hours a day. Consequently, we learned that circadian rhythms are internal and self-sustaining, existing in their own right. Circadian rhythms are not driven by external cues (e.g., they remain stable as external temperature varies). *True circadian rhythms are those that persist when external cues*

Light–dark circadian cycles provide a time cue for both diurnal and nocturnal animals.

have been removed. However, external stimuli can somewhat adjust the period and phase of circadian rhythms. For instance, circadian rhythms can be modified by up to two hours (as by changing the light–dark cycle in a laboratory).

Given that circadian rhythms are internally driven, just what are the mechanisms for that? The answer would specify the nature of endogenous internal biological clocks that are physiologically self-sustaining.

Circadian rhythms occur within the body regardless of the nature of external stimulation.

BIOLOGICAL CLOCKS

The Superchiasmatic Nuclei (SCN) as a Daily Clock. A major problem occurs when people must work during hours that are contrary to their biological clock. Performance is most efficient when the body temperature is at its height; it is then that people feel awake. However, when body temperature is low, especially around 4 or 5 A.M., people's performance is relatively inefficient. An inordinate number of accidents occur at that time. Efforts are thus made to adjust the biological clock through such techniques as exposing people to very bright lights at night or administering chemical substances such as melatonin. But what is a biological clock?

In research to understand the components of circuits that function to maintain circadian rhythms, Curt Richter systematically eliminated various regions of rats' bodies. These included the adrenals, gonads, pituitary, thyroid, and pineal glands. The rats were also given shock therapy and placed in alcoholic stupors, and lesions were made systematically throughout their brains. None of these operations disturbed circadian rhythms until a region in the anterior hypothalamus called the superchiasmatic nuclei (SCN) was lesioned. Lesions in the SCN destroyed the rats' daily rhythms of water consumption, physical activity, and adrenal corticosterone secretion. These results were then confirmed on other species including hamsters, cats, squirrels, and rhesus monkeys. Apparently, then, the SCN are a critical component of a biological clock. However, the SCN do not control all rhythms—lesioning the SCN did not affect the rhythms of core body temperature, urine potassium excretion, and REM sleep.

A Pause for Reflection on the Ablation Method. We emphasized the method's shortcomings in Chapter 8 along with some of its virtues. The research on the SCN emphasizes some of its virtues, namely by experimentally producing brain lesions in animals, we are often better able to investigate the numerous kinds of behaviors that are disrupted by neural insult, the course of recovery from injury, and, most important, factors that facilitate both neural repair and behavioral recovery. Indeed, we have learned an amazing amount by the use of the ablation method.

Human Data. Although we generalize cautiously from animals to humans, one case on humans yielded conclusions consonant with those on animals. An autopsy on a woman indicated that she had a tumor in her left brain ventrical that had virtually destroyed her SCN. Prior to death she had trouble sleeping and could be easily aroused, as was the case in the lesioned animals.

The superchiasmatic nuclei (SCN) in the anterior hypothalamus constitute a critical component of a biological clock in mammals.

More extensive research has implicated the SCN not only in regulating sleeping and waking, heart and pulse rates, feeding and drinking cycles, and sexual behavior but also in the secretion of a variety of hormones. These hormones include thyroid-stimulating hormone, testosterone, prolactin, thyrotropin, growth hormone, and pineal N-acetyltransferase (the enzyme involved in production of melatonin, the chief hormone of the pineal gland). The interactions among the hormonal, neural, and other systems to maintain circadian rhythms are complex, indeed.

Melatonin is secreted by the brain's pineal gland and is synchronized to the 24-hour light–dark cycle so that its levels increase at night.

   Importance of Melatonin.   When **melatonin** is released by the pineal gland, it acts on a small region in the posterior of the hypothalamus that apparently contains receptors for it. Melatonin production is controlled as follows: Light activates the retina to send information through the hypothalamus to the pineal gland to inhibit the production of melatonin. On the other hand, lack of light increases the secretion of melatonin. Consequently, large amounts of the hormone melatonin are released at night and small amounts are released in the daytime. The conclusion is that melatonin is a chemical stimulus that induces sleep. Administering melatonin may thus reset the biological clock to produce better sleep. In fact, research has indicated that melatonin treatment relieves the symptoms of jet lag. More specifically, people who were administered the hormone had a better quality of sleep and were more alert than comparison travelers who did not receive the treatment. Melatonin apparently is not toxic and is well tolerated by humans. It may be useful for treating other biological disorders too. For instance some data suggest that depressed people who are exposed to bright light and sleep scheduling have benefited therapeutically.

High levels of melatonin seem to be conducive to sleep and to counteract jet lag.

   Melatonin also inhibits sex hormone secretions, indicating that estrus and menstrual cycles are also related to SCN. Newborn rats with SCN lesions fail to develop estrus cycles and adult female rats cease to ovulate once there are SCN lesions. Irving Zucker suggests that SCN lesions interfere with the flow of luteinizing hormones to the pituitary gland. Luteinizing hormones function in complex circuits to affect the secretions of other hormones that trigger ovulation (see Fig. 9.1).

   Whether or not there are other biological clocks like the SCN is a controversial research issue. Some data suggest that there is one in the eyes of amphibians and in the pineal gland of lizards and birds.

INFRADIAN AND ULTRADIAN RHYTHMS

Infradian rhythms, like those for menstruation, have longer cycles than do circadian rhythms; ultradian rhythms, like respiration rate, are shorter than 24-hour cycles.

In addition to circadian rhythms, there are other rhythms of the body, some of them longer, some shorter. The longer cycles are called **infradian rhythms** and include menstrual and estrus cycles, hibernation, and seasonal gains and losses of weight. Rhythms that are less than 24 hours are called **ultradian rhythms** and include heart beat, electrical activity of the brain, and respiration. Some of these infradian and ultradian rhythms correspond to mood and performance fluctuations throughout the day.

   EEG rhythms are one class of ultradian rhythms especially germane to biological psychology. EEG tracings of the right and left hemispheres have suggested that there are rhythm differences between them. One hemisphere will have a particular rhythm for an average of about two hours when it shifts to the other hemisphere. One interpretation is that one hemisphere "dominates" for awhile, then the other "dominates." Some data indicate that when the ability to perform verbal tasks is high, the left hemisphere is dominant and spatial ability is low. Conversely when the right hemisphere is dominant, the spatial ability is high and verbal ability is relatively low.

SLEEP AND WAKEFULNESS CYCLES

Sleep in humans is a biological rhythm organized in a systematic circadian pattern of about 24 hours. Humans spend about one-third of their lives in sleep. Various species have different kinds of behavior patterns and many have unique sleep patterns that are fitted to their particular worlds. For some species such as rodents and carnivores, the sleep and waking cycles are ultradian (less than 24 hours). Elephants have to spend most of their time finding food and eating it so they sleep only about two hours a day. Gorillas and domestic cats sleep about 18 hours a day. Opossums and bats sleep about 80 percent of the time, rats and cats about 60 percent, chimpanzees about 45 percent, donkeys and cows about 15 percent.

One study of a volunteer indicated that there was an internal mechanism informing him when to sleep and when to awaken. He lived in a special room for two weeks with no clocks or lights and was allowed to sleep as much as he wanted. Still, he was able to discern when it was lunchtime, teatime, and bedtime, using only the cues within his body. Under these conditions he settled down to a regular rhythm of sleep and wakefulness.

While sleep–wake cycles follow a circadian pattern for humans, other species follow different patterns.

Some think that sleep is a condition of relaxation and inactivity, but electrical studies of the body indicate that it is a complex and by no means inactive state. Mammals show similar alternating periods of quiet and active sleep. Only monotremes (the lowest order of mammals) fail to show these alternating patterns of sleep activity.

Stages of Sleep and REM Periods. In the human adult there are four stages of sleep that cyclically occur sequentially throughout the night. Depth of sleep increases as one passes through stages 1, 2, 3, and 4. Rapid-eye-movement (REM) periods occur about an hour and a half after sleep starts and then at intervals of about an hour and a half thereafter. By waking sleepers immediately after an episode of REM sleep, dreams are typically reported. The large portion of our dreaming occurs during REM periods.

Sleepers dream almost exclusively during REM periods when the sleeper's eyes move rapidly in various directions.

While the muscles of the body have reduced **tone** (or **tonus,** low sustained contraction) during REM sleep, they are covertly quite active with rapid, **phasic responses** (phasic contractions are very rapid bursts of short duration). (For an illustration of the phasic activity superimposed on the sustained tonic activity of muscle during a REM period, see Fig. 13.12.) The reduced muscle tone in sleep appears to be attributable to a circuit involving the pons (Fig. 6.5); more particularly, the locus coeruleus is an important region within the pons that contributes to the reduced muscle tone.[2] Lesions made in the locus coeruleus have been found to free some muscles from their reduced tonic state.

The sleep of human and other primates is similar in that they all have stages of sleep that include REM periods. However, the sleep of other species is generally composed of two stages of sleep resembling stages 3 and 4 of humans. While REM sleep comes about once every 90 minutes in human beings, it appears about once every 25 minutes in cats.

Essentially all species have REM (dreaming) sleep, although the timing and the duration of REM periods vary with the species.

---

[2]*Locus coeruleus* is Latin for "blue place," so named because an elevated amount of copper therein gives it a blue appearance. Copper is involved in the synthesis of norepinephrine which functions as a neurotransmitter.

REM periods are important for us in many ways. When REM periods were reduced or eliminated in experimental research, there was REM rebound. That is, subjects increased the amount of REM sleep later when allowed to make up for their REM loss. As one psychiatrist has suggested, dreaming is necessary and beneficial in that it allows us to go quietly and safely insane each night.

Why Do We Sleep?

Sleep is important to us, maybe even for our survival. But why do we go to sleep and stay so for some eight hours? What causes us to awaken and why do we sleep in regular cycles? Although we have learned a tremendous amount through psycho-physiological sleep research, we still do not have good answers to these questions nor do we really understand what sleep is. Although there have been numerous notions advanced to answer these questions, they generally reduce to two rather vague theories: sleep as an adaptive response and sleep as a restorative process. As summarized by Webb, the adaptive response theory holds that

> Sleep developed, in particular forms and patterns it took in each species, as a behavior that increased the likelihood of that species' survival. The particular survival value associated with sleeping—that of reducing behavioral activity—was to protect animals (e.g., including humans) from dangerous or inefficient activities, both their own and others', particularly in relation to foraging or food gathering. Sleep, then, evolved in each species as a form of "nonbehavior" when not responding in the environment would increase survival chances. (1975, p. 158)

The adaptive response theory holds that the function of sleep is to conserve energy when the environment is hostile.

Thus, the adaptive response theory holds that sleep is an innate behavior and is evolutionary in nature. As we have evolved, we have developed a mode of behavior that conserves energy and protects us from a dangerous environment at night. Webb speculates that our ancestors found safety from prowling nighttime predators in caves, perhaps adding a fire at the mouth of the cave. If they could, they slept. Those who roamed and did not thus protect themselves, by this notion, did not pass their genes on to any progeny. Sleep, thus, could have originally been a "nonbehavior" that had such survival value. Webb suggests that sleep is necessary to inhibit behavior. It is thus an innate response pattern that helps to keep us out of danger. (The hibernation of bears during a hostile winter is another example of sleep's protective value.)

The Restorative Process Theory of Sleep. The commonsense notion is that sleep has a biological restorative function. We need to restore ourselves when fatigue builds up and sleep certainly helps, at least when we have good, effective sleep. However, just because we restore ourselves with sleep does not mean that the restorative function is the reason that we *do* sleep. Sleep may be biologically restorative, but it may only be something that we rhythmically do. Like feeding, sleep may only be part of an innate rhythm. We thus help our bodies by eating and sleeping at regular times during 24-hour periods. However, noting that eating and sleeping are rhythmical does not explain why we do them.

In Conclusion. Unfortunately we do not have sufficient data to decide between the adaptive response and the restorative process theories, nor to propose a different, superior one. Limited data support each theory. For instance, animals that can sleep securely wherever they wish, such as lions, sleep many hours during the day, while animals that are preyed upon and have no place to hide, such as cattle, sleep very little—perhaps they must constantly be alert to dangers. On the other hand, when organisms are deprived of sleep, there are indications that the brain does not function normally. Eventually, we trust, the accumulation of additional data will help to answer these important questions about why we spend one-third of our lives in a nonproductive process.

Do We Need Sleep?

Among the many factors that influence human performance is amount of sleep. Sleep deprivation, disturbance of circadian rhythms, and to a lesser extent ultradian rhythms affect human performance.

In one study, four students agreed to stay awake for 36 hours without sleep and then were tested. They performed well on interesting games like chess, but they were not good at boring, repetitive tasks; for example, when they had to recognize short musical notes from a series of long and short notes, they made more and more mistakes as time without sleep passed.

In general, the body can go without sleep for some time, provided it is given adequate rest and food. There seem to be no permanent adverse effects of sleep loss on how the body functions. Strangely, though, not everybody does need sleep. A man by the name of Lesley Gamble claimed that as a result of an accident, he never slept. When psychophysiologically tested by Wilse Webb, the recordings indeed showed that he was awake all night. His report was that he thinks most of the night, reflecting on happy events in his life which helps him to relax. At the time of the report he had gone for 11 years without sleep.

Normal humans do need to sleep, although the amount and the quality vary considerably among individuals.

DO MOON CYCLES AFFECT BEHAVIOR?

Among the different cycles that the human body has experienced for thousands of years, the moon has been thought to have special significance. Many conduct their lives according to the phases of the moon. Some farmers plant and harvest by lunar cycles and other people believe that the moon causes changes in human emotions, health, and mental status. Some have reported increases of violent and bizarre crimes, psychiatric emergencies, auto accidents, high-speed chases, births, suicides, and aggravated assaults during the new and full moons.

Arnold L. Lieber, a psychiatrist, in his book *The Lunar Effect: Biological Tides and Human Emotion,* says that humans, like the earth's surface, contain about 80 percent water and 20 percent solids. Consequently, he asserts that the gravitational force of the moon exerts an influence on the water in the human body just as it does on the oceans to produce tides. He concludes from his statistical studies that new and full moons create biological tides within the body that then have their greatest effects on behavior.

In *The Skeptical Inquirer,* a journal dedicated to separating fact from myth, scientists reviewed forty studies and concluded that they could find *no evidence of the moon's affecting human behavior.* They concluded that there is so little water in the human body that the gravitational forces of the moon cannot affect it — if the moon could affect that small amount of water, the puddles of water on earth would be sliding around during the full moon.

Although some believe that the position of the moon affects behavior, there are no reliable data substantiating such a causal relationship.

Yet, there could be some truth in the reported statistical relation between moon position and behavior. Centuries of unusual tales and beliefs indeed could have implanted the suggestion; and by believing that there is a relationship, perception and behavior could conform to that belief. Believing that something is true, even if it is false, still can exert a powerful influence on one's behavior. This is known as the **placebo** effect.

EMOTIONAL BEHAVIOR

Few concepts have been subjected to such extensive criticism as has emotion; some scientists even refuse to use the term. Nevertheless, like "motivation" and "instinct," "emotion" remains in psychology in some form, especially in physiologically oriented theories.

From a commonsense (nonscientific) point of view, emotions are subjective feelings of being happy, sad, angry, fearful, and so on. Emotions are considered mental states wherein one is aroused with feelings that are positive (euphoria, love) or negative (anger, fear). Taking such notions as a starting point, a scientific approach would attempt to define and measure emotions, a difficult task indeed.

To gain a better perspective, let us timidly approach this formidable area by first mentioning some of the various theories of emotion. Then we will sample some relevant neural, hormonal, and behavioral data that we will attempt to fit within the framework of our general cybernetic model.

Some Traditional Theories of Emotion

EVOLUTIONARY THEORY

Darwinian evolutionary principles hold that there are numerous emotions expressed in common by humans and other higher primates. For example, a frown by a human or an ape indicates emotional concern. An evolutionary theory seeks to determine the functions of emotional response patterns; that is, how did they help in the struggle for survival and what is their meaning today?

COGNITIVE AROUSAL THEORY

The cognitive arousal theory is dualistic, holding that emotions are mental processes different from physiological states. One form modeled on psychophysical interactionism holds that the specific parameters of bodily arousal determine the specific kind of emotion that one cognitively experiences. A classical example of this kind of theory is the famous **James-Lange** (pronounced "Longuh") **theory.** Developed independently by William James and the Dane, Carl Lange, it reversed the commonsense notion of the day. The prevailing view was that perception of an emotional event caused a physiological state of emotionality. In contrast, the James-Lange theory held that emotion is a mental (cognitive) feeling that followed directly from psychophysiological arousal (increased heart rate, muscle tension, etc.). James's famous example was that a person in the forest perceives a bear, runs, and *then* becomes afraid, in that temporal sequence. In contrast, the prevailing theory held that one perceives the bear, becomes emotionally afraid, and then runs. The James-Lange theory held that perception of feedback from physiological and be-

The James-Lange theory of emotions is a cognitive-arousal one. It holds that one perceives an emotion-producing stimulus and reacts to it, whereupon perception of feedback from the reaction leads to the appropriate emotion.

havioral events produces the cognitive emotional events. Perception of such feedback is compatible with a cybernetic model.

NEUROPHYSIOLOGICAL THEORIES OF EMOTION

Neurophysiological theories emphasize that emotional feelings are generated by different patterns of reaction in the nervous systems. There are two principal kinds of neurophysiological theories emphasizing the functions of the autonomic nervous system and the central nervous system respectively. The autonomic nervous system theory assumes that different emotions are produced depending upon the pattern of autonomic events. The central nervous system theory seeks to specify events in the brain that generate emotions.

Most theorizing has concerned the central nervous system as in Walter Cannon's conclusion that the thalamus and hypothalamus are important central structures for integrating emotions. He reasoned that the thalamus mediates emotions because it can be activated by sensory inputs from external receptors and by cortical impulses. Thalamic activity can interact with both the cortex and the viscera, involving the autonomic nervous system. Cannon hypothesized that cortical activation is responsible for the consciousness of emotions.

In 1934 P. Bard held that the hypothalamus was the major director of emotional expression since it regulates both the endocrine system and the autonomic nervous system.

The Limbic System Theory. In 1937 James W. Papez hypothesized that the limbic system (see Fig. 6.11) regulates emotion, in part because it has connections with the thalamus, the cortex, and the hypothalamus. The limbic system also has an input into the reticular formation, which provides another pathway for arousal through stimulation of the cortex.

Papez's theory assumes that there is a composite of forebrain structures that form a border around some midline structures. (The term *limbic* comes from the Latin word *limbus* that means "border.") As we saw in Chapter 6, depending on the authority, the hypothesized limbic system includes such structures as the hypothalamus, the hippocampus, the amygdala, the olfactory bulb, some areas of the thalamus, and the cingulate gyrus of the cerebral cortex as well as several other structures. All structures of the limbic system are closely connected with each other.

Papez knew that the limbic system receives considerable sensory input from the olfactory receptors so that it was understandable why smells are important in emotion. He hypothesized that the limbic system generates neural impulses that are transmitted to the cerebral cortex to add feeling tone to the ongoing activity of the cortex. He proposed that all sensory inputs are separated by the thalamus into three streams for different kinds of processing: movement, thought, and feeling. The stream of movement is sent to the basal ganglia; the stream of thought to the lateral cerebral cortex; and the stream of feeling to the hypothalamus and from there to the rest of the limbic system. After processing, they are reunited in the cerebral cortex which would then be "aware" of all aspects of an experience. The actual experience of emotion thus, by Papez's theory, depends on the cerebral cortex (as it did for Cannon). Recent findings that most of the areas that may be stimulated for reward or

Neurophysiological theories hold that emotional experiences are generated by patterns of reactions in the autonomic and central nervous systems.

Papez hypothesized a limbic system that regulates emotion. His anatomic data showed that it has connections with the thalamus, the cortex, and the hypothalamus, all of which have been implicated in emotion.

Papez's theory held that the limbic system generates neural impulses that are transmitted to the cortex to add feeling-tone to ongoing cortical activity. Messages about movement, thought, and feeling are reunited in the cortex whereupon subjective emotional experiences occur.

punishment are located in the limbic system and that most of the reward areas contain either catecholamines, norepinephrine, or dopamine synaptic transmitters are consonant with this theory.

Other Theories.   We mention some other theories in the next sections. In the meantime, if you, the reader, conclude that theories of emotions are vague, inadequate, and incomplete, you have a realistic perception of the state of research on emotional behavior, confirming our introductory remarks about the scientific status, or lack thereof, of emotion. However, there do seem to be some kinds of behavior that can be profitably defined in terms of objectively observable responses classified as emotional responses.

There is no commonly accepted objective definition of emotion nor is there an adequate theory to explain emotions.

Some Behavioral, Physiological, and Anatomical Data

ORIGIN OF EMOTIONAL BEHAVIOR

At birth and in early infancy there are consistent expressions commonly identified as emotional behaviors. Apparently an infant has an innate readiness to perceive and to emotionally respond to various social stimuli. John Watson concluded from his extensive research on infants that love, fear, and rage are basic inborn emotional reflexes. Within a year infants can reproduce emotional responses such as happiness by smiling back at a person. Infants are also capable of imitating various responses that are not considered to be expressive of emotions, such as head turning and tongue and finger movements. Behaviors such as these have basic communicative value; for example, when a social cue such as a mother's smile elicits a similar response in an infant, the infant begins to learn many things. For one, the infant seems to become aware of the distinction between itself and others, developing a concept of "me" that separates its body from other bodies. Another is that the infant learns the names of various emotional behaviors. Different patterns of emotional responses generate their unique afferent neural impulses from muscles (see pp. 428–430 in Chapter 13). The infant learns that each unique muscular facial pattern of responding with its neural feedback has a name — when muscles that control the mouth move it up to smile, the infant is told that it is happy and the response pattern is identified as the emotion of happiness; another facial response pattern is learned as that of sadness, and so forth. Infants then learn to emotionally respond in order to communicate their various internal physiological states (that they "feel" happy, sad, etc.).

Although some basic emotional behaviors appear to be innate, further emotional development is a learning phenomenon resulting from social interactions.

Several kinds of data are consistent with the thesis that some emotional expressions are inborn, a thesis developed by Darwin. First, there is a universality of emotional reactions such that adults from different cultures can match expressions to the situation that generates them. For instance, people in culture A can match pictures of emotional expressions (like a smiling, happy face) to a given environmental situation (like children at play), even though the stimuli came from culture B. Second, soon after birth, infants will differentially respond to various kinds of social situations with appropriate expressions of smiling, anger, or distress, depending on the situation depicted. Third, children who are blind and children who are sighted emit similar emotional expressions at approximately the same stage of development.

THE HYPOTHALAMUS AND EMOTIONS

A long and widely held consensus is that the hypothalamus is a site of neural integration for emotional behavior. Bard's 1928 classic demonstration that a decorticate (a cortex extirpated and thus a thalamic) animal is still capable of producing a complete display of emotional behavior is part of the evidence. If there is ablation of the ventromedial nucleus of the hypothalamus, there is explosive, biting attack behavior called "sham rage" in response to usually harmless stimuli. Further evidence is that stimulation of specific locations in the hypothalamus can produce a variety of integrated emotional behaviors that have been considered to be flight, anger, or defense patterns. Also, there is a hypothalamic influence on autonomic behavior which is similar to the autonomic responses that are present during emotional behavior.

Additional implication of the hypothalamus comes from the stimulation of an area referred to as the **hypothalamic controlling emotional response area (HACER).** Such stimulation reproduces cardiovascular responses that are part of a conditional emotional response pattern. When the HACER area is extirpated, there is a complete disappearance of those cardiovascular responses that otherwise would occur during the conditional emotional response. In accord with conclusions of Smith and DeVito (1984), the HACER appears to be a major component of an autonomic control system during emotional behavior. They suggest that the output of the HACER is designed to activate cells that guarantee total sympathetic nervous system discharge. They conclude that the HACER region stands at that critical junction between emotional responses and resultant autonomic responses. No doubt there is return afferentation so that circuits between the HACER and autonomic nervous system reverberate during emotional behavior.

Ablation and stimulation techniques have implicated the hypothalamus in emotional behavior. A specific area of the hypothalamus, HACER, functions with the autonomic nervous system during emotional behavior.

LATERALITY AND PROCESSING
OF EMOTIONAL STIMULI

Importance of the Right Hemisphere.   A classic observation by J. Babinski in 1914 was that patients with right cerebral hemisphere damage were often emotionally indifferent. Since then, considerable data indicate that the right hemisphere is especially important for processing emotional stimuli. For example, patients with right hemisphere disease have more difficulty than patients with left hemisphere disease in comprehending emotional facial expressions, such as those for sadness, or for emotionally toned speech. However, that does not mean that the left hemisphere serves strictly nonemotional functions. It is now clear in fact that both hemispheres can contribute to emotional experience. A consistent pattern of results shows that there is a heightened right hemisphere involvement in negative emotional states like depression; furthermore there is heightened activity of the left hemisphere while processing positive affective states. For instance, studies have generally shown that left hemisphere sedation or damage (which allows the right hemisphere to "dominate") results in excessive worry, pessimism, and crying. On the other hand, right hemisphere sedation or damage often results in inappropriate euphoria, indifference, or laughter. Furthermore, these emotional reactions are especially associated with damage to the frontal lobes. This finding is consistent with the existence of circuits between the frontal lobes and the limbic system as we discussed in Chapter 6.

The right cerebral hemisphere functions more in the processing of emotional stimuli than does the left cerebral hemisphere.

The two cerebral hemispheres do not function independently; however, the frontal lobes of the right hemisphere are primarily involved in processing negative emotional states, while those of the left hemisphere are more active in processing positive emotional states.

Cerebral circuits for processing emotional stimuli involve frontal lobes, subcortical structures, and those between the two hemispheres, as well as interactions with other systems throughout the body.

The right hemisphere is functionally connected to subcortical structures that are important for mediating cerebral arousal and activation. Thus, although we momentarily concentrate on cerebral functions in emotional behavior, we must not forget that these regions are but portions of extensive circuits running throughout the body.

FACIAL FEEDBACK FINDINGS

Darwin (1872) in his classic work *The Expression of Emotion in Man and Animals* proposed that emotions and emotional expressions have biological bases. He emphasized common facial expressions among higher primates such as that of frowning. Subsequent data indicate that such facial expressions are in fact biologically wired in. Other data also indicate that humans are biologically predisposed to interpret and appropriately respond to facial expressions of others (e.g., Buck, 1984).

It is possible that the expression of emotions is a feedforward process in which central commands are directed to the facial muscles. However, feedback from the facial muscles has been hypothesized as necessary for generating the subjective experience of emotions (see Manstead, 1988, for a review of relevant data).

Patterns of facial muscle tension generate feedbacks that differentially lead to different subjective emotional experiences.

Facial muscles react differentially and have sensory nerves that go directly to the hypothalamic region of the brain. Presumably internal feedback of afferent neural impulses from facial muscles carries information that then evokes emotions. Thus, facial expressions are produced by contractions of the facial muscles in various combinations that produce movements of the skin and connective tissue of the face (e.g., when the mouth turns up, afferent neural impulses presumably carry information that evokes subjective feelings of happiness). These facial expressions also communicate one's emotional state to others.

Data that show that internal feedback from facial patterns can shape subjective feelings have been gathered by two different methods: (1) indirect manipulation through instructions to express or hide expressions and (2) direct manipulation of facial muscles. Both strategies have been successful in generating various emotional experiences depending on the muscles contracted. However, spontaneous, as compared to voluntary, expressions of emotion influence subjective states more strongly. Examples of these kinds of research follow.

Volitional control exercised by a person over the facial muscles produces widespread changes throughout the body by activating circuits involving the hypothalamus, autonomic nervous system, and so on.

A number of studies have shown that various patterns of facial muscle activity are reliably associated with the subjective experience of different emotional states. For instance, Schwartz, Fair, Salt, Mandel, and Klerman (1976) found that when their subjects were instructed to imagine pleasant thoughts, the activity of the zygomatic muscle increases (as in Fig. 9.5, that muscle elevates the cheeks to form a smile). On the other hand, when the subjects were instructed to imagine unpleasant thoughts (e.g., an unhappy situation), the corrugator muscle activity increased (the muscle used for frowning). It is also been shown that subjects' corrugator muscles increased in activity when they were presented with angry faces and the zygomatic responses increased to happy faces; both reactions were extremely rapid (Dimberg, 1990). Dimberg also presents some data that indicate that even though facial expression of emotions is prewired, the muscles are also subject to learning so that there is a cultural effect on our emotional expression. These subtle covert responses can be electromyographically measured and often cannot be detected by the naked eye.

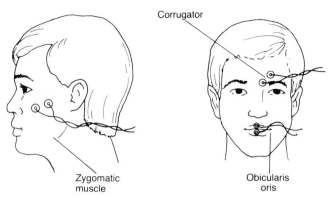

FIGURE 9.5 The muscles of the face differentially react according to the kind of subjective emotional experience.

For the second method, when subjects are asked to voluntarily change their facial muscles corresponding to such emotions as fear and anger, Paul Ekman found that they report the appropriate subjective emotional experience. Furthermore, he found that those facial muscle changes produce significant changes in heart rate and skin temperature. Thus those changes affect the autonomic nervous system which reacts differently during different emotions.

Jacobson (1938b, 1967) found that minuscule (covert) muscular contraction patterns are present whenever one experiences emotions. Furthermore, each pattern is a specific one that corresponds to how the person would overtly behave. For instance, if a person experiences the emotion of fear of being hit in the right leg with a rock, the muscles in the right leg would be covertly active. It can be seen that Jacobson's pioneering work laid the basis for research in studying facial patterns during various emotions. But as we emphasize in the next section, bodily activity during emotions is not limited to one system or region of the body — it is extensively represented throughout the body. As demonstrated in Figure 9.6, subjective emotional perception is a complicated network of neuromuscular patterns of virtually the entire organism.

Having established that muscular patterns are covertly, and sometimes overtly, present during a variety of emotions, Jacobson then established the reverse strategy as well. That is, he showed that it was impossible for patients to experience emotions when their muscles were well relaxed (Jacobson, 1938b). These and other data support a peripheral feedback hypothesis of emotions. However, there is a puzzlement. As Rinn (1984) summarizes, there are apparently no, or very few, muscle spindles (which would contribute to the generation of feedback) in the facial muscles. On the other hand, muscle spindles are plentiful in the tongue and masticating muscles in the jaws. We know that the tongue is covertly very active during mental activity. Perhaps it is the tongue and jaw muscles that carry the load for feedback for emotional experience.

Based also on extensive research cited herein and elsewhere (McGuigan, 1978, 1991, 1993b), the conclusion that the striated musculature is critically involved in the generation of subjective emotional experiences is inevitable.

Voluntary facial movements modify subjective emotionality and some of the physiological functioning of the body involved in emotional behavior.

Jacobson established that there are striated muscle responses that activate other systems and generate emotions; conversely, he found that when striated muscles are well relaxed, emotional experiences are eliminated.

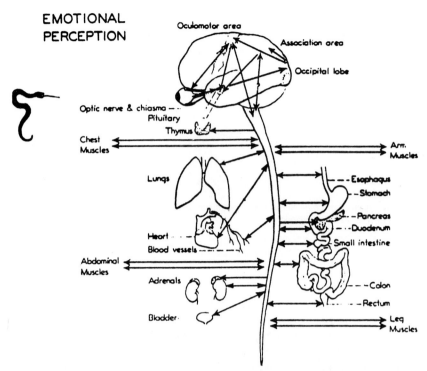

EMOTIONAL
PERCEPTION

FIGURE 9.6   Emotional perception is a reaction of virtually the entire organism and involves the ANS and the organs it supplies, the striated musculature, and the CNS. (From E. Jacobson, *The Biology of Emotions*, 1967. Courtesy of Charles C Thomas, Publisher, Springfield, Illinois.)

Verbal reports of subjective emotional experiences and emotional behaviors are generated when various systems of the body interact selectively as feedback from muscles activates reverberating cybernetic circuits.

In Conclusion.   We have seen that the autonomic nervous system, critical regions of the brain—especially the frontal lobes, the hypothalamus and other aspects of the limbic system—and the facial muscles among others are critically involved in emotional behavior. To say that various emotions are generated within any one system, such as the hypothalamus, or due solely to feedback from the facial muscles is unduly restrictive. Subjective emotional experiences, like all cognitive mental activities, are generated when various circuits of the body selectively reverberate and intimately interact.

BEHAVIOR GENETICS

Motivated and Emotional Behavior Is Influenced by Our Genes.   Because much of our behavior, be it motivated, emotional, or any other, is at least partially predetermined genetically, it is important to study the field of behavior genetics.

Behavior genetics is the study of the hereditary influences on behavior of all species.

The science of genetics properly began with the pioneering work of the monk Gregor J. Mendel. His research in 1866 involving breeding experiments with peas provided us with the basic principles of genetics. The more recently developed field of **behavior genetics** is the study of the hereditary bases of behavior of species throughout the phylogenetic scale ranging from bacteria to humans.

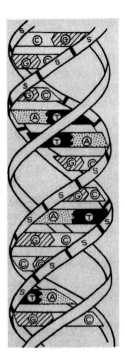

FIGURE 9.7
Strands of DNA — the
Watson-Crick Model of DNA.
DNA molecules have two
chains, each twisting about
the other in a double helix,
somewhat like two spiral
staircases that wind about the
same axis.

Genes and DNA

Genetic materials, **genes,** are functional units in the nucleus of cells of the body; they contain all the information that the cell needs to carry on its protein and energy production. In a sense, genes are chemical blueprints of all living things and determine whether an organism will grow into a plant, an animal, a bacterium, or a human. They also determine characteristics of organisms such as sex, the color of the hair, and, to a large extent, intelligence.

Composition of Genes. Genes consist of long, spiraling double strands of atoms made up of deoxyribonucleic acid (DNA). DNA is the master chemical of genes (Fig. 9.7). The DNA in a single cell would be six to seven feet long if its double strand were unfolded. Placed end-to-end, the strands of DNA in one human body have been estimated to reach to the moon and back 8000 times. Each strand of DNA is a chain of subunits called nucleotides. Each nucleotide includes one kind of chemical group called a base. The sequence of bases encodes the genetic information.

A gene is a stretch of DNA atoms subdivided into nucleotides that encode information.

Genes are arranged in linear sequences to form **chromosomes.** When two members of a species have offspring, their genes recombine to form new combinations of genes upon the chromosomes of the progeny.

Genotype and Phenotype

Genotype refers to the complete set of genes that the organism possesses. **Phenotype** refers to an overtly observable feature of an organism that is common among members of a species.

In the process of intentional selection for inbreeding, organisms with common phenotypes can be bred to increase the similarity of their genotypes. (*Inbreeding* is the mating of animals with common phenotypes that therefore are genetically similar.)

Some Accomplishments of Behavioral Genetics. Genetic analyses have helped us to understand physiological mechanisms underlying some motivational behaviors, as summarized by Wimer and Wimer (1984). Studies of genetically obese animals, for instance, have advanced our understanding of their feeding behavior, and different lines of animals have been genetically inbred to study addictive alcohol consumption.

Human Disease. Genetic characteristics of animals have been successfully used to study the causes of human disease and have facilitated searches for treatments. We have progressed noticeably by studying brain and behavioral phenomena in diseases that have a known or suspected genetic basis such as Down's syndrome, hypertension, obesity, and epilepsy. Indeed, more than 160 diseases that affect the nervous system or the striated muscle in humans have been given at least a tentative assignment for location on chromosomes. Biochemical techniques have been successful in mapping the majority of such assignments on such genes.

Psychopharmacology, which includes studying the effects of drugs on genetically different animals, is of importance in behavior genetics. For instance, animal studies of inherited epilepsy have indicated neurotransmitter abnormalities. As a result, anticonvulsant drugs for epilepsy have been successfully evaluated in animal research.

Alcoholism. In studies of genetically influenced dependence on alcohol, mouse models have been useful. Some strains of mice will consume substantial amounts of alcohol, while others will drink only water. The reason seems to be a genetically produced enzyme difference (greater alcohol activity involves the enzyme dehydrogenase in the liver of the alcohol-preferring strains). Possibly, there is a genetic basis for preferring alcohol, which could be a first stage of alcoholism in humans. With the exception of such findings on alcohol, efforts to specify genes that influence other drug behaviors, such as using opiates and barbiturates, have thus far been negative.

The Immune System. One possible disorder of the immune system is its failure to "recognize" one's own cells so that specific tissues become diseased. The result is a group of diseases known as autoimmune disorders (e.g., myasthenia gravis, rheumatoid arthritis). Such autoimmune diseases are more common in females than in males and may have some genetic basis. We do know that regulation of the autoimmune system is associated with sex hormones; for example, androgens provide protection against a disorder known as systemic lupus erythematosus (SLE). SLE affects the central nervous system and has various physiological and behavioral manifestations.

Some Negative Results. Mouse strains that live long versus short lives have been studied to identify genes controlling normal aging processes, but the research has not been very productive. The effort to find genetic effects on learning and memory have been similarly disappointing.

In Review. Research has established genetic influences in brain chemistry, brain structures, sexual behavior, alcohol preference, emotional and aggressive behavior, laterality, and more. It seems likely that genes influence many of these factors by regulating neurotransmitters. In sum, behavior genetics is a field of in-

creasing importance to biological psychology. As Wimer and Wimer (1984) conclude, the subtleties and complexities of hereditary influences on behavior "are
becoming increasingly well defined" (p. 106). The genetic influences on us are
extremely important.

Common genotypes and phenotypes among members of a given species are
accompanied by some unique behaviors they have in common. The study of such
behaviors that are specific to given species has increased in importance in recent
years.

SPECIES-SPECIFIC BEHAVIORS

On the premise that all species originated from a common ancestor, we can expect
much similar behavior among all species. Differences appear in **species-specific
behaviors**. Comparing behaviors among species helps us to better understand
human behavior.

Species-specific behaviors show common characteristics among members of a given species, while other species do not usually have those behaviors.

Some species-specific behaviors are adaptive; they develop in all members of a
given species regardless of their environmental experiences and thus typically do not
depend on learning to be acquired. Species-specific behaviors in humans appear
independently among all cultures. As Charles Darwin noted, humans in all societies
smile, frown, laugh, and cry under essentially the same kinds of environmental
conditions. Such behaviors also appear at an early age in children, even if they are
deaf or blind.

Some species possess a specialized capacity for learning certain kinds of behavior, but have little ability to learn other kinds of behavior. Those behaviors that a
species can easily learn are particularly beneficial to it. On the other hand, behaviors
that are difficult for it to acquire are not of much natural value. For example, rats can
learn well using the olfactory modality, but they are not very good at visually
discriminating among objects. One could surmise that for such nocturnal animals,
smell is especially useful for helping them manipulate through the environment at
night, while sight obviously is not.

Various species are geneti- cally predisposed to learn those certain behaviors that have specific survival value for them.

Species-specific behaviors that are inborn with a genetic basis remind us of the
old instinct doctrine, although this newer concept has a sounder empirical basis. In
contrast to the instinct doctrine, the concept of species-specific behaviors has considerably advanced our understanding of behavior throughout the phylogenetic
scale.

A SUMMARY OF SOME IMPORTANT ADVANCES IN THE STUDY OF MOTIVATED BEHAVIOR

Another major advance, as we point out in the next section, is that scientists now
more frequently follow a cybernetic model, wherein central and peripheral systems
interact. Their adherence to this model may be explicit or only implicit. Whalen and
Simon (1984) cite a change in investigative focus: Many investigators now study
"motivated behaviors" rather than motivation per se. Thus, they study ingestion
instead of hunger, mating behavior instead of sex drive, and flight rather than fear.

The importance of this advance is that it focuses on objective, observable, behavioral events instead of hypothetical states.

Yet another major advance has occurred with the development of the ability to observe the biochemistry of behavior. We are now able to perform sophisticated observations and manipulations of individual neurotransmitter systems involved in motivated behaviors.

To a large extent, the field has also evolved from a strategy of extreme environmentalism to now incorporate (recognized) inherited influences on behavior. Behavior genetics is the field that has led us to this view: "We now see an increased awareness, at least in some areas, that genotype is an important variable—rats are not cats, and even all mice are not created equal" (Whalen & Simon, 1984, p. 273).

EMPHASIS ON A CYBERNETIC PRINCIPLE— EVOLUTION OF A CENTRAL-PERIPHERAL MODEL OF MOTIVATED BEHAVIOR

Scientists are increasingly employing a model for motivated as well as for other kinds of behavior in which there are intricate two-way interactions between the brain and the periphery of the body. This thinking is quite compatible with a cybernetic model in which feedback circuits reverberate to control behavior.

As a consequence there has been a major change in how scientists view the regulation of motivated behaviors. The dominant view used to be a Cartesian model, derived from Descartes's conception that the soul acts on the brain to control behavior (p. 37). As we moved toward objective science, the Cartesian model evolved to one that held that centers in the brain control various response patterns. We have discussed the errors inherent in holding to such a one-way brain-centered conception of behavioral control. In summarizing how the field has changed from a brain-only control model, Whalen and Simon (1984) state that "Today we recognize that the brain is attached to the rest of the body and that the peripheral nervous system, either directly or through the control of secretion, plays an important role in regulation" (p. 273).

ENRICHMENT MATERIAL: PURPOSIVE BEHAVIOR AND HOMEOSTASIS
Purposive Behavior

Motivated Behavior Is Purposive.   Motivational conditions within an organism have been referred to as **purposes.** An organism may have a purpose to acquire food, for instance. Edward Chace Tolman emphasized the concept of purpose in his classic book *Purposive Behavior in Animals and Men.*

One application of cybernetics has been to understand the role of purpose in directing behavior, as Rosenblueth, Wiener, and Bigelow (1943) developed in a classic paper. **Purposive behavior,** so conceived, employs negative feedback whereby internal (purposive) signals modify and direct behavior to achieve a goal:

1. There is a certain existing condition of physiological need within the organism.
2. There are also strivings within the organism to satisfy the need.

3. Those strivings generate signals directing the organism to a goal that would satisfy the need.
4. There exists a difference between an existing need and the condition of satisfaction of the need.
5. The organism therefore purposively behaves to reduce that difference, as occurs in a negative feedback system.

In short, a negative feedback conception of the **goal-directed behavior** is that it is purposive behavior aimed at reducing the difference between an existing organismic condition of need and the condition of satisfaction of the need toward which the organism is moving. That difference is fed back into the organism's system so that behavior is modified. When the organism achieves its goal, the difference is reduced to zero. As in any negative feedback circuit, then, information is fed back to reduce/eliminate an error difference.

Purposive behavior occurs when an existing shortcoming within the organism deviates from a target (goal) value; behavior is then goal directed and negative feedback reduces that difference (error value) to zero by achieving the goal.

Homeostasis and Purpose

Deviation from Homeostasis Establishes Purposive Behavior. In Chapter 1 we introduced Walter Cannon's concept of homeostasis, which literally means "similar standing," as an example of how negative feedback circuits physiologically function. The concept is compatible with the cybernetic model of purpose. Thus, when physiological conditions of the body change from a standard level, a need exists. The organism then seeks a goal to return the condition of the body to that set level by ingesting whatever substance has become deficient. That seeking constitutes purposive behavior. When the goal is reached and consumed, the organism is returned to a stable homeostatic state. Disturbance of homeostasis thus serves as biological motivation to evoke such ingestive behaviors as the intake of food, water, and minerals; for example, if there is a physiological deficiency of salt, the organism will seek to consume salt (or if there is an excess, it will be excreted) so that homeostasis is restored. In general, then, physiological events act to purposively move and direct the organism in search of specific goals. When the difference between the need and the purposive striving becomes zero, a stable homeostatic state is again achieved.

Homeostasis is a process that maintains biological conditions about a constant, set value through the functioning of negative feedback circuits.

Negative feedback circuits function to maintain homeostasis by adding deficient substances to the body or by excreting them if they are in excess.

KEY TERMS

Addictive behavior—Repeated compulsive, uncontrolled responses, especially self-administration of drugs beyond medical needs.

Androgens—Male hormones, including especially testosterone.

Approach behavior—Behavior in which the organism moves toward an incentive—that is, leading to mating, food and liquid ingestion, and so on.

Avoidance behavior—Behavior in which the organism removes itself from stimuli and conditions. Humans report corresponding subjective experiences as painful, noxious, fearful, and so on.

Behavior genetics—The study of hereditary bases of behavior of species throughout the phylogenetic scale.

Catecholamines—A group of amines including dopamine, epinephrine, and norepinephrine which act as neurotransmitters; they are considered "feel good" chemicals.

Catharsis—The presumed relaxation of emotional tension or anxiety by an expressive reaction.

Chromosomes—One of the bodies in the cell nucleus that contains genes.

Chronobiology—The study of temporal phenomena within the body, for example, circadian rhythms.

Circadian rhythms—Daily rhythms of

24-hours' duration (e.g., body temperature).

Drive—A motivational concept implying that behavior, initiated by deviation from homeostasis, is directed to the attainment of a certain goal.

Endorphins—A class of neurotransmitters whose properties are similar to morphine. They are believed to function as natural narcotics (opiates) in the body.

Enkephalins—Naturally occurring opiates produced in the brain.

Estradiol—Of the estrogens, the major female hormone.

Estrogens—Female hormones, including especially estradiol.

Flight behavior—A response of avoidance and escape from a stressful stimulus.

Gate-control theory—Theory proposed by Melzack and Wall (1965) integrating, reconciliating, and generalizing both the specificity and pattern theories of pain sensation. It holds that pain is experienced when a pain gate is open, but not when it is closed.

Genes—Units of heredity that are on chromosomes.

Genotype—The complete set of genes that an organism possesses.

Goal-directed behavior—Behavior aimed at reducing the difference between an existing organismic condition of need and the condition of satisfaction of the need toward which the organism is moving.

Gonad—A sex gland. The gonads in the male are the testes, which produce sperm, and in the female the ovaries, which produce eggs (ova).

Hormones—Chemicals that are excreted by a gland and transmitted through the circulatory systems to influence other organs of the body.

Hunger drive—A hypothesized internal state due to shifts in physiological balance that directs the organism toward food.

Hypothalamic controlling emotional response area (HACER)—A component in the hypothalamus of a major autonomic control system for emotional behavior.

Infradian rhythms—Biological cycles longer than circadian rhythms, such as menstrual cycles and cycles for hibernation.

Ingestion—Eating behavior.

Instinct—A concept to attempt to explain the behavior of organisms discarded because of its circularity. It holds that there is an innate disposition of members of a species for some behaviors that are biologically adaptive.

James-Lange Theory of Emotions—Theory similarly developed by William James and Carl Lange that emotions are caused by states of the body (e.g., we feel sorry because we cry).

Melatonin—The chief hormone of the pineal gland that affects sleep.

Motivated behavior—Observable behavior whereby organisms advance toward or away from stimuli. Approach behaviors include ingestion of food and water, while avoidance behavior includes removal from noxious conditions.

Motivation—A concept meant to explain variability in behavior: why an organism will respond to a particular stimulus at one time, but not at another (see motivated behavior).

Nociceptor—A pain receptor.

Osmoreceptors—Receptors located deep in the brain that sense the movement of water across cell membranes.

Pain—Avoidance behavior that we report as noxious.

Pattern theory of pain—Holds that patterns of pain receptors and neural pathways are coded for carrying pain information to the brain.

Phasic response—A rapid, short duration event, as of the striated muscle.

Phenotype—In genetics, a category to which an individual is assigned on the basis of one or more observable characteristics.

Physiological need—A condition of a shortage of oxygen, water, or food that is found throughout the phylogenetic scale and in all human cultures and has a physiological basis.

Placebo—Preparation containing no medicine administered to cause the patient to believe he or she is receiving treatment.

Purpose—A determiner of behavior inferred when an organism persists in a series of acts until it reaches some specific environmental goal.

Purposive behavior—A cybernetic concept, it employs negative feedback whereby internal (purposive) signals modify and direct behavior to achieve a goal.

Sex drive—The desire to mate.

Species-specific behavior—Behavior that innately develops in all members of a given species regardless of their environmental experiences.

Specificity theory of pain—Holds that specific noxious stimuli act upon specific pain receptors.

Subjective experience—A commonsense term referring to presumed mental events like being happy, sad, and thoughtful. We can study objective verbal reports about what an individual says are her or his subjective experiences. We can also psychophysiologically measure covert reactions when a person has such experiences (e.g., when a person has the subjective experience of dreaming, he or she can verbally report on those experiences and we can also study them objectively by means of rapid eye movements recorded through electrooculography).

Substantia gelatinosa—A group of cells in the dorsal and lateral region of the spinal cord. It is hypothesized to have neural influences on nerve fibers so as to modulate the perception of pain.

Testosterone—Chief male hormone among the androgens. It is thought to affect sex behavior.

Tone (tonus)—Consistent muscle tension contrasting with phasic tension.

Ultradian rhythms—Biological cycles of less than 24 hours in duration, for example, heartbeat and respiration.

Vicarious learning—Learning by observation. Presumably it is because covert responses mimic the overt ones being learned.

Vicious circularity—A reasoning by which an antecedent condition of a statement is used to explain the consequent condition, while the consequent condition is also used to explain the antecedent condition.

Yohimbine—Originally obtained from bark of the tropical tree corynanthe yohimbine; considered an aphrodisiac in folklore.

STUDY QUESTIONS

1. T or F. Organisms approach certain stimuli in order to restore homeostasis.
2. How is the hypothalamus involved in hunger?
3. T or F. The endocrine system is an exception to other systems in that it does not function according to cybernetic circuit principles.
4. Discuss techniques of contraception.
5. T or F. The catecholamines act as stimulants in the brain.
6. "Pain, and the avoidance of pain, is the most intense motivator of all." Discuss the nature of pain and what the experience implies.
7. Discuss the specificity theory and the pattern theory and their incorporation into the gate-control theory of pain.
8. Outline some characteristics pointed out by John P. Scott as distinctive for human warfare.
9. T or F. Daily rhythms are not synchronized, self-sustaining, and automatic.
10. Discuss theories of sleep.
11. Discuss theories of emotion.
12. Are emotions differentially related to the right and left hemisphere?
13. What is behavior genetics?
14. Summarize changes in how regulation of motivated behavior is viewed.

FURTHER READINGS

This book presents an effective statement that the nature of human aggression is learned rather than innate:

Groebel, J., and Hinde, R. A. (eds). (1989). *Aggression and War: Their Biological and Social Bases*. Cambridge University Press.

The following book presents a theory of such differential emotions as fear, anger, and joy with their specific neural substrates:

Izard, C. (1991). *The psychology of emotions*. New York: Plenum Press.

CHAPTER 10

Learning
and
Memory

MAJOR PURPOSES:	1. To learn basic behavioral principles of conditioning and learning
	2. To understand how we measure memory
	3. To sample some theories about how memory functions
	4. To explore physiological aspects of learning and memory
WHAT YOU ARE GOING TO FIND:	1. How organisms acquire conditional responses through classical and instrumental conditioning procedures
	2. Phenomena related to conditioning, including generalization, discrimination, experimental neurosis, extinction, and spontaneous recovery
	3. Other learning phenomena, including ethological learning and learning in the natural environment
	4. How we study memory and why we forget what we have learned
	5. The psychophysiology of learning and memory, including methods of study used, the biochemistry of learning and memory, various theories of memory, and a cybernetic model
WHAT YOU SHOULD ACQUIRE:	A good foundation of behavioral and physiological principles of learning and memory, and how these phenomena are viewed within a cybernetic model

CHAPTER OUTLINE

PRINCIPLES OF LEARNING
  AND MEMORY FORM THE
  BASIS FOR SCIENTIFIC AND
  APPLIED PSYCHOLOGY
THE NATURE OF LEARNING
MEASURES OF LEARNING
THE ACQUISITION OF CONDI-
  TIONAL RESPONSES—TWO
  PROCEDURES
  Classical (Pavlovian, Respondent)
    Conditioning
  Instrumental (Operant) Condi-
    tioning
    Measuring operant conditioning
    *The operant conditioning proce-
      dure*
    *Positive and negative reinforce-
      ment vs. punishment*
    Successive approximation
  Classical and Operant (Instru-
    mental) Conditioning Con-
    trasted
  A Brief Note on Pavlov

SOME ADDITIONAL CONDI-
  TIONING PHENOMENA
  Stimulus Generalization and
    Transfer of Learning
  Stimulus Discrimination
  Experimental Neurosis
  Extinction of Responses
  Spontaneous Recovery
HOW MANY KINDS OF
  LEARNING ARE THERE?
CYBERNETIC CIRCUITS AND
  THE BIOLOGIC VALUE OF
  CONDITIONING
ETHOLOGICAL LEARNING
  AND SPECIES-SPECIFIC CON-
  STRAINTS
  The Primary Concepts of Ethology
    Cue recognition
    Fixed action patterns
    Endogenous (internal) control
    Selective learning
  Learning in "the Field," the Nat-
    ural Environment

Nonassociative learning
Classical conditioning
*Trial and error learning and cog-
  nition*
Ethological Criticisms of Psycho-
  logical Research
SOME LEARNING QUESTIONS
  WITH SOCIAL SIGNIFICANCE
Is There Prenatal Learning?
How Are Addictions Learned?
Can the Immune System Be Con-
  ditioned?
  The conditioning theory
  The selection theory
MEMORY
  Interference Theory of Forgetting
  Learning and Memory in Lower
    Animals
THE PHYSIOLOGICAL PSY-
  CHOLOGY OF LEARNING
  AND MEMORY

PRINCIPLES OF LEARNING AND MEMORY FORM THE BASIS FOR SCIENTIFIC AND APPLIED PSYCHOLOGY

Our strategy in this chapter is first to understand the *behavioral* principles of learning and memory, which will be approached from a classical psychological viewpoint. Then we will inquire (more specifically) into the biology of learning, which will take us into the neurophysiology and neurochemistry of learning and memory processes. Within a biological framework we will seek to specify the changes that occur within bodily systems as learning progresses. We assume that a memory trace, called an **engram,** is established in the brain when learning is concluded.

Learning Principles Are Applicable Throughout Psychology.   The topic of learning is the most basic underpinning in the field of psychology. Learning phenomena permeate every aspect of behavior and therefore serve as a basis for understanding behavior in essentially all subfields of psychology. As an example, learning is of special importance to clinical psychology and psychiatry because the scientific study of how behavior systematically and permanently changes explains much aberrant behavior. Indeed our greatest advances in clinical psychology have been based on the scientific study of learning processes. Examples abound, as in Pavlov's work on experimental neurosis; Edward Guthrie's clinical applications for habit breaking; B. F. Skinner's research that led to behavior modification (therapy); and Edmund Jacobson's Clinical Progressive Relaxation and Joseph Wolpe's method of systematic desensitization.

The result of learning is an engram which is generally assumed to be established in the brain as a memory.

Behavioral principles of learning have given us considerable understanding and control of behavior, both normal and abnormal.

THE NATURE OF LEARNING

Principles of Learning Explain Much Behavior.   The general goal of psychology is to understand behavior as it is broadly defined, including both overt and covert responses. Psychologists are continuously seeking general principles (laws) to help them accomplish this purpose. Although psychology has far to go, considerable

Important steps toward discovering general principles (laws) of behavior have been made through learning research.

After a number of appropriate associations of a stimulus, response, and reinforcement in that sequence, the strength of association between the stimulus and response becomes greater.

progress has been made by isolating some major determinants for various kinds of behavior. One of the most important sets of determiners of behavior are learning variables. As psychological research progresses, our present principles of learning are being modified to fit more closely with complex behavioral phenomena. That is the process of all science — as we learn more about phenomena, our scientific laws become increasingly more precise and probable.

Three Factors in Learning.   For the moment, analyze any of a number of learned behaviors that you have observed. For example, you might ask yourself how it came to be that your dog approaches you when you call it. First, you presented a stimulus — the auditory stimulus of saying its name. Then, in spite of its failure to approach you a number of times when you repeated this stimulus, eventually the dog did come to you. When the approach response was made, you administered some type of **reinforcement** or reward (it may have been food or a pat on the head). In brief, these are the crucial factors for basic learning: a stimulus (you call the dog's name), a response (your dog approaches you), and a reinforcement (you feed the dog). Each time that these three factors, known as a trial, were closely associated, there was an increase in the likelihood that the stimulus would evoke the response. Unless your dog is a genius, the increase was only slight for each trial, so that as these three factors occurred repeatedly, learning progressed. The statement that "If a stimulus systematically precedes a response that produces reinforcement, that stimulus acquires the capacity to evoke that response" is an example of a law that has wide applicability.

The Theoretical Learning Curve.   A graphic representation of this learning process, a **learning curve,** is plotted as the increase in the tendency of a stimulus over trials to evoke a response (Fig. 10.1). The fact that the amount of learning generally decreases with each successive trial is typical of the learning process. More is usually learned in the early trials than in the later trials. Eventually, an ideal

FIGURE 10.1   A theoretical learning curve. As the number of trials increases, the strength of learning increases as indicated on the vertical axis; habit strength varies from 0 to approach an asymptote (a theoretical physiological limit that can never be reached) at 1.000.

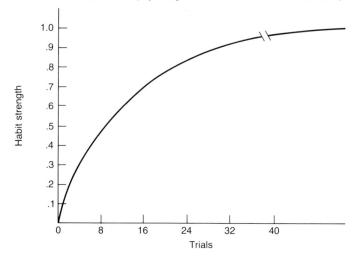

physiological limit of learning may be approached (but is never reached). In any practical situation it is impossible for one to acquire that maximum amount of learning, which, as indicated in Figure 10.1, is reached only after an infinite (∞) number of trials.

A physiological limit is the maximum amount of learning that is theoretically possible.

MEASURES OF LEARNING

Learning Is Measured Through Responses. The first step in understanding a phenomenon is to adequately define and thereby to measure it. The learning process, however, must be indirectly defined and measured because we cannot directly observe learning as it progresses. Consequently, we must infer learning from changes in performance. It would now be helpful for you to review the section in Chapter 8 on overt response measures (p. 221). As applied to learning, response measures include increases in rate of responding, the probability of a correct response being made, speed of responding, the amplitude (intensity or vigor) of responding, decrease in latency (the time between the presentation of stimulus and the initiation of a response), time required to complete a task, number of errors made in learning to perform a task, and resistance to extinction. Let us emphasize that from such observed measures of performance we infer an internal process of learning. In efforts to understand these internal states wherein an engram (a memory) is established, we must study physiological aspects of learning. The laying down of an engram in physiological systems establishes the permanency of learning. **Learning** therefore is defined as a relatively permanent change in behavior as a result of experience. However, before we can study physiological research, we must construct a behavioral foundation of learning on which physiological research is based.

We infer that learning has occurred from changes in responses.

Learning is a relatively permanent change of behavior as a result of experience wherein engrams are established.

THE ACQUISITION OF CONDITIONAL RESPONSES—TWO PROCEDURES
Classical (Pavlovian, Respondent) Conditioning

History. The experimental operations for **classical conditioning** were first systematically studied at the Imperial Institute of Experimental Medicine by S. G. Vul'fson, who was working on his doctoral dissertation under Pavlov.[1] As Pavlov reported to the Society of Physicians of St. Petersburg in 1898, Vul'fson had found that dried food placed in a dog's mouth produced greater amounts of salivary secretion than did wet food. But both foods presented at a distance produced saliva, and in about the same amounts. *The mere sight of food evoked salivation.* Based on these observations, Pavlov and his associates then conducted a number of experiments over the decades that had revolutionary significance for physiology, psychiatry, and psychology.

---

[1] The names of the great Russian physiologists are spelled in various ways. For instance, Pavlov is the usual spelling in English, but other spellings such as "Pawlow" are used ("w" is pronounced as a "v" in German). Similarly, Sechenov is sometimes spelled "Stechenev" or "Setschenow" and Bechterev as "von Bectherew." A little reflection will explain that the sounds of a Russian's name can be variously transcribed into other alphabets so that there is no single correct spelling in English. In the Cyrillic alphabet used in Russia, Pavlov is written: Павлов.

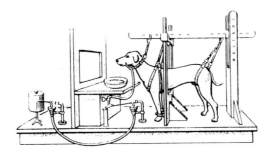

FIGURE 10.2
Pavlovian apparatus to measure response amplitude through salivation flowing through a glass tube.

Classical Conditioning Procedure.   One starts with an **unconditional reflex,** which is an unlearned stimulus–response connection. Higher organisms have a large number of unconditional reflexes; for example the **unconditional stimulus** (US) of a light in the eye evokes the **unconditional response** (UR) of pupillary contraction, and a tap below the knee at the patellar tendon is a US that evokes the UR of a knee jerk. In Pavlov's dogs the US was the presentation of meat powder in the mouth which evoked the UR of salivation. The amount of salivation was a measure of **response amplitude.** To collect saliva, a fistula that contained a glass tube was placed in the cheek near the duct of one of the salivary glands (Fig. 10.2). The number of drops of the saliva that flowed through the glass tube was counted —the larger the number of drops, the greater the amount of saliva and thus the larger the response amplitude.

An unconditional reflex is innate and consists of an unconditional stimulus (US) that evokes an unconditional response (UR).

Next, a neutral stimulus was selected, which is one that does not noticeably evoke the UR being studied. Pavlov studied a number of neutral stimuli including the sound of a bell, a tone, the beating of a metronome, and the presentation of a light to the dog's eyes.

As shown in Figure 10.3, the neutral stimulus (e.g., a tone) was presented just *before* the US (about 0.5 seconds prior is generally optimal). After a number of associations of the neutral and unconditional stimuli, the neutral stimulus tends to evoke the UR by itself (Fig. 10.4). Eventually a new connection is formed (Fig. 10.5). The connection becomes quite stable so that the presentation of the neutral stimulus by itself evokes the UR. When conditioning is successful, the previously neutral stimulus becomes a **conditional stimulus** (CS) and the response becomes a **conditional response** (CR). But whenever salivation is evoked by the meat powder, it is still called the unconditional response. Whether or not salivation is a conditional or unconditional response depends on whether it is evoked by a conditional or an unconditional stimulus.

In classical conditioning, a neutral stimulus is presented prior to a US that evokes a UR; after a number of associations of the US with the neutral stimulus, the neutral stimulus becomes a CS that evokes the major components of the UR (those now become components of a CR).

S (Tone) ⟿⟿⟿⟿⟿⟿⟿⟿ ► R ("Ear twitch")

US (Meat powder) ───────────────► UR (Salivation)

FIGURE 10.3
The first stage in classical conditioning. A neutral stimulus (e.g., a tone) is presented before the unconditional stimulus. The neutral stimulus evokes an irrelevant response such as an ear twitch, but it does not evoke the unconditional response.

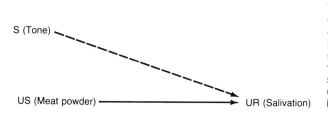

FIGURE 10.4
The second stage of classical conditioning. As the number of associations of the neutral stimulus and the unconditional stimulus increases, the tendency for the neutral stimulus to evoke the unconditional response increases.

Two Examples of Learning Measured by Response Amplitude and Response Latency. Anrep (1920), one of Pavlov's associates, conducted a classic study using two measures—response magnitude (number of drops of saliva) and response latency. Figures 10.6 and 10.7 show how the process of conditioning progressed over 50 trials—the neutral stimulus gradually became a CS. As the number of pairings (trials) of the unconditional and the conditional stimuli increased, the magnitude of the CR also increased until a limit was approached at about the thirtieth trial. To test the strength of the CR, Anrep presented the tone by itself to see how many drops of saliva would thereby be elicited. As shown in Fig. 10.6, after one trial the neutral stimulus did not evoke any saliva; after ten associations, it evoked six drops, and after thirty associations, it evoked sixty drops of saliva. Also (see Fig. 10.7), as the number of pairings of the conditional and unconditional stimuli increased, the latency of the conditional response decreased until a limit was approached at about the thirtieth trial.

Everyday Applications. By observing dogs, children, or other friends, examples of classical conditioning should occur to you. The following case, reported in Lope de Vega's play *El Capellan de la Virgin,* was probably written in 1615:

> Saint Ildefonse used to scold me and punish me lots of times. He would sit me on the bare floor and make me eat with the cats of the monastery. These cats were such rascals that they took advantage of my penitence. They drove me mad stealing my choicest morsels. It did no good to chase them away. But I found a way of coping with the beasts in order to enjoy my meals when I was being punished. I put them all in a sack, and on a pitch black night took them out under an arch. First I would cough and then immediately whale the daylights out of the cats. They whined and shrieked like an infernal pipe organ. I would pause for awhile and repeat the operation—first a cough, and then a thrashing. I finally noticed that even without beating them, the beasts moaned and

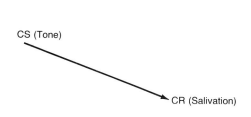

FIGURE 10.5
The final stage of classical conditioning. After the neutral stimulus has been associated with the unconditional stimulus a sufficient number of times, it can evoke the unconditional response by itself. At this point we denote the previously neutral stimulus as the conditional stimulus (CS) and the response that it evokes as the conditional response (CR).

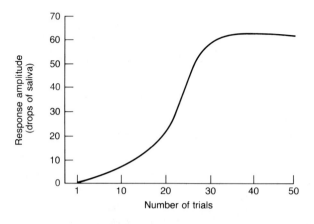

FIGURE 10.6
A learning curve using amplitude of response as a measure of learning.

yelped like the very devil whenever I coughed. I then let them loose. Thereafter, whenever I had to eat off the floor, I would cast a look around, If an animal approached my food, all I had to do was to cough, and how that cat did scat! (Bousfield, 1955, p. 828)

You should have been able to identify the crucial conditioning aspects in this example. The US was the thrashing of the cats, the UR was their attendant misery and pain, as evidenced by their whining, shrieking, and running away, and the CS was the cough (Fig. 10.8).

Operant (Instrumental) Conditioning

It was in 1935 that the future eminent psychologist Burrhus Frederick Skinner distinguished between instrumental and classical conditioning. He referred to them as operant and respondent conditioning, respectively. His early experiments on **operant conditioning** used the "Skinner box," as shown in Figure 10.9; however, he called it a "free experimental space" (a term that never caught on), not wishing to be remembered as the inventor of a box.

When a hungry rat is placed in the apparatus, it makes a variety of responses. It will sniff in the corners, explore the walls by standing on its hind feet, walk about

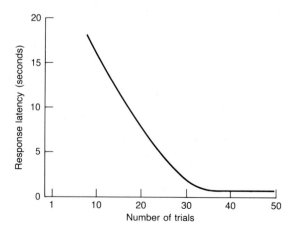

FIGURE 10.7
A learning curve using response latency as a measure of learning.

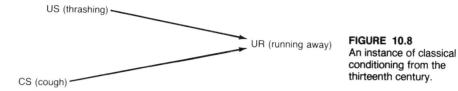

FIGURE 10.8
An instance of classical conditioning from the thirteenth century.

extensively, and eventually depress the bar that projects into the box. The rat may bump into the bar backwards or sideways, fall on it or push it with its nose. But whatever the accidental manner in which the first bar press occurs, the action of the bar releases a pellet of food into the food tray where it is eaten. After another period of wandering around, the animal, eventually, presses the bar again, usually in the same way that it pressed it before. The food pellet is again delivered and consumed; the "wandering" behavior starts again, but the irrelevant responses drop out. The animal then moves immediately to press the bar after it has finished eating a pellet, and rapidly makes a number of bar-pressing responses.

BURRHUS FREDRICK SKINNER
(1904–1990)

Professor B. F. Skinner was influenced to a great degree by John B. Watson, Edward L. Thorndike, and Ivan P. Pavlov in his development of contemporary behaviorism. Skinner relied heavily on Pavlov's principles of conditioning, but more so on Thorndike's principles of trial-and-error learning which emphasized the importance of reinforcement for "stamping in a response." He considerably extended conditioning principles in his scientific experiments, following which he applied them in

many ways for the betterment of society. His principal scientific work was entitled *The Behavior of Organisms: An Experimental Analysis,* published in 1938. Especially in his classic *Science and Human Behavior* he showed how positive reinforcement principles could be applied for improving society through its existing economic, religious, and other institutions. His famous *Walden Two* was a behaviorist's design for a utopian culture. This book was widely taught in the departments of English throughout the country. Skinner had been an English major as an undergraduate and spent the year after college writing fiction, but soon, as he put it, "discovered the unhappy fact that I had nothing to say." The next year, he was influenced by an article by H. G. Wells who praised Pavlov over playwright George Bernard Shaw. Skinner thereby abandoned literature for psychology.

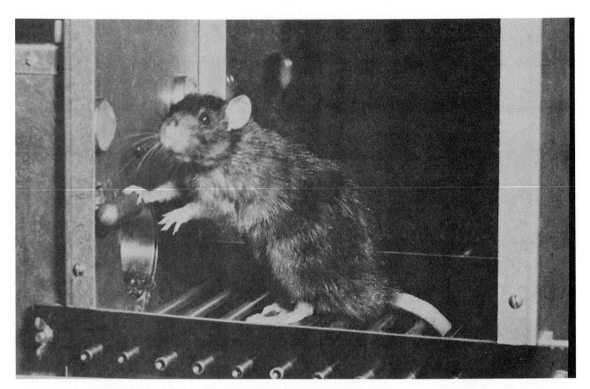

FIGURE 10.9 A Skinner box wherein a rat is operantly conditioned by being reinforced with food contingent on each bar press. (Photo courtesy of Med Associates, East Fairfield, VT.)

MEASURING OPERANT CONDITIONING

The strength of the bar-pressing response is measured by frequency per unit time, which is the *rate* of responding. An ink pen makes a moving record to automatically record response rate (Fig. 10.10). Each bar depression activates a mechanism that moves the ink pen one unit in the upper direction. Consequently, the number of responses is indicated along the vertical axis; the horizontal axis indicates the amount of time that the animal is in the box. After the pen moves up to indicate that a

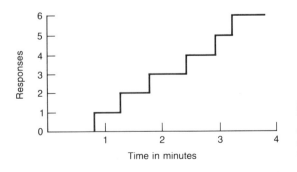

FIGURE 10.10
The construction of a cumulative record for conditioning a bar-pressing response.

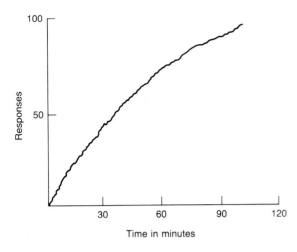

FIGURE 10.11
A cumulative record of a rat's food-getting response (bar pressing for pellets) during a daily eating period.

response has been made, it continues its movement to the right until another response is made at which time it moves up again, and so on. This is a **cumulative record,** such that the total number of responses is accumulated for the entire period of time that the animal is in the box. For a longer period of time, a smoother curve results, as in Figure 10.11 where after 90 minutes, approximately 90 responses had been made. After any given period of time, the number of responses made until then may be read from the vertical axis (e.g., in Fig. 10.10, one response was made after about 50 seconds, three after 2 minutes, and six after 4 minutes).

A cumulative record is one that records the total number of responses made by an organism as a function of time since conditioning commenced.

THE OPERANT CONDITIONING PROCEDURE

Emitted vs. Elicited Responses. The response in an operant conditioning procedure is called an **operant.** The operant is *emitted,* which means that we do not specify the stimuli that produced it. In contrast, in classical conditioning, the UR and CR are *elicited* ("caused") by specified stimuli (the US and CS).

Reinforcements Are Contingent on the Appropriate Operant. In operant conditioning, reinforcements are **contingent** on the organism making the correct response (*contingent* means that a reinforcement is given if and only if the appropriate response is made, Fig. 10.12). As the number of bar-pressing responses with contingent reinforcement increases, **response rate** (the number of times that the response occurs within a given period of time) increases. When the rate of responding is high,

An elicited *response, as in classical conditioning, is evoked by specified stimuli while the operant in operant conditioning is emitted with antecedent stimuli unspecified.*

FIGURE 10.12
The first stage in operant conditioning. The question mark indicates that we are not able, or do not bother, to specify the stimulus that produced the bar-pressing response. Once the response occurs it is followed by reinforcement.

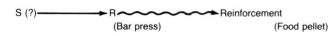

S (?) ──────────► R ∿∿∿∿∿∿► Reinforcement
　　　　　　　(Bar press)　　　　　　　(Food pellet)

FIGURE 10.13
A rat in a Skinner box about to press the bar says to the other rat "Boy, have I got this guy conditioned! Every time I press the bar he drops in a piece of food." Originally from the Columbia *Jester* at a time when the Columbia University psychology department was a mainstay of the experimental analysis of behavior.

In operant conditioning, reinforcements are contingent on the appropriate response being made.

operant conditioning has become quite stable, and we infer that learning has occurred.

The characteristic of operant conditioning fitting a negative feedback model is illustrated in Figure 10.13. From the rat's point of view, it has the experimenter conditioned such that the rate of delivering pellets and the rate of bar-pressing stabilize at a given target value.

Discriminative Stimuli Set the Occasion for Operants. Although the emphasis in operant conditioning is on the operant response, stimuli that precede the operant (and contingent reinforcement) later become important. Although it did not originally evoke the operant, the sight of the lever that the animal presses, for example, becomes associated with the response. It can then set the stage for the response to be made ("evoke" it). The presence of the lever indicates that the occasion is appropri-

A stimulus presented prior to the occurrence of an operant response may become a discriminative stimulus, which sets the occasion for the operant to be make in the future.

ate for the response to occur. Such a stimulus is a **discriminative stimulus (S^D).** In operant conditioning, as in classical conditioning, a stimulus–response relationship is formed, as indicated in Figure 10.14.

POSITIVE AND NEGATIVE REINFORCEMENT VS. PUNISHMENT

Positive reinforcement is the presentation of a reinforcing stimulus; negative reinforcement is the removal of an aversive stimulus. Both are contingent on the occurrence of a given response.

Operant conditioning may occur not only through **positive reinforcement,** but also through **negative reinforcement.** Positive reinforcement occurs when a stimulus that an organism will approach is presented contingent on the operant being made. Negative reinforcement occurs when an aversive stimulus is removed, contingent on the occurrence of the response. Thus, operant conditioning can occur through such positive reinforcements as food or water or through such negative reinforcements as the withdrawal of painful or harmful stimuli. For example, if a parent is hitting a child and ceases when the child starts to cry, the child's crying response is negatively

FIGURE 10.14
The final stage of operant conditioning. Discriminative stimuli (S^D), such as sight of the lever, set the occasion for bar pressing. The frequency with which the response (R) is made in the presence of S^{D}s increases as number of reinforcements increase.

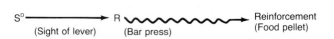

S^D ⟶ R 〜〜〜 Reinforcement (Food pellet)
(Sight of lever) (Bar press)

reinforced. The child is conditioned to cry since that response was reinforced by the withdrawal of pain caused by the hitting. Note that negative reinforcement is *not* punishment. **Punishment** is the administration of a noxious stimulus contingent on a given response (e.g., hitting a child as soon as he or she steps into the street is an effort to teach the child to stay out of the way of automobiles).

Operant Conditioning Is Very General. The importance of operant conditioning cannot be overemphasized. Even though much of our learning follows the principles of classical conditioning, more of it occurs according to the laws of operant conditioning. Instances of operant conditioning include learning to drive, type, draw, write, read, and shake hands. When we learn to drive a car the steering response and the responses of putting on the brakes and depressing the accelerator (remarkably similar to the bar-pressing response of the rat) are all responses that are learned according to the operant conditioning principle — they are all emitted, rather than elicited, and are all followed by reinforcement when properly made.

Punishment is the administration of an aversive stimulus contingent on the occurrence of a given response.

SUCCESSIVE APPROXIMATION

In operant conditioning, **successive approximation** to the desired response is required. The rat, for example, might only slightly touch the bar for its first response but still is reinforced. After reinforcing the animal for barely touching the bar several times, the experimenter then would require a more vigorous bar press before reinforcement is administered. By thus requiring more and more of the animal on successive responses, the experimenter can eventually get the animal to depress the bar with vigor. Eventually, a highly vigorous or refined response can be obtained. By following this procedure, Skinner (1938) was able to get a rat to depress the bar with a force of 100 grams, about one-half the animal's body weight. When an infant is learning to say "milk," the first response emitted may vaguely resemble "milk" and will only be understood by a loving, and especially perceptive, parent. On successive trials, increasingly precise responses occur so that eventually a well-spoken "milk" is emitted that can provide the infant with reinforcement (milk) from others.

In successive approximation, a response that is close to the desired response is first reinforced; however, the organism must then improve its approximation to the desired response since reinforcements are contingent on improved responding.

Classical and Operant (Instrumental) Conditioning Contrasted

Table 10.1 emphasizes the characteristics and differences of classical and operant conditioning. Diagrams of the two processes are shown in the first level while level 2 specifies the way in which the response occurs. Thus, in classical conditioning, the response is elicited by a certain known stimulus, but in the initial stages of operant conditioning the response is emitted. In Skinner's terms, a response that is elicited is a respondent, while an emitted response is an operant (level 3). In level 4, for classical conditioning, the organism is somewhat passive in that the US is "put in" so that a UR "comes out." The emphasis is on the stimulus. In operant conditioning, the organism is more active and operates on its environment to produce reinforcement. The emphasis is on the response.

At level 5, in classical conditioning the CS is "substituted" for the US so that a new connection results: that between the CS and CR. In operant conditioning, however, there is no substitution of stimuli. Rather, the strength of an operant is increased and certain stimuli in the environment become S^Ds that set the occasion for the operant to be made.

TABLE 10.1   Classical and Operant Conditioning Contrasted

Level	Classical Conditioning	Operant Conditioning
1. Diagram of Process	US ⟶ UR CS ⟿ R	$S^D \to R \rightsquigarrow$ Reinforcement
2. Way in which R occurs in initial stage of conditioning	Elicited by US	Emitted by unidentified stimuli
3. Name of response	Respondent	Operant
4. Requirement on part of organism	Organism is "passive," merely responds to input stimuli. Emphasis thus on stimuli.	Organism is active, operates on environment to obtain reinforcement. Emphasis thus on response.
5. Nature of learning	CS is "substituted" for US forming a new reflex CS ⟶ CR	No stimulus substitution. A discriminative stimulus becomes associated with the response.
6. Synonyms	Pavlovian, respondent, or type S conditioning	Instrumental, or type R conditioning

At level 6 there are some synonyms for the two types of conditioning: "Pavlovian," because of the importance of Pavlov; "classical" because some thought it was used earlier than instrumental conditioning; "Type S," Skinner's term, emphasizes the stimulus; "instrumental" and "operant" indicate that the organism operates on the environment and is instrumental in producing reinforcement; "Type R" indicates the importance of the response.

A Brief Note on Pavlov

Pavlov's primary purpose in the study of conditioning was to use it as an index of higher nervous activity in the brain.

Pavlov's interest in conditioning was to use it to study the brain. Higher nervous activity of the brain, he thought, allows the organism to interact with the external environment. In contrast, lower nervous activity, as of the autonomic nervous system, functions to integrate the body's organs. Pavlov used conditioning of the salivary reflex as a methodological basis for studying higher nervous activity. Variations in conditioning phenomena, he reasoned, provided an indirect index of central nervous system activity. As early as 1912, he believed that extirpation was too crude and that injuries to the brain produced unstable experimental results.

Why he selected salivation is an interesting instance of **serendipity.** The story is that as Pavlov studied digestive phenomena, the topic for which he received the Nobel Prize, he noticed that his dogs were "erroneously" secreting juices. Considering this phenomenon as an artifact, he reportedly studied it to eliminate it. Pavlov observed that the artifact started when the man who fed the animals approached them; he reasoned that the man had become associated with feeding and consequently with the secretion of various gastrointestinal juices. This led Pavlov to conceive of the man as a CS.

Pavlov held that classical conditioning allows the organism to better adapt to a constantly changing world because the CR extinguishes so easily.

After decades of research Pavlov, in 1933, proposed what amounts to a two-factor theory of learning based on classical and trial-and-error (instrumental) learning paradigms. (Pavlov was very favorably impressed with Thorndike's work on trial-and-error learning.) He concluded that the CR in classical conditioning is not

---

IVAN PETROVICH PAVLOV
(1849–1936)

Pavlov was born in Ryazan, a small city just south of Moscow. Eventually he became director of the department of physiology of the Institute of Experimental Medicine in St. Petersburg. Pavlov received the Nobel Prize in 1904 for his research on the physiology of digestion. His later research on conditional reflexes stemmed from his observation of salivary and gastric secretion which, as the story goes, was an unwanted phenomenon that occurred when the person who fed the dogs came to them with food. The sight of the man with food, he concluded, caused the secretion. Pavlov, his students, and colleagues conducted extensive research for over 30 years on conditioning.

Pavlov was greatly influenced by Sechenov's theory of the reflex mechanisms of psychic activity. He applied the conditional reflex method for understanding mechanisms for the acquisition of language and symbolic thought (referred to as "higher nervous activity") and toward the end of his life, abnormal behavior in psychiatric settings.

---

permanent because it is so easily extinguished. Classical conditioning thus allows the organism to adapt to an ever changing environment. However, associations established with trial-and-error learning are much more resistant to extinction. Resistance to extinction occurs because the organism's response has a *causal* relationship to environmental events (e.g., the response produces reinforcement). He thought that trial-and-error learning forms the basis for acquiring knowledge and thus was of great importance in human affairs. We develop scientific relationships (laws) among natural events through trial and error, he thought, and those laws are the basis of knowledge for understanding our world.

Trial-and-error (operant) learning forms the basis for knowledge because causal relationships with reinforcement produce a relatively permanent response, according to Pavlov.

Pavlov's research was extensive and included his introduction of the conditioning phenomena of extinction, spontaneous recovery, stimulus generalization, and differentiation. He studied sleep, hypnosis, conflict situations that resulted in experimental neurosis, and instincts in both humans and animals. He developed the concept of a **second-signal system** to incorporate language, developed a typology of temperaments, and repeated Wolfgang Köhler's transpositional experiments on insight in primates. Although he received the Nobel Prize for his gastrointestinal research, his later research on conditioning phenomena was of even greater importance. We now summarize some of these other conditioning phenomena.

SOME ADDITIONAL CONDITIONING PHENOMENA

Stimulus Generalization and Transfer of Learning

Generalization Occurs to Similar Stimuli.   Pavlov found that certain stimuli other than the CS also acquire the capacity to elicit the CR—this is known as **stimulus generalization.** Organisms generalize certain characteristics of a CS such that the higher the organism, the greater the generalization.

Organisms generalize CRs from the CS to other novel stimuli along a similarity dimension such that the more similar the novel stimulus is to the CS, the greater the generalization.

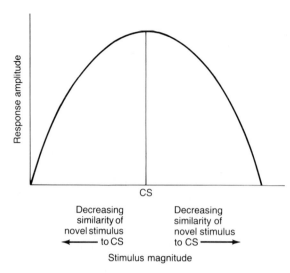

FIGURE 10.15
The greater the similarity of a novel stimulus to a conditional stimulus, the greater is the stimulus generalization from the conditional stimulus to the novel stimulus.

In a study Anrep did with dogs, the CS was a tone that had a frequency of 637.5 Hz (cycles per second). After the 637.5 Hz tone became a CS, a tone of 700 Hz also evoked the CR; this generalization occurred even though the 700 Hz tone had never been associated with the US. The dog generalized from the CS to a novel one.

But an important question is, "What was the amplitude of the salivary response when elicited by a tone of 700 Hz—was it greater than, less than, or the same as that elicited by the CS (the 637.5 Hz tone)?" The 700 Hz tone evoked the CR to a lesser degree than did the CS. Furthermore, the amplitude evoked by a 725 Hz tone was even less than that evoked by the 700 Hz tone. As in Figure 10.15, *the greater the similarity of a novel stimulus to the CS, the greater the amplitude of the CR when evoked by novel stimuli.*

Stimulus generalization also occurs in operant conditioning; (for example, the S^D of a larger lever than that originally used in a Skinner box would still evoke the bar-pressing response. The organism would generalize to other levers.

The Importance of Stimulus Generalization in Everyday Life. Without stimulus generalization, in a world in which there are so many stimuli, a fantastically large number of separate learning instances would have to occur in order for us to function effectively. For example, a person who learns to move a certain light switch generalizes from that specific S–R connection to a wide variety of light switches that vary in size, color, and kind (some are toggle switches, others are push switches, etc.). If a person's first experience in turning on lights was operating a small brown toggle switch, considerable stimulus generalization would occur to a larger white toggle switch because of their similarity. When the person comes to a push-type switch after learning on a toggle switch, however, generalization would not be as great. With the push switch, one would have "the general idea," but a certain amount of additional learning would have to occur before the response was made efficiently. Even less generalization would occur to a touch switch or one activated by heat from a hand.

Other everyday examples of stimulus generalization should occur to you with little effort—although you learned to read with a certain style and size of type, you

Stimulus generalization also occurs in operant conditioning such that there is generalization from the discriminative stimulus to other similar stimuli.

Stimulus generalization reduces the amount of learning necessary because similar responses are made to different but similar stimuli.

Through both classical and instrumental conditioning, we acquire numerous S–R connections from which there are many stimulus generalizations.

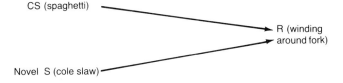

FIGURE 10.16
When stimulus generalization occurs, two different but similar stimuli evoke essentially the same response.

generalized to other styles and sizes of type and even to cursive writing (with some additional learning).

Once a two-year-old girl seated at the dinner table struggled with some cole slaw, attempting to wind it around her fork, not a normal occurrence. After a little thought the reason became apparent. She had been accustomed to eating spaghetti in this manner, and the similarity between cole slaw and spaghetti, if not apparent to an adult, was certainly real to the two-year-old. Stimulus generalization from one "stringy" substance to another had taken place, producing the "spaghetti eating" response to the cole slaw (Fig. 10.16).

Stimulus Discrimination

Stimulus Discrimination Is the Antithesis of Generalization. When stimulus generalization is inappropriate or ineffective, as for the child's winding cole slaw around her fork, one must learn to discriminate between different but similar stimuli. For example, one must learn that one response (winding around the fork) is appropriate to one stimulus (spaghetti), but that a different response (scooping) is appropriate to a different but similar stimulus (cole slaw). **Stimulus discrimination** is a process of "breaking down" stimulus generalization.

Stimulus discrimination occurs in both classical and operant conditioning when a response to the original stimulus continues to be reinforced, but a response to a similar stimulus is not reinforced.

An organism may learn to discriminate between two similar stimuli if the appropriate response to the original stimulus is reinforced but reinforcement is withheld if that response is made to a similar novel stimulus. For example, for the dog to discriminate between the original CS and a similar one, we continue reinforcing salivation to the 637.5 Hz tone; then, when the dog salivates to the 700 Hz tone, no meat powder is put in the mouth. After a number of trials, the dog will cease salivation to the 700 (but not to the 637.5) Hz tone. The dog then has learned to discriminate between the two stimuli.

The development of discrimination in an operant conditioning situation is analogous. We merely reinforce the animal when it responds to one stimulus, but not to a similar one.

Experimental Neurosis

Late in life Pavlov attempted to apply conditioning principles to psychiatric cases. One of his paradigms was to establish **experimental neurosis.** Pavlov had found that in establishing stimulus discrimination, if the discrimination required for reinforcement was beyond the dog's perceptual capacity, the dog was in conflict as to whether or not to respond. Being unable to determine which of two stimuli would result in reinforcement and because accurate discrimination was required for reinforcement, the dogs became "neurotic." Horsley Gantt (1944), Pavlov's last living student contributed sizably to the understanding of neurotic behavior as with his famous neurotic dog Nick.

Experimental neurosis occurred when the dog was unable to discriminate between two similar stimuli, yet the discrimination was important for the dog to make.

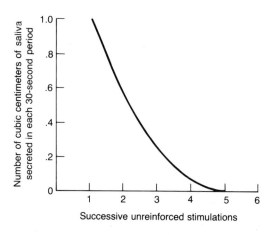

FIGURE 10.17
Results of an experiment that produced experimental extinction, performed by Babkin (1928) in Pavlov's laboratory.

Extinction of Responses

Extinction is accomplished by withholding reinforcement (the US) and is complete when a CS ceases to evoke a CR.

After successful conditioning, if the CS is presented for a number of trials by itself (without the US accompanying it), the CR ceases to be made to the CS — **extinction** of the CR has occurred. Babkin (1928), in Pavlov's laboratories, conditioned a dog to salivate to a CS, then stopped reinforcing the CS by no longer presenting the US. The data in Figure 10.17 show the amplitude of the CR on successive trials for which only the CS was presented. As the number of unreinforced responses increases, the amplitude of the CR decreases until, by trial 5, no salivation was forthcoming — the CR had been extinguished in the animal.

In a cumulative response curve, the steeper the slope, the faster the rate of responding, but when the curve becomes horizontal, no responses are being made, indicating extinction.

In rats, if we cease presenting reinforcement for the bar-pressing response after operant conditioning has become stable, there is a sizable burst of responses — an animal presses the bar quite rapidly, even though it does not receive food pellets (Fig. 10.18). After about a half-hour, the curve begins to slope off; few additional responses are added to the cumulative record; and the curve becomes almost horizontal. Thus, at the end of an hour, the operant has become extinguished.

With a little reflection you can see how important extinction is in your everyday life. Think of some undesirable response that you have learned. Some, like supersti-

FIGURE 10.18   A typical cumulative response curve for extinction of bar pressing by a white rat following about 100 reinforcements. (After Skinner, 1938)

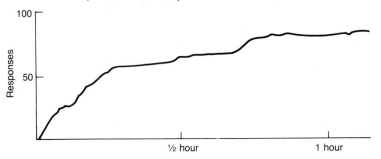

tions, were acquired because they were "accidentally" reinforced. Some undesirable or unnecessary responses may not have undergone extinction, although you may want to extinguish them. You may extinguish those responses that do not facilitate your adaptation to your environment by withholding the reinforcements that maintain them, as discussed here.

Spontaneous Recovery

Pavlov observed that when the CS was once more presented to the dog, about two hours after extinction the animal salivated 0.15 cc (cubic centimeters) of saliva; that amount was about one-sixth of the maximal strength of the CR. This phenomenon is known as **spontaneous recovery** — as time passes, a response that had been extinguished recovers a portion of its previous strength. Since Pavlov's original observations, spontaneous recovery has been observed in a wide variety of situations for both classical and operant extinction.

After spontaneous recovery, response strength is greater than that at the end of extinction, but less than that at the peak of conditioning.

If the spontaneously recovered response is again extinguished after the passage of time, it can recover strength again. However, amplitude of this second spontaneously recovered response is less than after the first spontaneous recovery. We can continue to obtain some spontaneous recovery following repeated periods of extinction, but the amount of recovery gradually decreases after each extinction. Eventually, there is no spontaneous recovery at all whereupon the response, either CR or operant, is completely extinguished. The implications for breaking personal habits are clear. If you extinguish a bad habit, there will be spontaneous recovery; therefore, you must *thoroughly* extinguish the response by repeated extinction periods until there is no spontaneous recovery. For example, you might break out in a cold sweat (CR) when you have a certain thought that originally was conditioned by a scene in a violent movie. You might extinguish that CR by repeatedly imagining the scene. But after the CR extinguishes, allow spontaneous recovery to occur and extinguish the CR again, and again, and again.

CRs spontaneously recover strength after extinction; but after repeated extinction, there will eventually be no spontaneous recovery at all.

HOW MANY KINDS OF LEARNING ARE THERE?

A Bit of History. Long ago, it was thought that there was one kind of learning process, association. Before psychology became a science, the philosophers spoke of the association of ideas. With the prominence of Pavlov, Thorndike, Watson, and other scientists, the mentalistic concept of association of ideas was replaced by the objective concept of association of observable stimuli and responses.

Throughout history, association of elements has been held to be the primary principle of learning, first by the association of ideas, then by stimuli and responses.

In the 1940s, Clark Leonard Hull held that there was only one principle of learning, an associative one based on reinforcement. According to Hull's view, instrumental and classical conditioning differ primarily because of the differences in the methods used: Reinforcement is presented in different ways and according to different schedules, but the same basic principle governs them both. Another view postulated by Pavlov, then by B. F. Skinner among others, was that classical (respondent) and instrumental (operant) conditioning were two different kinds of learning.

A two-factor theroy of learning is that classical and instrumental conditioning occur according to different laws.

One argument against the two-factor theory is that both kinds of conditioning occur in any conditioning experiment; for example, when there is operant conditioning involving food as a reinforcer, the organism also salivates according to a classical conditioning procedure. In any conditioning experiment more than one kind of response is conditioned. Pavlov merely selected salivation to study as one out of a pattern of responses.

Contrary to much popular belief, Pavlov and his colleagues and students used both kinds of learning procedures. Movies of experiments in Pavlov's laboratories in the 1920s show such procedures as putting an early Russian version of today's M&Ms into the mouth of a retarded child when the child made the appropriate response, quite like Skinner's operant conditioning procedure. Similar procedures were used on elephants.

In the 1950s, Edward Chace Tolman postulated that there were seven kinds of learning processes. One wit extrapolated from the one, then two-factor theory through Tolman's seven-factor thesis and inferred that by the year 2000 there would be several hundred different kinds of learning. How many there actually are is not going to be answered satisfactorily soon. But it is clear that the two different kinds of learning procedures are at the basis of the psychology and biology of learning. These are the classic learning paradigms of Edward Lee Thorndike formulated as instrumental learning (trial-and-error, or trial-and-success learning) and Ivan Petrovich Pavlov's classical (sometimes called Pavlovian) conditioning.

Classical and instrumental conditioning procedures form the basis for understanding learning phenomena throughout the phylogenetic scale.

CYBERNETIC CIRCUITS AND THE BIOLOGICAL VALUE OF CONDITIONING

The CS Signals the US.   We have seen that such processes as conditioning and generalization facilitate our behavior in many ways and thus have survival value. For example, in conditioning, a CR is elicited prior to the occurrence of a US, which is biologically important for the organism. Thus, the CS is a signal to salivate (the CR), which prepares the organism to process food in the mouth (the US, which is reinforcing to the dog). More generally, the organism uses the CS to predict the US and thereby to effectively respond to that biologically important stimulus.

On the basis of a CS, organisms predict and prepare themselves for the occurrence of the US, which is a biologically important event; consequently the entire CS–CR–US sequence has survival value.

Feedback from the CR Carries Important Information.   For such adaptive functioning, intimate relationships occur between neural, muscle, and other systems of the body. Over many decades, circuits that relate these systems, especially neuromuscular circuits, have been the object of Russian experimentation and theorization. Prominent among these is Peter Anokhin's theory of **functional systems,** which he developed in the early 1930s. Along with the early work of the Soviet scientist Nikolay Bernstein (Bernshtein), his theory antedated Wiener's cybernetics. Bernstein's profound theoretical analysis using an ingenious method of cyclographic registration was the first attempt by a Soviet physiologist to understand the importance of cybernetic concepts for physiology. Bernstein introduced such principles as *sensoril correction* and *reafference* prior to their uses in cybernetics. Wiener, in fact, probably was influenced by Anokhin during his visit to Russia prior to writing his book *Cybernetics.*

During conditioning, overt and covert responses, as well as neural, hormonal, and other events, occur in the body so that a simple notion of CS–CR–US must be modified to understand the complexity of interactive behavioral and physiological events.

Anokhin recognized early that the mechanical Cartesian concept of a single, unique response component of a reflex is excessively simplistic — that there is more than one important stimulus in the organism's environment and that the organism makes many responses. One cannot ignore relationships among these events, especially the informational consequences of responding. This error was at least partially corrected by Pavlov's research on conditioning. Anokhin, relying on Pavlov's research, explained how information carried in feedback from a response is critical in understanding behavior.

Harmonizing Information from the External and Internal Environments Leads to Purposive Behavior.   Anokhin's (1974) thesis was that conditional reflexes depend on the combination of two kinds of stimulation. The first is input from the external environment (the CS and US), and the second is internal feedback from responses, which he called reverse or return afferentation. **Reverse afferentation** is response-produced feedback carried by neural impulses that are generated when muscles contract (in Chapter 7 we studied how afferent neural impulses from muscles function as feedback). These two inputs, those from stimuli in the external environment and from muscles in the internal environment, produce preparatory reactions that facilitate responding. According to Anokhin, such preparatory reactions constitute the conditional reflex itself (as the CS evokes the CR that prepares the organism for the US).

Anokhin held that conditional and unconditional stimuli prepare an organism to respond; also reverse afferentation (feedback) from muscles facilitates adaptive behavior and thereby helps the organism to survive.

Such adaptive behavior depends on the formation of an "action acceptor" that harmonizes the input from the external with the internal environments (Fig. 10.19). When the action acceptor in the brain harmonizes information from the CS and US with feedback from the muscles, it generates a purposive program of action. The organism's purposive behavior then predicts the US. Anokhin's functional system thus is a composite of negative feedback circuits whereby conditioning occurs as information is transmitted between the muscular responses and the brain.

A hypothesized action acceptor in the brain harmonizes information from the external and the internal environments to activate the organism to behave purposively.

Anokhin's work and that of others have led to our current advanced understanding that behavior is influenced by stimuli from both the external and internal environments. Consequently, behavior is best understood by incorporating the basic concepts of cybernetics.

Having covered some of the major phenomena of conditioning, let us now consider some other views of learning, especially ethological learning.

FIGURE 10.19   Anokhin's concept of an action acceptor that harmonizes input from the external environment (CS) and the internal environment (e.g., a muscle); through reverse afferentation, the muscle sends information to the action acceptor. The organism then develops a purposive program of action wherein the US is predicted.

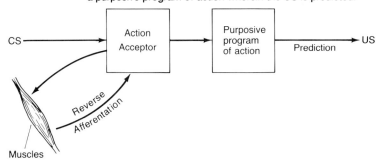

KARL VON FRISCH (1886–1982), KONRAD LORENZ (1903–1989), AND NIKOLAS TINBERGEN (1907–1988)

These three scientists received the Nobel Prize in 1973 for their research on organization and elicitation of individual and social behavior patterns. The awarding of the Prize recognized the importance of studying behavior of animals in their natural habitats.

Von Frisch, a German zoologist born in Vienna, eventually settled at the University of Munich. His study of the language of bees showed that the pattern of their flying dance could inform the swarm of the direction, distance, location, and quality of food (see his books *The Dancing Bees,* 1961, and *The Dance Language and Orientation of Bees,* 1967).

Lorenz, an anatomist and animal psychologist, became director of Animal Sociology of the Austrian Academy of Sciences. Lorenz studied how innate behavior patterns can be modified by the environment and by social contacts, as in "imprinting." Imprinting is a rapid form of learning that is possible only at a critical period of life, as when the greylag goose becomes permanently attached to a human as a parental object and follows the person about. Lorenz also discovered innate release mechanisms that condition an animal's reaction to environmental and social stimuli.

Tinbergen, born in the Netherlands, contributed to the new science of ethology by studying innate behavior of insects, fish, and birds in their natural habitat and how such behavior is influenced by sensory and social factors.

ETHOLOGICAL LEARNING AND SPECIES-SPECIFIC CONSTRAINTS

Ethologists study behavior and learning in natural environments.

Ethology is the study of the behavior of organisms in their natural environments. Contemporary interest in ethology stems primarily from the work of the three Nobel Prize–winning ethologists — Karl von Frisch, Nikolas Tinbergen, and Konrad Lorenz (see accompanying box). All three began their research by studying learning. Von Frisch's earliest work was on the classical conditioning of goldfish to sound and of honey bees to color. Tinbergen's earliest research was of the memory of hunting wasps, while Lorenz began his career studying imprinting and learned social recognition.

The Primary Concepts of Ethology

The conceptual framework used by most ethologists derives from four general principles put forth by Lorenz and Tinbergen. As discussed by Gould (1986), these are cue recognition, fixed action patterns, endogenous (internal) control, and selective learning, which includes imprinting.

CUE RECOGNITION

The principle of **cue recognition** holds that animals innately recognize important events, objects, and individuals in their environments because cues called **sign stimuli** are **releasers** that trigger specific behavior patterns. One releaser, for example, automatically triggers a response pattern in some birds that build their nests on the ground. Thus, an egg outside of the nest of a greylag goose is a releaser, so that the goose innately recognizes the egg. The goose then extends its neck over the egg and gently rolls it back to the nest with the bottom of its bill (this is the innate response pattern). The same response pattern can also be evoked by some similar stimuli, such as batteries, beer bottles, and baseballs, but not by other stimuli.

Animals thus are "prewired" to recognize important objects, individuals, and events in their environments. Apparently, visual, acoustic, and olfactory cells in the central nervous system (called feature-detector cells) are coded to react to sign stimuli so as to trigger these specific recognition responses. These innate stimulus–response connections have survival value so that presumably members of species that lacked such wired-in connections failed in the struggle for survival.

In cue recognition, sign stimuli release specific innate response patterns that are appropriate responses to objects, individuals, and events.

FIXED ACTION PATTERNS

The response pattern elicited by sign stimuli is so stereotyped and rigid that it is completed even if the sign stimulus that triggered it is removed. For instance, if the egg that the greylag goose retrieves is removed, the goose continues to "retrieve" the nonexistent egg. Apparently, specific proprioceptive feedback from each movement evokes the next response in the patterned chain of behavior (the **fixed action pattern**). One can thus observe a goose "rolling an egg" that is not actually there. Once started, it continues to run off the wired-in behavioral unit.

A fixed action pattern is a wired-in behavioral unit that is released by sign stimuli, each component of which is elicited by feedback from the previous response in the chain.

ENDOGENOUS (INTERNAL) CONTROL

Endogenous control is innate control of behavior through varying internal conditions. Consequently, some wired-in fixed action patterns are performed only during certain periods of an animal's life. For instance, egg rolling occurs seasonally, appearing about a week before incubation begins and lasting until about a week after hatching. The conditions that lead an organism to emit a motor program to the sign stimulus for eggs is absent at other times. According to Gould, research has not yet been able to help us understand the mechanisms underlying such motivated behavior. However, it is behavior under endogenous control and may be influenced by hormones or other factors that ebb and flow.

The principle of endogenous control holds that sign stimuli trigger and direct wired-in motor programs that, due to varying internal conditions, may only be performed during certain periods of an organism's life.

SELECTIVE LEARNING

The baby herring gull is born with the ability to peck at sign stimuli such as a horizontally moving vertical bar and at a moving red spot. It also selects out other features of a stimulus complex and learn to respond to them too. For example, while it is responding to a sign stimulus such as a moving mother, through **selective learning** it also responds to the shape of the head and beak of the mother.

Imprinting Is a Kind of Selective Learning. With **imprinting,** there is a certain

Selective learning is learning to respond to features associated with sign stimuli.

In imprinting, there is a sensitive (critical) phase during which specific stimuli come to trigger specific responses.

critical period during which the organism attaches a response to a given stimulus. That stimulus contains sign stimuli to which the organism responds so that associated aspects of the stimulus are selected out and also responded to. A famous example is that of ducklings that, during an early critical period of their lives, learned to follow Lorenz in a parade, just as they would follow the mother duck.

Selective learning is adaptive in that it helps a naive animal to learn an effective response that will have value for its later life. Selective learning is quite resistant to extinction and apparently occurs in the absence of external reinforcement.

Learning in the "Field," the Natural Environment

Some organisms are specialists in that they can only emit one response to a certain stimulus, while others are generalists that can make varied responses to a given stimulus.

Species may be located on a continuum from specialists to generalists depending on their ability to learn complex processes.

Specialists and Generalists. Some organisms are specialists in the sense that they are prewired to run off a certain motor program in response to a certain stimulus. Others, however, are generalists in that they are able to make a number of different responses to the same stimulus. In the acquisition of food, for instance, some species run off specific motor programs for harvesting a specific kind of food. Thus, the digger wasp is born able to recognize, capture, and paralyze particular prey—one species is specialized for honey bees, another for crickets, and so on. A generalist, such as a bee, on the other hand, is programmed to memorize the odor, color, and shape of all the species it forages.

Four Kinds of Learning That Vary in Complexity. We can conceive of a continuum between specialists and generalists on which we can locate various species. Gould specifies some categories of learning for such a continuum. Some organisms are capable of only the simpler kinds of learning while others can use higher processes. These kinds of learning, ranked from simple to complex, are (1) nonassociative learning, of which habituation and sensitization are two types; (2) classical conditioning; (3) trial-and-error learning; and (4) higher order, cognitive trial-and-error learning. Like all distinctions and classifications, these have shortcomings, but they are also useful, as we will now see. But we should also follow Lloyd Morgan's (1906) canon of **parsimony**—we should not ascribe a higher mental process to a species if the behavior can (more parsimoniously) be explained by a simpler process. In this instance, we should explain behavior through simple wired-in connections in preference to a complex cognitive learning process.

Nonassociative learning is the simplest learning process, followed by classical conditioning and trial-and-error learning; the most complex learning process is cognitive trial-and-error learning.

Morgan's canon of parsimony holds that animal activity should be interpreted in terms of psychological processes lower in the scale of psychological evolution and development in preference to higher ones, if that is possible.

In habituation, the repeated presentation of a stimulus diminishes the strength of the response that it evokes.

NONASSOCIATIVE LEARNING

Habituation and Sensitization. In **nonassociative learning,** the organism does not associate stimuli or stimuli and responses. **Habituation** is a waning of an individual's response to a repeatedly presented stimulus. Aplysia, for instance, withdraws its gills when stimulated by a jet of water. When repeatedly triggered by a jet of water, however, the withdrawal response becomes increasingly difficult to elicit (it habituates). One interpretation is that the threshold for receiving stimuli is adjusted in accordance with the background level of relevant stimuli; that is, the gill of the Aplysia in calm water is very sensitive to stimulation; however, in rough water it is less sensitive so that it is not continually withdrawn; only an unusual stimulus can then trigger the behavior of withdrawing the gill.

In contrast, **sensitization** heightens responsiveness. It can thus reduce or eliminate habituation when a novel stimulus is encountered. Sensitization occurs if the Aplysia that has habituated its gill-withdrawal response is poked in the tail—it will once again respond to a previously ignored water jet.

CLASSICAL CONDITIONING

For the ethologist, the UR is a motor program and the US is a sign stimulus. Through associative learning, a sign stimulus can be replaced with another stimulus that becomes a CS. Accordingly, the CS may allow an animal to anticipate the arrival of an individual of interest, such as when it hears or smells a predator. This is another example of the biological survival value of conditioning. Such conditioning is dependent on certain preexisting innate neural pathways so that some kinds of conditioning are relatively easy while others are extremely difficult. Thus, organisms are predisposed to acquire certain CS–CR associations and these involve what is known as alpha conditioning. However, **alpha conditioning** is not actual conditioning at all; it is the tendency of some animals in some situations to show a slight UR to a neutral stimulus before pairing it with a US, as Pavlov's dogs salivated slightly to the stimulus of a tone. However, when the tone and the US were paired, salivation became a CR that was of much greater amplitude than prior to conditioning. This tendency of animals to slightly respond to a stimulus before any conditioning (i.e., alpha conditioning) indicates that they are well prepared to learn the CS–CR association. For example, at birth, neural pathways in organisms are activated by a certain neutral stimulus and evoke a specific UR such as tone → salivation. Consequently, when the CS and US pathways are active simultaneously, the CS–CR connection is easily formed.

TRIAL-AND-ERROR LEARNING AND COGNITION

Much animal learning is of the trial-and-error (instrumental or operant conditioning) variety. We have already discussed these principles and need not elaborate on them here. In fact, habituation, sensitization, associative learning, and trial-and-error learning seem to account for most of animal learning. Yet, there may still be a higher kind of learning involving cognition, such as the concept of **cognitive maps** extensively developed by Edward Tolman. There is the possibility that animals, in some sense, think about a problem. They may evaluate behavioral alternatives or formulate plans. A rat may be thought of as solving a maze problem by cognitively mapping its behavior and later referring to this map as it makes choices in running the maze. The animal has learned what leads to what—that "if I turn left in this maze, I will get out." By trial-and-error, the organism cognitively formulates hypotheses and tests them. Thus, hypothesized cognitive trial-and-error learning is the ability to use cognitive maps. Over many years Tolman and his associates conducted important experiments on hypothesized cognitive abilities in rats and other animals. The research, in fact, laid the groundwork for what later came to be known as "cognitive psychology."

Whether or not the data justify a concept of cognitive trial-and-error learning, or whether or not cognitive processes should even be ascribed to animals, is controversial. Much research in the middle decades of this century was devoted to this issue. Many psychologists, holding to Morgan's canon, believed that traditional conditioning principles adequately accounted for animal learning. Others, like Tol-

Sensitization is a process by which presentation of a stimulus increases the likelihood that a response will be made.

Alpha conditioning is a tendency to show a slight UR to a neutral stimulus, thus facilitating the learning of a CS–CR association due to innate neural pathways.

The concept of cognitive trial-and-error learning embodies the notion that animals develop cognitive maps from which they form hypotheses as to sequences of events.

man and his colleagues, held otherwise. Only continued research will settle this issue.

Ethological Criticisms of Psychological Research

Ethological criticisms of traditional learning theory have questioned the generality of principles derived from animal experiments in the laboratory.

Ethologists hold that animals have evolved in such a way that they are predisposed to learn specific responses that are relevant to their unique environments. Some suggest that these **species-specific behaviors** preclude the possibility that there are *general* principles of learning; consequently, they deny that there are conditioning principles that are applicable to many species throughout the phylogenetic scale. Only by studying the animal in its natural environment can we understand how specific animals learn. No single set of traditional learning principles, they hold, has adequately coped with the complexity of human language or adequately handled such phenomena as selective attention and learning, conditional food aversion, complex problem-solving behavior, and the nature of reinforcement. They even question whether psychological learning theory has a future.

There Are Species-Specific Variables in Learning. To its credit, research *has* established that there are some biological constraints on learning — some species are relatively incapable of learning certain responses. Furthermore, some specific stimuli can be readily associated with some specific response while the association of others is more difficult. Some species can easily select out particular characteristics of a stimulus pattern to which to respond (this is selective attention) while other species cannot. In imprinting and song learning, for instance, there are unlearned predispositions. Thus, in song learning, birds favor certain sounds and learn them better, depending on the species. Such species-specific predispositions influence rates of associative learning that vary depending upon the particular species. Genetic influences are clearly important in imprinting, song learning, and language acquisition in humans. These three phenomena and others have critical (sensitive) periods in development wherein certain responses are more easily learned than at other times.

Comparative studies in the field have demonstrated differences in learning processes among species, but those differences have not always appeared under laboratory conditions.

In Short. Ethologists have established a sound data base for the argument that species variables influence the ease of associating certain stimuli and responses. They influence recall processes too.

A primary function of science is to criticize scientific principles and findings and thereby modify them to more closely approximate the "truth." The influence of ethology on psychological learning theory has been constructive and has accomplished that.

Although criticisms by ethologists have been valuable, they do not deprecate the tremendous accomplishments in psychological learning research.

How General Are Our Principles of Behavior? This question has long been with us. The psychologist Frank Beach (1950), in his article "The Snark Was a Boojum" takes off on Lewis Carroll's "The Hunting of the Snark" and criticizes the limited approach of comparative psychologists of that day. As illustrated in Figure 10.20, the white rat is misleading psychologists and their artificial laboratory equipment. He compared them to the baker who had the unfortunate experience of meeting a dangerous snark that was a boojum, unlike typical harmless snarks. The baker suddenly vanished. Beach's point was that comparative psychology too had vanished and that the focus had shifted to the laboratory study of the white rat *(Rattus norvegicus)*. As Beach said, his research in comparative psychology "compelled me to realize that dogs are not large rats which bark." His plea was for a return to a true

FIGURE 10.20 The snark was a boojum—Frank Beach's criticism of the limited approach of the study of the white rat in unnatural laboratory conditions. By concentrating on the white rat, the psychologists are failing to understand how species differ as they behave in their natural environments.

comparative psychology that studied organisms all along the phylogenetic scale in their natural environments wherever possible. A major issue raised by Beach and later by ethologists thus concerned the extent to which general principles of learning can be shown to be applicable throughout the phylogenetic scale. To answer this question, as Beach requested, lower animals now have been extensively studied to ascertain the degree of generality of conditioning principles. Conditioning principles have been shown to be quite general, but comparative psychology establishes that in addition, there are important differences among species. For example, rats and dogs obey the same general conditioning principles, but dogs have additional capabilities that rats do not have.

One major strategy has been to seek general principles through the study of simplified systems and learning processes. Consequently, researchers have analyzed simple forms of learning in animals with simple nervous systems. That is the rationale of laboratory research — to bring a complex phenomenon into the labora-

FIGURE 10.21
Honey bees were successfully conditioned to consume water as a conditional response to an odor or color.

tory and simplify it, so that, once dissected, it can be better understood. Once laws of learning are established for simpler organisms, the resulting principles could then be tested to see if they apply to higher species, including humans.

Bitterman and his colleagues (e.g., Couvilon and Bitterman, 1984) have followed this strategy extensively with the honey bee. The honey bee has good sensory capacities; its behavior is well motivated; and it has sufficiently variable behavior. The honey bee brain is about 1 mm wide and contains about 850,000 neurons. Bitterman points out that most of what we know about learning is based on **vertebrates** (organisms with spinal columns). This concentration on vertebrates in the upper regions of the phylogenetic scale was based on scientists' search for evidence of continuity among the species, as implied by Darwin's theory of evolution. Yet only about 5 percent of animal species are vertebrates while about 95 percent of all animal species are **invertebrates.**

An example of a learning study with honey bees follows: The organisms made the response of consuming a sugar solution in the presence of a certain stimulus (the odor of jasmine or a color such as yellow). The bees were then tested for a learned response to the associated odor or color. For this, number of trials to extinction was measured by replacing the sucrose with water, but leaving the odor or color. A relatively large number of responses were made to the water in the presence of the odor or the color, indicating that extinction was prolonged when the odor or color was present. Indeed, the bees did learn CRs to such CSs as odors and colors, as depicted in Figure 10.21.

Bitterman has employed other conditioning paradigms and other responses (e.g., extending the proboscis [similar to a "nose"]). His general conclusion from many studies is that both simple and complex learning in invertebrates is similar to that of the vertebrates. In fact, Bitterman concluded that *the conditioning data on vertebrates found by Pavlov are essentially the same as data from honey bees.* As Bitterman points out, there should be considerable generality along the phylogenetic scale

There are common behaviors among different species because of similar synapses. One reason for the greater complexity of behavior in higher organisms is the increased complexity of their neural networks.

because synapses of lower and higher animals are similar—they all derive in common from ancient metazoan. The greater complexity of behavior of organisms higher in the phylogenetic scale thus is due to the greater complexity of their neural networks (the patterns of neurons), as well as interactions with muscles, and so on, and not in differences among synapses.

Despite the great differences among species, conditional response learning is similar in all of them. This may be because of similar synaptic mechanisms.

Associative and trial-and-error learning, along with the nonassociative learning processes of habituation and sensitization, form the foundation for understanding learning throughout the phylogenetic scale. Yet, there is much to add to our understanding. To sizably advance our knowledge about learning and memory, ethologists, psychologists, and others need to effectively collaborate. We will soon consider the contribution of physiologically oriented scientists to our knowledge of learning. For now, let us sample some issues that are important for society.

SOME LEARNING QUESTIONS WITH SOCIAL SIGNIFICANCE

Is There Prenatal Learning?

It is commonly thought that there is learning before birth because the senses are functioning then. Some research by Anthony DeCasper indicates that there can be prenatal learning through the auditory modality. For instance, newborn infants were presented with regular cycles of beeps and silences through earphones. If they sucked during the beeps, they started a tape of their mother's voice. But if they sucked during the silences, they set off the tape of another woman's voice. In general, they sucked more frequently to produce their mother's voice, suggesting that they had learned the reinforcing sounds of their mother's voice while in utero. They also preferred nursery rhyme books that had been read aloud to them in utero over books that had not been presented to them. The control subjects, two-day-old babies, did not show a preference for fathers' voices over other male voices and they preferred to suck to hear a recorded sound of the mother's heartbeat over a male voice reading nursery rhymes. Apparently, human infants learn speech and heart sounds of the mother during the prenatal period.

Similar studies indicate that rats can develop odor preferences in utero that later are manifested behaviorally. Elliot Blass exposed some rats in utero to citral, a liquid with a lemonlike smell but no taste. After birth, the rats preferred to suckle other mothers whose bedding had been painted with citral over their own mothers' nests that did not contain citral. Similarly, rats exposed prenatally to citral later tended to choose mating partners that smelled of citral. Studies such as these indicate that organisms in utero have sensorimotor systems capable of learning to respond to some stimuli.

Stimulus–response relationships can be prenatally learned for some sensory modalities.

How Are Addictions Learned?

Through Operant Conditioning. Consider two stages of learning. The first stage occurs when a person tries out an addictive substance for whatever reason (e.g., peer pressure or need for escape). Euphoria then develops. But after the euphoria wears off, the learner may crave the substance. To relieve the unpleasant state of craving, the individual may consume more of the substance, which is further reinforcing. Thus begins a vicious (cybernetic) cycle:

Consume the drug ⟶ develop euphoria ⟶ experience the pain of the craving ⟶ consume more of the drug . . .

Viewed this way, addictive behavior is an operant maintained by both positive (euphoria) and negative (removal of pain) reinforcement. Such behavioral learning of addiction no doubt also has a biological component, perhaps involving changes in how neurotransmitters function.

Operant Conditioning as a Cybernetic Model. Addiction to chemical substances fits a cybernetic model that maintains the behavior as follows: Feedback from consuming the substance is both positively reinforcing (euphoria) and negatively reinforcing (relief from craving). Often these function as a positive feedback circuit

A cybernetic circuit for operant conditioning of addictive behavior: taking a drug → positive reinforcement of euphoria → noxious stimulation of craving → consuming more of the drug. There is positive (a high) and negative (relief from the craving) reinforcement.

wherein the addict goes out of control by repeatedly consuming the substance. This is the ultimate consequence of all unrestricted positive feedback circuits.

Multiple Addictions. The euphoria of drugs may be a coping mechanism for stress or pain. But as consumption continues, there is progressively less euphoria (tolerance increases) so that larger amounts of the substance are consumed. Relief from craving also becomes more difficult to achieve. Eventually, there may be inadequate euphoria and/or no relief from stress or pain which may lead to shifts to other substances permitting several addictions to develop and coexist. But they all fit the same operant conditioning–cybernetic pattern.

Addictive Behavior Becomes Self-perpetuating. Motivated behavior that is learned is called **secondary motivation** or **functional autonomy.** It has been learned because it has been associated with the reduction of physiological needs. For instance, an organism may be motivated to approach food because consumption of food reduced its physiological status of hunger. Similarly an organism is motivated to avoid noxious stimuli because it has learned in the past that they were harmful. We learn what is beautiful and desirable because it is associated with positive reinforcement just as we learn what is noxious and undesirable because it is associated with pain and discomfort. Similarly, the original *cause* of addictive behavior becomes unimportant, just as initially the cause of the operant in operant conditioning is irrelevant. Neutral stimuli that were associated with the reinforcing effects of consuming drugs acquire the power to motivate the addict to engage in addictive behavior — drinking coffee can evoke a cigarette-smoking response.

The concepts of secondary motivation and functional autonomy hold that organisms seek previously neutral stimuli because they were associated with the reduction of primary physiological needs.

Addictive behavior can continue on its own, functionally autonomous of the original conditions that started it.

Can the Immune System Be Conditioned?

The **immune system** comprises blood cells and molecules that perform various functions. One function of the immune system is to discriminate between the body itself and what is attacking the body: It then attacks and inactivates whatever is perceived to be the attacking agent. There are two views as to why the immune system functions in this manner: a conditioning theory and a selection theory.

THE CONDITIONING THEORY

The nervous system participates in regulating activity of the immune system, which is consonant with the theory that the immune system can be conditioned.

This theory holds that when a particular virus invades the immune system, the immune system learns to make a specific antibody to rid the body of that particular virus. (Antibodies come from a variety of lymphocytes and include T cells that derive from the thymus.) Traditionally it had been thought that the nervous and immune systems are functionally independent, but numerous studies now indicate that the nervous system can regulate the activity of the immune system.

Conditioning studies have tremendous importance for clinical intervention in the immune system.

Support for the learning interpretation also comes from direct conditioning studies (Brittain & Wiener, 1985). For instance, in a number of studies, a novel taste, usually saccharin, was used as a possible CS; the US were drugs that are aversive to the taste and also suppress immunological responses. Both saccharin and the US were jointly administered to experimental animals. The saccharin was then added to drinking water, to which there were impaired immune reactions and taste aversion. Conditioning was thus successful in suppressing the immune system through a CS, saccharin, and also producing a noxious taste for saccharin. In another conditioning study, the sight of the color of a vial was conditioned to enhance tuberculine reactions in tuberculine positive subjects. With conditioning procedures, behavioral medicine practitioners can regulate the immune system at least to some extent and even contribute to the treatment of some kinds of cancer (e.g., some data indicate that relaxation therapy and a positive psychological outlook can beneficially affect the course of this disease).

THE SELECTION THEORY

The selection theory holds that the immune system functions when an invading virus selects and acts on an appropriate antibody. The immune system does not learn to make a specific antibody to rid the body of a particular virus. Rather, already existing antibodies interact with the invading virus. Consequently, the immune system is formed by Darwinian principles of selection and not of learning. There are data supporting the selection theory (e.g., Cunningham, 1978).

In view of the evidence supporting both theories, it is wisest to conclude that until further research establishes otherwise, the immune system functions in accord with both theories.

Until further research is available, we conclude that the immune system functions by both selective and conditioning processes.

MEMORY

The general topic of forgetting and retaining information is extremely important to all of us. We frequently get irritated with ourselves because we forget something that we know we have learned — a telephone number or the year Constantinople fell, for example. On the other hand, we should often be thankful for the fact that we do forget material, since forgetting is adaptively useful to us. Think of all the material that you learn in a day: license numbers; facts about different kinds of deodorants; snap, crackle, and pop characteristics of breakfast foods, and so on. One person who had the unusual capacity to remember almost everything reported that he frequently thought he was going "mad." Fortunately, the material that is most important to us is used and reviewed rather frequently, so that it is constantly available — we do not forget where we live.

Memory was first systematically investigated by Hermann Ebbinghaus in 1885. To eliminate differences in ease of learning various verbal units ("cat" is easier than "nov"), he memorized numerous lists of meaningless nonsense syllables (zed, nov, bek) to which people had seldom been exposed. He then tested himself to see how well he remembered the lists after various periods of time. In Figure 10.22 we can see that he retained about 53 percent of the nonsense syllables after 20 minutes, about 34 percent after one day, and so on. The striking characteristic of Figure 10.22 is that most of the material is forgotten shortly after it has been learned. However, we will soon see that this conclusion does not apply generally.

Ebbinghaus developed non-sense syllables to reduce the degree of association (meaning) with already learned material.

Interference Theory of Forgetting

Why We Forget. We have experimentally produced forgetting in the laboratory and systematically varied the phenomenon. As a result of a number of such laboratory studies, we have developed the **interference theory of forgetting** to understand and explain forgetting. This theory asserts that we forget material because other material interferes with its recall. Furthermore, the more similar the other

We forget previously learned material because other learned material interferes with (inhibits) it.

The evidence indicates that the interference theory is the best single psychological theory to account for forgetting.

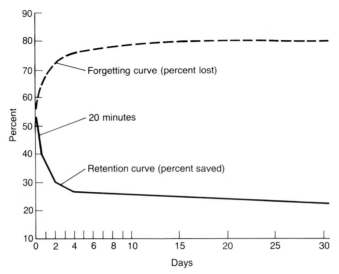

FIGURE 10.22   Curves of retention and forgetting for nonsense syllables obtained by Ebbinghaus.

The greater the similarity between two sets of material learned, the greater the interference and thus, the greater is the forgetting.

material is to the material that we wish to retain, the greater is the forgetting—material from *The Prophet* and *The Rubaiyat* would interfere with retention of each other more than would material from *The Prophet* and *TIME* magazine.

There is a constant state of competition of learned information to be recalled. Whatever is recalled at any given time is dominant. If the information is not recalled, we say we have "forgotten" the desired information at least temporarily.

Now we can see why Ebbinghaus's forgetting curve falsely indicates that only one-third of what we learn is retained by the next day. First, note that Ebbinghaus learned verbal material consisting of numerous lists of nonsense syllables. Consequently, in recalling any given nonsense syllable list, other similar lists interfered with that particular list. With such a large amount of competition among similar lists, there is considerable forgetting. If Ebbinghaus had memorized but one list of nonsense syllables and then tested himself for retention the next day, he would not have forgotten 66 percent of that list. Rather, later research indicates that the forgetting would have been only about 25 percent of the list. Furthermore, there are many other types of material that we learn—we learn motor tasks or abstract concepts, for instance. And forgetting of such tasks is considerably less rapid than is that for verbal material like words. Once you learn to ride a bicycle, you never forget how to do it.

Ebbinghaus's forgetting curve overestimates the amount of forgetting because there was considerable interference among the numerous nonsense syllables he memorized.

Verbal material is often forgotten, but motor skills seldom are.

Learning and Memory in Lower Animals

Our task as psychologists is to understand behavior in all of its complexity throughout the phylogenetic scale. The importance of studying lower species for understanding human behavior has been well demonstrated. Yet, it is also important in its own right to understand how lower species behave. We have become increasingly aware that various species inherit behavioral characteristics that make them especially efficient in learning and remembering things that are particularly relevant for them. For instance, many birds are extremely apt in learning the songs that are their species' specialties. Rats have special abilities to remember spatial locations just as bees remember the location of flowers. Animals easily learn the survival-valued behavior of avoiding noxious foods. A study that is illustrative of those seeking to establish unique capacities in species was conducted by Shettleworth (1983). He sought to determine whether or not there was a special kind of memory in food-hoarding birds. A nutcracker, for instance, retrieves as many as 33,000 pinon-pine seeds in caches of four or five seeds that it has buried. Throughout the winter it returns and digs up thousands of caches. Researchers have considered that these birds do not rely on memory. One reason is that their memory would have to be fantastically large in order to remember the sites of hundreds or thousands of individually hoarded items. Furthermore, the memory would have to be long term in nature. Even a short-term hoarder such as the marsh tit does not recover its stores until hours or days after they have been deposited. A long-term hoarder such as Clark's nutcracker does not return to a hoard for months.

Species inherit behaviors that have survival value, such as a predisposition to learn and remember avoidance of noxious foods.

Invoking Morgan's canon, it is possible to explain this behavior without postulating memory; for example, perhaps the hoarder stores food only in certain kinds of sites, such as south-facing slopes or holes in bark. It would not have to remember the specific sites but would only need the capacity to search in sites of a particular kind.

As a test for a true memory, researchers hid seeds in storage sites that were quite similar to those employed naturally by marsh tits. They found that the seeds hidden by the marsh tits themselves were retrieved earlier than the seeds that were hidden in the false sites by the investigators. The conclusion was that the marsh tits went first to the sites that they remembered, and not to the similar sites, which were less than a meter away from the true sites. They did have very special kinds of memories! These conclusions were then confirmed in the laboratory in studies reported by Shettleworth (1983).

Animals with simple brains, such as birds, show rather remarkable memory capacities for things that are especially important for them.

Through natural selection, birds and other animals that did not have good memories have probably been extinguished. Those that maintained memories that helped them in the struggle for existence have survived.

With this basis of behavioral principles, we can now turn to physiological, biochemical, and other characteristics of learning and memory.

THE PHYSIOLOGICAL PSYCHOLOGY OF LEARNING AND MEMORY

Physiological Psychology Relates Behavior and Internal Functions. While psychologists study behavior, physiologists study internal processes, including biochemical phenomena. It is the physiological psychologist, an important scientist in the area of biological psychology, who relates the two areas. For a complete understanding of an organism, we need to include both behavioral and physiological events and their relationships, which are complex and interactive. That is, we can influence physiological events (e.g., establishing an engram) by manipulating behavior (e.g., through conditioning). Similarly, we can influence behavior (e.g., generating euphoria) by influencing physiological processes (e.g., the administration of chemicals). Physiological research on learning and memory has concentrated on the brain, but peripheral events and central-peripheral interaction are also critical.

The Kinds of Questions Asked

Engrams are assumed to be in the brain as critical components of brain–muscle circuits, but there is no consensus as to how or where they are stored.

Some questions that have guided research strategies seeking neural characteristics of learning and memory include the following:

1. What happens in the brain during learning? Presumably a representation of new learning is encoded and stored there as an engram. But how?
2. How is an engram accessed and retrieved when we remember a past event?
3. Why do we forget something for the moment, but the memory is later accessible?
4. When memory for an event seems permanently lost, have the engrams been destroyed or have they just become unretrieveable?

Although these questions focus on the central nervous system, we must maintain the perspective that all brain activity is influenced by numerous peripheral events in the body, and vice versa. Therefore, to reach an adequate understanding of memory we must focus not only on the brain but also on the relationships between central neural events as they interact with bodily systems through cybernetic circuits. This broad perspective leads us to focus on another question:

The engram can be influenced by various systems of the body, especially muscular and hormonal ones, so that biopsychological studies of learning and memory include peripheral as well as central neural events.

5. In conditioning, how do we discover just what systems within an organism are conditioned?

There are more synapses in one human being than there are known stars.

To emphasize the complexity of the problems of understanding the role of the human brain in learning and memory, it is estimated that there are about 12–15 billion neurons in the cerebrum and that these neurons make perhaps $5^{14} \times 10$ (that is 500 trillion) synapses in the cortex; there are about 70 billion neurons in the cerebellum and 1 billion in the spinal cord. Add to this the complexity of peripheral systems with which the brain interacts (e.g., some 1030 muscles). We can thus understand why, after many decades of vigorous research, specifying the nature and location of the engram still constitutes one of the most baffling questions that we face. We have few firm answers, but let us start.

The general approach to answering the first question about what happens in the brain during learning is to condition members of subhuman species. Their brains are then carefully examined by means of various neurophysiological techniques in order to ascertain any neural changes that persist. Inferences follow about the involvement of such neural changes in the engram that resulted from conditioning. Before we discuss the results of such studies, we should first see how some methods discussed in Chapter 8 have been used in conditioning and memory research for seeking neural changes in the brain.

Methods for Studying Neurophysiological Changes During Learning

The most frequently used techniques have been those of extirpation, electrical recording from microelectrodes, and clinical approaches.

EXTIRPATION

First, the organism learns something, such as through conditioning. Then, a part of the brain is destroyed through stereotaxic surgery (Chapter 8). Using this highly refined technique, a microelectrode can be inserted into a precise spot in the brain and a small lesion is produced by electrically cauterizing brain cells. The lesion may also be made by introducing neurochemicals into the region of interest; this method is becoming increasingly popular in lesion research. Finally, the behavior of the organism is carefully measured to see if there has been a change in the learned response. If so, the extirpated brain region could be implicated as an important site for storing the memory.

Extirpation (ablation) is the experimental production of a brain lesion to learn the function of a brain region; however, the conclusions reached must be accepted with caution.

As we discussed in Chapter 8, however, the control problems with this technique are immense. For instance, any change in the learned response could result from a variety of reasons other than the fact that the specific targeted brain region was destroyed. In addition, if the learned behavior is *not* disturbed, it would not necessarily mean that the structure destroyed has no function in the storage of the memory. Perhaps it *could* function for the storage of the engram, but just is not necessary. Conclusions about the nature of the engram that result from extirpation, as Pavlov warned us, must be accepted with great caution.

EEG AND ELECTRICAL RECORDING FROM MICROELECTRODES

Electrical recording methods have traditionally been EEG measures, but more analytic electrical study has resulted from the insertion of microelectrodes into single neurons. In this way the electrical activity of a single neuron can be studied as learning progresses.

Insertion of microelectrodes into a single neuron allows the study of electrical activity in the neuron as learning progresses.

One problem in using this technique is that of determining exactly which cells are in fact active during the conditioning process. One may intend to insert the microelectrode into one cell but actually hit another cell. By using a biochemical technique in which certain chemicals can be injected, the precise cell that has been penetrated can be identified.

ELECTRICAL STIMULATION

Microelectrodes may also be inserted into the brain in order to deliver an electrical current to stimulate neurons. The strategy is to see if the stimulation of certain areas of the brain can affect the conditioning process. For instance, the hypothalamus has been electrically stimulated during classical conditioning. The CS is presented before the US. Following the US, hypothalamic stimulation has been found to accelerate the conditioning process.

The rate of acquisition of conditional responses is accelerated with hypothalamic stimulation indicating that it may be part of a neural process during conditioning.

Limitations of Correlational Strategies. Although some brain regions have been implicated in the search for the engram, these techniques yield but limited conclusions because they are only correlational ones—they do not establish causal connections. For instance, although there may be a correlation between the locus of a brain lesion and a change in behavior, that does not mean that the lesion, itself, caused the behavioral change (see pp. 240–241 and 241–242).

With this review and extension of methodology, let us now consider some findings from samples of research relevant to the locus of learning and memory.

Some Classic Research

Pavlov's Theory of Conditional Neural Connections Disproved. To understand higher nervous activity, Pavlov sought neural connections within the brain that mediated conditional stimuli and responses. In Lashley's classic research, series of experiments were conducted to seek those neural connections. Lashley's famous search for the engram systematically extirpated all reasonably possible regions of the rat brain. After the animals *still* retained the learning, he reluctantly and facetiously concluded that perhaps the only thing he had proven was that learning simply is not possible. But, obviously a more realistic conclusion was that learning is not just a matter of establishing specific neural connections between a stimulus and a response. Consequently, Lashley advanced his two major principles of brain organization.

The Principles of Mass Action and of Equipotentiality. The **Principle of Equipotentiality** holds that all neurons are equal in their capacity to store memories so that various regions of the cortex are capable of contributing equally to the performance of complex tasks. Equipotentiality denies that there is specialization of function within the cortex as far as memory for complex learning tasks is concerned.

The **Principle of Mass Action** holds that the cortex functions as a whole, integrated system such that the more of the cortex remaining intact, the better the performance of the complex learned task. To the extent to which a portion of the cortex has been destroyed, there is reduced efficiency of performance.

Lashley disproved Pavlov's theory of specific neural connections for conditional reflexes, but his Principles of Mass Action and Equipotentiality are no longer widely accepted.

Today the Principles of Equipotentiality and Mass Action are not universally accepted by researchers, nor are the extreme positions of equipotentiality and localization universally rejected as untenable. The body of research supports, as the most tenable, a model of specific complex circuits that function among specific areas to carry out specialized functions. The Principles of Equipotentiality and Mass Action retain some limited validity.

Lashley's presidential address to the American Psychological Association in 1929 was based on his conclusion that learning did not establish specific neural connections as Pavlov theorized. Pavlov had come with Gantt to the United States where he heard Lashley's vigorous attack on his reflex theory. Pavlov was immediately ready for a rebuttal. Pavlov so heatedly attacked Lashley's arguments that the interpreter lost track. Finally, after some 20 minutes, the interpreter gave up and summarized the argument: "Professor Pavlov said: No!"

Contemporary research indicates that both of them were wrong with regard to specific conclusions. However, these two scientific giants established the foundation for the many decades of research that followed.

Some Electrophysiological Research

Jasper, Ricci, and Doane's (1958) classic study employed the strategy of inserting microelectrodes into particular neurons and recording from those neurons during the conditioning process. These researchers reported that when an overt CR was made to a CS during conditioning trials, single cells sampled in the parietal cortex increased their firing rate. On the other hand, when the CR failed to occur to the CS during conditioning, these cells did not increase their firing rate.

The Hippocampus Is Important for Memory. Jasper and his colleagues also found that latency and amplitude of firing of cells in the hippocampus changed prior to the occurrence of the CR. Consequently, latency and amplitude measures of those cells were actual indications of the growth of the strength of the CRs. Rate of firing changes in single neurons there during learning has also been established. Later research showed that the hippocampus, and indeed the hippocampal formation of which the hippocampus is a part, participates intimately in the storage of memory. It is believed that the hippocampal formation interacts with the cerebral cortex over an extended period of time as engrams are established.

Larry R. Squire recorded images in the brain through a PET scanning while subjects recalled recently seen words. When the subjects were *forming* memories, most of the brain activity was in the hippocampus. He thus confirmed previous findings that the hippocampus plays a crucial role in processing events into memory. While *recalling* specific words, however, activity was localized in the hippocampus and in the frontal cortex. Squire held that information must pass through the hippocampus if it is to become a conscious memory. The hippocampus binds together information that is stored in various regions of the brain.

However, although changes in the hippocampal formation are important for learning and memory storage, remember that it functions with other regions of the brain for those purposes. Indeed various data indicate that engrams are spread over broad regions of the cortex. As Lashley (1929) had shown in advancing his Principle of Mass Action, more than 90 percent of the cells had to be removed before a visually mediated learned behavior was disrupted. Jasper, Ricci, and Doane (1960) used operant conditioning and found that when the discriminative stimulus was presented, there were different latencies for events over various regions of the cortex. First, there was activity at the central cortex and then events from the motor cortex, and finally they reported other activity at the motor cortex that just preceded performance of the learned conditional response. These findings have been confirmed and extended to other kinds of conditioning. Similar results from a task for humans are reported in Figure 10.23 (McGuigan & Pavek, 1972). Without worrying about the specific conditions of this study, during a cognitive task a number of events were almost simultaneously recorded from over the left temporal cortex, in the nonactive arm, in the lips, in the neck, and in the eyes. Following that there was an event from over the left motor cortex and a covert event in the active arm (the one that was going to be used to overtly report on a cognitive event). The fact that a number of events occurred almost simultaneously during the cognitive event indicates that widespread neuromuscular circuits were involved at that time. Eventually, circuits between the active arm and motor cortex were activated to report on the nature of the cognition.

Two-Way Connections as Components of Cybernetic Circuits. Clearly, neural circuits in the brain are numerous and interactive. These circuits function as information is transmitted from one region to another while information is returned in the opposite direction. Merzhanova (1988) empirically documented the Soviet physiologist E. A. Asratyan's thesis that *two-way connections are a basic principle of neurophysiology*. More particularly, she reported that increases in visual–motor coordinations occurred primarily because of an increase in neural connections between the motor cortex and the visual cortex. After conditioning, two-way connections also increased between the visual neurons and neurons in the lateral hypothalamus. These increased interactions occurred because of the acquisition of conditional responses and these connections decreased after extinction of the conditional response. Apparently, feedback from muscular reactions during conditioning had an influence on the development and extinction of these two-way phenomena.

Data indicate that neural circuits like these function extremely rapidly. For

Latency, amplitude, and rate of firing of cells in the hippocampus indicate the growth of the strength of the conditioning process.

Extensive evidence indicates that engrams are represented in many neurons distributed in circuits over broad portions of the human brain.

There are two-way neural connections in conditioning.

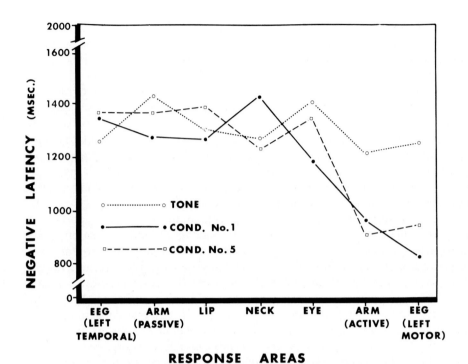

FIGURE 10.23 Relative mean latencies of responses identified in various bodily regions. (The higher the data point on the vertical scale, the earlier the response followed stimulus termination.) Ignoring the various conditions of the experiment, the important point is the large number of different responses that occurred simultaneously, indicating simultaneous cybernetic circuits.

example, when an auditory CS that evokes a conditional blink response is presented, an event occurs in the motor cortex with a latency of 13 ms, then at the eye muscles with a latency of 20 ms.

Combined Strategies. Valuable findings have resulted from numerous animal studies in which (1) essentially all brain regions were extirpated; (2) electrical recording was made from microelectrodes and surface electrodes over numerous regions; and (3) stimulation techniques were widely applied. The general conclusion is that engrams are encoded in sets of interrelated neurons. Just how widespread these sets of neurons are depends on the species and on the complexity of the learned behavior. In invertebrate animals, small networks of nerve cells that are responsible for integrating sensory information have been specified. The neural circuitry underlying simple reflexive behavior in invertebrates has also been successfully determined — there are sensory pathways that evoke neural circuits that store memories. When stimuli activate such sensory pathways and engrams are retrieved, motor pathways deliver information to the effectors. In turn, effectors feed information back to the central circuits. Once conditioning has occurred, the sensory component of a specific S–R circuit will retrieve information stored in the engrams and activate the central–peripheral circuits to carry out the conditional behavior.

Results from various studies have led to a consensus that engrams are represented within neural circuits spread throughout the brain.

Illustrative Clinical Data

Clinical data also indicate that the hippocampus plays an important role in the normal functioning of memory. A famous case, H. M., had his hippocampus and amygdala in both hemispheres removed in order to relieve symptoms of severe epilepsy. His symptoms disappeared but he was practically unable to form new memories and was unable to recall some of his older ones.

When a specific section of the hippocampus is destroyed, profound memory loss can be triggered.

Zola-Morgan, Squire, and Amaral (1986) confirmed and extended the findings on H. M. Another patient, R. B., had severe memory loss. When he died his brain was sliced into 5200 sections that were carefully examined under a microscope. The only relevant damage was in a specific region of the hippocampus (referred to as the CA1 region). The neurons in that region were totally lost. Apparently, the cells in that region died over a period of days when there was a loss of blood to the brain. It is thought that circuits going through that region of the hippocampus were blocked so that all neural impulses going into and out of it were stopped.

The general interpretation from clinical and other data is that the hippocampus plays some essential role at the time of learning for the development of memory of new experiences. It apparently helps to organize and retrieve information for perhaps months after it is learned. By interacting with the cortex where permanent engrams probably lie, the hippocampus seems to be a central processing center that helps to process various bits of information into coherent thought. Without the hippocampus, one may retrieve fragments of information, but not in any meaningful, coherent pattern.

Neural Encoding and Memory

The Neurobiotaxis Hypothesis. Assuming that results of learning are stored in neural circuits, how might it be encoded in those neurons and/or synapses? One hypothesis from the early part of this century is that of neurobiotaxis. In its simplest form, **neurobiotaxis** held that as learning progressed, the relevant neurons grew closer together, decreasing synaptic resistance to the passage of neural impulses. There is some contemporary evidence that when two adjacent sets of neurons are simultaneously active, they tend to become associated in some primitive way. As a result, if one is excited the other is too.

The hypothesis of neurobiotaxis holds that during learning, there are increases and decreases in how effectively certain synapses transmit impulses.

Deutsch (1973) provided some support for a hypothesis about chemical change at synapses. By administering certain drugs he increased the effectiveness of some kinds of synapses, for example, synapses that transmit impulses with ACh were altered with drugs that antagonize ACh enzymes. The effectiveness of some memories was thereby strengthened or weakened. Accordingly, neurons could encode learning experiences by chemical changes at synapses.

An enormous amount of research has been conducted to ascertain synaptic changes. For instance, a phenomenon known as **long-term potentiation (LTP)** occurs when repetitive stimulation of certain excitatory (vs. inhibitory) synapses increases their efficacy. LTP seems to be due to both pre- and postsynaptic changes. LTP has been established in two regions of the hippocampus known as CA1 and CA2. LTP has been considered as a candidate for explaining learning by changes in neurons and their synapses.

The selection hypothesis holds that during learning there is a selection of neural connections among existing neurons whereby an engram is encoded.

The Selection Hypothesis.   Some findings indicate that there are crucial stages of development in the brain so that as the brain matures, the number of synapses increases. As one learns, there could be a *selection* of the neural connections among existing neurons to encode a memory. Therefore, rather than forming new connections, learning could involve changes in the strength of (selected) neural pathways that already exist.

A Combination Hypothesis.   Perhaps new neural connections are formed during learning, although they do not initially encode information. Then, as learning progresses, some of the newly formed circuits are selected in which to store the information.

In Conclusion.   Whether new circuits are formed or selected during learning, they function *throughout the brain.* For integration of all modalities, especially important components of those circuits apparently exist in the prefrontal cortex association areas. In some way, electrical and/or chemical events interact to encode engrams and to establish neural networks. Only continued research will show us how. Especially promising is growing knowledge about the biochemistry of learning.

Engrams may be represented as changes in the functioning or in the structure of neurons or synapses, or in some as yet undetermined way.

Biochemical Studies of Memory

NEUROTRANSMITTERS AND NEUROMODULATORS

Neurotransmitters and neuromodulators that have been related to learning phenomena include the catecholamines, acetylcholine (ACh), the endogenous opiates, glutamate, and antidiuretic hormone (a vasopressin). Biochemical reactions when an organism is reinforced have been hypothesized to include the release of dopamine, seratonin, and endorphins. Epinephrine (adrenaline), which is generously secreted in an emergency, is thought to help us encode certain memories when we are emotionally aroused. This would help explain why we remember emotional events so well.

Many neurotransmitters and neuromodulators have been firmly related to learning phenomena, including dopamine, glutamate, acetylcholine, the catecholamines, and the endogenous opiates.

ACh clearly plays a role. As ACh synapses receive various drugs, memory is affected. Furthermore, as loss of memory in Alzheimer's disease increases, there is a correlated reduction in the number of ACh-secreting neurons.

Calcium Increases in Snail Neurons.   Another example of how we have learned much about higher organisms by studying lower ones is the research of Alkon (1983). He studied biochemical changes during learning in the marine snail *Hermissenda* whose anatomy and physiology is relatively amenable to our understanding. He reported that calcium ions accumulate within neurons during the acquisition of a CR. Prolonged elevation of intracellular calcium helps to reduce the outflow of potassium, which makes the cell membrane more excitable. In the presence of light, the cell depolarizes more readily, leading to the opening of more calcium channels to enhance the flow of calcium. When more calcium enters the cell, the number of open potassium channels is reduced. This process of increasing intracellular calcium and reducing channels for potassium to flow into the cell continues in a positive feedback cycle. Alkon concluded that this was the first evidence for any animal, vertebrate or invertebrate, that lasting associative learning is a direct result of a change in the excitability of particular identified neurons. Although synaptic changes may occur during associative learning, he found no evidence for such changes. The changes that Alkon found were at cell bodies and along axons, not at synapses.

Alkon speculated that the billions of neurons in the human brain may have the same potential as the snail cells to become more excitable or more inhibited. Just as the excitability of photoreceptors is altered when the snail learns, so the relative excitability of neurons in the human brain may undergo long-lasting shifts determined by conscious experiences. Perhaps the biophysical and biochemical changes responsible for storing learned information are similar in human beings to the mechanisms specified for the snail. As hypothesized earlier, the difference between what humans can learn and what a snail can learn may be due to differences in wiring diagrams in the more complex neural circuits. Differences would thus not be due to any special properties of the cell membrane or any special biochemical control mechanisms that would uniquely distinguish human neurons from those of a snail. If so, we can learn a remarkably large amount about the human brain by studying processes in lower organisms, as when we saw that synapses are similar among species, including humans.

The apparent similarity between human neurons and synapses and those of other species suggests that brain differences are due to complexity of neural networks and not to individual neuron and synaptic characteristics.

STATE-DEPENDENT LEARNING, DRUG-INDUCED DISSOCIATION, AND MEMORY

There has been considerable research with different drugs on state-dependent learning in humans. In **state-dependent learning,** if you learn something under the influence of alcohol, for instance, your recall is said to be better in a later similar state (when you have again consumed alcohol) than when in a sober condition. The notion is that the administration of certain drugs will cause a person to dissociate into a unique state. Consequently, what occurs during that state is dissociated from other states of the organism. Some supporting research has shown that there is a state-dependent condition for learning when sodium pentobarbital (an anesthetic "truth serum") is administered in sufficient dosage to put one to sleep. But at best, such positive conclusions are controversial. The notions of dissociated states and state-dependent learning as unique physiological phenomena have not been generally supported by research. More parsimonious explanations are to be preferred.

State-dependent learning means that learning under the influence of a drug is better recalled later if under that same condition. However, there is controversy as to its validity.

CYBERNETIC CIRCUITS AND MEMORY

Although it is widely assumed that the engram is localized in the brain, it would be unreasonable to assume that the brain functions for memory in isolation from the rest of the body. Some studies have indicated that memory retrieval may be facilitated or impaired by a variety of peripheral manipulations (see Fig. 10.26), for example, the peripheral action of hormones, neurotransmitters, and other chemicals throughout the body influences memory storage and memory retrieval. Critical links between such peripheral actions and central actions must be further studied, as did Vernon Mountcastle (1967) who found that specific inputs into the somatosensory system affect vertical neural columns in the parietal lobe.

It is highly likely that memory storage and retrieval in the brain are facilitated or impaired by peripheral events such as the actions of hormones and muscles.

IN CONCLUSION

A general conclusion on the neurochemistry of learning and memory is that even though we have made some progress, we have much further to go. If successful, the biochemical strategy could help us understand individual differences in learning ability (perhaps because of different conditions in the biochemistry of people's brains), and to control mental illness (certain chemicals such as serotonin vary in amount and are distributed differently in mentally ill people than in others). The possibilities for the betterment of humanity are limitless.

Neurons that are not used frequently may tend to lose their ability to function properly.

Use It or Lose It.   Whatever the precise mechanisms, apparently to maintain your memory, you must continue to use it. Wherever and however memory functions, it involves the continued use of the "little gray cells." Neurons in the brain need to be used in order to maintain them in good functional status. Neurons activated by stimuli change their chemistry and their form, especially as they develop. For example, in classic research by Hubel and Wiesel (p. 170), kittens were deprived of vision in one eye. Among their findings was that neural tissue that transmits information to the visual cortex for that blinded eye did not develop effectively.

Difficulties in Research

Confounding in Conditioning.   Learning and memory are such complex phenomena that it is not surprising that we do not better understand them. Even the physiology of the simplest forms of nonassociative learning (sensitization and habituation) baffle us. Furthermore, they have roles in conditioning that **confound** our efforts to understand associative learning. That is, the mere presentation of a stimulus by itself can result in nonassociative (sensitization, habituation) learning when our intent is only to use it as a CS. In studying and seeking the engram, then, we need to first specify changes due to nonassociative learning and then seek additional changes in neural cells due to associative processes.

Nonassociative processes of sensitization and habituation occur during conditioning and are confounded with the conditioning process.

Limitations of Lesion Research.   In attempting to pinpoint brain circuits that contain engrams, the production of lesions has been a major method. We saw that if the lesion produces a change in the learned behavior, the lesioned region may be part of the circuitry, or the lesioned structure may influence the circuit but not be a part of it. If there is no change in behavior, the region may still play a role but it is just part of one or two or more redundant circuits—activation of the region may be sufficient but not necessary to evoke an engram. For instance, the inferior olive is not a seat of engrams, although it is a relay station that conveys information to the cerebellum that does contain circuits for conditioning engrams.

Electrical Stimulation.   An advantage of electrical stimulation over surgical techniques is that it can only disrupt circuits temporarily. Still, if one electrically stimulates a region and there is disruption of learned behavior, an engram may be in that region, or the memory that is stored elsewhere may be influenced by stimulation in that region.

Results from extirpation, electrical stimulation, and electrical recording research provide useful information, but alone none yields conclusions that are definitive.

Electrical Recording.   Recording from microelectrodes has led to the conclusion that changes in a neuron's activity may mean that the neuron is part of a memory circuit. However, as in lesion and electrical stimulation, the implicated neuron may only incidentally be influenced by other parts that really are integral to the memory circuit.

A Way Out.   The combination of lesion, electrical stimulation, and electrical recording techniques can help to solve these general problems of what influences what. An example of this strategy would be to first condition an animal. Then, by recording from microelectrodes implanted in the cerebellum establish that certain neurons change their firing rate during the conditioning process. Next, produce a lesion in that area in the cerebellum to abolish the CR. Then, using other animals elicit the same CR through stimulation of that same region. Finally, by electrically stimulating neurons in the second group of animals, the CR should be abolished. The conclusion from the combined use of these three techniques would be that the region contains neurons that are actually responsible for the CR. In fact, research by Richard Thompson has led to the sound conclusion that an important locus of engrams is in the cerebellum. This conclusion is quite reasonable considering the cerebellum's important motor functions for integrating muscles and thus as a component of the neuromuscular circuits for memory.

But does that mean that muscle activity is *necessary* for learning? It is commonly held that a response is necessary during the original learning, but it becomes reduced in amplitude as learning progresses. Whether the response remains at a covert level or "recedes" into the cerebellum and does not occur during memory has been a major point of contention. For example, ask a two-year-old for his or her age and he or she will tell you "two" while simultaneously holding up two fingers. But by the time the child is five years of age, he or she no longer holds up fingers to accompany the oral answers (although the child covertly activates five fingers). These considerations lead us to concentrate on these questions.

Is Muscle Activity Necessary for Learning and Cognition?

CONDITIONING STUDIES

The Problem of Relationships Among Multiple Events.   Although Pavlov measured changes in the salivary response during learning, changes also occurred in other systems of the body. Conditional salivation was but one of a complex of conditional response patterns and neural changes, among others. In fact, Pavlov held that salivation was the consequence (and index) of more important higher nervous activity. It is possible that only brain events mediated the "conditional response" of salivation. However, others have argued that muscle events were necessary during conditioning, just as are brain events. The two positions, first that only brain events are conditioned and mediate salivation and second that both brain and muscle events are conditioned and that both thus mediate salivation, are depicted in Figure 10.24.

The Issue Is a General One.   Actually, this issue applies to more than just conditioning. Empirical tests of feedback-circuit models of conditioning and cognitive processes address the same issue, one that is critical for the sciences of physiology and psychology. The basic problem has been posed under many rubrics, but it all comes down to the question of whether or not muscular activity and consequent neural feedback to the brain are necessary or even sufficient for the body's various physiologic/psychologic functions. Can conditioning and cognition occur in the

The conditional salivary response may be the consequence of brain events or of brain and muscle events that mediate salivary changes.

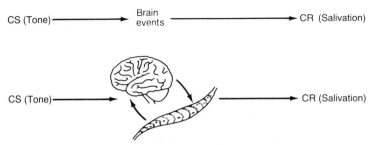

FIGURE 10.24 Two models of what is conditioned in Pavlov's conditional salivation studies. The top model indicates that conditioning is located totally in the brain, while the bottom indicates that brain–muscle interaction is necessary.

It has been argued that autonomic learning such as galvanic skin response conditioning and cardiovascular conditioning are artifacts of striated muscle response conditioning.

absence of muscular responses? Because of the abundance of relevant data during conditioning, we focus on these conditioning data.

Muscle Responses Can Control Brain and Autonomic Activity.   Researchers have called changes of heart rate, galvanic skin response, brain waves, and so on "conditional responses." But what actually were the critical conditioning changes? The striated muscle position hypothesis is that brain–muscle responding constituted the critical controlling events that mediated what researchers erroneously referred to as "*the* conditional response." For example, in one study conducted by B. F. Skinner, a subject said "contract" whereupon a gun was fired to produce strong vasoconstriction as measured in blood vessels of an arm. Eventually vasoconstriction followed the stimulus of saying "contract," resulting in apparent conditioning:

S (say "contract") $\longrightarrow$ r (vasoconstriction)

But it was later found that the subject was controlling the amount of blood flow in the arm by changing the amount of residual air in the lungs. Respiratory activity, which is controlled in part by the intercostal muscles of the chest, apparently generated feedback (s) that controlled the smooth muscles in the blood vessels (r). The depth of breathing was thus the actual CR that mediated blood volume of the arm:

S (say "contract") $\rightarrow$ r (breathing change) $\rightarrow$ s $\rightarrow$ r (vasoconstriction)

Breathing has been similarly implicated as a mediator in other conditioning studies. For example, changes in respiration have been considered to mediate the nonspecific galvanic skin response.

We can control brain waves by means of muscles so that alpha wave conditioning is apparently mediated by antecedent conditional muscular activity.

Rapid striated muscle components of neuromuscular circuits can mediate and thereby control what has been called autonomic, cardiovascular and electroencephalographic conditioning.

The problem of whether or not brain waves can be instrumentally conditioned has long been considered to be an important one. By furnishing subjects with feedback, they can learn to control the presence or absence of alpha waves, a phenomenon called *alpha wave conditioning*. However, we control alpha waves indirectly by certain muscular responses. Knott (1939), for example, concluded that the tension of muscles with attendant increases in peripheral stimulation blocks alpha rhythms during "attention." Blocking can also occur merely by opening the eyes, as illustrated in Figure 10.25.

In a more dramatic instance, alpha brain waves were voluntarily controlled by eye muscles to send Morse code signals of thoughts by means of electroencephalograms (Dewan 1967, 1968)—short bursts of alpha activity were the dots and longer

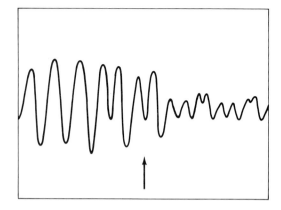

FIGURE 10.25
Alpha waves to the left occur in a resting subject with eyes closed. On opening the eyes as indicated by the arrow, the alpha waves are blocked.

bursts, the dashes. Feedback from other peripheral systems also can influence brain activity. In numbers of studies, induced muscular tension has enhanced evoked potentials from various brain regions. Various types of autonomic activity such as the galvanic skin response and cardiovascular activity have been mediated by conditional muscle activity (cf. McGuigan, 1978, for summaries of studies throughout these sections).

The Problem of Specifying Mediators. In electroencephalographic, autonomic, and other types of conditioning, specifying mediators is obviously a difficult problem. But it is clear that a large number of bodily events do occur during conditioning and that these events are intimately interrelated. The circuits of which they are components can only be adequately studied by taking a large number of psychophysiological measures during the conditioning process. In any given instance, which events control which is difficult to decide. However, it is clear that the striated muscles are always very active and in many studies it has been established that they do control other bodily events.

This important issue of possible muscle mediation of other bodily systems has been addressed in three other classes of studies: (1) efforts to eliminate muscular activity and consequent feedback by *paralyzing* the striated musculature with pharmacologic agents such as curare (usually d-tubocurarine); (2) clinical studies of extensive bodily insult, such as cases of quadriplegics; and (3) **deafferentation** studies in which efforts are made to completely eliminate neural feedback to the brain by severing all afferent pathways from the relevant skeletal musculature. Let us discuss these three topics in turn.

THE CURARE STRATEGY

Paralysis Through Neuromuscular Junction Blocking Agents Is Incomplete So That Covert Behavior Remains. Attempts have been made to completely paralyze the striated musculature pharmacologically by administering neuromuscular junction blocking agents such as curare. (A natural form of curare has been used on arrow heads by South American Indians to paralyze their enemies.) Presumably, conditioning and cognition could thus be studied with the role of the skeletal musculature eliminated.

The assumptions upon which this strategy of paralysis is based are that the curare used (1) is actually effective in producing total paralysis of the skeletal mus-

Strategies to ascertain the role of striated muscle and feedback therefrom during conditioning and cognition include (1) measuring its presence; (2) paralyzing it; (3) studying quadriplegics; and (4) deafferentation.

The strategy of paralyzing agents such as curare is based on the assumption that they totally paralyze the striated muscles and function only at the neuromuscular junction. Neither assumption is justified.

culature and (2) acts only at the neuromuscular junction and thus does not affect other systems such as the central nervous and autonomic systems.

Continuing awareness and successful conditioning while curarized may occur because of a still functional motor system that generates covert behavior.

A widely accepted (although unjustified) conclusion is that individuals remain conscious and can "think" under total muscle paralysis due to curare. Smith of Smith, Brown, Toman, and Goodman (1947) earned his position as first author by being curarized, reported that he remained acutely conscious throughout the experiment and that his memory was unimpaired. Therefore, the notion is that muscle activity is not important for thought processes. Although one must greatly admire this pioneering research, the experiment using one subject must be realistically evaluated in light of its methodological inadequacies. Six shortcomings of such studies as by Smith et al. (1947) on which this conclusion is based are cited by McGuigan (1966), the most immediately relevant is that curare does not totally paralyze the skeletal musculature, a point that could be easily decided through appropriate EMG monitoring. Hence, although there are no overt responses in the curarized state, important minute (covert) responses still occur. Some researchers did monitor EMG when they used curare during autonomic conditioning, but the sample electromyograms offered show covert behavior of perhaps as much as 20 microvolts in amplitude in presumably paralyzed animals. Such covert behavior could have important consequences because it and its consequent feedback may be sufficient to maintain cognition and for conditioning to occur (probably through what is called the high threshold gamma-efferent system).

Conditioning and cognitive research in which the role of muscle activity is tested should employ sensitive electromyographical monitoring procedures.

In Conclusion. To determine whether or not the striated muscle system is actually paralyzed, it should be extensively monitored with sensitive electromyographic apparatus. Then, to test the hypothesis that a neuromuscular blocking agent effectively eliminates the striated muscle activity, the subject should be instructed to maximally contract muscles; or preferably a mild electric shock could be administered. Only if the EMG recordings show amplitude of 0.0 microvolts throughout the body could we firmly conclude that the neuromuscular blocking agent totally eliminated muscle activity. Only then could one properly test the proposition that muscles are or are not necessary for conditioning and cognitive activity. As in the Smith et al. study, we should also be admonished against the uncritical acceptance of subjects' reports.

Curare Also Affects the CNS and ANS. The second assumption stated at the beginning of this section as being necessary for successful application of the curare strategy is that d-tubocurarine affects only the striated musculature. However, evidence establishes beyond doubt that d-tubocurarine is capable of modifying central nervous system activity, as indicated by EEG measures; for example, there is an increase in the latency of evoked potentials in curarized animals. Curare also releases histamine, which causes widespread bodily changes, including increased permeability and dilation of cerebral blood vessels and changes in cholinergic synapses and the autonomic nervous system.

Paralyzing drugs such as curare have not excluded the striated muscles as a mediator in conditioning studies or during consciousness, nor do the drugs function only at the myoneural junction.

In Summary. The conclusion with regard to the two assumptions for the curare strategy are

1. Striated muscle responding has not been excluded by the curare strategy as a possible mediator in studies of brain conditioning and autonomic and other activity. Nor has it been shown that thought processes or awareness are or are not affected through injection of curare or similar drugs.
2. The requirement that d-tubocurarine or similar drugs not affect the brain is not

satisfied since evidence indicates that it does have central and autonomic nervous system effects.

THE QUADRIPLEGIC QUESTION

Some have argued that since quadriplegics, those overtly paralyzed from the neck down, still think, muscles are not necessary for cognition. The straightforward answer is that although quadriplegics may not overtly respond, they are capable of covert muscle responses. Electromyographic recordings have indicated that muscles of quadriplegics in fact are often quite functional if only at a covert level.

Limitations of Clinical Data. As we have observed elsewhere, clinical observations can be suggestive sources of hypotheses, but seldom can they furnish a valid foundation for definitive conclusions about how any single system of the body functions. The extent and precise nature of damage to the neural and muscular systems in clinical cases is typically unknown. Therefore, we should not use clinical data to assert or deny causal relationships between muscle activity and thought processes (or any other causal relations). Several variables are confounded in clinical cases, such as that bodily damage that an individual suffered from an accident or surgery was undoubtedly accompanied by emotionally traumatic events. The post-shock state of the patient may thus be a function of the bodily damage, of the emotional trauma that led to and/or followed the injury, or of a complex interaction between these two variables.

One cannot reach unambiguous conclusions from clinical data about the effects of bodily damage on cognitive processes.

In Conclusion. The pharmacologic and clinical studies are methodologically deficient for the purposes of isolating systems of the body during conditioning and cognition. For instance, pharmacologic agents fail to completely eliminate muscle activity, leaving covert responses intact. They also do not function exclusively at the neuromuscular junction. Their effects are widespread, thus preventing definitive conclusions. Similarly, clinical studies are deficient because muscles still function; also, the lack of precise knowledge of which bodily systems have been incapacitated and to what extent and the confounding effects of emotional trauma prevent sound causal conclusions.

THE DEAFFERENTATION STRATEGY

The Deafferentation Strategy Has Not Been Successfully Implemented. We have seen that Edward Taub and his associates (e.g., 1980) conducted a series of deafferentation studies with considerable ingenuity. One early finding was that monkeys could still use their limbs after they were deafferentated. It was thus demonstrated that even though sensory feedback apparently was eliminated, the monkeys could still walk and exhibit other coordinated behavior. However, we have also noted that the problem they attacked is immense. The intricacy and complexity of the numerous parallel channels for simultaneously processing information between the muscles and the brain are fantastic. The primate organism is so marvelously redundant that even if most channels, including all normal channels, are successfully deafferentated, minor collateral channels may still exist that can take over critical functions. Recall that there are exceptions to the Bell-Magendie Law (which holds that afferent neural impulses enter the dorsal horn of the spinal cord and exit from the ventral horn), in that some afferent neurons are in the efferent nerves just as some efferent neurons are in the afferent nerves. Consequently both afferent and efferent nerves would have to be severed before there could be complete deafferentation, in which case the organism's limbs would be completely dysfunctional.

The issue can be settled decisively only by monitoring all conceivably relevant afferent neural activity through sensitive electrophysiologic techniques. In addition, precise and extensive electromyography could be used to ascertain whether any relevant active neuromuscular units remain functional (were not successfully deafferentated). Perhaps only then could we be sure that there is in fact no relevant muscle feedback anywhere in the body. The enormity of the task becomes apparent when we recognize that the 1030 skeletal muscles of the human body comprise about 45 percent of the body's weight. The intricate interaction of this mass of fibers with some 10 billion cerebral neurons is humbling indeed. If a typical nerve contains 25,000 to 100,000 fibers with some afferents and efferents, we can appreciate why the task of complete deafferentation is staggeringly difficult.

Deafferentation studies have eliminated considerable, but not all, sensory feedback from muscles so that the studies are not decisive.

What can we conclude at present with regard to the findings of the deafferentation studies? Deafferentation studies may succeed in eliminating most, but not all, feedback and so, considering the great redundancy of processing circuits, results remain inconclusive. Furthermore, these studies have necessarily been conducted on animals, and it is possible that animal circuits are more limited and sufficiently different from human circuits to make conclusions based on animal studies for this purpose inadequate for the human level.

IN CONCLUSION

The abundance of data obtained from observations in the normally functioning human justifies the generalization that muscle activity plays an important, perhaps critical, role in all conditioning and cognitive functions (McGuigan, 1978). The fact that the pharmacologic, quadriplegic, and deafferentation studies have failed to eliminate the muscular component in conditioning and cognition studies leaves this positive generalization in place.

Biological Theories of Memories

To conclude our consideration of memory, we sample some of the theoretical attempts to understand this complex phenomenon.

GRANDMOTHER CELL THEORY

The grandmother cell theory holds that each memory is individually stored in a single neuron, but this theory has been discarded.

The **grandmother cell theory** has held that each memory is stored in a single neuron. The name is derived from the notion that the face of a grandmother, for instance, would be encoded within a single neuron. But through research it has become clear that there are no single neurons devoted to storing single memories, as in one memory per neuron. Not only are specific neurons not devoted to specific memories, neurons that do function in circuits for the storage of engrams also are used for other functions. Even after discarding this theory, though, there remain numerous conflicting theoretical views of memory, especially of the neurology of memory.

CONSOLIDATION THEORY

Another classical theory of memory storage is that memory traces are consolidated over time. An early hypothesis by Müller and Pilzecker (1900) suggested that neural activity responsible for storing an engram persists for some time after the learning experience. As the neural activity perseverates, the physical changes in the neurons become more firmly fixed. This progressive fixation with time is called **consolidation.** However, if the reverberating neural activity is disrupted, consolidation of the engram should be prevented and amnesia for the event should occur, according to the hypothesis.

Two kinds of amnesia are supportive of the consolidation hypothesis. These are retrograde and anterograde amnesia, concepts similar to retroactive and proactive inhibition, respectively. **Anterograde amnesia** means that an individual is amnesic for events occurring soon after an incident — an accident that causes brain injury can produce unconsciousness and coma; the person awakens later and is disoriented, confused, and unable to remember events happening at that time (this is analogous to proactive inhibition).

Retrograde amnesia occurs when one is unable to recall events immediately before and connected with an incident, such as a traumatizing accident. As in retroactive inhibition, retrograde amnesia of events acts backward in time from the precipitating incident to produce forgetting. There may be amnesia for events that preceded the trauma by hours, days, or months.

The consolidation hypothesis suggests that in anterograde and retrograde amnesia, the consolidation of memories for events is prevented by a traumatic incident and the threshold is raised for the recall of older memories. Research testing the consolidation hypothesis has continued over the decades with evidence accumulating both for and against the hypothesis.

The consolidation theory holds that neural activity after learning perseverates during which time a memory is consolidated, but the status of this theory is controversial.

Memory has been classified into that for facts (remembering words) and for skills (motor activities such as playing tennis). People who lose their memory, amnesiacs, typically lose their recall of facts while they retain their skill memories.

SHORT- AND LONG-TERM MEMORY

A dual memory hypothesis proposes a short-term memory and a long-term memory. **Short-term memory** persists but briefly; that is, the storage time of short-term memory for visual input was estimated to be 250 msec. Apparently, information is received in a buffer storage mechanism where it persists for a short period of time, presumably within reverberating neural circuits. The circuits would include the receptor organs with afferent and efferent pathways involving the brain and the skeletal muscles. If reverberation of the circuits continues for a sufficient period of time, there could be a permanent structural change creating **long-term memory.** When the long-term reverberation ceases, the structural change stops and the memory remains at the strength attained. Information stored in the buffer is erased as new information enters.

One hypothesis is that information is received in short-term memory where, if it persists for a sufficient period of time, it may be transferred into long-term memory.

Another hypothesis proposes a very short-term memory that functions for less than 250 ms. In research, specific characteristics of long-term, short-term, and very short-term memory traces are sought.

EMOTIONAL BEHAVIOR AND MEMORY

Our memories are coded on a value scale varying by degrees from good to bad.

We have seen that the entire body activates itself for emergencies of fight or flight and during pleasant and unpleasant activities. We also rate emotional behaviors as good or bad. For instance, we have pleasant memories of a loved one, but unpleasant memories of having been sick.

Charles Osgood's findings that words such as "mother" or "injury" have common rated values among different cultures, even though languages differ, substantiates this conclusion (Osgood's rating scales, though, were more sophisticated than just evaluative and included other dimensions as well).

A value system for memory may be genetically transmitted, having evolved over millions of years.

Memories Are Emotionally Coded. Organisms learn that some things are noxious and code them at the bad end of the memory scale so as to avoid them. Similarly, organisms are reinforced and learn to approach those things coded at the good end of the scale. The good–bad emotional character of memories thus may facilitate the struggle for survival. Perhaps because these value ratings have functioned for millions of years, through principles of evolution, some are genetically transmitted. Objects that satisfy physiological needs or are deleterious are probably most clearly coded in memory.

Encoding through ACh may occur because of its muscular functions.

Emotional behavior may be physiologically encoded through chemical, CNS, muscular, and autonomic events in value systems of good or bad memories.

How we might physiologically encode memories is another matter. Because neural, muscle, endocrine, and autonomic systems are all very active during emotional behavior, in some way coding must be accomplished by their complex interactions. Chemical events seem to have important roles in encoding emotional processes. For instance, acetylcholine, epinephrine, and norepinephrine have traditionally been implicated in emotional states. They and other chemicals could be specific agents for encoding memories as good or bad. Depending on their activity, an organism would tend to repeat or avoid a specific object that evokes some aspect of these chemicals. We make muscle responses when emotional, and ACh is involved in numerous muscle activities. For instance, ACh is a transmitter at the myoneural junction, it is present in certain parts of the neuromotor system, and it is in the muscle itself. Norepinephrine could serve a coding function in value systems for memories because it plays an important role in the brain so that it may be active in the central components of neuromuscular circuits.

HOLOGRAPHIC THEORIES

A holographic model of memory is that a learning experience is ingrained throughout the entire brain and may be retrieved when a portion of the original stimulus is presented; however, there are serious shortcomings to this model.

Some have hypothesized that memory works according to holographic principles. A hologram is a photographic-like record whereby one piece may be used to reproduce the entire picture. To the naked eye, a hologram is meaningless, but if it is illuminated with part of the wave front that produced it, the rest of the wave front will automatically emerge.

The notion is that a learning experience "zaps" a memory onto the entire brain like the taking of a hologram. Apparently Beurle (1956) was the first to employ an analogy between this widespread representation of long-term memory with holography. The analogy has been followed by others, e.g., H. C. Longuet-Higgins and also Pribram (1971).

Longuet-Higgins attempted to account for how a portion of memory fed into the brain can evoke memory as it was originally laid down. For instance, seeing one component of an original context can evoke recall of the original scene. Longuet-Higgins held that stored memory is activated when external input (such as audible speech) enters the cortex for recognition. However, the analogy is pressed too far for technical reasons later detailed by Willshaw, Buneman, and Longuet-Higgins (1969). They abandoned holography as an analogy with a model that better accounts for human memory called a correlograph and associated nerve nets.

MEMORIES ARE CATEGORIES

Since we recognize better than we recall, one theory is that we categorize things in memory. Consequently, we recognize category items, not a specific item. We do not recall specific objects, such as how a particular person was first seen and experienced. Rather, we recall that person in general, not the specific experiences we had of that person. Through specific experiences we form a general category that is our concept of the person. Memory is thus an ability to organize particular experiences into categories, categories that vary in their generality. Therefore, there are no specific mental images stored in the brain that can be specifically recalled. One implication of this theory is that research for memory molecules and specific engrams in the brain may be fruitless because they may just not be there.

The hypothesis that memories are categories formed from particular experiences implies that being general they do not consist of specific mental images, specific molecules, and so on.

DECLARATIVE AND PROCEDURAL MEMORIES

Squire (1982, 1987) describes two anatomically different memory systems: a declarative memory that contains information and a procedural memory that contains habits. The procedural memory corresponds to learned S–R habit sequences, and the declarative memory has perceptual (stimulus representation) and cognitive functions. Although neuroanatomically distinct, these two systems are hypothesized to normally work in parallel and close harmony.

This view of memory is compatible with a common distinction between the contents of learning (the information acquired) and how the organism acts upon the contents of learning. If you wish to recall some specific bit of information such as the name of a friend, you employ declarative memory. It is a memory that is tapped volitionally. We maintain habits such as riding a bicycle in procedural memory, which is not typically subject to voluntary retrieval.

The hippocampus and amygdala (see Fig. 6.11) are intimately involved in declarative memory. Typically, extensive brain damage does not impair procedural memory, which suggests that its storage components in the brain are widespread.

Hypothesized declarative and procedural memories for information and habits, respectively, are neuroanatomically distinct.

CONTEXTUAL MEMORY

A Widely Held Concept of Memory. When we remember something, that process is considerably facilitated if the context in which the event was originally experienced is present. When we attempt to analyze what this means, we can assume that the stimuli present when something was learned extensively evoked covert processes throughout the body whereupon encoded engrams were laid down. When one returns to the original context, those stimuli retrieve engrams with consequent awareness of the original learning experience. Part of the retrieval process could be the individual's bodily orientation evoking complex covert muscular responses. Very often memories are retrieved by making the appropriate muscular response toward an item.

The context theory holds that memories may be reinstated by the context in which they were originally learned: Perhaps stimulus components of that context evoke muscular response patterns that generate afferent neural impulses that retrieve engrams in the brain.

The posture of the body has long been considered a variable that can initiate selective memory. Fisher (1964, 1972) has held that sensations from different regions of the body are capable of influencing perceptual-cognitive functions. Fisher actually mechanically vibrated different portions of the body and found that those vibrations influenced perceptual and other cognitive processes. This notion was implicit in Rorschach's view that when an individual attributes movement of human figures perceived in inkblot stimuli, he or she is projecting his or her own kinesthetic sensations. This reasoning is consistent with Titchener's context theory of meaning which held that kinesthetic attitude is a factor in determining the meaning attributed to stimuli. In sum, when localized covert response patterns are evoked, they generate afferent neural coding that accesses selective memories stored in the brain. For example, people forget where they put their wallet. However, once they walk into a room where they had inadvertently placed it, they unconsciously move toward the location. Thereupon the afferent neural impulses generated by the orientation movement retrieve the centrally stored memory resulting in the "aha" phenomenon — "aha, that is where I put it." We can exercise volitional control over memory to some extent by thus placing ourselves into the original context. Relevant here are Ebbinghaus's concepts of voluntary and involuntary recollection. Ebbinghaus (1885) distinguished among various types of memory, among them voluntary recollection, by which he meant that we can exert the will to call back into consciousness a previous experience, and involuntary recollection, by which he meant that previous experiences (mental states) spontaneously appeared in consciousness without any act of will.

Ongoing Research

We have seen that the earliest systematic research on memory started with verbal material. Scientists are now extending their research far beyond verbal memory. Some research has indicated that there may be different kinds of memory codes for pictures, for faces, and for words. Other concepts in memory research, too numerous to elaborate on fully, illustrate how memory research abounds. Some areas of current research include concepts of spreading activation, depth of processing, episodic versus semantic memory, working versus reference memory, declarative versus procedural knowledge, schemas, scripts, and cognitive maps. We must await the outcome of further research to see which of these are viable concepts that should be maintained.

EMPHASIS ON A CYBERNETIC PRINCIPLE — RESPONSE RETRIEVAL OF AN ENGRAM

As learning progresses, a representation of that learning, an engram, is presumably established in the brain; quite possibly in the cerebellum, as suggested by Knight Dunlap, by John Eccles, and others. When the intricate interaction of brain circuits reverberates in highly specialized ways, there presumably is remembrance of the original learned response.

The circuits that constitute a given engram (as represented by the circuit A in Fig. 10.26) might be activated by any of a variety of antecedent stimulating conditions. In general, though, they may be set off either by preceding brain activity (B in

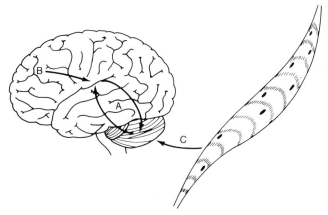

FIGURE 10.26   An engram represented by circuit A may be retrieved when evoked by prior neural activity (B) or by feedback from prior muscle responding (C).

Fig. 10.26) or by feedback from muscular contractions (C). If the engram is evoked by B, we can speculate that the activity itself is an engram that is associated with a response. If the engram is activated by feedback from muscular contractions (C), those contractions probably constitute the original learned response when it was made again. However, the response need not occur in its complete form in order to evoke the engram. Rather, a covert, incipient component of the original response may suffice to generate sufficient afferent neural activity to retrieve the engram. For example, if you had hit a home run, a memory (circuit A) of that highly favorable event would be laid down in your brain. Later if you recall the event, we know that complex covert responses would be generated throughout your arms, legs, and other parts of your body. Those covert responses generate afferent neural impulses (C) which, when they retrieve the engram, recreate the subjective experience (recall) of the earlier motor activity involved in hitting the home run. The evidence that such covert responses do occur when we remember various experiences is substantial. The tremendously complex patterns of covert responses throughout the body and the resulting complex patterns of afferent neural impulses presumably are uniquely coded to retrieve particular engrams, such as the memory of hitting the home run.

In analyzing a relationship between the muscles and an engram in the brain, it is important to emphasize that neither a response nor the recovery of an engram is an instantaneous phenomenon. As a muscle contracts in the act of responding, there is successive shortening of the muscle fibers contained therein. As each set of fibers contracts, afferent neural impulses are generated. Those impulses ascend over a finite, if brief, period of time to the brain to activate the neural circuits that compose the engram. Efferent neural activity then returns to influence the musculature to the ongoing contraction. Continuous bombardment from muscles to the engram occurs as each additional set of muscle fibers contracts. This muscle–brain bombardment and its efferent consequences continue until the response (be it overt or but the covert component of it) is completed, a matter of some milliseconds.

If it is a verbal memory that is retrieved, the engrams may be organized like a dictionary on the basis of initial phonetic sounds like "T" and "P." There is evidence that verbal phonetic coding is carried by afferent neural volleys from the speech musculature to the linguistic regions of the brain (see Chapter 13). We conclude that centrally stored verbal memories are thereby "retrieved" by the speech mechanism to produce verbal perception. (The importance of these considerations for the generation of cognitive activity will be enlarged on in Chapter 13.)

KEY TERMS

Alpha conditioning—The occurrence of a slight UR (motor program) to a stimulus before pairing the stimulus with a US so that it is not conditioning at all.

Anterograde amnesia—The inability to remember events happening soon after a traumatic event that caused a brain injury.

Classical (Pavlovian, respondent) conditioning—The process by which an originally neutral stimulus repeatedly paired with an unconditional stimulus comes to elicit a response. The neutral stimulus becomes the conditional stimulus (CS); the unconditional stimulus (US) is a reinforcer; the unlearned response is the unconditional response (UR) and the learned response is the conditional response (CR).

Cognitive map—A construct originally formulated from animal research by Tolman. The organism learns what leads to what so that behavioral alternatives are evaluated and plans are formulated.

Conditional response—Response that appears or is modified as a consequence of the occurrence of a conditional stimulus in association with a US.

Conditional stimulus—Previously a neutral stimulus that acquires the power to evoke a response through the process of conditioning.

Confound—The presence of an extraneous variable, systematically related to an independent variable, that might differentially affect the dependent variable values of the groups in the investigation.

Consolidation—A progressive fixation of memory storage over time.

Contingency—In operant conditioning, reinforcements are given if and only if the appropriate response is made.

Critical period—A period in early development of some organisms wherein experience has a major or maximal impact on subsequent behavior. The term *sensi-*

tive has replaced *critical* in the work of some researchers.

Cue recognition—An innate recognition by animals of important objects or individuals in their environments.

Cumulative record—In operant conditioning, a continuous record in which the total number of responses made since the start of the experiment is indicated.

Deafferentation—A research strategy in which the effort is to remove afferent neural pathways from muscles, usually surgically.

Discriminative stimulus (S^D)—A stimulus in operant conditioning that has preceded a reinforced response and has thereby come to set the occasion for the response's being made in the future.

Endogenous control—Control due to internal conditions such as those that generate physiological needs.

Engram—A memory trace established as a result of learning.

Equipotentiality, Principle of—The generalization that any portion of the cerebral cortex can function for any other part in learning.

Ethology—The study of behavior in natural, uncontrolled environments.

Experimental neurosis—A concept advanced by Pavlov that resulted from his research on stimulus discrimination. He found that when an organism was forced to make an important discrimination beyond its perceptual capacity, the organism developed a neurotic-like pattern of behavior.

Extinction—The withholding of reinforcement following a response. It results in gradual diminution in response strength.

Fixed action patterns (effector organization)—Behavior triggered by a sign stimulus.

Functional autonomy—A term developed by Gordon Allport that is approximately synonymous with *secondary motivation*. Both concepts indicate that an activity that was originally motivated by a primary, physiological drive or need has come to be made for its own purposes. For example, a sailor originally went to sea to satisfy basic needs but learned to love the sea for its own sake.

Functional systems—Anohkin's discovery of composite negative feedback circuits whereby conditioning occurs as information is transmitted between the muscular responses and the brain.

Grandmother cell theory—A discarded theory holding that each memory is stored in a single neuron.

Habituation—The diminution in response parameters as a result of repeated presentation of a stimulus.

Immune system—The system by which the body protects itself from invaders. It is capable of discriminating between the body itself and what is attacking the body. The invading infection generates white blood cells that produce antibodies to attack the invader.

Imprinting—A behavioral response acquired during a critical period early in life, not reversible, and normally released by a certain triggering stimulus.

Interference theory of forgetting—The theory holding that the greater the similarity between two sets of learned material, the greater the interference between them; considered the best psychological theory to account for forgetting.

Invertebrates—The large division (approximately 95 percent) of the animal kingdom that lacks a backbone.

Learning—The permanent acquisition of new behavior due to experience.

Learning curve—A graphic representation of the learning process. It is plotted as the increase in the tendency of a stimulus to evoke a response as the trials increase.

Long-term memory—Relatively stable memory.

Long-term potentiation (LTP)—The increased responsiveness of a neuron due to rapid bombardment by synaptic excitations.

Mass Action, Principle of—Holds that the cortex functions as an integrated system such that the more of the cortex remaining intact, the better the performance of a complex learned task.

Memory—The retention of information, responses, and so on that were previously learned.

Negative reinforcement—The withdrawal of a noxious stimulus contingent on the organism's making the appropriate response.

Neurobiotaxis—A notion about systematic decreases of synaptic resistance to account for a variety of psychological phenomena such as learning.

Nonassociative learning—Changes in behavior that occur due to the repeated presentation of a stimulus; includes habituation in which the intensity of the response decreases and sensitization in which the intensity of the response increases.

Operant—A response that is identified by its consequences and for which eliciting stimuli have not necessarily been determined.

Operant (instrumental) conditioning—Conditioning wherein reinforcement is contingent upon the organism's response; for example, an instrumental conditional response (an operant) such as a rat's lever-pressing response, may be conditioned by reinforcing it with a pellet of food.

Operant level—The rate of occurrence of an operant before it has been reinforced during conditioning.

Parsimony, Canon of—The principle that we prefer to explain phenomena with simpler principles than with more complex ones when either will suffice.

Physiological limit of learning—The maximum amount of learning theoretically possible.

Positive reinforcement—In instrumental conditioning, a stimulus object or event that, when presented contingent upon the performance of a specific behavior, increases the probability of occurrence of that behavior.

Punishment—The administration of a noxious stimulus contingent on a given response.

Reinforcement—The process by which a stimulus that is contingent on a response increases the response rate. In positive reinforcement the stimulus is presented, while in negative reinforcement the noxious stimulus is withdrawn.

Releaser—A specific stimulus that initiates species-specific behavior.

Response amplitude—A quantitative measure of one dimension of a response, its intensity or power.

Response rate—The number of response instances occurring per unit time (e.g., 5 responses per minute).

Retrograde amnesia—Reduced ability to remember events that happened prior to a traumatic event such as a brain injury.

Return (reverse) afferentation—A concept advanced by Peter Anohkin which is similar to the concept of feedback from muscles within a cybernetic circuit. Thus, it holds that response-produced feedback occurs when neural impulses are generated as a result of muscles contracting. The concept is an important component of Anohkin's functional system.

Secondary motivation—A motive that has been learned through association with the reduction of a primary (physiological) need (see Functional autonomy).

Second-signal system—Pavlov's concept of a higher system of processing which provides humans with the ability to use language.

Selective learning—Learning to respond to secondary features of sign stimuli.

Sensitization—The process of an enhancement of response parameters as a result of repeated presentation of a stimulus.

Serendipity—A concept deriving from Walpole's three princes of Serendip. It is the finding of something unexpected that is more valuable than the original purpose of the research.

Short-term memory—Immediate memory for sensory events that may or may not be consolidated into long-term memory.

Sign stimuli—Stimulus patterns that serve as cues for action leading toward a specific goal.

Species-specific behaviors—Behaviors that species are predisposed to learn and that are especially relevant to the environment of the species.

Spontaneous recovery—The recovery of response strength as time passes after completion of extinction. Recovery of response strength is less than that occurring during the height of conditioning.

State-dependent learning—The hypothesis that something learned while the organism is in a certain state or condition can best be recalled only when that organism is in that condition again. It is applied especially to the consumption of drugs, such that if one learns an item while under the influence of alcohol, recall is best when the organism again consumes alcohol. The hypothesis is at best controversial.

Stimulus discrimination—The process by which an organism learns to respond to one stimulus that is reinforced and not to other similar stimuli that are not reinforced.

Stimulus generalization—The evocation of a response that was conditioned to one stimulus by a different but similar stimulus.

Successive approximation—A procedure by which an organism learns to acquire a complex behavior pattern by small steps. Thus, the first response made only approximates the desired terminal behavior but is still reinforced. Increasingly the response must improve in order to be reinforced to eventuate in the desired terminal behavior.

Unconditional reflex—An unlearned stimulus–response connection which is innate and consists of an unconditional stimulus (US) that evokes an unconditional response (UR).

Unconditional response—An unlearned response.

Unconditional stimulus—That stimulus in classical conditioning that evokes an unconditional response and hence serves as the reinforcing agent.

Vertebrate—A division of the animal kingdom consisting of all animals having spinal columns.

STUDY QUESTIONS

1. Analyze the nature of learning in some behavioral events that you have observed.
2. Can learning be measured through resistance to extinction?
3. Summarize Clark Hull's view of learning.
4. Outline and contrast the basic principles of classical and operant conditioning.

5. Give some examples of stimulus generalization.

6. How do we measure forgetting and retention?

7. Summarize interactions between ethology and learning theory.

8. Why do conclusions from the method of extirpation for studying neurophysiological changes have to be accepted with caution?

9. Discuss the hippocampus's role in the normal functioning of memory.

10. Discuss the role of muscle activity in conditioning and cognitive functions.

FURTHER READINGS

This book considers developmental changes in memory and cognition in children during their natural activities:

Fivush, R., & Hudson, J. (Eds.). (1990). *Knowing and remembering in young children.* Cambridge, England: Cambridge University Press.

This book includes an assemblage of important facts and problems for future research relating to the biological basis of human, individual, and group behavior from an ethological point of view:

Eibl-Eibesfeldt, I. (1989). *Human ethology.* New York: Aldine de Gruyter.

CHAPTER 11

The Biology of Language and Lateral Systems

MAJOR PURPOSE:	To understand the nature of language, how linguistic information is processed, and the anatomy and physiology of lateral systems of the human organism
WHAT YOU ARE GOING TO FIND:	1. A definition of "language"
	2. Evidence of laterality for left cerebral hemisphere dominance for language
	3. How the left hemisphere extensively interacts with the right side of a person, including the auditory system, during language processing
WHAT YOU SHOULD ACQUIRE:	A concept of how cybernetic circuits function between the brain and body to generate the uniquely human phenomenon of language

CHAPTER OUTLINE

WHAT IS LANGUAGE?

As with any word, definitions of *language* are arbitrary. Because of its unique yet staggering importance in human endeavor, the term is used in many ways. We have natural languages such as Italian, and formal languages such as geometry. We communicate with each other through speech, writing, and body language using a variety of modalities (auditory, visual, kinesthetic, etc.). Consequently, there are many different definitions of language. To arrive at a useful one, let us consider some characteristics of language.

Is Language Communication?

A basic characteristic of language is that we use it to communicate with each other (and internally within ourselves). Our communications can be expressed on many levels from the eloquent language of Shakespeare's plays to the grouchy spouse who merely grunts a reply on a dreary Monday morning. Does a grouchy grunt or even the bark of a dog for its supper actually constitute the use of language?

Animals Communicate Specific Information. Much has been made of dolphins communicating with each other in a sophisticated manner through sounds. Ants have a highly elaborate system of communicating by making paths of chemicals so that other ants may follow them to food. Bees dance to tell other members of the hive the location of food. Whales send messages encoded as complex tones to each other over long distances through water. Birds sing and chimpanzees scream to tell each other that danger is approaching. Some communications emitted by animals are quite distinct, as in the alarm calls of vervet monkeys — an alarm call warning of a python evokes the response in other monkeys of rising to look in the grass around them; when one monkey hears another emit the sound of an "eagle alarm" it looks skyward; and the alarm call that signals an approaching leopard causes others to climb into the trees. Do such instances of communication constitute the use of language? Some people would answer that they do, but linguists prefer a more demanding set of criteria than that language is merely communication.

Mere communication does not by itself define language.

Is Language Speech?

The primary means of human communication is talking. Can we define language as speech? If so, Polly the Parrot is using language when she proclaims that she wants a cracker. But defining language as speech is excessively restrictive because we use language in many other ways. We write words; we signal them by semaphore flags; we transmit them by Morse code; and we use sign languages. We have to look further for an adequate definition of language.

Although we use language to communicate through speech, language is more than speech.

Is Language Verbal Responding?

Verbal refers to the use of words and we have just seen how words may be communicated in ways other than through speech. We have oral verbal communication but we also have nonoral verbal communication, as in writing letters. But do we use language to communicate in other than verbal ways? That is, is there nonverbal communication through language?

Verbal communication may be oral through speech and nonoral as in the written word.

Consider gestures. Is a goodbye wave a use of language? Do we use language that communicates nervousness when we clench our hands, fidget, and tap our feet? Compare these examples with those of animal communication. Is a goodbye wave in principle any different from a chimpanzee's scream that danger is approaching? On reflection, animal communication and human nonverbal communication by themselves do not define language. Although language does involve the use of words and is used for communication, the essential characteristics of language are still more demanding.

Communication through words or gestures does not define language.

Language Defined

Natural languages, such as French and Japanese, are distinguished from formal languages, such as algebra and symbolic logic.

Natural languages (e.g., English) consist of discrete linguistic units (e.g., words). But more important, we use discrete linguistic units in many different ways. Words may be placed in a specific order; they may be reordered; they may be combined and divided according to the rules of language that specify, for instance, how to form a proper sentence. The mynah bird that repeated "I am an organism, I am an organism . . ." did use words. However, the mynah bird could not rearrange (transform) those words to say "An organism am I." Nor could it add that "you are an organism too" or form plurals by adding the letter "s" to words. Parrots and mynah birds are not capable of using true language. A basic characteristic of human language is that the user has an ability to form an indefinitely large number of well-formed sentences from discrete units. The user can transform and modify words in an endless number of different combinations.

A language consists of discrete verbal units that may be endlessly combined according to rules for the primary purpose of communicating.

Yet there are other characteristics of language that we should consider. Human languages are naturally spoken and need not be taught to children as they mature. Children develop a facility for using the language of their culture on their own, merely by listening and talking according to their own schedule; this cannot be said of any other species. Although chimpanzees, for instance, may be able to use language, it must be painstakingly taught to them.

Finally, it is possible to represent all languages symbolically in writing. The symbols, such as letters, are combined to form the discrete units, words. Those units can then be systematically compiled in dictionaries.

In Review. One purpose of language is to communicate, which we may do merely with a grunt or gesture. Similarly, animals can communicate through chemicals that a certain path leads to food. However, communication does not constitute an adequate definition of language. Linguistic communication may be oral (through speech) or nonoral (as in writing). It is communicated in the form of sentences, and children come to speak it without being formally taught. Its units can be compiled in dictionaries. The essential defining characteristic of **language** is that *it consists of units (e.g., words) that may be transformed in an indefinitely large number of ways according to rules (a grammar)*. No doubt about it, the natural use of language is uniquely human—it is specific to the species *Homo sapiens*. Can it be taught to other species?

Language is essentially a species-specific class of behavior, uniquely used by humans in a natural way.

Human language is learned by children on their own; it can be written; its words are formed and transformed into sentences; and the words can be compiled in dictionaries.

CAN OTHER SPECIES BE TAUGHT HUMAN LANGUAGE?

If we examine the anatomical characteristics of other primates, many aspects of their oral systems resemble the speech systems of humans. If the anatomical characteristics of the vocal tract, the richness of the speech muscles, and some of the characteristics of the brain were modified to some extent, other primates might, indeed, be physiologically capable of producing speech. Some of the other primates do have anatomical precursors to human speech, and speaking, of course, is the original use of human language. We have noted that other species naturally communicate orally, even though that communication is limited, fixed, and **stimulus-bound** (the response is unalterably evoked by specific stimuli and cannot be varied—the parrot cannot vary "Polly wants a cracker" nor can the dog vary its bark for food). The characteristics of the oral–anatomical system of apes present the possibility that they could be taught some elements of human speech.

Clever Hans

A Caution.   Before we approach research on the question of the learning of human language by other primates, we should be aware of the possibility that animals can use subtle cues to make it appear that they have higher mental abilities than they do. For instance, we unwittingly condition dogs to respond to certain subtle distinctions between words we use. But the dog's response is only reflexlike (stimulus-bound). It only appears as if the dog has fine discriminative cognitive abilities when it does not. One famous case was that of Clever Hans (Der Klüver Hans), a horse exhibited throughout Germany early in the nineteenth century. Hans was billed as a brilliant animal. When he was presented with problems in addition, subtraction, multiplication, and spelling, Hans answered by stomping his foot the correct number of times. The audience could count with Hans and check to make sure that he was performing the cognitive task correctly. But then Oskar Pfungst, something of a psychologist before there was a psychology, designed a series of ingenious studies to determine just how Clever Hans performed these feats. Rather than actually performing arithmetic operations, Pfungst found that Hans was responding to very subtle visual cues that were unintentionally provided by the horse's trainer. The trainer, knowing the number of stomps that should be made, unconsciously moved his head slightly when the number of stomps was sufficient. Hans would stomp away in a mechanical fashion until he perceived the very slight head movements made by the trainer, whereupon he stopped stomping to provide the right answer. Thus, although horses can do many intelligent things, mathematical operations are beyond their cognitive abilities. Research designs must eliminate subtle cues that may mislead us into thinking that animals cognitively understand to the extent that they can use language.

The ability of animals to respond to subtle cues should be considered before concluding that they have linguistic or other cognitive abilities. This is an application of the Principle of Parsimony.

Attempts to Teach Primates Oral Language

A Theoretical Issue.   Whether primates other than humans can be taught human language has been a major issue throughout the history of psychology because its answer could shed light on a possible continuity of mental processes throughout the phylogenetic scale. Comparative psychologists have long studied the mental abilities of various species to determine where in the phylogenetic scale there might be a discontinuity. One issue concerned the species with which "mind" developed. If primates below *Homo sapiens* could be taught human language, this could be taken as evidence of a continuity indicating that they have something akin to a human mind, as Charles Darwin believed. That is, Darwin had concluded that the difference in mind between humans and the higher animals, great as it is, is one of degree and not of kind (at the molecular level, humans and chimpanzees have been estimated to be at least 98 percent identical, which on a biochemical scale accords with Darwin's assessment).

Early Attempts.   Efforts were made to teach primates to vocalize words. The first serious study by psychologists was in 1933 when the W. N. Kelloggs raised the chimp Gua for nine months with their own child, Donald. The study started when Gua was seven-and-one-half months old, two months younger than Donald, and the two became close companions. Gua was dressed in human clothing and was kissed, cuddled, and otherwise treated like Donald. As a result of being raised in a human environment, Gua acquired some human behaviors such as walking upright, skipping, kissing, eating with a spoon, drinking with a glass, and controlling the bladder and bowels. Gua matured much more rapidly than did Donald and was considerably superior in those psychomotor skills. Gua was also superior in strength, sound localization, and following verbal commands. However, her success in vocalizing words was almost nonexistent.

During the period from 1932 to 1950, there were a number of other efforts to teach apes to speak human language. They were essentially unsuccessful. Then, in 1951, Keith and Cathy Hayes raised Vicky, a female chimpanzee, also in a home environment. After six years of patient training and manual manipulation of Vicky's lips to help her produce sounds, Vicky learned to speak only three words: "papa," "mama," and "cup." Vicky said "cup" to ask for a drink of water, but "mama" and "papa" were more generally used to refer to anything else that she wanted. Vicky did learn some concepts, such as discrimination between pictures of people and animals. Her human experiences apparently led to a human self-concept—she placed her own picture with a group of people, rather than classifying herself as an animal. Like Gua, Vicky acquired many human behaviors, such as spontaneously imitating someone else who sharpened a pencil, applying cosmetics to her face and lips, and prying lids off cans with a screwdriver. Vicky was able to solve some mechanical problems after a single demonstration, which caged chimpanzees could not do. Unfortunately, Vicky died of a virus infection before the limits of her ability to be humanized were ascertained.

Patient teaching of primates has led to the conclusion that their limited anatomic apparatus precludes an ability for vocalizing fluent human speech.

Primates and Nonoral Language

Gestured Language Is More Successful. If, then, apes do not have morphological (anatomic) systems sufficient for producing fluent human speech, perhaps a system for using language that is more appropriate for them would be successful. In 1927 the famous psychologist Robert Yerkes suggested that apes might learn a gestured language since gestures are a more natural means of communication for them. However, it was not until 1971 that Beatrice and Allen Gardner employed that strategy for apes. The Gardners used the American Sign Language that deaf people use in which gesture signs stand for whole words rather than letters. They raised their subject, Washoe, in her own house trailer in their backyard. The trailer was fitted out like a home with cribs, highchair, bibs, wash cloths, and toothbrushes. Washoe experienced considerable human interaction, although communication was solely by means of the sign language. By the age of four, Washoe had learned to *respond* appropriately to about 500 signs and could reliably *produce* more than 80 signs. More important than learning specific signs, she was able to generalize some of the signs to objects other than the ones used in training, and even to absent objects. For example the sign for "dog" was originally learned from a picture of one dog but was generalized to pictures of other dogs and to real dogs. She was also able to produce some new spontaneous combinations of words. For instance she named watermelon a "drink-fruit."

Chimpanzees learned to make signs, but that still was not human language.

Although Washoe displayed some skill in putting signs together in short grammatical sequences, she never showed any extensive ability to produce consistently grammatical sentences in varied situations—a **grammar** is a set of rules of a language; for example, a grammatic sentence includes a noun and a verb. Although Washoe did make progress, in later research young chimpanzees such as Nim were successfully taught hand signs at a much faster rate. However, Terrace (1979) extensively analyzed the hand signs of Nim and other apes and concluded that their productions were not truly linguistic—their signing was different from human language because they did not follow the rules of human grammar; their communications were short in length, highly repetitive, imitative of their human teachers, and lacked spontaneity.

There is thus no question that apes can be taught to communicate rather effectively with signs. However, the essential question is whether they are capable of transposition, that is, learning to use rules of a language in order to construct novel sentences. Once taught words in one sequence, can they construct other novel sentences using those words?

Chimpanzees Can Be Taught Nonoral Language.   David Premack (1979) used another strategy to answer the question of whether chimpanzees could be taught the transpositional characteristics of language. He taught the chimp, Sarah, to manipulate and associate different things with specific plastic chips. For example, one chip stood for Sarah, one for the experimenter, one for bananas, and one for chocolate. Other chips stood for relations or actions. Sarah was then successfully trained to communicate by placing the plastic chips on a magnetic board in various orders, such as "Mary give chocolate Sarah." Sarah was also able to use the chips to represent absent objects (e.g., to construct sequences that included chocolate when no chocolate was present). In other cases, she responded differentially, depending upon the sequence of the signs presented to her—she was able to respond one way to one sequence of symbols, and another way when the sequence was different. In short, Premack successfully demonstrated that chimpanzees are able to use true human language to a limited extent, if patiently trained in a response mode appropriate for them.

By transposing verbal units in various combinations (the essential defining feature of language), chimpanzees have indicated their ability to use human language nonorally.

Other positive findings have indicated that chimps can distinguish between different novel word orders once they have become familiar with one word order. For example, the chimp Lucy first learned to respond appropriately to the phrase "Roger tickle Lucy." Then Lucy responded correctly when the novel request "Lucy tickle Roger" was made.

Research at the Yerkes Laboratory for Primate Research by Emily Savage-Rumbaugh has shown that chimpanzees are able to acquire the use of language comparable to an average human child of about two years of age. For example, Kanji was able to make a toy snake bite a toy dog on command, to make the snake bite Linda (a human), to make the dog bite the snake, to go into the next room and get a can opener to open a can and select a potato out of a number of other vegetables.

Chimpanzees Can Also Use Symbols Representationally to Solve Problems.   An example of using a symbol representationally would be naming an item and also requesting it when it is not present, as did Sarah with "chocolate." In another case, a chimpanzee was presented with a problem that required a special tool in order to solve it. The chimpanzee was allowed to go to a different room and request the tool from another chimpanzee. The other chimpanzee then successfully selected the appropriate tool from among several on the table whereupon both chimpanzees went back to the problem situation to use the tool. They were even able to interchange roles in this procedure.

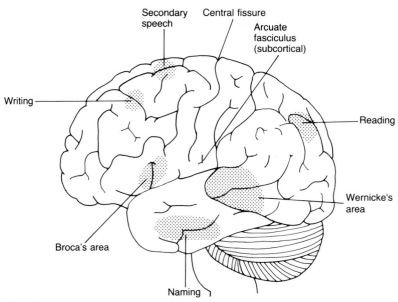

FIGURE 11.1 Some regions of the brain that serve language functions.

Although the natural use of language remains uniquely human, some transpositional and other aspects of it can be taught to apes.

In Review. It is clear that at least some rudimentary forms of communication that resemble human language have been successfully taught to apes. To some limited extent apes can transform the order of linguistic units and they can use symbols representationally. But we must remember that these are unusual and very limited instances of the use of human language. On the other hand, research indicates that apes *are* capable of more abstract conceptual thought than was suspected prior to these studies. Thus it confirms Darwin's theory that there *is* some continuity of linguistic and cognitive abilities in the upper regions of the phylogenetic scale.

Even though primates and humans share some physiological and anatomical bases for language, apes as presently constructed will never develop fluent human language or speech.

Still, apes would never use these latent linguistic and cognitive abilities in the jungle because there is no need for them—they survive quite well without rudimentary forms of human communication. Research and controversy surrounding these issues continue in linguistics.

Linguistic Regions in the Brain. Language development in children follows a predictable series of stages that depends on the maturation of critical brain and speech structures. These and other anatomical and physiological bases for language must have developed in *Homo sapiens,* but not in apes, according to principles of evolution. Linguistic functions in the human brain are identified in Figure 11.1.

EVOLUTION OF THE SPEECH SYSTEMS

Language development can best be understood in terms of evolutionary theory.

The Anatomical Bases for Speech Developed Simultaneously in the Brain, Oral, and Auditory Systems. The use of language no doubt facilitated adaptation to the environment, helping in the struggle for existence in many ways. Primitive speech sounds, for instance, could have helped coordinate hunters as they searched for large animals. As the anatomic bases for language developed, so did speech. As we saw in Chapter 2, brain size dramatically increased from about 400 to 1400 cubic centimeters within the last 5 million years. Within the last 2 million years the rate of brain growth and development has been especially remarkable. As the brain increased in size, the vocal and auditory systems also evolved. It is amazing that the numerous, highly refined anatomical structures required for the physiological production of speech all came together at the same time in a single unique species, *Homo sapiens*. No doubt, for the first time on this earth, organisms gained the ability to produce speech through complex coordination of the speech apparatus, to hear the speech of others through a complex auditory system, and to internally understand speech through circuits involving the brain and speech apparatus (Fig. 11.2).

Language became possible when the crucial morphological structures of vocal, auditory, and brain systems evolved and appeared simultaneously in Homo sapiens.

FIGURE 11.2 Unique physiological–anatomical characteristics of *Homo sapiens* necessary to produce and perceive speech depended on the simultaneous development of a speech apparatus, an auditory system, linguistic regions of the brain, and their complex interactions through cybernetic circuits.

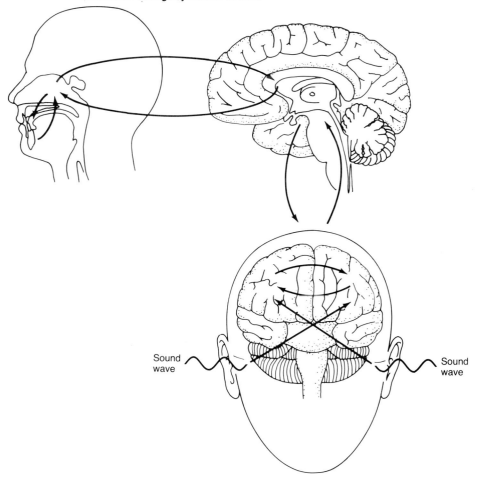

SIDE PREFERENCES OF THE HEAD AND BODY

Various regions of the body and head are specialized on one side (lateralized) so that we are typically "right-sided" or "left-sided."

Some Lateral Systems. In humans as well as in lower animals, one side of the body and head is almost always dominant, or preferred, to the other side. These preferences indicate **laterality.** They include handedness, facedness, footedness, and so on, but lateralization of the brain is of particular importance. The specialization of lateral cerebral regions for language is a crowning achievement in our evolutionary history. Lateralization of other systems is also used in language processing, although that for emitting speech through the mouth is centrally located and, thus, not lateralized. Since sensory systems like those for audition and vision are **bilaterally** represented in both hemispheres, only language processing systems in the brain are unique in that they are laterally represented.

The Evolution of Cerebral Laterality. Although some anatomic bases of speech occur in primitive form in other primates, only in humans are they all found so well developed and in the requisite combination. Among the most important characteristics of these anatomical and physiological bases for language is laterality (the dominance or preference for one side) of the brain and body. Early studies of the human brain, conducted with unaided vision, determined that some language regions appear larger in the left than in the corresponding area of the right hemisphere. This asymmetry is evident in the human fetus and in the newborn infant.

The study of the evolution of cerebral asymmetry (that the two hemispheres are structured and function differently) has been aided by the fact that the major fissures (cleavages) of the brain left imprints in the skull. In the study of human fossils it was thereby determined that Peking man, dating about 3 million years ago, had an imprint of the right lateral fissure that is higher than that of the left fissure. Neanderthal man (30,000 to 50,000 years ago) had the same asymmetry. Since this asymmetry is the same as that seen in modern humans, cerebral lateralization must have been present well before *Homo sapiens.* Fossil evidence suggests that left cerebral representation of language may go back to *Homo habilis (Australopithecus habilis)* 2 to 3 million years ago. Apparently, there was a very early but gradual evolution of speech cerebral structures that functioned for language processes.

Cerebral laterality has been found in animals, human fetuses, newborn infants, and in ancient humans as long as 3 million years ago.

Corballis (1989) holds that cerebral asymmetry is more marked and extensive in humans than in other animals and right handedness is a biological endowment that almost certainly is a universal human characteristic. Consequently, he believes that laterality of both right handedness and left cerebral representation of language provide a criterion for assessing human uniqueness. On that basis he concludes that a distinctively human mode of cognitive representation may not have emerged until perhaps 1.5 million years ago with *Homo erectus.* The evolutionary process probably culminated with the development of flexible speech in the last 200,000 years with *Homo sapiens.*

Cerebral laterality occurs in the upper regions of the phylogenetic scale indicating continuity of cognitive abilities.

Cerebral Laterality in Animals. Cerebral asymmetry has also been found in the great apes. Perhaps this means that apes possess some cerebral characteristics that could function for language processing. Alternatively, this cerebral laterality might have allowed some cognitive ability to develop that was a forerunner of the language that evolved in humans. Such a cognitive system could then later have become specialized for linguistic functions in humans.

Anatomical and physiological research on animals lower than primates indicates that some degree of brain laterality is present in many species. For example, injecting testosterone into the right hemisphere of young chickens results in the chick's increasing its copulatory behavior (but it does not if injected in the left hemisphere). In animals, as in humans, the right hemisphere is more involved with emotional behaviors than is the left. For instance, copulation, attack, fear, taste aversion, and muricide (mouse killing) are associated with the right hemisphere in animals. If the left hypoglossal nerve is severed in singing birds, the ability to sing is almost entirely eliminated, but this does not occur when the right hypoglossal nerve is severed. (The hypoglossal nerve is a cranial nerve that functions in a two-way circuit between the tongue and the brain.) Such research has advanced our understanding of laterality in both animals and humans. Such comparative studies of species add to our understanding of how morphologic characteristics of the human speech system evolved.

In Conclusion. Some characteristics of the speech system are present in animals, again indicating a continuity of linguistic–cognitive abilities in the upper regions of the phylogenetic scale.

Studies of Cerebral Laterality of Language

Considerable research has established that the left hemisphere of the brain is typically dominant over the right for the processing of language. Most left-handers also have the left hemisphere dominance for language. However, in about 40 percent of left-handers, Broca's area is either dominant in the right frontal lobe or is represented about equally in both hemispheres.

The large majority of humans are right-handed and have the left cerebral hemisphere specialized for linguistic (verbal) abilities.

EARLY CLINICAL CASES

In 1825 J. B. Bouillaud published a paper on the location of the speech center in the frontal lobes of the brain. Apparently the earliest systematic empirical conclusion that the left hemisphere functions primarily for linguistic processing was reported in 1836 by Marc Dax, an obscure practitioner in Montpellier, France. In autopsies of forty patients who had suffered from various speech disturbances, it was found that there was some damage in the left hemisphere but none was observed in the right.

BROCA'S AND WERNICKE'S APHASIA

A Lesion in Broca's Area Produces Broca's Aphasia. The next major step in implicating the left hemisphere in language functioning was taken in 1861 when the French surgeon Paul Broca ("Broke-uh") reported to the Société d'Anthropologie in Paris on his patient "Tan." Because of gangrene, Tan had been mute for 30 years with one exception; namely, he could speak the word "Tan," as he was so-named. Tan was intelligent, lacked psychiatric symptoms, and retained the ability to write normally and to comprehend both written and oral language. Shortly after Broca presented the case to the Société, Tan died. Broca's autopsy revealed a lesion localized in the *left frontal lobe* (now known as **Broca's area**). The correlation between that lesion and Tan's inability to produce spoken language suggested that this area is important for speech production. Broca proclaimed "On parle avec l'hemisphere gauche" ("People speak with the left hemisphere").

Numerous follow-up cases have confirmed that individuals who have difficulty in *producing* speech have some kind of damage in Broca's area (see Fig. 11.1);

Broca's area, typically located in the left frontal lobe, functions in concert with the rest of the speech system for speech production.

still, they can comprehend speech. The usual cause is a stroke wherein blood flow, specifically to that part of the brain, is interrupted. The inability to produce speech (as against comprehending speech) is known as **Broca's aphasia.**

Broca's aphasia, the inability to produce speech, results from an interruption of speech circuits due to a lesion in Broca's area.

A Lesion in Wernicke's Area Produces Wernicke's Aphasia.   In 1874 the German neurologist Carl Wernicke ("Vernickee") described a different kind of aphasia. Wernicke studied the inability to *comprehend* language in its oral and written forms, although his patients *were* capable of producing speech. However, although their speech was spontaneous, grammatically correct, and appeared to be fluent, it was meaningless. For instance, a patient might say "Before I was here I was there, and then they came and I was there and here."

After autopsy, Wernicke also described the locus of damage as being in the left hemisphere. But for his patients, the lesions were in the left temporal lobe in a rather diffuse, ill-defined area that has come to be known as **Wernicke's area** (see Fig. 11.1). The syndrome of patients with the inability to understand language is known as **Wernicke's aphasia.**

Wernicke's area, typically in the left temporal lobe, functions for speech comprehension; a lesion there interrupts circuits and results in Wernicke's aphasia, the inability to understand speech.

After continued study, Wernicke concluded that there are a variety of aphasic syndromes associated with different lesions. However, he always found the lesion in the left hemisphere.

We will now elaborate on aphasias, emphasizing that this early research established the importance of the left hemisphere for linguistic functioning.

There Are Variations in Broca's and Wernicke's Aphasias.   The kind of aphasic errors that a patient develops depends on the nature of the lesion in the brain — no two lesions are precisely the same. Nor are two brains precisely the same. Broca's area, for instance, is located somewhat differently in each person's brain. Furthermore, the nature of the lesion in Broca's area may also lead to other kinds of bodily disorders such as limb **apraxia** (disorganized movement resulting in clumsiness). There are also different degrees of Broca's aphasia depending on the extent and locus of damage to the area. Some individuals are unable to speak at all while others can emit various phrases, for example, "I New York come," telegraphic speech that is shortened by omitting prepositions, conjunctions, and so on. Wernicke's area and Wernicke's aphasia have variations similar to these.

Wernicke's Theory of Aphasias.   Wernicke noted that the damage that he observed was located near the auditory cortex in the temporal lobe. Consequently, he reasoned that Wernicke's area may be involved in *transferring* incoming speech into auditory channels so that the speech sounds may be comprehended by the listener. He further noted that since Broca's area is located near the motor cortex in the frontal lobe, it may function to convert language into the motor activity that produces speech. Wernicke then wondered how the comprehension area (Wernicke's area) might be connected with the production area (Broca's area). He hypothesized that specific neural fibers (the **arcuate fasciculus;** see Fig. 11.1) connect them. Wernicke also thought that this system was connected with the visual and auditory areas of the cortex. Thus, damage to any of these neural connections among Broca's, Wernicke's, visual, and auditory areas should result in specific linguistic deficits. Consequently, Wernicke thought that different aphasic syndromes resulted from lesions in different areas. The specific language deficit depended on whether the lesion was in Broca's area, Wernicke's area, the arcuate fasciculus connecting those areas (lesions there would create a conduction aphasia), or in neural connections with the auditory or visual cortex.

Wernicke reasoned that different aphasias differentially result from lesions in Broca's area, Wernicke's area, or neural connections with them and with visual and auditory areas; however, the lesions were always in the left hemisphere.

IS THERE A CONDUCTION APHASIA DUE TO LESIONS IN THE ARCUATE FASCICULUS?

Research Indicates There Is Not.   One view of brain mechanisms of language that emerged from these findings is that discrete language centers in the brain interact through conduction pathways. Wernicke's and Broca's regions, for instance, interact through the arcuate fasciculus. An analogy is that of a map showing how cities connect through highways. According to this view, a lesion in the arcuate fasciculus between Broca's and Wernicke's area would cause conduction aphasia. **Conduction aphasia** would be when people are unable to relate what they say with what they hear. For example, one could be told to sit down but would respond that "the sky is blue." In conduction aphasia, the speech is reported to be mostly fluent but with poor repetition ability. However, the aphasic has been said to comprehend quite well. The lesion, independent of Wernicke's and Broca's areas, was thought to involve pathways that transfer information into the motor systems for producing speech.

Many textbooks continue to follow Wernicke and report that there *is* a kind of aphasia called "conduction aphasia" due to lesions in the arcuate fasciculus. However, after reviewing relevant data, Brown (1984) concluded that there are no documented cases of aphasia in which lesions were restricted to this pathway. On the other hand, there are cases with symptoms of so-called conduction aphasia with no lesions of that pathway.

Although there may be a behavioral syndrome that may be defined as conduction aphasia, it is not uniquely caused by lesions in the arcuate fasciculus.

CONTEMPORARY RESEARCH AND BEHAVIORAL ANALYSIS

The Brain Is Not Organized like a Road Map Because Regions Are Dynamic.   Of greater importance than the issue of conduction aphasia is that a fixed road map model of language areas and connections in the brain is inappropriate. Brown concludes that neural language structures are not fixed and immutable but undergo changes like a process in continual growth. According to this view, brain regions are not fixed and limited. For instance, there is growth (arborization) of dendrites in the region of Broca's area in the left hemisphere which does not occur in the comparable region in the right hemisphere. The changing character of brain cells implies that the analogy of fixed brain regions being connected like fixed cities on a road map is inappropriate. The neural bases of the aphasias are clearly more complex and varied than originally thought.

The language regions of the brain seem to be dynamic and thus are not fixed and unchanging.

Anatomic and Behavior Studies.   Using a radioisotope scan, Benson (1967) located various lesions in 100 aphasic patients and classified the lesions in the major quadrants of a hemisphere. The patients were then rated behaviorally for various features of aphasic speech. The behavioral measures included rate of speech, pronunciation, phrase length, pauses, and word use. There were two distinct clusters of these speech features in the majority of patients. The first behavioral cluster was related to lesions anterior to the central fissure (see Fig. 11.1). The second cluster was in patients who had lesions posterior to the central fissure. The speech of the anterior group was nonfluent, characterized by a low rate of verbal output. The posterior-lesion group had fluent speech, but it was abnormal because of the incorrect choice

There are numerous variations in the kinds of aphasias and in the nature of their associated cerebral lesions.

of content words. Benson concluded that there are different aphasic syndromes associated with different lesions in the left hemisphere, as suggested by Wernicke himself. Benson's study is typical of newer approaches in research in this fascinating area. The traditional method of autopsy for correlating lesions with speech pathology is seldom used anymore. By using computer tomography (CT), introduced in 1973, it has been possible to relate behavioral measures in the living person with brain lesions. Other valuable methods in the behavioral and neural analysis of linguistic performance have included neuropsychological assessment, analysis of regional cerebral blood flow, and neuroimaging techniques of positron emission tomography (PET) and nuclear magnetic resonance imaging (MRI) (see Chapter 8). Even though researchers of the last century have provided findings of inestimable value, no longer must we await autopsies to study these important language phenomena.

Early empirical conclusions of cerebral areas specialized for language in the dominant hemisphere have been confirmed with new methods. However, we still do not understand the principles by which the two hemisphere differentially function.

In Review. We have seen in this section that great advances in understanding the neural basis of language were made over a period of a century in which single-case studies were used to relate language deficiencies with lesions discovered at autopsy. These early conclusions have been abundantly confirmed with the development of new, more effective methods: There is a cerebral dominance for language and there are cortical areas that are specialized for linguistic processing. There has been a dramatic increase in our understanding of the neurological basis of language.

One Lingering Question. What is the physical basis for cerebral laterality? We have no sound explanation of differential hemispheric function. One generally unsupported theory to account for hemispheric differences in visual perception is that the two hemispheres differ in sensitivity to the frequency of signals. The theory holds that the right hemisphere is the more sensitive to low visual frequencies while the left hemisphere is more sensitive to high frequencies. To test the theory, visual stimuli with different frequencies have been directed through the eyes into the two hemispheres. However, the data are, at best, mixed in support of this theory, so we should search elsewhere for explanation.

SPLIT-BRAIN OPERATIONS

Research since the observations of Dax, Broca, and Wernicke has abundantly confirmed the correlations between brain lesions in the left hemisphere and speech disorders. However, it was not until the 1940s that experimental research, as opposed to mere correlational research (see p. 341), confirmed the importance of the left hemisphere for language processing. This experimental research has come to be known as the **split-brain operation.**

Contralateral and Ipsilateral Pathways. To set the stage, note in Figure 11.3 that information received by one side of the body generally crosses over to the other side of the brain. These direct paths to and from one side of the body and the opposite side of the brain are **contralateral pathways** and they generally occur below the cerebrum itself. In contrast, relatively few neural fibers go to and from one side of the body directly to the same side of the brain. Those that do transmit information along **ipsilateral pathways.**

Contralateral neural pathways transmit information from one side of the body to the opposite side of the brain; ipsilateral neural fibers transmit information to and from one side of the body to the same side of the brain.

Interhemispheric Transfer of Information Across the Corpus Callosum. Information that is received in one side of the brain is normally transmitted to the other side by means of the corpus callosum. Studies have indicated that information directed

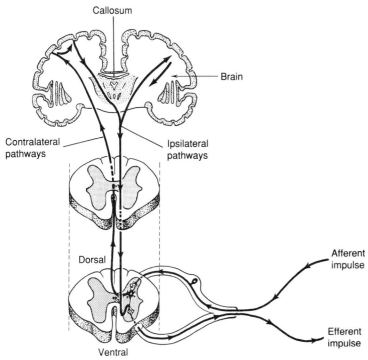

FIGURE 11.3   Most information received by one side of the body is transmitted to and from the opposite side of the brain along contralateral pathways. A relatively small amount of information is transmitted to the same side of the brain along ipsilateral pathways. In either case, information received by one hemisphere is transmitted to the other along the corpus callosum.

from one side of the body to the same side of the brain along ipsilateral pathways is processed faster than information that then must cross the callosum to be processed by the other side of the brain. The amount of time required to cross the callosum is called the interhemispheric transmission time. In a wide variety of studies, interhemispheric transmission times have been estimated to be as fast as 2.6 milliseconds and as long as 30 milliseconds. For instance, verbal information may enter the right hemisphere, but it then crosses the callosum to be processed by the left hemisphere, delaying its processing. But more of this shortly.

The interhemisphere transmission time across the callosum from one side of the brain to the other has been variously estimated to be from 2.6 to 30 milliseconds.

   The First Split-Brain Operations.   In the 1940s the callosum was severed on two dozen people by William Van Wagenen, a New York neurosurgeon. Van Wagenen had observed that tumors in the corpus callosum in epileptics sometimes seemed to reduce the severity of their seizures. He reasoned that because the corpus callosum bridges the two hemispheres, damage to it somehow limits the spread of the neural activity that was responsible for the epileptic seizure. Possibly, the damage to the callosum limited the epileptic activity to one hemisphere. Van Wagenen therefore attempted to isolate the two hemispheres by surgically severing the connection (which is called a commissure) between them at the corpus callosum (Fig. 11.4). However, the results of Van Wagenen's surgery were quite inconsistent and he eventually discontinued the operation.

The strategy for the split-brain operation assumed that neural epileptic seizures could be limited to one hemisphere by lesioning the corpus callosum.

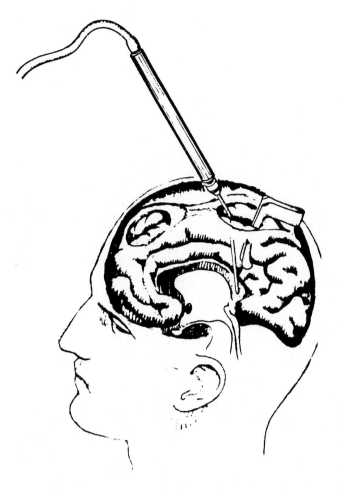

FIGURE 11.4
In the split-brain operations, the hemispheres were surgically separated by severing the corpus callosum. (From Gazzaniga, 1973)

Later, the surgeons Phillip Vogel and Joseph Bogen reviewed Van Wagenen's work and reached different conclusions. They noted that Van Wagenen had severed different regions of the callosum in different patients but that complete commissurotomies had not been performed (*otomy* means "severing"). In contrast, Vogel and Bogen did perform complete commissurotomies on some two dozen epileptic patients and had considerable success in reducing or eliminating epileptic seizures. Thus Van Wagenen had the right strategy, but the wrong tactics. In addition to being clinically valuable, these "split-brains" provided a wonderful opportunity to study the functioning of each hemisphere in isolation from the other. This gold mine of research opportunity merely awaited the appropriate researcher, Roger Sperry.

The Research Strategy. To understand how Sperry tested the split-brain patients with disconnected hemispheres, refer to the optic pathways in Figure 5.9 and Figure 11.5. The left side of each retina projects to the left cerebral hemisphere and the right half of each retina projects to the right cerebral hemisphere. A person's visual field (which includes the stimulus that a person looks at) is divided into left and right parts so that the left part impinges on the right half of each retina. Consequently, the left visual field in a person's environment, striking the right half of each retina, is projected to the right cerebral hemisphere. Similarly, information in the right visual field falls on the left half of each retina and is then projected to the

The split-brain operation has been clinically beneficial for epileptic patients and has also had considerable scientific value in understanding the different functions of the two hemispheres.

Information presented into the left visual field impinges on the right half of each retina and is transmitted to the right cerebral hemisphere; information presented in the right visual field impinges on the left half of each retina and is projected to the left hemisphere.

ROGER WOLCOTT SPERRY
(1913–)

Sperry was born in Hartford, Connecticut in 1913. The research for which he received the Nobel Prize in 1981 was on the specialized functions of each side of the brain. Studying the split-brain operation, Sperry and his students demonstrated that there was also a splitting of conscious awareness, which is developed in the text.

Around 1960, Roger Sperry was experimenting with the transfer of information between cerebral hemispheres of animals. He presented information that went to one hemisphere through one eye, Sperry found that the animal transferred a habit from the trained to the untrained eye. Thus, visual information is laid down in both hemispheres during training, even though it only entered one eye. The untrained eye makes connections with both hemispheres. It thus retrieves and uses the information (an engram) to guide correct responses. The next step was to study animals whose left and right hemispheres had been separated by severing the corpus callosum. His purpose was to study how the two hemispheres of the brain function when information cannot be communicated between them. Consequently, he was well prepared to recognize the magnificent research opportunity of studying human epileptics who had complete commissurotomies. The strategy used by Sperry led to important research that contributed to his receiving the Nobel Prize.

left cerebral hemisphere. If a picture is flashed in the left visual field, the information contained therein is carried by neural impulses to the right hemisphere. Similarly, information flashed in the right visual field results in neural impulses directed to the left hemisphere. Since the patient has experienced a commissurotomy, information that reaches one hemisphere cannot then be passed across the callosum to the other, as normally occurs. The question then is, "What are the experiences of patients who receive information in only one or the other hemisphere?"

Verbal Stimuli Are Processed in the Left Hemisphere. Research showed that if a patient is asked to report on the name of a stimulus that is directed only to the right hemisphere, the patient cannot name the stimulus. For instance, if a picture of a pair of scissors is presented only in the left visual field, the individual cannot identify the stimulus by naming it.

Patients who had their corpus callosums severed could not transfer information between hemispheres. Research confirmed that the left hemisphere is specialized for language while the right is specialized for visual, facial, and emotional functions.

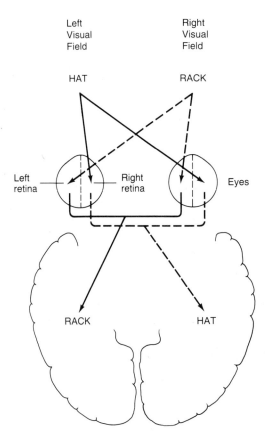

FIGURE 11.5
A split-brain patient would report only that RACK was presented since only RACK entered the left hemisphere. The word HAT that goes to the right hemisphere is not consciously perceived. In a normal person, the compound word HATRACK would be perceived because HAT would cross the callosum to the left hemisphere. (Adapted from Gazzaniga, 1973.)

Suppose a compound word such as "HATRACK" is visually presented precisely in the middle of the visual field of a split-brain patient (Fig. 11.5). The right hemisphere would receive "HAT" and the left would receive "RACK." Normally, a person would integrate the two components to form the concept HATRACK. However, commissurotomy patients report only that RACK was projected since that was the only information that went to the left hemisphere. The patient fails to report that HAT was received by the right (nonlinguistic) hemisphere because the right hemisphere has minimal language ability.

Linguistic stimuli are generally processed in the left but not the right hemisphere.

Information Is Processed Nonlinguistically Through the Right Hemisphere. If an embarrassing stimulus such as a nude picture is projected into the right hemisphere, a patient displays embarrassing emotions but is unable to report what the emotions are about. On the other hand, stimuli projected from the right visual field into the left hemisphere can be readily identified with their verbal labels.

In general, emotional stimuli are perceived more accurately when they are presented to the right hemisphere.

We presented data in Chapter 9 indicating that there are lateral cerebral functions for emotions. To a large extent the right hemisphere is involved in emotional processing, although the left hemisphere has some emotional functions too. People are better at behaviorally identifying emotions portrayed in cartoon drawings of faces when those cartoons are directed to the right hemisphere than to the left. However, even though the emotions portrayed can be understood in the right hemisphere, they cannot be verbally labeled unless the left hemisphere can function.

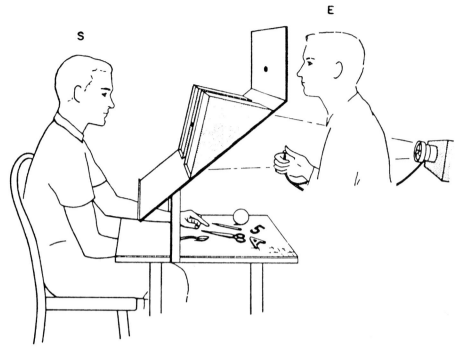

FIGURE 11.6   Testing apparatus. A slanting shield prevents the subject from seeing test items on the table, his hand, or the examiner. After hemisphere disconnection, the patient can identify an object by touching it with the right hand, which cannot be done if the left hand is used.

In short, the right hemisphere is dominant for the reception and expression of emotions. Furthermore, as Victor Denenberg concluded from his research, brain laterality for emotions is not a uniquely human attribute; rather, strong emotional responses in the rat are also mediated by the right hemisphere.

Circuits Process Information Between Each Hand and the Contralateral Hemisphere.   The split-brain patient has also been studied with regard to the sense of touch. As illustrated in Figure 11.6, a person may feel visually hidden objects with either hand. If felt with the left hand, the patient typically cannot verbally identify them because information about the object is projected contralaterally to the right hemisphere. However, if the patient feels the object with the right hand, verbal identification can be made rapidly.

Interaction of Vision and Touch Modalities.   For this, the split-brain patient feels several objects with the left hand. Then the name of one of the objects is projected to the right hemisphere, instructing the individual to select the specific object named. The individual can select the object named from among the several other objects, even though the patient cannot report the name of the object that was flashed.

In Review.   Research on disconnected hemispheres indicates that they generally function in circuits with eyes and hands (and presumably with face, legs, feet, etc.) for different kinds of tasks. Primarily, the left hemisphere carries out verbal

The ability of the split-brain patient to verbally identify objects with the right hand but not with the left hand indicates linguistic circuits function between the right hand and the left hemisphere.

functions while the right hemisphere carries out spatial–visual and emotional functions. Words can be understood when projected to the left hemisphere, but not understood when received only by the right.

Nonverbal information, such as the picture of an object, projected to the right hemisphere *can* be reacted to meaningfully. For instance, one can correctly arrange wooden blocks into certain patterns according to the pattern presented to the right hemisphere. However, the individual still cannot verbally label anything about these spatial tasks. The processing of visual–spatial and emotional information by circuits between the right hemisphere and left side of a person is indeed complex.

PARALYZING A HEMISPHERE WITH THE WADA TEST

The Wada Test, which can temporarily paralyze one hemisphere by means of an injected barbiturate, can identify the dominant hemisphere for language.

In preparing to remove a tumor that may be the focus of epileptic discharge in an epileptic patient, it is important to confirm prior to the operation that the left hemisphere is the one that is dominant for language for that patient. Juhn Wada in 1960 developed a technique for this purpose. Injecting a barbiturate such as sodium amytal into the artery feeding one side of the brain will temporarily paralyze that hemisphere. For a period of several minutes the patient may be tested for ability to speak. Typically, when the left hemisphere was so anesthetized, the ability to use language was diminished or eliminated. Then, as the drug is carried away from the hemisphere by the circulatory system, linguistic functions return.

Wada Test Results Confirm Those from Split-Brain Research. With the **Wada Test** the patient can be studied when either the right or the left hemisphere is functioning. When the left hemisphere is paralyzed and information is presented to the right hemisphere, as with the split-brain patient, that information can be used even though the patient still cannot verbally describe it. For instance, when a picture of an apple is transmitted into the right hemisphere of an individual whose left hemisphere has received the drug, that patient can select an apple out of a number of alternative stimuli but still cannot name the apple. The results with this additional experimental preparation thus confirm the conclusions from commissurotomy patients.

Tests similar to the Wada Test using animals provide results similar to those on humans.

Cognitive Functions in Animals. Some interesting results have been obtained using a technique similar to the Wada Test. Normal functions of an animal's cerebral hemisphere can be temporarily altered, as with the Wada Test. A spreading depression of neural activity is started over the brain with a small amount of potassium chloride solution. The solution is applied locally through a small hole in the skull to the surface of the dura mater membrane surrounding the cortex. The normal electrical activity of the treated hemisphere of the cortex then becomes depressed and lasts for as long as the chemical solution is applied. When the solution is removed, neurons resume firing, as indicated by resumption of electrical activity. Hemispheres that are depressed in this manner temporarily give no sign of retaining habits that were learned when they were intact. Apparently, access to the memory of the habit is blocked by the chemical depression. Results on chemical dissociation of hemispheres in animals are thus consonant with those for humans, although linguistic functions have yet to be tested.

While we are discussing chemical dissociation, we might mention that there are certain chemical asymmetries that occur naturally. Just why this is so is not currently understood. As an example, it has been found that LSD (lysergic acid diethylamide) acts primarily on the temporal lobe in the right hemisphere. Perhaps the bizarre visual hallucinations produced by LSD are related to its peculiar stimulation of the right hemisphere that serves special visual–spatial functions.

DICHOTIC LISTENING TASKS AND AUDITORY LATERALITY

During normal hearing, information is received and processed by both ears. The primary pathway from each ear is to the contralateral hemisphere, as shown in Figure 11.7. Thus information put into the left ear is processed primarily by the right

FIGURE 11.7   In the dichotic listening task, the two inputs primarily cross to the opposite (contralateral) hemispheres, although they then are transmitted to the other hemisphere through the corpus callosum. Thus, verbal information put into the right ear has an advantage over and blocks verbal information put into the left ear. But when music, which is processed primarily in the right hemisphere, enters the left ear, it has an advantage over and blocks music placed in the right ear.

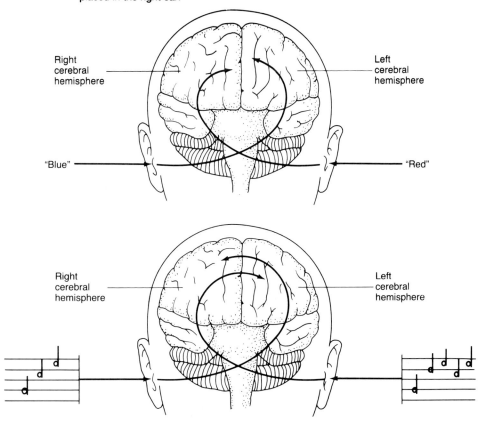

hemisphere, just as information from the right ear goes mainly to the left hemisphere. Therefore, the anatomical arrangement specified in Figure 11.7 allows for the study of the two hemispheres independently, just as is done with the eyes and with the Wada Test.

The Right Ear–Left Hemisphere Circuit Has Priority for Processing Verbal Information. In the **dichotic listening test,** different stimuli are simultaneously entered into the two ears (*dichotic* is from the Greek *dicha* meaning "in two, apart"). For instance, the word *red* may be spoken into the left ear and *blue* into the right. Since *blue* is coded and transmitted directly to the left hemisphere, it is dominant over *red* so that only *blue* is heard. Research using the dichotic listening task once again implicates the importance of the left hemisphere for processing language, at least in the large majority of people. The relatively small number of people who have the right hemisphere specialized for language have a priority for information placed into the left ear over information simultaneously sent into the right ear. For them, *red* spoken into the left ear is heard in preference to *blue* entered into the right ear.

On the other hand, nonverbal stimuli like musical sounds presented dichotically are better identified when they enter the left ear because those signals go to the right hemisphere. Apparently, music is processed more by the right than by the left hemisphere.

Dichotic and other auditory studies have also shown that there is left ear superiority in most of us for the judgment of emotions. Thus if emotional verbal material is simultaneously entered into both ears, it is transmitted primarily to the right hemisphere where it is processed over the other stimuli entered into the right ear.

Consequently, we add the auditory system and its relation to the hemispheres to our list of sidedness (laterality) of the head and body.

What happens in the dichotic listening task with split-brain patients? Information placed in the left ear is not verbally processed because it is transmitted to the right hemisphere and cannot cross the commissure into the left hemisphere. Once again there is further evidence of the dominance of the left hemisphere for language in the large majority of people.

LEFT HEMISPHERE SUPERIORITY
FOR THE *COMPONENTS* OF LANGUAGE

Even though the left hemisphere is typically specialized for processing language, "language" is still a complex concept. One conventional way of analyzing language is to separate it into phonologic, syntactic, and semantic elements. In **phonology,** we study the sounds of speech. Phonological analysis of speech specifies the physical characteristics (frequencies, intensities) of sound waves that are emitted from our mouths. **Syntactic** factors of language concern the processing of grammar, of how linguistic units such as words are combined to form sentences in accordance with rules of language. Such rules tell us just what is and what is not a properly formed sentence. **Semantics** has to do with meaning, with the understanding of linguistic utterances.

Analytic studies of language have generally shown that the left hemisphere is far superior to the right for all three of these characteristics of a language. All aspects

Different verbal information simultaneously spoken into the two ears is typically heard from the right ear only.

Verbal information entered into the right ear has priority over that entered into the left ear for those whose left hemisphere is dominant for language; but the reverse is true for those whose right hemisphere is dominant for language.

Music that is dichotically entered into both ears is better identified from the left ear.

Language can be analyzed into phonologic (speech sounds), syntactic (grammar), and semantic (meaning) factors, all three of which are processed primarily in the left hemisphere.

of language processing, be they phonologic, syntactic, or semantic, are specialized in the left hemisphere, at least for most of us.

ARE THERE TWO BRAINS OR ONE?

Some have referred to individuals as being "right-brained" or "left-brained," suggesting that they are verbally or visuospatially oriented. Although some people do have relatively more verbal ability than others, that does not mean that they are "left-brained." Neither hemisphere has an exclusive function. To some limited extent, the left hemisphere serves spatial and emotional functions and the right hemisphere serves language functions. The important generalization is that both hemispheres function intimately together in the normal person and there is no such thing as a "right-brained" or "left-brained" person. Descartes and many since him have concluded that there is but one brain that functions in the generation of a single, undivided individual. Although there are many specialized regions of the brain, it still is a single, integrated organ that functions intimately with the rest of the body, as we now develop.

The two hemispheres function together in an integrated manner and with lateralized relations throughout the head and body.

Since most of the nervous system and body relations are symmetrical, so are most of those brain–body relations. Such bilateral symmetry has considerable survival value as in facilitating our locomotion (if the nerves on one side of the body were larger and more active, we would have a hard time not turning in that direction as we attempted to walk in a straight line). But the lateralized systems have considerable survival value too, as we will now see.

Handedness

A simple test for **handedness** is to offer a pencil directly at the center of a person's body. Most will accept it consistently with one particular hand. About 65 percent of the population is completely right-handed, and only about 4 percent is completely left-handed. Being completely right-handed means that the right hand dominates for two-handed tasks like hitting a baseball and for one-handed operations like brushing teeth. About a third are not completely one-handed, which means that they use their left hand for some tasks (e.g., writing), but their right hands for other tasks (e.g., using scissors). We do not know why such complexities exist, but they indicate that there are aspects of our nervous and muscular systems yet to be understood. One finding is that the corpus callosum is larger in those who tend to use their left hands for many tasks. Just how this finding fits into the jigsaw puzzle is not clear, but once we attain more pieces perhaps this question will be answered too. A larger corpus callosum in left-handed individuals could contain more neural fibers to allow greater communication between the hemispheres. Or, there may simply be more space between the fibers so that its mass is not really greater, which, if true, would compound the puzzle.

A cognitive finding related to handedness is that when one listens to someone else speak, electromyographically measured activity in the preferred arm increases. Preferred-arm covert behavior is evident even when one is silently thinking and imagining language activities (McGuigan, 1978).

The Hand Used to Gesture Is Related to the Hemisphere Dominated for Language. The relationship between the hand with which we gesture and the preference for right versus left hand is germane here. We all make hand gestures, particularly when we speak. Right-handed individuals make more gestures with their right hand than with their left, which suggests that there is an interaction between the right hand and the left ("verbal") hemisphere. This conclusion is buttressed by findings for left-handers since they show more right-handed gestures if their left hemisphere is dominant for language. On the other hand, left-handers whose right hemisphere is dominant for language show more gestures with the left hand.

Circuits between the left hemisphere and the right hand function linguistically for those who are right-handed.

The rich interaction between handedness and speaking has also been shown with studies in which individuals balanced a stick on one hand or the other. When right-handed individuals balance a stick on the right hand, their speech facility is decreased. On the other hand, their speech facility is not interfered with when they balance a stick on the left hand. In contrast, left-handed individuals have their speech interfered with about equally when the stick is balanced on either hand. This close relationship between speech and hand activity is consonant with a widely held hypothesis that hand gestures were a first step in the evolution of language. McNeil (1985) argues that gestures and speech, in fact, are part of the same psychological structure. He holds that overt speech and gestures are united by means of inner (covert) speech. On reviewing various kinds of evidence, McNeil reached the following conclusions: (1) Gestures occur only during speech; (2) they have semantic and pragmatic functions that parallel those of speech; and (3) they are synchronized with linguistic units in speech. Gestures develop along with speech as children acquire language and they dissolve together with speech in aphasia.

Linguistic processing circuits reverberate between the speech muscles, the preferred hand, and the left hemisphere.

In General. The right arm in right-handed individuals is covertly active while processing language stimuli, again suggesting that circuits between the left hemisphere and right hand function for cognitive activities. It is as if we covertly write something about the linguistic components of our thoughts. Like the child who overtly raises fingers to signal age, the adult covertly responds with muscles in the preferred hand.

Asymmetries Have Been Documented in Animals. We have seen that animals also have cerebral and other important lateralities. Many animals show a preference for one or the other of their paws. Many also have a preferred direction of rotation, either clockwise or counterclockwise. These findings suggest a subtle asymmetrical bodily system that has survival value. Such an internal asymmetry of the body can provide internal cues to indicate which direction is left and which is right. Such cues may help animals learn and remember important aspects of their spatial world such as where they have stored food.

While body asymmetry may be valuable for locating stored food, it may also have greater value than that. Body asymmetry may also help animals communicate with each other so that they interact in uniform ways. Perhaps evolutionary processes led all members of a given animal group to be asymmetrical in the same direction — they all prefer to move clockwise. Left-footedness in parrots, for instance, may predispose them to uniformly turn to the left as a group. Such group harmony could be biologically adaptive since the entire group would sharply veer to the left together when the occasion calls for movement. Deviant individuals, those who have the tendency to turn to the right, probably did not survive because they were overwhelmed by the group — similar to someone's walking into an oncoming crowd in Times Square.

Eye Dominance and Hand Preference

Although it is necessary to treat these lateralities separately, we must not lose sight of the fact that the eyes and hands, like the other systems of the body, are intimately interrelated. People have a preference for using one eye over the other—the preferred eye being the dominant one. Usually the dominant eye is on the same side as the preferred hand. Arm preference intimately involves systems of the eyes and speech. For example, while circuits function between the left cerebral hemisphere and the right hand, they also function between the left cerebral hemisphere and the eyes to generate rightward turning of the eyes. Similarly the right hemisphere interacts with the left hand and generates left eye turning and functions especially in spatial–visual–temporal tasks.

Eye and hand lateralizations are positively correlated.

Development of Eye–Hand Coordination. Arnold Gesell, who extensively studied infants, found that one-year-old infants typically manipulate objects with the right hand and use the left hand to hold the object. The operating hand appears as early as four weeks of age and eventually becomes the preferred hand; at that age the head turns to the infant's preferred side when the infant is lying on its back. Gesell indicated that this activity was fundamental to eye–hand coordination. In developing eye–hand coordination, one eye is the active one and the other is subordinate. That active eye usually develops into the dominant eye, which is typically the right one. Thereupon the right eye and right hand become coordinated.

A number of studies indicate that tracking a target with the eyes is influenced by arm activity and vice versa. Circuits must function between the preferred arm and the dominant eye interacting through the brain.

Lateral Eye Movements

When people answer a question requiring momentary reflection, they briefly make **lateral eye movements,** either to the left or to the right. There is no good understanding of why some people make eye movements to the left while others do to the right, or in fact why there are lateral eye movements at all. One hypothesis is that those who make left lateral eye movements tend to engage the right hemisphere during thought while they are processing the question. Conversely, the hypothesis holds that those who make movements to the right especially employ their left hemispheres as they are processing the question. This hypothesis is anatomically based on the fact of neurological pathways from the left side of both eyes to the right cerebral hemisphere and that pathways from the right side of both eyes are represented in the left hemisphere (see Fig. 11.5). Further support comes from the findings that selective stimulation of parts of the left hemisphere can produce movements of the eyes to the right, as such stimulation of the right hemisphere can produce movements of the eyes to the left. Although it is clear that we *do* make these lateral eye movements when silently answering questions, the data are not at all clear that such a directional hemispheric function is involved. Directional lateral eye movements may or may not be related to the relative use of one hemisphere over the other while processing the answer to a question. Only with further research may we explain why some people make them to the left and others to the right and how that directionality might be related to laterality in the brain and elsewhere in a person. Nevertheless, since laterality of eye movements is a fact, we will maintain lateral eye movements as an additional component of brain–body sidedness. Lacking a better

Lateral eye movements are made either to the right or to the left while individuals are reflecting on how to answer a question, but we do not know why they occur.

It is possible that left lateral eye movements function in circuits with the right hemisphere just as right lateral eye movements are components of circuits interacting with the left hemisphere.

notion, we will suppose that eye movements to the right function in circuits with the left hemisphere and that left eye movements function in circuits with the right hemisphere.

Footedness and Leggedness

Footedness refers to a preference for using one foot and leg **(leggedness)** over the other. Right-handed humans generally also have a right-foot bias for activities that require skilled manipulation. Footedness and leggedness are important for athletes and dancers and for using some musical instruments and operating some machines. Some individuals deprived of the use of their hands write with the toes of their preferred foot. Circuits between the left hemisphere and the preferred leg and foot carry out important processing functions, even some linguistic ones. Peters (1988) concluded that foot motor performance should be a routine part of neuropsychological evaluations because it can provide information about neurological insults.

There are right-foot and right-leg biases for the large majority of people wherein circuits with the left cerebral hemisphere carry out numerous processing functions.

Even though humans generally have a right-leg bias, their left leg tends to be longer and heavier than the right leg. One interpretation is that the left leg gets more exercise because it supports the body as one advances the right leg in various activities. The opposite tends to be true for left-handers, although to a lesser extent.

Facedness

One side of the face is, like handedness, more active and expressive than the other.

A considerable amount of research has indicated that individuals have distinctive expressive patterns with one side of the face or the other. Like handedness, **facedness** seems to be present at birth and most humans are right faced. However, musicians tend to be left faced suggesting that facedness is related to hemispheric dominance. Most of us are right-faced and have our left hemisphere dominant, which may help account for why many of us are not good musicians. Apparently, expressiveness of the right side of the face is a linguistic one and that of the left side is nonlinguistic. Consonant with this interpretation is the conclusion of Bryden and Ley (1983) that the left side of the face is more involved than the right in the expression of emotion. Emotional stimuli directed to the right hemisphere, as we have seen, are more accurately perceived than when directed to the left hemisphere. Bryden and Ley determined that there are specialized processes in the right hemisphere that are particularly involved with the processing of emotional stimuli. Any emotional stimulus or emotional thought would thus activate events that are especially prominent in the right hemisphere. Cybernetic circuits between the left side of the face and the right hemisphere would thus be especially active in most of us when we process emotions and express emotional behavior.

Circuits between the left hemisphere and right side of the face are thought to function linguistically, while circuits between the left side of the face and right hemisphere function for processing and generating emotional behavior.

Electrodermal Laterality

Right-handed responders show higher electrodermal activity on the right hand, while left-handed responders show higher electrodermal activity on their left hand. In addition, left-handed responders have a slower habituation rate on their left than on their right hand. Most research on bilateral electrodermal activity has assumed that differences in electrodermal asymmetry are related to differential hemispheric activation (see especially Hugdahl, 1984).

EMPHASIS ON A CYBERNETIC PRINCIPLE— A REVIEW OF INTERACTIONS OF BRAIN LATERALITY WITH OTHER HEAD AND BODY SYSTEMS

In Review. Considerable research has established that there are various asymmetries in the head and throughout the body:

1. Cerebral laterality—the left hemisphere of the brain is typically specialized for language while the right hemisphere is specialized for visual–spatial and emotional functions.
2. Auditory laterality—there is lateralization for hearing such that stimuli presented simultaneously into the two ears will consistently be processed by one ear over the other, depending on whether the input is linguistic or nonlinguistic (e.g., musical or emotional stimuli).
3. Handedness—the right hand is generally preferred over the left.
4. Eye dominance—there is lateralization for the eyes in that one eye is typically preferred over the other.
5. Lateral eye movements—lateral eye movements occur involuntarily immediately on being asked a question. Presumably, eye movements to the right function in circuits with the left hemisphere while eye movements to the left function in circuits with the right hemisphere.
6. Footedness and legedness—the right foot and leg are usually preferred over the left foot and leg.
7. Facedness—most of us are verbally right-faced, but we typically express emotions more with the left side of the face.
8. Electrodermal laterality—handedness is related to electrodermal laterality such that right-handed individuals have greater electrodermal activity on the right hand and left-handed people have greater electrodermal activity on their left hand.

This constitutes a fair summary of various lateralities that exist in the typical human.[1] Following our general cybernetic principles, we have depicted in Figure 11.8 circuits through which systems and regions interact. For simplicity, we have illustrated only the left hemisphere–right-hand and body circuits. The decussation of neural fibers to and from the left hemisphere and the right side of the body helps us to better understand how these interactions occur. In particular, neural impulses from the right side of the body run along neural tracts to the left hemisphere and from the left hemisphere to the right side of the body; as these circuits reverberate they often carry out language functions.

Neural tracts between the right hemisphere and the left side of the body constitute circuits that are similar anatomically in ways we have just discussed. However, it is likely that circuits to and from the right hemisphere and the left side of the body are especially active when we covertly engage in spatial–visual and emotional activities.

Other circuits that we have discussed in the context of laterality are also simultaneously active. Thus, the right side of the face interacts with the left side of the brain during language processing as the right hemisphere interacts with the left

Complex neuromuscular circuits are constantly interacting between the right side of a person, especially the right face, arm, and hand, and the left hemisphere of the brain during linguistic processing.

---

[1] There is also a possible laterality for mustaches—for right-handed individuals, the mustache grows more vigorously on the right side of the face. However, systematic data have apparently not been collected on this hairy issue.

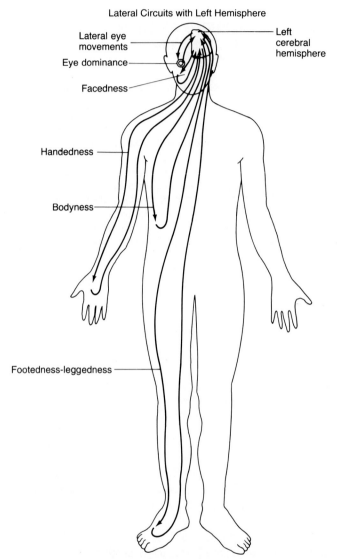

Lateral Circuits with Left Hemisphere

Lateral eye movements

Eye dominance

Facedness

Left cerebral hemisphere

Handedness

Bodyness

Footedness-leggedness

FIGURE 11.8   Cybernetic circuits interacting among lateralized systems to integrate and generate physiological/psychological functions of the body. Only circuits between the left hemisphere and the right side of a person are illustrated.

side of the face during emotional processing. Other circuits include those involving the left hemisphere and the right leg, and so forth, as depicted in Figure 11.8.

In Review. From a broad perspective of language and of complex neuromuscular circuits, we can see why the entire body is covertly active during any kind of cognitive processing: The right side interacts with the left hemisphere during internal linguistic processing. Neuromuscular circuits simultaneously reverberate between the right hemisphere and the left side to generate cognitive processes that involve visual, spatial, and emotional components. Thus, our cognitive processes, which generally have linguistic, visual, spatial, and emotional aspects, involve information that is simultaneously processed in our various sensory modalities. There must be thousands of channels of those information processing circuits simultaneously reverberating. Indeed, the entire body is covertly quite active as we generate cognitive activities that we call thinking, imagination, and emotions, as we develop in Chapter 13.

KEY TERMS

Apraxia—Inability to perform a series of purposeful movements often due to lesions in the motor areas of the cerebral cortex.

Arcuate fasciculus—Connection between Wernicke's and Broca's areas made up of subcortical neural fibers.

Bilateral—On both sides of the midline of the body.

Broca's aphasia—Inability to produce speech resulting from a lesion in Broca's area.

Broca's area—Functions for speech production and is typically located in the left frontal lobe.

Conduction aphasia—Inability to relate what is said with what is heard. Although speech is generally fluent, the individual has limited ability to repeat. The person can comprehend quite well. Originally thought to be due to a lesion in the arcuate fasciculus between Broca's and Wernicke's areas, that notion has been disconfirmed.

Contralateral pathways—Neural tracts by which information received by one side of the body crosses over to the other side to and from the brain.

Dichotic listening task—The entering of different information simultaneously into the two ears. The result is that verbal information entered into the right ear enters the left hemisphere and thus has priority over verbal information entered into the left ear.

Facedness—One side of the face is more active and expressive than the other.

Footedness (and legedness)—A preference for using one foot (and therefore also that leg) over the other.

Grammar—A system of rules of language used to construct sentences. The rules specify how to use discrete linguistic units in many different ways—how to combine and divide words, how to form proper sentences.

Handedness—The hands are specialized on one side (lateralized) so that we are typically "right-handed" or "left-handed."

Ipsilateral pathways—Neural fibers that transmit information from one side of the body to and from the same side of the brain.

Language—Consists of discrete units that may be transformed in an indefinitely large number of ways according to rules. We use language to communicate through speech, writing, signaling, and so on.

Lateral eye movement—Movements made by eyes either to the left or to the right while reflecting on how to answer a question. The data are not clear as to why this phenomenon occurs.

Laterality—Various regions of the head and body are asymmetrical, specialized on one side, and thus are lateralized. In contrast, many systems are bilateral in that they are equally represented on both sides of the body and head (e.g., the spinal nerves).

Phonology—The study of the sounds of speech.

Semantics—The study of the meaning and understanding of (linguistic) sentences.

Split-brain operation—Lesioning of the corpus callosum. The belief was that neural epileptic seizures could thereby be limited to one hemisphere. Experimental research started in the 1940s confirmed the importance of the left hemisphere for language processing.

Stimulus-bound response—A response that is involuntarily and inalterably evoked by specific stimuli.

Syntactics—The study of formal relations between language units abstracted from meaning and language users.

Verbal—Refers to language. Communication may be oral as in speech and nonoral as in the written word.

Wada Test—The temporary paralysis of one hemisphere by injecting a barbiturate into it to determine dominance.

Wernicke's aphasia—Inability to understand speech due to a lesion in Wernicke's area in the left temporal lobe.

Wernicke's area—A region in the left temporal lobe that functions for speech comprehension.

STUDY QUESTIONS

1. Give the defining criterion of language and explain some of its essential characteristics.
2. T or F. If we examine the anatomical characteristics of primates, many aspects of the subhuman oral systems are completely different from the speech systems of humans.
3. At least some rudimentary forms of communication that resemble human language have been successfully taught to apes. Discuss these studies.
4. Discuss the work of the French surgeon Paul Broca as it relates to the left hemisphere.
5. Discuss the importance of the left hemisphere for linguistic functioning.
6. List the different kinds of tasks performed by the two hemispheres.
7. The phenomena of aphasia are very complex. List and discuss them.
8. What is the reasoning for the hypothesis that hand gestures were a first step in the evolution of language?
9. Summarize the various lateralities that exist in the typical human body and how they might interact.

FURTHER READINGS

This is a highly speculative, but interesting, account of the origins of language:

Bickerton, D. (1990). *Language and species.* Chicago: University of Chicago Press.

The following book discusses the broader psychological and biological aspects of language, including aphasia, speech and language pathology, brain theory, the phylogenesis of language, and animal communication:

Newmeyer, F. J. (1988). *Language: Psychological and biological aspects* (Vol. 3). Cambridge, England: Cambridge University Press.

See also:

Geschwind, N., & Galaburda, A. M. (1984). *Cerebral dominance.* Cambridge, MA: Harvard University Press.

Miller, G. A. (1981). *Language and speech.* San Francisco: Freeman.

CHAPTER 12

The Psychophysiology of Aging

MAJOR PURPOSE: To understand the important aging changes that occur throughout the body

WHAT YOU ARE GOING TO FIND:
1. That the problems of the elderly constitute an increasingly important concern for society
2. A specification of some of the characteristics of the aging process
3. That we can measure biological age and probably slow aging down through exercise and systematic relaxation

WHAT YOU SHOULD ACQUIRE: Knowledge of the aging process, how to retard it, how to treat it, and the importance of further understanding it

CHAPTER OUTLINE

THE IMPORTANCE OF STUDYING THE AGING PROCESS

Realizing That We Are Aging. What makes us grow old? This is a question that seldom occurs to young people or to older ones who have always had good health. Part of the reason is that when we are energetic and in good health, we blithely assume that our good fortune will continue forever. An elderly man, in reviewing his life, said that the one thing he would do differently is to start a retirement plan earlier. He explained that "when we are young it is inconceivable that we will grow old and die."

In a sense, aging starts at the instant of conception. From then, you, I, all of us age each moment of our lives, even as we read these words. Often, on reaching thirty, this point is brought home to us with alarm. Middle age makes it worse. We all recognize the stereotype of the middle-aged man with a pot belly and receding hairline. His stamina has decreased so that he puffs while climbing the stairs and his sex life is not what it used to be. He panics at the thought that his youth has escaped from his grasp and he increasingly becomes preoccupied with the aging process. Like Ponce de Leon, he joins the widespread search for "the fountain of youth." Multi-billion-dollar businesses thrive on selling wrinkle creams, hair restorers, and rejuvenating pills.

People are living longer and the proportion of the elderly in the United States is sizably increasing.

Our Population Is Aging.   The rapid increase in the number of the elderly is focusing our attention more and more on all aspects of the aged. Major successes in medical science have contributed to a record life expectancy for us. Although statistics vary, an estimate by the National Center for Health Statistics is that the life expectancy for newborn female babies in the United States is a record 78.3 years. The life expectancy for males is now 71.3. If increases in life expectancy continue on this scale, the average American can expect to live into his or her eighties by the year 2050.

As a consequence of living longer lives, the number of people over 65 years of age in the United States has greatly increased. Coupled with a reduced birthrate, the *proportion* of elderly people has increased sizably. One prediction is that there will be 35 million people over 65 years of age in the United States by the year 2000. Such a dramatic change dictates radical modification in many aspects of our society. Certainly, life-styles have changed. With more healthful living, older people now enjoy many aspects of life that previously were reserved for the young. People in their sixties, seventies, and beyond now jog, roller-skate, bicycle, and take fitness classes. We even have national tennis tournaments with divisions for those above 70 years of age. The winner of a recent national tennis championship for senior men was 82 (he won 6–2, 6–3).

On the other hand, many of the aged have not survived so successfully. For them, we have increased the number of nursing homes and engineered special environments for their enfeebled capacities. What is it that distinguishes those "youthful" oldsters from their biologically aged fellows? We are seeking answers through specialized scientific research.

Gerontologists seek to understand and retard the aging process as well as to solve the problems of the aged.

The Science of Gerontology.   One of the most vigorous endeavors of biological science, one that has recently mushroomed, is **gerontology,** the study of the aging process. Gerontology, a multidisciplinary field involving anatomists, physiologists, biochemists, psychologists, and physicians, focuses on the problems and triumphs of the aged.

The prime goals of gerontology are to (1) identify "normal" aging processes that are *common* among people, with the goal of preventing them, and (2) identify the *unique* characteristics of people who have successfully coped with the aging process. If we can specify the reasons that aging is retarded in such people, perhaps we can preserve these characteristics in others and thereby maintain them into very old age. More of us can thus stay "youthful" for a longer period of time. In this chapter we discuss these two general goals of gerontology in turn. But before we do, let us broaden our perspective by introducing the following term.

LIFE SPAN DEVELOPMENT

Fields of psychology that had to do with early development used to be called "child psychology" and "developmental psychology." These fields studied somatic and intellectual growth during infancy, childhood, and adolescence. However, the recent surge of interest in aging has now expanded these fields so that they have been replaced by that of **life span development.** There has been a tremendous increase in the amount of research at both ends of the life span, in the abilities of infants and the aging processes of the elderly. Neurological impairment has become especially important at both ends of the life span.

Life span development is the study of life processes from conception to death and is now the term used instead of "child psychology" and "developmental psychology."

NORMAL AGING CHANGES—WHY DO WE GROW OLD?

The changes that are common among us as we age constitute the **primary aging processes.** Some examples of the physiological and anatomical aspects of these "normal" aging changes are as follows: As aging increases, the amount of REM and of stage 4 (deep sleep) decreases. There is a decrease in the amount of water in the body so that some chemicals, such as lithium, become more concentrated; as a consequence, the effects of drugs change with age. Similarly, the fat/muscle ratio increases so that there is more fat per unit of muscle. Therefore, drugs stored in fat have a different effect. As one grows older, blood pressure typically increases, the vital capacity of lungs decreases, hearing acuity decreases, and kidney function decreases.

Primary aging processes are normal age changes and include changes in sleep patterns, increases in amount of fat per unit of muscle, increases in blood pressure, and decreases in vital capacity of lungs, hearing acuity, and kidney function.

Tissue Changes in the Central Nervous System

Does the Brain Age?. It has been traditionally thought that the brain deteriorates with age. Past research has indicated that there is loss of neurons, general atrophy, and decline in the functioning of neurotransmitter and synaptic systems. There is also markedly reduced blood flow in the aged human central nervous system. Along with this is a reduction in the use of oxygen to only three-quarters of that in younger persons. Such important deprivation of neural tissue must be detrimental. However, more recent research indicates that the story is not all that simple. Although it is clear that there typically are declines in brain functioning as one ages, these declines are not universal nor are they inevitable. For instance, there is neuronal loss in some regions of the brain as one ages, especially in the cerebellum and cortex. Other regions, however, have no loss of neurons at all, such as in the inferior olive (Fig. 12.1).

It used to be thought that once neural tissue was lost, it was never replaced or regenerated. We now know however that the brain does have some regenerative capacity, which is greatest in young organisms. As age increases, regenerative capacity in some brain regions remains constant. Such regeneration occurs with the formation of new dendritic and axonal material and even of new synapses. We can generalize as follows, although we need to continue research to better specify relevant parameters: At any given stage of aging, some regions of the brain are degenerating while other regions are actually regenerating. There is thus a kind of balance from one region to another.

One specific kind of change in the brain deserves a special section. That change concerns dopaminergic neurons.

As organisms age, there is loss of some neural tissue, but regeneration occurs in other neural tissue; regenerative capacity of brain tissue is greatest in young organisms.

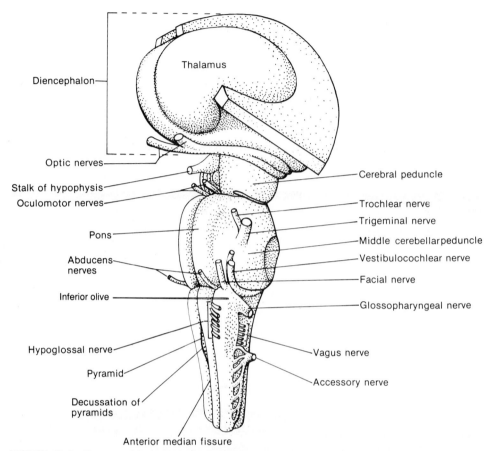

Diencephalon—

Optic nerves—

Stalk of hypophysis—

Oculomotor nerves—

Pons—

Abducens nerves—

Inferior olive—

Hypoglossal nerve—

Pyramid—

Decussation of pyramids—

Anterior median fissure

Thalamus

—Cerebral peduncle

—Trochlear nerve

—Trigeminal nerve

—Middle cerebellar peduncle

—Vestibulocochlear nerve

—Facial nerve

—Glossopharyngeal nerve

—Vagus nerve

—Accessory nerve

FIGURE 12.1   The brain stem indicating the location of the inferior olive.

Decline in Dopaminergic Function in the Basal Ganglia

Clinicians used to employ the concept of "hardening of the arteries" as the main reason for the aging of the brain, but this concept has been abandoned. Axons that project up to the basal nuclei ganglia (Figs. 7.6 and 12.2) from the substantia nigra of the midbrain progressively lose their function of secreting the neurotransmitter dopamine. If these neurons do not provide sufficient dopamine, they apparently contribute to **Parkinson's disease.** The substantia nigra of a 25-year-old person contains about 400,000 dopaminergic neurons while only about 200,000 are present in an 80-year-old person. There is thus a loss of synapses where dopamine is secreted which substantially reduces the number of neural circuits. There are then widespread effects on other bodily systems.

Basal nuclei of the corpus striatum contribute to the coordination of body movements by integrating neural impulses. When the dopamine content of the corpus striatum falls to less than 30 percent of the level in earlier life, clinical symptoms of aging appear. This decrease in dopamine content is associated with progressive loss of motor speed between ages 45 and 85.

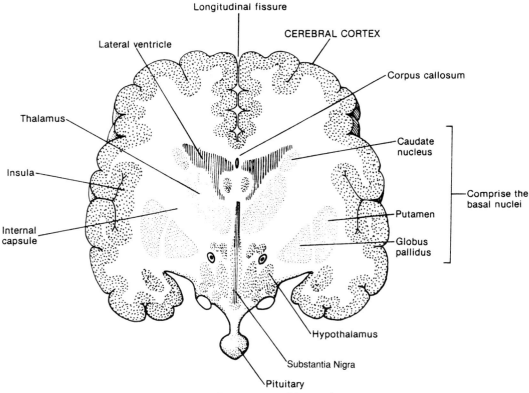

FIGURE 12.2   Frontal section of the white and gray matter of the cerebrum showing the location of substantia nigra. The basal nuclei are located in the midbrain within the cerebrum.

Some research indicates that motor function is restored or preserved in aged animals by administering dopamine. Dopaminergic therapy for slowed motor function in adults can also have favorable results. Dopamine implants have improved the status of Parkinson's patients.

As aging progresses, there is a loss of dopaminergic neurons whereby the decrease in dopamine content in the brain apparently contributes to symptoms of aging.

Decline in Muscular Strength and Speed

As aging increases, the mass of skeletal muscle decreases because there is a decrease in the number of muscle fibers and in their size, leading to a decrease in muscular strength. There are also decreases in the number and percentage of fast-twitch muscle fibers and their associated motor neurons during aging, which may help account for decreased speed of action and endurance. Fast twitch muscle fibers, which apparently are white muscle fibers, produce fast contractions but they quickly fatigue. Slow twitch muscle fibers, which apparently are red muscle fibers, produce less vigorous contractions without fatiguing so rapidly.

Presbystasia, a decrease in ability to maintain equilibrium, is a good index of aging. The older the person is, the greater the tendency to sway from side to side. The ability to stand on one leg shows a 100 percent decline with age; the elderly can lose the capability completely. Presbystasis may occur because of a decline in the func-

Decreased strength during aging results from the decreased quantity of muscle. There are also decreases in speed, endurance, and performance of psychomotor tasks.

tioning in the vestibular mechanism and/or peripheral nerve loss, along with atrophy of the muscles. There is thus decreased efficiency of central–peripheral circuits between the vestibular mechanism and skeletal muscles.

There is a consistent decline in the ability to perform such simple tasks as writing (especially in the speed of writing) and removing clothing. The WAIS (Wechsler Adult Intelligence Scale) Digit Symbol Substitution Test, which is a psychomotor test, provides one of the most highly correlated measures of declines of such functions with increasing age. A **psychomotor test** is one in which psychological functions are measured by means of motor activities such as making discriminations and then responding in some way. As we will see, measures of these abilities are quite consonant with the findings that simple reaction and choice reaction times (see pp. 392–393) are sensitive measures of the aging process.

The decline in neural activity and in muscle tissue during aging leads to decreased functioning of cybernetic circuits between the muscles and the brain.

Decreased activity of the central nervous system, decreased functioning of motor neurons, and subsequent loss of motor neurons lead to reduced nerve impulse activity and atrophy of muscle. All of this in turn reduces the afferent neural activity back to the central nervous system. Aging in part, then, occurs because of a decline in the functioning of neuromuscular circuits. The disuse of muscle and of neural tissue as they fail to interact leads to a deterioration of both. There is a consequent reduction of cybernetic neuromuscular activity throughout the body that leads to a general decline in effective functioning.

Sensory Changes

HEARING DECREASES

Approximately 80 percent of those with hearing problems are over 45 years of age. Significant hearing loss occurs in 55 percent of people over 65 years of age; and 75 percent of those between 75 and 79 years have hearing problems of some sort.

Changes that occur in the ear include the following: The middle ear becomes ossified at the tympanic membrane and there can be a loss of elastic tissue there; the inner ear loses hair cells on the basilar membrane (which is exaggerated by extended listening to loud sounds such as rock music); and there is a change in inner ear metabolism. The result is a loss in ability to detect sounds of high frequency. Such hearing changes are not as great in women as they are in men.

Presbycusis, one of the major sensory changes that occurs with aging, is a loss of ability to perceive or discriminate sounds. Presbycusis includes impairment of pure tone thresholds, frequency discrimination, auditory temporal discrimination, sound localization ability, impairment of speech discrimination, and impairment of ability to recall long sentences. A decline of the ability to locate sounds seems to be due to a decreased ability to integrate sounds that arrive at slightly different times at the two ears. Failing to achieve this neural integration, the aged can lose the ability to perceive a unified sound and to infer its locality.

A number of auditory abilities, including ability to perceive speech, commonly decline as aging increases, apparently due to a decreased functioning of the auditory system.

Important aging changes seem to occur in the neural auditory system, leading to a decrease in ability to discriminate between tones. This finding suggests that there are sensitive brain processing changes that function for speech reception. In fact, changes in the ability to perceive speech seem to be a good index of biological age. Specifically why this occurs is not clear, but it may involve a decrease in the functioning of the auditory nerve, of related cochlear nuclei, of higher level nuclei, or even the auditory cortex itself. Auditory evoked potentials from these structures have been used to potentially diagnose Alzheimer's disease before it becomes apparent, but more research is needed before we can say anything definitive about the value of this approach.

DECLINES IN VISUAL ABILITIES

Among the visual changes that occur with aging, one of the most common is senile miosis (excessive contraction of the pupils of the eye). This decrease in the diameter of the pupils is due to changes in the tone of the iris muscles. (The iris muscles contract and relax to regulate the amount of light that enters the eye.) Various other visual changes occur so that older people require much longer to identify faces than do younger people. There are retinal function changes with age as there are for visual evoked brain potentials. There is a decline of visual acuity throughout the adult years, especially when the lighting is poor. The effective visual fields of older people are also reduced in size so that some have less ability to perceive events that occur at the periphery. Consequently, the intensity or size of stimuli, particularly those for peripheral vision, need to be increased in order to be perceived.

Probably because of reduced visual acuity, there is progressive decline in stereopsis (depth perception) after the forties. Consequently, there is a loss of ability to make fine judgments of distances.

There is a general decline in such visual abilities as acuity, stereopsis, and peripheral vision as components of the visual system deteriorate.

OTHER SENSORY CHANGES

Other decreasing abilities include sensitivity for taste and smell and impaired balance of the body due to changes in the vestibular sense.

Declines in auditory and visual sensitivity are accompanied by decreases in sensitivity of other sensory systems including those for taste, smell, and balance.

Endocrine and Other Biochemical Functions

Estrogen and Testosterone Decrease in Women and Men. It is well established that there is a decrease in the amount of estrogen in the aging female, especially after menopause. It can be counteracted by estrogenic intervention, but the side effects of the available estrogens can be toxic and carcinogenic (cancer producing).

For men, there is a significant decline in testosterone levels starting from about age 20 and continuing through later life. In one study it was reported that there is a 35 percent decrease in plasma testosterone content between the ages of 21 and 85. Testosterone blood levels during midlife and beyond do not seem to correlate with sexual activity.

Other Biochemical Aging Changes. Animal and human clinical studies indicate a decline in effectiveness of the immune system with age so that there generally is reduced resistance to infection. There is also a declining renal (kidney) function that typically begins in the middle of the fourth decade. The decrease in efficiency of processing urine has biochemical effects that can deleteriously affect other bodily systems.

There is a normal increase in the level of sugar in the blood with aging. Two hypotheses are that there is a progressive decrease in the amount of insulin in the blood and/or that the amount of insulin does not decrease but merely becomes less effective. Insulin functions to maintain the appropriate level of sugar in the blood through a negative feedback system. Diabetics must receive extra insulin to maintain

The amount of estrogen decreases in women, particularly around menopause, while levels of testosterone start decreasing in men at about age 20 and continue through life.

The immune system generally becomes less effective in the aged, accompanied by declining effectiveness of the kidneys.

There is a normal increase in blood sugar level with aging because of the decreasing effectiveness of insulin.

their proper sugar level. Research has confirmed the second hypothesis—that the amount of insulin does not decrease with aging, but its effectiveness does.

Effects of Aging on the Respiratory System

The human respiratory system has completely developed by about 19 years of age. In general, its maximum level of functioning occurs between the twentieth and twenty-fifth years, after which there is a progressive decline.

In a number of studies, it has been demonstrated that total lung capacity (TLC) decreases with age. However, this is but a correlational relationship and may occur because height decreases as we grow older. The decrease in height results because the space between the vertebrae in the spinal cord decreases. When TLC data are normalized for the decrease in height, TLC does not change with age. So, although at first glance TLC could appear to be a major cause of aging, it is not. We must look for other possible changes in the respiratory system.

Vital Capacity Decreases with Age. Vital capacity is defined as the volume of gas (air) expired in a maximal expiration starting after a maximal inspiration. Perhaps you remember performing this task during a medical examination. An instrument with a meter is placed in the mouth and the goal is to exhale to maximal capacity, to raise the hand on the meter as far as possible. Because air is forced out of the lungs to the maximal capacity, this measure is called **forced vital capacity.** It is regarded as one of the most important indices of aging because it summarizes a number of physical changes. Levitsky (1984) holds that as you age, anatomical changes include a loss of alveolar elastic recoil (alveoli are air sacs in the lungs that decrease in their elasticity with aging so that less air is expelled). These changes in alveolar elastic recoil change the structure of the chest wall with an accompanying decrease in chest muscle strength. The decrease in the strength of the respiratory muscles also contributes to a decreased lung volume. Reduced vital capacity also may be due to a loss of surface area of alveoli with decreased efficiency of air circulation in the lungs. The loss of alveolar surface area and changes in circulation of air in the lungs also result in decreased capillary blood volume as well as a decreased surface for exchanging gases between alveoli and capillaries of the bloodstream. All of these structural changes result in a decreased ability of the lungs for expiratory flow rate and contribute to a decreased ability for muscular exercise (as measured by maximum amount of oxygen that can be taken in).

Forced vital capacity, the maximum amount of air that can be forced out of the lungs, decreases with aging probably because the alveoli (air sacs in the lungs) become less effective in exchanging gases with the capillaries of the bloodstream.

Pulmonary changes with age were also shown in the famous Framingham, Massachusetts, heart study in which the population of the town was studied over many decades. Forced vital capacity was a good predictor of the 20-year mortality rate. More particularly, low vital capacity predicted a high death rate regardless of gender, smoking versus nonsmoking, or age. Those with low vital capacity died more frequently due to all major causes of death, although cardiovascular disease was the major cause. The effect of age on vital capacity is apparently related to those changes in the chest that we have enumerated.

Cardiac Functions

The Cardiovascular System Decreases in Efficiency in the Aged. Postmortem studies have revealed significant coronary artery disease with increasing age in over

Deterioration of the Knees

The life expectancy in the United States is now over 75 years; yet the human knee has been estimated to be good for about 40 years as it is used in modern life. Thousands of times a week we pivot, lean, jump, kneel, and so on. One estimate is that about 50 million Americans have experienced a knee injury or knee pain. One thing that happens is that the ligaments and tendons that hold the joints together weaken and stretch because the cartilage that cushions the contact between the bones deteriorates.

The primary function of the knees is for flexion and extension of the leg as in walking, sitting, and standing. Although the knee can also rotate slightly from side to side, its range of rotary motion is limited by ligaments that are not strong enough to withstand twists and turns that are extreme and abrupt. It served us well before we stood on two feet. But on two legs, we subject it to strong forces, and thus to injuries. The padding of cartilage between the leg bones can also be damaged especially when shear forces are severe or when the cartilage is repeatedly pounded as in years of jogging, especially on hard surfaces. Sports subject the knees to a force many times the weight of the body. Squatting and excessive stair climbing put a force four to seven times your weight across the surface of your knee cap. High heels or thinly soled shoes also are hard on the knees. Moderation of such activities as well as maintaining a normal body weight can help prevent knee problems.

The knees deteriorate earlier than other bodily regions, indicating that earlier in life we should not misuse them.

QUANTIFYING THE AGING PROCESS

Chronological Age Is Not Biological Age.   The most obvious characteristic of aging is the great variability among people. You probably know someone who looks, thinks, and acts young, although that person may be 70 years old. Such a person is chronologically old, but biologically rather young. On the other hand, you may have been surprised to discover that an elderly-looking man was in his early forties. This person is chronologically young, but biologically (functionally) old. It is important for us to distinguish between **chronological age** and **biological (functional) age.**

We Need a Measure of Biological Age.   We have a ready measure of chronological age, but not of biological age. The development of a scale of biological aging is thus a top research priority. Such a scale could be analogous to that for mental age — in intelligence testing we measure mental age regardless of chronological age. With a scale for biological age, we could assess where a person is in his or her life span. With that knowledge, we could predict how long a person will live, barring getting a terminal disease or being hit by a truck, of course. Although we know little about the differences between biologically young and biologically old persons, we are beginning to accumulate such valuable information especially for the cardiovascular, neuromuscular, and central nervous systems.

As the great psychologist E. L. Thorndike said early in this century, "If a thing exists, it exists in some amount. If it exists in some amount, it can be measured." How might we apply his principle to **explicate** biological aging and specify stages of the process? (Explication means to replace an ambiguous concept, one that usually comes from everyday language, with a systematically analyzed, objective set of measurements.)

Chronological age differs from biological age in that a person can be old on one scale but younger on the other.

By measuring changes in bodily systems we can develop an effective scale of biological age that thereby advances our understanding of the aging process.

How fast a person reacts to a stimulus can inform us of how efficiently the sensory, neural, and muscular systems are functioning within integrated cybernetic circuits throughout the body.

Reaction Time Can Measure Biological Age.   One of the most promising approaches to the direct measurement of aging is to use a **reaction time** task. In a simple reaction time task, time is measured from the onset of a stimulus, such as the flashing of a light, to the onset of a response, such as pressing a button as fast as possible. Measurement of reaction time tells us something about the functional status of the systems of the body; in particular, it is an index of how effectively the receptor, nervous, and effector systems are integrated. Research does in fact indicate that biological age *is* indexed by reaction time. For example, in one study it was found that two tapping and two hand reaction tasks were significantly related to a person's length of survival — those who were slower in these tasks (i.e., biologically older) died at a relatively young chronological age (Borkan & Norris, 1980). Conversely, biologically younger individuals (those who reacted rapidly) lived longer, regardless of chronological age.

Theodore Bashore has reported that older joggers have reaction times similar to those of young adults and that older racket ball players have even shorter mental reaction times. Older nonexercisers had the slowest times of all. Biological age is thus inversely related to reaction time. However, we must always be careful in interpreting results from such correlational studies that are not experimental. Thus differences other than biological age exist between groups of people. Other unspecified or unknown differences could have been responsible for the differences in reaction time. Chronologically older people may merely need more practice on reaction time tasks. It is possible that reaction time differences between biologically old and young individuals may disappear in the aged with extensive practice.

Correlational studies indicate that the faster the reaction time, the younger the biological age.

In another study of performance on three psychomotor tasks that required considerable information processing and fine motor control, it was found that speed was predictive of life span — the faster individuals lived longer (Botwinick, West, & Storandt, 1978). Psychomotor speed tasks are also valuable as an index of ability to process stimuli and to carry out motor functions.

A large number of measurable events occur between the stimulus onset and the overt response.

When we react to a stimulus, we do so with systems throughout our whole body, even though reaction time is usually indexed by only one overt response, such as pressing a key with a finger. In measuring reaction time, then, it is important that we study several components of the complex bodily response pattern to a stimulus. This can be done very effectively through psychophysiological methods, including several measures of motor activity using electromyography (Fig. 12.3). It can be seen that the responses occurred very early in the brain, tongue, and passive arms, followed later by activity in the active arm.

Brain Reactions.   Research on electrical activity in the brain during aging has concentrated on sensory evoked potentials and the contingent negative variation (CNV). CNV amplitude from over the frontal lobes, for instance, was found to be significantly lower in older than younger people. This finding suggests that frontal lobe functioning changes in the aged. Cortical areas should be electrophysiologically mapped to determine which regions do and do not deteriorate as a function of aging. Then, patterns of electromyographically measured reaction times throughout the body (as in Fig. 12.3) could be related to relevant cortical areas. The strategy here is to longitudinally measure (vs. mere cross-sectional research) changes in psychophysiological profiles as a function of increasing biological age. Resulting data could elaborate considerably on the classical finding that reaction time slows during aging.

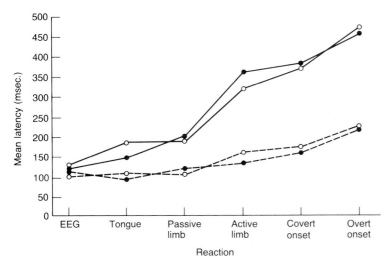

FIGURE 12.3 Results of a reaction time task psychophysiologically specifying several measures during processing prior to the overt response. The top two traces are for complex (choice) reaction time, while the lower two traces are for simple reaction time. Filled circles are reactions to linguistic stimuli, while unfilled circles are for nonlinguistic stimuli.

Cardiovascular Fitness as an Index of Biological Age. To measure how physically fit a person is, researchers often assess the degree to which that individual is free from cardiovascular disease. Research has indicated that those who have cardiovascular disease or high blood pressure are excessively slow in performing psychomotor tasks. There is, in fact, a strong correlation between degree of cardiovascular disease and poor psychomotor performance. As with all correlations, we must interpret this one cautiously. We cannot, for instance, assert that cardiovascular disease causes poor psychomotor performance, or vice versa. It may well be that both are simply components of the aging process. But the immediate point is that those who are physically fit by cardiovascular measures also have faster psychomotor speed.

As research adds to the relevant variables, we can develop profiles of biochemical, behavioral, and psychophysiological changes that can lead to a refined scale of the aging process.

We can also improve the effectiveness of interventions on aging and thus the quality and length of survival. Using animals as our model of a biochemical–psychophysiological syndrome of aging processes, we have succeeded in delaying the process somewhat, a topic to which we now turn.

Potential measures of biological age include reaction time, speed of performing psychomotor tasks, brain reactions, and cardiovascular fitness.

WHAT KEEPS US YOUNG?

Secondary Aging Processes Advance Aging. With this overview of the changes that occur within us as we normally age, let us consider how we might retard the primary and secondary aging processes. **Secondary aging processes** are unique kinds of illnesses (pathological conditions) that facilitate aging; that is, pathological (diseased) disorders take a toll on our bodies, causing us to age more rapidly. For example, a cardiovascular disorder such as high blood pressure retards proper functioning of many systems of the body and advances the aging process. Similarly, a respiratory (pulmonary) disease may cause muscular weakening that is characteristic of aging. Most people over 65 have some kind of pathological condition, however minor it might be. It has been said, for instance, that anyone who lives long enough will develop arthritis.

Normal aging is free of disease. Secondary aging is facilitated by various diseases.

Normal Aging. **Normal aging** is aging that is free of the pathological disorders of secondary aging processes and occurs as a result of primary aging processes.

Those who have normally aged and have remained biologically youthful despite advanced chronological age have preserved at least four functions: (1) certain nervous system structures that are crucial to motor functions; (2) an enhanced endurance capacity; (3) relatively skilled motor performance; and (4) freedom from bodily tremors and rigidity of the parts of the body (Mortimer, Pirozzolo, & Maletta, 1982).

How can we maintain such characteristics so that we can stay younger longer? We know of two programs. The first is to *maintain physical fitness* and the second is to *successfully cope with the stresses of life.* Combined, these approaches should help to retard motor and mental deterioration.

Aging can be retarded by maintaining physical fitness (good endurance, motor performance, flexibility, and freedom from tremors) and successfully coping with stresses of life.

Maintaining Physical Fitness

Disuse Leads to Atrophy. Aging of cells and tissues is a subtle phenomenon common to all living things. Even parrots grow old. All cells require active stimulation in order to optimally function. When they are not sufficiently active, they deteriorate both functionally and structurally with consequent deterioration of the organ systems that they compose. When we are active, every bodily system participates, including especially the nervous, muscular, receptor, and cardiovascular systems. Conversely, disuse of the bodily systems can result in behavioral slowing down and illness. Much illness and changes in the body that are attributed to aging actually may be the result of disuse.

A general principle for prolonging a healthy life is expressed in the often-heard phrase "use it or lose it."

The degeneration of the musculature, which occurs because of a loss of muscle fibers and decrease in their size, can be counteracted through physical exercise.

Maintenance of Physical Strength and Endurance. A common characteristic of aging is known as **senile muscular atrophy. Atrophy** (degeneration) of the musculature occurs from the decrease in muscle size as the number and size of muscle fibers decrease. There is a corresponding loss of functioning motor units with increasing age that is dramatic: Less than half of the previously used motor units typically remain functional in the aged. Furthermore, as we have noted, this loss in motor units is selective. That is, although slow-twitch fibers (those that contract relatively slowly) are maintained, fast-twitch fibers apparently are lost. In fact, any kind of muscular disuse causes a loss of fast-twitch fibers that is similar to the loss seen in aging.

Continual mental, aerobic, and other exercise deters declines in cognitive functioning, vital capacity, and cardiac efficiency.

In Short. We can expect some muscular deterioration when we age, regardless of what we do. But by exercising muscles, we can at least delay their deterioration. Daily endurance training has been shown to prevent the attrition of both slow- and fast-twitch muscle fibers, which suggests that those who establish a life-style of daily exercise are more likely to maintain their ability to recruit fast-twitch fibers. This may contribute to the faster reaction time in the biologically young.

Physical fitness apparently enhances the general functioning of the systems of the body in an integrated fashion. Regular aerobic exercise delays the decline in vital capacity seen with aging. Cardiac and respiratory fitness are related to such regular intense physical activity. Regular physical exercise seems to help maintain proper functioning of the cardiovascular and neuromuscular systems and even seems to help prevent the decline of cognitive functions. Susan Dottl, in studying a large number of men, concluded that frequent use of a specific cognitive function helps to maintain that function. The mental abilities that people expect to decrease with age can actually be maintained into late life if they are regularly used.

Important cognitive skills that are frequently used are maintained throughout aging.

Some Large-Scale Research.   Some data have strengthened our belief that physical activity does, indeed, extend longevity. For example, Steven Blair studied 13,000 men and women for an eight-year period and found that inactivity is related to the likelihood of dying. Inactive men were almost 3.4 times more likely to die during the eight-year period than active men; inactive women were 4.6 times more likely to die. Subjects were classified by treadmill tests according to their level of fitness. Those physically unfit were at greater risk for all causes of mortality, but especially for heart disease and cancer, which accounted for the majority of the excess deaths. Only smoking seemed to have a greater effect than being physically unfit.

In another study, the physical activity and other life-style characteristics of 16,936 Harvard alumni, aged 35 to 74, were examined (Paffenbarger, Hyde, & Wing, 1986). Exercise was measured as amount of walking, stair climbing, and sports play. Of that number, 1413 died during the years from 1962 to 1978. An inverse relationship was found between amount of exercise and mortality, which was primarily death from cardiovascular or respiratory causes. That is, the greater the amount of exercise reported by these alumni, the longer was their life. More specifically, as the amount of energy expended on exercise increased from about 500 to 3500 calories per week, death rates steadily declined.

Earlier studies for this population had shown that the risk of coronary heart disease was affected significantly by histories of hypertension, cigarette smoking, overweight, and habitual physical inactivity. By taking the factors of hypertension, cigarette smoking, extremes or gains in body weight, or early parental death into account and removing their effects from the data, alumni mortality rates were still significantly lower among those who had been physically active. The highest death rates were for individuals who both smoked cigarettes and had hypertension. By the age of 80 years, adequate exercise seems to have extended life by from one to more than two years. Indeed, the thesis was confirmed that exercise does in fact add extra years to life. However, although these two studies were well conducted, they were not experiments.

Research using large populations of people indicates that exercise increases longevity.

Another possible limitation is that Harvard alumni may not be typical of the general population. In 1980 their death rate was about half the rate of white males in the United States, with suicide excepted. (These Harvard alumni had a 50 percent higher suicide rate than did the general population.)

Nevertheless these data are among the soundest that are available. Rosenbaum and Barr (1986), noting a fitness boom in some 24 million people, surveyed nurses engaged in aerobic dance. They concluded that aerobics increases vital capacity (ability of the lungs to take in oxygen and expel waste carbon dioxide) and decreases residual volume (amount of air remaining in the lungs at the end of maximum breathing out—such stale air may increase lung disease). Decreased residual volume indicates how stiff the chest wall is versus how elastic is the lung. Other findings were that there was a strengthening of chest muscles due to heavy breathing; resting respiration rate increased, as did mucus flow, which washes the lung surfaces making the exchange of oxygen and carbon dioxide more efficient; triglycerides and **LDL (low-density lipids,** "bad cholesterol") decreased; **HDL (high-density lipids,** "good cholesterol") increased; female hormone metabolism improved, which, in turn, causes recalcification of bone, making the bones more elastic; and there was a 30 percent increase in sexual activity, perhaps because of better blood circulation in nipples and genital erectile tissue, and of hormone regulation.

Survey findings indicate that aerobic exercise increases vital capacity, decreases residual lung volume, promotes favorable changes in blood lipid levels, improves female hormone metabolism, and increases sexual activity.

Although research does not allow us to unambiguously assert that physical fitness prolongs life, it is a good bet that there *is* a causal relation here. It probably is to our advantage to behave as if regular exercise does help us to live longer.

In Summary.   While we must settle, for now, for data gathered with nonexperimental methods, what data we do have strongly indicate that exercise is generally beneficial and that it prolongs life in the ways we have indicated.

Good Nutrition.   Good nutrition probably helps to retard the aging process by reducing the incidence of age-associated degenerative diseases. An individual who reduces intake of total calories of fat and uses **polyunsaturated fats** (which tend to increase high-density lipoproteins, HDL) helps to prevent circulatory problems due to the accumulation of cholesterol plaque within the blood vessels.

One aspect of good nutrition is reduced food intake. Some years ago the pathologist Roy Walford showed that he could increase the life span of rats and primates by restricting their food intake. A hypothesis was that one of the "Methuselah" genes (genes that help to prolong life) functions in the same way as does the process of caloric restriction. The relevant Methuselah gene provides a blueprint for an enzyme that destroys highly reactive molecules called free radicals. Free radicals form naturally in the body and are thought to break down normal cells and thus speed the aging process. Radicals are formed when food is digested so that by restricting food intake, one should be able to prolong life.

Research indicates that genetic engineering and other biological methods for destroying free radicals generated by food intake can increase life span.

Other research has been consistent with the conclusion that by breaking down age-inducing free radicals, life span can be increased. By restricting the amount of food that fruit flies eat, it was found that not only were their life spans extended, but they had an unusually high concentrate of an enzyme called superoxide dismutase (SOD). (SOD is an enzyme that breaks down free radicals and comes from one of the Methuselah genes.) Working along the same lines, the molecular biologist James E. Fleming applied genetic engineering methods to insert extra copies of the gene for SOD into the embryos of fruit flies and found that the fruit flies increased their life span by about 80 percent.

Controlling the Stresses of Life

Excessive Stress Kills.   The stressors of everyday living may kill us suddenly or slowly. The most dramatic and devastating instances are those of sudden cardiac arrest, which is the leading cause of death in industrially developed countries. In the United States, sudden cardiac arrest causes 1200 deaths daily, about one death per minute. About one-fourth of those who die suddenly have had no previous symptoms of heart disease. The median age of sudden cardiac death in men is about 59 years. The failure to effectively cope with the stresses of life can produce any of a wide variety of other bodily disorders as well, as we will see shortly.

Stressors come from a variety of sources, such as when an ill-prepared student takes a test or receives a low grade or a person is fired from a job and/or is involved in an argument. Furthermore, stressors are often unique to a person so that what is stressful for one person may not be stressful for another. Nevertheless, no one is immune to some life stress.

The problem of how to react sensibly to the stresses of life is not a new one. Although earlier and simpler cultures apparently were less tense, their stresses were more concrete and immediate and were quickly resolved. Even animals in their native environments exhibit excessive tension, as shown by their sometimes agitated and even neurotic behaviors (recall from Chapter 10 Gantt's neurotic dog Nick). Yet stress–tension levels in contemporary life set an all-time record.

As a result of failing to cope with stressors, we develop a wide variety of pathological behaviors and disorders, as we discuss in Chapter 14. This happens because when one faces a stressful situation, the muscles of the body immediately tense. If that tension becomes chronic and is carried around 24 hours a day, the other systems of the body are overtaxed. It is a sound principle in the field of clinical relaxation that a chronically overtense body will eventually experience a breakdown in some system, be it cardiovascular, gastrointestinal, or cognitive.

We Exercise Self-Control with Our Skeletal Muscles. To deal with stress, one should properly relax the body when stress strikes. The most effective way to achieve that desired state of bodily tranquility is Edmund Jacobson's (1938b) method of progressive relaxation. Jacobson's clinical observations over seven decades suggested to him that those of his patients who learned to relax may well have added 20 years to their lives. His clinical observations make good physiological sense in that there is a dramatic slowdown of many critical functions in a relaxed body. Instead of a racing heart and rapid, erratic breathing, one competent in relaxation may normally breathe at a rate of 8 respirations per minute and have a pulse rate of 40 per minute. During a state of total relaxation, all cognitive processes are reported to cease.

As encouraging as Jacobson's clinical observations are, only sound experimental data would definitively tell us if relaxation prolongs life. Difficult as it might be to obtain, a longitudinal study in which psychophysiological profiles of the aging process are measured over a number of years would answer the question and be a gold mine for the advancement of gerontology.

We can never escape from stressors and some amount of stress is critical for productive living. We need challenges to be productive. But in meeting stress, we should learn to control our bodies for optimal performance. The goal is to learn when to behave vigorously, when to relax our bodies, and when not to be emotional. Some situations call for vigorous behavior, others for relaxed reactions. Such self-control comes with the wise use of our voluntary muscles, which once again involves using feedback from neuromuscular circuits.

Conclusion

In short, by learning to use our muscles to relax and control our bodies appropriately for the situation, by following exercise programs to maintain physical fitness, and by

Everyone experiences stress, which, if ineffectively coped with, can result in pathological behaviors that can reduce the quality and length of life.

By learning how to relax one's muscles when excessive stress strikes, one can maintain the body's serenity and avoid damaging it.

Through the method of progressive relaxation, we can learn to control the systems of our bodies so as to rationally regulate ourselves to adjust to the situations in life that we meet.

incorporating other self-control procedures such as maintaining a proper nutritional diet, we should be able to live longer with qualitatively better lives.

Yet, research findings presented in this chapter emphasize that we have much to learn. The extensive and intricate changes that occur throughout the body, especially in the cardiovascular, muscular, visceral, and central nervous systems need to be better understood. As we saw early in this chapter, this research requirement is especially pressing from a practical point of view because of the great increase in the number of the elderly and in their needs. Through preventive medicine, especially behavioral medicine, we can expect further progress in retarding primary aging processes and in alleviating or preventing secondary aging processes. But in the meantime, what can be done for those already afflicted with the ravages of advanced age?

TREATMENT OF THE ENFEEBLED ELDERLY

The elderly who have developed pathological conditions present special problems. (Alzheimer's disease, which we discuss shortly, deserves special attention.) The data indicate that two approaches can be applied.

1. *Pharmacologic therapies intervene with medication.* There is some evidence that effective chemicals can help to treat the pathogenesis of aging. Some research indicates that administration of testosterone to elderly men increases muscular strength. Chemicals have been studied to attempt to restore youthful characteristics in older mice; for example, the administration of L-Dopa in rats beginning at 8 weeks of age increased their average survival rate and maintained spontaneous motor activity as they aged. We must be careful here, though, and recall that drugs act differently in the aged than in younger people, and the aged may be more susceptible to false or misleading advertising claims.

2. *Behavioral retraining techniques may help the elderly to compensate for reduction of some abilities.* Thus, one may develop new strategies for dealing with situations in which effectiveness of performance has decreased. One may learn to avoid situations that now cause dangers. Or one may pay increased attention to certain stimuli to which they previously responded automatically. For instance, as peripheral vision decreases with age, an elderly person may learn to move the head to a greater extent to better perceive what is in the peripheral field of vision.

ALZHEIMER'S DISEASE

Extent of the Illness.   In 1907, the German neurologist Alois Alzheimer described this disease, although its major characteristics traditionally constituted senile dementia. **Alzheimer's disease** is the most common cause of increasing decline of mental abilities in the elderly. It mainly afflicts people in their forties or fifties. Estimates are that from 750,000 to perhaps 3 million Americans are afflicted with Alzheimer's with perhaps 100,000 dying from it each year.

Symptoms and Signs.   Memory loss is usually the first difficulty experienced. An inability to remember names of close relatives and friends occurs first, followed by deterioration of language and visual–spatial skills. Motor and reflex functions, sensory perception, muscle strength, and consciousness remain relatively intact. Late in the disease, language disturbances progress to aphasia and often to mutism with the patients becoming increasingly unaware of their surroundings. Eventually they become incontinent of urine, which progresses to fecal incontinence. In the final stage, speech consists of but several words and often dwindles to one word repeated in response to all questions. Finally, the one word is lost; then there is a loss of ability to walk, followed by the loss of ability to sit up. The last response to go is the ability to smile.

A patient can retain eyesight but still not visually perceive because of an inability to interpret retinal images. Perhaps perception is precluded because of neural degeneration.

An autopsy has been required for a definitive diagnosis of Alzheimer's. Microscopic examination of brain tissue can reveal pathological changes such as neuritic plaques and neuronal tangles in the hippocampus and the cerebral cortex. However, PET scans are now successful in diagnosing Alzheimer's by establishing decrements of cerebral blood flow and oxygen and glucose metabolism in the parietal and temporal lobes. The association cortex, limbic structures, and some subcortical nuclei are most severely involved with relative sparing of the primary sensory and motor areas along with the brain stem and cerebellum. The earliest stages are in the parietal cortex bilaterally 13 months before clinical diagnosis of probable Alzheimer's.

In Alzheimer's, there is a decrease in neural transmission in cholinergic pathways in the cortex.

Research on Alzheimer's. Research was rare until the mid-1960s when it was found that choline acetyltransferase (ChAT), the enzyme that synthesizes acetylcholine (ACh) in cholinergic pathways, is markedly diminished in the cerebral cortex of patients with Alzheimer's. Perhaps, it was reasoned, ChAT deficiency could explain the cognitive deficits so that cholinergic therapy might be effective. However, such therapy has not yet been successful.

A major characteristic of Alzheimer's is that 60–70 percent of acetylcholinesterase (the enzyme that acts on ACh) and ChAT is depleted in the limbic system and in the cortex; in contrast there is no such depletion in the striatum and the thalamus. Such depletion can be detected as early as one year after onset of the disease.

A related finding is that cells that produce ACh are destroyed in patients, so that ACh levels are low. Consequently, one therapy has been to replace or protect ACh in the brain. The analogy is with treatment for Parkinson's patients wherein L-Dopa is a substitute for a low supply of dopamine. However, the replacement experiments have not been successful, which may be because more than one chemical transmitter is lost in Alzheimer's; that is, other cortical transmitters such as serotonin, norepinephrine, dopamine, and somatostatin are also depleted in some patients. Even if decreased cholinergic function is not the prime cause, it probably contributes substantially to memory and learning deficits.

Apparently acetylcholine is deficient in the brain of Alzheimer's patients, although there are also shortages of other neurotransmitters.

Critical cortical–cortical connections apparently are lost, perhaps because of the loss of the neurotransmitters. Loss of these connections is another theory that opposes the cholinergic-deficit theory. Thus, the chemical losses would be secondary to the neural connection losses. If the connection theory is true, therapy would try to prevent the neural connections from being destroyed.

The sizable amount of research on Alzheimer's has increased our understanding of the gradual decline of memory in normal aging processes. The age-related decline in memory in rats has been reversed by means of cholinergic therapy. Perhaps memory loss of aging reflects a gradual decrease of cholinergic transmission. If so, this may be prevented or reversed by the appropriate drug therapy, which would be a substantial accomplishment.

There may be a genetic predisposition toward Alzheimer's in a relatively few cases. For instance, in some families covering five generations, dementias of the Alzheimer's type have been found. However, most cases are of unknown and probably diverse causes.

FALLS

Falls are the second leading cause of accidental death in the United States after those due to motor vehicle accidents. Among the elderly, falls rank first. About 6300 people annually die in falls at home in the United States, about one-half of all home-related deaths. Of these, some 4900 are 65 years or older. Falls account for two-thirds of deaths at home among people age 75 and older. Elderly people have health problems that increase their likelihood of falling, and they are also more susceptible to severe injuries such as hip fractures because their bones are often weakened by osteoporosis.

Physical, psychological, and environmental factors all increase the chances of falling. As vision becomes impaired, and if areas are not well lighted, the elderly may fail to see obstacles or steps in time. The elderly are also more sensitive to the disorienting effects of alcohol. As one ages, gait and balance deteriorate. Because blood pressure to the head does not rise fast enough, they are more likely to get dizzy when standing up after they have been lying down or bending over. Patients who are receiving drug therapy for high blood pressure, tranquilizers, antidepressants and antianxiety drugs are often similarly victimized by dizziness and falling.

To prevent or diminish the chances of falling, everyone, but especially the elderly, should look at his or her feet and hold on to a handrail on stairs. Dangerous obstacles in the living environment should be removed, including uneven floors and steps, slippery floors or rugs, unexpected door thresholds, obtrusive furniture, and wires.

THEORIES OF AGING

The Additive Insult Theory. This theory holds that you get old because errors and damages accumulate in the body over time. For example, oxidation accumulates molecules that cannot be broken down; or aged pigment cells in the skin accumulate to interfere with the effective functioning of other cells.

The Aging Gene Theory. This theory holds that a code is built into our genes that dictates that a cell dies after it divides a certain coded number of times (perhaps 50). The process of aging is thus genetically programmed in all of us. With considerable individual variability, genetic programs determine that some organs and systems progressively deteriorate more than others. With such deterioration, we reduce our ability to withstand threats from our environment. In a sense, the body self-destructs because its components can no longer reproduce and replenish themselves.

Immune System Degeneration. One of the most vulnerable physiological changes in our bodies occurs in the immune system. One theory holds that the immune system degenerates, resulting in diseases of aging such as arthritis. In all mammals that have been studied, including humans, immunologic functions decrease in effectiveness with age. The elderly become increasingly susceptible to infections. The result is physical degeneration over time. The aging changes include loss of cells, changes in the proportion of kinds of cells, and changes in quality of cells. Two types of cells are called helper and suppressor cells, which activate and suppress our immune system in response to infection. As we age, the helper cells no longer are as dynamic in response to infections. Researchers have apparently isolated chemicals that the helper cells normally secrete to activate immune reactions. When these chemicals were administered to old mice who had been exposed to infectious agents, the chemicals brought the immune system back toward normalcy. The long-range hope is that a way can be discovered to keep the immune system dynamically responsive to infections, and degenerative diseases can be held in check so that we can live a higher quality of life for a longer period of time.

As we age, our immune system becomes increasingly unresponsive to infections and makes us increasingly vulnerable to diseases.

EMPHASIS ON A CYBERNETIC PRINCIPLE— A BENEFICIAL NEGATIVE FEEDBACK SYSTEM IN AGING

Why Do People Want to Avoid Growing Old? The answer generally is that being old implies being feeble and a deterioration in the quality of life. Aging typically restricts the number and frequency of activities in which one can engage and thus the reinforcements available. Even though a person can play tennis at 80, he or she cannot play the same as at age 20; nor can such a person engage in contact sports such as football. Nevertheless, the elderly who are healthy enjoy many aspects of their lives. The robust octogenerian Horsley Gantt said that he "could do everything that he ever did in life but not quite so much." In contrast the enfeebled person finds few reinforcements in day-to-day living. In fact, reinforcing enjoyments frequently become so rare that the enfeebled person just gives up. Finally some refuse to eat, eventually resemble inmates of Nazi concentration camps, and die.

What distinguishes these two kinds of elderly? No doubt, genetic inheritance and environmental influences both play great roles. Nevertheless, as we develop in Chapter 15, we need not be total victims either. Through wise techniques of self-control and self-management, we can impede or prevent falling prey to destructive environmental influences and pathological genetic predispositions. Through such biobehavioral engineering, a person can often maintain a high quality of life until close to death — as we age, we often can effectively maintain reinforcements that are important to us. By retarding primary aging processes and preventing secondary aging processes, we can enhance the ability to enjoy life. The result is that the enjoyments of life beneficially affect our health and the maintenance of good health allows us to continue enjoying life. Indeed, we have another general application of a negative feedback system in which stable, peaceful aging can be achieved and maintained.

In many ways we can adjust to and avoid the stresses of life. By exercising wise self-management procedures, we can enhance the reinforcements of everyday living.

A negative feedback system can function between good health and enjoyment of life for the mutual benefit of each condition resulting in a better quality of aging.

KEY TERMS

Alzheimer's disease—A form of premature senility marked by memory loss resulting from brain deterioration.

Atrophy—A wasting away, such as may occur in paralyzed muscles.

Biological (functional) age—A measure of the effectiveness of the body that does not necessarily correspond to chronological age.

Chronological age—The age in years and months of an individual.

Explication—Replacement of an ambiguous concept, one that usually comes from everyday language, with a systematically analyzed objective set of measurements.

Forced vital capacity—The maximum amount of air that can be forced out of the lungs; decreases with age probably because the alveoli (air sacs in the lungs) become less effective in exchanging gases out of the bloodstream.

Gerontology—The science that studies the aging process, including the problems of the aged.

HDL (high-density lipids)—Fatlike substances of high density ("good" cholesterol).

Intentional recollection—Trying to recall a person's name; declines with age.

LDL (low-density lipids)—Fatlike substances of low density leading to buildup of placque in blood vessels ("bad" cholesterol).

Life span development—A field of study of life processes from conception to death; has largely replaced terms such as "child psychology" and "developmental psychology."

Maximum oxygen uptake—The amount of oxygen that one can breathe in at any given time; a measure of cardiovascular function.

Menopause—The period of life in a woman around 50 years of age at which menstruation ceases and there are complex hormonal changes.

"Normal" aging—Aging free of the pathological disorders of secondary aging processes.

Osteoporosis—Disorder of the skeletal system, which becomes increasing fragile due to loss of calcium, often resulting in "dowager's hump."

Parkinson's disease—A neurological disorder characterized by rigidity, tremor, and difficulty in controlling movements believed to be caused by a dopamine deficiency in the nigrostriatal fibers.

Polyunsaturated fats—Fats that help to increase HDL.

Presbycusis—Loss of ability to perceive or discriminate sounds; part of the aging process.

Presbystasia—Decrease in ability to maintain equilibrium that may occur because of a decline in the functioning in the vestibular mechanism and/or peripheral nerve loss, along with atrophy of the muscles.

Primary aging processes—Normal physiological and anatomical changes in human bodies due to aging.

Psychomotor test—Psychological functions are measured by means of motor activities such as making discriminations and then responding in some way.

Reaction time—Measurement from onset of a stimulus, such as the flashing of a light, to the onset of a response, such as pressing a button as quickly as possible.

Secondary aging processes—Pathological conditions that facilitate aging.

Senile dementia—A gradual deterioration in intellectual, judgmental, and particularly memory processes, found in some elderly individuals (see Alzheimer's disease).

Senile muscular atrophy—Degeneration of the musculature due to a decrease in muscle quantity.

Unintentional memory—Spontaneous memory in which the name of an item "just pops into one's head" for no apparent reason. This type of memory does not decline with age.

STUDY QUESTIONS

1. Discuss the prime goal of gerontology.
2. Why do muscles decrease in size with aging?
3. Distinguish between chronological and biological age.
4. List some functions normally preserved by those individuals who have

remained youthful despite advanced chronological age.

5. Is there any correlation between degree of cardiovascular disease and poor psychomotor performance?

6. Summarize some of the findings on the effects of exercise on the body.
7. Discuss stress management.
8. Give an overview of theories of aging.

FURTHER READINGS

This book describes the demographics of the aging population, presents important findings in the study of aging, and outlines contemporary issues in the aging society:

Belsky, J. K. (1990). *The psychology of aging: Theory, research, and interventions* (2nd ed.). Pacific Grove, CA: Brooks/Cole.

This book presents personal narratives about the aging process that maintain interest, and it has a rich reference list:

Sherman, E. (1991). *Reminiscence and the self in old age.* New York: Springer.

This book provides a compendium of information about these topics:

Light, L. L., & Burke, D. M. (1988). *Language, memory, and aging.* New York: Cambridge University Press.

CHAPTER 13

Cognitive Psychophysiology

The Biology
of Higher Mental Processes

MAJOR PURPOSE:	To understand the nature of "mind" through a biological explication
WHAT YOU ARE GOING TO FIND:	1. The commonsense concept that mental events (cognitions) are physical processes that originated as overt behaviors
	2. Illustrations of psychophysiological measurements of cognitive activities presumed to be components of cybernetic circuits that generate mental events
	3. Psychophysiological events recorded during various "mental processes" are similar; they have different names only because they occur under varied environmental and organismic conditions
	4. A discussion of cognition throughout the higher levels of the phylogenetic scale
WHAT YOU SHOULD ACQUIRE:	An understanding that mental events (cognitions) are generated through the selective interaction of cybernetic circuits composed of central and peripheral structures

CHAPTER OUTLINE

MIND AND COGNITION

Are There Real Mental Processes?

Mental Events Are Materialistic Phenomena. Psychology has traditionally sought to understand the concept of *mind*. It is usually thought of as having both functions and contents. Its functions include the ability to program one's own behavior. **Mental events** are the contents, the phenomena referred to when people tell us that they have "immediate experience," that they are "aware and conscious" or that they are "thinking." Mentalistic (cognitive) terms like these have been inherited by contemporary psychology from the first scientific psychologists, such as the father of psychology Wilhelm Wundt. Professor Wundt (pronounced "Voont"), in turn, had inherited such mentalistic terms from philosophers and from the vernacular. Wundt and his colleagues attempted to study consciousness by directly observing its contents (introspecting on them) as immaterial (nonphysical) phenomena. Although Wundt thereby started psychology as a science, his dualistic approach was doomed to fail, as we saw in Chapter 3.

The original and continuing problem of psychology is to understand mental phenomena that constitute the nature of mind.

Nevertheless, no one can deny the subjective experiences that we verbally describe as conscious awareness. As Lashley said, if we deny that there is a consciousness, we at least have to explain why we have an *illusion* that there is a consciousness.

We assume that mental phenomena do have a real, physicalistic existence, that they are not illusions. But then we must establish a scientific status for mentalistic notions so that we can objectively study them.

What Is Cognition?

Much of Cognitive Psychology Is Only "Old Wine in New Bottles." Today psychologists often speak of **cognitions** rather than mental events. The contemporary use of the term *cognition* stems primarily from the research of Edward Chase Tolman, who behaviorally studied cognitive processes in rats. The research of Tolman and his colleagues and students led to the development of such concepts as **cognitive maps.** The model is that organisms learn *what leads to what.* For instance, when you are driving to school, you specify your goal, but you may take any of several routes. Your driving would not be merely a matter of mechanically turning left or right at various choice points along one specific route. Rather, it is one of purposively getting from home to school regardless of the route. Research since Tolman's day has built on the cognitive model. It has been applied to many phenomena, such as explaining conditioning. Unfortunately, though, in psychology today, the term *cognition* has become vastly overused so that because it means so many things, it means nothing unique. We can use words such as *mental* for cognition without losing any information.

The term cognition *is essentially the same as* mental event, *although it is often used in an information processing context.*

It has been said that the more things change, the more they remain the same. If you compared the topics in the classic book *Experimental Psychology* by Robert Woodworth (1938) with those of a more recent popular book entitled *Cognition,* you would find them essentially the same. There are chapters in both books on perception (including sensation and attention), memory, concepts, learning, language, problem solving, imagery, reasoning, decision making, and individual differences. In short, what we call "cognitive psychology" is largely old wine in new bottles, dressed up with terms from computer science, information processing, and so on. But there is a difference in that some cognitive psychologists espouse a dualistic approach. For instance, B. F. Skinner held that cognitive psychologists study overt behavior and imagine nonphysiological cognitive processes that could account for and cause behavior. However, there is nothing inside the behaving organism but the organism itself—cognitive psychologists look in the wrong place in the wrong way. There is nothing to the mind but what is under the skin of the organism.

Difficulties in Studying Cognitions

The First Problem. Cognitive (mentalistic) terms such as *ideas, images, thoughts, dreams, hallucinations, fears, depression,* and *anxiety* are so vaguely defined in everyday usage that it is hard to know even how to start to analyze them. But that problem is not a new one. In science we often take such commonsense notions as our starting point and through the process of **explication** (a term used by the eminent philosopher Rudolf Carnap) replace the ill-defined, vague terms with relatively precise statements.

The Second Problem. Mentalistic terms generally refer to as **private events,** events that are not observed by others. *A prime requirement of science is that the phenomena studied are objectively observable.* This means that more than one person can observe an event so that they can agree *that* it actually occurred as well as about its characteristics. We can agree that a particular object is a tree, and even that it is a pine, which we do not do for a pain in the stomach that a person says s/he feels. What we do about private events is verbally report on them, as when you tell your physician "it hurts here." When we have an experience that we call consciousness about something (like a pain or a thought), we can at least tell others about it. We can, then, talk about many private (internal) events just as we can about external (public) ones. *The difference between private and public events is that others do not observe private ones.* Is there a strategy for others to directly observe mental events, a way of making private events public?

Cognitions Originated in Behavior

To approach the problems of the nature of mental processes, let us ask how the notion of such states of mind arose in the first place. Professor Skinner held that the concept of mind arose through behaviors, responses to things. Words that refer to states of mind (cognitive processes) originally referred to overt behaviors (or to the environmental settings that stimulated the behavior).

Skinner, like Watson, held that thinking is simply behavior, that "mind" only means "do." Although thought may be verbal or nonverbal, covert or overt, it is not some mysterious process responsible for behavior. Rather, thought is behavior itself together with the physiological events that generate it. In a similar vein, Charles Osgood (1957) held that words represent things because they produce in people some replica of the actual behavior toward the things. The word *baseball* for instance evokes covert responses in the throwing arm and **mediational processes** (his r_M which he held was in the brain). Osgood and others, such as Jerome Bruner and Hans Werner, have thought that the immature language user makes overt responses that result in the cognitive "meaning" of words. The meaning of the word *eating* originates in the responses that one makes while ingesting food, just as the meaning of "two" to the two-year-old originates in the overt response of holding up two fingers. As learning progresses, the overt response becomes abbreviated in the mature language user and becomes a covert representation of meaning (Osgood's r_M). That is, as in Figure 13.1, the total overt response (R_T) becomes r_M, a representa-

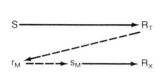

FIGURE 13.1
Overt behavior (R_T) to things
(S) results in covert meaning
reactions (r_M). The meaning
reaction then produces
stimulation (s_M) that can evoke
other overt behavior (R_x).
(Modified from Charles
Osgood's theory)

tion that means R_T. A series of studies was conducted by Osgood and McGuigan to determine if r_M was totally a brain event or whether it also had muscular components (cf. McGuigan, 1978, pp. 194–201). One finding was that there was significantly elevated tongue EMG when subjects became aware of meanings of words, suggesting that r_M had muscle components.

The word *experience* is an example of a mental term that originally referred to public behavioral events that one had undergone. *Experience* thus used to refer to overt acts of *doing* something, which constituted public behavior that others could witness and then even engage in themselves (e.g., they could behaviorally learn ice skating by watching and mimicking others). Such observational learning led them to "mentally" (covertly) experience the event they witnessed. Gradually, words that once labeled behaviors evolved into references to "mind" and its functions. For example, in the nineteenth century the word *experience* changed from witnessing behaviors to a description of what was felt or introspectively observed.

This reasoning as to the origin of mentalistic words is consonant with how children originally learn the proper use of a word. The teacher (father, mother, etc.) and pupil define words by means of **ostensive definitions,** wherein they behaviorally point to events and objects and attach terms to them. For example, we learn that the object to which we are pointing is a table and we agree to use that term in common. Dogs in the home easily pick up this learning process too. At rock bottom, all scientific definitions are ostensive definitions.

An ostensive definition is one by which we point to objects or events and agree on the use of a specific term applied to them.

Learning to Name Mental Phenomena

Through ostensive definitions, we also learn to name various internal events with mentalistic terms. As Keller and Schoenfeld (1950) point out, this happens when other people tell us what we are doing. A boy who is trying to solve a problem may be told by his parents that he is thinking. He then learns to attach the label "thinking" to that state of his body, one in which he senses covertly the activity of muscles, just as we can tell that our bodies are tense. In a similar way we learn to attach names to other conditions of the body such as when we are sad and crying. What apparently happens is that the muscular events generate afferent neural impulses (the Muscle Sense of Bell) that are uniquely coded and become symbols for the word spoken to name our state—we generate stimuli that come to stand for mentalistic words; we have seen this process at work in such conditioning studies as those of Hefferline (see p. 422). We thus directly, internally, sense and label what is happening in our muscles when we are thinking, crying, imagining, and so on. A person who learns that he or she is "thinking" thus does not have immaterial ghostly thoughts. Rather,

We internally observe the neuromuscular activity generated when muscles contract. Those events are coded for words naming various internal conditions. We then interpret the codes and can report that we are in a specific state, such as thinking or depression.

there are measurable events in the speech muscles, the brain, the eyes, and indeed throughout the body.

In Review. The meanings of words originate in children as overt behaviors, but through learning and use those behaviors become abbreviated as covert events. Although no longer overt, the responses still remain as covert physicalistic processes within the adult who names specific ones with mentalistic terms.

Measuring Mind

What happens within our bodies when we experience conscious mental events has a physical reality that can be objectively measured.

Mental events are covert processes that are the contents of the mind. They are psychophysiologically measurable as components of cybernetic circuits.

Given that we have learned to name various internal conditions as specific mental states, as scientists we can measure each of them using psychophysiological parameters. Our strategy for studying the mental processes that are the contents of mind is to measure those responses and neurophysiological events that occur when we have the subjective experiences referred to as "thinking," "imagining," and "dreaming." Such mental phenomena mainly refer to covert events because they typically occur when people are silent and not overtly behaving. Sometimes, though, mental events are overt as when we "think out loud."

Our position of materialistic monism, that mental events are actual, physicalistic phenomena, leads us to use the empirical electropsychological methods for measuring covert processes presented in Chapter 8. With this approach we seek to explicate commonsense cognitive terms. To illustrate, we have sizably advanced our understanding of nocturnal dreams through the scientific study of psychophysiological variables (e.g., dreams include sequences of patterns of EEG reactions, covert speech responses, covert eye responses, and contractions of the colon). When these bodily events interact through circuits, they generate the subjective experiences that we have learned to call "dreams." By observing rapid eye movements, we can objectively tell when a person is dreaming and, if awakened, the individual can verbally report on the dream content. We are thus able to furnish sound information about dreams and to some extent even ascertain dream content from psychophysiological measures. Science thus benefits from dispelling such old myths as that dreams occur in the flash of a second. The scientific study of dreams has also helped in understanding sleep disorders and has led to therapeutic interventions (Chapter 14).

In Review. Mental processes (like dreams) are generated by sequences of bodily events within cybernetic circuits that occur under specifiable external and internal conditions and *nothing more.* In principle, once we have measured *all* of those bodily events, we have completely specified the mental processes in question. That would constitute a scientific explication of the contents of mind.

Consciousness and Unconsciousness

We can name some internal events, but not others. By our model, this ability to name what is happening within us occurs because the speech system is a component of the interacting circuits. That is, when circuits involving the speech musculature and the linguistic regions of the brain and body are activated, the individual can become aware (conscious) of the psychophysiological events that are components of mental activities (see Fig. 13.2). One may then verbally report on the thoughts generated by neuromuscular circuits if asked, "What is on your mind?" If, though, the individual

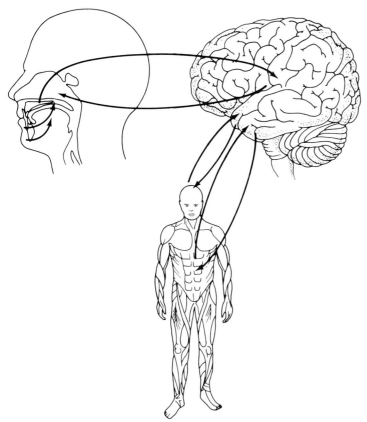

FIGURE 13.2 When the neuromuscular circuits that reverberate to generate cognitive events include the speech musculature, the person can orally report on those events; that ability can make the cognitions conscious.

cannot name (is not aware or conscious of) certain internal activities, there may only be nonspeech information processing. Without interaction with speech circuits, these nonlinguistic events cannot be reported (Fig. 13.3). This line of reasoning is consonant with that of traditional behavioristic approaches to consciousness and unconsciousness. Thus, internal events that a person is able to name are conscious events while those on which he or she cannot report are unconscious events. Skinner adds, however, that "all behavior, human and non-human, is unconscious; it becomes 'conscious' when . . ." there is occasion for one to engage in self-observation (1989, p. 63).

Conscious bodily events are those that can be talked about because the circuits that generate them include the speech system; we have no verbal labels for unconscious events because the circuits that generate them do not include the speech system.

Functions of Mind

In our efforts to explicate "mind," we have concentrated so far on mental events that constitute its content. In addition, many abilities and powers have been ascribed to mind as a causative agent. Following our materialistic approach we of course dismiss nonphysicalistic conceptions such as those espoused by some cognitive psychologists and physiologists. As Skinner has said, there is nothing to the mind but what is

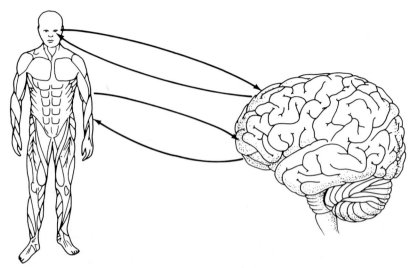

FIGURE 13.3   In contrast to circuits in Figure 13.2, when the speech musculature is not involved in the generation of cognitive events, the person is unable to report on them. Consequently, they are unconscious cognitions.

Our model holds that humans have the ability to control much of their behavior by the judicious use of selected neuromuscular circuits.

The human mind is the functioning of interacting bodily systems that program behavior and generate mental events.

under the skin of the organism. Our search is for how the organism controls its body in terms of cybernetic principles. More particularly, it is the striated muscle components of neuromuscular circuits, especially the speech and eye muscles, that are the main instruments of self-control. Through self-instruction by means of the speech musculature and visualization processes using the eye muscles, we can guide much of our behavior. Our explication of the functions of mind then starts with the following definition: The human **mind** is the functioning of the interacting systems of the body. As those systems selectively interact, they program both overt and covert behavior. Principal programming is carried out by the circuits that include the eye and speech musculature. As they reverberate, the mental events on which we may behaviorally report are generated.

We have developed a theoretical basis for the important concept of self-control on pp. 504–506; furthermore, because of the technological importance of self-management procedures, we devote much of Chapter 15 to control of behavior.

ILLUSTRATIVE PSYCHOPHYSIOLOGICAL EVENTS DURING SOME COGNITIVE ACTIVITIES

Following a cybernetic model we will sample psychophysiological data obtained when individuals were engaged in various mental processes. Covert responses are especially prominent components of cybernetic circuits as they are electromyographically measured. Although it is critical to understand the nature of the brain components of these circuits, their complexity precludes a detailed presentation at this stage of neurophysiological research.

Thinking

Mental Activity Engages the Striated Musculature.   Terms such as *thinking, reasoning,* and *imagination* are applied to such activities as problem solving, combining old experiences in new ways, and being free of controlling external stimuli, respectively. When people were instructed to silently engage in a number of such activities, they emitted covert speech behaviors of the tongue and lips, as electromyographically measured (McGuigan, 1978).

Covert Speech and Muscle Behavior.   In a thinking task (one technically called a **verbal mediation paradigm**), the tongue was especially active. When subjects solved a nonverbal mediation task, the arms and eyes were covertly active, possibly for nonverbal mediational thought (Fig. 13.4). Similar results have been obtained in many other tasks in which the subjects were engaged in thought.

Covert Language Behavior in the Deaf.   Whereas the speech muscles are active during thoughts of individuals who speak, many deaf people who cannot speak communicate with sign language using their fingers. Consequently, as shown in Figure 13.5, the dorsal arm muscles, which control the fingers, are especially active

FIGURE 13.4   Relatively heightened tongue electromyograms (EMG) were recorded during verbal mediational thought. Relatively heightened arm (and also eye, not shown) activity were recorded during nonverbal mediational thought. Both tongue and arm EMGs for the verbal and nonverbal tasks were of significantly greater amplitude than during a control condition. (From McGuigan, Culver, & Kendler, 1971)

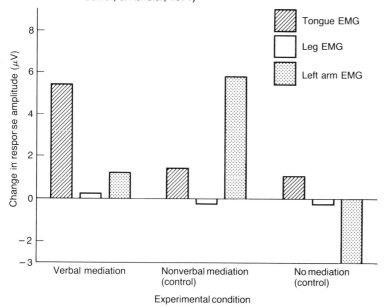

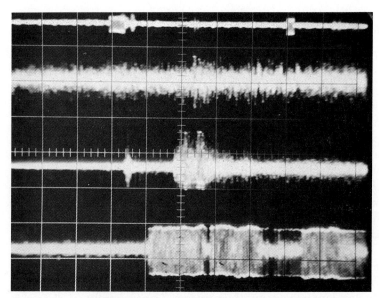

FIGURE 13.5 The first event in the top trace indicates presentation of a problem and the second is the subject's report that it was solved. Deaf children who engaged in problem solving manifested increased EMG in the left and right arms (bottom two traces respectively).

Hearing individuals engage their speech musculature while thinking. However, deaf children who communicate with sign language covertly activate their fingers when they think.

when deaf children solve problems (McGuigan, 1971). The speech musculature of deaf children is not covertly active, unless they are capable of oral speech.

Another fruitful area of research has been the psychophysiological study of silent reading. When we read, we think about the words that we are processing. The understanding of how we perceive speech will help us to also understand how we comprehend during silent reading because reading apparently depends on the perception of speech. However, we should note that the relationship between speech perception and reading is debated by linguists, psychologists, and others.

Speech Perception

One line of reasoning compatible with our cybernetic model is that because speech perception and speech production are learned together, they are one and the same phenomenon. For instance, the eminent linguist C. Cherry said that the representations of speech sounds that we carry in our heads are likely to be formed of data based on speech muscle configurations and other physiological speech events. Thus, "when we listen to someone speaking, we are also preparing to move our own vocal organs in sympathy . . . our imitative instincts of childhood never leave us" (Cherry, 1957, p. 293). Lashley (1960) agreed by holding that "the understanding of speech involves essentially the same problems as the production of speech . . . comprehension and production of speech have too much in common to depend on wholly different mechanisms" (p. 513). We thus perceive the speech of others during listening, in part because the incoming information evokes speech

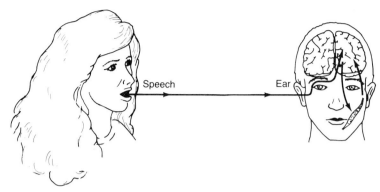

FIGURE 13.6 During speech perception, information that enters the ear is processed in speech muscle–brain circuits enabling us to understand the words that are being spoken to us.

muscle patterns whereby we covertly reproduce with our mouths what we hear. One can often observe listeners moving their lips as they are processing the speech of others, a phenomenon known as "shadowing." For instance, in the Osgood and McGuigan studies (McGuigan, 1978) tongue EMG significantly increases in two experiments, one in which subjects were listening to Gilbert and Sullivan operettas and the other in which subjects trained to pronounce the Finnish language listened to Finnish prose. In this process, the muscles code information that is carried in neural trains of impulses to and from the brain. As numerous speech muscle–auditory brain circuits reverberate, we perceive what is spoken to us (Fig. 13.6).

During listening, we covertly say what we hear, then we hear what we reproduce.

The way coded information carried by the afferent neural trains generated by the speech musculature is processed in the brain must be amazingly complex. But in some way semantic processing, understanding, involves the extensive activation of cerebral circuits within the cortex together with subcortical loops and efferent components (see McGuigan, 1978, Chapter 9, for a specific model of how this happens). In any event, we now have a basis for understanding information that enters the auditory modality.

We now can return to the question of how we perceive visually inputted information. Written words that enter through the eyes must be transferred from the visual to the auditory modality. Let us expand on this process.

Thought During Silent Reading

Silent reading is an important cognitive activity that has a particular advantage for the researcher — the reader's thought processes are largely controlled by the words being read. Consequently, the researcher knows what the reader is thinking.

When our ancient ancestors learned to write down symbols that represented their speech sounds, major cultural advances resulted. We were able to accumulate knowledge over the years, and we learned to symbolically manipulate our world — for example, we could plan the construction of bridges.

When we write, we encode speech sounds on paper. When we read those symbols, we interpret them back into spoken language. Reading is thus a process of decoding written symbols into their original speech sounds. Many centuries ago,

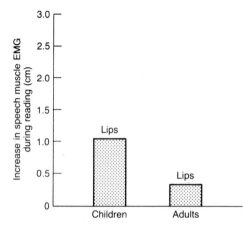

FIGURE 13.7
Amount of lip movement measured in children while silently reading is greater than that measured in adults.

reading was always overt (aloud), but it eventually became silent with speech responses becoming covert.

Subvocalization Naturally Decreases in Amplitude but Still Remains in the Adult. Covert speech behavior, sometimes called "subvocalization," has especially interested educators and psychologists because of the reading process in particular and cognition in general. It is common to observe children moving their lips while they are silently reading.

The amount of such covert speech activity during silent reading is larger in children than in adults (Fig. 13.7), but it naturally decreases in amplitude as children grow older. In Figure 13.8 we can see that the increase in lip and chin EMG was

FIGURE 13.8   Amplitude of covert speech responding decreases naturally as children practice reading and grow older. Yet it stabilizes at a level typical of adults, which is significantly above 0.0.

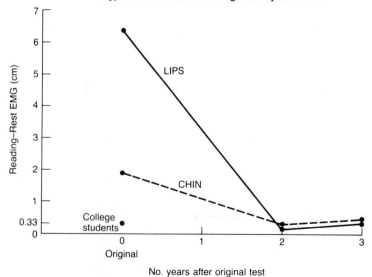

considerably higher during silent reading than during resting in children during the original test. When they were tested two and three years later, the amplitude had naturally decreased. Yet it stabilized at a level approximately that of college students, a level that was significantly greater than zero. When first learning to read, the child necessarily makes large articulatory movements while attempting to pronounce the written word. As with motor skills like swimming, when proficiency increases, the amount of muscular activity is reduced and efficiency increases — as one learns to read or swim, initial large-scale and erratic movements become woven into smooth, coordinated sequences of responses. In silent reading, these response sequences are efficiently run off at the covert level.

Covert speech responses during silent reading are large in children and persist in the adult at a reduced level.

Apparently these covert responses are made as part of the process of interpreting (decoding) the text being read. While reading, one orally reproduces words. Consequently, as one speaks words overtly or covertly, one hears them as auditory images and thus understands them. In this way, visual information is transferred to the auditory mode. Thus, one says what one sees and then hears what one says (Fig. 13.9). According to our model, the feedback from the speech-muscle responses during subvocalization carries information that allows us to interpret linguistic symbols in a meaningful fashion. Data indicate that the feedback information is a verbal code. The reader interprets (understands, comprehends) what is read by decoding the code when it reverberates in circuits between the linguistic regions of the brain and the muscles.

Reading is the oral decoding of the previously encoded speech sounds (the words being read).

Consistent with a principle of behavioral efficiency, the accomplished reader typically generates a minimal amount of verbal information that is afferently carried from the speech muscles to the brain. But the poorer reader, or the good reader under distracting conditions, requires a greater amount of afferently carried verbal information, perhaps needing to send a redundancy of information to the brain. Presumably, the poor reader and the person reading under demanding conditions thus

During silent reading, the speech muscles generate a verbal code that is carried through neuromuscular circuits to the brain; the code is thereupon decoded, which constitutes understanding of the text that enters the eyes.

FIGURE 13.9   In reading, the visually inputted information is initially processed in circuits between the visual regions of the brain and the eyes. That information is then transferred to an auditory modality by means of circuits between the speech muscles and the brain. Following this intermodal transfer from the visual to the auditory modality, information is processed during reading just as it is during listening. Thus, when one reads, one says what one sees following which one hears what one says; thereupon there is understanding of the text. In listening, one needs only to say covertly what one hears.

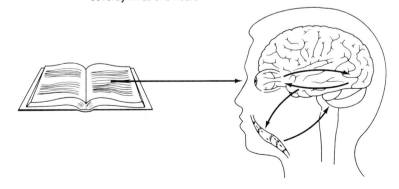

enhance the interpretation processes by exaggerating the amplitude of their covert speech behavior. This increases feedback from the muscles to the brain. Sometimes covert speech even bursts into overt speech to enhance understanding, adding overt speech sounds to the feedback complex.

One implication for teachers is that they should not tamper with the child's subvocalization. The child needs to subvocalize to understand what is being read and, in any event, the subvocalization naturally becomes reduced in time (see Fig. 13.8).

In Conclusion. Even though terms from everyday language, such as *thinking*, are vague, they have some scientific value in providing us with a starting place for explication. We have been successful in psychophysiological measurements of what goes on in the body when people are instructed to perform such activities. We know that when we "think," we engage in covert speech responses, covert nonspeech responses, and more, as we will develop soon. A sound generalization is that electromyographically measured covert behavior occurs when people are thinking. If the thought processes involve language, the speech musculature is especially active. But if the thought processes are nonverbal, regions of the body other than the speech mechanisms, such as the arms, are covertly responding.

Rapid Information Processing: "Speed Reading" and "Speed Listening"

Scanning Is Not (Thorough) Reading. In reading, the eyes fixate on selected words, whereupon information from the written symbols is received, processed, and interpreted. Perceptual interpretation of that information occurs when it is processed in circuits that include especially the eyes, the brain, and the speech musculature. When we subvocalize what we read, we internally hear and understand it. However, if the eyes do not sufficiently fixate on selected words, some of the visual information fails to be received. If one attempts to read too rapidly, the eyes simply will not receive and process all of the information in the text. If the text is complex, as in technical or scientific works, rapid reading with complete comprehension is simply not possible. Even reading each word aloud does not guarantee complete comprehension of the meaning of a sentence. Sometimes one must read each word carefully, perhaps even aloud, to enhance the intake and processing of information to comprehend the meaning of a sentence. Even under ideal conditions we simply are not perfect in processing any kind of information. In simple auditory processing, for instance, there is a sizable loss of information due to the physical degradation of signals from the speaker to the listener. There also are physiological limits in the rate at which humans can process information. In silent reading some research suggests that there is a loss of comprehension beyond about 1000 words per minute. Beyond this physiological limit, "reading" becomes merely "scanning" or "skimming." This physiological limit exists because of the inability of circuits between the eyes, brain, and speech muscles to function more rapidly. Perhaps the interchange of information at the myoneural junction and the mechanical contraction and relaxation of speech muscle fibers are responsible for this physiological limit. Yet, we can approach that limit. As we do, we *increase* muscle activity in order to more rapidly process the information being read. In three separate experiments (Fig. 13.10), two

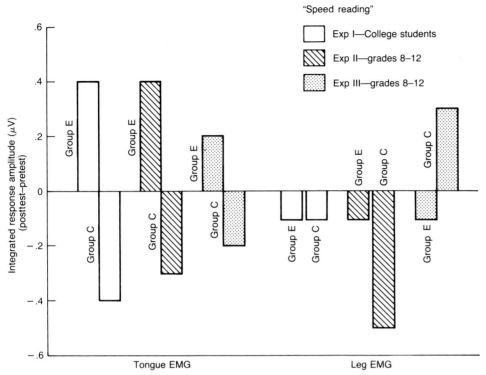

FIGURE 13.10 Electromyographically measured covert speech responding ("subvocalization") increases as reading rate increases.

using teenagers and one using college students, subjects were trained to increase their reading rate in "speed reading" courses (McGuigan & Pinkney, 1973). As reading rate increased from the beginning to the end of the courses, all three trained groups (Groups E) significantly increased the amount of tongue EMG during silent reading. The increase in each case was significantly greater than for control groups who were not trained. In no case did leg EMG (a comparison measure) significantly change. That is, as reading rate increases, one covertly says words more rapidly which generates more muscle activity.

However, as one attempts to read extremely rapidly, the components of the speech-muscle–brain circuits cannot respond beyond their physiological limits. Consequently, as we increase our efforts to read very fast, we understand less. Claims of "reading rates" of 10,000 or 25,000 words per minute would more accurately be called "scanning" or "skimming" rather than reading. In scanning (what some call "speed reading"), the scanner ("reader") selects certain words out of each page to process and uses those words to infer what the material is about. Sometimes the inference is erroneous or minimal. As expressed by Woody Allen: "I took a speed-reading course, learning to read straight down the middle of the page, and I was able to go through *War and Peace* in 20 minutes. It's about Russia" (cited by Carver, 1972, p. 22).

There is a limit to the amount of prose that can be understood within a given time period. This limit to reading rate is perhaps 1000 words per minute.

One may apparently speed read using selected words that evoke recall of previously acquired and stored information (e.g., by selecting the words *Mary* and *lamb*, the entire nursery rhyme, "Mary had a little lamb whose fleece was . . . ," can be reinstated). A learned professor thus does not need to *read* the new textbook along with the students, but only to scan it. By selecting critical words, a professor can reinstate what the introductory students must diligently acquire for the first time. A comprehension test given to the professor who thus scans an introductory textbook for the first time at the rate of 30,000 words per minute would show little loss in comprehension. When reading novel or difficult material, though, the physiological limits do constrain the rate of information processing.

Moderate increases in reading rate increase amplitude of covert speech behavior, indicating that those muscular responses function in understanding the text being read.

The strategy in some commercial speed-reading courses is to eliminate "subvocalization" so that the reader supposedly engages in strictly "visual reading." But if the speech-muscle component of the neuromuscular circuits involved in reading were eliminated, comprehension would be prevented. In several experiments, we used various techniques that have been traditionally used in education for this purpose. The subjects engaged in silent reading with the tongue placed between the teeth or wrapped around a pencil. We also sprayed lidocaine on the tongue and lips to attempt to reduce speech-muscle activity. In each case, however, the speech musculature continued to respond, even at an exaggerated level, during silent reading (see McGuigan, 1978, pp. 214–220). Furthermore, Edmund Jacobson's subjects who were instructed to read with their speech muscles totally relaxed comprehended nothing about the text; without covert speech behavior, the prose was meaningless.

Efforts to inhibit or interfere with subcocalization during reading are ineffective because the speech musculature still responds.

In Conclusion.   Subvocalization is useful to the reader. Parents and teachers should recognize that children *need* to subvocalize in order to understand what they are reading and that as the need fades, so does the amount of lip movement.

Information Processing During Cursive Handwriting

Writing is another kind of cognitive behavior in which there is complex linguistic functioning. When the written output is internally generated, as in composition, the writer's speech musculature is covertly activated (McGuigan, 1970a). We can expect that covert speech behavior also increases in similar linguistic processing activities, such as typing, sending Morse Code by means of a telegraph key, inputting instructions to a computer, or operating an abacus. Handwriting and similar activities are other cognitive activities that may be known to the researcher through overt behavior. Information processing during the cognitive event can also be directly indexed psychophysiologically prior to the overt behavior.

Language processing activities such as cursive writing involve increased covert speech behavior.

Nocturnal Dreams in the Seeing and Blind

Dreams.   In everyday language, *dreams* are series of sleep thoughts or images, states of mind that are marked by a release from reality. Through the centuries dreams have been variously interpreted as temporary departures of the soul to guide armies and omens to determine political destinies of nations. In Freudian terms, dreams involve symbolic systems—the latent content (the meaning) of the dream presumably becomes understandable through the symbols of the dream's manifest content (what you recall).

Certainly, dreams are among the more curious of our cognitive processes and have generated many folk tales (e.g., that some people never dream, that dreams are extended episodes compressed into instants of time, that we dream but once a night, that dreams are expressions of wish fulfillment, that dreams are directed by external events, that we understand latent content, and that the mind shuts down at night during sleep). One of the major accomplishments of psychophysiology has been to falsify such erroneous beliefs. More positively, psychophysiology has precisely defined the dream state in an objective manner.

Early Psychophysiological Dream Research.   It has long been known that there were rapid eye movements during dreaming (e.g., by George Trumbell Ladd in 1892; see also McGuigan, 1966, pp. 143–144 and Jacobson, 1938a). Consequently modern dream researchers have concentrated on electrical recording of eye and brain activity. However, as with all mental activity, widespread activation of other systems was also found during nocturnal dreams. During the REM state, for example, there are changes in brain waves, increases in pulse and respiration rates, widespread changes in cardiovascular activity, galvanic skin responses, striated muscle responses, and activation of the sexual organs in both males and females. Penile tumescence is especially prominent, as the sexual organs participate intimately in the dream state. Approximately 91 percent of all tumescent episodes at night occur during REM periods.

Researchers often measure EMGs from the neck and chin and report that tonic (sustained) responses are suppressed during the REM period. However, phasic (rapidly changing) activity is quite prominent in these regions and indeed throughout the body during dreaming. In fact, dreams involving bodily movements are often accompanied by covert activity in the corresponding locations in the body. For instance, E. A. Wolpert electromyographically recorded sequential covert responses in one arm then in the other, and then in a leg. In later interrogation, the dreamer reported that he picked up a bucket with one hand, transferred it to the other and then started walking. Many such correlations between dream content and electromyographic measures have been established, allowing us to ascertain, to some extent, the content of dreams (e.g., covert speech behavior [lip and chin electromyograms] is elevated during conversational dreams relative to only minor changes during visual dreams as in Fig. 13.11) (McGuigan & Tanner, 1971). Localized changes in the speech region suggest that covert speech behavior serves a linguistic function during conversational dreams just as it does during the waking performance of linguistic activities.

Hypnotically Induced Dreams.   Like nocturnal dreams, suggestions during hypnosis that one will engage in specific activities produce the appropriate, corresponding covert behavior. For example, "leg dreams" resulting from the suggestion to hypnotized subjects that one is riding a bicycle have been accompanied by heightened EMG in the legs. In contrast, "relaxation dreams" evoked by suggestions to do nothing are not accompanied by increased covert behavior. When oral dreams such as silent recitation of the "The Lord's Prayer" were induced, tongue EMG dramatically increased as shown in Figure 13.12. As it is in night linguistic dreams,

Bodily locus of psychophysiological reactions is often related to dream content, including heightened covert speech behavior during conversational dreams.

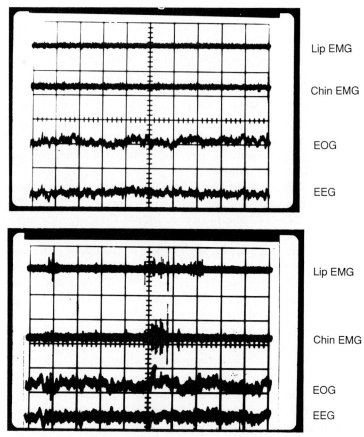

FIGURE 13.11   Illustration of signals during a nondreaming period (top) and a
conversational dream (bottom). Notice the phasic speech
muscle activity during the conversational dream that is not
present during the nondreaming period (McGuigan & Tanner,
1971).

the speech mechanism is also covertly active in hypnotically induced dreams. In comparable nonoral dreams there was no increase apparent in covert speech activity.

DOES EVERYBODY DREAM?

People successfully report dreams when awakened after REM sleep but often do not recall them when questioned the next day. Individuals who claim that they do not dream merely do not recall their dreams. Consequently, we should classify dreamers as "recallers" versus "nonrecallers." However, if a person is queried more than about 15 minutes after the termination of the REM stage, he or she typically has no memory of dreaming. As Raul Hernandez-Peon reported, every species that is

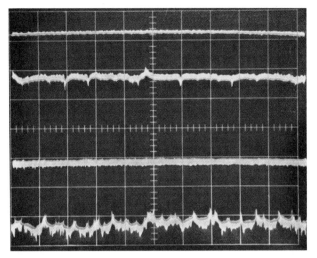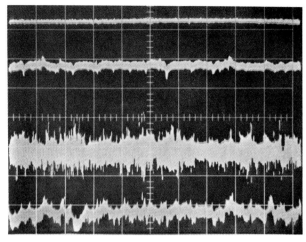

FIGURE 13.12 Sample tracings typical of college students while resting when hypnotized (left). When hypnotic verbal dreams were induced, tongue EMG dramatically increased. Tracings from top down: left arm EMG, horizontal EOG, tongue EMG, and frontal lobe EEG.

physiologically capable of making rapid eye movements does so during sleep; presumably they also dream.

Mental activity is also present during non-REM periods, although it is of a less vivid nature than during dreams. Sometimes dreams, which are really nocturnal hallucinations, seem vividly real.

All humans dream and the occurrence of rapid eye movements throughout the phylogenetic scale suggests that lower animals dream too.

DO BLIND PEOPLE HAVE VISUAL DREAMS?

EOG Findings. As summarized by McGuigan (1978), people who become blind later than early childhood typically report visual imagery in their dreams. As they age, the amount of their reported visual imagery progressively decreases. After about 40 years of blindness, only a few subjects report some visual imagery. Some people who were congenitally blind (i.e., blind since birth), and some who had been blind for as long as 30 or 40 years, reported no visual imagery in their dreams, nor did they have REMs.

Normal REMs apparently do not occur in congenitally blind people or those who have been blind for some decades, nor do such individuals report visual imagery in their dreams.

Hallucinations

Hallucinations Defined. Hallucinations are regarded as "false" perceptions that are confused with "real" perceptions. They may involve any modality (visual, auditory, olfactory) and they may be **positive hallucinations** (e.g., perceiving a cross of fire that is not there) or **negative hallucinations** (e.g., failing to perceive obvious external stimuli that occurs when one fails to react to stimulation, as when a child does not perceive a constantly nagging parent).

Motor hallucinations are a kind of negative hallucination in which one believes that one has overtly behaved when one has not (there probably were only covert behaviors). One patient thought that he overtly ordered breakfast and became upset when the waitress failed to bring it. The reverse also occurs as when one confuses overt with covert speech — one may speak and think overtly, believing that the thinking is silent. We see this in mentally ill persons who walk the streets talking to themselves. A more common instance occurs when one "remembers" either mailing a letter or having thought of mailing it and is not sure which occurred. Such covert motor phenomena during hallucinations are instances of the more general phenomena of muscle activity in neuromuscular circuits during thought.

An obvious kind of normal hallucination are the visual images of dreams. During waking life, a normal person may also hallucinate during a highly emotional state, when deprived of sleep, or in periods of deep preoccupation.

Causes.   Hallucinations may occur with such pathological conditions as schizophrenia and brain tumors. Auditory hallucinations are especially frequent in paranoid schizophrenia. The patient may hear one or several voices simultaneously "emanating" from such different locales as their stomach or the walls of the room. A common finding in the literature on sensory and perceptual deprivation is that subjects report a variety of hallucinations that often occur in front of them rather than in the head. Similarly, patients treated for poliomyelitis in tank-type respirators have reported hallucinations. Hallucinations can be produced experimentally by means of drugs, hypnosis, and conditioning. There is an extensive literature on hallucinations produced by mescaline from the plant *Anhalonium lewinii,* from LSD (lysergic acid diethylamide), nitrous oxide, and alcohol.

Naturally occurring hallucinations may develop in any modality. They may be experimentally induced with conditioning procedures and drugs.

How are auditory hallucinations generated? Subvocal speech and heightened speech EMG have been measured by different researchers when patients experienced auditory hallucinations. Figure 13.13 shows increased amplitude of chin EMG and pneumograms immediately prior to the overt report of having heard voices (McGuigan, 1966). Subvocal speech of slight whisperings corresponded roughly to the content of the hallucinations (e.g., the patient reported overtly that the voices had told him "I am in prison in Kansas City"). On playing back the tape recording of the subvocalization sounds that issued from the patient's mouth one could hear in a whisper "I am in prison in Kansas City." The durations of the chin EMG increases were positively correlated with the durations of the reports of the verbal hallucinations. Furthermore, the loudness of the verbal hallucination was positively related to the amount of the EMG increases. The interpretation was that the patient produced the auditory hallucinations by covertly activating his own speech musculature.

Auditory hallucinations in paranoid schizophrenics are apparently produced in part by covert speech behavior.

Conditioning Hallucinations.   Ralph Hefferline and associates (1958) showed that feedback from muscular contractions can carry information to produce hallucinatory images. They repeatedly associated the proprioceptive feedback from a naturally occurring thumb twitch with a tone. Then, whenever the thumb twitched, the subject reported hallucinating the tone. Some years later one of the subjects *still* experienced hallucinations whenever the thumb twitched. One might replace the tone in this paradigm with an orally administered language stimulus like "ali oop," as one of my students tried. He then looked for hallucinated speech behavior imme-

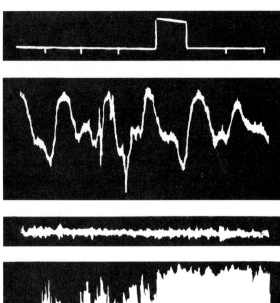

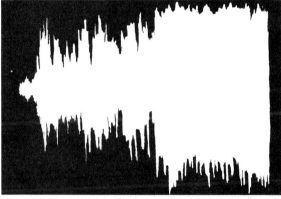

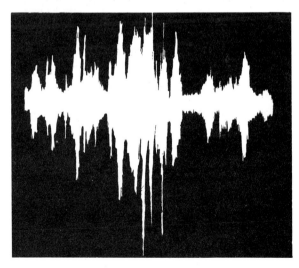

FIGURE 13.13
Covert events during an auditory hallucination. Two-second intervals before and after the report of a typical hallucination are marked on the event line at the top. Next in descending order are the pneumogram, arm EMG, chin EMG, and the highly amplified sound record.

diately following the thumb twitch but had to discontinue the research when the semester ended and the subject was no longer available.

Hallucinations have also been successfully conditioned by pairing a light and a tone and later testing subjects without the tone. Subjects indicated that they "heard" the tone when only the light was presented.

In a similar conditioning approach to produce hallucinations, a click was associated with a diamond drawn on a piece of paper. Later the click alone was presented; the report was that there was a visual hallucination of a diamond on a blank paper. EOG research would probably establish increased eye activity during such visual hallucinations, just as there is increased covert speech activity during auditory hallucinations.

General Interpretation.   Hallucinatory experiences of psychotic individuals are probably generated by complex responses to internal stimuli. Those internal stimuli are mistakenly ascribed to external sources by the hallucinating individual. One consequence of this reasoning is that if the covert speech response is interfered with, the patient should fail to report auditory hallucinations. Evidence, consistent with this prediction, shows that when a patient engages in various kinds of oral activities such as brushing teeth or swallowing, there are reports that hallucinations are eliminated or reduced in frequency. Hallucinations, like all cognitive activities, occur during selective activation of neuromuscular circuits. Visual hallucinations would be generated as circuits reverberate between the occipital lobes and the eyes and ocular muscles. Auditory hallucinations would similarly involve circuits among the various auditory and linguistic regions of the brain, neural and muscle components of the auditory system, and the speech musculature. Similar reasoning would apply for other classes of hallucinations, including the most interesting motor hallucinations discussed earlier.

"Lie Detection" (Detection of Deception)

One kind of cognitive activity that has great social significance occurs when a person undergoes a "lie detector test."

TECHNIQUES OF ANTIQUITY

One **lie (deception) detection** procedure used by the ancients called on supernatural powers to reveal whether or not a suspect was guilty. Thereby intimidated, a frightened and guilty man was convinced that he was caught and would incriminate himself.

Perhaps the first record of lie detection was that of wise King Solomon who had to decide which of two women was really the mother of an infant claimed by both. His test was to threaten to cut the infant in half and divide it between the two claimants. He decided in the favor of the woman who was so upset that she pleaded to let the other woman have the infant. The deceptive woman calmly concurred.

Assuming that those who lie are frightened and therefore have a dry mouth, ancient psychophysiological lie detection techniques measured salivation by placing cotton or rice in the mouth. In ancient China, suspects were forced to chew rice powder and spit it out. If the powder was dry, the suspect was judged guilty. During the Inquisition, a suspect was made to swallow a slice of bread and cheese; if the food stuck in the palate or throat, the suspect was judged as not telling the truth. With a similar approach, Bedouins of Arabia required conflicting witnesses to lick a hot iron. The one whose tongue was burned (presumably due to decreased salivation) was thought to be lying.

Ancient methods assumed that the guilty could be detected because being fearful during lying reduced the flow of saliva.

EARLY SCIENTIFIC STUDIES

About 250 B.C. Erasistratus apparently was first to associate the emotions with psychophysiological changes by concluding that emotions alter pulse rate. Consequently, heightening of pulse rate could indicate an emotional state of lying.

Probably the first scientific investigation of deception was by the Italian criminologist Cesare Lombroso, who reported reliable differences in blood pressure changes between guilty and innocent suspects. V. Benussi (1914) concluded that a respiration ratio was indicative of truthful versus false answers. W. M. Marston (1917), a student of Hugo Münsterberg's, added the important concepts of making several different but simultaneous psychophysiological measurements and of establishing the reliability of those measurements. J. A. Larson (1932) was apparently the first to employ a **polygraph** to measure blood pressure, pulse rate, and respiration changes. Chester Darrow (1936) studied the GSR as a measure of emotional reaction to the possibility of being detected. The widely used Keeler (1930) polygraph added GSR and in 1945 the Reid polygraph added an electromyographic channel. Reid had noted that individuals undergoing interrogation tensed the muscles of their arms during questioning. We will soon see that this measure is indicative of whether or not a person is silently answering a question as "yes" or "no."

These were the major steps in the development of the contemporary polygraph. Today the polygraph, which has not changed noticeably from some decades ago, is widely used for such purposes as detecting industrial or political espionage and the identification of criminals.

CURRENT POLYGRAPH TECHNOLOGY

The "Lie Detector" as Normally Used Lacks Reliability and Validity. The usual paradigm for the polygraph procedure is to mix control (irrelevant or neutral) questions with probing, relevant questions. For instance, an irrelevant control question in a series of questions for one suspected of having stolen a ring out of a desk could be: "Did you ever lie before the age of 19?" A probing question would be: "Was there a ring in the desk?" Liars, it is thought, are aware of their lying which in turn causes emotional reactions that are measurable with contemporary lie detection methodology.

Contemporary detection techniques assume that neutral and probing questions evoke different involuntary emotional reactions that can be psychophysiologically differentiated.

The standard psychophysiological measures taken are cardiovascular reactions including pulse rate and blood pressure, electrodermal measures (especially skin resistance) and respiratory measures (especially breathing amplitude and rate).

ERASISTRATUS OF CEOS

Erasistratus of Ceos (c. 250 B.C.), a Greek anatomist and physician in Alexandria, was regarded by some as the founder of physiology. Known especially for his studies of the circulatory and nervous systems, Erasistratus noted the difference between sensory and motor nerves, but he thought that the nerves were hollow tubes containing fluid. He believed that air entered the lungs and heart and was then carried through the body in the arteries, and that the veins carried blood from the heart to the various parts of the body. He correctly described the function of the epiglottis and the valves of the heart. He was the first major exponent of pneumatism, which was based on the premise that life is associated with a subtle vapor called the pneuma.

Polygraphers typically use a global technique in which they look at all measures to reach a decision about whether or not the individual is lying. However, the evidence indicates that polygraphers have high error rates: There are numerous **false positives,** in which an excessive number of people are falsely classified as being guilty (having lied); there are also **false negatives,** those who are falsely classified as innocent (they lied but were not detected). The false positive errors have been as high as 50 percent (innocent suspects were identified as guilty), which is no better than the results obtained by the toss of a coin. When the test is administered idiosyncratically (in ways unique to the interrogator), as it usually is, validity and reliability are at best low.

Another problem is that such measures as systolic and diastolic blood pressure, pulse rate, and palmar conductance do not reliably correlate within a given person. This means that on any given question one measure may indicate guilt while another suggests lying. Thus, none of these psychophysiological responses can be representative of a general, uniform psychophysiological activity of the body.

No doubt most individuals are emotional when they are taking a test, but these emotions may have nothing to do with deception. Just because the psychophysiological measures increase during questions does not necessarily indicate guilt. On the other hand, some individuals know they are lying but it is not picked up on a polygraph because they are not emotional about it.

Another error made by contemporary polygraphers is the assumption that lying is a simple response, that one lies or one does not lie. However, lying is more complex than that. It can involve subjective experiences of excitement, of psychopathic humor about the situation, special purposes, and so on. Clearly, the simplistic polygraph is an unreliable and ineffective tool for such a complex problem.

Successful Uses. When the polygraph technique *is* successful, it is due to the experience and procedures of individual examiners, making it essentially a "clinical art." Such successes as do occur are usually with naive suspects who, confronted with "scientific" methods, may be induced to confess—the interrogator says "we know you are lying and the machine shows you are guilty." Thus, as Martin Orne has put it, a good interrogator aided by a polygraph is probably more effective in detecting deception than a good interrogator without a polygraph.

Counter Measures.   Even if the polygraph were more reliable, one can be successful on the test by mentally relaxing, by engaging in self-deception or distracting thoughts, by using muscular control to change breathing and heart rates, and by self-inducing pain such as by biting the tongue. Those who are well trained in physical counter techniques such as tongue biting can increase the success rate of beating the test by about one-third. Individuals silently engaging in such cognitive responses as multiplying numbers increase success by about one-fourth.

Conclusion.   Psychophysiological changes *are* recordable in emotionally loaded situations, but those changes have not been sufficiently well established to differentiate between lying and telling the truth with the polygraph. The field of deception detection technology currently lacks adequate generalized validity. Yet polygraphs (as "lie detectors") continue to be extensively used, especially by the federal government. As the Congressional Committee on Government Operations pointed out long ago, in one fiscal year some 20,000 polygraph tests were administered in spite of the committee's conclusion that "there is no 'lie detector,' neither machine nor human. People have been deceived by a myth that a metal box in the hands of an investigator can detect truth or falsehood" (1976, p. 1).

The societal implications of deception detection systems are enormous, which is why the polygraph is so popular with law enforcement agencies, private corporations, and the government. It is only because many laypersons and law enforcement personnel believe that the polygraph works that people continue to be intimidated into confessing. Current lie detection procedures thus have the same basis as the ancient use of the belief in the supernatural. The difference is merely the substitution of "scientific instruments" for "supernatural powers" to get the suspect to confess. As Kleinmuntz and Szucko (1984) conclude from their survey, contemporary polygraphic practice relies on reasoning that is similar to primitive supernatural techniques—for example, intimidation.

There is insufficient scientific evidence to establish the validity and reliability of polygraphy.

WHAT IS THE FUTURE OF DECEPTION DETECTION?

There Could Be a Better System.   Past technology has been almost exclusively based upon the Keeler polygraph, so measures other than respiratory, cardiovascular, and GSR have received little systematic attention. Our science of covert processes does contain sufficient knowledge on which to develop effective deception detection systems. One strategy would be to employ such psychophysiological measures as EMG, EOG, and EEG (especially evoked potentials). Even research conducted many years ago illustrates how this strategy could improve the success rate. For example, Cutrow, Parks, Lucas, and Thomas (1972) measured eye blink latency and rate, breathing amplitude and rate, heart rate, GSR, and voice latency when subjects were instructed to always answer "no" to questions. Eye blink rate and latency significantly increased during deception. Cutrow et al. concluded that each measure is useful for the detection of deception, but a combination was even better. McGuigan and Pavek (1972) were successful in diagnosing whether a subject si-

Psychophysiological data using EMG, EOG, and EEG measures could be used to develop an effective system for detection of deception.

lently answered questions as "yes" or "no" using selected EOG and arm EMG parameters. That these scientific approaches have not reached the necessary technological level is but one more instance of cultural lag.

CAPABILITY OF SPEECH MUSCLES FOR REFINED DIFFERENTIAL ACTIVITY

Linguistic components of thought, we have held, depend on the generation and transmission of a refined verbal code to the brain. A critical question for our cybernetic model is whether the speech (and other) musculature can actually generate sufficient coded information that is transmitted to the brain. For this, the musculature must be able to function in a highly differentiated manner. That is, some muscle fibers need to contract as other nearby ones are simultaneously relaxing (lengthening) while yet other close-by muscle fibers are contracting. Various combinations of highly differentiated contractions and lengthening like a myriad of keys on a gigantic piano are required to send precisely coded feedback information to the language regions of the brain. Can the speech musculature do that?

The evidence suggests an affirmative answer. Sussman (1972), in an article entitled "What the Tongue Tells the Brain," considered the nature of the information carried by the afferent pathways from the tongue. He concluded that

> Not only can the higher brain centers be kept informed as to the *initiation* of a high-speed consonantal gesture of the tongue but also as to the *attainment* and subsequent *release* of that gesture. . . . The neuromuscular system of the tongue has been shown to be a built-in *feedback system* that can signal the length and rate of movement of a muscle. [Consequently] it is logical to assume that the *afferent discharge pattern emanating from the tongue should contain high-level distinctive information.* Such discriminative information can be provided by the differential frequency discharge patterning of the muscle spindles due to the orientation of the extrafusal fibers relative to the direction of movement. (1972, pp. 266, 267, italics added)

The tongue, the most important of the speech muscles, can do the job. The lips, chin, and other speech muscles, research shows, intimately cooperate during cognitive activities.

The Speech Muscles Do Function in the Generation of a Verbal Code. Another line of research also supports this hypothesis. We know that patterns of speech-muscle behavior are related to a linguistic system during the performance of various cognitive processes as in Fig. 13.14 (McGuigan & Winstead, 1974). For instance, when one is silently reading words like "Bob" and "Mom" that would mainly require overt speech movements of the lips, lip EMG is especially (and significantly) heightened. And similarly, the tongue is especially active when silently reading "tongue words" like "Dad" and "none." More amazingly, the speech muscles also differentially respond during silent reading of individual letters as against words. Thus, covert responding of the lips is relatively large when one silently reads "P" just as is that of the tongue when one reads the letter "T." In particular, as indicated in Figure 13.15, the lips had a significantly greater amplitude of responding when reading "P" than when reading "T"; similarly, lip response was significantly greater when reading

The speech muscles generate a verbal (phonetic) code that interacts with the brain for understanding what we read and hear. Thus, the tongue reacts to words like "nine" and the lips to "peep."

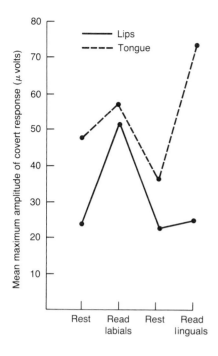

FIGURE 13.14
The speech musculature differentially responds depending on the kind of prose that is being silently read. For instance, when one reads labial material like "Mom," the lips are especially active and the tongue is especially active when reading lingual words like "Dad."

"P" than during a control (C) condition. On the other hand, the tongue responded to a significantly greater extent when processing "T" than when processing "P" and when processing the control figure. Such highly differentiated activity of the speech musculature argues well that it does indeed generate a verbal code. (More precisely, the code is called a phonetic one since it carries distinctive phonetic information for instances of phonemes, e.g., the lips send neural impulses to the brain phonetically coded for [P] when reading the letter "P", see McGuigan, 1978; McGuigan & Dollins, 1989.) This afferently carried code interacts, by our model, with the linguistic regions of the brain whereby we comprehend what is being read or spoken.

Facial Muscles Generate Emotional Experiences. More than 100 years ago, Edgar Allan Poe said that

> When I wish to find out how wise or how stupid or how good or how wicked is anyone, or what are his thoughts at the moment, I fashion the expression of my face, as accurately as possible, in accordance with the expression of his, and then wait to see what thoughts or sentiments arise in my mind or heart, as if to match or correspond with the expression. (cited by Ekman et al., 1990, p. 382)

Following this strategy, Ekman and his associates (e.g., 1990) instructed subjects to produce specific facial patterns that were typical for anger, disgust, fear, happiness, sadness, and surprise. These volitional expressions on their faces generated the reports of subjective experiences appropriate for those facial activities. Furthermore,

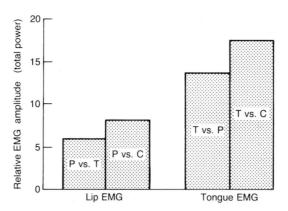

FIGURE 13.15
When silently reading labial letters such as "P," the lips are especially active, as is the tongue when reading lingual letters such as "T." The implication is that the speech musculature functions in generating neural impulses that are verbally coded for instances of phonemes such as for [P] and [T]. When that information reverberates with the speech regions of the brain, there is understanding of what is being read.

the specific facial appearance generated emotion-specific patterns of autonomic activity that were appropriate for those facial expressions. For instance, when the subjects were told to move their facial muscles that portray the facial expression for anger, the subjects reported subjective experiences of feeling anger; furthermore, their patterns of autonomic activity were those associated with the experiences of anger.

AN ILLUSTRATION OF SELF-CONTROL WITH A CYBERNETIC MODEL—RELAXATION AND MENTAL PRACTICE IN SPORTS PSYCHOLOGY

Using a cybernetic model, an individual can exercise self-control by intervening within the cybernetic circuits that reverberate between the brain and effectors. That intervention is accomplished by controlling the voluntary (striated) muscles and the attendant feedback transmitted in those circuits. In the following section we illustrate an application that has special relevance for cognitive activities.

Covert Response Practice Can Substitute for Overt Response Practice. A line of research that began in the 1930s has demonstrated that we can improve overt performance of various motor skills through mental practice (summarized by McGuigan, 1978). For instance, subjects mentally practiced dart throwing by imagining throwing darts at a visible target. Results indicated that they improved their accuracy as effectively as if they had overtly practiced. Other research showed that subjects without previous experience mentally learned such gross bodily skills as gymnastics and juggling without overt practice.

The reason for the effectiveness of mental practice has been attributed to the fact that imagining movement results in actual, if minimal, contraction of muscles.

Sports Applications. In athletic training programs, coaches can help their athletes to "mentally reinstate" past successful performances. For example, the basketball player who is about to attempt a free throw can mentally reinstate a time in practice when the shot was successfully made. One can mentally rehearse each

Mental (muscle-brain circuit) practice improves movements used in overt motor skills.

aspect of the event, imagining all activities down to how one is breathing, how the feet feel on the floor, and so on. The mental rehearsal should be in real time. Sports psychologists routinely record electromyograms during the mental reaction as for the skier who imagined himself in the process of jumping and had electromyographic bursts of activities in all relevant muscles.

Another application is in the form of stress–tension control by differentially relaxing to just "let the play happen" (see Chapter 15). Otherwise, the athlete often "chokes" due to excessive tension. In choking, one tenses irrelevant, interfering muscles and can "blow" the shot. In differential relaxation during any athletic performance, the athlete maintains peak arousal of skills without pushing excessively. Such optimal performance is especially difficult to maintain when the pressures of the event are great (recall achieving optimal mental activity in Chapter 1).

An athlete's attention must also be focused on the task at hand and he or she must be free of distracting thoughts. During irrelevant thoughts there are actual covert speech responses that interfere with optimal performance. In tennis one must, for instance, concentrate on getting *this point* and forget about the error just past — many matches have been lost merely because the player continues to think about past mistakes or misfortunes like a bad ball call so that the covert muscle activity of the interfering thought causes a bad swing. Interestingly, the reverse also occurs as shown by McGuigan, Hutchens, Eason, and Reynolds (1964). In particular they showed that motor activity immediately following knowledge of results retroactively interfered with the knowledge of results. That is, the cognitive activity of knowledge of results that was being processed was interfered with when the ensuing motor activity generated afferent neural impulses. One can see that this is the reverse of what happens in athletics when a person's thoughts interfere with ensuing motor performance.

DO ANIMALS THINK?—EVOLUTION OF COGNITION AND INTELLIGENCE

In Chapter 11 we considered the question of whether animals can use language as well as the relationship of language to cognitive processes. To maintain our perspective of behavior along the phylogenetic scale from an evolutionary point of view, we here consider the question of whether animals think.

Frustrated Expectation Is Indicative of Mental Processes. As summarized by M. E. Bitterman, one of the ten most important experiments in animal learning was a study by M. H. Elliot (1928) that demonstrated a **negative contrast effect.** The negative contrast effect occurred when rats that were used to finding wet mash at the end of a maze suddenly found sunflower seeds. Expecting wet mash, but finding seeds, the animals became very active. According to Tolman's cognitive model, that activity indicated "frustrated expectation" — an indication of cognition.

The negative contrast effect has been confirmed many times with different tasks, conditions, and rewards. When Otto Tinklepaugh's chimpanzees did not receive the reward that they expected, they became frustrated and aggressive, even when the reward to which they were shifted was more desirable.

Researchers since then continued to test down the phylogenetic scale until the negative contrast effect was *not found*. Finally, it was concluded that goldfish are incapable of cognitive expectation. Apparently goldfish represent an important transition in the phylogenetic scale.

Another concept used for studying cognition in animals concerns the relationship between amount of reward in learning and resistance to extinction. The relationship is an inverse one such that the larger the amount of reward given for a learning task, the fewer the number of responses before the learned response extinguishes. Like the negative contrast effect, "frustrated expectation" is thereby produced. That is, as the animals that learn under a large amount of reward are shifted to no reward, they have frustrated expectations. On the other hand, animals who learn with small amounts of reward and then are shifted to no reward conditions, manifest lesser amounts of frustrated expectations. The enhanced amount of frustrated expectation is taken as an indication of cognitive functioning. It is concluded that rats and pigeons do show cognition by this criterion. However again, as researchers proceeded down the phylogenetic scale, the effect was not found in fishes and turtles; Bitterman concluded that they are precognitive animals while birds, rats, and monkeys are cognitive animals. Figure 13.16 shows that birds, rats, and monkeys had a common ancestor that had cognitive abilities. Perhaps it was some kind of crocodile.

Research indicates that animals above the level of goldfish show cognitive abilities because they objectively demonstrate a frustrated expectation; therefore, goldfish represent an important transition in the phylogenetic scale.

Another type of experiment concluded that very young rats do not show the inverse relation effect and thus behave like the precognitive animals. Older rats, however, do show that effect, indicating that at this phylogenetic level cognition develops with maturity.

Bitterman concludes that there are two major learning mechanisms in all cognitive animals: (1) a primitive reinforcement mechanism and (2) a cognitive mechanism. Precognitive animals have only the primitive reinforcement mechanism.

PSYCHOCHRONOLOGY

Psychochronology is the study of mental phenomena as inferred from response times. Duncan Luce (1986), for instance, applied the strategy of using the time it takes to make a response as a source of information about how the mind is organized. This strategy is an old one, originally advanced in 1868 by F. C. Donders. Donders attempted to infer the time required for a mental process by employing various reaction time tasks. For instance, a task requiring a decision between stimuli **(complex reaction time)** takes more time than when only one response can be made to a stimulus **(simple reaction time).** The two reaction time tasks indicate that different mental processes are used. Furthermore, the difference between two amounts of time indicates how much time the complex mental event (the decision) took.

Luce follows the pathways of Joseph Jastrow who, in 1890, examined response times for the following reason:

If the processing of information by the mind is highly structured, as most psychologists believe, then different paths through that structure will entail different time courses,

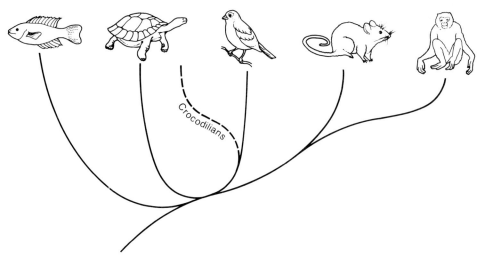

FIGURE 13.16 Some evolutionary relationships suggesting that birds, rats, and monkeys had a common ancestor with cognitive abilities. The dotted line suggests that it might have been some kind of crocodile that branched off into contemporary crocodiles. (Adapted from Bitterman, 1975)

and those differences will be reflected in response times. Thus, perhaps, one can infer back from the pattern of response times obtained under different experimental conditions to the structures involved. To the extent this is possible, response times are valuable. (Luce, 1986, p. 1)

From this strategy, as Luce points out, we should be able to learn something about the overall organization of the mind, but very little about the details. To find out more about the details, we need to use physiological approaches that allow us to look inside the "black box."

We have learned much about mental processes and their organization by response times, but we still have far, far to go using this strategy. The importance of a psychophysiological approach has thus been emphasized by the limitations of psychochronology.

EMPHASIS ON A CYBERNETIC PRINCIPLE— CONCLUSIONS ABOUT THE NATURE OF MENTAL PROCESSES

There are a variety of words in everyday language that refer to mental processes. But, following our analysis, they all refer to bodily events that have measurable psychophysiological components. If we looked at the psychophysiological variables measured when engaged in each, would those measures differ? Is what we call "thinking" a different internal information processing phenomenon than "dreaming"? Or, is the psychophysiology of a waking hallucination different from a dream hallucination or a rational thought? Certainly such mental processes occur under a variety of environmental and organismic conditions. The night dream occurs during sleep in contrast to the daydream. The nocturnal dream also differs from waking thought processes in that it generally lacks guiding control from external environmental stimuli. A diseased temporal lobe produces hallucinations, the congenitally blind lack visual contents in their dreams, and a person who has never heard of or seen snow does not dream about snow. Are there different psychophysiological events that generate these variously named mental processes?

There are environmental and organismic differences in mental events, but they are not psychophysiologically different.

The data surveyed in this chapter and elsewhere indicate that these events have common psychophysiological parameters and thus do not involve uniquely different kinds of internal information processes. Visual imaging occurs when eye–brain circuits reverberate, regardless of whether imaging occurs in dreams or in waking imagination. Various commonsense terms *(thinking, hallucinations, dreams)* all involve activation of cybernetic circuits within the brain and throughout the entire body.

Mental events with different names (nocturnal dreams, hallucinations, daydreams) are held to be generated by similar psychophysiological processes that occur under different environmental and organismic conditions.

As depicted in Figure 13.17, the components of the cybernetic circuits between the brain, eyes, and so on may be psychophysiologically recorded as they generate subjective experiences of night dreams, visual hallucinations, and visual images.

The scientific value of various commonsense mentalistic terms is to provide a starting point for systematic analysis. As we become increasingly successful in explicating these commonsense terms, they can be replaced by statements about which bodily systems are psychophysiologically activated, to the degree that the various parameters change the pattern of their activation and the conditions under which they are activated.

Regardless of the term, all mental events occur when sensory - neural - muscular circuits that carry feedbacks interact in a highly integrated, selective fashion.

Granted that the same kind of circuits reverberate as we internally process information that generates cognitive processes, how do the *contents* of our cognitions differ? Most cognitive processes have three components: (1) **speech imagery,** wherein we subjectively experience linguistic components of our thoughts—this involves contraction of the speech musculature and its feedback to the linguistic regions of the brain; (2) **visual imagery,** which involves the visual aspects of our cognitions—the activity of the eyes and eye musculature in conjunction with events in the visual regions of the brain; and (3) **somatic imagery,** wherein we subjectively feel various events in our bodies—this involves differential reactions throughout the body in conjunction with events in the somaesthetic regions of the brain. Thus, a thought about an apple would involve cybernetic circuits between the brain and (1) the eyes (to generate visual imagery), (2) speech muscles (for speech imagery) as you say "apple" subvocally, and (3) somatic imagery (perhaps as you feel the apple in your hands). In short, the contents of our cognitive activities depend on the relative contributions of these three kinds of imagery and on the specific engrams retrieved as these three classes of circuits reverberate.

Although all three kinds of imagery are usually present in cognitive activities, sometimes we only process information in one or two of these categories. Mental processes can be *conscious* when circuits engaging the speech muscle are activated for speech imagery; the verbal information allows us to verbalize about such cogni-

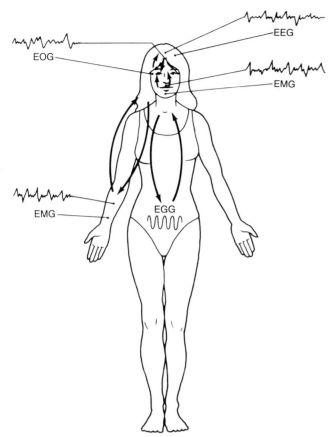

FIGURE 13.17 When systems interact in a specialized and integrated fashion, mental processes are generated. Psychophysiological measures of components of those cybernetic circuits are illustrated.

tions. Unconscious cognitive processes are generated by those circuits that do not involve (are independent of) speech-muscle responses.

We have generally been discussing normal cognitive events; abnormal ones require clinical intervention for control purposes. To develop control over mental processes, one would usually start with the speech and eye muscle components. Once we have the ability to verbalize about bodily processes, we have a start on the ability to control them. Phobias, anxieties, and depressions are topics we consider in Chapter 14 and whose control we consider in Chapter 15.

KEY TERMS

Cognition—Following Tolman's theories, there are processes involving expectations by which organisms learn cognitive maps of what leads to what. The term now is essentially synonymous with "mental processes" (see Mental events).

Cognitive map—The way that organisms know what leads to what (i.e., a "road map" that allows you to know how to perform a task).

Complex reaction time—The time required to respond when a decision must be made.

Explication—The process of replacing vaguely defined, ambiguous notions with precise, objective, and scientifically based statements.

False negatives—In detection, those who are falsely classified as innocent.

False positives—In lie detection, a person who is falsely classified as being guilty.

Lie (deception) detection—The use of the polygraph and related techniques for espionage detection and the identification of criminals. Contemporary technologies lack sufficient validity.

Mediational processes—Events that occur between two observable events (e.g., phenomena (X) that mediate stimuli and responses: S–X–R).

Mental (cognitive) events/processes—Sequences of bodily events that occur under objectively specifiable external and internal conditions that generate subjective experiences as in dreams and thinking.

Mind—The human mind is the functioning of the interacting systems of the body. As those systems selectively interact, they program both overt and covert behaviors. Principal programming is carried out by the circuits that include the eye and speech musculature. As they reverberate, the mental events on which we may behaviorally report are generated.

Motor hallucination—A type of negative hallucination; one believes that one overtly behaved when in actuality the behavior was only covert.

Negative contrast effect—Organisms used to finding a certain reward find a different one and become very active,

evidencing a "frustrated expectation." Tolman considered this phenomenon as evidence of cognition.

Negative hallucination—Failure to report an external object when it is present.

Ostensive definition—Definition by pointing to objects or events and agreeing on the use of the term thereby applied.

Polygraph—Instrument first used to measure blood pressure, pulse rate, and respiration changes to determine if the subject was being truthful; now used for purposes such as detecting espionage, job screening, and identifying criminals. (It lacks reliability and validity.)

Positive hallucination—A reported perception of an external object when no such object is present.

Private events—A term used by Skinner referring to conscious events beneath the skin that are not observed by others.

Psychochronology—The study of mental phenomena as inferred from response times.

Simple reaction time—The time required to make a single response to a single stimulus.

Somatic imagery—Reports of subjective experiences produced by reactions throughout the body in conjunction with events in the somaesthetic regions of the brain.

Speech imagery—Reports of subjective experiences produced by contraction of the speech musculature in conjunction with processes in the linguistic regions of the brain.

Verbal mediation paradigm—A paradigm in which a verbal process intervenes between a stimulus and a response to facilitate solution of a problem.

Visual imagery—Reports of subjective visual experiences generated by activity of the eyes and eye musculature in conjunction with events in the visual regions of the brain.

STUDY QUESTIONS

1. According to a cybernetic model, when does an individual become conscious of activities?
2. Do you think the increased amplitude of covert speech behavior facilitates silent reading? Discuss!
3. One of the major accomplishments of

psychophysiology has been to further our understanding of the dreaming process. Explain.
4. Discuss visual and auditory hallucinations from a psychophysiological point of view.
5. T or F. Some empirical research suggests

that in reading beyond about 1000 words per minute, there is a loss of comprehension, which suggests that there is a physiological limit beyond which reading becomes merely "scanning."

6. Describe some of the ancient methods for detecting lying based on reduced flow of saliva.

7. T or F. By relaxing all of the muscles of the body all mental processes can be brought to zero.

8. What is "thinking" according to John B. Watson and B. F. Skinner?

9. Point out the differences in learning due to a primitive reinforcement mechanism versus a cognitive mechanism.

FURTHER READINGS

This book presents general concepts of psychophysiology and issues in data analysis:

Cacioppo, J. T., & Tassinary, L. G. (Eds.). (1990). *Principles of psychophysiology: Physical, social, and inferential elements.* New York: Cambridge University Press.

The following book is a study of the mind–body problem from a biological point of view, although the book limits the mind to the brain, ignoring the mind's other components:

Eimas, P. D., & Galaburda, A. M. (Eds.). (1989). *Neurobiology of cognition* (2nd ed.). Cambridge, MA: MIT Press.

Part IV
Pathological Conditions and Clinical Applications

CHAPTER 14

Biology of Pathological Behavior and Disease

MAJOR PURPOSE: To specify and assess a sample of the psychobiological problems that contemporary humans face

WHAT YOU ARE GOING TO FIND:
1. A statistical assessment of the kinds of detrimental behaviors in which we engage
2. A sample of various behavioral disorders and medical diseases to which we fall victim, including psychiatric, psychosomatic, cardiovascular, immunologic, and oncologic (cancerous) diseases

WHAT YOU SHOULD ACQUIRE: A broad perspective together with specific knowledge about behavioral and medical disorders that can be prevented, alleviated, or otherwise controlled through principles of biobehavioral engineering

CHAPTER OUTLINE

ENGINEERING BEHAVIOR FOR A BETTER LIFE

We are all going to die! As the prominent U.S. Senator Jacob Javits said when he was nearing death: "We are all terminal, the only difference is when."

True enough, but most would agree that the later, the better. It has been said that "It is better to be rich than poor, healthy than sick," to which we add that it is better to prolong robust life than to hasten death. Yet many people behave in ways quite contrary to this simple truth. Why do so many seek their own premature destruction?

To enhance our perspective of the causes of our demise, we can recognize that we die because (1) we do something harmful to ourselves or (2) a truck falls on us (or some similar disaster).

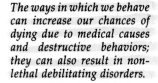

By rationally controlling our behavior, we can better our lives and those of others about us.

In this chapter we assess these pitfalls that await us. Then, in Chapter 15 we consider ways of reengineering our behavior to eliminate the prime cause (self-inflicted damage) and also to attempt to stay out of the way of trucks. As a result we can prolong life and make the inevitable pathway to death more productive and enjoyable.

NATURE AND EXTENT OF OUR PROBLEMS

Medical/Behavioral Causes of Premature Death.   Each year in the United States, we have been losing fewer adult lives to premature deaths (those before 65 years of age). Yet, major medical causes of premature death indicate that we have a long way to go; for instance, premature deaths due to cardiovascular disease number 12 million and 4.8 million are due to cancer, according to the World Health Organization in 1990. Figure 14.1 shows the percentages of these deaths, some of which could be prevented. Specific kinds of behaviors that can lead to premature death include smoking cigarettes, consuming drugs, and riding motorcycles.

The ways in which we behave can increase our chances of dying due to medical causes and destructive behaviors; they can also result in non-lethal debilitating disorders.

Premature death of young Americans (those under 35 years of age) is primarily due to accidents and deliberate injuries, which claim some 143,000 lives per year,

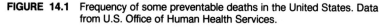

FIGURE 14.1   Frequency of some preventable deaths in the United States. Data from U.S. Office of Human Health Services.

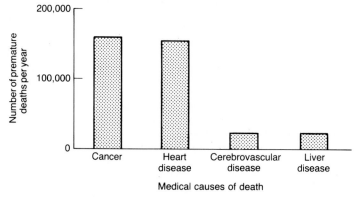

more than deaths from illness. About half of the deaths of children under 15 years are due to injuries; the rate rises to about 80 percent for the 15–24-year-old bracket.

Suicides Have Increased. Among Americans between the ages of 15 and 25 years, the suicide rate is epidemic. It rose from 5.2 per 100,000 in 1960 to 12.3 in 1980, doubling within a single generation. This rate translates into 100 successful suicides per week, although there are about a half million attempted suicides per year among young Americans. About 90 percent of suicide attempts are by young females. However, young males are the more successful so that the absolute number of young men who kill themselves is greater. The rate of suicide among young people has also dramatically risen throughout the world, particularly in Australia, Japan, Sweden, Denmark, and Hungary.

Debilitating Conditions. Debilitating disorders from which Americans do not die are even more numerous. For instance, brain damage leaves many people permanently in vegetative states. Although mental illnesses do not necessarily shorten the life span, they certainly reduce the quality of life. About one-fifth of adult Americans are victimized by psychiatric problems.

The most prevalent mental disorder is anxiety, which, including phobias and panic disorders, affects from 7 to 15 percent of the U.S. population. Alcohol and drug problems afflict about 7 percent; about 6 percent of adults are affected by depression, mania, and other affective disorders. Schizophrenia afflicts about 1 percent of Americans.

These statistics emphasize that the ways we behave cause various kinds of diseases, disorders, and even death.

THE IMPORTANCE OF BIOBEHAVIORAL CONTROL

By controlling our behavior, we can prevent many catastrophes that prematurely terminate life. The major strategies are to intervene chemically or behaviorally within the cybernetic circuits that generate maladaptive behaviors. One example of behavioral control is the beneficial use of exercise: 102 million Americans swim, 40 million bowl, 30 million roller skate, and 25 million play tennis!

By carefully engineering one's behavior, life-style can be improved.

To specify some of our control problems, let us sample psychiatric and other biologically related disorders and diseases that we develop.

KINDS OF DISORDERS
Stress and Its Effects on the Body

"Stress" Has a Negative Connotation. The word *stress,* which entered the English language as early as 1410 A.D., has been especially related to negative experiences, including applying physical force to an object or person. An example is the use of thumbscrews as a method of physical torture known as "compression stress." Today's meaning of the word is often similar, as when people say that their day "stressed them out."

A stressful situation (a stressor) evokes the startle reaction, wherein we rise on the balls of our feet and tense the striated muscles as we hunch forward to prepare for fight or flight.

Stressful Events Evoke the Startle Reaction Pattern.   Although the term *stress* is variously used, we define it here as an external stimulus (a stressor) that evokes an emergency startle pattern that includes covert and overt responses. Within milliseconds, the body hunches forward as the entire striated musculature contracts. We rise on the balls of the feet, bending the knees, with a tightening of the abdomen. Afferent neural impulses from the contracting striated musculature then initiate many other events that lead to hormonal reactions, emotional experiences, and so on. If the danger is a tiger in the jungle, the reactions are quite overt for fight or flight. But if the danger is more subtle, as in the stresses of the contemporary concrete jungle, the startle pattern may be only covert. In either case the body becomes very active.

The startle reaction is useful for us in many ways; for example, the body's adaptive mechanisms produce endorphins that can prevent the feeling of pain during a stressful situation. The flow of endorphins also leads to a sensation of calmness and lowered blood pressure, respiration, and heart rate. Adrenalin and cortisone are also secreted, both of which may make us "feel good."

Pathological Stress.   But if the startle pattern becomes prolonged, excessive, and inappropriate, we chronically overtense our muscles with autonomic changes. These constant widespread bodily patterns of muscular overtension due to stresses of life lead to many disorders. As with a mechanical system, prolonged or sudden excessive stress can cause weak systems of the body to malfunction. Muscular overtension is a major component of psychiatric and psychosomatic disorders. Clinical, epidemiological, and experimental studies have confirmed that stressful situations lead to a number of unfortunate psychiatric and medical consequences. Sustained stress combined with increased sodium intake has been shown to produce hypertension in animals. Emotional stress may facilitate illness because of a depressing effect on the immune system. Claude Bernard told us that a necessary condition for maintaining life is the maintenance of a constant internal environment. This constancy (homeostasis) must be maintained in spite of continuous changes in the external environment that influence internal systems. If the stresses of life disrupt this internal constancy, serious health consequences may develop.

Chronic tension of muscles can lead to numerous bodily disorders.

The stresses of life do not seem to lead to any single, unique pathology. Rather, they increase the probability that the individual may develop such illnesses as gastric intestinal disorders, hypertension, myocardial infarctions, cancer, tuberculosis, pneumonia, or more minor afflictions such as colds, headaches, or insomnia. Some individuals are uniquely predisposed to such diseases.

Subjective Experiences.   What some describe as "feelings of stress" are no doubt the result of the muscular tensions that occur in reaction to stressors. As discussed in Chapter 13 (e.g., p. 407), increased muscle tensions give rise to sensations that are essential elements of the sensation of stress. This thus follows the James-Lange Theory of Emotion, holding that peripheral components of emotions are essential for generating the emotional experience, quite as we developed in Chapter 13.

Stress, Blood Sugar Level, and Diabetes.   Children with juvenile diabetes mellitus who are impatient, aggressive, or competitive have been shown to react to stress with increased levels of blood sugar. (High levels of blood sugar are dangerous for the diabetic.) The stressor releases stress hormones such as adrenalin which increase the level of glucose in the blood. In contrast, those diabetic children who are more passive and relaxed do not show that increase. Diabetics are particularly vulnerable to the stresses of life and should take special care to learn to relax.

Does Stress Cause Voodoo Deaths? Voodoo practices that cause instant death have apparently been observed in many cultures throughout the world. One possibility is that a psychological process of suggestion can lead to death. Thus, extreme fright could disrupt the sympathetic nervous system and paralyze vital bodily functions. One research project studied individuals who experienced great fear after committing such acts as adultery or homicide. Fear exacerbates gastrointestinal and other disorders. In contrast, another theory is that some "voodoo deaths" are merely due to the cessation of water and food intake. Possibly such great fear then caused these people to believe that they should die, whereupon they ceased eating and drinking. In some primitive cultures the relatives assemble around the perpetrator of crimes, depriving them of water and food so as not to nurture the evil spirits that inhabit them. Accordingly, some voodoo deaths may not be due to suggestion or paralyzing fear but to dehydration.

Some Psychiatric Disorders

In this section we sample some of the classic "mental" disorders (which are really behavioral). Everyone experiences adjustment problems to some extent. Sometimes they are distracting for us and for those with whom we relate, but they seldom are sufficiently severe to seriously disrupt our lives. Temper tantrums, mood variations, and so forth are common but temporary. When behavioral disorders become severe enough to interfere with our everyday functioning, they have classically been referred to as **neurotic disorders. Psychotic disorders** are extremely disruptive. However, authorities disagree about the various diagnostic categories. For example the ICD-9 (the International Classification of Diseases) continues to use the term *neurotic disorders* while the DSM-III-R (the Diagnostic and Statistical Manual of Mental Disorders) no longer uses the term *neurosis*. Some authorities even refuse to use standard classifications. Therefore, our later discussion will illustrate only some classic syndromes, for example, neurotic disorders, which have included anxiety state, obsessive-compulsive disorders, phobic disorders, and hysteria.

It is normal to have minor, temporary adjustment problems, but sustained behaviors that interfere with everyday functioning have traditionally been referred to as neurotic or, if extremely disruptive, psychotic disorders.

Psychoses have been classified as various kinds of schizophrenic disorders and affective psychoses (especially manic and depressive disorders). Psychotic disorders are believed by many to have a biological basis—they are typically alleviated by chemotherapy. The major advance in psychiatry in recent decades, in fact, has been the development and application of effective chemical substances that alleviate some neurotic and psychotic disorders. We will enlarge on the use of drugs for these control purposes in the next chapter. For now, let us survey some common disorders.

NEUROTIC DISORDERS

Anxiety State

Fear Is Critical for Survival. Fearfulness often saves us from harm by anticipating some threat or danger. The fear may concern our own security and future welfare or it may be about threats to others who are close to us. By anticipating a threat to our well-being, we can plan ahead to meet or avoid it. We may use fear to rationally behave to prevent disorders, diseases, and being hit by a truck.

Fear helps us to survive if we use it to rationally deal with threats to our welfare.

When you experience pain or the threat of pain, your body naturally tenses throughout its striated muscle system, including especially the eye muscles as one visualizes such things as the cause of the pain. If you hear that somebody has suffered injury, the muscles of your body also tense (contract) in empathy. Tensing is a natural reaction that is part of the primitive startle response pattern that prepares you for fight or flight. Tensing helps to meet or to avoid danger and is thus protective and adaptive. However, if the tension becomes excessive and/or prolonged beyond the threat, it becomes pathological. Although it is realistic to be afraid of a mugger in front of you, a continuous fear of muggers when they are not present is not reasonable and may develop into a minor pathological behavior called nervousness. A nervous person is continuously anticipating some future threat. A more severe condition of sustained fear can qualify as an anxiety state. It has long been held that excessive anxiety is the hallmark of neurosis. Symptoms of **anxiety states** include heart palpitations, irregular and difficult breathing, excessive fatigue, dizziness, and always extreme fear. Panic disorder is one kind of anxiety state.

If muscular tension becomes chronic and excessive, it is maladaptive and may develop into a neurotic disorder.

Anxiety is generated as we chronically tense our striated muscles in anticipation of danger and threats.

Anxiety state is a condition wherein fear is represented by unique patterns of excessive tension of the striated muscles, including rapidly tensing eye muscles as one visualizes the threat.

Fearfulness Is Represented by Body Tensions.   A person who fears flying in an airplane represents that fear by tensing the muscles as he or she imagines flying. In imagining, the individual clutches the arms of a seat in fear ("the white knuckle syndrome") as he or she visualizes the scene with rapidly tensing eye muscles.

The Esophagus Contracts as a Component of Fear Reaction.   The esophagus, containing a mixture of striated and smooth muscle, responds to threat by contracting. The contraction is the peripheral part of the neuromuscular circuits that generate the emotion felt as one thinks about a threat to well-being. The esophagus can be in mild spasm for hours, weeks, or months. In a prolonged condition of fearfulness known as **globus hystericus,** there is chronic muscular spasm of the esophagus so that an individual feels something like a ball, lump, or clutching in the throat region.

Fear and anxiety are represented in part by constriction of the esophagus.

The relation of a contracting esophagus to the subjective experience of fear and thus of anxiety is revealed in the origin of the term *anxiety. Anxiety* was introduced into the English language from the thirteenth-century French *anguisse*, which meant a "a painful sensation in the throat." A person who was particularly emotional referred to the feeling as that which one gets when a fishbone is caught in the throat. Similar terms in other languages are *ansia* in Italian and *angst* in German.

We Covertly Visualize Difficulties with Our Eyes.   The representation of anxiety is also especially carried in the eye muscles as one visualizes specific matters of concern. No doubt many of our conditions of exaggerated fearfulness are learned through the visual modality. As Berger (1962) showed, people can vicariously acquire emotional responses merely by observing the pain of others. In fear, we visualize threats and relive past dangers. By tensing the eye muscles, we activate cybernetic circuits between the eyes and the brain to generate visual images that are components of our anxieties, just as we do in other emotional states (see Chapter 9). We can electromyographically measure covert eye responses that uniquely occur as one engages in such visual imagery (see Chapter 13).

We can empathically experience emotions by observing and covertly reacting to the pain viewed in other people.

Specific anxieties are represented by unique regions of the muscle system, including the esophagus and the eyes.

To treat anxiety, the patient learns to seek out tension arising throughout the entire striated musculature, especially in the esophagus and eye muscles, and then to relax them.

Therapy for Anxiety

If anxiety is represented in the striated muscle components of neuromuscular circuits, relaxation of the striated musculature should tranquilize those circuits and relieve the anxiety that they generate (see Fig. 14.6). Research has shown that when the esophagus becomes relaxed, the individual reports that fear and distress have disappeared. Numerous studies have indicated that this strategy for relieving anxiety is highly successful (e.g., Jacobson, 1938b; 1970). The patient first learns through Progressive Relaxation (cf. McGuigan, 1990, 1993b) to locate the relevant muscular tensions wherever they are in the body. With that highly cultivated ability to internally observe the world under the skin, the individual systematically relaxes those body tensions. As tensions are relaxed, the neuromuscular circuits of which they are the peripheral component cease to reverberate and the states of anxiety generated by the tensions are correspondingly eliminated (e.g., relaxation of tensions discovered in the arms and hands while imaging flying can help eliminate the white knuckle syndrome).

Obsessive-Compulsive Disorders

Obsessions (recurrent undesired thoughts) and **compulsions** (ritualistically repeated responses) are not uncommon. The usual diagnostic criteria for "compulsive personality disorder" include trying to be perfect, being rigid, workaholism, indecisiveness, strict compliance with rules, and excessive organization. In trying for impossible perfection, obsessive-compulsive individuals are unhappy with themselves. Indecisive behavior may result from the fear of failing to make correct choices in difficult situations.

Obsessive-compulsive disorder is characterized by obsessions (involuntarily repeated thoughts) and compulsions (rigidly recurring responses). The individual strives for excessive orderliness and perfection.

There are many diverse examples of obsessive-compulsive behaviors. Some people hoard things so that their rooms are cluttered; in a desire for perfection, some worry continuously about whether or not their behavior is ethical or moral; others have repeated sexual thoughts or frequently wash their hands or continuously check to make sure their doors and windows are locked.

There is some evidence of a biological basis for obsessive-compulsive disorders (e.g., there are reduced levels of serotonin in the blood of those so diagnosed, implicating a serotonin deficiency). The drug chlorimipramine, which modifies the serotonin level in the blood, has been successful in treating the disorder.

Many kinds of **compulsive behaviors** may seriously disrupt an individual's life. They are identified with the suffix *mania*. For instance, common stealing is kleptomania (*klepto* means steal; *mania* means mad or insane). Some other compulsive behaviors that have widespread significance for society include gambling, drug and alcohol abuse, and some eating disorders.

COMPULSIVE GAMBLING

Compulsive gamblers continue gambling regardless of whether they are winning or losing. However, lack of control is more serious when they are losing, perhaps because they are obsessed with the notion that a big win is just one bet away. Gamblers typically believe that the laws of probability, which are certain to lead to losses, do not apply to them. But even if they understand that they will eventually lose, their control is less than that of noncompulsive gamblers.

Destructive Behaviors. Compulsive gamblers often destroy their families as family needs are ignored and money is lost to gambling. The compulsion to make up for their losses frequently leads them to steal or run up large debts. The compulsive gambler is often self-destructive too. For example, in one survey, one-third of the compulsive gamblers sampled had serious weight problems, 42 percent were drug abusers, 38 percent had cardiovascular problems, and 50 percent had violated laws.

The compulsive gambler rigidly repeats gambling responses in spite of destructive consequences.

Compulsive gambling behavior is held to be learned and maintained because of powerful intermittent reinforcement schedules; as such, behavior therapy has had some success in controlling the behavior.

Destructive gambling often extends beyond race track betting and the like to include actions by financially successful business entrepreneurs. Why someone who has millions or billions of dollars breaks laws to achieve even more constitutes a behavioral control problem for society. The United States lost upwards of $500 billion in the savings and loan failures. Perhaps some of that loss could be accounted for by executives who gambled with other people's money.

Compulsions Are Learned.   Compulsive gambling is typically learned by age 20, but there are gender differences — women generally prefer lotteries, bingo, and slot machines, while men prefer sports betting. Like other behaviors, gambling is maintained through reinforcement. Because the reinforcements are intermittent, the conditioning is very powerful (i.e., those who receive only occasional, intermittent reinforcements for a response take longer to extinguish the response than those who are continuously reinforced for each response). Reinforcements include not only money, but also the excitement of placing bets and anticipating winning.

Therapy.   Our general therapeutic principle is that control of both normal and aberrant behavior can be achieved by controlling the muscular components of neuromuscular circuits. Two examples for gambling follow. If learned, gambling behavior can be controlled through conditioning. For example, mild electric shocks administered to the fingers as the gambler played a slot machine, read a racing form, and so on has been moderately successful. Relaxation therapy has also been somewhat successful — the individuals visualize themselves approaching the gambling situation, then relax their muscles. Through such relaxation therapy, they may get control of the muscles they use to engage in gambling behavior.

DRUG ADDICTION AND DRUG ABUSE

Drug abuse is an extremely serious problem in the United States, just as it was in precommunist China in the 1940s. Especially alarming is the dramatic increase in the number of infants whose bodies and brains have been damaged due to the use of drugs by their mothers during pregnancy. While many of these children die shortly after birth, those who live face difficult problems that society has to deal with as well.

Accidents Correlated with Drug Use.   Psychiatric patients taking one or more medications have two to three times more accidents than psychiatric patients who are not taking drugs. Valium is extensively used and impairs a driver's ability to stay in a lane, to maintain an even speed, and to navigate exits, and it increases the time and distance needed to stop a car. Allergy sufferers taking medication have 50 to 100 percent more accidents and time loss from work because of accidents, relative to nonallergy sufferers.

Catastrophes Due to Alcohol Abuse.   In the United States about 18 percent of one sample of nighttime drivers had some alcohol in their blood and about 7 percent exceeded the legal limits. Half of all car accidents in the United States involve the use of alcohol. Of drivers who are fatally injured, about half have blood alcohol levels over the legal limit.

Numerous calamities result from users of a variety of drugs including valium, alcohol, and psychoactive drugs.

Some studies estimate that alcohol is associated with about half of all murders, and about a third of rapes, suicides, and arrests. More than half of all production problems in society are drug related; about 14 percent of the American work force is affected by drug and alcohol problems and $70 billion is lost in production per year (about two-thirds of that due to absenteeism). Absenteeism among alcoholics is two to three times greater than the norm. Each employee with a drinking problem loses

22 work days a year as a direct result of drinking or related health problems. Alcoholics use health care benefits three to four times more than the norm. Problem drinkers have been found to function at about two-thirds of their work potential and are repeatedly involved in grievance proceedings. Work accident rates among alcoholics are three to four times above the norm with five times more compensation claims for alcoholics.

A Great Variety of Drugs are Abused.   Psychoactive drugs, which provide escape by reducing anxiety or creating a "high," are variously classified. One system classifies them according to their effects on the central nervous system; these include narcotics (e.g., heroin), antipsychotics (e.g., chlorpromazine), hallucinogens (e.g., LSD), and general depressants and stimulants. Antipsychotics, and perhaps others, have been thought to be effective because they, in part, relax muscular components of neuromuscular circuits.

Other classifications include opiates, which alleviate pain and anxiety; sedatives, which induce relaxation and sleep; stimulants, which increase activation of the central nervous system; tranquilizers, which relax muscles and thereby reduce anxiety; analgesics (pain killers), and hallucinogens and psychedelics, which activate fantasy and imagination.

Tolerance and Dependence.   All drugs can lead to tolerance and dependence. **Tolerance** occurs when a substance becomes less effective with repeated administration, requiring larger doses to achieve the initial effect. **Dependence** is a kind of compulsion that requires periodic or continuous administration of a drug to produce pleasure and avoid the discomfort of withdrawal symptoms. Once one develops **drug dependence,** removal of the drug can be catastrophic for the abuser.

Definitions of Addictions.   The classic definition of **addiction** includes substance abuse with withdrawal symptoms and tolerance. However, many authorities now prefer to define addiction as a compulsion for consuming a substance wherein there is loss of control and continued use despite aversive consequences.

How Drugs Affect the Brain

Drugs enter the bloodstream where they are widely distributed to affect various organs throughout the body, although most drugs have their greatest effect on the brain. One way that drugs change the way neurons in the brain chemically communicate with each other is by acting at synapses. Drugs such as heroin, marijuana, alcohol, LSD, PCP, and nicotine are direct-acting drugs because they function like neurotransmitters. They travel across synapses; when they arrive at the postsynaptic region in the next neuron, they fit into receptors there like a key into a lock (see Figs. 4.21 and 14.2). The behavioral consequences are changes in mood and behavior. For example, when tetrahydrocannabinol (THC), the active ingredient in marijuana, binds to (fits into) neural receptors on the postsynaptic neurons, the consequences of smoking marijuana occur—people may enter a dream-fantasy state, heart rate increases, thought processes change (are often distorted), and so on.

Drugs also affect neuronal activity, although we do not understand very well how they do so. Some evidence indicates that when drugs enter the bloodstream, they may cause **astrocytes** (a type of glial cell) to release potassium that concentrates outside of neurons; changes in potassium concentration are important in dilating cerebral arterioles (small blood vessels widely spaced throughout the brain). Since the arterioles are widespread, potassium defuses to them rather slowly, which may

The drug addict can develop tolerance, which occurs when a substance becomes less effective with repeated administration, and dependence, which requires repeated dosage to prevent withdrawal symptoms.

The classic criteria for addictive behavior are withdrawal symptoms and tolerance, but some authorities have replaced that definition with one of consumption compulsion and loss of control.

Many drugs produce behavioral changes as they are transmitted across synapses where they fit into receptors on postsynaptic regions.

When drugs enter the bloodstream, they may release potassium from astrocytes in the brain. Potassium concentration outside of neurons may cause neurons to increase their actions.

account for the slow activity of drugs. A consequent altered activity of neurons may partially explain the effects of drugs.

Alcohol Abuse

No doubt alcohol is the most widely abused drug. There is an old saying that alcohol causes one to become jocose, next bellicose, then lachrymose, and finally comatose. While low doses of alcohol only impair coordination, high doses also impair memory.

Characteristics of Alcoholism.   There are millions of alcoholics in the United States. The exact number depends on how one distinguishes alcoholics from problem drinkers. The defining characteristics of an alcoholic are varied and numerous. They include memory blackouts, problems in everyday living, tolerance, and alcohol withdrawal symptoms. Sudden discontinuance of alcohol may cause shakiness or DTs (delirium tremens). Among drugs, only alcohol produces blackout amnesia.

Predisposing Factors.   The alcoholic syndrome is typically viewed as an outgrowth of the interaction of a variety of biological, psychological, and social factors. Research has indicated that the main factors contributing to alcoholism are social pressure, as in peer sanction of heavy drinking, and ready availability of alcohol.

Some **dipsomaniacs** are held to have a character disorder called antisocial personality (sociopath). Often alcoholism develops in someone who has been drinking moderately for years but, perhaps because of sudden stresses, increases alcohol consumption to an excessive level. Individuals differ in their degree of susceptibility. The signs that characterize alcoholism and problem drinking show progressive changes as the problem develops.

Some research suggests a genetic predisposition to alcohol dependency. This seems to be especially true among some peoples in the colder northern regions, such as Ireland and Scandinavia. More than 100 studies published in this century indicate a familial basis for alcoholism, although this no doubt could reflect both genetic and environmental factors. According to one notion, the brain generates chemicals called THIQ that cause addiction. These chemicals are thought to be created when the by-products of alcohol react with dopamine neurotransmitters. The presence and amount of THIQ in a person could be genetically determined. Other biologically oriented research has shown that the average evoked potential, particularly P300 (see Fig. 8.13), is different in alcoholics and in their relatives than in nonalcoholic individuals. Yet, even if there is a genetic predisposition to alcoholism, one need not succumb to alcoholism any more than to other diseases to which one may be predisposed, such as tuberculosis. If forewarned, one can forestall or prevent the disorder or disease.

When Should Alcohol Not Be Used? Research has indicated that small amounts of alcohol may produce protective effects against cardiac disease. One theory is that alcohol increases HDL cholesterol. On the other hand, alcohol consumption in excess of two drinks per day seems to increase blood fat levels, including triglycerides and LDL cholesterol. There are a number of conditions in which alcohol is definitely contraindicated (e.g., if it interferes with the everyday functioning of a person or with the family, or if it deleteriously affects the person's body). One objective sign of alcohol impairing health is that the liver is unable to cope with the amount of alcohol being ingested. This may show up in the blood as an abnormality of amino acid ratios, plasma lipoproteins, or hepatic enzymes.

Behavioral definitions of alcoholism and problem drinking emphasize difficulties in everyday life (marital, job, social, or health problems) as a direct result of alcohol.

The main factors contributing to alcoholism are social pressure and easy availability of alcohol.

Some evidence suggests that there is a genetic predisposition to alcoholism, but if so, that is no different from a predisposition to other diseases/disorders.

Patients with gout can probably drink moderately with no ill effects, even though it had been thought for many years that alcohol causes gout. Patients with gastritis, gastric cancer, and bleeding in the upper digestive tract clearly should not drink. Nor should individuals with pancreatitis, cirrhosis, or hepatitis. Authorities disagree about whether patients with gastric and duodenal ulcers should consume alcohol (symptoms of peptic ulcer were diagnosed in only 5 percent of 430 alcoholics, which is approximately the frequency of peptic ulcer in the general population). But whatever the body's condition, it is clear that alcohol should not be mixed with certain other agents such as barbiturates, for these combinations can be disastrous.

There is a lively controversy as to whether alcoholics should consume any alcohol at all. Total abstinence is required in the Alcohols Anonymous (AA) programs while others espouse limited, controlled drinking. AA has been held to be effective for certain kinds of alcoholics. Research supporting controlled drinking programs has employed such poor methodology that its positive conclusions cannot be accepted. The issue is complex and unsettled.

Korsakoff's Syndrome—Characteristics.   Some alcoholics develop **Korsakoff's syndrome,** so named after the Russian physician Sergei Korsakoff's work in 1889. The main symptoms are apathy, confusion, and difficulty in forming new long-term memories (anterograde amnesia, inability to learn new information). The patient may recall events of long ago but may have difficulty entering new information into long-term memory. Confabulation and reduplication are characteristics of Korsakoff's syndrome. **Confabulation** is the production of incorrect information. It may be mild, such as exaggeration or weird fabrication. Confabulation may be due to frontal lobe disease. In **reduplication,** the patient can say what is true, such as his or her own names but does not believe that the information *is* true. Such delusions may be maintained even if confronted by evidence that the information is true.

Causes.   The alcoholic who goes several days without eating while drinking only alcohol is at risk for a severe thiamine (vitamin B1) deficiency. Glucose, which is converted from most foods and used for brain metabolism itself needs to be metabolized by means of vitamin B1. Consequently, vitamin B1 deficiency can lead to a long-term inability of the brain to use glucose. While consuming nothing but alcohol, much of the brain will gradually deteriorate. Specifically, there is a shrinkage of neurons in the dorsal-medial thalamus, in the mammalary bodies, and the hypothalamus as well as diffusely throughout the brain. Korsakoff's syndrome can be treated effectively if vitamin B1 is administered early. About 5 percent of all alcoholics eventually develop Korsakoff's syndrome.

Brain scans show some generalized atrophy of the right hemisphere and frontal lobes of the alcoholic brain. Yet, a sound causal connection between alcohol itself and brain damage has not been established.

Norman Butters has accumulated evidence that patients with Alzheimer's disease (p. 398) and Korsakoff's syndrome have similar memory and brain disorders. Butters concludes that the critical area of the brain affected in Korsakoff's and Alzheimer's is the **nucleus basalis of Meynert (NbM),** named after its nineteenth-century discoverer, W. Meynert; the NbM is located in the basal forebrain. The number of neurons in the NbM of Alzheimer's patients is about 79 percent fewer than normal individuals. Consequently, the reason that Korsakoff and Alzheimer's patients have similar cognitive (memory) defects may thus be because the NbM, which secretes **acetylcholine (Ach),** is deficient in both cases. This conclusion is

Whether alcoholics should totally abstain or whether they can engage in controlled drinking programs remains a controversial issue.

Korsakoff's syndrome involves apathy, confusion, and difficulty in forming new long-term memories and is probably due to the vitamin B1 deficiency common in alcoholics. Confabulation and reduplication are also common symptoms.

Korsakoff's syndrome and Alzheimer's disease share similar psychological symptoms and have common neurological defects, particularly in the nucleus basalis of Meynert, which produces considerable acetylcholine.

strengthened because patients with different brain defects, like Huntington's disease, have cognitive deficiencies that differ from those of Korsakoff's and Alzheimer's patients. It is presently believed that when cells in the NbM cannot produce sufficient acetylcholine, senile plaques may form to break down neural transmission from the NbM to the cortex. Apparently, circuits between the NbM and the cortex are very important for cognitive processing.

There is a common belief that alcohol prematurely ages the brain, but the pathology of the aged and alcoholic differ. For example, there is but a mild memory loss in alcoholics and excessive drinking does not affect long-term ability to use language—the verbal performance of alcoholics remains about normal. Butter's interpretation is that alcohol does not age the brain.

Apparently, alcohol does not prematurely age the brain.

Cocaine Abuse

Cocaine is one of the most powerfully addictive and reinforcing drugs which has contributed to cocaine abuse becoming an epidemic in the United States.

The Biochemistry of a Cocaine "High." Normally, neurotransmitters (such as dopamine) cross the synapse and are reabsorbed into the liberating neuron (Fig. 14.2). However, cocaine and amphetamines block this retrieval process so that the neurotransmitters remain in the synapse, repeatedly stimulating the neighboring neurons. It is thought that the body senses these stimulations as reinforcing ("pleasurable") events. Correspondingly, the body becomes aroused as heart rate and blood pressure increase. As the reabsorption of dopamine back into the liberating neuron continues to be blocked, the dopamine in the synapses is metabolized (broken down). Consequently, the emitting neurons become depleted of the neurotransmitter—they cannot produce dopamine fast enough to make up for the loss, so that the reinforcing effects of cocaine cease. The receptor cells, lacking dopamine, become overly sensitive, which is thought to create the feeling of craving. The user then may ingest more cocaine to relieve the craving.

Neurotransmitters are normally reabsorbed in the synapse; drugs like cocaine and amphetamines block the reabsorption process. Consequently, neurotransmitters remain in the synapse repeatedly stimulating neurons to produce a reinforcing effect.

As the liberating neuron is depleted of dopamine, the receptor cells become supersensitive, creating a craving that leads to more ingestion of the substance. This constitutes a positive feedback circuit that may eventually send the system out of control.

This unhealthy cybernetic circuit can continue for some time: It starts with the ingestion of cocaine (amphetamines, etc.), which blocks the reabsorption of dopamine, producing the "high" effect; then, with the breakdown of dopamine in the synapses, a need to inject more substance is created; with ingestion of more cocaine,

FIGURE 14.2   Neurotransmitters such as dopamine normally cross a synapse to communicate with receptors on receiving neurons whereupon they are reabsorbed by the emitting cell (left). However, cocaine blocks the reabsorption so that dopamine remains in the synapse to repeatedly stimulate the receptor cells, producing a "high" (middle figure). Eventually the dopamine is metabolized (depleted), producing a craving for more cocaine (right).

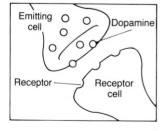 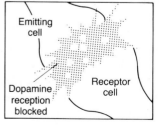 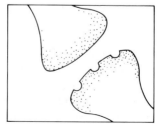

the craving is relieved and a high returns. The vicious (positive feedback) cycle may continue until the body collapses.

Negative Consequences of Cocaine Use. There are many detrimental effects of cocaine use. Paranoid perceptions can lead to violence. Tactile hallucinations are common, such as feeling that insects are crawling under the skin. Visual hallucinations, "snow lights," may be perceived, probably due to neural stimulation of the retina from somewhere in the visual pathways.

Manic behavior with flight of ideas, restlessness, and irritability are common, as are stereotyped behaviors (pacing, bruxism, scratching the skin, etc.), and disinterest in sex, often with loss of ejaculatory ability. **Anhedonia** (inability to enjoy the usual pleasures of life) often exists for days or weeks in serious users. Insomnia is common.

Cocaine deleteriously affects the cardiovascular system perhaps by releasing large amounts of adrenaline which stresses the heart and lungs (e.g., the heart may twitch wildly as in the ventricular fibrillation that caused death for the famous basketball and football stars Len Bias and Don Rogers).

Considerable body weight may be lost by not eating during an extended coke-run, resulting in serious protein and vitamin B deficiencies. Use of cocaine by pregnant women can retard fetal growth causing neurological abnormalities, and in extreme cases loss of the small intestine and brain-damaging strokes. Some of the worst effects occur during the first three months of pregnancy, when the mother often does not know she is pregnant and the baby's organs are forming. Cocaine-exposed babies have ten times greater risk of crib death than nonexposed babies. Death usually occurs because the baby stops breathing for abnormally long periods.

Crack Is More Dangerous. Certainly, an informed, reasonable individual would not even start cocaine use. Yet, the epidemic continues and expands with the even more dangerous form of cocaine called crack. Crack is a mixture of cocaine with baking soda and water that is heated, allowed to harden, and then cracked into little pieces. By smoking it in cigarettes or water pipes, crack provides a quicker high than snorted cocaine. However, the high is of shorter duration and the crash is more dramatic. As little as 30 or so seconds after taking crack the high may turn into depression that leads to another hit. The positive feedback circuit gains in momentum.

Cocaine can seriously damage the brain by disturbing its delicate biochemical state of homeostasis. Neural functioning with muscles then becomes unpredictable and behavior may go out of control. In studies of rats fed cocaine, 60 percent of the nerve cells related to motor skills were destroyed, leading to ataxia, as in Parkinson's disease.

Treatment requires absolute abstinence from cocaine and other psychoactive drugs, detoxification, possible pharmacologic therapy, and nutritional assistance. Behavior therapy may also be applied.

Tobacco Addiction

History. The first report of tobacco use came from Christopher Columbus in 1492, courtesy of the natives of San Salvador who had been using the leaves for centuries. Tobacco was then distributed throughout the world over the next 150 years by Portuguese sailors. Tobacco was smoked as cigars, in cigarettes wrapped in

Negative effects of cocaine include paranoid perceptions, tactile hallucinations of itching, visual hallucinations of "snowlights," maniclike behaviors, poor decision-making ability, disinterest in sex, and moderate to life-threatening cardiovascular disorders.

Weight loss, and even anorexia, is the rule in frequent cocaine users.

Crack, a mixture of cocaine with baking soda and water, produces a quicker high than snorted cocaine, but the high is shorter in duration, the crash is more serious, and the danger is greater to the brain, heart, and effectors.

corn husks, in pipes and used as a syrup to be swallowed or applied to the gums. It was chewed, snuffed, and used rectally as a ceremonial enema. In 1574, Nicholas Monardes recommended tobacco as a remedy for 36 different ailments, describing tobacco as a healing herb sent by God to humans. However, some disputed its medical value and held that tobacco was sent by the devil. In the 1600s, the sultans in Turkey executed subjects who were caught smoking; the Romanov tsars in Russia publicly tortured smokers; and the Chinese decapitated smokers. Still the frequency of tobacco use spread, in large part, because of technological advances in mass-producing cigarettes.

While tobacco was originally thought to be beneficial, eventually its harmful effects were recognized. Nicotine addiction presents another problem of self-control.

Hazards. Smoking, the single most preventable cause of death, has been called the only industry in the United States that routinely kills 390,000 of its best customers. Through lung cancer, heart disease, and other illnesses, cigarettes are implicated in one out of every six deaths in the United States. A smoker has three times the risk of sudden cardiac death compared to a nonsmoker. People who smoke two packs of cigarettes a day have a lung-cancer rate twenty-five times greater than that for nonsmokers.

Tobacco Is Addictive. Nicotine is officially recognized in the United States as an abused drug and a drug of dependency, apparently due to a need to maintain a certain nicotine level in the body.

Marijuana (Cannabis) Use

Psychological Effects of Marijuana. Marijuana produces negative consequences that include distortion of various perceptual and cognitive processes and impairment of recall, psychomotor performance, and peripheral vision. Sometimes there are illusions and hallucinations, and paranoid thinking is not unusual.

Marijuana seriously distorts cognitive and performance abilities.

As a consequence, smoking marijuana, like other drugs, can deleteriously affect performance of duties important to the public (e.g., those of bus, train, and truck drivers and even experienced airplane pilots). For instance, some pilots who smoked a strong social dose of marijuana tended to increase the size and frequency of their maneuvering responses and showed a greater likelihood of missing a simulated runway center line.

Marijuana Can Become Addictive. Repeated use of cannabis produces tolerance and withdrawal symptoms in many species with behavioral and physiological changes.

Harmful physiological effects of marijuana include damage to the lungs and heart and to the fetuses of pregnant women.

Physiological Effects. Negative effects of marijuana persist for months after discontinuance. Abnormal EEGs and behavioral and structural brain changes have been identified in animals. Marijuana also interferes with energy processing (e.g., of energy-rich sugars used by testicular cells in humans and animals). Newborn female rats given THC during their first five days of life never developed female cycles; and after ten months their ovaries were insufficient in egg production.

Pregnant women who smoke pot pass THC to their fetuses along with various potentially permanent damage, especially to their reproductive abilities.

Marijuana smoking is also especially harmful to the lungs; it increases the likelihood of contracting bronchitis and lung cancer. One joint delivers much more tar to the lungs than a cigarette in part because smokers inhale deeply to maximize the effects. Carbon dioxide in the blood also increases four to five times more after smoking one joint relative to the increase after smoking one cigarette. Finally, tachycardia regularly accompanies marijuana use and cholinergic responses in the hippocampus diminish, which may account for memory deficit for recent events.

Some argue that marijuana is no more harmful than alcohol. However, the components of marijuana are stored in the body for very long periods of time, with effects that we do not adequately understand. On the other hand, thousands of years of alcohol use indicate that in "proper dosages" it is liberated relatively rapidly as harmless substances with no significant deleterious effects on the body. If there is a proper dosage for marijuana use by healthy people that can avoid its harmful effects on society, that dosage and mode of use have yet to be established.

Beneficial Medical Effects. For more than 1000 years the hemp plant, from which *cannabis sativa* comes, has been recognized as having beneficial medicinal properties. Marijuana reduces the intraocular pressure that occurs in glaucoma; it is a broncodilater that helps relieve asthma; and it reduces the nausea and vomiting that often occur with chemotherapy.

Tranquilizer Abuse

Young ambitious females and middle-aged housewives have been stereotyped as abusers of valium. Actually, though, about 71 percent of long-term users are age 50 or older and they are people who suffer high levels of emotional stress and chronic health problems. Furthermore two-thirds of tranquilizer users use them less than one month in a whole year. Abuse of tranquilizers used to be a major problem, but it no longer is because of greater caution by physicians in prescribing them.

Abuse of tranquilizers, especially valium, has been reduced probably because physicians have become more aware of their misuse.

Abuse of Performance-Enhancing Drugs

Humanity has long sought drugs to increase strength. In the late 1880s the famous neurologist Brown-Sequard prepared an extract of animal testosterone which he administered to himself and reported feelings of increased vigor. Synthetic and extracts of testosterone have anabolic (nitrogen-saving and protein-building) properties. It is thought that Russian athletes used such drugs in the early 1950s and the practice spread to the United States in the late 1950s.

Anabolic steroids are used mainly for muscle building and have serious side effects. Reports are that in males they cause atrophy of the testicles, resulting in the appearance of feminine characteristics. Decreased male hormone activity decreases the secretion of pituitary hormones which, in feedback circuits, further decreases testosterone production. Anabolic steroids also damage the liver, cause difficulty in urination because of modification of the prostate seminal vesicles, decrease sperm production, increase impotence, and enhance the male breasts. One famous case was that of Lyle Alzado, the outstanding professional football player who used body-building steroids. The National Football League physician specializing in this area held that those steroids caused his brain cancer, adding that anabolic steroids depressed the immune system and lymphocytes.

Anabolic steroids have been widely used to increase muscle mass, but they all have serious side effects.

A new menace threatens us in the form of a genetically engineered drug called recombinant Erythropoieten (rEPO), which is used to combat anemia associated with kidney failure. However, it is being increasingly used by athletes to enhance their stamina and performance. Authorities agree that it is indeed effective and is able to decrease a 20-minute running time by 30 seconds. The drug is produced naturally in the body so that there is no known test to determine its illegal use. Consequently, its increased use among athletes seems assured. Yet, like other drugs, its abuse can be quite serious. It is thought to have first been used by cyclists in Belgium and Holland starting about 1986. Within the next four years eighteen Dutch cyclists mysteriously died due, some experts concluded, to abuse of rEPO.

Addictive Behavior and Intoxication

Many common themes run through the various kinds of compulsive substance abuse disorders that we have surveyed. For one, addicts and nonaddicts alike typically become intoxicated when they take drugs. During intoxication, the metabolism of the brain is distorted with far-reaching peripheral effects. The intoxicated individual often makes improper decisions; is impulsive, irritable, and confused; and has impaired psychomotor functioning. Extreme intoxication can cause delirium, and even death.

Intoxication may be induced by alcohol and sedatives resulting in motor deficiencies including gait ataxia, slurred speech, trembling, poor coordination, and nystagmus (a quick, jerky movement of the eyes, followed by a slower return). It can also be produced by stimulants like cannabis and the hallucinogens that distort cognitions.

Addicts often seek an enhanced high by sharply increasing the concentration of the drug in the brain, producing rapid changes that maximize pharmacological effects.

To enhance a drug's "high," addicts often inject their drug into the bloodstream instead of taking it orally. A substance such as heroin injected into a vein can be lethal — 20 milligrams of heroin can reach the brain and other organs within 10 seconds where it stimulates susceptible cells in 1 to 3 seconds. Similarly, alcoholics may gulp drinks, and heavy smokers deeply inhale cigarette smoke.

Why Do People Seek Highs? Some people seek escape from depression or stressful problems through drugs. Drugs decrease inhibition so as to remove responsibility for one's behavior. Getting drunk often has high social value — young men think they are being macho and grown-up. Also, the immediate reinforcing effects of drugs obscure the long-term, negative effects.

Although people may be genetically predisposed to addictive behaviors, it is a learned phenomenon often controlled by environmental cues.

Addictive Behavior Is Learned. Because drugs are noxious it is not easy to acquire an addiction. Children and animals do not need or like the taste of drugs, alcohol, tobacco, caffeine, narcotics, and so on. Not only are they noxious, but they may induce nausea and dizziness. Although there may be genetic predispositions to addictions, people still must learn to tolerate and even crave drugs.

Addictive behaviors are learned and maintained because of their immediate reinforcing effects and are often evoked by associated cues.

Environmental Stimuli Acquire Control of Addictive Behavior. Once learned, addictive behavior can be evoked by cues associated with the taking of a drug. For instance, addicts who were discharged as "cured" have been seized with an intense craving when they returned to their home environments. Cues there evoked the craving. The tobacco addict often has a hard time refraining from smoking when drinking coffee. Such learned cues form the basis of much advertising as when an ice-cold beer or some delicious food presented on television sends us to the refrigerator.

Easy Availability of Substances Contributes to Addiction. Technological "advances" have often contributed to addiction by making the substance readily available. The ease with which college students obtain beer, often contributed by the beer companies themselves, has been identified as increasing beer consumption. The epidemic of alcoholism that followed the introduction of gin in the eighteenth century is another example (Fig. 14.3). Similarly, the introduction of the hypodermic

FIGURE 14.3 An engraving entitled "Gin Lane" by William Hogarth depicting an early epidemic of alcoholism.

needle in the nineteenth century contributed to an epidemic of narcotic addiction just as the mass production of cigarettes in the twentieth century was followed by an epidemic of smoking.

Difficulty of Assessing the Extent of the Use of Drugs. Often, laboratory tests are ineffective in determining drug use. For instance, checks on the laboratories throughout the United States that test urine have indicated that about 90 percent of them have unacceptable error rates for detecting barbiturates, amphetamines, cocaine, and morphine. As a result, we may get a false picture of how effective our programs are in combating drug abuse. Clearly, we need to improve the validity of assessment.

COMPULSIVE EATING DISORDERS

There Are a Variety of Behavioral Eating Disorders. The most common disorders are compulsive eating and obesity, although anorexia nervosa and bulimia have received increasing attention. A less common disorder is **pica,** which is the eating of substances that provide no nutrition. Pica is most prevalent among children over the age of about 18 months; however, it also occurs in adults. Another disorder is **rumination,** which is chewing and swallowing food that was previously eaten and regurgitated. Rumination is rare, occurring mostly in infants, although it is found in adults too. Conditional food aversion occurs when a food stimulus signals the onset of aversive consequences if the food is ingested. It has survival value when, through conditioning, we learn to avoid toxic substances. But it is an eating disorder when we learn to avoid safe food or become ill after ingesting safe food.

Behavioral eating disorders include anorexia nervosa, bulimia, pica, rumination, and obesity.

Compulsive Eating and Obesity

An estimated 34 million adult Americans are sufficiently obese that therapy is appropriate for them. Not only do obese individuals tend to overeat, they also tend to underexercise. Many compulsive eaters diet frequently, which can harm their health. As has been said, one may well lose a hundred pounds through dieting, but it is the same ten pounds lost over and over again.

The definition of excessive weight is somewhat arbitrary. However, obesity increases the risk of disease and shortens the life span. Research has shown that it contributes to diabetes, high blood pressure, high levels of blood fats associated with heart disease, some cancers, and a number of other health-threatening conditions. Obese males have higher death rates from cancer of the colon, rectum, and prostate, while obese females have higher death rates from cancers of the gall bladder, breast, and sexual organs. It should be emphasized also that an obese or overweight individual can still be malnourished.

The location of excessive fat differs for men and women and is relevant to health complications. For men, fat is concentrated in the waist, abdomen, and upper body which is more unhealthy than the concentration in the hips and thighs more common to women. However, we do not know what accounts for these different locations.

Causes of Obesity. Compulsive eating behavior typically is learned in youth and is associated with eating for reasons other than satisfying hunger. Compulsive eaters thus often fail to distinguish between their need for food and learned wants. Consequently, they eat even though they are not hungry. Some learn to eat to reduce stress, just as one learns to abuse chemicals. Having been learned, successful treatment has focused on controlling the overeating response through behavioral conditioning techniques.

On the other hand, some people are physiologically predisposed to overeat due to hormonal malfunctioning. One theory of obesity is that the infant has a specific number of fat cells that can increase to a genetically predetermined size as they absorb nutrients. If there is overeating after that, new fat cells form that can lead to obesity.

The Set Point Theory of Body Weight. The **set point theory of body weight** holds that healthy people have an innate mechanism centered in the hypothalamus that fixes and monitors body weight. The mechanism "controls" the body at a stable weight by modifying appetite, activity, and metabolic rate. However, those with an excessively high set point gain too much weight. If they successfully diet, eating later returns their body weight to its set point. One reason may be that an enzyme called adipose tissue lipoprotein lipase (AT-LPL) helps fat cells to fill up with fat. The amount of this enzyme in the body increases when an obese person loses weight and it returns to its previous level if the weight is regained. In a sense, AT-LPL instructs the body to regain the lost weight and return to the set point for body fat. The solution to successfully losing weight is to lower the set point. This can be accomplished by drugs such as amphetamines and nicotine (nicotine increases metabolic rate and thus burns more calories). But if the drugs are discontinued, the set point returns to normal, which again leads to a gain in weight. Regular exercise can keep the set point at a low setting by increasing metabolic rate. Vigorous exercise burns calories at a relatively high rate for perhaps 15 hours.

According to the set point theory of body weight, a mechanism in the hypothalamus specifies how much fat the body should store and directs the body to remain at that normal, steady weight; a high set point leads to obesity.

Obese people see and think more about food than do slender people. This is similar to a conditional anticipatory response that may arouse an intense appetite when obese people are exposed to food stimuli. More generally, we all have learned such conditional anticipatory responses that influence us to seek various substances. This is a major basis of much advertising — the appearance of a desirable product on television often influences us to go to the refrigerator.

Anorexia Nervosa

Signs of Anorexia Nervosa. **Anorexia nervosa** occurs throughout the world but has no single recognized cause. It most commonly afflicts young women with onset generally in early adulthood. Often the onset follows important events in life such as the start of menstruation, sexual maturation, or illness. The disorder is characterized by being underweight, having an extreme fear of being obese, and the misperception that a thin body is fat. The amount of food eaten is minimal often with bizarre eating patterns — only certain foods are eaten, food is sneaked and picked at, it is thrown away when no one can see and often hidden. Anorexics usually exercise vigorously (jogging, etc.) to reduce their misperceived overweight. Frequently they are depressed, deny that they are anorexic, and resist treatment.

Anorexia nervosa is a behavior disorder manifested by extreme aversion to gaining weight and results in life-threatening weight loss; it most frequently occurs in young women.

Theories. There are many efforts to account for anorexia nervosa and other eating disorders. Cultural learning no doubt contributes, as in pressure on young women to be thin for physical attractiveness. Apparently, environmental influences are greater in young women than young men, such that women are more sensitive to being fat.

FIGURE 14.4   A representation of avoidance conditioning. A noxious stimulus is terminated and then avoided for a period of time if the relevant response (R) is made. The organism eventually learns to repeatedly respond to prevent the noxious stimulus from reoccurring.

Biological theories include that it is an addictive behavior perhaps caused by an endogenous opioid or that it is genetically determined.

A behavioral analysis considers that the sight and smell of food may become noxious conditional stimuli. Consequently, when one receives them, one avoids food and thus does not experience those noxious stimuli. Continued avoidance of those noxious conditional stimuli provides the reinforcement that maintains the anorexic response. Furthermore, the thought that by not eating one is losing weight is also reinforcing. The more the anorexic loses weight, the greater the reinforcement, constituting a positive feedback circuit that often leads to severe illness and death. So conceived, the learning of anorexia fits an avoidance conditioning paradigm (Fig. 14.4). Although avoidance behavior in general is difficult to extinguish, understanding anorexia according to these principles provides a start on controlling it. We do know some ways of reconditioning such avoidance behavior (see Chapter 10).

Avoidance of food by an anorexic can be understood in terms of avoidance conditioning principles in that the restraint from eating is reinforced by avoidance of noxious stimuli and the thought that weight is being lost.

As summarized by the Harvard Medical School Mental Health Letter, there is little agreement on how professionals treat anorexia nervosa. It concludes that individual psychotherapy has had a poor rate of success. Most anorexics recover with or without treatment, although as many as 5 percent die from suicide or physical illnesses.

Drug therapies, primarily using tricyclic antidepressants and antipsychotic medication, have also had some success.

Bulimia

An individual with **bulimia** rapidly consumes large amounts of food, usually in secret. Such binge eating often is followed by self-induced vomiting and excessive use of laxatives. Those who vomit may go through the binge/purge cycle from twice a week to twenty times a day. Bulimics typically restrict their diet following a binge and often exercise excessively.

Bulimia is a binge eating disorder often followed by intentional vomiting, and it typically occurs in young females.

Bulimia typically occurs in adolescence or in the twenties and is much more common in females and in the upper socioeconomic classes. One survey indicated that 13 percent of the college population exhibited the major symptoms of bulimia. Of this number 87 percent were female.

Bulimia is much more prevalent than anorexia nervosa. It differs from anorexia in that bulimics typically have normal menstrual periods, normal sex drives, and average body weights. However, like anorexics, they often tend to be depressed.

The duration of bulimia varies, lasting from a couple of weeks or months to many years. Behavior therapy coupled with drug therapy has had some success.

Phobic Disorders

While rational fears have survival value, unreasonable fears may be sufficiently debilitating to be classified as **phobic disorders.** There are two broad classes of phobias: fearing something that can pose absolutely no danger, such as the color yellow; or exaggerating a fear of something that it is reasonable to have a minor concern about, such as consuming germs from a glass in a restaurant.

A phobic disorder is an irrational fear of something that is harmless or an exaggerated fear of a minor threat.

There is an obsessive characteristic about phobias in that the victim dwells excessively on the feared object. The phobia may be sufficiently intense that the individual is immobilized with a high level of anxiety.

It has been estimated that there are perhaps 11 million individuals in the United States who suffer from phobic disorders. People have learned to fear almost everything imaginable, as depicted in Table 14.1.

An illustrative neurotic fear is dental phobia. Numerous people delay their visits to dentists or refuse to go because of fear of treatment. This constitutes a serious problem for dentists as well as patients. Research shows that both dentists and patients overestimate the discomfort so that the anticipation can be more distressing than the treatment itself.

Phobias are learned according to conditioning principles wherein a nonthreatening stimulus is associated with one that evokes a fear response (Fig. 14.5). Having been conditioned, a phobia can be alleviated through conditioning paradigms, relaxation, and other behavior therapies.

Conditioning techniques, clinical relaxation, and other behavior therapies are effective in controlling phobias.

PSYCHOTIC DISORDERS

Overview

Traditionally, a defining characteristic of a **psychosis** is that the individual has lost touch with reality. No amount of reasoning or objective data can convince the person that, for instance, he or she is not an agent of God. However, this, as in all other attempted definitions of psychosis, is insufficient and lacking in some respect (e.g., some people classified as psychotic *are* in touch with reality). The definitions of psychosis are imprecise. What we can say with confidence, though, is that psychoses encompass a number of disorders that are more severe than neuroses. In the case of both neuroses and psychoses, the individual has difficulty functioning in everyday life. However, in a psychosis, the disorder may be so severe that the individual is institutionalized.

Psychotic disorders are more disruptive than are neurotic disorders. They are classified as organic, for which there is a specified physiological/anatomical cause, or functional, for which there is no known organic cause.

Organic Versus Functional (Nonorganic) Psychoses. **Organic psychoses** are those in which there is a specified physiological/anatomical cause. In contrast, **functional psychoses** have no known organic cause. Often organic psychoses begin with mild symptoms of fatigue, headache, or moodiness. The organic cause is some dysfunction of the brain due to infections such as meningitis, head traumas, tumors, or the thiamine deficiency that produces Korsakoff's syndrome. Endocrine disorders and Alzheimer's disease may also lead to psychotic disorders. The victim develops such difficulties as depression, disorientation, hallucinations, memory confusions, and **dementia** (dementia is a decrement in intellectual abilities that is sufficiently severe to interfere with everyday functioning).

A major kind of functional psychosis is the affective psychoses, which have

TABLE 14.1   Kinds of Phobias

Name	Fear
Acrophobia	High places
Agoraphobia	Going out of the house
Arachnophobia	Spiders
Amaxophobia or hamaxophobia	Vehicles
Androphobia	Males
Autophobia	Self
Automysophobia	Being dirty
Belonephobia	Pins
Bromhidrosiphobia, osphresiophobia, or osmophobia	Odors
Claustrophobia	Closed spaces
Cynophobia	Dogs
Cypridophobia	Venereal disease
Electrophobia	Electricity (getting shocked)
Entomophobia	Insects
Ergasiophobia or ponophobia	Work
Gamophobia	Marriage
Genophobia	Sex
Gephyrophobia	Crossing a bridge
Graphophobia	Writing
Gynephobia	Women
Heliophobia	Sun
Hodophobia	Traveling
Hydrophobia	Water
Hygrophobia	Dampness
Hypnophobia	Sleep
Ichthyophobia	Fish
Kakorrhaphiophobia	Failure
Mysophobia or rhypophobia	Dirt
Ombrophobia	Rain
Panphobia	Everything
Pathophobia	Disease
Peniaphobia	Poverty
Pharmacophobia	Drugs
Phobophobia	Phobias
Siderodromophobia	Trains
Spectrophobia	Mirrors
Thanatophobia	Death
Vaccinophobia	Vaccination

FIGURE 14.5
Through classical conditioning, a nonthreatening stimulus can acquire the power of evoking a fear response which can lead to a phobic disorder.

been variously classified according to whether they have manic or depressive characteristics.

Depressive Behavior

Types of depression vary greatly in intensity, duration, and frequency of occurrence. On the one hand, we all experience periods of depression to some extent. That is only a normal aspect of life. Living involves meeting a wide variety of stresses, some of which are so demanding that some degree of discouragement is only natural. Short periods of depression are realistic after severe losses or illness onset. Sometimes we feel depressed even though there is no identifiable cause — we just wake up in a strange mood that seems only to be controlled by an unusual flow of our hormones. However, these moods do not endure, nor do they interrupt our everyday living to any great extent — before long they evaporate and are forgotten.

At the other end of the continuum are depressive disorders classified as **depressive psychoses.** The depressive with psychotic features may lose contact with reality, possibly become delusional with hallucinations and poor motor coordination. Those who have **manic-depressive** (bi-polar) **psychoses** will break out of a depressive phase into a manic episode or vice versa.

Diagnosing Depression

Symptoms often include reported feelings of sadness, hopelessness, lack of enthusiasm for life ("I just don't want to do anything," "the world is empty, without meaning"), and irritability (especially in children and adolescents). Extreme feelings of guilt and/or hopelessness may develop into suicidal ideation or intent. Somatic complaints often include changes in appetite, identified by significant weight change, changes in sleeping patterns (hypersomnia or insomnia but particularly early morning awakening), psychomotor agitation or retardation, and excessive fatigue. Headaches and gastrointestinal problems are not unusual. Diminished ability to think or concentrate is also frequently reported.

The Depressive Has Poor Perspective. By focusing on negative events and short-term consequences, depressed individuals tend to judge themselves with excessive hardship and take excessive blame for their failures. With appropriate therapy they may develop more realistic perspectives.

A number of (objective) **signs** (vs. symptoms) of depression facilitate diagnosis: changes in appetite, fatigue and lack of energy with decreased activity, or conversely, agitation with increased activity, withdrawal from daily activities, difficulty in sleeping (especially awakening too early), poor eating and sexual performance, and inability to concentrate. Somatic disturbances such as headaches and gastrointestinal disorders are also frequent.

The depressed individual often reports feelings of sadness, hopelessness, worthlessness, guilt, and self-reproach, often the basis for suicidal ideation. Somatic complaints are also evident with changes in sleeping and eating patterns most common.

Symptoms are expressions of complaints by a patient whereas signs are objective characteristics that can be used to diagnose a condition.

Signs of depression include agitated or decreased activity, lack of energy, and retreat from participation in daily activity.

FREQUENCY OF DEPRESSION

The problem of depression is severe. One estimate in the United States is that some 10 million Americans each year suffer from depression with relatively few of them getting treatment. As many as 15 percent of them are eventually driven to self-destruction. The World Health Organization estimates that more than 100 million people throughout the world are clinically (severely) depressed. Among famous individuals who had periods of depression were Abraham Lincoln, Winston Churchill, and Ernest Hemingway, who committed suicide by shooting himself.

The frequency of depression is higher among women, blacks, people who live alone after divorce or death of a spouse, the poorly educated, and the financially poor. In the physician's office, the frequency of major depression is often underdiagnosed or diagnosed incorrectly when the symptoms are ascribed to another physiological cause.

COLLEGE STUDENT SUICIDE AND DEPRESSION

Depression that leads to self-destruction is especially hard to understand in college students — they are privileged, young, intelligent, and educated. Yet they commit suicide at a greater rate than their noncollege peers.

Research by Richard Seiden has shown that suicidal students are differentiated from their classmates on the variables of age, class standing, nationality, major subject, academic achievement, and emotional condition. Compared to the student population at large, the suicidal group is older, contains a greater proportion of language majors and foreign students, more frequently reports the experience of emotional disturbance, and demonstrates academic achievement superior to that of their fellow students.

Contrary to the popular belief that suicides frequently occur during final examinations week, studies have indicated that the peak danger period for student suicides is the beginning (first 6 weeks), not the middle or end, of the semester. Most suicidal students give recurrent warnings of their suicidal intent. Many of them have a similar pattern marked by loss of appetite, insomnia, and periods of despondency. Among the major precipitating factors are worry over schoolwork and chronic and bizarre concerns about physical health. They often have difficulties with interpersonal relationships because of emotional withdrawal, social isolation, and romantic rejections.

MANIC-DEPRESSIVE (BI-POLAR) BEHAVIOR

Estimates are that marked mood swings of an extreme nature affect 1 to 2 million Americans and about 100 million people worldwide. Depressives may become hyperactive in a socially acceptable fashion, or in a more extreme way by becoming physically destructive to themselves or to others. Although we do not understand how lithium functions, in some way it stabilizes manic-depressive reactions.

Theories of Depression

It is understandable why some poor or sick people may be depressed. But why do others with similar life situations not become clinically depressed? Furthermore, why are some people clinically depressed for no apparent reason? Theories abound, and they come from numerous disciplines within psychology and psychiatry. In general, they can be classified as (1) genetic (2) psychological, and (3) biochemical theories.

Theories of depression can be classified as genetic, psychological, or biochemical.

Genetic Theories

To unambiguously implicate specific genetic causes of depression is an exceedingly complex research task that requires separation of inherited vs. environmental (learned) influences on behavior. For instance, the Amish, a nonviolent sect who isolate themselves and eschew modern technology have severe depression and suicide rates that run in specific families. At first glance it seems reasonable to conclude that the disposition toward depression and suicide is genetically passed down from one generation to the next, particularly in such a homogeneous and isolated community as the Amish. That is, with all families having similar divorce, separation, loneliness, and nonalcoholic factors, environmental variables would seem to be largely eliminated. Genetic factors apparently are implicated. Yet, intimate family environmental influences can have important effects. Children learn from their parents and can pass on to their own progeny unique behavioral patterns that can exert powerful influences beyond those of the community. It seems likely that genetic factors predispose some to depression but environmental factors also contribute in extremely complex and subtle ways.

Genetic factors seem to predispose some to depression, particularly as they interact with environmental learning factors.

Psychological Theories

Behavioral interactions with environmental and social variables can cause depressive behavior. Learning influences can be severe indeed. Since the stresses of life can cause depressive behavior, psychological techniques are often appropriate for alleviating the disorders; for example, the depressive typically visualizes and verbalizes problems so that we can often deal with them through behavioral manipulation, as we discuss in Chapter 15.

Depressives typically visualize and verbalize their difficulties, indicating that psychological techniques to control those kinds of imagery can often be effective in alleviating depression.

Biochemical Theories

These theories focus on the influence of various kinds of naturally occurring chemicals in our bodies. For a variety of reasons, there is substance to this strategy — clearly, our moods are influenced by the biochemical composition of our bodies (neurotransmitters, hormones, etc.). Yet the issue is so complicated that a well-established, clearcut biochemical theory seems far off. Each year new research implicates additional factors and forces us to reevaluate old conclusions. Norman Cousins, for instance, reported that as depression decreases, the level of interleukins (which help activate the immune system) rises sharply. Some other conclusions have been that brain deficits of various substances (serotonin and 5-HT) are implicated and that sodium and potassium in the nervous system are inappropriately balanced (as in the balance maintained between these two electrolytes in the resting state of neurons). Research is increasingly indicating that there is decreased serotonergic

Biochemical factors no doubt influence our mood states such as in manic and depressive reactions, although we lack a sound theory with sufficient generality to explain how they function.

activity in the development of affective disorders. Reduction of serotonin may thus contribute to such common disturbances as depressed mood, poor sleeping habits, disturbed circadian rhythms, and abnormal endocrine function. Another theory is that the levels of various hormones (such as amount of adrenocorticotrophic hormones relative to corticotrophic hormones) are out of normal balance.

The effectiveness of lithium and other medications for manic-depressive disorder lends much credence to a biochemical theory. No doubt the impressive biochemical research that is underway throughout the world will continue to make major contributions to the alleviation of depressive and other disorders.

Schizophrenia

The term *schizophrenia* was proposed by Eugen Bleuler in his 1911 classic book *Dementia Praecox or the Group of Schizophrenia.* In a 1908 paper, he had renamed **dementia praecox** as **schizophrenia.** The reason was that actual dementia did not generally occur in the 647 cases on which he reported.

Schizophrenic behavior usually becomes apparent during adolescence or early adulthood and may afflict the individual for a lifetime. Symptoms of auditory hallucinations, bizarre ideas, delusions of grandeur, paranoia, and so on appear at various times and in various combinations. Estimates suggest that about 1 percent of the population develops schizophrenia.

In schizophrenia, there are disturbances of thinking involving a distortion of logical relations among ideas. There is characteristically a separation between rational thinking and emotional behavior. Consequently, the patient behaves inappropriately in social situations. The patient usually retreats from social involvement into an internal fantasy life ("out of touch with reality") characterized by delusions and hallucinations.

Kinds and Characteristics
of Schizophrenia

There are a number of classifications of schizophrenic disorders. Traditionally, four forms have been recognized: simple, paranoid, catatonic, and hebephrenic. The **simple** variety of schizophrenia is characterized by a lack of a sense of responsibility. These individuals are often very pleasant and socially popular. **Paranoid schizophrenia** is characterized by **delusions of persecution** and is typically accompanied by hallucinations. **Catatonic schizophrenia** is extremely rare; its main symptom is a waxy flexibility of the limbs. For example, the limbs of a true catatonic can be moved by another person to various positions where they remain for extended periods of time. **Hebephrenic schizophrenia** is characterized by silliness and bizarre laughter, although this type is not commonly referred to today.

Schizophrenia, originally called dementia praecox, has traditionally been classified as simple, paranoid, catatonic, and hebephrenic.

Characteristics of schizophrenia have been classified as "positive" or "negative." Positive characteristics are those that are present, such as hallucinations, delusions, and incoherent speech. Negative characteristics are not present and include social isolation, withdrawal, and poverty of speech. Researchers have found that schizophrenics respond differently to antipsychotic drugs depending on whether they have predominantly positive or negative characteristics.

Like most of our terms depicting mental disorders, schizophrenia is an ambiguous one that is loosely applied. In mental hospitals it is often a "garbage can" category meaning that diverse cases are often diagnosed as schizophrenia because they fit no other syndrome. Consequently, we should realize that individuals classified as schizophrenic are likely to differ in many ways. Therefore, we should not expect to find a single cause for schizophrenia. At best, we can only hope to find causes for specific subcategories or for specific symptoms and signs.

Biochemical Approaches.   The speech of schizophrenics during psychotic episodes, often referred to as "word salad" and gibberish in which words and ideas do not fit together in any coherent fashion, has been biochemically studied. An inability to control speech results in errors such as intrusions of associations the person has with a word. For instance, when talking about pigeons, one might intrude with the word *peace*. Drugs such as thorazine are commonly administered to schizophrenics to reduce disordered speech and other psychotic symptoms. One interpretation is that the drugs affect the neurotransmitter dopamine, suggesting that schizophrenic speech is a linguistic problem created by a biochemical imbalance. Indeed, neuropharmacological research has indicated that there is heightened dopaminergic activity associated with schizophrenia. Antipsychotic drugs reduce the heightened dopaminergic activity.

There is some evidence that schizophrenia has a major brain disease component. This conclusion is based on the finding that statistically reliable differences have been found between schizophrenics and those who have been diagnosed as not psychiatrically impaired. Yet there is a considerable overlap between schizophrenics and normals with regard to brain metabolism rates, ventricular size, genetic relationships, and neurotransmitter functions.

Genetic Studies.   To study a possible genetic basis for schizophrenia, identical and fraternal twins have been compared. Genes of identical twins are identical. But the genes of fraternal twins are no more alike than those of siblings born years apart. Because they are usually reared together, environmental influences on both kinds of twins are somewhat equated. Thus, if fraternal twins share mental illness as often as do identical twins, environmental influences should be the major factors influencing the development of the disorder. On the other hand, if identical twins share mental illness more frequently than do fraternal twins, genetic factors would seem to be indicated.

Most studies of twins with mental illness have found that both identical twins suffer more frequently from a mental illness than do both fraternal twins. The implication is that there is a genetic basis for the mental illness, although there is still some environmental confounding (e.g., identical twins who look alike may be treated more similarly by family and friends than are fraternal twins; consequently, both twins might be influenced to behave similarly whether normally or abnormally). To solve this problem and to further separate environmental parenting and hereditary influences, adoption studies have been useful. Children who are adopted receive their genes from their biological parents but are raised by their adoptive parents. Thus, evidence for a genetic influence would occur if adopted children of schizophrenic parents also develop schizophrenia even though they are raised in normal homes. The results have been in that direction: Significantly more of the adopted children of parents with schizophrenia have been diagnosed as mentally ill than were those of normal parents. However, *most* children of schizophrenic biological parents did *not* develop schizophrenia, indicating that environmental factors also were influential.

While there are no well-established known causes of schizophrenia, neuropharmacological findings implicate some kind of biological basis for it, particularly involving the neurotransmitter dopamine.

Studies of identical and fraternal twins and twin-adoption studies have indicated that there is a genetic predisposition toward schizophrenia, although learning factors are also influential.

Researchers have identified several chromosomal sites as potential genetic bases for Alzheimer's and for manic depression; similarly, chromosome number five has been implicated in schizophrenia. Other genetic markers are expected to be determined, although more than 200 possibilities remain to be studied.

In Conclusion. The twin-adoption studies have indicated that there *is* a genetic predisposition toward mental illness, especially for schizophrenia. However, twin-study methodology does not lead to unambiguous conclusions and the studies also indicate that environmental influences are important. The long historical nature–nurture controversy continues. It is clear that both genetic and environmental (learned) factors influence the development of personality. The relative contribution of each in any given person diagnosed as schizophrenic no doubt depends upon a large number of special variables. One environmental factor associated with the development of schizophrenia concerns when individuals were born. More persons who develop schizophrenia were born in the winter months, proportionately, than at any other time of the year. Why that is so is difficult to determine, although the diet of the expectant mother has been thought to be relevant.

CRIMINALITY, SCHIZOPHRENIA, AND GENETIC PREDISPOSITIONS

Research suggests that genes may play a role in criminal activity.

Sarnoff Mednick agrees that there is convincing evidence that genetic influences are important in the development of schizophrenia, which forms the basis for determining whether genes are also involved in criminality. Nine studies conducted since 1929 indicate that identical twins are about twice as likely to engage in criminal activity than are fraternal twins. In a study of 7172 twins born in Denmark, 35 percent of the identical twins, compared with 13 percent of the fraternal twins, showed similar criminal activity. However, since identical twins are treated more alike than are fraternal twins, perhaps the cause was due to similar environment and not genetic factors. If the identical twins are adopted at birth by different parents, however, they would not share such similar environmental influences.

Two studies in Denmark of 5483 and 14,427 adoptions respectively do indicate some genetic basis for criminal behavior. In general the sons of parents who had criminal records and who had been adopted early in life themselves had criminal records to a greater extent than sons of parents who did not have criminal records. Mednick concludes that a genetic predisposition plays an important role in criminality. He suggests that any biological predisposition the adoptees inherit must be of a general nature such as an incapacity to conform.

In general, we inherit genetic predispositions toward a variety of normal and abnormal behaviors; but through behavioral engineering, those predispositions can be influenced and often counteracted.

Eysenck and Gudjonsson (1989) agree in principle with Mednick about a genetic component for criminality. More generally, they summarize a large body of evidence from twin and adopted children's studies that "leaves little doubt that genetic factors are at least as powerful as environmental ones and that we now know a good deal about physiological and hormonal mediators in this field" (p. 408). However, Gottfredson and Hirschi (1990) question this conclusion, claiming that the scientific evidence favoring a substantial genetic component to crime is extremely weak.

In Conclusion. It certainly is true that we have genetic predispositions toward a wide variety of disorders and diseases. Whether we actually develop pathologies depends largely on environmental factors and how we behave toward them. Just as people may be genetically predisposed toward lung cancer, if they do not smoke cigarettes, they may never contract it.

AUTISM AND SCHIZOPHRENIA

Autism, from the Greek word *autos,* meaning "self," is a disorder of childhood, occurring mainly in males with a frequency of about six in 10,000 births. Infantile autism is the most serious psychological disorder of childhood. Some authorities consider autism to be a kind of schizophrenia while others regard it as different. However, they do have some symptoms and signs in common.

The main characteristic of autism is a general withdrawal that typically occurs within the first year of life. Use of language is limited. The autistic child does not play with other children or toys, has trouble paying attention, and may even appear to be deaf or blind. The child is usually hostile, often having temper tantrums. Self-mutilation is common as when they hit their heads against the wall, strike themselves in the face, or bite their own flesh. Repetitive behaviors are frequent (e.g., they may jump up and down or tap their teeth for long periods of time).

Their intelligence scores are often in the retarded region, but perhaps 10 percent of them are savants (formerly known as idiot savants or *savant idiot* in French). For example, some autistic children have amazing artistic, musical, or memorizing abilities.

Research has indicated there is a definite biological basis for autism in that there is a mutant gene on the "male" chromosome responsible for a missing enzyme (possibly adenylosuccinate lyase) that triggers the autistic behavior. More specifically, this enzyme seems to trigger a metabolic defect that results in the accumulation of purides (which are toxic substances in the blood and in other tissues). Purides can be detected in cerebral spinal fluid, blood, and urine, but most easily in urine tests. Genetic therapy could eventually insert the normal gene into these patients.

Autism resembles schizophrenia and occurs most frequently in boys; its behavioral characteristics are withdrawal, aggression, self-mutilation, and repetitive behaviors; apparently it is due to a mutant gene on the male chromosome.

In spite of the biological bases for autism, behavior therapy has been impressively successful, as will be discussed in Chapter 15.

Psychosomatic (Somatoform) Disorders

Mentalistic Conception.   **Psychosomatic disorders** are commonly thought of as those physiological disorders for which the cause and course are due to "psychic" (mental, cognitive) stresses. For example, one who chronically worries ("psychic stress") develops the physiological illness of a peptic ulcer. The "psychic" causes "somatic" (body) disorders, as in psychophysical interactionism (Chapter 3). Other disorders with a psychosomatic component include asthma, high blood pressure, headaches, rheumatoid arthritis, hyperthyroidism, colitis, and neurodermatitis.

Materialistic Conception.   Our model is that mental (psychic, cognitive, psychological) processes are actually bodily events. Hence, we interpret *psycho* in *psychosomatic* as "behavior," which is the common interpretation in contemporary psychology. And behavior, of course, is an activity of the body. *Soma* in the term *psychosomatic* literally means "body."

A Cybernetic Model.   Frequently, the originating system is muscular, as in a state of chronic overtension (e.g., increases of striated muscle tension can overdrive the gastrointestinal systems, the cardiovascular system, and so on, with pathological

Psychosomatic (body – body) disorders result because some systems of the body pathologically affect other systems or organs.

WHEN WE MANIPULATE
SKELETAL MUSCLE

WE MODIFY
AUTONOMIC ACTIVITY

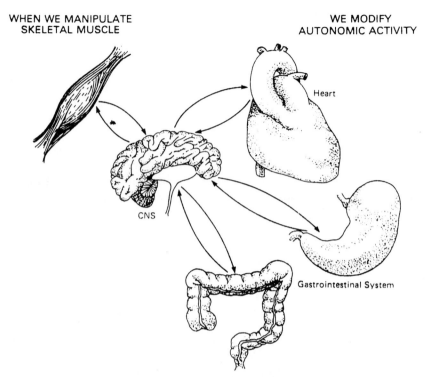

FIGURE 14.6 A model of the functional relationship between the striated musculature and other bodily systems. As tension increases, the central nervous system is aroused. In turn, activity of autonomic and other systems is heightened. Conversely, relaxation of the striated musculature produces a tranquil state throughout the body.

Effective treatment for psychosomatic (body–body system) illnesses is to reduce overtension of the striated musculature.

consequences; (Fig. 14.6). To briefly follow our cybernetic model, systematic relaxation of the striated musculature should bring a state of tranquility to other systems such as the autonomic. Psychosomatic illnesses thus often can be treated when the body relaxes (e.g., relaxation can reduce gastric activity and the secretion of hydrochloric acid so that an ulcer may heal). This model is consonant with a basic principle of medicine: Do not unnecessarily intervene into the body's functions, and give the body the opportunity to heal itself. Successful tests of the model are developed in the next chapter.

GASTROINTESTINAL DISORDERS

Functions of the Digestive System. The digestive system transports food, absorbs nutrients, and excretes waste products. Stimuli, such as food, activate the digestive system and cause it to secrete products. The physiology of gastrointestinal reactions involves smooth muscle fibers, nerves within the bowel walls, and hormonal factors. Much of the motor behavior of the gastrointestinal tract is carried out through networks of excitatory and inhibitory neurons that involve many receptors. There is a rich supply of afferent nerves to the central nervous system so that central and visceral mechanisms interact through cybernetic circuits.

Disturbances of the Gastrointestinal Tract. Gastrointestinal (GI) tract disturbances are among the most frequent stress–tension complaints. Patients offer a wide variety of reports that are understandably quite vague because they have had little training in precisely describing internal states. Consequently, the patient may merely be able to refer to vague feelings of "lumps and choking sensations in the throat," "tightness in the chest and abdomen," or "bloated stomach and intestines." More precise reports can be made with training in Progressive Relaxation (see Chapter 15).

Signs of digestive disturbances include diarrhea, constipation, vomiting with heightened temperature, and hemorrhoids. More serious conditions include mucus colitis, spastic colon, and ulcerative colitis. Some of these gastrointestinal disorders may have an organic, non–tension-related basis, but many are directly due to chronic muscular overtension.

The Esophagus

Physiology. The upper part of the gastrointestinal tract, the esophagus, contains both skeletal and smooth muscle. We can use the skeletal muscles to volitionally contract the esophagus, as when we swallow at will. The smooth muscle responds involuntarily. There is a swallowing center in the medulla that receives input from the cerebral cortex and from sensory fibers of cranial nerves. The esophagus contains sensitive receptors that detect changes in volume and acidity, sending afferent information to the central nervous system through sensory fibers of the vagus nerve.

Reactions of the Esophagus. The esophagus involuntary constricts in a moment-to-moment fashion as we meet and emotionally evaluate our daily life problems. Loud noises and stressors cause a small but measurable increase in the intensity of contraction waves. Excessive contraction can lead to a loss of coordination of its normal function in swallowing. There is a high correlation among fear, anxiety and affective disorders, and contraction abnormalities. Recall that in *globus hystericus* there is reported to be the feeling of a ball in the throat. Such extreme states of esophageal contraction often interfere with the passage of food.

The Stomach

In the early nineteenth century, gastric fistulas were used to study the effects of psychological stress (fear, anger, and depression) on gastric motility. Illustrative findings included delayed gastric emptying and suppressed gastric secretion. Since then, numerous studies have confirmed that stressors can deleteriously affect the condition of the stomach by delaying gastric emptying and suppressing gastric secretion. On the other hand, hostility, resentment, and other such emotions increase stomach motility.

The Colon

The lower part of the gastrointestinal tract contains only smooth muscles so that the intestines cannot be directly controlled volitionally as can skeletal muscle. Rather, they can be controlled indirectly by neuromuscular circuits (see Fig. 14.6), especially involving the complex layers of skeletal muscle over the abdomen. The stressors that you encounter thus can produce excessive skeletal muscle tension, which in turn can lead to various kinds of gastrointestinal distress. Abdominal pains, for instance, can

Cybernetic circuits between the CNS components of the GI tract may malfunction to produce a variety of pathologies such as spastic esophagus, spastic colon, and ulcers. Less serious disturbances include diarrhea, constipation, and hemorrhoids.

develop suddenly, as when one has intestinal cramps in tense social situations. An overtense person always has some degree of spasticity of the digestive tract. In the extreme, a spastic colon may assume an extensively malformed shape. Some 90 percent of the constipation and diarrhea cases are estimated to be due to overtension. Hemorrhoids are frequently caused by tension. Complaints of pain and of being bloated are often to be understood in terms of an excessive amount of air brought into the gastrointestinal tract. The overtense individual may unconsciously swallow so that air pressure is literally increased within the body. With relaxation, air can exit through the rectum and the mouth in an easy, relaxed fashion. Efforts to force flatus and to belch are ill advised because they add tension and defeat the purpose. Similarly, elimination should be conducted in a relaxed fashion rather than being forced. The excessively tense colon, with forced evacuation, results in misshapen, small, pencil-like stools. Larger, well-formed stools are indications of a relaxed colon. Spastic (overtensed) colon, inflammation of the colon (colitis), and other tension maladies of the gastrointestinal tract apparently can only be permanently relieved through the sensitive application of clinical relaxation principles. People often try in vain to solve such gastrointestinal problems with patented medicines or altered diet. Prescribed medication can effect some temporary relief, but, once again, medication does not permanently solve the problem. Nothing can be very effective if the condition has become so advanced that it is irreversible. Ulcerative colitis for instance, may well require surgical intervention.

Since overtension of the gastrointestinal tract contributes to a number of disorders, the appropriate therapy is to relax the striated muscles.

Ulcers

These are small, round, raw indented areas about 4 to 5 inches in diameter. They vary from being a slight depression to a hole through the walls.

Kinds and Frequency of Ulcers.   Esophageal ulcers usually occur at the lower end of the esophagus near the stomach. Gastric ulcers occur in the stomach, and duodenal ulcers occur in the duodenum, that portion of the small intestine near the stomach.

Approximately 12 percent of the population of the United States has been estimated to suffer from ulcers at any given time. Duodenal ulcers are most frequent, followed by gastric ulcers; esophageal ulcers are relatively rare.

Duodenal and gastric ulcers occur much more frequently in men than in women. Gastric ulcers come on mainly between the ages of 45 and 55, while duodenal ulcers usually start in the 35 to 45 age range. The onset of ulcers usually occurs in the spring or fall regardless of type. The large majority of them heal adequately if not further antagonized.

Causes of Ulcers.   The precise reasons that ulcers develop are unclear. But we do know that there are *aggressive factors,* which include secretion of hydrochloric acid and the enzyme pepsin (two natural substances used to digest food) and *defensive factors,* which include the production of acid-neutralizing chemicals such as bicarbonate. Most research has been on aggressive factors and has indicated that excessive acid produces ulcers by eroding the gastrointestinal lining. As a result, ulcer drugs can prevent histamine from exciting the acid-producing cells. For this purpose, Tagamet has become the best-selling prescription drug in history. On the other hand, most ulcer patients have normal or low amounts of acid. For them, a deficiency of defensive factors such as bicarbonate apparently constitutes an important factor in the development and maintenance of their ulcers.

Bacteria may also play a role in duodenal ulcers. Research has indicated that antibiotics help to alleviate ulcers, suggesting infection as a causal agent. Patients with chronic gastritis (inflammation of the stomach) often have unique bacteria in the stomach lining. The bacteria apparently infect cells that are eroded by stomach acid to cause gastritis and perhaps ulcers. However, the physiology must involve other factors too such as stress because that unique bacterium is also common in people who have no digestive problems.

Perhaps there are genetic predispositions — children and siblings of ulcer patients are three times more likely to develop ulcers than people not related to an ulcer patient.

Cigarette smoking also significantly increases a person's chance of developing an ulcer — the frequency is relatively greater in heavy smokers, next in light smokers, and least in nonsmokers. Smoking promotes gastric ulcers and impedes their healing by allowing the flow of duodenal juices back into the stomach and by reducing the amount of acid-neutralizing secretions produced by the pancreas.

Behaviors such as smoking and reactions to stressors influence aggressive and defensive factors to cause ulcers.

Food and diet apparently do not contribute — vegetarians, meat-eaters, and people who eat highly spiced foods develop ulcers at about the same rates.

Whatever the complex physiological events that produce ulcers, there is no doubt that muscular overtension as a reaction to stress is a major precipitating cause. Consequently, ulcers can usually be behaviorally controlled through relaxation.

HEADACHES

Tension and Migraines.   Among the different types of pain experiences, headaches rank among the most frequent. Headache specialists classify numerous kinds of headaches, the most prominent being the migraine and tension varieties. The tension headache often has a primary locus at the back of the head or about the eyebrow region. Tension headaches can by definition always be treated through relaxation.

Headaches are caused or exacerbated by overtension.

Migraine headaches are distinguished by their severity and localization on one side of the head. The word *migraine* derives from the Latin *hemicrania*, meaning "pain on one side of the head." Migraine headaches occur when arteries in the head dilate and thus press against nerves that can produce pain. They, like any kind of pain, are exacerbated by the excessive tension evoked by stress. By relaxing the smooth muscle of the arteries, relief can often be gained. Research shows that the drug sumatriptan is effective in reducing the pain of the migraine.

TEMPORAL MANDIBULAR JOINT SYNDROME (TMJ) AND MYOFACIAL PAIN DYSFUNCTION (MPD)

Myofacial pain dysfunction (MPD) is a more general term that includes **temporal mandibular joint syndrome (TMJ).** TMJ implies that the joints in the jaws are malfunctioning, whereas MPD implies that facial pain may result from other causes as well.

TMJ syndrome is often caused by complex muscle contractions around the temporomandibular joints. TMJ can be produced by a normal person's yawning and opening the mouth wide, or the person can use the muscles of the face in abnormal ways. Sometimes TMJ pain results from a habit of biting fingernails or clenching

Myofacial pain dysfunction including temporal mandibular joint syndrome and bruxism is often caused by excessive muscle tension.

teeth together, habits that put stress on the jaws. In other cases, improper bites (the way upper and lower teeth come together) can play a part. It used to be thought that bad bites were the primary cause of TMJ dysfunction. However, the problem is not so much that of a bad bite as the individual's behavior of grinding or clenching the teeth, known as **bruxism.** Frequently, bruxism becomes so intense that the teeth are worn down, which in turn may lead to a variety of other disorders.

The pain is often in the joints and muscles of the jaws, but it may be referred to other parts of the face and the head. Sometimes TMJ pain is experienced as a headache between the eyes and the forehead, near the temples, or as pain in the shoulders and neck. TMJ pain may even be referred to the ears and experienced as earaches even though there is nothing wrong with the ears. Other symptoms are popping or clicking sounds in the jaws. Chronic TMJ pain often can be debilitating and can lead to depression.

One way to diagnose TMJ syndrome is to place the knuckles of the three middle fingers vertically in your mouth. If you can open your mouth wide enough to accommodate all three, you probably do not have TMJ syndrome.

Treatment is usually to relax especially jaw muscles and breaking the pain cycle (see Chapter 15). In relaxing, patients should avoid excess tension and not chew gum, clench their teeth, bite their fingernails, or yawn excessively. Eating soft food may help as might applying moist heat to relieve sore muscles. Patients who do not respond to behavior therapy may use a splint, which is a device placed over the teeth to keep the teeth from grinding.

RHEUMATIC DISORDERS

A rheumatologist treats such conditions as arthritis, bursitis, neuritis, rheumatism, neuralgia, stiff neck, headache, sciatica, backache, and chest pains. One theory is that overtension in relevant muscles leads to muscular fatigue and spasm (cramp). Since muscles are relatively insensitive, some cramping may persist for months or years without significant symptoms. When pain symptoms do occur they are apt to appear first in the neck and shoulder muscles, or in hip and lower back muscles. Eventually tightened joints, tendons, and bursae evidence signs of excessive wear and tear (inflammation). When mild and chronic, this is called osteoarthritis (*osteo* means bone) or "wear and tear" arthritis.

Treatment.   Clinical work suggests that most antirheumatic drugs relieve symptoms by suppressing inflammation and relieving muscle spasm. Unfortunately, though, this often results in further weakening of muscle, leading to more difficulties.

Relaxation has been effectively applied to treat arthritis, stiff neck, and backache without the muscle-weakening side effects of drug therapies.

Nondrug therapy includes rest, exercise, physical therapy, and intensive training in recognition and correction of maladaptive muscular tightening. Primary attention is placed on the relaxation of those muscles used in "the instinct to fight or flight." The "fight" muscles are primarily in the arms, shoulders, neck, and chest, while "flight" muscles are in the hips, back, and legs. Although a relaxation approach requires a great deal of time and diligence on the part of both patient and therapist, it has been an effective way to achieve long-term gains.

Muscle spasms invariably cause pain and joint inflammation. For patients who have chronic pain, it is often too difficult to begin relaxation training immediately because the pain is so great. For them, physical therapy is prescribed, such as heat, cold, massage, and vibration to loosen up the muscles and force blood circulation into the afflicted area. Once the pain has been temporarily alleviated in this manner, relaxation training can be used to control the tension and the pain more permanently.

Cardiovascular Disease

HEART ATTACKS

Heart attacks (myocardial infarctions) strike an estimated 1.5 million people in the United States each year. About 500,000 of them die, 350,000 before they get to a hospital. It is estimated that about 200,000 of these could have been saved had they been given CPR (cardiac pulmonary resuscitation). However, of those who do survive, estimates are that 80 percent eventually die of a second heart attack. On the positive side, the frequency of death from heart attacks that reached a peak in the mid-1960s has steadily declined since then for a total reduction of over 25 percent by 1980.

ATHEROSCLEROSIS

The terms *ischemic heart disease, coronary heart disease,* and *arteriosclerotic heart disease* are roughly synonymous, all denoting clinical manifestations of atherosclerosis. **Atherosclerosis** is the obstruction of the flow of blood through the coronary arteries that nourish the muscle of the heart. The process involves the growth of plaque in the layers of the arterial wall. Atherosclerosis is facilitated by a high fat diet and is responsible for numerous heart attacks. In its early stages plaque contains smooth muscle cells and cholesterol; later it contains fibrous tissue and deposits of calcium. Figure 14.7 shows how plaque decreases the diameter of the blood vessels. A portion of the coronary artery is shown on the left. When an acute clot forms, it

The slow course of atherosclerosis may result in a clotting of blood and then in heart attack.

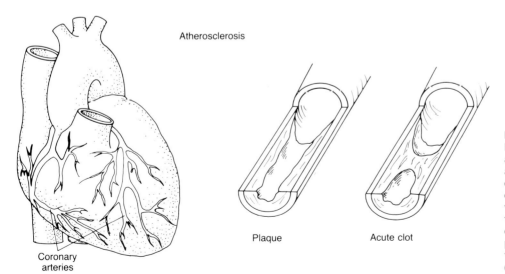

Atherosclerosis

Plaque   Acute clot

Coronary
arteries

FIGURE 14.7
Development of atherosclerosis. Coronary arteries in the heart are depicted at the left. An enlarged view of one artery in which plaque is built up is in the middle. The plaque can enlarge to block the artery preventing the flow of blood, thus causing a heart attack (right).

may completely block one or more coronary arteries and that particular portion of the heart muscle is deprived of its blood supply, producing a myocardial infarction (heart attack).

Various drugs have been used to attempt to dissolve the blood clots that cause heart attacks. When they are successful, the arteries may return to their earlier state.

Behavioral control can help prevent excessive atherosclerosis and thus prevent heart attacks by reducing LDL cholesterol and high fat diets, particularly if begun early. This is because thickening of the walls of the arteries begins early in life and slowly progresses over decades.

PREDICTION OF HEART ATTACKS

Quiet Heart Attacks. About 30 percent of all heart attack victims do not realize they have suffered one. Results of the long-running Framingham Heart Study indicate that more than a quarter of the heart attacks in male participants and about a third in female participants were not recognized when they occurred. Routine electrocardiogram tests administered later revealed that the attacks had occurred. About half of the victims could not remember suffering pain at all, whereas the remainder were misdiagnosed as having ulcers, gallstones, hiatus hernia, or some other noncardiac problem. A number of these individuals who had "quite heart attacks" died, indicating that coronary heart disease can be unrecognized and yet lethal.

Some Predictor Variables. A high-priority research goal is to assess variables that can predict a heart attack. One problem is that we lack complete explanations for their causes. Some well-established variables that are associated with cardiovascular disease are high levels of low-density lipoprotein (LDL) cholesterol, high sodium (salt) levels, cigarette smoking, obesity, stress-tension and high levels of iron in the blood of men. Data are conflicting with regard to hypertension (high blood pressure), some studies indicating that it is not related to heart attack mortality at all. Psychological factors such as unsatisfactory sexual behavior, fatigue, sadness, depression, excessive worry, and stress-tension have been shown to be predictive of and even to help precipitate some heart attacks. Much research is under way in this area and it is likely that psychological measures will eventually be quite useful in screening for potential heart attacks.

Echocardiograms, which are obtained by means of ultrasonic heart scans, have indicated that people with an enlarged left side of their heart, called ventricular hypertrophy, are two to three times as likely as others to have heart attacks or strokes. The left ventrical is the main pumping station that sends blood through the body's arteries. Its mass (its size and thickness of the muscle) is what is correlated with increased risk. The condition is thought to be caused by high blood pressure and being overweight. It has been estimated to be as powerful a risk factor as high LDL cholesterol, blood pressure, and smoking.

Factors that have been related to heart disease and can predict its onset include high levels of LDL cholesterol, sodium, iron in males, DHEAS, ventricular hypertrophy, cigarette smoking, obesity, excessive stress-tension profiles, and peripheral arterial disease.

People with peripheral arterial disease (PAD), which can indicate general atherosclerosis, have more than seven times the death rate of people without PAD. To detect PAD one can use ultrasound to measure the velocity of blood flow in the leg and compare pulse and the blood pressure in the lower extremities.

The circulating steroid hormone **DHEAS (dehydroepiandrosterone sulfate)** has been predictive of the risk of dying or incurring cardiovascular disease. For instance, in a sample of men aged 50–54 years, DHEAS levels were nearly three times higher than those of men of the same age who had died of cardiovascular disease. Studies in laboratory animals have shown that the administration of DHEAS appears to delay aging, prevent obesity, and lower serum cholesterol levels. Its natural amount is a predictor of longevity independent of age, smoking, obesity, plasma, cholesterol and glucose levels, and familial heart disease. DHEAS levels in plasma steadily decrease as individuals age but those with higher DHEAS baseline levels regardless of age have lower death rates and less cardiovascular disease. The precise functions of DHEAS are uncertain. Perhaps DHEAS is an indicator of another substance that determines longevity and cardiovascular disease, or it is possible that it confers protection against death in general and thus only incidentally against cardiovascular disease in particular. We do not know how to control the level of DHEAS with medication or behavioral techniques.

Studies show that hair in the ear canal and a crease on the ear lobe are associated with heart disease in men. The association between ear canal hair and coronary heart disease may be due to a long-term exposure to androgens which could cause both ear-canal hair growth and coronary heart disease.

Heart disease has now become the number 2 killer in Japan, with cancer continuing to be the leading cause of death. About 49,000 Japanese people died of heart disease in 1947 but by 1985 the figure jumped to 136,000. Many Japanese have changed their traditional diet of rice, fish, and vegetables since the end of World War II to one of Western foods that contain large amounts of animal fat. Many American fast food chains serving hamburgers, French fries, pizza, and now tacos are thriving across that country.

STROKES

In a stroke, a blood vessel may burst or occlude in the brain possibly causing widespread paralysis and loss of speech. Typically, there are such warning signs as loss of vision, dizziness, speech impairment, and numbness in the face, arms, or legs. About one-third of those who experience such warning signs are likely to suffer a stroke within three years.

The movement of blood in the arteries leading to the brain has been studied with ultrasound with some success in predicting strokes. Blocking of arteries diminishes blood flow, increasing the likelihood of stroke. Endarterectomy, a surgical procedure to unblock arteries, has been reported to have a 95 percent success rate and takes about an hour to complete.

HIGH BLOOD PRESSURE (HYPERTENSION)

About one in four Americans has high blood pressure. For a majority, the condition is very serious. High blood pressure is defined as systolic pressure exceeding 140 mg Hg or diastolic pressure greater than 90 mg Hg: (mg = milligrams; Hg = mercury). If each heart beat pushes blood against the blood vessels with pressure that exceeds 140/90 and it is chronic, a stroke, heart attack, or kidney disease may well result.

EFFECTS OF TOBACCO SMOKE

Adverse health effects for nonsmokers who are subjected to passive smoke apparently include increased risk of heart disease and diminished lung capacity.

Passive Smoke. Exposure to cigarette smoke of others increases coughing and diminishes lung capacity. For example, there was a 14 percent incidence of coughing or markedly reduced lung capacity of young nonsmoking athletes who had been passively exposed to tobacco smoke. In comparison, the frequency was only 3 percent of athletes from smoke-free homes. Girls were more severely affected than were boys. Diminished lung capacity of athletes prevents maximum performance.

A summary of ten studies by Stanton Glantz that he considered nonbiased concluded that nonsmokers who live with smokers have an increased risk of 20 to 30 percent of dying from heart disease. This is relative to the risk for nonsmokers who live with nonsmokers. In one study, nonsmoking women who inhaled smoke from their husbands' cigarettes had a 2.5 times greater risk than women whose husbands did not smoke. Of 203 wives of nonsmokers studied, only 2 died of heart disease, while of 492 wives of current or former smokers, 17 died of heart disease. Other research indicates that children with smoking parents suffer higher rates of lung impairment and respiratory disease than do children of nonsmoking parents.

Active Smoke. Women who smoke have a two to three times higher rate of developing cardiovascular disease and of dying suddenly from heart disease than women who do not smoke. If they use birth control pills, death rate from heart disease increases by a factor of ten. Osteoporosis, bone loss, and fractures are far more common among women 40 and older who smoke than women who do not smoke. Facial wrinkles are more prominent among women who smoke. When women try to quit smoking, they report more withdrawal symptoms than men, including headaches, drowsiness, irritability, and lack of energy. A major deterrent to quitting is the fear of gaining weight.

How Does Cigarette Smoking Affect Cardiovascular Disease? One long-term study indicates that smoking alters the production of two hormones that regulate blood clotting and expansion of blood vessels. Changes in these hormone levels were found only in chronic smokers; no changes occurred in nonsmokers after they inhaled high nicotine cigarettes. Apparently, the damage is not immediate but occurs only after the passage of considerable time. Perhaps a slow change in hormone production facilitates the development of atherosclerosis. Consequently, when blood vessels are constricted or obstructed by blood clots or plaque deposits, blood flow is impaired, which can result in stroke or heart attack. One possibility is that it is the hormone thromboxane that constricts blood vessels and stimulates the aggregation of platelets.

Inhaling cigarette smoke, whether actively or passively, reduces the ability of the heart to receive unused oxygen and to convert oxygen to ATP, perhaps by production of hormones that regulate blood clotting and expansion of blood vessels.

Smoking also reduces the ability of the heart to receive and use oxygen. Carbon monoxide in cigarette smoke binds with hemoglobin in the blood, reducing its capacity to furnish oxygen to the heart. The smoke also reduces the ability of cells in the heart to convert oxygen to **adenosine triphosphate (ATP),** which provides energy to the heart muscle as it does to neurons and other muscles. Consequently, the heart has a reduced capacity to pump and to use what oxygen it does get. Extended exposure to cigarette smoke can thus reduce ability to exercise, thus facilitating pathology.

Children under 18 years of age in the United States annually consume some 1 billion packs of cigarettes. Extrapolating from these data, the Surgeon General has estimated that 5 million of today's children will thereby die of coronary heart disease, cancer, and other diseases in their later years, unless changes are effected.

EFFECTS OF SODIUM (SALT) AND POTASSIUM

Salt, found in numerous foods such as hamburgers and French fries, affects blood pressure, but we do not know exactly how. The diet of prehistoric humans must have been low in sodium and high in potassium since they ate only foods that they could hunt or gather. Through evolutionary forces, some 4 million years of our prehistoric history probably led to the survival of humans who could function most efficiently on high potassium and low sodium diets. But as food processing developed, sodium was added to foods and the amount of potassium decreased. This has contributed to an increase in strokes, heart attacks, and kidney disease.

Potassium seems to reduce the negative effects of sodium. Rats genetically predisposed to high blood pressure did develop high blood pressure when administered sodium. However, when fed higher than normal amounts of potassium, rates of stroke and kidney damage decreased. Somehow, potassium seems to help protect arteries from atherosclerosis. One serving of potatoes, citrus fruit, or melon provides about a tenth of the suggested daily amount of potassium.

STRESS AS A CAUSE OF HYPERTENSION

We saw that as one reacts to the stresses of everyday living, the striated muscle component of the startle reaction increases cardiovascular responding. Contraction of smooth muscles in the arterioles (small blood vessels) then causes an increase in the pressure within those arterioles. In turn blood pressure increases throughout all of the blood vessels of the body. If one continually tenses the striated musculature in facing ever-present stresses, the increased cardiovascular activity can become relatively permanent.

Excessive chronic muscle tension can also produce coronary vasospasm, in which the smooth muscles of the coronary arterioles are restricted, even cutting off the flow of blood. Extreme stress has been thought to affect the coronary vessels dramatically, such as in sudden and unexpected cardiac death. Another example is when a person whose spouse has just been killed in a traumatic accident suddenly "gives up" and dies too. In seemingly healthy adults it has been found that the heart can stop beating for periods of up to nine seconds during a dream. It is possible that this could cause a serious cardiac event, even sudden death. Cardiac deaths during sleep are proportionately higher than during waking hours.

Stressors might interact with genetic factors to regulate blood pressure. In one study, sons of hypertensive parents had higher systolic blood pressure and higher heart rate while performing a frustrating cognitive task than did sons of parents with normal blood pressure. However, the children could have learned such elevated cardiovascular responses from their parents.

Prevention. To prevent heart disease, people need to stop doing many things they like to do, such as smoking cigarettes and eating inappropriately. Furthermore, they need to do some things they do not like to do such as taking antihypertensive drugs and exercising. This requires behavioral engineering. If an individual learns to

Momentary stressors temporarily increase blood pressure as part of an emergency reaction, but continued contraction of the striated musculature can produce chronic constriction of the arterioles, resulting in consistent high blood pressure.

Untimely deaths may occur due to chronic neuromuscular hyperactivity throughout the body that results in excessive neural stimulation and finally coronary vasospasm.

A partial answer to the problem of high blood pressure and coronary heart disease can come from effective tension control of muscles when we meet stress and from changing other habits.

relax the striated musculature and thus stops overreacting to the stresses of life, he or she can relax the smooth muscle in arterioles, decrease high blood pressure and risk of vasospasm, and often prevent organic damage to the cardiovascular system.

People do seem to be learning to behave more wisely for blood pressure control. For example, between 1976 and 1980 the number of individuals whose high blood pressure was adequately controlled doubled from 17 to 34 percent. Associated with the increase was a decline by more than 40 percent in stroke mortality and about 30 percent in heart attack mortality. In addition, more factors to prevent the disease will no doubt be found through research.

Premenstrual and Menstrual Problems

Most women experience a variety of symptoms prior to their menstrual period.

About 82 percent of menstruating women become aware of at least one behavioral change in the week or so prior to menstruation. About 12 percent experience positive symptoms, such as increased energy and heightened desire for sex. On the other hand, about 70 percent have negative symptoms that include blemishes on the face, tenderness and swelling of the breasts, bloated abdomen, irritability, depression, and fatigue.

IS THERE A PREMENSTRUAL SYNDROME (PMS)?

Premenstrual syndrome is perhaps experienced by 3 to 10 percent of women who have undesirable symptoms such as painful and sensitive breasts, some characteristics of asthma, diabetes, arthritis, ovarian cysts, mood swings and feelings of depression that can disrupt their lives for a week or two each month and strain social relations.

Alternative Interpretation of PMS Reports.   Many women who seek treatment for menstrual disorders report wide mood changes throughout the month. When women charted their mood changes daily, moods were not cyclic. Typically the women who sought treatment, and they are a small minority of women in general, reported that they were depressed and anxious most of the time during the premenstrual period. Some researchers thus disagree that there is a PMS at all, although there may be a premenstrual magnification (PMM) of ongoing moods. Those who do not refer to PMS use such terms as *premenstrual tension, menstrual disorder,* or *menstrual distress.*

There is no generally accepted clinical definition of PMS, there is no standard way to diagnose it, and there is no consensus about what causes it or how to treat it.

There are many biological changes prior to menstruation so that it is difficult to isolate any particular changes that could produce menstrual symptoms. Unpleasant and disruptive symptoms often appear when a woman is in her thirties. Frequently they follow an interruption of the menstrual cycle that may occur through pregnancy, hysterectomy, or the use of birth control pills. Research directed at treatment found that placebo treatments have been as effective as progesterone. Although there is no effective treatment that is validated, almost any treatment seems to provide some temporary relief (e.g., the mere suggestion of treatment may release natural brain opiates, endorphins, that temporarily relieve pain and anxiety).

PMS was thought to result from a progesterone deficiency, but progesterone is now thought to be ineffective.

Possible Causes.   Perhaps PMS (or PMM) results from an excess of endorphins in the brain that are then acutely withdrawn. According to this notion, just as estrogen and progesterone levels are cyclic, levels of the brain opiates also rise and fall; they peak about a week before menstruation and then fall off abruptly, producing distress.

TOXIC SHOCK SYNDROME

Toxic shock syndrome is a disease caused by a toxin released by the bacterium *Staphlococcus aureus* ("staph") identified in 1978. It was found in children aged 8 to 17 and was related to menstruation. The onset was sudden and characterized by flulike symptoms. Toxin from the bacteria rapidly accumulates, leading to shock and sometimes death. In the United States, of 2625 reported cases of toxic shock by August 1984, 114 resulted in death. About one-fifth who survive an episode eventually experience a reoccurrence. The staph infection is treated with antibiotics to prevent reoccurrence. The wearing of tampons has been implicated as a causal factor. However, in many cases of the syndrome the women did not wear tampons. Although a single cause remains elusive, complex legal battles involving the manufacturers of tampons followed the outbreak of the disease. Further research is required to understand this phenomenon.

MENOPAUSE

This natural cessation of menstruation generally occurs between the ages of 45 and 50. Symptoms may include depression, anxiety, fatigue, mood swings, irritability, hot flashes, dizziness, numbness, nausea, heart palpitations, insomnia, and backaches. Treatment includes proper nutrition and exercise; hormonal replacement therapy, such as with estrogen, has some advantages and disadvantages and remains controversial.

Psychoimmunology and the Immune System

CLASSICAL RESEARCH

The function of the immune system is to destroy bacteria and viruses that enter the body. If it is not effective, the body may succumb to disease. **Psychoimmunology** is the study of how the immune system is influenced by psychological factors and how, in turn, diseases develop. Behavior, our so-called "life-style," has long been implicated in such disease development (e.g., since the times of Hippocrates and Galen, emotional factors have been thought to contribute to disease).

Russian Precedents. An early instance of psychoimmunology and "behavioral medicine" in the nineteenth century is the Russian scientist S. P. Botkin's belief that fever is a useful physiological defense mechanism. Consequently, Botkin did not advocate the excessive use of drugs to combat fevers, although that was fashionable medical practice in his day. Rather, he suggested that we study how the organism combats disease in order to arrive at methods of facilitating recuperation.

Another nineteenth-century predecessor of psychoimmunology was Il'la Mechnikov, a distinguished Russian pathologist and contemporary of the physiologist I. P. Pavlov. Mechnikov developed the concept that immunity is a major factor in maintaining health. In 1883, Mechnikov reported to the Society of Physicians and Scientists in Odessa, Russia, on the role of phagocytosis. **Phagocytosis** is a process by which bodily cells destroy foreign matter, especially bacteria (*phago* means "eat";

Psychological factors have long been related to psychophysiological pathologies such as ulcers, heart disease, and cancer.

Psychoimmunology is the study of the influence of psychological factors on the immune system and is closely related to the field of behavioral medicine.

cyte means "cell"). In phagocytosis the cell can surround and consume the invading body, much like an amoeba does in ingesting foreign matter. Phagocytosis, Mechnikov held, is a defense mechanism used by organisms in combating infectious diseases. For this significant contribution to the development of the concept of immunity, he, along with Paul Ehrlich, was awarded the Nobel Prize.

Another important development occurred in 1891 when the Russian scientist I. G. Savchenko demonstrated that the brain influences resistance of the body to disease. By extirpating parts of the brain, the course of the infectious process was modified. Follow-up experiments confirmed that the nervous system influences immune reactions, but the specific mechanisms involved had yet to be specified.

The brain was further implicated in immunology when research established that substances that inhibit cerebral functions, such as soporific (sleep-inducing agents) and narcotic drugs, also decrease the effectiveness of the immune system; in part they do so by decreasing the phagocytes and the antibodies that fight infection. Conversely, it was found that by stimulating the central nervous system, the effectiveness of the immune system was increased. Much work was performed by Russian physiologists in efforts to regulate immune reactions by means of conditional reflexes. However, the results have been both positive and negative so that the issue remains controversial.

TWO RESPONSES OF THE IMMUNE SYSTEM

The Humoral Response.   The humoral response is made through blood and lymph fluids (*humoral* refers to such fluids of the body). Through it, B cells are generated by bone marrow, and antibodies are also released that combine with and neutralize bacteria. Antibodies released into fluids of the body also may coat bacteria so that the bacteria can be ingested by scavenger cells of the immune system.

Cell-Mediated Responses of the Immune System.   These are usually carried out by T cells that are generated by the thymus, a body located in the throat region. The cell-mediated response is slower than the humoral response and fights slower diseases such as cancer. It also assists in fighting viruses and helps to accept transplants.

VARIABLES THAT AFFECT THE IMMUNE SYSTEM

Research classically has studied the effects of various drugs on the immune system by administering them to healthy, normal animals. The possible effects on the immune system are often measured by lymphoid organ weights (the spleen, the thymus, etc.), the capacity of phagocytes to destroy foreign bodies, and condition of the lymph nodes. Research with these measures has shown that the immune system is affected by increasing age, poor nutrition, uncomfortable temperatures, irradiation, various drugs, genetic characteristics, and circadian rhythms. There is increasing evidence that psychological stresses deleteriously influence the immune system, as well as the progress of cancers. Those influences come about as a result of variations in CNS, neurotransmitter, and hormone activity. Since the immune system deteriorates with stress and age, the restorative effects of drugs might be more

---

Early research indicated that brain activity influenced the body's ability to fight infections; since conditioning was thought to be a brain phenomenon, Russian physiologists sought to control immune reactions by developing relevant conditional reflexes.

In general, CNS excitation stimulates immune processes whereas CNS inhibition reduces them.

The immune system has millions of different kinds of antibodies that are produced in response to foreign substances so as to protect the body against invading organisms. All animals are born with a complete repertoire of antibodies.

The immune system fights disease by humoral responses wherein B cells are generated from bone marrow and by antibodies that may combine with and neutralize bacteria. Slower cell-mediated responses carried out by T cells fight slower diseases such as cancers.

Variables that have been shown to affect the immune system include increasing age, poor nutrition, and psychological reactions to stress that apparently affect the CNS through neurotransmitter and hormone activity.

easily detected in stressed or aged animals than in normals. Research has indeed indicated that neurotropin (NSP) has a restorative effect on depressed immune systems of stressed and aged mice. NSP apparently has a broad range of effects such as analgesic and antiallergic actions.

As we have seen many times, the development of instruments and methods has led to major advances in a field. Psychoimmunology is no exception in that the development of powerful new methods (e.g., laser flow cytometry) has allowed several subtypes of immune system cells to be simultaneously measured within a single study.

HOW DO STRESSORS AFFECT THE IMMUNE SYSTEM?

Distress

The perception of stressful events is followed by a complex set of internal processes. When threatening information is received by way of the receptors, we have seen that the entire body is activated in the startle reaction. Complex neuromuscular circuits direct messages between the muscles and the brain. Especially the circuits between muscles, the cortex, the limbic system, and posterior hypothalamus of the limbic system are activated.

In these interactions, the body is in a state of **distress** (perception of negative, threatening stressors) that reduces the effectiveness of the immune system. The hypothalamus secretes neuropeptides that affect the pituitary gland. The pituitary gland in turn releases hormones, principally adrenocorticotropic hormone (ACTH), which acts on the cortex of the adrenal glands to release corticosteroids. The corticosteroids depress the immune system by inhibiting the action of scavenger cells and various types of lymphocytes (cells from the lymph nodes) as well as their abilities to reproduce. When distress situations are chronic, there is atrophy of lymph node tissue and enlargement of adrenal glands.

Survival Value of a Suppressed Immune System

Why have we evolved with this apparent disadvantage that distress suppresses the immune system? If organisms biologically prepare themselves to meet emergency situations, one might think that the immune system should become more effective then. One speculation is that when organisms are injured in a fight, for instance, they need not immediately fight off infections. Rather, they mobilize their energies. The immediate reduction in the effectiveness of the immune system may thus actually be adaptive because the slow threat of disease that could result from injury is not immediately demanding—time is required to multiply threatening bacteria or viruses. After one has survived, then there is time for the immune system to increase its effectiveness. A more effective immune system could then attack bacteria and viruses that may have entered the organism during the injury. One can further speculate, in accordance with principles of survival of the fittest, that those organisms whose immune systems increased effectiveness either too early or too late to optimally combat such bacteria and viruses failed to survive.

Eustress

While distress (deterious stress) generally suppresses the immune system, positive stress (eustress) may actually facilitate the immune system.

Eustress may liberate beta endorphins to create pleasant feelings and beneficial physiological effects by activating opiate receptors that mimic opiate drugs (morphine, heroin, etc.).

In addition to the depressing effects of distress on the immune system, there probably also are positive factors. Hans Selye called positive factors **eustress** (as against distress). Stresses related to what we call "hope," "love," and "happiness" may have beneficial effects on health. In his book *Anatomy of an Illness*, Norman Cousins tells how he discharged himself from a hospital and went home to care for himself. His treatment included encouraging himself to laugh by watching old comedy movies. A similar finding is that people significantly put off dying until after an important event, such as Christmas or a birthday. Perhaps laughter, pleasant occasions, and other such factors release endorphins that have a beneficial physiological effect. One possibility is that when we are happy, the body releases beta endorphins (a neuropeptide created in nerve cells from amino acids) that mimic drugs like opium. (Specific opiate receptors can be activated by beta endorphins just as they can by opiatelike drugs such as morphine, codeine, and heroin.)

THEORIES OF IMMUNE SYSTEM FUNCTIONING

There are two theories of immune system functioning, one based on selection of antibodies and the other on conditioning or instruction processes. An analogy to the conditioning theory is instructing a tailor to make a suit that closely fits the body of a buyer. An analogy to the selection theory is a buyer's entering a department store and selecting a pretailored suit that fits.

The Selection Theory

The selection theory, suggested in the 1950s by MacFarlane Burnet and Niels Jerne, holds that an antibody present in the body combats a virus or bacterium that enters the bloodstream by attempting to fit and bind itself to the invader. If the fit is adequate, the antibody cell then divides and makes thousands of copies (clones) of itself. The body can thus rid itself of the virus or bacterium.

This model of the immune system is consistent with principles of selection and of survival of the fittest. If the invading organism selects an appropriate antibody, the individual may survive. But if a person does not have the appropriate antibody that can bind the virus or bacterium, that person may die. Also, if the body cannot reproduce appropriate antibodies, the immune system may be unable to kill foreign cells. Cunningham (1978) summarized evidence that supports this theory. G. M. Edelman and Rodney Porter received the Nobel Prize in 1972 for developing the selection theory and for empirically confirming it.

The Conditioning Theory

In 1940, Linus Pauling suggested that there was one basic kind of antibody molecule in the body that would mold itself around an intruder, thus acquiring a specific shape. That mold was then to be copied many times and released into the bloodstream where the modified antibodies could bind onto invading bacteria. In this way, the system learned from the bacterium what shape it was to assume.

A variation of the conditioning theory is that invading bacteria condition the immune system to increase the number of natural killer cells so as to combat the invader.

One line of evidence that behavioral medicine can influence immune functions derives from research indicating that the immune system can be conditioned. In 1926 the Soviet scientist V. I. Metalnikov first demonstrated that changes in immune responses could be classically conditioned. Since then there has been success in conditioning an increase in natural killer cells of the immune system that may control the spread of tumors. In 1975, Robert Ader tried to instill in rats an aversion to saccharine flavored water. For this, he fed the rats saccharine, then injected them with cyclophosplamide which made them nauseous. Cyclophosplamide suppresses the immune system but after consumption, the system quickly reverts to normal. Ader found that he conditioned the rats not only to avoid saccharine but to suppress the immune system whenever they drank saccharine. In such successful conditioning studies, neuroendocrines may be the physiological mediators responsible for linking the conditional stimulus (e.g., sensory stimuli deriving from the saccharine) to the immunological conditional response (suppressing the immune system), that is, CS (saccharine) — CR (immune system suppressor).

Both the selection and the conditioning theories of how the immune system functions have support, although the selection theory seems to be favored. Nevertheless, both are maintained as viable at this time. Through further research, we may definitively decide in favor of one or the other, or that both serve different functions for the immune system.

In Conclusion

Behavioral variables do have physiological effects on the immune system, but the effects are extremely complex. The immune system is integrated with other systems to maintain homeostatic conditions. There are complex interactions among immune, genetic, neural, and endocrine systems with behavioral–emotional responses. Behavioral interventions through stress management, conditioning, and so on can alter specific and nonspecific aspects of immune function. These are important findings that can help in control of the immune and related systems (see Chapter 15).

Two theories of immune system functioning are viable: The selection theory holds that antibodies combat invading organisms by surrounding and consuming them; the conditioning theory holds that killer cells are increased to combat the invader.

Changes in behavior may alter immune functions which may mediate the development and progress of some disease states.

ACQUIRED IMMUNE DEFICIENCY SYNDROME (AIDS)

It is held that AIDS viruses (the human immunodeficiency viruses, HIV1 and HIV2) decrease the immune systems ability to resist disease. There are progressive behavioral–cognitive and neurological complications that are due to disease of the brain. A worldwide epidemic threatens large regions of the world, especially Africa.

AIDS was first discovered in a few homosexual men during the summer of 1981. It first spread through sodomy by homosexual men as well as through sharing of needles by drug addicts. Some people contracted AIDS through contaminated blood transfusions and heterosexual activity, including sex with prostitutes.

The first patients with AIDS died from a variety of infections and malignancies including pneumonia and sarcoma, a cancer of the lining of blood vessels. The infections and cancers had been seen previously only in people born with certain defects in their immune system and in patients whose immunity had been impaired by chemotherapy or by immunosuppressive drugs given for organ transplantation. The inference was that AIDS killed its victims by destroying their immune system.

Causes.   The causative agent was presumably identified in 1983 as a virus of the retrovirus family. It was called LAV (lymphadenopathy associated virus) and synonymously HTLV-III (human T-lymphotropic virus type III). While the consensus is that AIDS is produced by a virus, some authorities question this hypothesis, reasoning that many infected people do not contract diseases and that infected chimpanzees do not develop AIDS. If so, treatments with expensive drugs may not be needed.

The loss of immune defenses in AIDS stems primarily from a reduction in the number and change in the function of T4 lymphocytes, one of the many kinds of cells in the immune system. The loss of T4 cells from the blood, lymph nodes, spleen, and other tissues in which they are normally concentrated is consistently found in AIDS patients. T4 cells may normally constitute three-fourths of the circulating T cells in normals, but in many AIDS patients they often cannot even be detected.

It is presumed that the AIDS virus attacks and destroys the body's immune system, causing the victim to be susceptible to infection. Consequently, people do not die of AIDS, but of other diseases such as pneumonia.

The AIDS virus is thought to avoid destruction by destroying the immune system itself. That phenomenon is similar to that of other viral infections such as in measles where immunity is temporarily weakened.

Diagnosis.   Lymph-node disruption is characteristic of AIDS, which is an early clue that one is infected with an AIDS virus. A precursor of lymph-node disruption is AIDS-related complex (ARC), which has symptoms of fever, night sweats, weight loss, chronic cough, and diarrhea. AIDS itself then follows. The lymph nodes swell because their regular structure is changed, but it is not known how the AIDS virus causes those anatomic changes.

Several studies have found that behavioral signs may indicate AIDS before any symptoms occur. In particular, researchers have found that impaired coordination and cognitive difficulties, especially of memory, indicate neuropsychological impairment. First there are subtle cognitive changes that progress into gross dementia in some patients. AIDS patients are slower in information processing and have difficulty in maintaining attention and functioning in a task that requires divided attention.

The results of neuropsychological examinations indicating brain impairment had an agreement rate of 74 percent with direct brain diagnosis through magnetic resonance imaging. Although we do not adequately understand how AIDS affects the brain, it does seem clear that the AIDS infection enters the brain and remains there, sometimes causing AIDS dementia. The typical prognosis for a patient with active AIDS is death in four years.

In Conclusion.   From a survival-of-the-fittest criterion, one can predict a long-term trend in which the disease will have a dramatic effect on such practices as sodomy, intravenous drug use, prostitution, and casual sex.

Cancer, Behavior, and the Environment

Malignant (cancerous) cells are distinguished from benign (noncancerous) cells because they can invade and disrupt the functioning of organs. Malignant cells grow to produce malignant tumors, which are classified as carcinomas (epithelial cancers in tissues in the outer layers of the body or in linings of organs), which account for approximately 85 percent of all cancer in adults; sarcomas (cancers in connective tissues such as tendons), which comprise about 2 percent; the remainder are leukemias and lymphomas (cancers that stem from immature red and white blood cells).

Lung cancer is the most frequent cancer followed by colorectal cancer. Ninety-eight percent of all colorectal cancers occur in adults 40 years or older. Approximately 130,000 new cases occur in the United States each year. Of those about 40,000 could be helped with early detection.

NUMEROUS CAUSES OF CANCER

Most disorders and many diseases have a variety of causes. In part this is true for cancer because there are different kinds of cancers. Clearly there are genetic predispositions to cancer (e.g., fair-skinned Caucasians are more likely to develop skin cancer). However, there is considerable variation due to environmental and behavioral factors, which is the area of concern for biobehavioral medicine. Behavior is important; as early as the second century Galen observed that women who were melancholic (e.g., depressed) were more likely to develop cancer than were sanguine (e.g., cheerful) women. We will discuss several behavioral factors through which we can at least partially control the likelihood of developing cancer. Even though we know of a number of environmental variables that can produce cancer, behavioral engineering can often prevent them from becoming active.

A multicausal principle is that there is no single cause of a disease or disorder, but there are many contributing factors. It is applicable to most disorders and many diseases such as schizophrenia and cancer.

A variety of behavioral, environmental, and genetic factors can increase the likelihood of developing cancer.

STRESS AND CANCER

There is no evidence that stressful events can cause cells to become cancerous. However, since stress does affect the immune system, the immune system in turn may affect the growth of tumors. It is thought that stressful events influence existing tumors through central and peripheral neurotransmitter activities and the secretion of hormones. In this way, stressful events may affect other disorders too. Through feedback circuits, stress can influence the development of psychiatric illnesses which in turn may influence the immune system, perhaps facilitating the development of cancer.

Laboratory research has confirmed that experimentally induced tumors in animals can be influenced by specific environmental and behavioral variables. It is now possible to predict to some extent how an already existing tumor will respond to stress. Stress can cause viral tumors to grow faster, and stress may inhibit the growth of nonviral tumors. Perhaps the immune system affects only viral tumors, which are not the most significant kinds of cancers for humans.

BEHAVIOR, THE SUN, AND SKIN CANCER

Excessive exposure to the sun can cause skin cancer. It is estimated that some 500,000 Americans develop skin cancer every year. There are three varieties: basal cell, squamous cell, and malignant melanoma. Malignant melanoma is the most dangerous because it may spread to other parts of the body; this variety is doubling in frequency every decade or so, striking about 26,000 each year and causing 5000 deaths annually. Through behavioral intervention, we could reduce that number. On the other hand, we should not forget that the sun has positive effects too, as in providing vitamin D. As with most things, the proper dosage is what is important.

DIET (WHAT SHOULD WE EAT?)

The jury is still out on whether diet contributes to risks of cancer. Because cancer *may* be associated with diet, experts recommend eating fibers, vegetables, and fruits to help prevent cancer in part by moving feces in the intestines so that carcinogens have minimal effect on the gastrointestinal lining. Vitamins A and C themselves may also have beneficial effects.

Obesity apparently is a risk factor for certain kinds of cancer, such as of the breast, perhaps by increased hormonal action. It has been recommended that no more than 30 percent of a person's diet be fat intake (a typical American diet has about 50 percent fat intake).

Barbecuing apparently produces carcinogens when fat from meat burns on hot coals and generates smoke containing these hydrocarbons.

Diet may influence the likelihood of developing cancer such that smoked meat may increase risk, and fruits, vegetables and fiber may decrease risk.

SHOULD WE AVOID MICROWAVES AND MAGNETIC FIELDS?

Microwave radiation is emitted by many sources including radar installations, satellite ground stations, relay towers for long-distance telephone links, television transmitters, microwave ovens, and citizens band radios. Increased rates of leukemia, headaches, dizziness, memory loss, and fatigue have been reported among power-station operators, aluminum workers, power and telephone line workers, and others repeatedly exposed to electric and magnetic fields. Magnetic fields created by electrical current as in the 60 Hz fields generated in our homes, have become suspect (e.g., children living in homes with relatively strong magnetic fields from electrical systems had significantly higher rates of cancer). Whereas these findings come from correlational studies on humans, experiments on animals have more firmly implicated microwaves.

We can only speculate as to how electrical fields might affect us. Even though the fields are too weak to cause chemical reactions, they might rhythmically bend enzymes to speed up certain metabolic processes. In turn, deleterious chemicals could accumulate in cells over an extended period of time.

Although the final answers are not in, serious study of the problem is underway in many laboratories throughout the country. In the meantime, we probably should protect ourselves, for example, by avoiding the use of electric blankets and staying at least 28 inches away from VDTs (video display terminals).

Limited research has suggested the possibility that microwaves and magnetic fields caused by electrical currents can cause, or increase the rate of, growth of cancers.

SMOKING

Tobacco smoke has been implicated as a causative agent in lung cancer.

Cigarette smoking has been estimated to be responsible for 75 percent of lung cancer cases among women and 85 percent among men. The higher cancer rates for men reflect the fact that in the past more men than women smoked, and they smoked more heavily. However, the gap between male and female smoking is narrowing. Accordingly, lung cancer deaths among women 55 and older quadrupled from 1960 to 1982 and continue to increase. Lung cancer has thus become the number one killer of women, surpassing breast cancer. Rate of death has also increased for those in every other age group who smoke. Cigarettes are implicated in this increase because for comparison, breast cancer mortality rates remained essentially unchanged through those years. The increased rate of lung cancer in women started during

World War II when smoking became more socially acceptable. The effects of smoking during pregnancy include intrauterine growth retardation, congenital defects, and perinatal death.

One study of the effects of coffee drinking and smoking cigarettes showed that men who smoked a pack or more a day and also drank five or more cups of coffee a day were seven times more likely to die from lung cancer than men who smoked but drank no coffee at all. Smoking alone increased the risk of lung cancer tenfold. But smoking along with drinking coffee increased the rate of lung cancer to 40 times higher than that for men who neither smoked nor drank coffee.

On the other hand, nonsmokers are six times more likely than smokers to develop ulcerative colitis. How smoking might protect against ulcerative colitis, though, is unknown. We do now know that nicotine alters the balance between prostacyclin and thromboxane, causing prostacyclin levels to fall and thromboxane levels to rise. Each action accelerates the other in a positive feedback cycle resulting in constricted blood vessels and accumulation of platelets. But how that helps remains the subject of future research. In any event, ulcerative colitis is sufficiently rare that one would not smoke just to prevent it.

PHYSICAL ACTIVITY RELATED TO CANCER

Men who have sedentary jobs such as bookkeepers and bus drivers, have a greater colon cancer risk than do active workers. The risk is nearly three times greater for the descending colon, the major section toward the end of the gastrointestinal tract. Apparently, physical activity stimulates the colon to contract and propel feces. Carcinogens in the feces thus have greater contact with the lining of the colon in sedentary people because of their less frequent expulsion, among other reasons. Surface contact is greatest in the descending colon where feces remain longer. However, physical activity and risk of rectal cancer are not related, probably because feces are not in contact with membranes there for long periods of time.

Colon cancer is more frequent in sedentary than in active people such that the greater the physical activity, the less the likelihood of colon cancer.

The behavioral implications are that those who are sedentary should increase their physical activity and probably thereby decrease risk of colon cancer (among other positive effects). However, since these data are only correlational (not causal) there could be confounding effects (e.g., sedentary workers could also have a more cancer-producing diet, they could be genetically predisposed to cancer, etc.).

Carcinogens in feces may contribute to colon cancer in sedentary people; however, there could be other causes such as cancer-producing diets or genetic predisposition.

Motor Diseases

BASAL GANGLIA DISORDERS

The neurological disorders of basal ganglia (Fig. 7.6) typically include the signs of postural changes (such as an exaggerated stoop or a leaning forward of the body), involuntary movements of the trunk, gait disturbances (such as shuffling of the feet), articulatory (speech) disorders, and some kinds of emotional disturbances.

All basal ganglia disorders probably involve a malfunctioning of neurotransmitters, possibly with alterations in the metabolism of catecholamines. Five clearly identified diseases of the basal ganglia are Parkinson's disease, Huntington's disease, progressive supernuclear palsy, Wilson's disease, and sydenhamchorea.

Basal ganglia diseases have a number of signs in common and are probably caused by disturbances in the functioning of neurotransmitters.

Parkinson's Disease

In 1817 James Parkinson described patients with shaking palsy. Their intellectual abilities were normal, but they were emotionally depressed and even wished for release from their illness through death.

In Parkinson's disease, there is generally a tremor and weakness of the muscles which is chronic and progressive, muscle stiffness, memory loss, visual and speech problems, as well as a general slowing of activity, and the body leans forward. Delirium is characteristic in the final stages.

Parkinson's disease afflicts more than 500,000 Americans, usually individuals over 60 years of age. Normally, the basal ganglia have a rich dopaminergic innervation. However, there is a dopamine deficiency in Parkinson's patients. One effective therapy is to increase the amount of dopamine by administering L-Dopa. Unfortunately, the large amounts of L-Dopa that must be administered cause adverse effects such as nausea.

Brain transplants of fetal tissue that increase the amount of dopamine have markedly reduced the symptoms of Parkinson's, although so far the improvement has lasted for only several years at best. Vigorous research on brain transplants is underway, largely because of the extent and seriousness of Parkinson's.

Symptoms of Parkinson's have also been caused by the ingestion of bad batches of synthetic heroin that is made in illicit laboratories and sold inexpensively. The use of synthetic heroin has reached epidemic proportions. The symptoms last for days, weeks, months, or more than a year, leaving some users paralyzed.

Huntington's Disease

In 1872 George Huntington described a disease characterized by involuntary movements and intellectual decline with insanity and a tendency to suicide. There are major emotional disorders, with early symptoms often including irritability, aggressiveness, irresponsibility, promiscuity, alcoholism, and schizoid behavior. Initially, such changes are typically subtle and might be observed only by those very close to the patient. A genetic marker has been discovered for Huntington's disease. Current treatment includes GABA (gamma-amino-butyric acid, an inhibitory neurotransmitter).

Progressive Supernuclear Palsy

In this unusual disorder of the basal ganglia, there is paralysis of some eye movements with dysarthria (speech disorders), mild dementia, apathy, and depression.

Wilson's Disease

This is characterized by involuntary movements, rigidity, dysarthria, and emotional overreaction, which occurs when patients are engaged in spastic smiling.

Sydenhamchorea (St. Vitas Dance)

Sydenhamchorea (St. Vitas Dance) occurs in childhood and involves involuntary movements of the face, trunk, and extremities. The etiology is due to rheumatic fever with the typical onset between 5 and 15 years of age. There is apathy, intermittent irritability, and sometimes thought disorder.

MUSCULAR DYSTROPHY

Duchenne muscular dystrophy is one of about ten forms of muscular dystrophy and is marked by destruction of muscle tissue. Its victims normally have some difficulty walking by ages 3 to 5, are frequently confined to a wheelchair by ages 9 to 12, and usually die in their late teens or early twenties when their respiratory muscles fail.

Duchenne muscular dystrophy is caused by a defect on the X chromosome. It is possible that Becker muscular dystrophy may be caused by the same defect. Genetic diseases that are linked to the X chromosome appear only in males whose mothers carry the defect but do not have the disease. Fetuses can be tested for the presence of the genetic defect.

There is a strain of mice with a disease that resembles the most common form of muscular dystrophy and may be caused by the same kind of genetic defect, located on a particular region of the X chromosome that causes Duchenne muscular dystrophy. Mouse and human X chromosomes are very similar so that a mutation that shows up in a mouse will probably be found to be identical to a human mutation.

MULTIPLE SCLEROSIS (MS)

Roughly 250,000 Americans, usually young adults, have one of the two forms of multiple sclerosis: the relapse version, characterized by periodic attacks followed by quiet periods, and the chronic version, wherein the symptoms are steady and unrelenting.

MS is linked to a virus that causes the body's defense system to attack myelin, the fatty sheath that surrounds and insulates some nerve fibers. Without this protective covering, neurons in the brain function abnormally for seeing, walking, talking, and other motor activities. In severe cases, it can also trigger bladder and bowel problems and sexual dysfunction.

Injection of interferon, an antiviral agent naturally produced by the body, has caused some decrease in the number of flare-ups associated with MS. Perhaps in some way, interferon slows down degenerative brain processes.

EPILEPSY

It has been estimated that 500,000 to a million Americans suffer from some form of epilepsy. The patient may have focal (limited) brain damage or a more widespread form of cell damage. About 70 to 80 percent of people with focal epilepsy can be helped by medication, but the rest have seizures so frequently that they cannot lead normal lives. Surgery in which the tissue causing the epilepsy is removed is effective for about half of those for whom medication is not helpful.

Attention Deficit Disorders (ADD) with Hyperactivity

Attention deficit disorder (ADD) is also known as hyperkinesis or hyperactivity. The preferred term by the psychiatric profession is *attention deficit disorder with hyperactivity.* However, attention deficit disorder without hyperactivity is now also recognized by some. Symptoms include increased activity and restlessness, distractibility, impulsiveness, lack of response to punishment, occasional outbursts of fighting, and often problems with school work. It is usually noticed early in childhood, during kindergarten or first grade. About 80 percent of hyperkinetic children are boys. There may well be a genetic basis for the condition leading to impaired maturation of the nervous system, perhaps associated with catecholamine abnormalities.

Children diagnosed with ADD are hyperactive, have difficulty paying attention, and often are aggressive. ADD generally responds favorably to drug therapy with amphetamines.

Drug therapy, such as with amphetamines, is usually effective but presents a paradox because amphetamines are stimulants. Yet in ADD they decrease activity and arousal. Stimulant drugs have been the preferred treatment for ADD since the mid 1960s and typically calm the child's disruptive behavior.

Hyperactivity may be related to neurotransmitter imbalance. A basis for this conclusion is that MAO (monoaminoxidase) inhibiters improve hyperactive children's behavior as dramatically as does Dexedrine. MAO is a brain chemical that breaks down the neurotransmitter norepinephrine. However, using MAO inhibitors has been confined to research because a very restrictive diet, difficult to conduct with children, is required.

Head Injuries

EXTENT

Approximately 7 million people experience head injuries each year in the United States. Approximately 500,000 require hospitalization. Perhaps 300,000 of that number have permanent physical or mental disabilities.

Adolescents and young adults are the most vulnerable; 30 percent of all head injuries in one year occur in those 15 to 19 years of age. Males are two to three times more likely than females to be injured. Automobile and motorcycle accidents produce half the cases; other causes include being assaulted, shot, stabbed, or seriously beaten.

TRAUMA TO THE BRAIN CAN OCCUR
IN VARIOUS WAYS

Following a blow to the head, there is bleeding around and within the brain that can cause blood clots. The blood is being compressed in the cranium and presses on sensitive tissues. Brain swelling can cause brain cells and nerve pathways to be stretched and sheared, disturbing neural transmission.

Brain damage occurs most frequently in young people and may result in loss of cognitive abilities and emotional instability. The brain insults in head injury cases are generally not well localized.

The pressure on the brain from blood clots can be relieved through surgery. But the brain cells that die often leave the victim with permanent brain impairment and perhaps in a coma. Comatose patients who awaken do so slowly and often have severe disabilities. Generally, the longer the coma the greater are the disabilities. On the surface, such patients may look normal and thus are expected to behave normally. However, there are cognitive deficits (memory losses, impaired judgment, etc.). They may have unstable emotional responses, including outbursts that occur with little provocation, and they may be very agitated. Rehabilitation, if at all successful, requires months or even years.

The Vietnam Head Injury Study of more than 1200 Vietnam veterans who survived brain wounds was headed by Andres Salazar and sponsored by the U.S. National Institutes of Health. It linked aspects of behavior to specific parts of the brain. Most of those injured in the right side of the brain remained conscious or had only momentary blackouts following their injury. On the other hand, those who were unconscious for a prolonged period had damage to their left hemisphere and experienced speech problems later. There was thus a relationship between consciousness and the hemisphere damaged, which implicates language functioning (see Chapter 11).

Findings have indicated that there is more of a relationship between the reticular formation and the left hemisphere in maintaining wakefulness than there is with the right. Injury to the left hemisphere could thus disrupt the reticular formation, leading to unconsciousness, but a comparable injury to the right hemisphere would not.

Frontal Lobe Damage.   When damaged, the frontal lobes, which encompass almost 40 percent of the cortex, often have lesions, tumors, or hemorrhages. The results of injuries to the frontal lobes, particularly from gunshot wounds, have been described as a behavioral syndrome that may include lack of judgment and foresight, facetiousness, childish behavior, disinhibition, and euphoria.

However, specific behavioral deficits involving frontal lobe damage vary because there is typically injury to other brain areas too. Huntington's disease is one disorder that used to be thought to be due to a frontal lobe disorder but now primarily, if not exclusively, is known to involve subcortical structures. Similarly, multiple sclerosis has often been said to involve significant frontal abnormalities, but we now know that this disease has many pathological locations.

Damage to the right frontal lobes causes difficulty in recognizing specific facial features. Those Vietnam veterans with damage to the right temporal lobe had problems matching up unfamiliar faces, while those with left temporal lobe damage had trouble identifying famous faces. Perhaps the left hemisphere functions in the retrieval of memories of familiar faces and puts them into context.

A behavioral syndrome due to frontal lobe damage has included lack of judgment and foresight, facetiousness, childish behavior, disinhibition, and euphoria.

The right frontal and parietal lobes seem to function in discriminating among different facial features. The right hemisphere may help to interpret facial features while the left may retrieve memories associated with those features so that complete face-to-face recognition depends on both functioning. Damage to both areas would result in complete failure to recognize faces, known as **prospagnosia** (inability to verbally identify a face).

SOME SPECIAL PROBLEMS OF YOUTH

Youth and Sex

Sexual behavior is increasing the problems for young people because they reach puberty at earlier ages than before. Females in industrialized countries now typically have their first menstruation before their thirteenth birthday, which is one year earlier than their mothers and two years earlier than their grandmothers.

Adverse consequences of sexual behavior include AIDS, herpes simplex, unwanted pregnancy, birth and postnatal complications for both the mother and the infant, abortions, gonorrhea, syphilis, and other sexually transmitted diseases. In developed countries more than two-thirds of all reported cases of gonorrhea occur among persons younger than 25 years. It has been estimated that 12 – 20 percent of females with untreated gonorrhea will eventually develop salpingitis, which can lead to serious complications including ectopic pregnancy, tubo-ovarian abscesses, and infertility. In the Dominican Republic and Japan teenage mothers are more likely than mothers in their twenties to die in childbirth due to complications during pregnancy and delivery.

The World Health Organization has concluded that sexual education does not lead to promiscuity, as some critics have suggested. On the contrary, they have found that sound information about sexuality seems to encourage postponement of sexual intercourse. They recommend that contraceptive services be made more widely available.

Noise Pollution

Special problems of youth in industrialized countries include adverse consequences of sexual behavior, destruction of their auditory system due to noise pollution, and skin diseases.

The excessive noises in our environment constitute a major pollution problem that increases the stresses of life. Anatomically, it is increasing the rate of deafness. Some music from traditional Chinese operas is even louder than Western rock music coming out of "ghettoblasters." The increasing frequency of deafness in teenagers is due to the chronic exposure to loud noises that kills the hair cells on the basilar membrane.

Tight Jeans

Inflamed cutaneous nerves with chronic pain have been thought to be due to wearing tight jeans, which place pressure on the cutaneous nerve. The cutaneous nerve, which runs from the lower spine to the thigh, sometimes becomes inflamed in overweight adults and pregnant women because of the excessive pressure weight puts on it. Although the symptoms are well known, the cause has been elusive.

Skin Disease

Skin diseases such as acne, psoriasis, hives, eczema, and herpes can be aggravated by stress. Students report, for instance, that just before an examination, job interview, or new date their acne or psoriasis suddenly worsens. In one case study when a woman was relaxed, nothing would happen when a copper penny was placed on her arm. But if she was subjected to stress, she would break out in hives under the penny.

Subtle interplay between skin problems such as acne, psoriasis, and eczema and emotional behaviors fits a positive feedback model such that a skin condition flares up as emotional behavior increases which worsens the skin condition, and so on.

Skin problems, like health problems in general, tend to have cybernetic characteristics. For instance, people may pull out their hair or scratch themselves badly because of an emotional disorder. In turn, the more they physically hurt themselves, the worse the emotional behavior becomes. The skin condition shingles (herpes zoster) is a good example—it may lead to emotional problems that in turn feed back to worsen the shingles.

Environmental factors such as temperature, humidity, cosmetics, toiletries, and clothing can also contribute to skin problems. However, their effects are more severe when an individual experiences environmental stresses. Allergens such as dust in the house, for instance, seem to trigger asthma attacks primarily if the individual is emotionally stressed. We have seen how stress works to depress one's natural level of immunity, thereby making people more susceptible to infections such as various kinds of herpes.

Relaxation or even distractions such as working at hobbies have been shown to sometimes help clear the skin.

DISORDERS OF INITIATING AND MAINTAINING SLEEP

The seriousness of sleep disorders is indicated by the estimate that in one form or another they affect every person every year. Approximately 10 million Americans take prescribed or over-the-counter sleeping aids each year. There may be transient sleep disorders that can last for days or weeks as a result of various temporary stressors, or sleep disorders may be chronic and relatively long-lasting. More than 100 centers throughout the United States study the two major categories of sleep disorders: dyssomnias and parasomnias. **Dyssomnias** include insomnia disorders and maladaptive sleep/wake schedules. **Parasomnias** include sleep terrors, nightmares, and sleep walking. Nightmares usually occur in the REM stage of sleep. In contrast, night terrors typically occur when dreams are absent. In night terrors, the individual often panics and wakes up screaming. Although it is thought by some that anxious people have more nightmares than nonanxious people, a study by James Wood indicated the opposite. He had 220 men and women keep logs of their dreams for two weeks and found that the average number of nightmares was about one with no relationship to degree of anxiety. It may be that anxious people are more likely to remember or more likely to complain about nightmares.

Sleep disorders are often associated with other behavioral disorders such as worrying, obsessive-compulsive disorder, and anxiety state and with such organic conditions as Parkinson's.

Three disorders of initiating and maintaining sleep are (1) falling asleep, defined as taking more than 30 minutes for sleep onset; (2) maintaining sleep, defined as awakening for more than 30 minutes; and (3) terminal insomnia—awakening early in the morning and not getting back to sleep. All three types may occur together or singly, but they all contribute to daytime fatigue. A sleep problem is serious when it starts to affect daytime performance.

Causes. Many sleep disorders are due to excessive stress. The overly tense individual thinks about problems and carries the stresses of life over into bedtime. Excessive muscular tension is incompatible with good sleep. Other contributing factors are biological predisposition, drugs and alcohol, medical problems (produced by arthritis, ulcers, angina, migraines, asthma, irregular heart beat, and sleep apnea, in which there are brief bouts of breathing cessation). Drug and alcohol dependency has been established as the primary cause in 12.4 percent of patients with chronic insomnia.

Sleep disorders often follow a positive feedback model in which physiological arousal (rapid heart beats, high bodily temperature etc.) decreases sleep and poor sleep leads to worry and increased physiological arousal.

How Much Sleep Is Enough? As much as the body requires—people should sleep as long as their body will allow. Some people get along on only a few hours of sleep quite effectively while others need more. But if one is deprived of sleep too long, the body may suffer profound metabolic changes.

Negative Conditioning. The stimuli associated with nights of lying awake in

Sleep disorders or dyssomnias include insomnia and parasomnias (e.g., nightmares) that often contribute to such behavioral disorders as anxiety state.

bed can be conditioned to keep one from sleeping. Consequently, since people can learn to not sleep well, they can also learn good sleep habits.

To acquire effective sleep control, one should associate the bedroom primarily with sleep. If you do not readily go to sleep at night, leave the bedroom and come back only when you are sleepy.

The conditioning typically develops when people associate bedroom cues with worries that are incompatible with sleep. For prevention, one can strengthen the association between stimulus properties of the bedroom and sleep by eliminating cues that are incompatible with sleep.

To treat sleep disorders, professionals are moving from drugs to behavioral therapy, including Progressive Relaxation.

Other treatments include medication, which is not a permanent solution, and Progressive Relaxation. Thoughts, sometimes described as a "racing mind," interfere with sleep. By learning to relax, especially to relax the speech musculature that is involved in generating the thoughts, the racing mind can be relaxed, as we learned in Chapter 13.

DYSLEXIA AND LEARNING DISORDERS

Many different kinds of learning disorders are commonly referred to as *dyslexia*. Five to 15 percent of children are referred to as dyslexic. Such children scramble words and/or numbers so that "d" looks like a "b," or "6" looks like "9." Some have difficulty determining which direction is right and which is left.

Dyslexia, like so many of our terms, is vague and ambiguous. Anatomical, electrical, chemical, and genetic research is aimed at systematically subdividing learning disorders into biological categories. For instance, brain tissue of deceased dyslexics, EEGs of hyperactive children, and family trees are studied. The emerging view is that genetic, prenatal conditions, drugs, hormones, infections, and injuries are variables that affect changes in brain structure and function that can lead to learning disorders.

Anatomical Abnormalities. One classic study revealed that the brain of a dyslexic man who died in an auto accident had misaligned cells, especially in the left side of the brain. Similar abnormalities have been identified in other dyslexic brains. In other research, unique electrical activity has been found in the left hemisphere of dyslexic children.

Structures leading to learning disorders are thought to be formed during fetal development.

Congenitally underweight infants have excessively high rates of learning disorders, so that causes of the underweight may also cause the disorder. The mother's use of drugs or malnourishment can possibly cause brain disorders. One view is that during pregnancy neurons grow from the center of the brain through white matter to form the outer cortex. In this complex development of billions of cells, some fail to reach the cortex, thereby causing learning disorders. Another interpretation is that as the fetal brain grows, neurons compete for space. In the normal process, many fail to survive but some cells die in abnormal ways to cause the disorder.

Some other facts may provide some hints about the causes of learning disorders. For one, boys are more likely than girls to develop learning disorders. The left side of the rat brain has been found to develop more slowly than the right. These facts implicate the male hormone testosterone. Only in boys is there fetal testosterone so that testosterone may slow the growth of the left hemisphere of the male brain. This could help account for the fact that boys develop language so much later than do girls. Other data indicate that the frequency of learning disorders in extreme left-handers is ten times higher than in extreme right-handers. People whose right brain is dominant for language are usually left-handed. Also, left-handers have an elevated rate of immune system disorders.

Genetic factors may predispose some children. For instance, research indicates that more than 90 percent of identical twins shared similar learning problems. Furthermore, more than half of the children diagnosed as dyslexic had family members with a history of the disorder. There is also evidence of a dominant gene on chromosome 15 that appears in some cases among dyslexic family members. Certainly, environmental influences also play their role in the development of learning disorders.

As has been long recognized, children who have learning disorders typically also have emotional/behavioral problems. Learning to read is critical for their proper functioning in life so that if they fail, they meet many embarrassments. Following a positive feedback model, the more they fail, the greater the negative impact on their behavior which, in turn, discourages their attempts to read. On the other hand, when their learning disorders are corrected, their emotional adjustment improves considerably.

EMPHASIS ON A CYBERNETIC PRINCIPLE— ADDICTIVE BEHAVIORS HAVE SOME CHARACTERISTICS OF A POSITIVE FEEDBACK MODEL

Recall that input is consistently added in a positive feedback system, whereupon the system eventually goes out of control. Similarly, in addictive behaviors the victim starts the system by inputting a certain amount of the substance. Ingestion of it leads to additional inputs, one after the other over varying periods of time until the user loses control (e.g., the cocaine addict may die; the alcoholic experiences blackouts). In contrast, normal consumption resembles a negative feedback system in which ingestion ceases when the system reaches a target value (e.g., most individuals stop eating or drinking alcohol "when they've had enough"; Fig. 14.8).

Addictive behaviors often fit a positive feedback model wherein there is repeated ingestion of the substance until the abuser's system goes out of control, contrasted with controlled consumption.

FIGURE 14.8 Addictive behavior follows a positive feedback model in which continuous ingestion of a substance leads the abuser's system to go out of control. In contrast, controlled consumption resembles a negative feedback system wherein ingestion ceases as a standard reference value of the system is achieved.

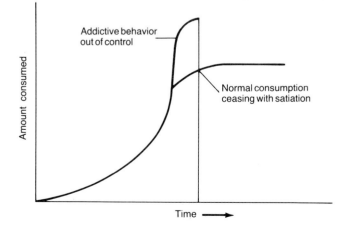

A behavioral criterion for addictive behavior thus emerges—ingestion of a substance continues as in an exponentially increasing growth curve until there is a dramatic cessation. However, if ingestion levels off, as in an S-shaped curve, it approaches an asymptote wherein a negative (instead of a positive) feedback system begins to function. (An asymptote is a straight line that a regular curve constantly approaches but reaches only at infinity.)

KEY TERMS

Acetylcholine (ACh)—One of many vital neurotransmitters found in the brain and other tissues.

Addiction—Classically defined as the production of withdrawal and tolerance symptoms when a substance is not consumed. An alternative definition is a compulsion for consuming a substance wherein there is loss of control and continued use despite the adverse consequences.

Adenosine triphosphate (ATP)—Chemical substance providing the energy for muscular as well as neural activity.

Anabolic steroid—Chemical substance comprising hormones, vitamins, etc. that is converted into living substances, often used for increasing striated muscle mass.

Anhedonia—Loss of the capability to enjoy ordinary pleasurable events.

Anorexia nervosa—A behavior disorder manifested by extreme aversion to food, resulting in life-threatening weight loss. It usually occurs in young women.

Anxiety state—A psychophysiological condition which is represented by excessive tension within the striated muscle; other components typically include heart palpitation, irregular and difficult breathing patterns, constricted esophagus, excessive fatigue, dizziness, and always the report of extreme fear.

Atherosclerosis—Thickening and hardening of the arteries due to the accumulation of plaque.

Astrocyte—A star-shaped glial cell found in the brain that serves a supportive function to cerebral neurons.

Autism—From the Greek *autos* or "self," a disorder of childhood mainly affecting males; often there is withdrawal, hostility, and self-mutilation.

Bruxism—Grinding or clenching of the teeth especially during sleep.

Bulimia—Eating disorder characterized by rapid ingestion of large portions of food in a brief time span, often followed by self-induced vomiting, use of laxatives, and abdominal distress.

Compulsive behavior—The tendency to repeat over and over a certain kind of behavior; despite its inappropriateness, the person does not inhibit the behavior.

Confabulation—Production of incorrect information, often a distinctive feature of Korsakoff's syndrome.

Delusions—False beliefs such as persecution.

Dementia—A decrement in intellectual abilities that is sufficiently severe to interfere with everyday functioning.

Dementia praecox—A term used (principally under Kraepelin's influence) to denote a group of deteriorating mental disorders commencing mainly between the ages of 15 and 30; now called schizophrenia.

Dependence—Compulsion in which the drug user requires periodic or continuous administration of the substance in order to produce pleasure and avoid the discomfort of withdrawal symptoms.

Depressive psychosis—Subclass of affective disorders in which the psychotic is inaccessible to stimulation and has poor initiative with gloomy thoughts.

DHEAS (dehydroepiandrosterone sulfate)—The most abundant steroid hormone found in human blood; seems to be related to frequency of heart attack such that the higher the level, the less frequent is the heart attack.

Dipsomania—A compulsion to consume alcohol.

Distress—A state of the body that includes reduction of immune system effectiveness produced by the perception of negative, threatening stressors.

Dyssomnia—Sleeping disorder characterized by a maladaptive sleep/wake schedule.

Drug dependence—Bodily condition

wherein continued administration of the drug is required to prevent uncomfortable withdrawal symptoms.

Eustress—The type of stress Selye called positive factors, stressors that we call "hope" and "happiness" that may have beneficial effects on health.

Functional psychosis—A severe behavioral disorder not related to any specific organic disorder, as is organic psychosis.

Globus hystericus—A condition in which there is the sensation of having a lump in the throat due to overtension of the esophagus.

Korsakoff's syndrome—A mental disorder marked by disturbances of memory and orientation often occurring in alcoholics due to vitamin B deficiency.

Manic-depressive psychosis—Psychosis in which the individual manifests both depressive and manic (bipolar) phases, but at different times.

Neurotic disorders—Sufficiently severe behavioral disorders characterized by anxiety that disrupt the individual's everyday life (e.g., anxiety reactions, obsessive-compulsive reactions). The designation *neuroses* is not recognized by some authorities.

Nucleus basalis of Meynert (NbM)—Cerebral region that is the main supplier of certain neurotransmitters to the cerebral cortex and the hippocampus, which are involved in memory.

Obsessive-compulsive disorder (obsessions, compulsions)—Neurotic disorder characterized by persistent obsessions (thoughts) to carry out irrational stereotyped acts (compulsions).

Organic psychosis—Severe behavioral disorder in which there is a known and specifiable organic dysfunction associated with disturbed mental and overt behavioral functioning.

Parasomnias—Sleep disorders that include sleep terrors, nightmares, and sleep walking, occur in the REM stage.

Phagocytosis—Process by which bodily cells destroy foreign matter especially bacteria (*phago* = eat; *cyte* = cell).

Phobic disorder—Strong persistent and irrational fear usually elicited by a nonthreatening stimulus.

Pica—Depraved or perverted appetite in which there is a hunger for nonfood substances.

Premenstrual syndrome (PMS)—A hypothesized syndrome not universally accepted, in which women experience such symptoms as painful and sensitive breasts and sometimes feelings of depression.

Prospagnosia—The inability to identify a face by means of words.

Psychoimmunology—A new field that studies the ways in which the immune system is influenced by psychological factors and how, in turn, various diseases of the body develop.

Psychosomatic (somatoform) disorders—Those physiological disorders in which the cause and course are due to behavioral (mental) factors, including stresses.

Psychotic disorders—Severe behavioral disorders characterized by disorganization of the thought processes, disorientation, and hallucinations, often losing touch with reality (e.g., schizophrenia).

Reduplication—Distinctive feature of Korsakoff's syndrome resulting in the incapacity to accept information as real, although recognizing that the information is often correct.

Rumination—Habit of chewing and swallowing food that was previously eaten and regurgitated.

Schizophrenia (kinds of)—General name for a group of psychotic reactions characterized by withdrawal, disturbances in emotional and affective life, presence of hallucinations, delusions, and negativistic behavior. Simple schizophrenia is characterized by a lack of a sense of responsibility. Paranoid schizophrenia is characterized by delusions of persecution and is typically accompanied by hallucinations. Catatonic schizophrenia is characterized by a waxy flexibility of the limbs. Hebephrenic schizophrenia is characterized by silliness and bizarre laughter.

Set point theory of body weight—Theory that holds that a mechanism in the hypothalamus specifies how much fat the body should store and directs the body to remain at that standard weight.

Sydenhamchorea (St. Vitas Dance)—Neurological disorder of the motor system characterized by spasmodic movements, delirium, and restlessness; caused by rheumatic diseases.

Symptoms/signs—Symptoms are expressions of complaints by a patient; signs are objective characteristics used to diagnose a condition.

Temporal mandibular joint syndrome (TMJ) — Discomfort often caused by excessive tension in the jaw muscles involving the TMJ joints at the jaws. The more general term myofacial pain dy-

function (MPD) is increasingly being used.

Tolerance — Occurs when a substance becomes less effective with repeated administration, requiring larger doses to achieve the initial effect.

STUDY QUESTIONS

1. List some bodily disorders and diseases that Americans suffer and specify which are fatal.
2. If anxiety is represented in the striated musculature, relaxation of these muscles should relieve the anxiety. Discuss this subject.
3. Discuss some specific examples of compulsive disorders such as gambling, drug and alcohol abuse, and eating disorders and explain their etiology.
4. How would you suggest that depression be controlled? Discuss theories of depression.
5. What is schizophrenia?
6. Address the relationship between psychosomatic illnesses and systematic relaxation of the striated musculature.
7. What are cardiovascular diseases and what might be the causes of a heart attack?
8. Discuss causes of cancers.
9. What is psychoimmunology and what might be its link with the immune system and stress?
10. Discuss and specify ways in which behavioral control can alleviate or prevent various behavioral disorders and medical diseases.

FURTHER READINGS

This is a highly recommended book for students, clinicians, and researchers, presenting a valuable British perspective on schizophrenia research:

Bebbington, P., & McGuffin, P. (Eds.). (1988). *Schizophrenia: The major issues.* Oxford, England: Heinemann Medical Books/Heinemann Professional.

The author presents a compelling case that there is no valid syndrome of schizophrenia, although there may be a number of unrelated schizophrenic symptoms:

Boyle, M. (1990). *Schizophrenia: A scientific delusion?* London: Routledge.

This is a treatise for the health professional and for the layperson with some basic information in biochemistry. It includes presentations of neurotransmitters and neuropeptides with emphasis on opiate peptides, although the neural chemistry of addiction is not well known:

Cohen, S. (1988). *The chemical brain: The neurochemistry of addictive disorders.* Irvine, CA: Care Institute.

This book presents a comprehensive summary of theories of alcoholism including

biological, psychological, and social theories. It is a well-organized, edited book that is relatively advanced in its exposition:

Chaudron, C. D., & Wilkinson, D. A. (1988). *Theories on alcoholism.* Toronto, Canada: Addiction Research Foundation.

This book presents considerable information on etiological, diagnostic, and treatment issues concerning the affective disorders. The physical and biochemical bases and treatment of depression are explored. This is a valuable book both for reading and as a sourcebook:

Flach, F. (1988). *Affective disorders.* New York: Norton.

This book is about the harm that can befall people because of such toxic hazards as atomic tests and accidents, poorly constructed or managed waste sites, accidental spills of toxic substances, and so on:

Vyner, H. M. (1988). *Invisible trauma: The psychological effects of invisible environmental contaminants.* Lexington, MA: Lexington Books.

CHAPTER 15

Therapy and Control of Pathological and Normal Behavior

MAJOR PURPOSES:

1. To emphasize that we *do* have considerable control over both normal and pathological behavior
2. To learn how to apply principles and techniques of control

WHAT YOU ARE GOING TO FIND:

1. Development of the thesis that there is a materialistic "free will" in the sense that we can apply self-management procedures to control much of our behavior
2. A survey of methods used for self-management
3. Applications of some biobehavioral, biomedical, and psychiatric methods to normal and abnormal problems faced by humans in a complex society

WHAT YOU SHOULD ACQUIRE:

Knowledge of biobehavioral principles of control and how to apply them for yourself and for others.

CHAPTER OUTLINE

OUR SEARCH FOR HAPPINESS

Most people would agree that their primary goal in life is to be happy, although the ways to achieve happiness are as varied as what "happiness" means to different individuals. For some, happiness is seeking power; for others it is accumulating money, loving, and being successful in their careers. Those who suffer from mental disorders may seek pleasure in bizarre, abnormal ways such as inflicting pain on

499

themselves or on others. It has been said that the ultimate in happiness is a marriage between a sadist and a masochist.

Factors That Contribute to Happiness and Unhappiness.   Happiness is often measured by life-satisfaction scales on which people indicate how contented they are with their friendships, sex life, work, and health. Research has identified some factors that specify about one-third of what is satisfying and dissatisfying (the remaining two-thirds are unknown and thus are the subject for ongoing research). Health is the most important factor. Presumably, happiness could be increased by increasing the frequency and kind of exercise in which one engages, thereby improving health. Other factors are having a full social life, an adequate income, a fulfilling marriage, and comfortable housing. Strangely, achieving long-held goals yields but little satisfaction, perhaps because when they are achieved, people raise their levels of aspirations even further and thus delay reward.

Good health, a full social life, adequate income, a fulfilling marriage, and comfortable housing account for about one-third of what makes us satisfied with life.

Being neurotic, sick, poor, and lonely contributes to dissatisfaction with life. The amount of time that a person spends avoiding undesirable feelings is a predictor of unhappiness. When we recall our inappropriate behavior or when we feel guilt, embarrassment, fear, and shame, we are not satisfied with our life.

That most of the factors that contribute to happiness are unknown is made evident when we witness the many disadvantaged people who still cope well and are satisfied with life. Experiencing hardships or being poor does not always cause dissatisfaction. Such self-control is very important for happiness, a matter that we must further consider.

Positive Feedback Between Eustress and Health.   Health and satisfaction appear to be related by positive feedback circuits. That is, good health makes people feel content and the feeling of contentment feeds back to benefit people physically, e.g., some research has indicated that when people feel good, their immune system is stronger and the stronger their immune system the better their health and good feelings. However, there must be a leveling off of the mutual facilitation at some point to establish a stable negative feedback circuit—there are limits to our good health and happiness.

Positive moods interact with health for the improvement of both.

There are relevant data on the effects of eustress which is stress that produces a positive outcome—it derives from the Greek *eu* meaning "good," as in "euphoria." An example of eustress is a positive pleasant psychological state that results from satisfaction with a job. Edwards and Cooper (1988) define eustress as a positive discrepancy between what a person perceives a situation to be and what that person desires it to be, assuming that the discrepancy is important for the person. One thus perceives things to be better than they really are.

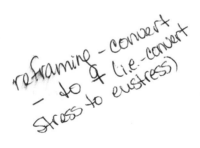

Evidence indicates that eustress may be directly beneficial for health by stimulating the production of anabolic hormones, HDL cholesterol, and other biochemical substances that enhance health (Edwards & Cooper, 1988). There is much evidence of an anecdotal nature for this proposition, such as Norman Cousin's recovery from a paralyzing collagen illness by taking massive doses of Vitamin C and inducing laughter in himself; another is a case in which clowns brought a catatonic girl out of her stupor. Laboratory experiments have confirmed that the physiological components of laughter favorably affect health. Some evidence indicates that this occurs because of temporary increases of the arousal of the sympathetic nervous system and of lowered serum cholesterol.

In efforts to be happy and avoid being unhappy, people seek all kinds of solutions. Too often these "solutions" are not solutions at all. Rather they are unsound, fast "cures" and "quick fixes," like drugs used inappropriately. About one-fourth of the population in the United States spends about $2.24 billion per year on dietary supplements and other scientifically unproven treatments in their quests.

[handwritten note: along w/ drugs do mental work or physical activity.]

QUACKERY

"A sucker is born every minute, and there are two more people to take him." Although this famous quotation is inaccurately attributed to P. T. Barnum (it was actually made up by a newspaperman who wrote about him), it *is* characteristic of humanity. The quackeries that have been perpetrated on us throughout our history and indeed even today stagger the imagination. We only fool ourselves when we are gullible enough to buy get-rich schemes, "quick cures," and other unsound practices. There is an endless list of unproven, unsound, or deleterious treatments that people use for stress, skin rejuvenation, pain relief, disease prevention, and cholesterol reduction and to increase strength, reduce cancer risk, stop smoking, eliminate body poisons, slow the aging process, promote hair growth, enhance memory or intelligence, remove cellulite, improve sexual performance, increase bust size, and on and on.

The problem is not unique to the United States. In modern Singapore ancient Chinese "remedies" still in use include the following: Grumbling children can be soothed with guinea pig soup; live lizards, swallowed whole, are good for mumps; crocodile meat can provide a tonic for the digestive system; the flesh of fruit bats alleviates asthma; the fresh heart of a python is a tonic for an aging man, as are snake gall bladders; the boiled skin of a python is a cure for sore eyes, and soup made from its flesh is a blood and kidney cleanser.

Nor are our most hallowed institutions immune. For example, around 1930 the practice in some of our medical schools to "cure" schizophrenia was to cut out several feet of the lower intestine. A classic book by the famous physician Weir Mitchell was *Fat and Blood and How To Make Them,* which prescribed, among other things, staying in bed and eating a dozen eggs a day.

Even though these practices seem outrageous to us, many are still engaged in by millions of people. But we also knowingly engage in many other behaviors that are obviously detrimental.

THE COSTS OF DETRIMENTAL BEHAVIOR

The destructive effects of various behaviors on the length of life have been calculated. To gain some perspective on what destructive behaviors do to us, consider specific behaviors that can add to or subtract from our life expectancy. Richard Wilson has computed amount of life lost by engaging in the following behaviors. An average 30-year-old reduces the estimated time yet to live by

Smoking one cigarette	minus 12 minutes
Drinking a diet soft drink	minus 9 seconds
Driving one trip without a seat belt	minus 6 seconds
Being an unmarried male	minus 1800 days

Since most things we do involve some risk, another way of computing the detrimental effects of behavior is to view them as equal in principle but differing in amounts. For example, the following have been estimated to increase the likelihood of death by one chance in a million; if you do a million of them, presumably you are dead.

> Drink half a liter of wine
> Spend three hours in a coal mine
> Live two days in New York
> Travel 6 minutes by canoe
> Ride 10 miles on a bicycle
> Drive 300 miles in a car
> Fly 1000 miles by jet

Behavioral Engineering.   A wise person rationally specifies goals and modes of behavior to achieve them. Those goals include maintaining good health and avoiding quackeries, smoking, and feeling bad. How can we engineer our behavior to achieve happiness, to engage in beneficial behaviors and to avoid destructive ones that lead to the deleterious conditions discussed in Chapter 14?

HOW TO ACHIEVE WHAT WE WANT— SELF-CONTROL AND THE DEVELOPMENT OF WILL POWER

By controlling one's behavior, a person can more effectively achieve goals in life, improve living conditions, and prevent disease and premature death.

Behaviorally Engineered Life-Style Changes Can Often Prevent Disease.   Behavioral technologies can be applied to control early risk factors for disease and help us to adapt to chronic illness. Most of the major causes of premature death and morbidity have behavioral antecedents (e.g., smoking causes cardiovascular disease and lung cancer; abusing alcohol contributes to accidents, homicides, and cirrhosis of the liver). These antecedent factors (smoking and abusing alcohol) can be controlled through behavioral methods. Prevention saves human suffering and could reduce high medical costs.

The U.S. Prevention Services Task Force, after five years of work, concluded that influencing health-related behaviors is more likely to reduce morbidity and mortality in this country than any other category of clinical intervention. They emphasized that patients need to change behaviors that jeopardize their health and to increase behaviors that reduce their disease risk. Seven out of ten leading causes of death in this country are largely behaviorally determined and thus can be reduced through changes in behavior.

Even though behavioral intervention can help achieve such goals as being happy and avoiding disease, certainly we do not have complete control of our lives—there are constraints on our adaptability. For instance, we have genetic predispositions that can strongly influence us in the direction of happiness or unhappiness. But beyond genetic constraints on us, are we volitionally capable of determining our own behavior? Or is our behavior all determined for us? This question of the extent to which we can intervene and control our own destinies has been argued for centuries.

Is There Free Will?

A popular philosophical position on this issue is yes, we do have **free will.** In fact many societal institutions such as our penal systems are based on this premise. Our laws assume that individuals are responsible for their own behavior—if they volitionally *decide* to commit a crime, they will be *liable* for punishment. Thus, society assumes that people choose whether or not to break the law. In many other ways, we are constantly assigning responsibility to ourselves or to others as in "it's my fault" or "well, don't blame me."

A common societal assumption is that citizens have a free will and should employ their willpower to behave in a rational and nondestructive manner.

On the other hand, some deny that there is free will and hold that behavior is completely determined; consequently, we are not responsible for what we do (e.g., "that's the way that I was raised, so blame it on my parents"). Some people who commit murder are judged insane because they could not control their behavior. This position holds that the individual has no choice.

Why Do People Lack Self-Control? As you look at people about you, you see some who in various ways may lack self-control. Some are excessively obese, weighing perhaps 400 pounds, and some smoke cigarettes. Why does an individual smoke cigarettes or consume an excessive amount of food? If you ask in a sufficiently diplomatic way, you might get some answers, although they probably would not be very enlightening. According to statistics, people overwhelmingly state that they wish they *could* lose weight and that they *could* stop smoking. However, they cannot explain their lack of control over their behavior. We saw that pathological obesity, for example, may be an instance of a positive feedback system wherein each additional food intake leads to further intake until the system goes out of control.

Arguments have waged over the centuries as to whether humans have free will or whether behavior is determined.

Instructions to "Use Your Willpower" Are Ineffective. How *can* one intervene to regain control over undesirable behavior? The assumption of free will gives you a straightforward answer—to better yourself, exercise your willpower. Unfortunately, such a vague formula is not only ineffective, it is also circular. It does not tell you just *how* to use your willpower. The recipient of the advice to stop smoking cigarettes by "using willpower" would be well justified by responding: "Thank you for nothing." At rock bottom this is a tautology that tells you that to stop smoking, you should stop smoking! You are not told *how* to do it.

In a similar vein, Carl Duncan conducted a study that showed that it is useless to give instructions in a general way. He found that it is ineffective to just tell children that to solve a problem they should think. What you have to tell them is *how* to think. That is, you need to present them with a behavioral program of exactly what to do. Similarly, it is useless to tell somebody to "just ignore your problem" because the instruction does not specify *how* to ignore the problem. The mother who tells her child to "be careful going to school" should specify how to be careful—telling the child to look both ways when crossing the street and so forth. Many slogans are valuable in principle but they need to be translated into precise behavioral programs that specify "If you do such and such, *then* you can control such-and-such behavior." But just *what* are specific responses that can bring about desired behaviors? The answer to that question answers our more general question of whether or not there is free will.

Instead of vague statements, specific behaviors are required to produce desired outcomes.

Establishing an Antecedent Variable
to Control Behavior

The major strategy for exercising volition (willpower) is to provide an individual with a *causal variable* by which specific behavior can be controlled. The great Russian physiologist Sechenov suggested in 1863 that sensory stimulation (neural feedback) that results from muscle activity could be used as such a causal variable. A muscle response (R_1) thus produces sensory stimulation (afferent feedback, s) that can control a later response (R_2):

$$R_1 \longrightarrow s \longrightarrow R_2 .$$

To produce or otherwise control a given response R_2, one needs to learn to produce it by an antecedent response R_1 that generates sensory stimulation s. Consequently when one performs R_1 one evokes R_2.

In essence, Sechenov proposed a cybernetic neuromuscular circuit model such that the feedback (s) from an antecedent response (R_1) goes to the central nervous system whereupon efferent neural stimulation returns to evoke a consequent response (R_2). With repeated practice of that circuitry, the response R_2 can come under voluntary control by instituting R_1. In short, R_1 can produce R_2. For example, if you want to always remember to take a book to school (R_2) you could place it in your way out of the door (R_1) for the next morning. In such ways we can tidy up our lives and thereby accomplish Benjamin Franklin's general principle that there should be a place for everything and everything in its place.

A Bit of Relevant History. Sechenov's paradigm has been advocated by many. For example, his conception fits well with the model advanced about the same time by Alexander Bain (1855). Bain's basic notion was that the striated (voluntary) muscles are the instrument of the will and only through them can volitional control be exercised over other mental and bodily processes. By judiciously manipulating them, you can control yourself.

William James emphasized that voluntary behavior is learned. His view was that feedback (s) from a muscular response (R_1) produces an image (which is an idea of the response to be performed). The image consists of memories of feedback, an initiating stimulus (s). By instituting R_1, the image s can then cause (volitionally will) the voluntary behavior (R_2) to occur: $R_1 \longrightarrow s \longrightarrow R_2$.

IVAN MIKHAILOVICH SECHENOV

Ivan Mikhailovich Sechenov (1829–1905), the founder of the Russian reflexology school, laid the basis for Russian physiology that was followed by such eminent scientists as Pavlov and Bekhterev. His extensive research has made important contributions to psychology, neurophysiology, and physiological chemistry. His major work, *Reflexes of the Brain* (1863) viewed mental activity as a function of the brain as manifested by muscle responses that control verbal and other physical behavior. He sought to establish physiological bases for psychological processes. Sechenov is regarded as a forerunner of physiological cybernetics. As Melvin Marx pointed out, Sechenov's work in 1863 was truly amazing in that it was a philosophical and methodological position nearly identical to Watson's in its objectivity.

The famous German psychologist Oswald Külpe stated that voluntary recollection never takes place without the assistance of movements. For instance, he said there are movements of the body (R) that help us to recall a rhyme and that movements of speech muscles are the most important.

"Sensations from eye movements play a predominant role in the control of the memory image" (so observed Moore, 1903, cited by Jacobson, 1938b, p. 184).

Tuke (1884) described cases of voluntary control over pupillary movements, gastrointestinal activities, and the like (e.g., he cites Professor Beer who was "able in the same light to contract or dilate his pupils at will"). Changes in the size of the pupil were caused by certain ideas that he conjured up. When Professor Beer thought of a very dark space, the pupil dilated but when he thought of a very light place, the pupil contracted. By our model the controlling "ideas" would consist of initiating covert responses, here principally of the eye muscles.

We are fortunate that vegetative (autonomic) functions are already automatically carried out, for it would be excessively demanding for us to have to willfully cause our heart to periodically beat, our intestines to digest our food, or our lungs to breathe. Nevertheless, these involuntary functions can be brought under some form of voluntary control. A psychologist who performed at parties could voluntarily let tears flow when things got dull and his friends asked him to "turn them on." When the friends had enough, he would stop the tears at will.

Voluntary responses, particularly from the eye and speech musculature, and the afferent neural impulses that they generate can, through learning, come to control a variety of mental/bodily processes.

The early behaviorist Walter Hunter similarly developed this theme by holding that verbal processes (language responses) are the antecedents for controlling voluntary behavior. He concluded that these verbal processes consist of conditional responses that are under the control of self-excited receptors.

Covert Behavior May Be Used to Control Overt Behavior or Other Covert Behavior.   It has been theorized by many that muscular responses, especially of the speech musculature, constitute a causal variable $R_1 \longrightarrow s$. With $R_1 \longrightarrow s$ we can then learn to control a desired response R_2. However, the controlling response need not be overt, but as previously developed, it may be covert (r). The fact that the causal instruction (r_1) may be silently (covertly) issued, as against overtly spoken aloud, does not change the control principle. As we developed in Chapter 13, when you think to yourself that you want to perform a given act, the muscles of the lips, tongue, cheeks, jaws, throat, and so on actually tense to a slight degree. These small-scale speech-muscle responses also occur when you instruct yourself to follow the steps that constitute R_2. We may thus think of what we want to do. The thought includes r_1, which is principally a speech-muscle response (although eye responses that produce visual guidance are also effective). Those covert speech movements ($r_1 \longrightarrow s_1$) can thereby be used to "will" the desired response (R_2) or other "thoughts," "sensations," or "ideas" (r_2); that is, $r_1 \longrightarrow s \longrightarrow r_2$ or R_2.

Many laboratory studies have been successful in using covert responses for controlling other covert responses. For example, the subvocal saying ("thinking") of words and nonsense syllables has produced pupillary contraction, heightened electrodermal responding, vasodilation, vasoconstriction, and pulse retardation (McGuigan, 1978).

The covert speech-muscle response is a major antecedent controlling variable for the behavior to be modified.

Using Speech to Guide the Development of a New Habit.   Any complex act to be brought under control can be analyzed into a sequence of steps. Then one can verbally guide the sequence of those steps so as to better perform the act R_1 (or r_1); in this case R_1 is a sequence of speech instructions to guide the performance of the

Speech responses can verbally guide the learning of a complex act that is to be brought under voluntary control.

desired act R_2. For example, small children may first verbalize that their shoes need to be tied and in the process of learning, carefully verbalize each step of tying shoes. Similarly, in first learning to serve a tennis ball, each step of the process is verbalized and one attempts to follow the self-instructions to learn the entire act.

Developing Automaticity. With repeated practice of instructing one's self to perform the steps of the desired response and then following those instructions, the response R_2 can often come to *automatically* follow those self-instructions. This is the development of a new, automatic habit of $R_1 \longrightarrow s \longrightarrow R_2$. In the method of Progressive Relaxation one learns to recognize the very slight contraction of speech (and other) muscles during thought. By repeatedly instructing oneself, observing the signals from covertly contracting muscles ($r_1 \longrightarrow s$) and then carrying out the desired act (R_2), automatic control over behavior can be acquired. Many acts that at first have to be carefully verbalized become highly habitized and reflexive after repeated performance. Well-practiced automobile driving habits in getting from place A to place B are carried out unconsciously. Unfortunately, though, sometimes you start from place A with the goal of going to place C, but without thinking, you run off the previously habitized chain of behaviors and end up at place B. In such cases you need to verbally inhibit acts that are incompatible with the one to be controlled, thereby making the volitional process more efficient.

By repeatedly instructing oneself either overtly or by thinking the instruction covertly and carrying out the desired response, a new automatic habit can often be acquired.

Using External Variables for Control. Even though self-control can come through verbalizations, be they overt or covert, the verbalizations must lead to well-specified response sequences in order to be effective. For instance, one may specify a goal of exercising. Consider two alternatives available: The individual self-instructs (1) to engage in calisthenics, to jog, and so on or (2) to enroll in an organized exercise class. In the first case, the goal must be continuously verbalized and steps followed in order to achieve it, a difficult task indeed — many excuses can be found to skip or shorten the exercise. In the second case, however, once the individual enrolls in a class, external variables can control and maintain the behavior, at least until the termination of the class.

To Summarize. To practice **self-control,** you need to manipulate antecedent variables that can control the behavior to be learned. By activating the speech muscles (R_1 or r_1), nerve impulses (s) are generated that are directed to and from the brain to evoke the desired behavior (R_2). With this paradigm, self-control can be applied to such problems as weight reduction and improving sleep and nutrition. Furthermore, we can apply these principles to control mental (behavioral) events such as fears, depressions, emotions, and anger.

These considerations thus suggest an answer to the question of whether humans have free will. In the sense that people are capable of controlling much of their behavior, there is free will. But such free will is based on the use of materialistic, lawful relationships. Free will thus can exist to the extent that there is determinism in nature.

Determinism

Determinism holds that there is lawfulness (order) in nature so that phenomena are caused by antecedent variables. Consequently, events can be predicted and controlled. Indeterminism holds that phenomena have no specifiable causes.

Determinism is the principle that there is order (lawfulness) in the universe. To the extent that the universe is orderly, researchers may find lawful relationships among variables. The statements that specific variables are related in such a manner constitute our storehouse of knowledge. To the extent that there is lack of order in nature, there is **indeterminism.** On a determinism–indeterminism continuum, then, complete determinism represents a universe in which there is 100 percent order so that, in principle, all phenomena can be understood by specifying variables to which they are related. On the other hand, complete indeterminism would be a state of randomness in which there are no reliable empirical relationships. The application of our laws, such as $R_1 \longrightarrow s \longrightarrow R_2$ for free will, therefore, is possible to the extent that there is determinism. If the sequence of responses is well learned and has become automatic, the probability of controlling R_2 with R_1 is high. Yet none of our laws is perfect, meaning that they all have some degree of probability (McGuigan, 1993a). Just why none of our laws is perfect in the sense of being absolutely certain (rather than only probabilistic) constitutes a complex philosophical problem that has been debated for centuries. On the one hand, the fact that we must settle for probabilistic laws may be because of a certain amount of indeterminism in nature. On the other hand, that limitation may be because we have not yet discovered all of the relevant variables for a given law. In any event, we do have a probabilistic concept of free will and we do know that when other variables intervene, our control of behavior may be less than perfect.

The theoretical limit of the extent to which we can control our behavior (exercise a free will) is limited by the degree to which there is determinism in nature.

A Confusion. Some hold that determinism and free will are opposite phenomena. That is, behavior is either determined by events beyond a person's control or behavior may be controlled by free will. From our analysis we can see why this is a confused philosophical position. The opposite of determinism is indeterminism, not free will. Determinism and free will are thus compatible. To the extent to which there is indeterminism, behavior cannot be brought under volitional control.

Punitive Control Techniques in Society

A major problem with society is that it is primarily run by punitive control techniques (e.g., we attempt to keep people honest by threatening them with prison for dishonest behavior). In contrast, control could be vastly improved by using positive reinforcement. A society designed on the basis of wise and effective behavioral engineering principles (in which punitive techniques are largely replaced by positive psychological principles) would have numerous favorable consequences indeed. One consequence could be that we would no longer have overcrowded mental hospitals, prisons, and psychological clinics, as B. F. Skinner extensively developed, particularly in his novel *Walden Two.*

Control for the benefit of society can be improved by the judicious use of positive reinforcement with only limited punishment of behavior in highly specific situations.

Approaches to Self-Management

BIOBEHAVIORAL PRINCIPLES

Progressive Relaxation—Learning
How to Control Ourselves

Learning to Relax. The method of **Progressive Relaxation (PR)** was developed and applied by Edmund Jacobson (1938b) for over 70 years. He was empirically guided through electromyographic and clinical records resulting in the most effec-

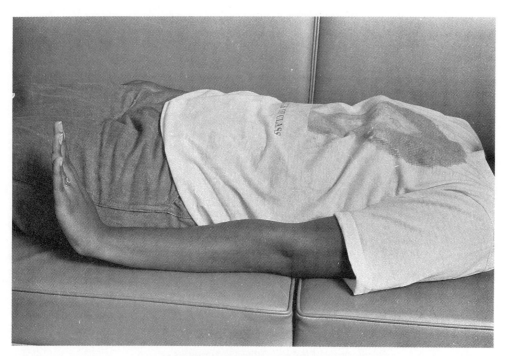

FIGURE 15.1   In learning Progressive Relaxation one starts by bending the hand back to produce a slight tension in the upper (dorsal) surface of the forearm. The tension is then studied and relaxed away, where upon the process is repeated throughout the body.

tive method for relaxing and controlling the entire body. Tension is defined as contraction of striated muscle fibers while relaxation is the lengthening of those fibers. The principles of the method are to (1) identify and study a localized signal of tension (the muscle sense of Bell) that is produced by muscular contraction; then (2) allow the tension signal to relax away; and finally, (3) study the contrast between the previous state of tension and the ensuing state of relaxation. Once the learner has that basic notion, it is simply a matter of systematic repetition throughout all regions of the body.

The first region of the body to be controlled is the arms. As shown in Figure 15.1, the hand is bent back at the wrist; the position is held for a minute or two while the tension signal is studied. The tension signal is produced when muscles contract and generate afferent neural impulses, as discussed in Chapter 7. This particular localized tension signal is found in the dorsal surface of the forearm and is the first time that the learner has ever specifically recognized what localized tension feels like. Once there is a good clear image of tension, the hand is allowed to relax like a limp dishrag—the hand simply collapses when support is removed. The learner thus allows the striated muscle fibers to elongate by "letting go." With practice, the tension signal can be relaxed or tensed to an appropriate degree at will at which point it becomes a **control signal.**

The method calls for thoroughness; as detailed in McGuigan (1992; 1993b), there are a number of control signals in each arm that need to be studied. After sufficient practice with the arms, the learner proceeds with the legs in the same thorough manner, up through the buttocks, the trunk, the abdominal region; and through the chest, back, shoulders, neck, eyes, and the speech region. The muscles of the jaws are particularly vulnerable to tension control problems of bruxism and TMJ, and control of the tongue is effective for helping individuals to relax and go to sleep.

Upon completion of this phase of training, the learner has studied all of the 1030 muscles of the body in groups while learning to relax lying down. But to generalize control into everyday living, through successive approximation, the learner relaxes while sitting, reading, writing, standing, and so on. The essential concept is Differential Relaxation. **Differential Relaxation** is learning to *optimally* contract (tense) only those muscles that are necessary for performing the act at hand.

Clinical Goals of PR Therapy. The clinical applications of Progressive Relaxation fall into two general categories, psychiatric and psychosomatic disorders. In Figure 14.6, we illustrated how overtension of the striated muscle can overdrive the central nervous system and in turn cause psychosomatic disorders such as in the autonomic system. In Figure 15.2, we similarly illustrate how excessive chronic tension can lead to such psychiatric disorders as phobias, depression, and anxiety and to various psychosomatic disorders. In either case, the appropriate therapy is to reverse the process by relaxing the striated muscles. The therapeutic process to change behavior, both overt and covert, has three stages.

Stage one: In this stage the patient specifies some contingent relationships between muscle responding and a complaint. This is achieved by identifying tension signals that control particular maladaptive thoughts or other disorders (e.g., one may relate tension in the abdomen with gastrointestinal problems such as colitis, ulcers, diarrhea, and constipation).

Stage two: The patient achieves control over the difficulty by relaxing the relevant control signals. If he or she has disturbing visual images such as crashing in an airplane, control can largely be obtained by relaxing the eye muscles so that the visual image is relaxed away. When the eyes are totally relaxed, there is no visual imagery, or visual perception either. The eyes must move before there can be visualization or perception, just as covert speech behavior is necessary for understanding what is being read (McGuigan, 1978). (Other research in which the visual image is stabilized on the retina has also confirmed that when the image on the retina does not move, there is no visual perception.)

Stage three: The contingent relations between the therapeutic control of the problem are generalized to behavior in the external environment through differential relaxation. If the problem is pain in the abdomen due to a spastic colon that occurs in social situations in everyday life, one learns to relax the abdominal muscles, along with muscles throughout the body, when entering into such social relationships.

By systematically repeating the process of identifying localized tensions and relaxing them away, one can effectively control muscular tension.

The final stage of Progressive Relaxation is to differentially relax 24 hours a day, including during sleep.

With totally relaxed eye muscles, there are no visual images or perceptions.

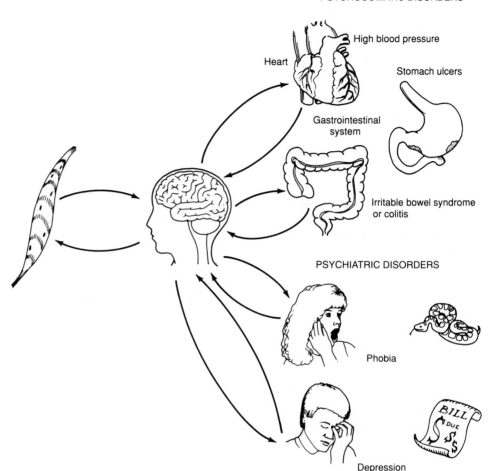

FIGURE 15.2
Overtension of the striated
muscles can lead to a variety
of psychiatric and
psychosomatic disorders.
Therapy is to reverse the
process through relaxation.

Behavior Therapy (Modification)

*In Clinical PR, the learner
identifies tension signals that
control the psychiatric or somatoform complaint and then
learns to relax those controlling tensions away.*

*In behavior therapy, mental
disorders are viewed as physical covert processes that can
be behaviorally controlled.*

As the result of many decades of research to develop laws of learning, we have
arrived at powerful principles of instrumental and classical conditioning. They have
been effectively applied for clinical purposes in **behavior therapy,** sometimes referred to as **behavior modification.** The basic strategy is that many psychiatric and
somatoform (psychosomatic) disorders that have been learned can be modified
through relearning or new learning. Traditional "talk" psychotherapy which only
discusses problems and possible solutions contrasts with behavioral approaches.
Instead of discussion, the goal in behavior therapy is to change the way the patient
acts and thinks.

Mental (cognitive) disorders are viewed as physical phenomena that include
small-scale muscular behaviors. Such covert behaviors can thus be systematically
manipulated by learning principles to alleviate pathological conditions. Clinical

conditioning procedures that have been successfully applied include covert sensitization, covert positive reinforcement, covert negative reinforcement, and covert extinction. Clinical relaxation is also used, as in the treatment of a phobia: The patient imagines fearful acts of increasing intensity, then relaxes the musculature to relax the fear away. In a classic case treated by Jacobson in 1934 (see Jacobson, 1957), a patient who feared heights was told to imagine a feather dropping and then to relax the muscles. Gradually, he proceeded up a scale to imagining looking down from tall heights. Eventually, the patient rented an office high up in a skyscraper, having totally relaxed away the fears that were represented in his muscles. Behavior therapy has also been especially effective in the treatment of autism.

Behavioral Medicine

The field of **behavioral medicine** applies behavioral procedures, principles, and techniques for health-related problems that fall within the traditional context of medicine. There is a rich interplay among the principles of medicine, psychophysiology, physiology, biochemistry, and learning. Journals specialized for the field include *Annals of Behavioral Medicine, The British Journal of Medical Psychology,* and *Psychological Medicine.* There thus is considerable overlap among behavioral medicine, behavioral therapy, Progressive Relaxation, and exercise medicine.

Neal Miller offered an example of how behavioral variables can be used to understand etiology and for pathophysiological treatment. In this case, instrumental learning principles were applied for a woman who had been bedridden for months. Her problem was that when she was brought upright using a tilt table, she became faint, even when the raising was gradual. A behavioral analysis indicated that the nurse would raise her slightly on the tilt table and then leave the room. As soon as the woman complained of being faint, the nurse hurried back, reassured the woman, and lowered the table. Fainting behavior was thus actually being reinforced by the nurse so that, by operant conditioning, fainting became strengthened. The appropriate therapy was to reverse the procedure so that the woman was raised slightly on the tilt table while the nurse talked with her and reassured her. If the woman grew faint, the nurse lowered the table but left the room. Fainting was thus no longer reinforced, and in fact it was punished by the loss of contact with the nurse. The result was that the woman quickly recovered.

In behavioral medicine, behavioral principles are applied for pathological conditions that have traditionally fallen within the context of medicine.

Applications of learning and other behavioral principles to different kinds of medical and behavioral disorders are so numerous that we mention only a small sample from a recent program on behavioral medicine: AIDS, asthma care, cancer, cardiac rehabilitation, neurological trauma, chronic binge eating, obesity, and pain management.

Exercise and Exercise Medicine

Exercise has been beneficially used to help rejuvenate the elderly and for cardiovascular, neurological, pulmonary, gastrointestinal, renal, metabolic, endocrine, and genital-urinary disorders.

People with moderate levels of fitness have been shown to be protected to some extent from premature death due to cancer or cardiovascular disorder (King, Blair, Bild, & Dishman, 1992). Cardiovascular and respiratory training benefit us in part because the heart becomes a more efficient pump by beating slower, both during exercise and rest; and the slower the heart rate, the longer cardiac muscle can rest between beats. The pumping chamber also may enlarge due to systematic exercise and thus beat more forcefully so that more blood is pumped out with each heart beat; blood pressure also may rise less when exercising. Peripheral muscles can benefit by an increase in blood volume in the muscle capillaries by as much as 60 percent; this facilitates the extraction of oxygen from the blood by muscle cells and also primes enzymes to combine oxygen and ATP thus generating additional energy.

Exercise medicine is a field in which specialized exercise training has been applied to improve cardiovascular functioning and a number of other disorders.

In general, studies have shown that men who exercise regularly have a considerably lower chance of dying from sudden heart attack than do sedentary men. Older athletes who continued to exercise over the years maintained their good condition, muscle mass, ability to use oxygen, and strong bones. Mild exercise seems to prevent the bone loss that normally accompanies aging and susceptibility to fracture. Exercise also seems to help protect against disease. For example, some studies have shown that exercise elevates high-density lipoprotein (HDL) levels, possibly alleviating atherosclerosis because HDL functions to remove fat and cholesterol from the walls of arteries.

How Much Exercise Is Beneficial? It is a matter of dosage. You should not push yourself too hard too fast. Excessive exercise could well reduce longevity. In a study of some 17,000 Harvard alumni, it was found that those who exercised heavily actually had a slightly shorter life expectancy than more moderate exercisers (although, of course, that does not establish a causal connection). Men were also more likely to have cardiac arrest during a workout than at other times.

The greater the level of habitual exercise, the lower the risk of cardiac arrest during exercise but the odds of suffering cardiac arrest are still relatively higher during vigorous exercise.

Unfortunately, only 8.2 percent of 25,000 adults surveyed exercised sufficiently frequently and vigorously to improve their physical fitness. More than 25 percent never exercised at all. To improve health of people through appropriate exercise presents yet another problem in behavioral engineering.

But exercise has limited value — it does not seem to protect us against colds, flu, and other infectious diseases. This is because exercise only slightly and temporarily stimulates certain factors in the blood or serum responsible for defense against these diseases.

The Science of Laughter (Gelotology)

Laughter is a topic for serious empirical study. The field of **gelotology** received a lift when Norman Cousins reportedly used laughter to relieve pain and break a cycle of negative emotions. Apparently, his pain caused him to increase muscular tension which in turn increased the pain, as in a positive feedback circuit. The cycle was broken because, he observed, 10 minutes of belly-laughter had an anesthetic effect that would give him two or more hours of pain-free sleep. Laughter also increases heart rate and blood pressure. Circulation of blood is thus enhanced, increasing the amount of oxygen and other metabolic and nutritional components that are carried to various parts of the body. Perhaps laughter also helps relieve pain through the release of endorphins into the bloodstream.

Gelotology, the science of laughter, has been applied to improve health.

Psychologist Blair Justice has found that laughing results in a significant increase in antibodies in the saliva, and that pleasant moods are associated with the level of such stress hormones as adrenaline.

In laughing, smiling, and chuckling, the facial, neck, scalp and shoulder muscles are active in neuromuscular circuits with the brain. Heavier laughter stimulates the intercostal (chest) muscles, abdominal muscles, and the diaphragm. The entire skeletal muscle system is involved in convulsive laughter. Feedback from the muscles to the brain can generate pleasant, euphoric subjective experiences. Paul Ekman showed that when a person's facial muscles assume positions representing happiness (or sorrow or anger), the person actually reports that he or she feels these emotions. This is another instance of how we can control our mental processes by skillfully manipulating our striated muscles. To eliminate unwanted emotions, then, one relaxes the muscles, especially those unique to the face that help generate negative emotional feelings.

Biofeedback Training

Biofeedback is a method by which people may learn to control internal events, such as brain waves, that they are not able to observe through regular sensory modalities. The first step is to sense the event. This is often done with electrodes that detect electrical signals. Then the event of interest is amplified and **transduced** — energy involved in the event is changed (transduced) to another form so that the event *can* be monitored by the learner (Fig. 15.3). Consequently, when transduced, one can see, hear, or otherwise monitor one's own muscle responses, brain waves, cardiovascular activity, galvanic skin responses, skin temperature, and any other bodily organ that generates signals.

As one observes the continuous activity of an internal event as it is readout from the instrument, efforts are made to modify it. For example, by monitoring activity of the muscles through an EMG instrument, one can decrease muscle tension by relaxing. As with all therapies, one seeks to generalize what is learned in the clinical situation to normal life situations. For instance, if one has learned to relax a

Biofeedback training uses instruments to sense and transduce internal events so that they can be monitored in an effort to control them.

FIGURE 15.3 A patient's use of biofeedback signals. Usually electrodes sense weak electrical signals that are transmitted to an amplifier. The patient may monitor the output of an amplifier visually or auditorally. The patient learns to use the feedback from the physiological signal to modify the internal event.

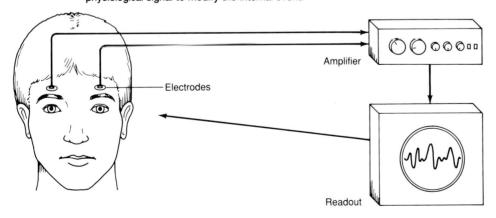

muscle while receiving EMG feedback, that muscle should then be relaxed outside the clinic.

Biofeedback has been used for scientific and clinical purposes. Scientifically, efforts involve advancing our understanding of how bodily systems function and developing principles of volitional control over them. As such, biofeedback holds great promise, but it has been used more for clinical purposes.

The goal of biofeedback training is to generalize volitional control over internal events learned in the clinic to everyday life.

History. The first clinical use of biofeedback was apparently by Edmund Jacobson (1957) in the early 1950s when he transduced electromyographic signals to attempt to facilitate the process of learning to relax the skeletal muscles. Jacobson displayed the signals on a cathode-ray oscilloscope that his patients could visually monitor. Even though they could control their signals in the clinic, he abandoned the approach because it did not facilitate generalized relaxation of the muscles of the body relative to what could be accomplished with Progressive Relaxation.

In the 1960s and 1970s there was widespread clinical application of biofeedback. Unfortunately this was often by individuals who were not professionally qualified as psychologists or other health professionals. Like many new developments, biofeedback became a fad with many "huxters" trying to make fast bucks. Simultaneously, though, there was a growth in research to better understand the possible value of biofeedback.

The early research on biofeedback was also scientifically important because its results were thought (erroneously) to disconfirm a widely accepted "two-factor" theory of learning. That two-factor theory held that autonomic responses could be modifiable only through classical conditioning while striated responses were modifiable only through instrumental conditioning. Some early, quite ingenious studies such as those by Neal Miller and his colleagues seemed to indicate that autonomic functions, however, *could* be modified through instrumental conditioning. The procedure was to instantaneously reinforce a response such as heart rate by brain stimulation (a kind of biofeedback). But these early studies were criticized because it could have been the striated musculature that was conditioned so that it mediated the autonomic responses (see Fig. 10.24). Curare was then used to "paralyze" the striated musculature and thus remove that possibility. However, paralysis was actually incomplete so that the striated musculature still functioned, albeit at a reduced level (see pp. 339–341). Furthermore, efforts to confirm those studies failed. In short, the striated musculature still could have been conditioned, so that the two-factor theory of learning remains viable. Nevertheless, this early research enhanced the prestige of, and advanced, biofeedback.

Biofeedback has been used to teach epileptic patients to use cues like slow cortical potentials to anticipate and prevent a forthcoming seizure.

Some Therapeutic Applications. Successes with biofeedback have been reported for cardiac arrhythmias, motor deficits in neurologically disabled patients, epilepsy, Raynaud's disease, and tension headaches. Epilepsy, for example, has no cure, but one strategy is to control it through biofeedback of slow cortical potentials (SCPs) which precede epileptic seizures. Some patients *have* successfully learned to identify these internal stimulus factors as early signals and thereby relaxed muscular tension to prevent the seizure from occurring.

Vaginal temperature feedback was an effective treatment for both physiological and psychological PMS symptoms.

Another example of a biofeedback application was David Van Zak's treatment of premenstrual syndrome. Using vaginal temperature biofeedback, patients increased mean vaginal temperature to thereby acquire self-control over such symptoms as bloating, aching pain, depression, lethargy, and irritability. However, we still lack understanding of the mechanisms underlying this physiological self-control technique.

Limitations of Biofeedback Training. Some experts hold that there is no reason to believe that biofeedback methods are effective for many disorders such as migraine headaches and anxiety. Even when successful in the laboratory or clinical setting, some major problems must be faced by biofeedback therapists. For one, the learner depends upon the external feedback signal so that control over the bodily event is learned in its presence. Perhaps the most difficult problem in biofeedback training is learning to control the internal event outside of the clinic without feedback from the instrument. In one study of muscle modification, when the biofeedback signal was withdrawn, the learners returned to pretraining levels (McGuigan, 1971). Progressive Relaxation, however, does not suffer that disadvantage because the feedback (control) signal is internal — the muscle sense of Bell is the result of muscular contraction and is monitored internally.

Another problem with muscle biofeedback training occurs because the striated musculature does not act as a unified system. That is, if through biofeedback one learns to relax muscles, such as the forehead muscle so often used in efforts to control headaches, the remaining skeletal muscles are not affected. No disorder is controlled by but one muscle alone, so others must then be relaxed in turn. It is not easy to control, transfer, and generalize from the clinic to everyday life situations.

Like many scientific techniques, biofeedback has its successes and failures. Further scientific and therapeutic investigation of the method will no doubt yield additional valuable findings. Yet it has become clear that the early enthusiasm for biofeedback was excessive and has faded so that we now are more realistic. The former Biofeedback Society of America, for instance, has substituted the term *applied psychophysiology* for *biofeedback* in its name.

Biofeedback techniques have had numerous psychotherapeutic successes, although a major problem is getting the patient to generalize the bodily change to everyday life independent of the biofeedback apparatus. Furthermore, muscle biofeedback treatment is limited to only one or a few of the 1030-odd muscles.

MEDITATION

There has been widespread use of various meditation techniques for a number of purposes. These techniques typically originated in Eastern religions but have spread to the Western world. Despite their variety, the general goal of meditation techniques is to reduce somatic (and "mental") arousal. In one technique, the meditator silently repeats a particular term (a mantra) to help induce a calm state. However, some techniques are designed to *increase* arousal (e.g., Maulavi, a dancing practice of the whirling dervishes, involves considerable body activity).

The word *meditate* derives from the Latin *meditari*, which means to actively think about, to reflect, or to consider. Consequently the term *meditation* indicates that some bodily activity is occurring. In particular, speech muscles are covertly active during silent meditation. Other research using brain wave criteria indicates that meditators often go to sleep.

Meditation has been clinically applied to treat psychiatric disorders, hypertension, asthma, inflammation of the gums, drug abuse, alcohol abuse, insomnia, and stuttering, among other disorders. Meditation is sometimes used as a psychotherapeutic technique because it is believed that it will facilitate the control of arousal in threatening situations. However, in an insightful review of the experimental evidence Holmes (1984) reached the following conclusions:

When the somatic arousal of meditating subjects was compared to the somatic arousal of resting subjects [there was no] consistent differences between meditating and resting subjects on measures of heart rate, electrodermal activity, respiration rate, systolic blood pressure, diastolic blood pressure, skin temperature, oxygen consumption, EMG activity, blood flow, or various biochemical factors. Similarly, a review of the research on the effects of meditation in controlling arousal in threatening situations did not reveal any consistent differences between meditating and non-meditating subjects. (p. 1)

On the other hand, positive effects of procedures like meditation and yoga are sometimes reported by people. The extent to which such techniques have been thought to be therapeutically beneficial is probably due to several causes. For one, merely taking time out of the day's activities and resting may help to restore the body, although as Jacobson (1938b) showed, instructions to rest were quite ineffective compared to applying Progressive Relaxation. Other reasons may be suggestive placebo variables and unsound methodology.

Though meditation is widely promoted, the evidence of its successful application therapeutically is limited. What successes are reported are probably due to the limited effectiveness of merely resting, placebo effects, and unsound methodology.

HYPNOSIS

The uses of hypnosis and self-hypnosis have varied widely and have included the treatment of neuroses, anxiety, personality problems, addictions, sexual dysfunctions, pain, criminal behavior, and fear of the dentist. What do we know about hypnosis?

Suggestion is a critical component in the contemporary use of hypnosis and in fact permeates every facet of psychology. Clinically, each subtle nod and variation in tone of voice, as well as direct instructions, carry the therapist's powerful suggestions. Similar suggestive effects flow from the industrial psychologist and the teacher and are especially powerful throughout the realm of social psychology. What is the role of such suggestive influence in hypnosis?

Some have held that hypnosis is nothing more than suggestion. In psychology classes, professors turn students into mute dummies and stiff boards and then demystify hypnosis simply by telling the entire class to stand up. When they do, they are told they were just hypnotized, which concludes the topic. Is there more to hypnosis than such mere suggestions as telling students to stand up?

History.   Artificial somnambulism, also called magnetic somnambulism, was a major discovery made by de Puysegur in 1782. In 1841 James Braid first witnessed two demonstrations of de Puysegur's artificial somnambulism and somewhat later Braid renamed the phenomenon as hypnotism or nervous sleep. Among Braid's conceptions of hypnotism were that it (1) is a state of concentrated attention, (2) can be established within about five minutes, (3) *is an all-or-none condition without degrees,* (4) appears like sleep, and (5) is always accompanied by spontaneous amnesia for all events transpiring during its presence. *Suggestion was minimally used by Braid!*

The process by which de Puysegur's and Braid's concepts of hypnotism eroded is a complex one. To a large extent it was transformed through the work of A. A. Liébeault and H. Bernheim from an all-or-none state to a graded one, and suggestion increasingly became a major tool for the production of hypnotic phenomena. De Puysegur's phenomenon is thought to occur in less than 1 percent of individuals, so what we now frequently encounter in the laboratory and clinic is not hypnotism at all in the original sense.

Contemporary Views of Hypnotism Are Chaotic.   Researchers today disagree about whether or not there is a unique state known as hypnosis — some assert that it is merely role playing. Hypnosis is not generally held to be just a state of concentration. Nor is it a state of relaxation, since the hypnotized person is mentally very active, as electromyographic records of the muscular condition attest. Two centuries after the discovery of artificial somnambulism the only consensus seems to be that if there is a unique state of hypnosis, it is *not* sleep. Yet hypnotic "experts" abound. Many just read a book and assume they are competent hypnotists. Lay hypnotists hold no bonafide degrees but use such titles as "clinical hypnotist." Records show that lay hypnotists arrive in a city, simultaneously hypnotize 50 or more persons in a one-session smoking clinic and then leave. They advertise that people can control such habits as smoking, dieting, and drinking and also be psychotherapeutically treated. But horror stories abound; for example, as reported by Frank MacHovec, a man with emphysema attended a one-session hypnosis clinic and required emergency medical attention because the suggestion that he relax his breathing deprived him of sufficient oxygen; a woman who was hypnotized by a stage entertainer was admitted to a hospital in a catatonic state and required intravenous feeding.

Hypnosis has been glamorized in our search for magical cures. Scientific study has been limited and its therapeutic use is poorly regulated. A scientific strategy for leading us out of the chaos would be to psychophysiologically or physiologically **explicate** the phenomenon. Some model research has studied alpha and beta brain waves and p300 amplitudes of evoked potentials (see Fig. 8.13). Through electromyographic study, changes of the neuromuscular system often result from a specific state of hypnosis. Sustained psychophysiological research using sound experimental methodology could eventually lead to an understanding of what hypnosis is, because we surely don't know now.

Although suggestion is a main component of contemporary hypnotism, it was not originally used.

There is no consensus as to what hypnosis is or even if there is such a unique phenomenon. Sound psychophysiological research is required to explicate the possible existence of hypnosis.

VERBAL PSYCHOTHERAPY

Psychotherapy is a method of relating with patients (clients) for the purpose of improving their behavior in everyday living. Usually, the patient's behavior interferes with his or her effectiveness, as it does in some psychiatric disorders. The purpose of psychotherapy may also be to improve an already satisfactory life.

There are numerous psychotherapeutic techniques, including psychoanalysis, client-centered therapy, and orgone therapy (the attempt to manipulate a biological energy named after *orgasm*) and over 460 other techniques. Traditionally, psychotherapies have used verbal techniques (sometimes referred to as "psychobabble"). Basically, regardless of the type, the effort is to *modify* the patient's behavior in some way. Consequently, psychotherapy is supposed to be primarily a learning experience, however it may be described.

The purpose of psychotherapy, of which there are over 460 techniques, is to improve effectiveness in everyday living. All techniques seek to modify behavior in some way that emphasizes the importance of principles of learning.

Freud and Verbal Psychotherapy.   An important early event in the development of psychotherapy was Josef Breuer's treatment of Anna O. — a case that influenced Sigmund Freud and the evolution of psychoanalysis. Freud had sought a university post in anatomy, neurology, and/or psychiatry. However, it became apparent that he would have a long wait, so he took his medical exams and entered private practice. He was soon helped financially, professionally, and personally by Breuer. Anna O. was described as a highly intelligent girl with multiple symptoms, including paralysis of three limbs, contractures, and dual personality. In the course of their work, Freud and Breuer concluded that if she was able to tell Breuer the origin of a symptom, the symptom would disappear. They thought that hypnosis helped the relating process. The method was christened the "talking cure" or "chimney sweeping" (it later became known also as catharsis). Eventually Breuer realized that he had developed a strong affection for the girl, so in 1882 he stopped treatment. Freud's acceptance came with his development of psychoanalysis, which was based on Breuer's method with Anna O. (Freud's lectures on hypnosis and hysteria, which he had studied in Paris with Charcot, had not been well accepted.) The thesis of psychoanalysis was that the symptoms represented feelings that Anna O. had originally repressed and that they apparently could be abolished with a free expression of those emotions. Freud has had tremendous influence on countless numbers of psychotherapists.

Contemporary Assessment of Freud's Cases.   Ellenberger's (1972) study of the case of Anna O. determined that Anna O. actually suffered from tuberculous meningitis and not from a hysterical illness as diagnosed by Breuer and Freud. She was not cured by Breuer but continued to suffer from the same symptoms for many years. Freud was well aware of her continuing suffering but pretended otherwise (see Thornton, 1983). Eysenck (1983) states that Freud was unable "to tell the truth" (p. 310). Masson (1985), in his book *The Assault on Truth: Freud's Suppression of the Seduction Theory,* attacked Freud's integrity because of Freud's change of heart with respect to the seduction theory. Freud had become impressed by the neurotic difficulties of his female patients to relate memories of sexual abuse in early childhood. He later abandoned this formulation and held that his patient's recollections were based on fantasies rather than on actual events. This was a shift of attention from an external trauma to internal fantasy as the causative agent in mental illness which, Masson holds, was not the truth. As Hans Strupp (1986b) states "In plain English, he [Masson] calls Freud a liar" (p. 293). Strupp refers to strong circumstantial evidence for this thesis. A broad examination of the alleged "malignant effect of Freud's theory on American thought and culture" is offered by E. Fuller Torrey (1992) in his book *Freudian Fraud.* See also Eysenck (1990) and Masson[1] (1990).

Contemporary Demand for Validation for Psychotherapy.   The increasing number of practicing psychotherapists includes those in psychiatry, psychology, social work, and numerous other professions such as religion and nursing. The extremely large number of people engaged in psychotherapy has led to its becoming a multi–billion-dollar-a-year industry in the United States alone. Its widespread use has emphasized the need to understand just what psychotherapy is and a demand for data to validate it as an effective approach. But as a leading psychotherapist assesses the status of psychotherapy, it lacks "clear boundaries, with hazy quality control and relatively vague ethical standards" (Strupp, 1986b, p. 121). As a result, he adds, psychotherapy is in a crisis situation.

Hans Eysenck (1983) expresses the issue as follows:

While Freud has had a tremendous impact on society and on psychotherapy, recent analyses have questioned his integrity and the effectiveness of his methods.

---

[1]Masson offers extensive criticisms of psychoanalysis and psychotherapy. As Stephen Appelbaum writes, Masson deplores the psychoanalytic practice of "taking authority as the main source of evidence."

Based on his own work, and that of numerous others, Eysenck demolishes any apparent scientific basis of psychoanalysis. Michael Lambert asserts that Eysenck thinks that "Freud was a drug-addicted fraud who consistently lied about his own work."

The popular image of psychology is inextricably mixed up with its clinical functions, with psychoanalysts and similar creeds. As psychologists, we will inevitably be judged in terms of our integrity and honesty, as far as claims for the success of the methods of psychotherapy are concerned. Every science has to pass through its ordeal by quackery, and on the outcome of this particular debate will depend the judgement of whether we are scientists or quacks. This is a vitally important question for the future of psychology, for the estimation of it in the eyes of "hard" scientists, and of administrators, officials, politicians and public in general. Even more important, from an ethical point of view, is the question of whether we have a right to make great claims for such practices as psychotherapy, demand exorbitant fees for performing an increasingly doubtful service, and train aspiring psychologists in the arcane and mysterious rites of the profession. (p. 319)

Methodological Problems in Validation.   A tremendous amount of research has been conducted to attempt to meet the demand to demonstrate the validity of psychotherapy. In part, because of the great complexity of the problem, however, the results have been disappointing. A large amount of psychotherapy research has been methodologically unsound so that there have been few valid conclusions. One problem is that the establishment of a legitimate control group is thought to be unethical because it may deny patients the help that they need. At issue is the question of whether doing nothing more than giving a placebo treatment is actually less effective than administering psychotherapy.

Another problem is that psychotherapies are so numerous and varied that a conclusion with regard to one may have nothing to do with the others.

To validate a method it must be shown that the particular method of therapy is more effective than a placebo treatment (one-third of patients improve whether or not they receive treatment). Also it needs to be established that whatever therapy is used (medical, behavioral, or verbal) is not harmful to the patient. For instance, as Irwin Berg pointed out, a psychotherapist may unintentionally reinforce maladaptive behavior expressed by the patient. A classical instance occurs when a bored psychotherapist listens to drudgery all day until suddenly a patient describes interesting sexual activities. The therapist lights up and listens intently, thus reinforcing the patient for discussing problems of that nature. Such reinforcement contingencies have been offered to explain why Freud was particularly interested in sex and why so many of Freud's patients expressed such frequent and peculiar sexual behaviors.

More generally, whatever the issue the patient may mention, if the therapist suddenly expresses interest, the therapist thereby reinforces the patient to continue to discuss and elaborate on that particular issue, even if it does not constitute a problem. Consequently, the patient and therapist reinforce each other and may develop a strong, false belief system, when only tentative thoughts were originally expressed by the patient. What happens is that the therapist and patient create a *folie à deux* in which they both develop and share the same delusional beliefs. The therapist is a very powerful reinforcing agent and can do great harm by misapplying learning principles. For example, psychotherapists have tragically influenced some clients to falsely "recall" instances of childhood abuse by their parents, even leading them to sue their parents. For instance, one woman was led to discover through "therapy" that she had repressed memories of being abused when she was three months old. The respected researcher Elizabeth Loftus says that there is no scientific evidence that these repressed memories are authentic. John Kihlstrom explains that

The multi–billion-dollar-a-year practice of psychotherapy is in a crisis because of the lack of validating data for its effectiveness.

The validation of a method of psychotherapy is methodologically extremely complex; at a minimum, it must be established that it is not harmful and that it is more effective than a placebo condition.

we do not remember much of anything from the first 5 – 7 years of life because before that the brain is not sufficiently mature enough to record memories.

This discussion does not in any way minimize the seriousness of authentic child abuse episodes. Certainly, any instance of child abuse should be dealt with sternly, and society should make a great effort to prevent the horrible mistreatment of children. The point here is that there have been an increasing number of "false positives" wherein unqualified psychotherapists have created problems when they did not exist, unethical activities indeed.

The psychotherapist must be extremely aware of suggestive and reinforcement influences so as to not create behavioral problems that did not originally exist.

Many such cases have been documented, for example see Wakefield and Underwager (1988) and Underwager and Wakefield (1990). Pamela Freyd at the False Memory Syndrome Foundation has developed considerable substantiating data for what has become known as "therapist abuse." Ralph Underwager at the Institute for Psychological Therapy has also accumulated data documenting the phenomenon and edits a relevant journal, *Issues in Child Accusation.* To illustrate, one prominent case was that of Alicia, a ten-year-old girl, who was kept from her family for 2½ years because authorities wrongly accused her father of raping her. As chronicled in the *San Diego Union,* October 20, 1991, Alicia, then eight years old, was brutally raped and sodomized as the family slept in their apartment. For more than a year, Alicia told police, doctors, social workers, and others in authority that a stranger had come through the window, taken her outside, attacked her and then returned her. The authorities were convinced that the story was a fabrication and focused on the father as the rapist. Alicia was then isolated from her family so that therapist Kathleen Goodfriend could work with her whereupon, in June 1990, Alicia changed her story and identified her father as the rapist. He was arrested and not freed until DNA and other evidence indicated that he was not the molester and the real rapist was found.

Eysenck (1983) summarized the results of a large number of studies aimed at validating various kinds of psychotherapy and concluded that

> behavioural therapies are reliably more effective . . . than verbal therapies . . . or developmental therapies. Behaviour therapies were particularly more effective than others for neurotics, complex phobics, and simple (monosymptomatic) phobics; verbal therapies were not reliably more effective for any diagnostic type. Behavioural therapies reveal larger average affects for measures of global adjustment. (p. 316)

One of the problems with psychoanalysis is that it is so lengthy and expensive. More than once psychoanalytic therapy was terminated because of the natural death of the psychoanalyst or the patient. It has been calculated that psychoanalysis costs from $55 to $150 per 50-minute session for four to five sessions per week for four to seven years or more. Consequently, each new patient represents an income to a psychoanalyst of perhaps $60,000 to $200,000 over a period of years. That might be acceptable if psychoanalysis was validated, which it is not.

In Conclusion.   A poll of 227 distinguished research scientists indicated that 96 percent of them thought that traditional psychoanalysis will be less used or scarcely used at all by the year 2000. Their consensus was that psychoanalysis is not really applicable to the major, serious causes of mental illness.

Although Freud's influence is inestimable, his method of psychoanalysis probably set psychology back a half century because of its ineffectiveness and inefficiency. His "talking cure" which started contemporary psychotherapy currently seems thoroughly discredited. The consumer must call into question the ethics of continuing to use verbal psychotherapeutic methods for which there are no validating data. The distinguished clinician Raimy (1950) referred to verbal psychotherapy as an "unidentified technique applied to unspecified problems with unpredictable outcomes" which often remains applicable today.

Biomedical and Behavioral Approaches

PSYCHOSURGERY

Background. **Psychosurgery** is the procedure of destroying apparently healthy brain tissue in order to relieve seriously debilitating psychiatric disorders. Archaeological evidence has indicated that **trephine operations** (drilling holes in the skull) were performed as early as 2000 B.C. Archaeologists have found trephine operations of special value in providing cues for the nature of various cultures. In some cultures, they were performed to release evil spirits that were thought to inhabit the brains of insane people. In the late 1930s, psychosurgical procedures started to be widely applied for psychiatric disorders, reaching their peak in the 1960s. Over 100,000 patients were treated with destructive lesions in the frontal lobes during the 1940s and 1950s. The frequency of these procedures has declined since the 1970s but they are still performed today.

Methods. At first, medical **frontal lobotomies** were performed by bilaterally cutting fibers in the frontal lobes. For this, holes were drilled laterally through the skull and then a surgical instrument was inserted. Later, the surgery was performed by insertion through the bony orbits above the eyes. In the 1950s with the development of stereotaxic instruments (see p. 240), well-localized lesions could be made by using electric currents or radio frequency waves delivered through electrodes. More recently amygdalectomies (surgery on the amygdala) have been performed.

Psychosurgery, principally frontal lobotomies, has been used to relieve serious psychiatric disorders; although the practice has become relatively rare due to the emergence of pharmacological and behavioral therapies.

A Theory. One notion was that a severing of connections between the frontal lobes (used for anticipation) and subcortical areas involved with emotions (such as the amygdala, the thalamus, and hypothalamus) severed "reasoning" from "emotion." Consequently worry and other such behaviors could be eliminated. Part of this thinking for performing frontal or prefrontal lobotomies resulted from observations of behavioral changes following head injuries. A classic case in the latter part of the last century was that Phineas Gage, whose personality dramatically changed when a crowbarlike instrument went through his frontal lobes during a dynamite accident.

Consequences. In general, prefrontal lobotomies have been said to result in decreased drive, decreased self-concern, and shallow affective life. The major signs following psychosurgery have been described as (1) vegetable-like qualities of inertia, lack of ambition, indifference to the opinions of others, poor judgment, purposelessness, a slowness of thinking and acting, a lack of emotional expression and decreased interest; and (2) maniclike behavior—lack of restraint of behavior and increased motor activity as in restlessness and euphoria.

On the other hand, such changes have not always been clearly documented. For example, Donald Hebb held that psychosurgery has not yielded interpretable evidence. Most studies suffer from two serious defects: First, there was little or no formal testing of emotional status on a before-and-after-surgery basis. Second, patients already had a serious personality defect that led to the surgery, confounding any interpretation.

Much controversy has surrounded the use of psychosurgery and involves ethical, scientific, and legal concerns. Once again this is an instance of wide use of a procedure that has not been validated. In any event, the development of tranquilizers and other medication has largely replaced psychosurgery.

ELECTROCONVULSIVE SHOCK THERAPY (ECT)

Electroconvulsive shock therapy induces seizure in the brain by passing a brief high-voltage electrical current through it.

Method and History.   In **electroconvulsive shock therapy (ECT)** a brief high-voltage electrical current is applied to the brain to stimulate a seizure that lasts for about a minute. Two electrodes are placed on the patient's head. ECT, along with insulin and shock treatment produced by metrazol, started to be used in the 1930s to combat severe depression in the mentally ill.

The first patients treated with ECT were schizophrenics. At that time psychiatrists thought that since schizophrenia was rare in epileptics it was the spontaneous electrical epileptic seizures that protected them against schizophrenia. Thousands of schizophrenics have been treated with ECT but there is little evidence that it is effective for them.

Sixty thousand to 100,000 people per year now receive ECT treatments in the United States, perhaps half the number from several decades ago.

Patients who now receive ECT for depression are given general anesthesia and muscle relaxants to allow them to sleep through the procedure and to minimize convulsions that are intense enough to have caused bones to break. Oxygen is administered because muscle relaxants might stop breathing. Brain waves are also monitored. The procedure takes about five minutes and medical complications are said to be rare. Treatment is generally one to three times a week for from two to four weeks.

Effects on Memory.   Patients' thinking and memory are disrupted immediately following ECT treatment. They are often confused and disoriented and have difficulty remembering things that were presented to them just before and immediately after the treatment. Sometimes memories are lost for events occurring several months before and after treatment. Memory for events that occurred before ECT treatment starts to return in months, beginning with the oldest memories. But apparently recall of events a few weeks before and after treatment never returns.

Theories of Physiological Effects.   We do not know why ECT is successful. There is some evidence that it increases receptor sensitivity to both serotonin and the catecholamines. It also increases secretion of hormones from the hypothalamus and from the pituitary and weakens the blood–brain barrier, allowing these hormones greater access to brain cells. It has been reasoned that these hormonal effects on the brain play a major role in ECT's antidepressant effects.

ECT seems to alter EEG, cerebral blood flow, neuroendocrine levels, and inhibit neurotransmission. It also affects the concentration of serotonin, as well as its synthesis and its receptors by increasing postsynaptic binding sites.

Animal studies indicate that the seizure may cause the brain to release higher levels of inhibitory neurotransmitters, perhaps GABA, which sharply decreases activity in the brain. (GABA apparently raises seizure thresholds.) According to this notion, the seizure itself is not the critical feature; rather, it is the process of terminating the seizure that is important. The termination process is an anticonvulsant one that reduces the excitability of the brain tissue. Accordingly, some people are thought to be depressed because the brain does not release the proper chemicals to terminate the cerebral depression.

Another theory is that during depression, certain regions of the brain, including the right frontal cortex, are overactive. Following the seizure, brain metabolism decreases sharply to levels lower than those that occurred prior to the seizure. Accordingly, the previously overactive regions of the brain are made less active.

Effects on Depression. Results have indicated that ECT can help 70 to 80 percent of people with major depression. In studies that compared the effectiveness of ECT with standard antidepressant drugs such as imipramine, ECT was as effective or more effective in relieving major depression. Several controlled studies indicate that over 70 percent of seriously depressed patients improve significantly after ECT, compared to only about 50 percent who improve following treatment with MAO inhibitors or the tricyclic antidepressant drugs.

One study showed that more than 70 percent of the 190 patients who did not respond to antidepressant drugs improved when subsequently given ECT. Other research indicates that ECT's effectiveness is not due to fear or to a placebo effect—ECT produces greater improvement than does placebo treatment. The improvement, however, often does not last since between 30 and 60 percent of patients relapsed during a six-month follow-up. In another study no difference was found with a sham ECT group six months later.

Although ECT has always been controversial, it apparently is the most effective treatment for major depression when medication has failed and there is no evidence of persistent brain damage. Its advantages over drugs are its rapid onset of action and its effectiveness when drugs have failed. In a study of 166 patients, 74 percent described their improvement as satisfactory, with 65 percent saying that they would have the treatment again. Perhaps the earlier negative evidence should be replaced due to improved techniques. Nevertheless, ECT is a treatment of last resort and remains controversial. ECT might be appropriate for those for whom drug therapy has been ineffective, when suicide is possible, for a hopeless psychotic, for an extremely agitated patient, or for a depressed patient who refuses to eat, to cooperate with treatment plans, or to otherwise care for him- or herself.

A number of studies have shown that ECT has a beneficial effect on people with major depression, although it is a method of last resort after drugs have failed.

PSYCHOPHARMACOLOGY AND ANESTHESIOLOGY

The use of chemical agents has had a profound effect on science and clinical technology. One landmark advance was the invention of anesthetics, which perhaps had its greatest impact on surgery.

Anesthesiology

In 1799 Humphry Davy, an English chemist, studied nitrous oxide, which was used widely for amusement as a laughing gas. In 1840 nitrous oxide and ether were used in the United States during surgery. The discovery and use of anesthesia quickly spread throughout the world, producing major changes in surgical procedures. Its importance ranks with the finding that germs cause disease and the discovery and use of antibiotics. For instance, before the use of anesthesia, the mark of a great surgeon was speed and strength, which minimized pain to the patient and reduced bleeding. In the late eighteenth century, a record 35 seconds was set for amputating a leg at the thigh. However, in the surgeon's haste, the left testicle of the patient was also inadvertently removed.

After the use of anesthesia, the surgeon could be slower so as to study the patient more carefully in the process (and apparently save testicles). In this way much new knowledge about the body was gained, such as the development of the surgical remedy for appendicitis.

Early Psychopharmacology

Drugs with psychotropic characteristics have been used for therapeutic purposes from the beginning of recorded human history and no doubt long before that.

The use of such drugs as alcohol, opium, cannabis, Indian snake root (which contains reserpine), and henbane (which contains scopolamine and atropine) has been dated from 40,000 B.C. to 10,000 B.C. The Greeks used opium in rituals as early as 2000 B.C., and they used a popular drug, perhaps cannabis or opium, to relieve anger and depression from about 800 B.C. The Chinese used opium as medicine in 2737 B.C. The earliest known prescription for a psychoactive drug was in an Egyptian papyrus dated 3700 B.C. In a folklore instance dating from around 900 A.D., an Abysinian noted that his goats were very frisky after eating coffee beans.

Aztecs of Central America, borrowing much knowledge from the Maya, used at least 641 plant drugs, including LSD and marijuana, to help stay awake all night, to enhance memory recall, and to sedate victims for human sacrifices, among other uses.

Medieval witches used atropine to produce hallucinations and love potions; they used a broomstick to apply it on vaginal membranes and the skin.

The Development of Modern Psychopharmacology

Modern pharmacology developed out of chemistry in the later part of the nineteenth century. Emil Kraepelin, a student of Wundt's founded psychopharmacology when he published a book on the use of psychological methods in clinical pharmacology.

The term *psychopharmacology* was first used by Necht in 1920, although the term *psychopharmakon* was used by Reinhardus Lorichius of Hadamar in 1548 to refer to prayers of comfort for the dying.

In 1933 Albert Hofman, a Swiss chemist, accidentally discovered lysergic acid diethylamide (LSD), a major precursor to the development of modern psychopharmacology. He had synthesized a new substance, molecules of which he inhaled. As he was going home he became dizzy. Later he snuffed some of it up his nose whereupon he had bizarre feelings that led to six hours of hallucinatory activity. As a reward for thus putting his nose into things, Hofman became the discoverer of LSD.

The discovery of chlorpromazine increased the use of antipsychotic drugs to reduce psychotic symptoms, which has drastically reduced the chronic institutionalization that was typical of the mental hospitals in the 1950s and before.

During the 1950s the chemical study of the brain began to flourish. It was found that drugs like reserpine could penetrate the blood–brain barrier and have specific cerebral actions. In 1952 the French surgeon Laborit discovered the antipsychotic drug chlorpromazine by chance. This development revolutionized psychiatry, largely replacing psychoanalysis, electroconvulsive shock therapy, and psychosurgery. The treatment of schizophrenics and manic depressive and other affective disorders thus radically changed and the number of patients in mental hospitals was drastically reduced. For example, one hospital in the 1950s had 3000 inpatients, but by 1977 there were less than 400. Many psychotic patients are now largely handled in emergency rooms and stabilized in the community with their families, in nursing homes, or halfway houses. Unfortunately, however, a large number of mentally ill people "fall through the cracks" and wander the streets as homeless people.

Where Do Drugs Act?

When molecules of a drug fit (bind) into appropriate receptors on neurons, a drug's action commences (see Fig. 14.2). One strategy to establish where drugs act (and thence identify the location of their receptors) is to administer them and see if they increase or decrease the activity of neurotransmitters that have specified origins. Another approach is to directly inject a drug into specific brain regions to determine whether it has an effect.

Research has indicated that drugs may act at synapses, on the surface of nerve cells, inside axons and cell bodies, on cells of receptor organs, and at effectors (muscles and glands). One hypothesis is that potent drugs bind to specific neural receptors while weak drugs act more generally in their sites of action.

Agonists Versus Antagonists

An **agonist** is a drug that facilitates an action and an **antagonist** is a drug that opposes an action of an agonist. Antagonists can thus oppose and control the effect of a drug (e.g., naloxone is an antagonist that stops most actions of morphine and related narcotics). We now have antagonists for histamine, ACH, norepinephrine, dopamine, gamma aminobutyric acid (GABA), and other substances, although they have not yet been found for most other drugs.

Some Kinds of Psychotropic Drugs

Psychopharmacological agents have become the most frequently prescribed drugs in the world. The major classes of **psychotropic drugs** are antipsychotic, antidepressant, and antianxiety drugs.

ANTIPSYCHOTIC DRUGS

Antipsychotic drugs are also called **neuroleptics** (medications with antipsychotic properties). Their single most effective use is in the treatment of schizophrenia. They produce their main effects by altering neurochemical transmission (specifically, they reduce excessive dopamine in the mesolimbic striatum of the brain). All antipsychotic drugs seem to block dopamine transmission (dopamine is a primary neurotransmitter in several brain regions). The phenothiazines were the first modern psychotropic drugs developed. They include chlorpromazine (thorazine), thioxanthenes, and the butyrophenones, such as haldol and rauwolfia alkaloids (reserpine).

Relative to the effects of placebos administered as control conditions, antipsychotic drugs have significantly improved symptoms of delusions, hallucinations, and thought disorders in schizophrenics; the major improvement was shown in the first week of 13 or so weeks of treatment. However, often there is decreased initiative, with impaired social and vocational functioning. The antipsychotic drugs also effectively block bizarre behaviors induced in animals with amphetamine. They are also effective in the treatment of amphetamine psychosis in humans.

Drugs act by fitting into receptors that are contained in neurons, a process called "binding." Different drugs act at different sites on neurons, cells of receptor organs, and effectors.

The action of a drug (an agonist) can be terminated by administering its antagonist.

Chlorpromazine is used for both acute and chronic schizophrenia, although improvement is variable; some patients improve on oral doses of 150 mg of chlorpromazine a day while others require 3000 mg. For a crisis of psychotic behavior, chlorpromazine administered into the muscles can be effective within a few hours.

Clozopine has helped a number of schizophrenics for whom other drugs, such as haldol and thorazine, were ineffective.

Antipsychotic drugs were discovered by chance because we do not have a good understanding of the biological etiologies of psychiatric disorders; consequently we lack strategies for developing other antipsychotic drugs. Furthermore, the psychiatric syndromes lack sufficient homogeneity so that any particular drug could not be universally effective for all cases of any given syndrome.

Because antipsychotic drugs reduce activity in animals, it is thought that they protect the psychotic patient by decreasing responsiveness to the environment, thus decreasing the likelihood of exhibiting psychotic behaviors. By delaying responses, the antipsychotic drugs thereby can lead the patient to process stimuli more effectively and to arrive at more rational behavior.

Side Effects of Antipsychotic Drugs

Antipsychotic drugs (neuroleptics) such as chlorpromazine and clozopine have been most effectively applied for schizophrenia. Side effects include dystonia, muscle spasm.

The antipsychotic drugs differ markedly in their side effects. The earliest side effect in treatment usually is **dystonia** (muscle spasms) typically in the neck and face and lasting a few minutes to hours. Although dystonia is harmless, it is disconcerting to experience and to observe. It can be rapidly relieved with injection of anti-Parkinsonian drugs. A related possible side effect, pseudo-Parkinsonism, is characterized by muscular stiffness, stooped posture, shuffling gate, drooling, and akathesia (feeling restless). Prolonged use often results in tardive dyskinesia, which is characterized by chewing, smacking the lips, protrusion of the tongue, and twisting movements of body and legs. A serious side effect of clozopine is that about 1 percent of recipients are estimated to contract a blood disorder that cripples the immune system.

Patients in psychotherapy frequently are on medication. Psychotherapists thus need to be aware of drug side effects and of withdrawal symptoms as well as interactions with other pharmacologic agents. Furthermore, psychotherapy and drug-induced effects are thus confounded so that any behavioral improvement cannot be ascribed unequivocally to either factor.

ANTIANXIETY DRUGS

The benzodiazepines are the antianxiety drugs indicated for generalized anxiety disorders. They include valium, librium and imipramine.

The benzodiazepines are the only group of drugs that are indicated for generalized anxiety disorders. They are among the most frequently prescribed drugs, having been in use since 1957. The benzodiazepines, especially diazepam (valium), have quick onset because they rapidly bind to benzodiazepine receptors. Another subclass is chlordiazepoxide (librium). Imipramine, phenelzine, alprazolam, and clonazepam have been confirmed as effective for panic disorder. The benzodiazepines affect both norepinephrine and serotonin by decreasing turnover of those chemicals to synapses. They also impair neural discharges from the amygdala and decrease muscle activity, apparently because they affect the reticular formation. They also induce faster, low-voltage EEG activity.

Research on the neurobiology of anxiety has implicated neurotransmitter and neuromodulator systems. These include the noradrenergic system, the mesocortical dopaminergic systems, and central serotonin systems. How dopamine and these other neurotransmitters might be involved in the pathology of anxiety is unclear, although such a discovery may lead to more effective drug therapy in the future.

ANTIDEPRESSANT DRUGS

The major classes of drugs used in the treatment of depression are (1) the tricyclic antidepressants (TCA), which work by blocking uptake in the synaptic receptors and (2) monoamine oxidase inhibitors (MAOI), which help depression by blocking the breakdown of receptors in the synapses. However, the side effects of MAOIs, which sometimes lead to fatal hypertensive episodes, have caused them to fall out of favor. There is controversy as to whether the level of certain neurotransmitters in synapses is responsible for depression or whether there is a breakdown at the receptor site. Since both classes of drugs function in these two different ways, perhaps both are implicated in depression. We do know that many of the antidepressant medications function by increasing the amount of neurotransmitters at the receptor sites of synapses. Furthermore, neurotransmitters in the brain have important roles in depression (e.g., reserpine, which alleviates depression, lowers the level of norepinephrine in the brain).

The major antidepressant drugs are tricyclic antidepressants and monoamine oxidase inhibitors.

About 70 percent of those treated for unipolar depression have benefited from TCA therapy, which alleviated the depression and prevented relapse. Lithium salts, which decrease norepinephrine transmission, are used to treat bipolar manic-depressive psychotics. However, lithium is relatively ineffective for unipolar depressive disorder. One hypothesis as to how these drugs work is that psychotic depression may be due to a decrease in catecholamines at septal or other reward regions in the brain (Fig. 9.2). Another possibility is that there is an excess of serotonin in brain punishment areas.

How Long Should Antidepressant Drugs Be Administered? It usually takes one to two weeks for drugs to produce the desired therapeutic effect. If drug therapy is effective, the individual often improves quickly: Sleep and eating patterns improve and the person becomes less withdrawn and morose. If there are no indications of improvement after two to four weeks, the antidepressant should be discontinued. Many patients require long-term maintenance to prevent the return of symptoms. The medication usually should be taken for 6 to 12 months after a major depressive episode because the risk of relapse is high. Clinicians need to be vigilant for the onset of deleterious side effects of drugs. Undesirable side effects usually show up well before there is any improvement in behavior.

In Conclusion. Antianxiety and antidepressant drugs are used for such disorders as manic excitement, anxiety, and depression, as well as for behavior disorders of children and the elderly. Antipsychotic drugs should be regularly used only for schizophrenia or acute mania. Only if the benzodiazepines and the tricyclic antidepressants have failed should antipsychotic drugs be used for anxious or depressed patients.

Controlling Depression — Interactions Between Chemical and Behavioral Therapies

There are over one hundred psychotherapies, more than two dozen antidepressant drugs, and various ways of administering electroshock therapy to treat depression, which indicates that there is little consensus about the most effective treatment. All approaches seek to intervene into the depressive state, but in different ways. Several decades ago ECT was the primary treatment for severe clinical depression. Then when antidepressant medications were developed, depression was often rapidly alleviated, even though they were not effective in all cases. Furthermore, drugs help only as long as administered so that behavior therapy should also be employed to effect more permanent changes.

Biochemical and Muscular Interaction. One reason that tricyclic medication reduces depression, Arnold Gessel has suggested, is that it produces muscular relaxation. George Whatmore has recognized that thought, feelings, and emotions are in part activities of the muscles and that the maintenance of the waking state is in part dependent upon motor activity. Whatmore found that depressed patients had significantly increased elevations of jaw – tongue motor activity relative to other muscle groups in their bodies. Furthermore, the more severely depressed the patient, the greater was the amount of residual motor activity. His interpretation was that **hyperponesis** (hyper motor activity) produces emotional disturbances and predisposes individuals to depression. Conversely, relaxation of muscles can help depression, in part because adenosine triphosphate (ATP) is saved. ATP, the chemical substance derived from creative phosphate, provides the energy for muscular (as well as neural) activity. However, if the amount of ATP falls below a certain required level in any muscle group, relaxation fails. If ATP insufficiency is prolonged, muscle activity may be excessive so that external stresses are not adequately handled; a state of depression thus may develop.

Complex interactions between chemicals and muscular conditions influence depression.

Behavior Therapy. Depressive people often have difficulty learning and remembering, particularly dealing with abstract concepts. Depressed individuals have learned inappropriate ways of perceiving. Consequently, they misperceive and misunderstand their experiences and external events. Mainly, they focus excessively on a relatively few negative events, losing perspective for all of the good things in their lives. Traumatic experiences thus place excessive demands on such people. Lonely individuals probably experience the adverse affects of stress relatively more than others. With a relative lack of ability to experience pleasurable emotions, accompanied by feelings of emptiness and painful moods, these individuals become less sociable. Resultant decreased opportunities for pleasurable experiences leads to a complex feedback circuit. Thus, the more withdrawn depressives become, the more unpleasant they are to be with; then, because they are more unpleasant to be with socially, they are avoided by others, leading them to withdraw further into their depressive state — another positive feedback system.

Through behavior therapy one can intervene into positive feedback circuits for depressives in which social withdrawal makes them unpleasant and the more unpleasant they are the more they withdraw. Depressives may learn to behave to increase reinforcements, reducing unpleasant experiences.

To deal with the learned aspects of depression, the behavior therapist helps individuals learn how to behave in order to increase reinforcements. The individuals can often learn that their reasoning is faulty, thereby reducing negative perceptions and thereby the frequency and duration of painful emotional states. That accomplishment also increases the opportunity to experience and enjoy positive experiences. Such modification of behavior can at least be started through Progressive Relaxation.

The Amine Hypothesis of Drug Action in the Affective Disorders

The amine hypothesis states that depression is associated with a deficit of amine brain neurotransmitters at specific central synapses; conversely, mania is associated with an excess of amine neurotransmitters. Neurotransmitter catechol*amines* include norepinephrine, serotonin, and dopamine. The hypothesis resulted from a chance observation in the study of reserpine. First, many patients who used reserpine as a tranquilizer in the early 1950s experienced symptoms of depression. Then, laboratory research indicated that reserpine depleted nerve endings of serotonin, dopamine, and norepinephrine. These observations from the clinic and from the biochemical laboratory were associated, leading to the amine hypothesis of **affective disorders.**

The neurotransmitter systems for amines consist of neurons with very long axonal processes and a very large number of terminal branchings. Consequently, a single nerve cell can synapse with as many as 75,000 other neurons so that it receives input from many sources. These amine systems are concentrated in the brain stem and midbrain and project throughout the limbic system, cerebral cortex, neocortex, hypothalamus, and lower brain stem. They thus interact with the major areas of the brain. Because affective illnesses include such characteristics as cognitive, emotional, psychomotor, appetitive, and autonomic manifestations, these amine systems are the focus of much study.

The amine hypothesis holds that depression is associated with a deficit of brain neurotransmitters (known as amines) at specific central synapses; conversely, mania is associated with an excess of amine neurotransmitters.

A Lithium – Hormone Hypothesis

Lithium salts are among the most effective therapies for bipolar manic-depressive illness, a therapy discovered accidentally by the Australian researcher J. F. Cade. Cade believed that uric acid would be therapeutically useful for treating mania and depression. He mixed the uric acid with lithium salt to help it dissolve. The mixed solution did help the patients. Researchers then identified the effective agent as lithium, not uric acid. Lithium does not alter the amount of neurotransmitters in the synapse but acts at the postsynaptic receptors.

The amine hypothesis also holds that affective disorders result from neurotransmitter catecholamines (norepinephrine, dopamine, and serotonin) that affect neural impulses that are regulated at synaptic junctions.

One hypothesis is that lithium's therapeutic effects involve the hormonal systems because lithium affects endocrine organs (e.g., lithium inhibits thyroid hormone secretion and prolactin secretion from the pituitary, and it alters the way growth hormones respond). Related to this is that depression in women often starts around 40 to 50 years of age, which coincides with menopause. Women also often experience some depression around the time of menstruation when the levels of estrogen decrease.

The lithium – hormone hypothesis holds that lithium beneficially affects bipolar manic-depressive illness because it interacts with the endocrine system.

Drugs and Sleep

Medication for sleep disorders should be taken for only limited periods (one or two weeks) to start. It should also be a mild drug that has a low potential for being abused (e.g., flurazepam).

REM and Drugs. A central problem with hypnotic drugs (those for sleep), as with alcohol and barbiturates, is that they reduce REM sleep. Consequently, later there can be **REM rebound,** which is increased dreaming with the person often waking up during unpleasant dreams. The patient may therefore request more sleeping medication, which leads to habituation and a positive feedback cycle can develop.

Some drugs increase REM sleep (e.g., reserpine, chlorpromazine, tryptophane, 5HT, and methyldopa). LSD increases REM sleep early in the sleep cycle but without a marked effect on total REM time.

Narcolepsy. **Narcolepsy** is characterized by involuntary episodic attacks of sleep during normal waking hours. Amphetamines and tricyclic antidepressants have been effective for narcolepsy. Some symptoms such as cataplexy, sleep paralysis, and hypnogogic hallucinations can be controlled by moderate doses of imipramine.

Ineffective Drugs. A number of sleep disorders cannot be adequately treated by pharmacologic agents at present, for example, **sleep apnea,** a condition in which nocturnal insomnia and subsequent daytime **hypersomnia** occur. Sleep apnea is caused by the collapse of soft tissue in the back of the throat over the windpipe opening so that each time the patient falls asleep, breathing ceases. Consequently, people with apnea stop breathing (sometimes hundreds of times) during the night; they wake to choke and gasp for air. A lack of nighttime sleep leads to a tendency to sleep during the day. Similarly, nocturnal myoclonus, spontaneous movements of the legs with accompanying arousal, does not respond to medication.

Drugs and Sexual Behavior

The New Sexual Revolution. The Model-T Ford had a major impact in changing sexual mores, but the development of pharmacologic agents had an even greater effect. Drugs such as penicillin reduced the fear of venereal disease, and oral agents for controlling conception removed the fear of pregnancy.

Sexual Therapy. People also increased their frequency of seeking therapy for such sexual dysfunctions as impotence and premature ejaculation in the male and frigidity, orgasmic dysfunction, and vaginismus in the female. Sexual functioning and malfunctioning had been a subject for psychotherapy for many years, particularly because of the importance given it by Freud. However, taboos and restrictions limited research on this important problem until the pioneering studies of Kinsey in 1948 and Masters and Johnson in 1966. Since then, a variety of sex therapies have been developed. To prevent premature ejaculation, for instance, local anesthetics such as cocaine and procaine in cream form have been applied to the genital regions; the goal is to reduce sensation and thereby prolong the preorgasmic phase of sexual activity. Yet, controlled studies have not been conducted to validate the practice. In addition, many drugs have been found to have side effects that impair sexual function (e.g., guanethidine impairs erectile potency and ejaculatory ability in men).

The wide use of various drugs has contributed to a sexual revolution wherein sexual behavior has become more widely practiced and therapy for sexual dysfunction has become more widely accepted.

Sexual dysfunction can also be a secondary result of other diseases such as myocardial infarction, hypertension, diabetes, benign prostatic hypertrophy, and Parkinsonism. Therapy for those primary disorders often has improved sexual adjustment.

The Search for Aphrodisiacs. Drugs such as powdered rhinoceros horn have been sought throughout history to enhance sexual desire and activity. However, we have seen on p. 262 that only placebo effects have been found. Cocaine, amphetamine, marijuana, and hashish have a reputation for improving sexual performance, but well-controlled studies are lacking.

A number of drugs have been used as aphrodisiacs, but research in controlled studies has not validated them as effective agents on normal people.

Anaphrodisiacs. As Shakespeare said in *Macbeth* "alcohol provokes the desire, but takes away the performance." Alcohol does impair sexual reflexes in animals and alcoholics are frequently impotent. Such sedative agents as the barbiturates, the benzodiazepines, and neprobone also can depress the sexual reflex. The opioids (morphine, heroin, methadone) depress sexual functioning. In India opium has been used as a means of prolonging erection and delaying orgasm, but the practice is questionable at best.

Anaphrodisiacs have been sought to depress sexual functioning when such a behavior is impossible or undesirable. For centuries saltpeter (potassium nitrate) was used for depressing sexual desire by placing it in the diets of school boys, prisoners, and sailors. There is no evidence, however, that it has any effect on sexual behavior, although it does produce diuresis (increased urination). For their possible side effects, antipsychotic drugs have been used in efforts to decrease sexual desire in sexual criminals as an alternative to surgery or incarceration; thioridazine especially is thought to produce impotence by inhibiting ejaculation. Castration in the male reduces testosterone levels and sexual excitability, causing atrophy of the penis. Still, castrated male animals and humans can have some sexual functioning and may be able to produce an erection.

Neurotransmitters. Neurotransmitters function in cybernetic circuits with the autonomic nervous system for such sexual activities as secretion, tumescence, ejaculation, and orgasm. Dopamine seems to be the basic facilitator of sexual function while 5HT and dopamine-blocking agents such as pinozide have been shown to be sexual inhibitors.

Efforts have long been made to apply anaphrodisiacs to suppress sexual behaviors. However, those that have been used do not have a sound general basis and do produce unwanted side effects.

Drug Treatment of Hyperactive Children

Treatment with stimulant medication has been validated with double-blind control studies that show improvement in school performance and psychosocial adjustment. Of the central nervous system stimulants, Ritalin is most frequently prescribed, though it is controversial. The amphetamines are second in frequency. The tricyclic antidepressants show some promise.

CONTROLLING SOME DEBILITATING DISORDERS AND DISEASES

Relief of Pain

The problem of alleviating pain is staggering. It has been estimated that as many as 80 million people in the United States suffer from chronic pain. The most common types are recurrent headaches, low-back pain, and arthritis. Based on a Lou Harris national sampling of 1254 people, three out of four Americans suffer at least one headache during a year, 56 percent experience backaches, and 46 percent stomachaches. Chronic pain costs the United States some $60 billion annually in hospitalization, insurance, loss of work, legal costs, and disability payments. Contemporary efforts to treat pain include nerve blocks, acupuncture, hypnosis, physiotherapy, ultrasound, biofeedback, relaxation, and electrical stimulation.

PLACEBO EFFECTS

Throughout history people have pursued the prevention and removal of pain in many ways. Its origin has been thought to have been in evil spirits, angry gods, and sinful behavior. In some cultures it was thought that diseases and pain could be transferred from an injured living part to an inanimate model of that part. Metals have long been used — copper bracelets were worn to ease the discomfort of arthritis, and sometimes still are today.

Static electricity treatments generated by Rube Goldberg contraptions were used as early as 1743 to treat pain. Recognizing them as ineffective and dangerous, Benjamin Franklin denounced their use, but generally to no avail.

Why were (and are) such quack practices used? Even though they are totally ineffective, and sometimes even deleterious, a patient's belief in a cure may influence the course of a disease. The practice of medicine, or indeed of any kind of therapy, combines technology with belief. This is as much true for us today as it was for past cultures. The best explanation of the many quick and easy cures for pain offered today is probably the placebo effect. The analgesic effect of placebos could release endorphins, the opiate-like chemicals produced by the body that help to regulate pain. Even with Progressive Relaxation, which uniquely avoids the use of suggestion to the maximum extent to avoid such placebo effects, there is obviously some expectation (suggestion) on the part of the patient that relaxation will lead to beneficial results.

Many unvalidated practices to alleviate pain are effective only because of their suggestive effects so that they do not permanently or effectively alleviate pain.

BEHAVIORAL TREATMENT

To help control pain, individuals need to properly perceive and react to it. First they should understand that the purpose of acute pain is to warn them to seek to protect themselves, to stop what they are doing. Chronic pain (as in a tension headache), on the other hand, is not usually informative of immediate danger — it is not a symptom of disease or injury. Consequently, chronic pain must be dealt with behaviorally. Patients need to learn what behaviors increase and decrease pain so that they can behave to reduce or eliminate it. In a behavioral treatment program, complaints about pain should be ignored while toleration of pain should be reinforced. For instance, if patients are successful in not giving in to the first sign of pain they are praised. Others are taught to ignore the complaints of sufferers because attention to the complaints may reinforce not only the complaint behavior, but the pain experience itself.

A behavioral program could attempt to extinguish or punish pain behavior and reinforce successes in alleviating pain.

By first recognizing that one can control pain, one can behave in ways to reduce or eliminate pain and the anxiety generated by pain.

Since chronic pain does not signal immediate danger, sufferers should be as active as possible. If they are inactive and concentrate on pain, they exacerbate the sensation and the body may deteriorate. Active patients keep their bodies healthier and more pain resistant. Activity can often also mask pain by creating a distraction. Distraction is compatible with the gate control theory of pain (see pp. 273–275) in that only a certain number of messages can go through the gate at once. Consequently, pain messages will not reach the brain if other messages are already "filling" the gate. If a patient considers it hopeless to control pain, this idea of hopelessness has to be counteracted. This can be accomplished by applying the method of successive approximation, reinforcing slight successes followed by systematic increases in pain resistance.

Passive Therapies. In contrast to behavioral therapies in which the patient is active, passive therapies, such as acupuncture and ultrasound, not only seem to be ineffective in themselves, but what placebo relief they bring leads the patient to become dependent on them, a problem in common with drug treatments. Furthermore, suggestive placebo effects are temporary and thus do not come to grips with chronic pain. Acupuncture, experts hold, does not deal with the basic problem of pain, although the distraction may produce some temporary relief.

Sufferers who do something themselves, rather than have something done to them, are more often able to prevent and eliminate pain.

Treating Headaches. There are certain (myofacial) trigger points in the muscles of the head and neck that cause tension headaches. These trigger points can be specified by palpating (examining by feeling and pressing with the palms of the hands and the fingers). One palpates the muscle to identify a locally tender region, although that is not where the patient experiences the headache. The pain of the headache is reproduced by palpating or tensing the trigger point. The therapy is to allow the muscle to relax and resume its normal maximum length. This may be temporarily facilitated by fluorimethane spray or injecting procaine.

HYPNOTIC TREATMENT

Suggestion through hypnosis (see pp. 516–517) can block extremely intense pain in some people, but how it does so remains a mystery. Presumably, in some way hypnosis closes gates so that while pain messages are actually generated, the brain does not receive them. Consequently, the patient does not feel pain. Other possibilities are that the individual feels the pain but either forgets about it later or does not mind it.

About 20 percent of the general population seem to be capable of extreme anesthesis under hypnosis. They are instructed that the pain will be eliminated rather than simply to imagine that they are feeling good.

SURGICAL TREATMENT

Surgery is sometimes used to relieve severe pain, as in a **cordotomy** (dividing tracts of the spinal cord, by incision, radio frequency coagulation, and other methods). Most of the pain fibers in the spinal cord that ascend to the brain are destroyed. However, the pain usually returns about nine months later.

TREATING PAIN CHEMICALLY

Aspirin (Acetylsalicylic Acid). We can intervene and alleviate pain to some extent with chemical pain killers; for example, aspirin is effective because it inhibits the production of prostaglandins (we saw in Chapter 9 that this chemical stimulates nerve fibers when there is tissue damage, which is the beginning of a pain message). Aspirin was discovered in the bark of a willow tree more than 200 years ago. It has an analgesic effect in the peripheral nervous system by interacting with pain reception where the injury has occurred. Aspirin works in part by blocking the release of prostaglandins, which are released when tissue is injured. However, it has side effects that can promote ulcers and strokes. A positive side effect of aspirin is that in older men it decreases frequency of heart attacks because it reduces the ability of blood to clot.

Calcium Channel Blockers. Verapamil is one kind of **calcium channel blockers,** drugs that interfere with the cellular transfer of calcium, thereby preventing blood vessels from contracting. Verapamil thus prevents or lessens migraine headaches by controlling arteries in the head that constrict and dilate to press against sensitive nerves.

Verapamil has been used in treating angina chest pains, which are produced when constricted arteries cannot deliver adequate blood to the heart. One advantage of calcium channel blockers is that they have few unpleasant side effects relative to other medications that produce such side effects as fatigue, depression, lethargy, and heart irregularities.

Local Anesthetics. Novocaine deadens nerves by raising the threshold for their excitation. Barbiturates affect synaptic transmission in the CNS. Opium and other narcotics effectively relieve severe pain, but they have toxic side effects and are addictive.

Pain has been successfully treated with relaxation, hypnosis, surgery, and chemicals such as calcium channel blockers and local anesthetics.

Treating Pain Through Electrical Stimulation

Various techniques for electrically stimulating nervous tissue have been successfully used to inhibit the subjective feelings of pain. For example, a stimulator can be attached on the lower back to stimulate the spinal cord. Another common analgesic device to control pain is the TENS (Transcutaneous Electrical Nerve Stimulation device). The TENS unit consists of a power pack and electrodes that are applied to the area near the injury to electrically stimulate in a variety of impulse patterns. It is believed that the TENS stimulates further release of endorphins to inhibit the pain.

Another device is the Transcutaneous Cranial Electrical Stimulator (TCES). This technique has been successfully used to decrease the necessity for anesthetics by 60 percent, compared to an opiate analgesic. TCES is applied as a low-frequency current with high-frequency current pulses at the level of the mastoid bones behind the ears. With no side effects reported, it has been applied for periods of several days continuously. One finding has been that it hastens the detoxification of heroin addicts. Both human and animal studies confirm that it alleviates the symptoms of abstinence from opiates during treatment for addiction.

A last resort is to use electrical stimulation in the brain. The following presentation by Orlando J. Andy of a case history is illustrative.

Electrode Implant for Chronic Headaches. H. P., a 46-year-old man had encephalitis at age 35. He subsequently developed severe and incapacitating headaches and could not sleep because of pain. There was an abnormal tremor in the right leg and arm. At times he remained awake all night. Vomiting occurred with the headaches. At 43 years of age, he had a gastric ulcer, became depressed, and contemplated suicide. Shock therapy was given for depression at 44 years. Headaches, depression, and suicidal thoughts recurred two months after treatment. At age 45, electroshock therapy was repeated. Beneficial results only lasted 10–12 days after each treatment. In addition to headaches, he had increased stuttering, memory impairment, blurred vision, tremor in the right upper extremity, dizziness, clumsiness, stumbling, falling, dropping things, forgetting, disorientation, obsessive eating, and impotence. EEG studies revealed slowing with sharp waves on the left side.

Treatment: A left thalamotomy was done at age 46 for the intractable pain. The headaches and pain, in addition to the insomnia, depression, and suicidal thoughts were alleviated for about two years, but seizures developed.

Thalamic electrode implant: At age 51 a thalamic electrode was placed in the pontine reticular area just to the right of the midline, at the level of the seventh cranial nerve (Fig. 15.4).

Results: The patient stimulated himself 30 minutes daily just before going to bed and has been pain free, sleeping well at night, and no longer depressed and suicidal.

Comments: This patient's pain may be considered of central origin secondary to encephalitis which has caused brain stem and diencephalic abnormal electrical activity activating pain cells at that level. Electrical stimulation suppresses the abnormal pain and discharge.

Follow Up: This patient died recently but was in complete control of his chronic intractable pain and insomnia for over 10 years before coming down with cancer. Of major interest was his rhythm for pain control such that if he did not stimulate for 40 hours or more, the headache would burst through.

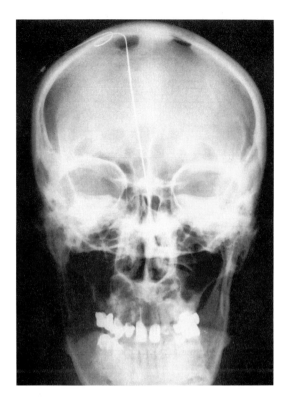

FIGURE 15.4
Repeated stimulation of the thalamic site prevents it from firing spontaneously and results in suppressing the spontaneously recurring attacks of pain. (Courtesy of O. J. Andy, The University of Mississippi Medical Center.)

Another of Andy's successful electrode implants was for seizures and chronic body pains in a 20-year-old female. While other methods were unsuccessful, the thalamic electrical stimulation suppressed both the pain and the seizures with no untoward side effects.

A successful method of last resort for alleviating pain is to implant electrodes into such regions as the thalamus so that the patient may deliver electrical stimulation when desired.

How to Control Cancer

BEHAVIORAL ENGINEERING

Appropriate Behavior Can Help to Prevent Cancers.   There are many things that people can do to avoid cancer—they can give up smoking; not overexpose themselves to the sun; have Pap tests, proctoscopic examinations, and mammograms; examine their breasts and testicles; avoid exposure to hazardous substances such as asbestos; and modify their diets. Through education, people generally are quite aware that they should do these things. However, there is a wide gap between making people aware of what they should do and getting them to actually do it. More than 90 percent of adult smokers say they'd like to quit if it were easy to do so and 60 percent claim they have tried during the past year. Thus, people do know that they should engage in self-examining behavior, give up smoking, and so on, but if they even start, they typically do not continue. Even though we have effective methods of self-control through contingent reinforcement (Chapter 10), society does not widely apply them. To prevent cancers, the consequences of desirable and

Behavioral technologies can be effectively applied to develop behaviors that prevent and retard the development of cancers, but they need to be more extensively applied.

undesirable behaviors need to be made immediate and relevant to the individual. If children are to learn that they should not smoke, it is ineffective to focus on long-term health consequences. Children do not plan too far into their future so that only immediate consequences have meaning for them. For instance, one study of seventh-grade children successfully emphasized consequences that they experienced with little time delay, such as bad health, exclusion from public areas, poor appearance, and rejection by other children.

Smoking cigarettes is the single largest preventable cause of death in the United States and the potential to reduce suffering and death is great. Even though tobacco is addictive, smoking can be stopped. Even individuals who have smoked as long as 50 years can show benefits within one to five years after quitting.

Moderately increasing the price of cigarettes through taxation has not seemed to cause many smokers to quit. However, there does seem to be evidence that increased cost has an effect on younger Americans who are not yet hooked. One study showed that if we were to reduce the cigarette tax, a million young people between the ages of 12 and 25 would start smoking or continue smoking. On the other hand when taxation is dramatically increased, as it was in Canada, the number of cigarettes purchased sizably decreased.

It *is* possible for one to quit smoking as shown by success with the more serious addiction to heroin (e.g., more than 70 percent of U.S. servicemen addicted to heroin in Vietnam stopped using the substance). Within a 20-year period, more than 30 million regular smokers quit. The percentage of male smokers in the United States dropped from 52 percent to 35 percent, but the percentage among teenage girls has increased.

EXERCISE

Ralph Paffenbarger reported the results of a long-term study of 50,000 people conducted since the early 1960s. He classified them according to their reports of how active they were. The results indicated that the moderately and highly active individuals had about half the risk of colon cancer relative to frequency among inactive subjects. Although these results were reported for men, a different study of 2500 females indicated a small possibility that there is a reduction in frequency of breast cancer among women who are relatively more active.

CHEMOTHERAPY AND BEHAVIORAL MEDICINE

Variables such as chemotherapy, vaccines, exercise, diet, and geographic location show some limited promise of affecting cancers, but research still has a long way to go to establish their effects.

Administering anticancer drugs is a method of last resort for cancer. Although chemotherapy has had some success in retarding the progress of cancer, its rate of effectiveness is low. Side effects frequently include protracted nausea and vomiting. These symptoms result from the drugs themselves but also are a result of classical conditioning. The patient learns to associate stimuli present during chemotherapy with side effects of the anticancer drugs. Consequently, those stimuli themselves can come to evoke the side effects. Approximately one-third of all chemotherapy patients develop conditional nausea and vomiting. Progressive Relaxation, hypnosis, and systematic desensitization have been effective in controlled studies for reducing the conditional side effects associated with cancer chemotherapy.

VACCINES

The most obvious approach to cancer prevention would be to vaccinate people against the disease. One reason that we have not been successful is that there are different kinds of cancer, so that a variety of different vaccines would be required. Of various types of cancer vaccines being sought, one uses cells from a cancer patient's own tumor to prevent recurrence. The purpose is to stimulate the person's immune system into action against tumor cells. The cells are treated by radiation to keep them from reproducing. Twenty patients in one study had their tumors removed by surgery and received three injections of a vaccine containing cells from their own tumors. This has shown encouraging results with individuals having colorectal cancer.

DIET AND GEOGRAPHIC LOCATION

A study indicated that 49 men who developed colorectal cancer also had a significantly lower dietary intake of calcium and vitamin D compared to other subjects. People living in geographical areas that are exposed to more sunlight, as in California, Arizona, and New Mexico, have a lower level of colon cancer than do people in New York, New Hampshire, and Vermont. Similarly, people in the northern latitudes are more prone to colon cancer than people in South America and Africa where there is sunlight for the greater part of the year. It could be that a diet including the grains, fibers, and milk, which contains Vitamin D, provides protection. However, in such studies in which the independent variable is geographic location and numerous extraneous variables are not controlled, the confounds are so enormous that other differences between those who are afflicted with cancer and those who are not could be responsible. Yet the correlations are provocative.

GENETIC ENGINEERING

Foreign substances (antigens) are found on the surfaces of cancer cells. Antigens cause an immune system response in which certain white cells produce antibodies. Antigens serve as a target for the antibody to seek out so that antibodies can lock onto antigens and immobilize them. Genetically engineered antibodies, such as one named 17-1A, can lock onto the antigens found on the cancer cell's surface. In a laboratory culture, the antibody 17-1A killed virtually all human colorectal cancer cells without affecting cells that lacked target antigens. Through genetic engineering it is possible to similarly attack other kinds of cancer cells. Promising research is also being conducted on methods of attacking selected regions of DNA that may be responsible for specific kinds of cancers.

Through genetic engineering we can attack human cancer cells. One process is to create antibodies that can immobilize antigens that are found on their surfaces.

Controlling Cardiovascular Disease

BEHAVIORAL CONTROL

Signals that warn of a heart attack include dizziness, nausea, extreme weakness, excessive perspiration, shortness of breath, and a steady feeling of pressure on the center of the chest lasting for two minutes or more; the discomfort spreads to the arms, especially along the left arm, the neck, and jaw. If an individual detects any of the symptoms the immediate response should be to stop what he or she is doing, to

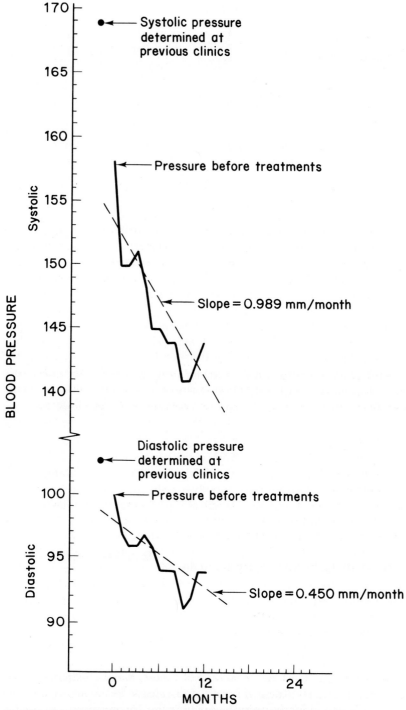

FIGURE 15.5 Mean decrease of blood pressure in selected patients treated with Clinical Progressive Relaxation. Follow-up data indicated that the decrease was lasting. (Data gathered by Dr. Edmund Jacobson at the Laboratory for Clinical Physiology; from McGuigan, 1978.)

relax, and certainly not try to fight the symptoms. To prevent any form of cardiovascular disease, people need to learn to relax the skeletal musculature and thus stop overreacting to the stresses of life. There is in turn a relaxation of the smooth muscle in the arterioles with a consequent lowering of blood pressure and decreased risk of vasospasm. In Figure 15.5 we can study a consistent decrease in blood pressure in selected patients treated with Progressive Relaxation. Values for the two components of blood pressure, systolic and diastolic, are plotted on the vertical axis. Amount of time spent in treatment and relaxation practice is plotted on the horizontal axis. For instance, we can note the average systolic blood pressure of these patients was about 158 when they began their practice. Twelve months later their systolic pressure had fallen to about 144. Similarly, diastolic pressure fell from about 100 to about 94 after 12 months of treatment. Follow-up measurements on these patients indicated that the decrease was a lasting one.

Unfortunately such decreases cannot be expected for all patients who have pathologically high blood pressure for two reasons: First, the muscular tension and other physiological reactions may have been so severe and so prolonged that the high blood pressure is irreversible. Many individuals have organically damaged their cardiovascular systems so that it is too late for relaxation to help. Second, although their bodies are not yet damaged, some individuals simply will not exercise the self-discipline required to practice relaxation.

Whether or not the reduction in blood pressure shown in Figure 15.5 was due to a direct, specific improvement in the cardiovascular system itself cannot unequivocally be answered, because by learning to relax the striated musculature you not only bring a restful condition to the cardiovascular system, but you also slow down the entire body. In an overly tense individual, the systems throughout the body are all racing excessively, including heightened pulse rate and blood pressure, an overactive stomach secreting hydrochloric acid, and tensed colon. When you relax the striated muscles you bring a more restful condition to the central nervous system and are indirectly able to slow down numerous autonomic functions. This set of relationships was expressed in Fig. 14.6 in which we saw how chronically contracted striated musculature indirectly drives various components of the autonomic system.

Other Factors. Diet seems to lead to a significant reduction in the risk of dying from heart disease. Saturated fat and low-density lipid cholesterol which can clog arteries that supply the heart muscle with blood should be reduced. Results of 130 different studies and reports indicated that reduction of blood cholesterol levels decreases the risk of dying from coronary artery disease by 30 percent. Actually the decrease should be in LDL such that the ratio between HDL and LDL is below 5; that is, if HDL ("good cholesterol") is 68 and total cholesterol is 243 the ratio is 3.57. Over half of the cases of high blood pressure can be controlled with drugs, and many can be controlled by loss of weight, lowering the intake of salt and alcohol, and exercising.

A long-term study of 50,000 men aged 40 to 75 has indicated that a limited amount of alcohol consumption is protective against heart disease in healthy moderate drinkers. Eric Rimm and his colleagues concluded that those who drank 5 to 30 grams of pure alcohol had a 26 percent reduction in the risk of heart disease (sudden and fatal heart attacks, nonfatal heart attacks, and clogged arteries) relative to those who drank 0 to 5 grams a day. A 6-ounce glass of wine has about 11 grams of alcohol, a 12-ounce can of beer about 13 grams. It was thought that alcohol renders its

Considerable control over cardiovascular pathologies can be effected by muscle relaxation, diet, medication, and exercise.

beneficial effect by increasing the level of high-density lipoprotein (HDL) in the bloodstream.

Panic Disorder

Sufferers of panic disorders are overwhelmed with intense anxiety sensations that something frightening is going to happen. There are sudden episodes of autonomic symptoms such as becoming flushed; shortness of breath; palpitating heart; feelings of being choked, dizzy, and light-headed; chest tightness or pain; nausea or abdominal discomfort; and sweating and weakness in the legs. There are often fears of having a heart attack. Four to 7 million people in the United States have such panic attacks with most of the sufferers being younger women. Those with panic disorder perceive their physical health to be poorer than comparison individuals. They tend to be frequent users of emergency, hospital, and ambulatory services. Accurate diagnosis of the presenting symptoms is difficult. It has been estimated that the average panic disorder patient may visit 10 physicians before an accurate diagnosis is made. The disorder may lead to agoraphobia. Although some family-history studies have suggested that there may be a genetic basis for panic disorder, that relationship has not been firmly established.

Successful biochemical research has indicated that panic disorder has a biochemical basis.

Since drugs often block or relieve panic attacks, it has been argued that the disorder has a biochemical basis. An observation in the 1940s was that strenuous exercise intensified the symptoms of people with chronic anxiety and also increased levels of lactic acid in their blood. When they were injected with sodium lactate, the panic stopped, apparently by reducing lactic acid. Further biochemical research indicated that three classes of drugs result in 65–90 percent of patients improving moderately or better: the antidepressants of monoamine oxidase (MAO) inhibitors, the tricyclics, and potent benzodiazepines (alprazolam and clonazepam). These medications act primarily in the central nervous system, which suggests that they control the disorder by modifying the central components of neuromuscular circuits. However, these disorders can also be controlled by modifying the peripheral components of neural muscular circuits. Thus, panic disorder, like phobias, is also treated quite effectively with behavior therapies, including relaxation therapy. Reviews of the literature have concluded that medication in combination with behavioral exposure to feared situations offers an advantage over pharmacological therapy or behavior therapy alone. Nevertheless, the advantages of adjusting the body through learning instead of taking medication are obvious. If one learns self-control to prevent and/or decrease the severity of the panic attack, the change may be considered permanent. The medication, however, must be continued indefinitely, with the disadvantages of side effects.

Bruxism ("Teeth Grinding")

We saw that a common tension problem is the habit of grinding the teeth, especially during sleep. Bruxism patients can practice clinching their teeth together for several seconds, and then relaxing the jaw. Repeating this procedure and continued practice with relaxing the entire body have successfully eliminated the grinding. In follow-up measures, the patients had not resumed the habit. In the application of Progressive Relaxation, special attention is paid to the relaxation of the masseter (jaw) muscle and as a result, bruxism is one of the earliest tension problems to be eliminated.

Gastrointestinal Disorders

Numerous successful applications of clinical Progressive Relaxation have been made for treating colitis, spastic colon, ulcers, constipation, and diarrhea. In treating such gastrointestinal problems, the clinician concentrates especially on abdominal relaxation, although one still relaxes the entire body. Edmund Jacobson estimated that perhaps 90 percent of the instances of constipation and diarrhea result from tension problems concentrated in the intestinal region.

Controlling Hallucinations

Since we have obtained objective data of psychophysiological processes (principally of the speech musculature) occurring during auditory hallucinations (see Fig. 13.14), one may speculate about how to control pathological hallucinations through conditioning or relaxation methodologies. The speech musculature is a critical component of the neuromuscular circuits that generate hallucinations. Elimination of that musculature component of muscle–brain circuits should eliminate the hallucinations. By conditioning the speech musculature to be otherwise involved or, perhaps more simply, by merely teaching the patient to relax the speech musculature, the patient's hallucinations could be eliminated through voluntary control. Heightened covert eye activity during visual hallucinations could also indicate that the same principle of control would apply to the eyes. That is, by relaxing the eyes, the visual muscle component of the relevant neuromuscular circuits would be removed, thus eliminating the visual hallucination.

Another method of eliminating auditory hallucinations could be to use incompatible behaviors to relieve them. For instance, some success has been recorded by having the patient count or listen to a radio program. One interpretation of these successes is that the auditory stimuli evoke echoic behavior incompatible with auditory hallucinations, or they simply drown out the stimuli that evoke the voices.

THE HEALING BRAIN — RECOVERY FROM BRAIN DAMAGE

Plasticity

Brain damage in humans typically destroys only certain neural circuits that function for specific behaviors. Recovery of the lost behaviors can occur because remaining, undestroyed neural circuits are reorganized. Perhaps through the formation of new circuits because of synaptic modifications, the reorganization known as **plasticity** occurs. Because of the great potential redundancy of neural circuits, only when there is massive destruction could there be no recovery of the lost behaviors.

Most plasticity research has been on animal models. For example, the sensory input to one brain region is altered to determine whether there are effects on other, associated brain regions. The brain regions thus associated have been modified in both developing and mature animals and have included the somatosensory, visual, and auditory modality areas. Cross-modality plasticity has also been demonstrated. For instance, when the afferent neurons for the visual modality were forced to innervate the somatosensory cortex in the hamster, neurons in this brain area often functioned like neurons in the visual cortex. Similarly, neurons in the auditory cortex

Plasticity is the phenomenon of neural reorganization that allows recovery of lost behaviors.

took on some of the characteristics of visual cortex neurons when they were innervated by afferent visual neurons; this occurred in ferrets.

Research on humans has included fetal brain transplants for brain lesions, the study of pathologic cells in Alzheimer's and Parkinson's diseases, and investigation about how the brain functions in immune disorders such as AIDS. We will sample some relevant phenomena concerning plasticity after which we will discuss reasons why it may occur.

Receptor or Peripheral Nerve Damage Affect the Somatosensory Cortex

Damage to a peripheral nerve or to receptors in an area of the skin affects the somatosensory cortex of mammals. The specific region of the cortex that then does not receive input from the corresponding part of the body undergoes reorganization. That is, the deprived regions in cortical somatosensory areas do not remain silent, but they are activated by inputs from skin areas near those destroyed. The part of the body that is affected is then represented elsewhere in the somatosensory cortex. Such reorganization of the somatosensory cortex after peripheral damage has been documented in rats, cats, raccoons, and monkeys. How this occurs is not known for sure. Perhaps changes in the cortex are the result of previously ineffective or unused connections; or gradual development of new representations may result when new or modified synapses form new neural connections.

After receptor or peripheral nerve damage, the somatosensory cortex apparently is reorganized so that other regions take over the missing function.

Regenerating Damaged Spinal Cord Nerves

About 500,000 Americans are paraplegics or quadriplegics. If spinal cord nerves could be regenerated for them, they could at least partially recover overt use of their limbs.

In general, the peripheral nerves have a better capacity to regenerate than do those of the brain and spinal cord. Axonal regeneration is common in the peripheral nervous system, as in cutaneous fibers that regrow to their original target. After a severe cut, sensation is lost in the tissue distal to the cut, but as the severed axonal nerve fibers regenerate, sensations can return.

Hemispherectomy

Hemispherectomy is the removal of a cerebral hemisphere as a last treatment resort. It is used for progressive neurological seizures involving only one cerebral hemisphere. The causes of such seizures include strokes, tumors, and viruses. After surgery, the patients function in a reasonably normal fashion, perhaps because certain brain functions migrate to the remaining hemisphere. Because plasticity is so much greater in young brains, hemispherectomies are best performed early in life.

One patient who had the left hemisphere removed was diagnosed as having Rasmussen's encephalitis, which is an inflammation of one side of the brain. Her first seizure was at 18 months of age, with the frequency progressing to 130 seizures a day. When she recovered from the hemispherectomy, her speech functions had apparently migrated to the right side of her brain. Within a month she was walking by herself in isolation from her parents. Other young patients have also successfully been treated this way.

Theories of Recovery of Brain Function

In the nineteenth and early twentieth centuries, people who were thought to have miraculously recovered from brain damage presented major challenges to neurologists and psychologists. Some of the interpretations of these apparent recoveries were noted by Marshall (1984):

1. *Alternative Strategies.* Patients achieve their goal with "tricks" by which they circumvent their lost capacities. For example, people who have damage in the visual cortex may compensate with especially active eye movements that scan the entire visual field; they thereby circumvent the missing visual fields caused by the injured brain regions. Apparent behavioral improvement thus occurs because of compensatory strategies and is not true neural recovery. In physical occupation therapy, patients seem to use their remaining brain more effectively, rather than modifying neurons. On the other hand, aphasic patients given speech training immediately after brain damage seem to improve more than when given the training after the first year; this does suggest true neural modification.

Some apparent behavioral recovery from brain damage probably involves behavioral compensation.

2. *Redundancy.* Considerable redundancy exists throughout the central nervous system so that even though there may be apparent recovery from brain damage, it is only because impaired behavior is mediated by alternative redundant, uninjured circuits. Redundant, surviving systems of neurons can function for behavior that otherwise would be lost.

3. *Vicarious Functioning.* This theory holds that brain regions surviving injury have a latent ability to carry out the function of the damaged system. Thus, neurons that were not previously involved in a particular function may assume that function after injury. This theory is distinguished from the redundancy theory because there must be relearning here. Work early in this century by Shepherd Ivory Franz and Lashley relied on this theory. They attempted to retrain certain uninjured regions of the brain to take over functions that had been performed by injured regions. The current thinking is that this is a rare event and when it does occur it seems to be in children with damage in the left hemisphere. The younger the child at the time of damage, the earlier speech is recovered and the greater is the degree of recovery. The right hemisphere may then regulate speech, but the right hemisphere would thereby also become less efficient at its own original functions (e.g., if the child becomes linguistically functional there could be a deficit in complex visual performance). Children with left hemisphere brain damage (and who apparently do have the right hemisphere take over the linguistic function) suffer from permanent deficits in complex visual–spacial abilities. There are some sound data that are consistent with this theory.

Spare, redundant neurons in circuits could provide a basis for behavioral improvement.

Franz and Lashley relied on a theory that other regions of the brain could be educated to take over the functions of a damaged area.

Removing Toxicity. Tissues surrounding a lesion are important for recovery so that not only is a group of neurons destroyed but the functioning of neighboring neurons is also impaired (e.g., chemicals in the blood from dead tissue may diffuse into nearby neurons, temporarily poisoning them). The temporary nonfunctioning of these surrounding cells adds to the behavioral deficit. But as time passes, the toxic materials are removed by glia or washed away in the bloodstream whereupon the

Recovery may occur when toxic materials are removed from the area around the lesion.

behavioral deficit, at least in part, disappears. Glial cells, which are ten times more common in the brain than are neurons, seem to nurse the injured brain area. Perhaps they also affect growth-inducing factors that may induce the nervous system to repair itself after injury.

Axonal Sprouting.   The dendrites and cell bodies of a neuron make junction with a large number of axons from other neurons. If one set of axons is destroyed, then the synaptic spaces become vacant. Within a few days to a few weeks the uninjured axons that remain in the surrounding area form new branches (collateral sprouts) that attach to the vacant synapses. This could account for some improvement; however, it could be disadvantageous too since axons could also sprout to occupy synaptic sites that are normally occupied by other axons. The different, improper connections could then retard behavior as in misconnecting wires in a TV set.

Some Data Relevant to These Theories

Evidence indicates that neural plasticity contributes to behavioral recovery after CNS injury.

Marshall holds that these theories have been resistant to experimental test. Relevant results for the older and traditional theories have been either disconfirming or equivocal. More recent research indicates that when lost behavior is restored, the CNS undergoes specific synaptic changes in response to injury. The evidence falls into two categories: (1) morphological, which emphasizes the ability of the injured CNS to form new synapses by axonal sprouting; and (2) neurochemical, wherein remaining synapses increase the synthesis of neurotransmitters, facilitating neural activity. Such neurochemical changes may thus facilitate recovery. After dopaminergic neurons in the brain are injured, there is synthesis of neurotransmitters with consequent recovery of some sensorimotor functions.

Axonal growth of immature nerve cells forms new functional neural circuits. The prenatal and neonatal brains are the most capable of growing and changing in response to damage.

Extensive axonal growth can occur following brain injury in the neonatal animal and also when fetal neurons are transplanted into the brains of adult rats. Replacement of axons in a severed pathway could then improve behavior. Sound data do indicate that this occurs; for example, sectioning of a cat's dorsal roots of the spinal cord innervating one hindlimb has led to an increase of other axons and an improvement in the use of a limb.

Infants typically recover from brain damage better than do adults, possibly because their axons are still growing. New connections may then be formed to compensate for some of those destroyed. The prenatal and neonatal brain is the most capable of growing and changing in response to damage. As the brain matures, it becomes more rigid and increasingly slow in replacing lost synapses.

BRAIN AND NEURAL TRANSPLANTS (GRAFTS)

The field of animal brain transplants is not new. A primitive brain transplant was attempted between a cat and a dog in 1873. Grafting of neuronal tissue to the mammalian CNS has been frequently attempted since the end of the last century, but the results were generally poor. In 1940 however, an embryonic neocortex was successfully grafted to the cortex of a six-week-old rabbit.

In 1979 it was discovered that grafted neurons are capable of interacting with a host brain. These findings have been substantiated in that many parts of the brain have been successfully transplanted into developing, adult, and aged animals. It is important, though, that the grafts come from neonatal tissue. Since 1979, neural transplants have increased exponentially and portend to lead to amazing clinical achievements. The most prominent in humans has been improvement of clinical signs in Parkinson's disease patients. Such brain transplants are not made with large pieces of brain but with pieces of tissue that have been gently broken up into a liquid solution of individual cells that are injected into a part of the brain. These transplants have relieved certain age-related motor and learning deficits but usually only for several years.

This experimental treatment for Parkinson's has followed successful transplantation of fetal dopaminergic cells into rats and monkeys that had Parkinsonian features associated with lesions of the dopaminergic tract. Transplants of fetal cholinergic cells have reversed learning, memory, and cognitive impairments experimentally induced by lesions to the brain. Fetal cholinergic cell grafting also improved the performance of aged rats relative to control rats in a water maze. Learning impairments in both short- and long-term memory induced by chronic alcohol administration to rats were reduced by grafting fetal cholinergic cells into the neocortex and hippocampus. The only primate in which cognitive recovery has been successful after transplantation is the marmoset. In disorders such as schizophrenia or Alzheimer's, the loss of nerve cells probably is so widespread that it would be impossible to treat the brain with transplants.

Mechanisms of Graft-Induced Recovery. Considerable research is aimed at discovering how fetal grafts facilitate recovery of lost behavioral functions. Sophisticated imaging techniques have indicated that grafts send messages to the host brain. It also seems that the host brain sends messages to a graft of fetal neurons. This was determined by research in which the nuclei of host cells were electrically stimulated and synaptic responses were found in the grafted nerve cells. To do this, the graft cells probably communicated with the host cells by extending their axons at least to the boundaries of the host territory. This phenomenon of a new two-way communication system only seems to work for neurons of fetal brain tissue; it has not been found in other grafts such as that of adrenal tissue. (The brain does not reject foreign tissue as do the heart and other parts of the body.) Apparently the grafted cells synthesize neurotransmitters that the host brain lacks, whereupon that chemical is sprayed into the host territory. For example, in Parkinson's disease, the brain lacks dopamine, a neurotransmitter essential for coordinating movements. The symptoms are often relieved by injections of the drug L-Dopa, a precurser to dopamine.

When transplants have been successful, the reason may be that the graft and the host brain have established new synaptic connections. The grafted cells probably emit specific neurotransmitters from their axons across synapses to the receptor sites of the host cells.

Total Brain Transplants? These may never be possible because of the millions of neurons that would have to be connected. Transplanting small parts of the human brain, however, is quite possible. Some day, too, it may be possible to modify regions of a person's brain. Perhaps the person's own regenerative powers can be increased biochemically. Tissue or even microchip implants might successfully replace lost nerve cells and the chemical neurotransmitters they produce.

However they work, brain transplants are very important, not only clinically, but because transplant studies also help us learn more about the brain's powers of regeneration.

CAN ONE LIVE WITHOUT A BRAIN?

We have considered the nature of living with impaired brains and ask this question in a sort of reverse strategy. It has been demonstrated that one can live without a hemisphere but can one live without a brain? John Lorber studied hydrocephalics who, because their cranium is filled mainly with cerebrospinal fluid, have severely reduced brain tissue. **Hydrocephalus** is associated with a disturbance of the circulation of cerebral spinal fluid through the ventricles of the brain. Pressure apparently develops so that the ventricles enlarge to many times their normal size and press the brain tissue against the cranium. The result is loss of brain tissue, sometimes essentially all of it. Although many hydrocephalics suffer intellectual and physical disability, a number appear to escape functional impairment in spite of grossly abnormal brain structure. In studying hydrocephalics, Lorber has asked: *Is your brain necessary?* One patient was a young university student with an IQ of 126 who won honors in mathematics and is socially normal, yet the boy has virtually no brain. A brain scan indicated that instead of the normal 4.5-centimeter thickness of brain tissue between the ventricles and the cortical surface, there was just a thin layer measuring a millimeter or so. This was not an isolated incident.

A WORD ABOUT STRATEGIES AND MODELS FOR RESEARCH

In constructing and testing our models, lower species and mathematical models for human diseases and disorders in conjunction with computers have served us well. However, it is impossible to avoid the use of mammals in medical, physiological, and psychological research. In trying to understand the brain, for instance, it would be impossible to use an alternative to a mammalian model. With nonmammalian, computer models we can only get out what we put in—computers cannot generate new knowledge. New knowledge about cybernetic circuits and their components can only be acquired empirically by studying animals and humans.

EMPHASIS ON A CYBERNETIC PRINCIPLE— MULTICAUSAL AND MULTIEFFECT MODELS MUST REPLACE SINGLE CAUSE–EFFECT MODELS OF BEHAVIOR

The traditional approach to understanding human functions and disease has been a one-to-one model in which a single cause is sought for a single disease. This model has served us well in many cases such as when it was found that a single class of bacterium caused a particular disease. In contrast, a much more effective strategy is required for complex diseases and disorders such as cancer and schizophrenia. For these, we need to employ a many-to-many model wherein scientists analyze the many components of a disease or disorder and then search the entire range of biological and psychological knowledge for applicable mechanisms. Any complex disease or disorder has many components and many contributing causes that interact (e.g., since there is little homogeneity among schizophrenics, it is likely there is no single cause of schizophrenia). How the causes and consequences interact constitutes complex cybernetic circuits. Just as we must abandon a linear nonfeedback model for biobehavioral phenomena, we must frequently abandon a single cause–effect model. A multicircuit cybernetic model in which there are numerous feedbacks among antecedent and consequent variables is the only approach that can be successful for understanding and controlling most of the phenomena considered throughout this book. The overriding strategy is that the various forms of behavior, both normal and pathological, are generated by the complex interaction of numerous neuromuscular circuits (see for instance Fig. 11.8). Control can often be achieved by intervening through the central components of those circuits, such as through medication, or behaviorally through their muscular components.

KEY TERMS

Affective disorders—Depressive and manic behavioral disorders with cognitive, emotional, psychomotor, appetitive, and autonomic manifestations. Neurotransmitter catecholamines (norepinephrine, dopamine, and serotonin) affect functions at synaptic junctions.

Agonists—Drugs that facilitate actions that can be terminated by administering antagonists.

Antagonists—Drugs that oppose and control the actions of agonists.

Behavior modification—See Behavior therapy.

Behavior therapy—Assumes that because many psychiatric and somatoform disorders have been learned, they can be modified through relearning or new learning. Therapy is designed to change the way the patient acts.

Behavioral medicine—A field that applies behavioral procedures and techniques for health-related problems that fall within the traditional context of medicine. There is a rich interplay among the principles of medicine, psychophysiology, physiology, biochemistry, and learning.

Biofeedback—A method by which events under the skin are transduced so that they can be monitored for the purpose of bringing them under volitional control. For instance, one can learn to control a muscle by observing its electrical activity on a cathode ray oscilloscope.

Calcium channel blockers—Chemicals that interfere with the cellular transfer of calcium to thereby prevent blood vessels from contracting.

Control signal—A muscular tension signal that helps us relax or tense so that one can effectively control behavior.

Cordotomy—Division of tracts of the spinal cord by such techniques as incision or radio-frequency modulation.

Determinism—Principle stating that there is order (lawfulness) in the universe, as in discovering cause–effect relationships.

Differential Relaxation—Learning to optimally contract (tense) only those muscles that are necessary for performing the act at hand.

Dystonia—Muscle spasms, typically in the neck and face lasting a few minutes to hours.

Electroconvulsive shock therapy (ECT)—Application of high-voltage electricity to the brain to stimulate convulsions for the purpose of combating severe depressions.

Explicate—To replace a vague concept usually from everyday language with a precise objective definition through scientific analysis.

Free will—Philosophical principle that people are capable of controlling their behavior.

Frontal lobotomies—Bilateral cutting of fibers in the frontal lobes. Early, holes were drilled laterally through the skull and then a surgical instrument was inserted. Later, the surgery was performed by insertion through the boney orbits above the eyes.

Gelotology—The science of laughter.

Hemispherectomy—Removal of a cerebral hemisphere as a treatment of last resort. It is used for progressive neurological seizures involving only one cerebral hemisphere.

Hydrocephalus—Condition marked by an excessive accumulation of fluid dilating the cerebral ventricles, thinning the brain, and causing a separation of cranial bones.

Hyperponesis—Hyper motor activity that produces emotional disturbances and may predispose individuals to depression.

Hypersomnia—Condition, probably toxic, in which one sleeps for an excessively long time but is normal in the intervals; it is distinguished from somnolence, in which one is always inclined to sleep.

Indeterminism—Lack of order in nature; a state of randomness in which there are no reliable empirical relationships.

Narcolepsy—Disorder characterized by involuntary episodic attacks of sleep during normal waking hours.

Neuroleptics—Medications with antipsychotic properties that function by altering neurochemical transmission in the brain.

Plasticity—Recovery of lost behaviors due to brain damage when remaining, undestroyed neural circuits are reorganized.

Progressive Relaxation—Developed by Edmund Jacobson, it teaches one how to relax and control the entire body.

Psychosurgery—The procedure of destroying apparently healthy brain tissue in order to relieve seriously debilitating psychiatric disorders.

Psychotropic drugs—Any of the classes of antipsychotic, antidepressant, and antianxiety drugs.

REM rebound—Increased dreaming due to previous REM deprivation, with the person often waking up during unpleasant dreams.

Self-control—Manipulation of antecedent variables that can control the desired behavior.

Sleep apnea—Condition that results in nocturnal insomnia and subsequent daytime hypersomnia. It is caused by the collapse of soft tissue in the back of the throat over the windpipe opening so that each time the patient falls asleep, breathing ceases. Consequently, the victim constantly awakens to resume breathing.

Transduce—To change one form of energy into another, a transducer may be employed to change electrical energy into mechanical energy so as to drive a machine with electrical signals from the body.

Trephine operation—Drilling of holes in the skull. It was an ancient practice to release evil spirits that were thought to inhabit the skulls of insane people.

STUDY QUESTIONS

1. Outline a brief history of determinism, free will, and how these concepts are related to Sechenov's view of volition and causal variables.
2. Discuss the relation of covert and overt speech to voluntary control.
3. "All events are stressful, even pleasant ones." Discuss this statement with examples.
4. Give a history of biofeedback, including its values and limits.
5. Trace the history of anesthesiology.
6. How does rehabilitation normally proceed for frontal lobe damage?
7. Discuss reorganization in the somatosensory cortex following peripheral nerve damage.
8. What is pain, and how is it treated?
9. Explain the relationship between stress and pain.

FURTHER READINGS

This is a good introduction to the research literature on ECT and how it is practiced:

Abrams, R. (1988). *Electroconvulsive therapy.* New York: Oxford University Press.

This is a presentation by five neuropsychologists designed to inform, stimulate, and educate psychologists from diverse backgrounds:

Boll, T., & Bryant, B. K. (1988). *Clinical neuropsychology and brain function: Research, measurement, and practice.* Washington, DC: American Psychological Association.

Two psychiatrists, one a cognitive scientist, the other a psychoanalyst, discuss the bankruptcy of psychoanalysis as a science:

Colby, K. M., & Stoller, R. J. (1988). *Cognitive science and psychoanalysis.* Hillsdale, NJ: Erlbaum.

This series, especially Volume 23, reviews behavioral and cognitive behavioral interventions and assessment techniques. Ex amples of treatment include those for bulimia, smoking cessation programs, and alcoholic behaviors:

Hersen, M., Eisler, R. M., & Miller, P. M. (Eds.). (1988). *Progress in behavior modification* (Vol. 23). Newbury Park, CA: Sage.

This is a comprehensive compendium of psychiatry that aims toward the development of a more behaviorally based science:

Kaplan, H. I., & Sadock, B. J. (1989). *Comprehensive textbook of psychiatry/V,* (5th ed., Vols. 1 & 2). Baltimore, MD: Williams & Wilkins.

This book explores clinical efforts to identify and evaluate therapeutic interventions that are appropriate to cocaine dependence, although there is no consensus on the most effective treatment modalities for this disorder:

Washington, A. M. (1989). *Cocaine addiction: Treatment, recovery, and relapse prevention.* New York: Norton.

Part V
Confronting Society's Problems Through Science and Technology

CHAPTER 16

The Future of Humanity as It Relates to Biological Science

MAJOR PURPOSE: To assess our future by sampling events that may be detrimental/catastrophic or beneficial and to consider ways to anticipate and control them

WHAT YOU ARE GOING TO FIND:
1. Illustrative developments leading to possible pessimistic or optimistic futures
2. Suggestions for how society can better engineer itself to enhance its future
3. How we *can* control and improve future human conditions through biobehavioral engineering
4. A sample of some scientific and technological advances that can serve as tools for biobehavioral control

WHAT YOU SHOULD ACQUIRE: A broad perspective for the present status of humankind, an enhanced ability for anticipating the long-term consequences of society's behavior, and a better understanding of how biobehavioral techniques of control can be applied for the betterment of society

CHAPTER OUTLINE

ANTICIPATING AND CONTROLLING
THE FUTURE[1]

Wise people have always benefited from their abilities to anticipate future events so as to better avoid defeats and achieve triumphs. Can we extrapolate to the future and apply principles of biological psychology for the benefit of biological science and of society in general?

In Chapter 14 we reviewed a number of the problems in biological science that we face and in Chapter 15 we applied principles of biological science for the purpose of solving some of those problems. In this chapter we sample broader issues that the human race faces. First, we assess a potential pessimistic future wherein humanity could fall victim to great disasters and lesser adversities. Then we consider applying control principles to achieve a more optimistic future wherein human rationality prevails and civilization flourishes.

In this effort we hope to enlarge our perspective as to how principles of biological psychology can be beneficially applied. To solve some of the numerous individual and group problems, positive reinforcement within negative feedback-like circuits can be judiciously applied. Stable systems (peaceful family and international relations, individual drug-free bodies, etc.) could thereby result. The achievement of such stable, homeostatic conditions can replace positive feedback systems that go out of control, as in drug addiction and escalating social aggression.

A PESSIMISTIC FUTURE

To establish a proper perspective to better understand our limits as human beings, we must recognize that there are future events that are largely uncontrollable. Humanmade calamities are, in principle, controllable, but some natural disasters are not.

When We Lack Control — Potential Natural
Disasters

THE BIG CRUNCH THEORY

It is commonly accepted that the universe began with a gigantic explosion and that the universe is continuously expanding. However, some data concerning the amount of visible and dark matter within the universe have led some scientists to conclude that there is sufficient gravity in the universe to slow and eventually stop its expansion. If true, the universe would then collapse back into its center with a "big crunch." Since that would occur in the extremely remote future, and since anything that could be done to prevent the big crunch would have to be left to far more advanced generations than ours, we will move on to more earthly matters. Nevertheless, recognizing a possible catastrophic future of our universe should sober us and provide perspective for recognizing our place in the larger scope of things. A less

A prominent theory is that the expansion of the universe that began with a "big bang" is eventually going to stop, whereupon the universe will start to collapse into its center with a "big crunch."

[1]We must be humble when we anticipate the future. Isaac Asimov gave an example of a futurist who predicts events when, early in his career, he wrote an article explaining why Mt. Everest would never be climbed. The next day that feat was accomplished.

remote possibility is that the species of the earth will become extinct. A model of this possibility is the well-studied death of the dinosaur some 65 million years ago.

THE EXTINCTION OF SPECIES

Theories. The traditional explanation for the extinction of dinosaurs has been that they died out in accordance with principles of evolution theory. The survival-of-the-fittest principle holds that as environmental conditions severely changed (climate, loss of regional food, etc.), some species became extinct while others were favored. Alternative theories with staggering consequences are that global happenings led to the extinction of much life on earth. Two possibilities are that there were catastrophic events from the skies or that there were gigantic volcanic explosions.

Natural Explosions — Comets, Comet Showers, and Volcanoes

Dinosaurs, as well as other species, could have become extinct because of the impact of comets, comet showers, and volcanoes.

Impact of Comets. Some of the twelve major extinction events that **paleontologists** have reported from fossil records have been related to the impact of comets. One explosion was estimated to be equivalent to 100 million megatons, which is 10,000 times as great as the combined explosive power of the world's nuclear weapons. The most recent major comet to hit the earth exploded in Siberia in 1908, releasing an estimated 20 megatons of energy (the equivalent of 20 million tons of TNT—the atomic bomb dropped on Hiroshima released 12 kilotons, which is one-thousandth of 20 megatons). Chemical and geological analysis of clay deposited at the end of the Cretaceous period about 65 million years ago yielded two samples that were selected from sites at opposite ends of the earth. The clay from both sites contained unique chemical signatures that could only have come from extraterrestrial sources, typically found in comets and meteorites. Minerals in the clay were "distorted" as if they had been shocked by a large impact.

Sixty-five million years ago a large asteroid or comet crashed into the earth, perhaps leading to the extinction of dinosaurs.

The astrophysicist Victor Clube holds that a violent collision between the earth and a swarm of comets is overdue and will certainly occur within one hundred years. The worst possible case, he predicts, would be the production on earth of effects similar to those of nuclear war.

Comet Showers. Comet showers occur when the solar system moves closer to a giant interstellar cloud of gas and dust in the Milky Way galaxy. The gravity from these immense galactic clouds disturbs the orbits of comets circling the sun. The sun, along with the planets, asteroids, and comets that orbit it, makes a complete swing through the galaxy every 250 million years. As the solar system so moves, it shifts up and down in relation to the plane of the galaxy and crosses the galactic plane every 33 million years. The immense clouds of gas and dust from which stars are formed are concentrated toward the plane of the galaxy. Consequently, the solar system would be expected to approach such a cloud roughly every 33 million years on the average. Research has shown that the earth has been punctuated every 26 to 36 million years by global events that have shaped continents, oceans, the direction of the magnetic field, and the course of life itself.

Research has confirmed a theory that the earth periodically passes through immense comet showers that trigger widespread impacts on the planet.

Volcanic Activity. The explosion of a large volcano could send enough ash into the sky to block out sunlight for months, cooling the earth's surface and extinguishing most life. Over the past 10,000 years about 1300 volcanoes have produced 6000 eruptions. The recent volcanic explosion at Mount St. Helens released 15 megatons of energy while other volcanoes have exploded with 100 to 1000 times that force.

A Death Star

The death star hypothesis accords with the approximately 12 distinct extinction events in fossil records separated by 26 or so million years.

Another theory is that there is a "death star" called "Nemesis," after the Greek goddess of vengeance and destruction. It is hypothesized to orbit the sun about once every 26 to 28 million years and to be responsible for the periodic, large-scale destruction of life on earth. The ages of 88 impact craters were grouped in periods that closely followed a 26- to 28-million-year cycle. This death star could explain why mass extinctions of life have occurred on earth at regular intervals during the past 250 million years at about the same time as large impact craters were made on the earth's surface. One hypothesis is that the death star's gravitation pulled billions of comets from their regular orbits and sent some onto earth to create large craters, enveloping the planet with clouds of dust and debris. Resultant freezing darkness could have wiped out numbers of species, including the dinosaurs.

OVERSPECIALIZATION OF SPECIES — BUT COULD INTELLIGENCE SAVE US?

We have considered natural catastrophes over which we presently lack control, calamities that could lead to the extinction of all species. That, however, would not be unique—it has been estimated that 99 percent of all species that have existed on the earth are now gone and that 50 percent of those in existence are in the process of dying out. As a general rule, all species that have overspecialized in some sense have become extinct; one instance is the ten-ton dinosaur triceratops that overspecialized by developing a huge skull with but a two-pound brain.

Our specialization in cybernetic systems of the brain and body that yield our relatively high intelligence have given us the ability to either destroy or improve ourselves.

However, one could argue that the species *Homo sapiens* has specialized in intelligence, which might be the one exception. We could use our intelligence to destroy ourselves as with nuclear war, or to help us survive. By astutely applying principles of biological science and more effectively using our frontal lobes, so to speak, we might avoid many potential disasters that we may face. An advanced civilization could conceivably exercise some control over natural disasters, with the probable exception of preventing the big crunch. Since mass extinction apparently occurs periodically, we could use the preceding theories to predict future catastrophes. For instance, we could predict the orbits of asteroids and comets that could hit the earth and design nuclear or other weapons to deflect or destroy such bodies before they arrive. It is also possible that we could take some steps to prevent explosions of volcanoes by tapping their magma to reduce the pressure.

With such hope and broad perspective, we now turn to disasters created by the human race which, by definition, could be totally under our control should we choose to exercise it.

What We Could Control — Humanmade Catastrophes

THE POPULATION EXPLOSION

A generation ago the world's population was 2.5 billion. It has more than doubled since then and is expanding geometrically. Estimates are that the world population will rise to 8.177 billion by the year 2025.

If these estimates are accurate, and some experts do hold that they are exaggerated, the consequences would be catastrophic. The disparity between the wealth of the "developed" and "underdeveloped" nations is widening. By the year 2000 it is estimated that 80 percent of the population will live in the underdeveloped countries and that their lives will be precarious at best. Africa and southern Asia have the lowest life expectancies, the highest mortality rate, and some of the highest birth rates. India's population of around 700 million is expected to increase to 1.8 billion by the year 2020, surpassing that of China.

Consequences of Overpopulation. Not only does overpopulation cause famine but also extensive destruction of the environment. An excessive number of individuals within a given region overuse resources, harm the atmosphere by burning fossil fuels, and destroy tropical forests and the protective ozone layer. Plants and animals suffer from poisoning of air, soil, and water, thus spreading deserts.

Human activities are exhausting natural resources and undermining the life support systems of the earth.

Possible Solutions. A truly major effort is required to solve the problem. To stop the population explosion we could just let nature take its course and, through natural selection, the "weak" will fail to survive. But that is precisely the kind of catastrophe that we seek to limit. It already is an international disaster on a widespread scale, with death rates due to hunger and inadequate medical care at a staggering rate. Steps could be taken to reduce the birth rate (e.g., China, with the world's largest population at more than 1 billion people, has decreased its fertility rate by 54 percent, though the measures have been stern).

Another alternative suggests that the planet does have sufficient resources to sustain a growing population, but that the wealth is unequally distributed. Enlightened policies could redistribute wealth to poorer countries to help them learn to feed themselves. More immediately, policies such as paying farmers to *not* grow food and the destruction of large quantities of food because of localized overproduction *could* be changed.

To prevent the spread of already existing catastrophes, world policies need to be dramatically changed, as in using military expenditures (about $1 trillion a year worldwide) to solve these problems.

More remotely, space travel could help to solve the population problem by sending our excess population to establish human settlements elsewhere in the solar system.

ENVIRONMENTAL POLLUTION

Chemical Pollution

Approximately 53,000 manufactured chemicals exist in our environment. They are contained in pesticides, drugs, food additives, cosmetics, and household items. However, as of this writing, the U.S. National Institute for Occupational Health and Safety has established presumably safe limits for only 588 chemicals, although few of these have been tested for their effects on behavior and/or for neurological damage. Most tests have been to identify potential carcinogens. This is unfortunate since some of these chemicals may well contribute to nervous system disorders, to Parkinson's and to Alzheimer's diseases, and perhaps to irritability, depression, sleeplessness, and memory deficits.

The toxic effects of lead have been known for 2000 years; we have known of the toxic effects of mercury for over 400 years. Yet only in the 1970s was the lead in gasoline removed. Removal of mercury from paint started only in 1990. Research established that there is a significant correlation between the levels of chemicals in people's bodies and their use of paints, solvents, cigarettes, building materials, and cleaning agents and their visits to gas stations or dry cleaners' stores. Specifically, there were reports that intellectual functioning of children was deleteriously affected; for example, children exposed to moderate levels of lead scored about five IQ points lower than children exposed to lower levels.

Although many chemicals in our environment may well contribute to various diseases and disorders, only recently have we attempted to control them as in removing lead from gasoline and mercury from paint.

In Japan in the 1950s mercury dumped in rivers was highly concentrated in fish, causing widespread death and neurological impairment among fishermen's families. In the early 1970s mercury caused at least 5000 deaths in Iraq after peasant families baked their bread with seed grain that had been treated with mercury.

Indoor Pollution.   High concentrations of chemicals in the home can be dangerous (e.g., the homes of smokers have thirty to fifty times more benzene [a known carcinogen linked with leukemia] than do the homes of nonsmokers). The "tight-building syndrome" has developed from office buildings that have been thoroughly insulated to save energy. Formaldehyde fumes escape from many sources such as carpets and copying machines. Photochemical reactions produce ozone. Eye irritation, nausea, respiratory discomfort, coldlike symptoms of the eyes and upper respiratory tract, difficulty breathing, allergies, asthma, skin rashes, headaches, and fatigue can result from dust, mildew, microorganisms, and other agents trapped in these energy-efficient buildings.

Asthma may be triggered by decayed bits of cockroaches that become mixed with house dust. In one study, half of the asthma patients tested in a hospital reacted negatively to cockroach dust.

Contaminated air in commercial jetliners poses potentially serious health risks from tobacco smoke, infectious germs, cosmic radiation, and ozone.

Exposure to Radon.   This odorless radioactive gas seeps into buildings from underground rocks and has been estimated to be responsible for about 13,000 lung cancer deaths annually. The risks from inhaling radon are greatly multiplied in cigarette smokers. In the United States it has been estimated that hundreds of thousands of homes have levels so dangerous that renovations should be undertaken.

In Conclusion.   The way that we pollute our earth has been called a blueprint for disaster. To clean up existing pollution requires a tremendously expensive, international effort. With sensible foresight, we could anticipate and prevent much serious environmental damage due to chemical (and other) kinds of pollution. The following are two examples of constructive efforts made within the field of biological psychology.

Psychology has biological instruments for detecting and controlling subtle effects of toxic chemicals within the subfield of behavioral toxicology.

Behavioral Toxicology.   The growing field of **behavioral toxicology** measures effects of chemicals on organisms by means of psychological tests to determine whether they are safe to be used. The goal is to prevent disorders such as motor deficits, paralysis, deafness, and blindness that chemicals can cause. Behavioral toxicology can also help prevent pollution by better designing our environment through behavioral engineering.

Behavioral Teratology.   **Behavioral teratology** is the study of possible prenatal damage caused by chemicals. It applies biobehavioral tests to study new food additives, medications, and drugs that affect the nervous and other systems. Until recently such substances have not been tested for their effects on the unborn. But the staggering problems created by the epidemic of infants addicted and deformed by cocaine, alcohol, and tobacco used by their mothers while they were pregnant has dictated this specialization.

Deforestation

Clearing of forests for farming and ranching has destroyed ecosystems and could extinguish some species. Some birds and pests are the fittest to survive because they easily reproduce and find ample food in such disturbed environments. Rats and cockroaches for instance suppress other species, further disturbing environmental balance. It has been estimated that a large percentage of the plant and bird species of the Amazon Basin is being lost.

Before many years there could be a dominant number of pests and weeds in deforested areas throughout the world.

Deforestation has caused floods, famine, and destruction of food sources such as fish. Increased flooding in Bangladesh has caused numerous deaths; in parts of Africa deforestation has led to devastating drought and famine. Estimates are that it would take 150 years to regenerate forests lost due to slash and burn farming and 1000 years for land that was cleared by bulldozers.

The Ozone Layer and the Greenhouse Effect

The stratosphere, that part of the atmosphere extending from about 9 to 30 miles above the earth contains ozone molecules that protect life on earth from the destructive ultraviolet radiation emitted by the sun. However, in 1979, British scientists discovered a hole in the ozone layer over Antarctica that is larger than the United States. The cause is chlorofluorocarbons used in refrigerators, air conditioners, and so on that remain in the stratosphere for as long as a century where they break down ozone molecules. It is estimated that by early in the twenty-first century the ozone layer will decrease by as much as 5 to 30 percent. That could increase skin cancer to epidemic dimensions. Skin cancer was rare in people under forty, but now it is prominent in people in their twenties.

The ozone layer surrounding the earth is being destroyed through the release of industrial gases into the atmosphere.

The decrease in the ozone layer is hypothesized to eventuate in the "greenhouse effect" that would devastate crops and ocean populations. Only a few degrees of difference in the earth's temperature can determine whether many species survive or become extinct.

The Automobile Crisis

Combustion of gasoline emits carbon monoxide, nitrogen oxides, reactive hydrocarbons (which form smog), methane, and carbon dioxide. An excessive number of cars waste billions of gallons of gasoline; pollute water, land, and air; degrade our environment; and contribute to the global warming problem. To control the automobile crisis, behavioral changes for society could include increasing fuel efficiency (which is the primary way to decrease automobile pollution in the immediate future); using cleaner burning alternatives to gasoline (natural gas, methanol, hydrogen, electricity, solar power, and fuel cells, etc.), and increasing the use of mass transit systems.

Gasoline combustion, especially in automobiles, contributes greatly to air pollution and global warming. The need for wider use of clean-burning alternatives to gasoline is necessary.

THE COUNTERATTACK OF BACTERIA

An Evolutionary Process. Antibiotic drugs are increasingly ineffective against new forms of bacteria. In accordance with principles of evolution theory, some bacteria have adapted, becoming resistant to all contemporary antibiotics. As antibiotics kill weak bacteria, stronger bacteria become more resistant. For example, if there are 1 million bacteria in an infected area and only one is resistant, 999,999 of them may be killed. However, the one surviving bacterium will multiply. Stronger and/or different antibiotics are then used against them, but the process continues so that eventually there are no effective antibiotics. Diseases can then attack the intestinal tract, lungs, skin, and other organs. Consequently, certain types of antibiotics are no longer effective against pneumonia and gonorrhea. For this same reason, tuberculosis, which was once thought nearly eradicated, is now making a major comeback.

Misuse of Antibiotics.   Throughout much of the world antibiotics can be purchased without a prescription; they are often overprescribed; and even livestock producers use them in animal food. In areas like the Philippines and Mexico, many prostitutes regularly take penicillin as a prophylactic agent. Consequently, antibiotic-resistant typhoid, gonorrhea, and shigella dysentery are widely found in these areas. Another problem is that although viral diseases do not respond to antibiotics, people still take them for viral infections.

Excessive use of antibiotic drugs is leading to strains of bacteria that are resistant to those drugs. The result is a limited ability to treat various diseases.

To prevent epidemics we need to be more conservative in our use of antibiotics while continuing to seek further pharmacological advances. One worldwide biological catastrophe that is much on our minds today is the AIDS epidemic.

ACQUIRED IMMUNE DEFICIENCY SYNDROME (AIDS)

AIDS is very difficult to transmit; otherwise it probably would have decimated the earth's population by now.

In Chapter 14 we saw how this fatal illness threatens to kill millions of people throughout the world. It is thought that the HIV virus prevents the body's immune system from repelling infection so that a number of diseases may be established. Fortunately, the virus is difficult to transmit from one person to another; otherwise, its effects on the human race probably would have already been even more disastrous.

THOUGHT CONTROL ("BRAINWASHING") AND SNOOPING

Controlling Thoughts

George Orwell's magnificent novel *1984* frighteningly depicted a closed society in which behavior was thoroughly controlled by an autocratic government. Most terrifying was effective thought control, some of which is with us today. "Brainwashing" techniques are used to change a person's belief system and perception of the world. Three critical elements are often used: (1) threats to an individual's well-being, (2) submerging the individual with misinformation so that he or she loses track of what is true, and (3) reinforcing beliefs that are incompatible with existing ones.

Phrased in terms of an operant discriminative stimulus training paradigm (Fig. 16.1), there is (1) punishment of the person's present beliefs (the response pattern to be suppressed), (2) presentation of misinforming stimuli to interfere with those existing beliefs, and (3) reinforcement when alternative beliefs are expressed (the low-strength response pattern to be made dominant). In Orwell's *1984*, slogans to misinform and confuse included "War Is Peace," "Freedom Is Slavery," "Ignorance Is Strength"; his concept apparently derived from Nazi Germany's famous "Work Makes Free" at the entrance to the Auschwitz concentration camp. People's belief

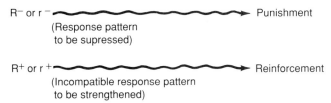

FIGURE 16.1   An operant discriminative stimulus training pattern that may be applied for changing a person's belief system. The plus and minus signs indicate the responses to be strengthened and weakened.

systems, loyalties, and affections can be significantly changed with the application of this methodology.

The Chinese brainwashed American prisoners during the Korean War by first persuading them to agree to an innocuous statement such as that the United States is not perfect. After elaborating on those flaws, they agreed to attach their names to the statements. The Chinese then got them to realize that they had not been co-erced; consequently, they experienced **cognitive dissonance** that needed to be resolved. To do so, they changed their belief so as to be consistent with their behavior of agreeing to the anti-American statements, resulting in what we call brainwashing.

Conditioning methods can be used in powerful ways. For instance, one could continuously monitor a target individual's thoughts through a thought-reading system and, when a specified thought appeared, electrically stimulate "pleasure centers" of the brain (like the septal region) for reinforcement and strengthening that thought.

Brainwashing by Cult Leaders.   Most cults seldom use physical force. Instead there is intense indoctrination. Typically, dependence on the cult leader is established by removing contact with friends and family and by inducing the victims to become lovers, employees, and so on. The victims often misperceive their world as when the brainwashed residents of Jonestown thought they were in paradise before they were led to commit suicide. The result often is traumatic, leading to suicide or even psychotic episodes. Philip Zimbardo held that the victims in cults put in more than they get out; they would not accept such an outcome if they understood it in advance. As he said, there is no contract up front that says "I agree to become a beggar and give up my family."

Effective thought control has been accomplished through various techniques that lead to control of the behavior of others.

Effective thought control techniques have been applied by cult leaders and others to manipulate people's behavior.

Snooping

Citizens in Orwell's *1984* were constantly under surveillance by two-way TV screens in their homes that could never be turned off. Today we have closed-circuit television sets that monitor us in banks, subway platforms, elevators, and so on. Employers often use video display terminals to monitor employees. They can use computers to count the number of key strokes, the number of items processed, and the amount of time that the employee is in the bathroom. Employers justify such behavior by saying that they thereby are better able to control fraud and waste. The reaction of

With the development of new technology, there is a major threat to the privacy of the individual in today's society.

employees to surveillance, as one can well expect, is typically negative. Reports are that stress-related diseases (e.g., headaches, rashes, nervous stomach, and insomnia) develop. Some workers have thought that companies send subliminal messages through their video display terminals urging them to work harder.

Our current data collection and storage systems provide useful information for society, but the dangers of misusing that information are great. The computer chip, which can store the statistics of one's life, can be tapped by anyone who knows the right code. Hackers are a great menace to society, having even broken into major military and business information systems. Not only do hackers retrieve information, they also alter it.

Computer Viruses

In computer terminology, a virus is a set of instructions implanted to spread among computer disks for the purpose of destroying files such as financial statements and students' grades. The presence of the virus may be detected when strange errors appear in programs or they may be intentionally diagnosed by other special programs. If there is extensive contamination, free flow of information can cease, making people very careful with whom they communicate by computer. To counter viruses, antidotes can be applied by writing special programs.

INTERNATIONAL WARFARE

Classical wars, those that do not use nuclear weapons, continue to be destructive, but the destruction is limited and reparable. Extensive biological and nuclear war would be another matter. Through the centuries, humanity *has* managed to progress in many ways but the real possibility of biological or nuclear holocausts has dramatically changed the rules. A nuclear war could cause debris and chemicals from burning forests and petroleum products to envelop the earth in a "global smog" that would drop temperature, stop photosynthesis, and kill plant life. Earth could be but a desolate radioactive hulk. The single reactor that had a near meltdown in Chernobyl in the former Soviet Union caused extensive radioactive fallout and destruction in Central Asia and Western Europe.

Biological warfare is not new. In ancient times, the Greeks and Romans used animal and human corpses to poison wells. Both before and during World War II, Japan used biological weapons. Bacteria and viruses could be effective weapons on an extensive scale, creating new diseases for which there is no known cure. Through genetic engineering, lethal diseases could target specific ethnic or racial groups (e.g., biological weapons could be based on a genetic characteristic to which blacks are especially sensitive). One study has suggested that geneticists could develop bacteria that attack specific organs such as the eyes of enemy soldiers.

No rational person or government would seriously undertake starting a biological or nuclear war. However, an irrational act by a madman at the head of a government, a terrorist leader, or an accident could start a nuclear or biological holocaust. Tight international control appears to be the only way to prevent such irrational acts. In an optimistic future, we would have an effective model for rationally controlling international tensions.

AN OPTIMISTIC FUTURE

Psychology's Critical Role

We have witnessed a sample of the numerous ways in which *Homo sapiens* can destroy the species of the earth, including themselves. A nuclear holocaust could do the job almost immediately, whereas pollution could lead to a lingering death. So long as we avoid destroying ourselves or being destroyed by forces beyond our control, we can expect science and technology to continue to contribute to our power to control our destiny through pure and applied knowledge. If we survive, it will be because psychology plays a central role. Many years ago Robert Oppenheimer, the physicist who was so important in the technological development of nuclear energy, prophesized the role of the future psychologist as follows:

> For him the acquisition of knowledge opens up the most terrifying prospects of control-ling what people do and how they think and how they behave and how they feel. . . . As the corpus of psychology gains in certitude and subtlety and skill, I can see that the physicist's pleas that what he discovers be used with humanity and be used wisely will seem rather trivial compared to those pleas which you will have to make and for which you will have to be responsible. (1956, p. 128)

The Japanese scientist Masanao Toda stated that,

> In the very distant future, psychology will be the master science. Psychology will be the most important of all the sciences. The reason? Very simple. Otherwise, mankind will not survive. And if no people survive, there will be no psychology . . . we will have to learn, somehow, how to live with our fellow men; and, in order to accomplish this very difficult task, our attention must inevitably be oriented toward the inner world within ourselves. (quoted in McGuigan, 1978, p. 441)

Let us now develop some of the ways in which biological science, including especially biological psychology, can contribute to the development of an optimistic future.

The key to an optimistic future and indeed to our very survival lies within the science and technology of psychology.

Science and Technology Interact

An optimistic future rests on the wise application of knowledge. The most rational process that society has developed for the acquisition of knowledge is through the scientific method. In **pure science,** knowledge is sought for its own sake. It has developed scientific laws such as the laws of thermodynamics and Einstein's famous equation $E = mc^2$. Scientific knowledge can solve practical problems; for example, the laws of thermodynamics were applied to develop a steam engine; and atomic energy was derived from $E = mc^2$ whereby mass (m) is converted to energy (E).

In the ongoing process of acquiring pure knowledge and solving practical problems, science and **technology** facilitate each other. Just as the fruits of pure science can often be applied for the solution of society's problems, research on technological problems may stimulate scientific advance. The existence of practical problems may make gaps in our scientific knowledge apparent and technological research can demand the development of new methods and principles in science.

Feedback between science and technology facilitate both enterprises.

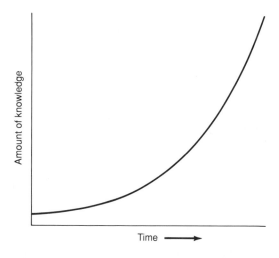

FIGURE 16.2
An exponentially increasing growth curve which, in this case, represents the geometrically increasing knowledge over the years.

Knowledge Explosion.   Scientific and technological knowledge has been expanding at an exponential rate (Fig. 16.2). At the same time, cultural lag , the interval between the acquisition of new knowledge and its incorporation into society, seems to be decreasing. For example, the wheel was invented about 5000 years ago, but it took many years for it to be widely used; but only four years and five months elapsed between the time that Einstein wrote $E = mc^2$ on the blackboard and Hiroshima was destroyed.

As Homer Dubs correctly noted long ago, increases in our knowledge result in still greater increases in the number of problems we can formulate. Being able to state a problem is the first step in its solution. In surveying a pessimistic future we stated a number of problems that have emerged through the development of knowledge. For instance without scientific advances, we could never have known that there was a hole in the ozone layer. Having stated that problem the next step is to engage in biobehavioral engineering in order to contain or eliminate the hole. More generally, it is critical that we anticipate threats to our survival and apply biobehavioral principles for social planning to prevent, or at least deflect, those dangers.

A Caution.   However, we should avoid premature applications of technology in efforts to solve threats that we face. For example, numerous malformed babies were born because mothers used thalidomide before it was adequately tested; and many infants were killed by injection of certain vitamins before the practice was validated. Humankind often walks a tightrope, making us wonder whether we do have the intellectual ability and the problem-solving capacity to really develop an optimistic future.

Biological Limitations

Do *Homo sapiens* have sufficient intelligence to solve their problems? Our genetic code (DNA) was laid down during the late paleolithic period and has remained essentially unchanged since then. The human brain itself is essentially that of some

50,000 years ago. There are no other major differences between modern and ancient humans in the striated musculature and other systems. Our genes constrain our development and we cannot wait for them to improve through evolution. We must thus rely on our existing capacities to attain an optimistic future. Humans do have remarkable anatomical–physiological systems that provide sufficient biological intelligence to solve the problems that we have brought on ourselves. Our ability to use abstract language to develop advanced scientific and technological knowledge is our primary hope.

The Value of Education

Granted that we have sufficient intellectual ability and knowledge to solve our problems, will we actually effectively apply what we know and what we learn to construct an optimistic future? Psychologists can make available the principles of learning and control that can facilitate the solution of our problems, but will society accept and apply them?

We have sketched out a sample of the numerous local, national, and international destructive acts that we commit. Well-educated citizens, supporting outstanding leaders who have sufficient discipline to react to our problems in a responsible and effective manner, could turn the tables. Government leaders who are insufficiently endowed in intellectual capacity and lack relevant knowledge only compound our problems. Why are the best minds not political leaders? Since it is the electorate who chooses leaders, better-educated and more objective and insightful voters could make wiser choices. Traditional modes of selecting leaders according to TV charisma and false promises are not enough.

Would a Multiple-Vote Concept Help Solve Our Problems?   The futuristic novelist Neville Shute in *On The Beach* sought to improve elections with the *multiple-vote* concept. Accordingly, each citizen's vote was weighted by the number of criteria (education, travel, etc.) that he or she satisfied. Because the better qualified citizens had more votes, the multiple-vote method led to the emergence of a superior nation.

Whether or not democracies of the world will be able to continue to exist with one vote for one person, weighting the qualifications of every individual equally is a question worthy of consideration. With one vote for each person, the assumption is that the opinion of a person with an IQ of 80 whose education terminated at the third grade or that of a psychopath is as valuable as that of a Plato. If the wiser individuals exercised more control over the development of society, perhaps uses of science would be better employed for improving the world. Those who engage in barbaric, destructive, primitive behaviors to the detriment of society could be more disenfranchised than at present. Gradually, with the power to control society being exercised by the more competent citizens, more people would receive more effective education, resulting in an increasing ability of society to correct its failures. At present, violence, gangs, and rampant drug problems are increasing according to the principles of positive feedback systems. Within past decades, for instance, the use of illegal drugs in the United States increased to epidemic proportions. In an optimistic future, we could intervene and replace such positive feedback systems with negative feedback systems that bring stability for the effective operation of society.

Contemporary humans are structurally almost identical with ancient humans. Only through genetic engineering might we eventually be able to increase our intellectual capacity within a short period. But we might still be able to solve society's problems.

Human systems have marked limitations due to unchanging genetic codes, but they still have amazing capacities.

Educational Interventions.   There are many educational scenarios to create an optimistic future. B. F. Skinner's astute applications of operant learning paradigms to the classroom are a start. We know that learning can be considerably enhanced if the learning task or material is (1) presented in small units that (2) evoke the appropriate response which (3) is followed immediately by reinforcement (e.g., the many subtle reinforcements traditionally used in education). The computer/electronic revolution presents fantastic possibilities for applying these and other effective learning methods. Computerized operant paradigms may sense what learners do not understand and guide them along. Electronic systems could deliver quality educational courses to schools and small rural areas, those in poor ghettos, and those in disadvantaged countries throughout the world; consequently learning effectiveness could be equalized with the more privileged regions. Life-size three-dimensional holographic images of teachers could be projected and engaged in programmed two-way conversations to enhance realism. Once such systems are in place, a wide variety of courses could be available economically, even for small classes.

A serious problem is that children are often unwisely raised by unqualified parents, so that they become a detriment to themselves and to society. If potential parents had to demonstrate that they are qualified to wisely raise children, birth rates could be sharply restricted and then only to competent, qualified parents. Society demands evidence of competence in many lesser respects, such as for operating an automobile. Might society analogously demand demonstration that parents have the requisite stability, temperament, knowledge, and ability to wisely raise children? Such demonstration could contribute to a more effective society by preventing child abuse, gangs of unwanted and unsupervised teenagers, and those born with the numerous disorders produced by drugs.

In Short.   For decades we have heard that "education could save us," yet our problems have become more numerous and often more serious. We need to intervene more effectively—if we increase the competence of our electorate, the competence of our leaders should increase, followed by increased competence of our children. We could then better apply the knowledge and tools that we have to solve

Education could be the key to an optimistic future.

our problems and develop a better world for all. This could be a favorable negative feedback system that corrects society until the stability of a peaceful, prosperous world is achieved. Education could save us if there is time.

Controlling Environmental Pollution

Considerable progress has been made on numerous fronts such as limiting cigarette smoking in public places and in decreasing smog. However, we are losing the battle on other fronts, such as controlling poisonous and radioactive substances that have been carelessly discarded worldwide. Untold billions of dollars are required to clean up the hazardous worldwide wastelands that we have created. It is difficult, but still possible, to be optimistic about pollution control.

We Need Imaginative New Programs.   For example, biological methods have been applied to poisonous material that would have been very expensive to clean up manually, as when it was eliminated by being aerated and mixed with mutant bacteria. Grease clogs in sewers have been removed by using a bacterial approach that was about one-third the normal cost. One can envision an environment in which numerous waste products disappear with the help of genetically engineered

Genetic engineering can design and use microbes for environmental cleaning.

microorganisms. If biological science solves such problems successfully, the potential could rival the applications in microcircuitry.

A Danger in Genetic Engineering. Unfortunately, we now know little about the behavior of microorganisms in the real world. The biological psychologist could contribute to research on them as a prelude to solving technological problems of genetic engineering of microorganisms that would make the approach widespread and practical. One issue is whether genetically engineered organisms pose a hazard if we lose control. Microorganisms could conceivably spread rapidly through host organisms with disastrous results.

Genetic engineering methods are potential effective means of microbial pollution control, but we need to learn more about their control

Pollution in an Optimistic Future. We would behaviorally control society to produce less waste; we would convert much waste into useful products and biologically control the rest. It has been said that what we now consider waste material is often just a resource not being used.

Biobehavioral programs could lead us to behave in ways that prevent environmental pollution.

The Miracle cf Computers

It is hard to estimate the impact of computers on society. In reviewing our major advances, we have to consider the computer along with the astounding developments of the use of fire, the wheel, and written language. We shall briefly mention how computers can help solve some of our problems. The most ambitious application of the computer is in the development of artificial intelligence.

ARTIFICIAL INTELLIGENCE (AI)

Artificial intelligence (AI), a field that overlaps psychology and computer science, is also contributed to by engineers, mathematicians, physiologists, linguists, and philosophers. The goal is to build and program computers that are able to carry out such human functions as perception, creativity, decision making and the production and comprehension of natural languages.

AI seeks to construct computers that are capable of human cognitive performances.

AI particularly seeks to improve our decision-making efficiency. If our vast knowledge was used to make important decisions in a relevant and organized way, our effectiveness in solving problems could stagger the imagination. Once again, though, we need an educated society in order to implement such wise decisions. Implementation constitutes a major problem as many decisions would run counter to what people believe or what is in their individual self-interest. However, the basic behavioral problem of how to implement new decisions with regard to AI is no different from others — we already know many unimplemented wise decisions that should be effected for the betterment of humankind.

AI seeks to program computers to think independently, one consequence of which is that decision-making effectiveness for numerous issues could be dramatically increased.

Perhaps people can have personalized computers that would be programmed for how and what they think and otherwise function. It could then anticipate one's program and efficiently achieve the goal and might even specify the goal with priorities. A simple example would be that a robot would sense your particular desires when you enter the kitchen in the morning and decide for you whether to cook a leisurely breakfast or hastily furnish a cup of coffee.

We saw how the Copernican and Darwinian revolutions pushed humanity further from being considered the center of the universe. As we increasingly recognize that thinking is no longer a unique human ability, humanity becomes increasingly but one aspect of a materialistic universe. The potential for computers seems endless. The next phase is for a fifth generation.

FIFTH-GENERATION COMPUTERS

In contemporary computers, information is transmitted between separate memory units and computing (processing) units and thus are limited because of the link between the processor and the memory.

The size and speed of computers is limited by the link between the memory and the processing units, a limitation that can be overcome with parallel processing in fifth generation computers.

In the **fifth-generation computer,** the semiconductor chips would themselves be miniature computers so that every chip would have its own processor and memory. A full-sized fifth-generation computer could have as many as 10,000 chips and each chip could work on various aspects of a single problem. This technology is known as **parallel processing.** Problems that present computers require weeks or months to solve could be solved by fifth-generation computers in fractions of that time. Applications for biological science should be impressive.

COMPUTER-RELATED DEVELOPMENTS

Neural Networks

Neural networks consist of units analogous to neurons that can be configured to accomplish tasks at which computers are slow, such as rapidly matching a large number of items.

Neural networks are not computers but consist of units analogous to neurons that can be configured to accomplish tasks at which computers are poor (e.g., neural networks can quickly match items, a task at which computers are very slow). Neural networks can compare an enormous number of patterns to find the best match for a particular stored pattern. For example, to find the person in the world who most closely matches your particular size, weight, and other characteristics, the computer would make some 5 billion comparisons, comparing you with each other person. To accomplish this, the computer would require perhaps eight minutes; it would take a neural network less than a second. A medical neural network stores information about symptoms, signs, treatments, and counterindications. By entering a patient's signs and symptoms into the system, it prints out the diagnosis and treatment. If there are questionable conclusions, the system can still provide alternatives with weighted probabilities.

Behavioral and Preventive Medicine

The reasons that people die unnecessarily are varied. Many deaths can be prevented without sophisticated behavioral engineering. For instance, many poor people throughout the world die of diarrhea, pneumonia, and measles, with most of the victims being children. Simple, straightforward measures such as better wells and toilets can prevent diarrhea and parasitic diseases. In China, family planning and vaccinations have cut infant mortality rates in half.

More advanced behavioral engineering is required in the developed countries. For instance, half of the deaths in middle age due to heart disease and cancer could be prevented by controlling tobacco and diet. We can prevent such problems in an optimistic future.

Length of Life Will Probably Continue to Increase. As we increase control over disease, normal life expectancy will no doubt continue to increase. Some estimates have been that we could live as long as 160 years on the average. Physicians will certainly need more training in geriatric medicine, as we concentrate on increasing the quality of life that deteriorates in old age.

Early Detection of Proneness to Diseases. Shortly after birth, genetic testing may assess who is susceptible to which illnesses. Someone who is susceptible to heart disease or to cancer could be behaviorally engineered to develop a preventive lifestyle.

Computerized Communication Systems. Immediate medical consultation throughout the world can help anticipate and solve medical problems. Computers can analyze massive data to present only relevant information to patients and physicians.

Self-Tests Will Become More Extensive. Today, individuals use home tests to diagnose blood in their stools, pregnancy, and sexually transmitted diseases. A variety of other tests will become more popular and more commonly used (but probably not do-it-yourself brain operation kits).

Scanning Methods Will Be More Extensively Used. Magnetic resonance imaging (MRI) is now used for the brain, spine, pelvis, and joints, but it could be applied to other regions of the body. With MRI, continuous three-dimensional visualization images can let us better study physiological functions such as heart beat. Thus we can move from stationary anatomical to continuous physiological diagnosis, with greater quantification and more precise localization.

Sonography (sound analysis) can determine normal baseline physiologic patterns that are unique for each individual. Any changes from the norm could indicate a pathological condition some place in the body. Such cues could then be followed up with other diagnostic techniques.

Some Other Future Developments. One cannot cease to marvel at the amazing advances that are occurring in biochemical and medical research. In the perhaps not-too-distant future, we will probably develop inhaling systems that protect the lungs against air pollution, antiaging drugs and hormones, and an artificial liver. Death rate due to cancer will probably decrease in part because of the development of vaccines specific for different cancers.

Medical practices now seen on "Star Trek," are well within reach in an optimistic future.

Genetic Engineering

The revolution in genetic engineering started in 1953 with the discovery of the structure of DNA. This and other milestones are presented in Table 16.1; Glossary appears in Table 16.2.

We can now identify many faulty or missing genes that predispose us to specific diseases and disorders.

GENE SPLICING

Recombinant DNA, which is known as "gene splicing," is closely aligned with what people understand as **genetic engineering.** In using recombinant DNA, scientists isolate pieces of DNA from a larger strand. Restriction enzymes are used to cut the genetic material at precise sites. The resulting pieces are then inserted into other pieces of DNA, which are usually short, circular pieces found in bacteria called plasmids. Plasmids carry genes for resistance to an antibiotic. After an isolated piece of DNA and a plasmid are recombined, the new plasmid is inserted into a host cell, which is usually a bacterium. The bacterium then clones as many copies of the recombined plasmid as the scientist specifies. Such genetically engineered bacteria have been used for manufacturing insulin to treat diabetics, to produce interferon for

Genetic engineering modifies genes in such ways as gene splicing (achieving recombinant DNA in which genetic material is inserted into pieces of DNA called plasmids).

A plasmid is a small, circular piece of bacterial DNA that carries a gene for resistance to some antibiotic.

TABLE 16.1 Major Stages in Genetic Engineering

1953 — The structure of deoxyribonucleic acid (DNA) is specified by James Dewey Watson and Francis Crick.

1957 — It is discovered that DNA reproduces itself into two strands.

1965 — It is discovered that sequences of nucleotides determine the structure of amino acids, thus deciphering the DNA code.

1970 — "Restriction enzymes" are used to dissect DNA.

1972 — Genetic material from two viruses is combined to form recombinant DNA.

1973 — Recombined genes are cloned by inserting them into host bacteria.

1975 — Pure (monoclonal) antibodies are made that can be targeted against specific antigens.

1978 — Recombinant DNA technology synthesizes human insulin as the first approved genetically engineered drug.

1989 — The U.S. courts approve the test of human gene transplants.

1990 — One form of a gene is exchanged for another in mammals and the modifications are bred through several generations.

treating cancer, for human growth hormone for dwarfism, and for many kinds of ongoing research. A number of products have also been developed for industry and agriculture, such as genetically engineered biodegradable insecticides that kill potato beetles, which are destructive worldwide.

MONOCLONAL ANTIBODIES

Monoclonal antibodies are purified natural antibodies cloned through genetic engineering for specific pathological functions such as diagnosing cancer.

Monoclonal antibodies are produced with a technique related to genetic engineering that involves cloning cells. We saw that antibodies protect an organism from disease by locking onto specific antigens (foreign invaders or "germs"). Monoclonal antibodies are highly purified versions of natural antibodies produced by a complex process that need not detain us here. But these monoclonal antibodies are developed for specific functions such as analysis of blood to diagnose pregnancy, heart disease, and some forms of cancer.

LOCATING GENES

The human genome is the genetic blueprint that scientists use to decode genetic information. It is encoded in DNA, which is composed of chromosomes that hold genes. The genome holds some 3 billion bits of information. About 100,000 genes in 23 pairs of chromosomes inside each human cell (except red blood cells) produce chemicals that affect every bodily function. Research seeks to chemically define all human genes and locate each gene on a map whereupon it can be copied (cloned). The result would be information about specific genetic diseases, genetic abnormalities, and predispositions for some diseases. Fewer than 2000 genes have been approximately located on chromosomes. Some of their specific tasks in the body have been identified as well (e.g., there are genes that program the making of insulin; without insulin, diabetes develops). Another example is the discovery of the approximate location of a gene that is a genetic marker for dystonia, a crippling brain disorder that affects at least 100,000 people in North America. Those affected with

TABLE 16.2 Genetic Engineering Glossary

Amino acids—The basic building blocks of protein.

Clone—A group of genetically identical cells or organisms produced from a common ancestor.

DNA—(deoxyribonucleic acid)—Strands that compose the gene and contain the basic unit of heredity.

Gene—Strands of DNA that carry blueprints for making amino acids, the building blocks of proteins.

Host cell—A cell into which external genetic information is inserted and from which a complete organism is regenerated.

Microbe—A one-celled microscopic organism.

Monoclonal antibodies—Identical antibodies derived from a single clone of cells.

Mutation—A change in DNA, that alters the genetic code.

Nucleic acid—Long chains of molecules composed of nucleotides as in deoxyribonucleic acid (DNA) and ribonucleic acid (RNA).

Nucleotides—The building blocks of nucleic acids.

Plasmid—A circular piece of genetic material found inside bacteria used for gene splicing.

Protein—Composed of amino acids, proteins serve as biochemical catalysts as well as structural elements of cells and tissues.

Recombinant DNA—A splicing together of new pieces of genetic material to form a single piece of DNA.

RNA—Ribonucleic acid, a nucleic acid that serves as a template for DNA.

dystonia have a distinctive variation in their genetic material on the long arm of chromosome 9, indicating that the gene involved in the disorder is located nearby.

If a gene is missing, malformed, or out of place, the chemical activity of the cell, and sometimes the entire organism, is affected. Such defective gene coding may cause more than 4000 human genetic diseases. These are thought to be caused by simple gene defects. Other diseases such as cancer are caused by multiple gene defects. Genetic engineering could prevent or alleviate these diseases by correcting defective cells. After success with animals, the therapy could be applied to humans either for the afflicted—somatic cell gene therapy—or for the progeny—heritable gene therapy.

Genetic defects can cause many disorders, diseases and deformities.

TWO KINDS OF GENE THERAPY

Somatic Cell Gene Therapy. **Somatic cell gene therapy** affects only the patient's body cells, not the reproductive cells. This noninheritable gene therapy helps patients whose defective genes cause serious diseases for which there is little or no treatment (e.g., to correct relatively rare enzyme deficiencies such as cystic fibrosis). One treatment is to remove cells from the patient's body and insert copies of healthy genes in place of defective ones; then the modified cells are returned to the body so that the new genes might function properly and correct the defect. Most applications to date have been of the somatic cell type.

One technique that has been successful in mice has been to inject genetic material into muscle tissue every few days or weeks. The genetic material is especially prepared to stimulate production of an enzyme or protein whose absence is the cause of the disease. The enzyme or protein is then carried by the bloodstream to body tissues where it is needed. The technique should be applicable for muscular dystrophy in humans. Healthy muscle cells from another person have been successfully transplanted into the muscles of patients with muscular dystrophy. The healthy cells began making the protein that is lacking in patients with the disease.

Genetic engineers have been successful in inserting foreign genes into plants and living animals.

Heritable Gene Therapy.   **Heritable gene therapy** affects the ova or sperm so that changes can be passed on to the patient's children. However, efforts to modify the genetic endowment of future generations have been attempted only on subhumans and plants. By transplanting the genetic properties of heartier life forms, they have been made more efficient and disease resistant. For example, a human growth hormone gene was transferred into a fertilized mouse egg. After the mouse was born, the human hormone helped it to grow to twice the size of a normal mouse. Also, a normal strain of mouse was produced by swapping one form of a gene for another and the engineered animals were bred through several generations.

Genetic engineering can affect a patient's body cells to correct genetically based diseases; heritable gene therapy could be applied to prevent diseases in progeny due to defective genes.

Beyond therapy, the heredity of human beings might be changed by removing or inserting genes into a fertilized human ova and then allowing those ova to mature into adults with new characteristics. Humans might be genetically engineered to be less susceptible to disease, more intelligent, stronger, faster, more agile, and so on. The technology is revolutionary with enormous consequences for humanity.

BEHAVIORAL CONTROL FOR GENETICALLY BASED CANCER

Cancers typically have a genetic basis in genes called **oncogenes** (*onkos* is Greek for "mass," as in the massing of malignant cells to form a tumor). A prominent theory is that everybody has at least one oncogene in every bodily cell. Environmental events then trigger oncogenes to produce chemical reactions that cause cells to divide and multiply uncontrollably. Millions of new cancerous cells are then formed to invade organs. More than twenty oncogenes have been discovered, such as one for bladder cancer. Behavioral engineering can prevent environmental events, like excessive exposure to the sun or smoking, from activating oncogenes.

Behavioral engineering could prevent much genetically based cancer.

"DNA FINGERPRINTS"

Each person's DNA is unique and can be identified through chemical and electrical processing that provides a record of dark bands. The technique is used in forensics to identify blood, semen, and tissue samples. Samples of blood stains and semen may be months or even years old and still identify an individual because DNA is so stable. The method has been used for such purposes as to settle paternity suits, to identify homicide suspects, and to identify rapists.

OTHER APPLICATIONS

Antihemophilic factor, the substance that helps blood to clot and is missing in hemophiliacs, has been successfully cloned. Genetic engineering is being applied to create endorphins and interleukin (a protein that helps regulate the body's immune system); for adenosine deaminase enzyme deficiency, a disease that inhibits the body's immune system; and for Lesch-Nyhan syndrome, another enzyme deficiency that leads to abnormal mental and behavioral symptoms. Research seeks to implant genetically engineered cells in the brain to treat neurological diseases by providing a source of certain proteins or enzymes. Disorders such as Parkinson's disease might thereby be eased.

FUTURE POSSIBILITIES OF GENETIC ENGINEERING

We have already witnessed amazing accomplishments and mentioned some possible future ones. Certainly, the revolution in genetic engineering has enormous consequences for humanity; even human cloning may be possible. Perhaps genes could be preserved so that, for instance, endangered species could be recreated at a later time. Some have even wondered whether retrieval of DNA from extinct species might be used to revive the species. What kind of world would we have if we recreated dinosaurs?

The future of gene splicing has tremendous medical potential such as to produce vaccines for AIDS, hepatitis, and herpes and to cure or prevent some forms of cancer, sickle-cell anemia, and hemophilia. For inherited diseases, the responsible genes could be replaced in the womb so that the child is born healthy.

By growing crops that resist disease and that thrive under bad weather and soil conditions, we could provide ample food to feed needy people throughout the world.

Continuing research is paving the way for genetic engineering to be used extensively to treat people and for human benefit in an optimistic future, but there are potential problems.

There have been numerous beneficial applications of genetic engineering, but the possibilities for the future are much greater. Those applications present a variety of ethical questions.

ETHICAL ISSUES IN GENETIC ENGINEERING

Before we could produce human genetic changes that can be passed on from generation to generation, society will have to make some difficult decisions. Somatic genetic therapy for inherited disorders that only affect individuals and not their offspring is in principle no different from other medical treatments and thus raises no new ethical issues. But to make genetic changes that are passed on to subsequent generations requires more thought and research before proceeding. There could be unfortunate unforeseen consequences. The transfer of a genetic trait from one mammalian species into the germ line of another unrelated mammalian species presents another major ethical question. We need to develop a good understanding of the processes for animals before we consider humans. One vehicle for that is a professional journal entitled *Ethics and Behavior*, which publishes articles on a wide variety of areas, including law, medicine, pediatrics, psychiatry, psychology, and public health. Problem cases concerning general issues has led to a new field called bioethics.

WARFARE—AN OPTIMISTIC FUTURE

The basic problem of international warfare is that it follows positive feedback circuits such as in the increasing buildup of war weapons between the Soviet Union and the United States as a result of increasing international tensions. Applying a general principle that we illustrate throughout this book, the solution is to intervene into such a positive feedback system and produce the stability that occurs with a negative feedback system, as in Charles Osgood's (1957) GRIT, Graduated Reduction in International Tension. A similarly based behavioral model was developed by McGuigan (1970b) in which professor Henry Kissenger indicated interest prior to becoming secretary of state and which resembles many aspects of his often successful detente.

BIOETHICS

In conducting research on humans and on animals, scientists have, over the centuries, made numerous remarkable contributions to knowledge. As a result, we better understand how organisms function and behave and how to alleviate and prevent numerous disorders and diseases. Countless lives have been saved. On the other hand, some scientists have violated basic principles of research, most notably the medical experiments by the Axis Powers before and during World War II. Atrocious and inhumane treatments were administered.

The main guideline to prevent unethical research is that the scientist assumes obligations for the welfare of the participants in the research. Having assumed that responsibility, the scientist seriously evaluates each aspect of the research in order to maintain the dignity and welfare of the participants.

This principle has served us well, there being almost no cases of violation of ethical principles in science considering the enormous number of studies that have been conducted. However, as new advances occur, novel issues are raised, leading to the development of a field called bioethics. **Bioethics** is the study of legal and moral issues raised by advances in biological science.

Standard guidelines for the ethical conduct of research have been well applied, but new advances have led to numerous new issues and to the developing field of bioethics.

Within bioethics, ethical principles are continuously considered as new problems develop. For instance, there are many questions when an individual loses capacity due to a nonfunctioning brain. Should the unconscious body survive or should life supports be withdrawn for hopelessly comatose patients? Should such decisions be made by a court, medical doctor, family, or someone else? Similarly, does a competent yet hopeless patient have the "right to die"? An understanding physician who has helped terminally ill patients use a "suicide machine" has been repeatedly charged with murder.

Many ethical issues are raised by new reproductive techniques such as in vitro fertilization, embryo transfers, surrogate motherhood, in utero therapy, artificial insemination from a donor, sterilization, and abortion.

In addition, what should be the ethics of control of the mentally ill? Issues include involuntary commitment and the competency of the mentally ill to consent to or refuse treatments such as ECT.

Other debated issues have included the case of the human Baby Fae who became the recipient of a baboon heart; a man with a fatal disease who sued to be removed from the artificial life support systems that kept him alive; and a cerebral palsy victim who unsuccessfully sued to force physicians to keep her comfortable while she starved herself to death.

Research on test-tube babies initially proceeded without any problems, but ethical questions were later raised. In one case in Australia, two test-tube embryos frozen in liquid nitrogen were orphaned after their wealthy parents were killed in an air crash. Should they have been thawed out and implanted in a surrogate mother so that they could inherit their fortune?

Research on embryos holds great promise for humanity, such as opening up new vistas for treating diseases. Embryos could be grown to provide tissue for transplants into adults. They could also be used for research for the first 14 days of life and new drugs could beneficially be tested on them during that period. Should such research be permitted?

Artificial "wombs" in which children could develop entirely outside their mother's bodies have been suggested. This would increase the freedom of women by providing them with nonbreeding life and work roles that do not retard their progress because of having children. It also would free them from active interaction with men, should that be their desire.

Not only do these issues raise questions for society in general but also for researchers themselves, who are asking for legislation so that they know where they stand before the law.

As additional advances are made in biological science, society needs to continuously formulate guidelines for such issues as we have sampled.

CONCLUSION

We have seen that our world is fraught with many dangers. Whether or not we will live in an optimistic or pessimistic future constitutes the primary problem for human behavior. Our goals are clear: We need to control aggression and reckless use of material things, to stop polluting, to stop excessive population growth. To achieve these goals, the nations of the world need to make Herculean efforts. It is comforting to know that we do have the requisite science and technology. The large majority of all scientific knowledge has been acquired in the past several decades and this knowledge will probably double in the next decade or two. B. F. Skinner has shown the power of the major controlling institutions of government, religion, economy, and others and how that power could be brought to bear for the solution of our problems.

The choice is not the scientist's. The choice is society's at large. If the composite of individuals throughout the world come to wisely apply our basic biopsychological principles, the fruits of science and technology can be effectively used for the benefit of the many and for our productive survival.

Will society wisely use our knowledge for determining the kind of world in which civilization can survive and flourish?

EMPHASIS ON A CYBERNETIC PRINCIPLE— INTERVENING INTO POSITIVE FEEDBACK SYSTEMS TO ACHIEVE STABLE NEGATIVE FEEDBACK SYSTEMS

Many potential calamities are based on unrestricted exponentially increasing growth trends. Predictions of the population explosion are one example (Fig. 16.3). In a comic vein, some predictions made in the *Journal of Irreproducible Results* illustrate

Extrapolations from data often indicate exponentially increasing growth curves that predict catastrophes.

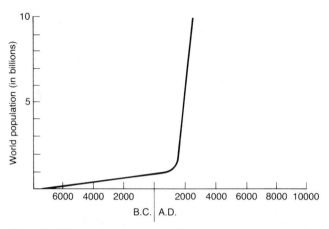

FIGURE 16.3   An exponentially increasing growth curve representing the population explosion.

the principle. Scientists pointed out that more than 6.8 million issues of the magazine *National Geographic,* each weighing two pounds, are sent to subscribers monthly and that not one copy has been thrown away since publication began about a century ago. Thus, if everyone keeps stacking *National Geographic* instead of throwing them away, it is predicted that the weight of the magazines will soon sink our continent 100 feet and we will all be inundated by the oceans.

Another prediction is that if beachgoers keep returning with as much sand clinging to them as do they now, 80 percent of the country's coastline will disappear in ten years.

Obviously such predictions are absurd, although they have sound data bases. What is wrong with them is that boundary conditions have not been specified so that in each case there may be limits to a growth curve; growth curves thus can slope off, reaching asymptotes, as in Figure 16.4.

Simple extrapolations about future problems by using past growth rates are typically inappropriate since exponential growth curves do not inevitably continue.

But how do we know whether a growth curve will continue increasing or whether it will slope off? At the present rate of population growth, there would be some 7 billion people on earth by the year 2000 and 25 billion long before the year 2100, which is about five times the present number. If 25 billion people drove five times more cars and walked on our sidewalks, there would be standing room for elephants only.

Doomsdays, based on extrapolations of growth curves, could occur unless other forces intervene, which they often do.

An extended period of time beyond an exponentially rising curve usually reveals that the growth curve is only part of an S-shaped curve.

Fortunately, our accumulated knowledge about growth curves leads us to apply a higher order prediction; that is, growth curves typically flatten out or even turn downward when growth comes up against some kind of barrier. When growth trends do slow down as they reach a limit, stable states often develop. Malthus's famous law is such a case. Malthus, we may recall, assessed that population growth increases geometrically, but the food supply only increases arithmetically. The limited food supply thus causes the population growth to reach a barrier and slope off. For example, bacteria grow exponentially, but as nutrients are consumed the colony stabilizes.

We can conceive of the growth portion of an exponentially increasing curve as the functioning of a positive feedback system. Eventually, the system can go out of

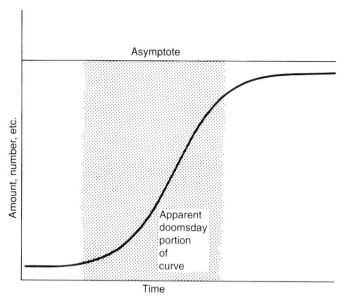

FIGURE 16.4 An S-shape growth curve that slopes off as it approaches its asymptote. By studying only the shaded portion one might incorrectly infer a "doomsday scenario."

control, which results in a doomsday scenario. The population explosion is an apt example — the greater the number of infants born, the larger the population; and the larger the population, the greater the increase in newborns. Similarly, with frequency of drug addiction, the more addicts there are, the greater the supply of illegal drugs; and the more drugs available, the greater the number of addicts.

A major premise of this chapter is that some rational social force needs to intervene into some growth systems to prevent catastrophe. If an external force intervenes, the growth curve may slope off. In cybernetic terms, we need to close the open circuit positive feedback systems so as to change them into negative feedback systems that can become stable. With adequate control for subtracting or adding to the population, for instance, to keep it at a standard target value, a stable population can result that is commensurate with the earth's ongoing resources. Events that can intervene on growth curves may be natural, as in catastrophes that reduce the population of a species in accordance with evolution principles. There may also be intentional intervention, such as we advocate through biobehavioral techniques of control. A behavioral analysis identifies such behaviors as we have discussed that deleteriously affect the environment. It also specifies how the environment in turn affects the behavior of people. For example, as environmental temperature increases, our forests are destroyed and people abandon land that is no longer usable. Large-scale cybernetic circuits function wherein people cause destruction of their environment and destruction of the environment causes them to change their behavior. Through behavioral engineering we can intervene into such circuits so as to eliminate the positive feedback effect that exists.

It is a major goal of this book to encourage wise control for the world's many individual and societal problems. It is hoped that we will replace potentially calami-

We can characterize the exponentially increasing section of a growth curve as fitting a positive feedback system that is going out of control.

tous personal and cultural positive feedback systems with stable negative feedback systems.

KEY TERMS

Artificial intelligence (AI) — An interdisciplinary science that seeks to empower a computer to perceive, create, reason, plan, imagine, and act.

Behavioral teratology — The use of biobehavioral tests in the study of possible prenatal damage caused by chemicals.

Behavioral toxicology — Measures the effects of chemicals by means of psychological tests to determine whether the chemicals are safe to be used.

Bioethics — The study of legal and moral issues raised by advances in biological science.

Cognitive dissonance — The assumption is that a person is motivated to maintain consistency or consonance among pairs of relevant cognitions such as thoughts or beliefs. If cognitions are dissonant one is "psychologically uncomfortable" so that there is pressure to reduce the dissonance by changing a behavior or belief.

Fifth-generation computers — Hypothesized computers containing chips that are little computers with independent processors and memories that make parallel processing possible.

Genetic engineering — An enterprise to modify genes in such ways as gene splicing (achieving recombinant DNA in which genetic material is inserted into pieces of DNA called plasmids).

Heritable gene therapy — An application of genetic engineering to prevent defective genes from being passed on to progeny.

Neural networks — Models of subsystems consisting of units analogous to neurons, configured to accomplish tasks at which computers are poor (e.g., matching data).

Oncogenes — Tumor-causing genes.

Paleontology — A science that deals with the life of past geological periods based on the study of fossil remains of plants and animals. It gives information about the phylogeny and relationships among modern animals and plants and about the chronology of the history of the earth.

Parallel processing — Technology in which several processors can run simultaneously. For example, humans can carry out a number of tasks at the same time as numerous neuromuscular circuits simultaneously reverberate.

Science (pure, basic) — The conduct of systematic inquiries only for the sake of knowledge itself, without regard to the solution of practical problems. Our universities are the primary agents for the search for knowledge for its own sake, and for the retention of that knowledge for society. (Contrast with *technology.*)

Somatic cell gene therapy — An application of genetic engineering to help patients whose defective genes have caused serious disease such as removing the defective cells and inserting copies of healthy genes.

Sonography — Sound analysis that can determine physiologic patterns that are unique for each individual. The results may be transcribed into phonetic symbols.

Technology — The activity of solving problems of immediate need in everyday life. Many of these problems can be solved by the application of the fruits of pure science whereas others require the conduct of empirical research "in the field." (Contrast with *science.*)

STUDY QUESTIONS

1. What is the Nemesis hypothesis?
2. Discuss the consequences and possible solutions of overpopulation in the world.
3. Describe environmental (including home) pollution and possibilities of controlling it.
4. Describe the potential dangers of "thought control."
5. "Every increase in our knowledge re-

sults in a greater increase in the number of problems we can formulate." Discuss this assertion by Homer Dubs.

6. List some "milestones" in genetic engineering.

7. Discuss perspectives and problems in genetic engineering.

8. What is bioethics?

9. What is your opinion of how society will use scientific knowledge in the future?

10. Consider how methods of biobehavioral engineering can be used to solve many of society's problems.

FURTHER READINGS

The following books make interesting reading for doomsday scenarios:

Gololsmith, D. (1986). *Nemesis: The Death Star and other theories of mass extinction.* New York: Berkeley Publisher.
Rave, D. M. (1986). *The Nemesis affair.* New York: W. W. Norton & Co.

Experts in their fields debate topics within the categories of foreign policy (e.g., nuclear war), domestic policy (e.g., pornography), and criminal justice (e.g., eyewitness testimony):

Suedfeld, P., & Tetlock, P. E. (Eds.). (1992). *Psychology and social policy.* New York: Hemisphere.

This book is a reasoned discussion of potential catastrophes:

Karplus, W. J. (1992). *The heavens are falling: The scientific prediction of catastrophes in our time.* New York: Plenum Press.

References

Adams, J. A. (1976). Issues for a closed-loop theory of motor learning. In G. E. Stelmach (Ed.), *Motor control—Issues and trends* (pp. 87–105). New York: Academic Press.

Akil, H., Watson, S. J., Young, E., Lewis, M. E., Khachaturian, H., & Walker, J. M. (1984). Endogenous opioids: Biology and function. *Annual Reviews of Neuroscience, 7,* 223–255.

Alkon, D. L. (1983). Learning in a marine snail. *Scientific American, 249,* 64–74.

Anokhin, P. K. (1974). Biology and neurophysiology of the conditioned reflex and its role in adaptive behavior. In A. C. Samuel (Ed.), *International series of monographs in cerebrovisceral and behavioral physiology and conditioned reflexes.* New York: Pergamon.

Anrep, G. V. (1920). Pitch discrimination in the dog. *Journal of Physiology, 53,* 367–385.

Babkin, B. P. (1928). *Die aussere sekretion der Verdauungsdrusen.* Berlin: J. Springer.

Bain, A. (1855). *The senses and the intellect.* London: Parker.

Bakal, D. A. (1982). *New perspectives on headache.* New York: Springer.

Bandler, R. (1988). *Modulation of sensorimotor activity during alterations in behavioral states.* New York: Alan R. Liss.

Bard, P. (1934). An emotional expression after decortication with some remarks on certain theoretical views. Parts I and II. *Psychological Review, 41,* 309–329, 424–449.

Beach, F. A. (1950). The snark was a boojum. *The American Psychologist, 5,* 115–124.

Beaumont, J. G. (1984). *Introduction to neuropsychology.* New York: Guilford Press.

Bebbington, P., & McGuffin, P. (Eds.). (1988). *Schizophrenia: The major issues.* Oxford, England: Heinemann Medical Books/Heinemann Professional.

Bell, Sir C. (1842). On the necessity of the sense of muscular action to the full exercise of the organs of the senses. *Proceedings of the Royal Society of Edinburgh,* pp. 361–363.

Bellissimo, A., & Tunks, E. (1984). *Chronic pain, the psychotherapeutic spectrum.* New York: Praeger.

Benson, D. F. (1967). Fluency in aphasia: Correlation with radioactive scan localization. *Cortex, 3,* 373–394.

Berger, H. (1929). Über das Elektrekehalogramm des Menschen. *Archiv für Psychiatrie Nervenkrankheiten, 87,* 527–570.

Berger, S. M. (1962). Conditioning through vicarious instigation. *Psychological Review, 69,* 450–466.

Berger, S. M., & Hadley, S. W. (1975). Some effects of a model's performance on an observer's electromyographic activity. *American Journal of Psychology, 88,* 263–276.

Berger, S. M., Irwin, D. S., & Frommer, G. P. (1970). Electromyographic activity during observational learning. *American Journal of Psychology, 83,* 86–94.

Berkowitz, L. (1989). Frustration-aggression hypothesis: Examination and reformation. *Psychological Bulletin, 1,* 59–73.

Berne, R. M., & Hoffman, J. F. (1984). Annual review of physiology. *Annual Reviews of Physiology, 46.*

Bertalanffy, L. von. (1968). *General systems theory.* New York: Braziller.

Beurle, R. L. (1956). Properties of a mass of cells capable of regenerating pulses. *Philosophical Transactions of the Royal Society. (London), 240,* 55–94.

Bitterman, M. E. (1975). The comparative analysis of learning. *Science, 188,* 669–709.

Bloom, F. E. (1988). Neurotransmitters: Past, present, and future directions. *FASEB Journal, 2,* 32–41.

Boll, T., & Bryant, B. K. (1988). *Clinical neuropsychology and brain function: Research, measurement, and practice.* Washington, DC: American Psychological Association.

Boring, E. G. (1929). *A history of experimental psychology.* New York: D. Appleton-Century Co.

Boring, E. G. (1942). *Sensation and perception in the history of experimental psychology.* New York: D. Appleton-Century Co.

Borkan, G. A., & Norris, A. H. (1980). Assessment of biological age using a profile of physical parameters. *Journal of Gerontology, 35,* 177–184.

Bortz, W. M. (1984). Executive health. *Scientific American, 250.*

Botwinick, J., West, R., & Storandt, M. (1978). Predicting death from behavioral test performance. *Journal of Gerontology, 33,* 755–762.

Bousfield, W. A. (1955). Lope de Vega on early conditioning. *American Psychologist, 10,* 828.

Bowman, J. P., & Combs, C. M. (1969). The cerebrocortical projection of hypoglossal afferents. *Experimental Neurology, 23,* 291–301.

Brittain, R. W., & Wiener, N. I. (1985). Neural and Pavlovian influences on immunity. *Pavlovian Journal of Biological Science, 4,* 181–194.

Brown, J. W. (1975). The problem of repetition: A study of *"conduction" aphasia* and the "isolation" syndrome. *Cortex, 11,* 37–52.

Bryden, M. P., & Ley, R. G. (1983). Right-hemispheric involvement in the perception and expression of emotion in normal humans. In K. M. Heilman & P. Satz (Eds.), *Neuropsychology of human emotion* (pp. 6–44). New York: Guilford.

Buchsbaum, M. S. (1984). The genain quadruplets. *Psychology Today,* pp. 46–51.

Buck, R. (1984). *The communication of emotion.* New York: Guilford Press.

Burish, T. G., & Redd, W. H. (1983). Behavioral approaches to reducing conditioned responses to chemotherapy in adult cancer patients. *Behavioral Medicine Update, 5,* 12–16.

Burtt, H. E. (1941). An experimental study of early childhood memory. *Journal of Genetic Psychology, 58,* 435–439.

Carlson, N. R. (1991). *Physiology of behavior* (4th ed). Newton, MA: Allyn & Bacon.

Carlson, J. N., & Glick, S. D. (1989). Cerebral lateralization as a source of interindividual differences in behavior. *Experientia, 45,* 788–798.

Carver, R. P. (1972). Speed readers don't read; They skim. *Psychology Today,* p. 22.

Chaika, E. (1985, August). Crazy talk. *Psychology Today,* pp. 30–35.

Chase, S. (1968). *The most probable world.* New York: Harper & Row.

Chaudron, C. D., & Wilkinson, D. A. (1988). *Theories on alcoholism.* Toronto, Canada: Addiction Research Foundation.

Cherry, C. (1957). *On human communication.* Cambridge, MA: MIT Press.

Cohen, S. (1988). *The chemical brain: The neurochemistry of addictive disorders.* Irvine, CA: Care Institute.

Colby, K. M., & Stoller, R. J. (1988). *Cognitive science and psychoanalysis.* Hillsdale, NJ: Erlbaum.

Constantine-Paton, M., & Law, M. I. (1982). The development of maps and stripes in the brain. *Scientific American, 247,* 54–62.

Corballis, M. C. (1989). Laterality and human evolution. *Psychological Review, 96,* 492–505.

Cotman, C. W., & McGaugh, J. L. (1980). *Behavioral neuroscience—An introduction.* New York: Academic Press.

Couvilon, P. A., & Bitterman, M. E. (1984). The overlearning–extinction effect and successive negative contrast in honeybees (apis mellifera). *Journal of Comparative Psychology, 98,* 100–109.

Culbertson, J. T. (1950). *Consciousness and behavior.* Dubuque, IA: Wm. C. Brown.

Culbertson, J. T. (1985). *Consciousness: Natural and artificial.* Roslyn Heights, NY: Libra.

Cunningham, A. J. (1978). *Understanding immunology.* New York: Academic Press.

Cutrow, R. J., Parks, A., Lucas, N., & Thomas, K. (1972). The objective use of multiple physiological indices in the detection of deception. *Psychophysiology, 9,* 578–588.

Damasio, A. R., & Geschwind, N. (1984). The neural basis of language. *Annual Reviews of Neurosociology, 7,* 127–147.

Damasio, A. R., & Van Hoesen, G. W. (1983). Emotional disturbances associated with focal lesions of the limbic frontal lobe. In K. M. Heilman & P. Satz (Eds.), *Neuropsychology of human emotion* (pp. 85–108). New York: Guilford.

Darrow, E. W. (1936). The galvanic skin reflex (sweating) and blood pressure as preparatory and facilitative functions. *Psychology Bulletin, 33,* 73–94.

Darwin, C. (1859). *On the origin of species by means of natural selection.* London: Murray. (New York: Appleton, 1960.)

Darwin, C. (1872). *The expression of emotion in man and animals.* London: Murray.

Darwin, C. (1874). *The descent of man and selection in relation to sex* (2nd ed.). London: Murray.

Dawson, G. D. (1947). Cerebral responses to electrical stimulation of peripheral nerves in man. *Journal of Neural and Neurosurgical Psychiatry, 10,* 134–140.

Dawson, M. E. (1990). Where does the truth lie? [Review of the *Polygraph Test: Lies, Truth and Science*]. *Psychophysiology, 27,* 120–121.

Denny, M. R. (1980). *Comparative psychology: An evolutionary analysis of animal behavior.* New York: Wiley.

Descartes, R. (1650). *Les passions de l'ame.* Amsterdam.

Deutsch, J. A. (Ed.). (1973). *The physiological basis of memory.* New York: Academic Press.

Dewan, E. M. (1967). Occipital alpha rhythm, eye position and lens accommodation. *Nature, 214,* 975–977.

Dewan, E. M. (1968). A demonstration of the effect of eye position and accommodation on the occipital alpha rhythm. *Electroencephalography and Clinical Neurophysiology, 24,* 188.

Dimberg, V. (1990). Facial electromyography and emotional reactions. *Psychophysiology, 27,* 481–494.

Divac, I., & Mogensen, J. (1985). The prefrontal cortex in the pigeon. Catecholamine histofluorescence. *Neuroscience, 15,* 677–682.

Dowling, J. E., & Boycott, B. B. (1966). *Proceedings of the Royal Society (London),* Series B, *166,* 80–111.

Duchenne, G. B. (1855). *De l'electrisation localisee.* Paris.

Dunlap, K. (1927). The short-circuiting of conscious responses. *Journal of Philosophy, 24,* 263–267.

Ebbinghaus, H. (1974). *Memory: A contribution to experimental psychology.* New York: Dover. (Original work published 1885; translated 1913.)

Eccles, J. C. (1967). Evolution and the conscious self. In J. D. Losansky (Ed.), *The healing mind* (pp. 3–28). Amsterdam: North Holland.

Eccles, J. C. (1973). *The understanding of the brain.* New York: McGraw-Hill.

Edelman, G. M. (1987). *Neural Darwinism: The theory of neuronal group selection.* New York: Basic Books, Inc.

Edwards, J. R., & Cooper, C. L. (1988). The impacts of psychological states on physical health: A review and theoretical framework. *Social Science and Medicine, 27,* 1447–1459.

Eibl-Eibesfeldt, I. (1989). *Human ethology.* New York: Aldine de Gruyter.

Eigen, M., Gardiner, W., Sehuster, P., & Winkler-Oswatitsch, R. (1981). The origin of genetic information. *Scientific American, 244,* 78–95.

Ekman, P., Friesen, W. V., & Levenson, R. W. (Eds.). (1990). Voluntary facial action generates emotion-specific autonomic nervous system activity. *Psychophysiology, 27,* 363–384.

Ellenberger, H. F. (1972). The story of "Anna O.": A critical review with new data. *Journal of the Behavioral Sciences, 8,* 267–279.

Elliott, M. H. (1928). The effect of change of reward on the maze performance of rats. *University of California Publications in Psychology, 4,* 19–30.

Eron, L. D. (1990). Understanding aggression. *The Bulletin of the International Society for Research on Aggression, 12,* 5–9.

Evans, W. F. (1983). *Anatomy and physiology.* Englewood Cliffs, NJ: Prentice Hall.

Evarts, E. V. (1973). Motor cortex reflexes associated with learned movement. *Science, 179,* 501–503.

Eysenck, H. J. (1983). Review of *The benefits of psychotherapy. Behavior Research Therapy, 21,* 315–319.

Eysenck, H. J. (1990). *Decline and fall of the Freudian empire.* Washington, DC: Scott-Townsend.

Eysenck, H. J., & Gudjonsson, G. (1989). *Causes and cures of criminality.* New York: Plenum Press.

Farley, J., & Alkon, D. L. (1985). Cellular mechanisms of learning, memory, and information storage. *Annual Review of Psychology, 36,* 420–479.

Feder, H. H. (1984). Hormones and sexual behavior. *Annual Review of Psychology, 35,* 165–191.

Fisher, S. (1964). Body awareness and selective memory for body versus nonbody references. *Journal of Personality, 32,* 138–144.

Fisher, S. (1972). Influencing selective perception and fantasy by stimulating body landmarks. *Journal of Abnormal Psychology, 79,* 97–105.

Flach, F. (1988). *Affective disorders.* New York: Norton.

Fulton, J. F. (1943). *Physiology of the nervous system.* New York: Oxford University Press.

Gantt, W. H. (1944). *Neurotic behavior.* Menasha, WI: George Banta Publishing Company.

Garmon, L. (1985, November). Of hemispheres, handedness and more. *Psychology Today*, pp. 40–48.

Gazzaniga, M. S. (1973). *Fundamentals of psychology*. New York: Academic Press.

Gazzaniga, M. S. (1985, November). The social brain. *Psychology Today*, pp. 29–38.

Gentner, D. R. (1987). Timing of skilled motor performance: Tests of the proportional duration model. *Psychological Review, 94*, 255–276.

Gilbert, C. D. (1983). Microcircuitry of the visual cortex. *Annual Reviews of Neuroscience, 6*, 217–247.

Gingerich, O. (1982). The Galileo affair. *Scientific American, 247*, 132–143.

Glick, S. D., Ross, D. A., & Hough, L. B. (1982). Lateral asymmetry of neurotransmitters in human brain. *Brain Research, 234*, 53–63.

Goldsmith, D. (1986). *Nemesis: The death star and other theories of mass extinction.* New York: Berkeley.

Goodwin, D. W., Powell, B., Bremer, D., Hoine, F. H., & Stern, J. (1969). Alcohol and recall: State-dependent effects in man. *Science, 163*, 1358–1360.

Gottfredson, M., & Hirschi, T. (1990). *A general theory of crime.* Stanford, CA: Stanford University Press.

Gould, J. L. (1984). Magnetic field sensitivity in animals. *Annual Reviews of Physiology, 46*, 585–598.

Gould, J. L. (1986). The biology of learning. *Annual Reviews of Psychology, 37*, 163–192.

Greene, E., & Naranjo, J. N. (1987). Degeneration of hippocampal fibers and spatial memory deficit in the aged rat. *Neurobiology of Aging, 8*, 35–43.

Groebel, J., & Hinde, R. A. (Eds.). (1989). *Aggression and war: Their biological and social bases.* Cambridge, England: Cambridge University Press.

Hatterer, L. J. (1984). Homosexuality. In R. J. Corsini (Ed.), *Encyclopedia of psychology* (p. 136). New York: Wiley.

Heath, J. E. (1984). Comparative physiology. *Annual Review of Physiology, 46*, 559–560.

Hebb, D. O. (1958). *Psychology*, New York: Saunders.

Hebb, D. O. (1966). *A textbook of psychology.* Philadelphia: W. B. Saunders.

Hefferline, R. F., Keenan, B., & Harford, R. A. (1958). Escape and avoidance conditioning in human subjects without their observation of the response. *Science, 130*, 1338–1339.

Heiligenberg, W., & Bastian, J. (1984). The electric sense of weakly electric fish. *Annual Reviews of Physiology, 46*, 561–583.

Heilman, K. M., & Satz, P. (1983). *Neuropsychology of human emotion.* New York: Guilford Press.

Herrnstein, R. S., & Boring, E. G. (Eds.). (1965). *Source book in the history of psychology.* Cambridge, MA: Harvard University Press.

Hersen, M., Eisler, R. M., & Miller, P. M. (Eds.). (1988). *Progress in behavior modification* (Vol. 23). Newbury Park, CA: Sage.

Hibberd, M. G., & Trentham, D. R. (1986). Relationships between chemical and mechanical events during muscular contraction. *Annual Review of Biophysics and Biophysical Chemistry, 15*, 119–161.

Hoffman, D. D. (1983). The interpretation of visual illusions. *Scientific American, 249*, 137–144.

Holmes, D. S. (1984). Meditation and somatic arousal reduction: A review of experimental evidence. *American Psychologist, 39*, 1–10.

Hopson, J., & Rosenfeld, A. (1984, August). PMS: Puzzling monthly symptoms. *Psychology Today*, pp. 30–34.

Horton, D. L., & Miles, C. B. (1984). Human learning and memory. *Annual Review of Psychology, 35*, 361–394.

Houk, J. C. (1988). Control strategies in physiological systems. *FASEB Journal, 2*, 97–107.

Hubel, D. H., & Wiesel, T. N. (1979). Brain mechanisms of vision. *Scientific American, 241*, 150–162.

Hudspeth, A. J. (1983). The hair cells of the inner ear. *Scientific American, 248*, 42–52.

Hugdahl, K. (1984). Hemispheric asymmetry and bilateral electrodermal recording: A review of the evidence. *Psychophysiology, 21*, 371–393.

Hunter, W. S. (1924a). The problem of consciousness. *Psychological Review, 31*, 1–37.

Hunter, W. S. (1924b). The symbolic process, *Psychological Review, 31*, 478–497.

Hunter, W. S., & Hudgins, C. V. (1934). Voluntary activity from the standpoint of behaviorism. *Journal of General Psychology, 10*, 198–204.

Huxley, A. F. (1988). Muscular contraction. *Annual Review of Physiology, 50*, 1–16.

Jacobson, E. (1930). Electrical measurement of neuromuscular states during mental activities: III. Visual imagination and recollection. *The American Journal of Physiology, 95,* 694–702.

Jacobson, E. (1938a). *You can sleep well.* New York: McGraw-Hill.

Jacobson, E. (1938b). *Progressive relaxation* (2nd ed.). Chicago: University of Chicago Press.

Jacobson, E. (1957). *You must relax* (4th ed.). New York: McGraw-Hill.

Jacobson, E. (1967). *Biology of emotions.* Springfield, IL: Charles C Thomas.

Jacobson, E. (1970). *Modern treatment of tense patients.* Springfield, IL: Charles C Thomas.

Jarvik, M. E. (1977). *Psychopharmacology in the practice of medicine.* New York: Appleton-Century-Crofts.

Jasper, H. H. (1983). Nobel laureates in neuroscience: 1904–1981. *Annual Review of Neuroscience, 6,* 1–42.

Jasper, H. H., Ricci, G., & Doane, B. (1958). Patterns of cortical neuronal discharge during conditioned responses in monkeys. In G. E. N. Wolsten Holme and C. M. O'Connor (Eds.), *Ciba foundation symposium, neurological basis of behavior.* (pp. 277–290) London: Churchill.

Jasper, H. H., Ricci, G., & Doane, B. (1960). Microelectrode analysis of cortical cell discharge during avoidance conditioning in the monkey. In H. H. Jasper & G. D. Smirnov (Eds.), *The Moscow colloquium on electroencephalography of higher nervous systems* (pp. 137–155). *Electroencephalography and Clinical Neurophysiology.* Supplement 13.

John, E. R. (1972). Switchboard versus statistical theories of learning and memory. *Science, 177,* 850–864.

Justice, A. (1985). Review of the effects of stress on cancer in laboratory animals: Importance of time of stress application and type of tumor. *Psychological Bulletin, 98,* 108–138.

Kaplan, H. I., & Saddock, B. J. (1989). *Comprehensive textbook of psychiatry* (Vols. 1 & 2, 5th ed.). Baltimore: Williams & Wilkins.

Karplus, W. J. (1992). *The heavens are falling: The scientific prediction of catastrophes in our time.* New York: Plenum Press.

Keeler, L. (1930). A method for detecting deception. *American Journal of Police Science, 1,* 38–51.

Keller, F. S., & Schoenfeld, W. N. (1950). *Principles of psychology.* New York: Appleton-Century-Crofts.

Kelly, R. (1978). Hemispheric specialization of deaf children: Are there any implications for instruction? *American Annals of the Deaf, 123,* 637–645.

Kelso, J. A. S., & Stelmach, G. E. (1976), Central and peripheral mechanisms in motor control. In G. E. Stelmach (Ed.), *Motor control, issues and trends* (pp. 1–35). New York: Academic Press.

Kelso, J. A. S., & Wallace, S. A. (1978). Conscious mechanisms in movement. In G. E. Stelmach (Ed.), *Information processing in motor control and learning* (pp. 79–111). New York: Academic Press.

King, A. C., Blair, S. N., Bild, D. E., & Dishman, R. K. (1992). Determinants of physical activity and interventions in adults. *Medicine-and-Science-in-Sport-and-Exercise, 24,* S221–S236.

Kleinmuntz, B., & Szucko, J. J. (1984, July). Lie detection in ancient and modern times. *American Psychologist,* 766–776.

Knott, J. R. (1939). Some effects of "mental set" on the electrophysiological processes of the human cerebral cortex. *Journal of Experimental Psychology, 24,* 384–405.

Kolb, B., & Tees, R. C. (1990). *The cerebral cortex of the rat.* Cambridge, MA: The MIT Press.

Langfeld, H. S. (1931). A response interpretation of consciousness. *Psychological Review, 38,* 87–108.

Langley, L. L. (Ed.). (1972). *Homeostasis: Origins of concept.* Stroudsburg, PA: Dowden, Hutchinson & Ross.

Larson, J. A. (1932). *Lying and its detections.* Chicago: University of Chicago Press.

Lashley, K. S. (1951). The problem of serial order in behavior. In L. A. Jeffress (Ed.), *Cerebral mechanism in behavior: The Hixon symposium.* New York: John Wiley.

Lashley, K. S. (1929). Learning: I. Nervous mechanisms in learning. In C. Murchison (Ed.), *The foundations of experimental psychology* (pp. 524–563). Worcester, MA: Clark University Press.

Lashley, K. S. (1960). Cerebral organization of behavior. *The neuropsychology of Lashley; selected papers.* New York: McGraw-Hill.

Leventhal, H., & Tomarken, A. J. (1986). Emotion: Today's problems. *Annual Review of Psychology, 37,* 565–610.

Levinthal, C. F. (1979). *Introduction to physiological psychology.* Englewood Cliffs, NJ: Prentice Hall.

Levitsky, M. G. (1984). Effects of aging on the respiratory system. *The Physiologist, 27,* 102–107.

Lieberman, P. (1984). *The biology and evolution of language.* Cambridge, MA: Harvard University Press.

Light, L. L., & Burke, D. M. (1988). *Language, memory, and aging.* New York: Cambridge University Press.

Lown, B. (1979). Sudden cardiac death: The major challenge confronting contemporary cardiology. *The American Journal of Cardiology, 43,* 313–328.

Luce, R. D. (1986). *Response times: Their role in inferring elementary mental organization.* New York: Oxford University Press.

MacLean, P. D. (1949). Psychosomatic disease and the "visceral brain." *Psychosomatic Medicine, 11,* 338–353.

Manstead, T. (1988). The role of facial movement in emotion. In H. L. Wagner (Ed.), *Social psychophysiology and emotion: Theory and clinical applications* (pp. 105–129). Chichester, England: John Wiley & Sons.

Marler, P., & Terrace, H. S. (1984). *The biology of learning.* Berlin: Springer-Verlag.

Marshall, J. F. (1984). Brain function: Neural adaptations and recovery from injury. *Annual Review of Psychology, 35,* 277–308.

Marston, W. M. (1917). Systolic blood pressure systems of deception. *Journal of Experimental Psychology, 2,* 117–163.

Martinez, J. L., Jr., & Kesner, R. P. (1986). *Learning and memory, a biological view.* New York: Academic Press.

Masson, J. M. (1985). *The assault on truth: Freud's suppression of the seduction theory.* New York: Penguin Books.

Masson, J. M. (1990). *Final analysis: The making and unmaking of a psychoanalyst.* Reading, MA: Addison-Wesley.

Masterson, R. B., & Imig, T. J. (1984). Neural mechanisms for sound localization. *Annual Review of Physiology, 46,* 275–287.

McGuigan, F. J. (1966a). Covert oral behavior and auditory hallucination. *Psychophysiology, 3,* 73–80.

McGuigan, F. J. (1966b). *Thinking: Studies of covert language processes.* New York: Appleton-Century-Crofts.

McGuigan, F. J. (1970a). Covert oral behavior as a function of quality of handwriting. *American Journal of Psychology, 83,* 377–388.

McGuigan, F. J. (1970b). Reduccion de la tension international por methodos Psicologicos (A behaviorist's suggestions for the reduction of international tension). *Revista Latino Americana de Psicologia, 2,* 327–341.

McGuigan, F. J. (1971). Covert linguistic behavior in deaf subjects during thinking. *Journal of Comparative and Physiological Psychology, 75,* 417–420.

McGuigan, F. J. (1978). *Cognitive psychophysiology: Principles of covert behavior.* Hillsdale, NJ: Erlbaum.

McGuigan, F. J. (1979). *Psychophysiological measurement of covert behavior: A guide for the laboratory.* Hillsdale, NJ: Erlbaum.

McGuigan, F. J. (1990). *Calm down—A guide to stress and tension control.* Dubuque, IA: Kendall Hunt.

McGuigan, F. J. (1991). Control of normal and pathologic cognitive functions through neuromuscular circuits. In J. C. Carlson & A. R. Seifert (Eds.), *International perspective on self-regulation and health* (pp. 121–132). New York: Plenum.

McGuigan, F. J. (1993a). *Experimental psychology: Methods of research* (6th ed.). Englewood Cliffs, NJ: Prentice Hall.

McGuigan, F. J. (1993b). Progressive relaxation: Origins, principles, and clinical applications. In P. M. Lehrer & R. L. Woolfolk (Eds.), *Principles and practice of stress management* (2nd ed., pp. 17–52). New York: Gilford Press.

McGuigan, F. J., & Ban, T. A. (Eds.). (1987). *Critical issues in psychology, psychiatry, and physiology.* New York: Gordon and Breach.

McGuigan, F. J., Culver, V. I., & Kendler, T. S. (1971). Covert behavior as a direct electromyographic measure of mediating responses. *Conditional Reflex, 6,* 145–152.

McGuigan, F. J., & Dollins, A. B. (1989). Patterns of covert speech behavior and phonetic coding. *The Pavlovian Journal of Biological Science, 24,* 19–26.

McGuigan, F. J., & Pavek, G. V. (1972). On the psychophysiological identification of covert non oral language processes. *Journal of Experimental Psychology, 92,* 237–245.

McGuigan, F. J., & Pinkney, K. B. (1973). Effect of increased reading rate on covert processes. *Interamerican Journal of Psychology, 7,* 223–231.

McGuigan, F. J., & Tanner, R. G. (1971). Covert oral behavior during conversational and visual dreams. *Psychonomic Science, 23,* 263–264.

McGuigan, F. J., & Winstead, C. L., Jr. (1974). A discriminative relationship between covert oral behavior and the phonemic system in internal information processing. *Journal of Experimental Psychology, 103,* 885–890.

McGuigan, F. J., Hutchens, C., Eason, N., & Reynolds, T. (1964). The retroactive interference of motor activity with knowledge of results. *Journal of General Psychology, 70,* 279–281.

McNeil, D. (1985). So you think gestures are nonverbal? *Psychological Review, 92,* 350–371.

Melzack, R., & Wall, P. D. (1965). Pain mechanisms: A new theory. *Science, 150,* 971–979.

Merton, P. A. (1972). How we control the contraction of our muscles. *Scientific American, 226,* 30–37.

Merzhanova, G. K. (1988). Neuronal manifestation of two-way connections in conditioning. *The Pavlovian Journal of Biological Science, 23,* 135–142.

Miller, G. A. (1981). *Language and speech.* San Francisco: W. H. Freeman.

Morgan, C. L. (1906). *An introduction to a comparative psychology* (2nd ed.). London: Walter Scott.

Morrison, A. R. (1983). A window on the sleeping brain. *Scientific American, 248,* 86–94.

Mortimer, J. A., Pirozzolo, F. J., & Maletta, G. J. (1982). Overview of the aging motor system. In J. A. Mortimer, F. J. Pirozzolo, & G. J. Maletta (Eds.), *The aging system* (pp. 1–6). New York: Praeger.

Mountcastle, V. B. (1967). The problem of sensing and the neural coding of sensory events. In G. Quarton, T. Melnechuk, & F. O. Schmitt (Eds.), *Neurosciences.* New York: Rockefeller University Press.

Mowrer, O. H. (1947). On the dual nature of learning—a reinterpretation of "conditioning" and "problem solving." *Harvard Educational Review, 17,* 102–148.

Müller, G. E., & Pilzecker, A. (1900). Experimentelle Beiträge zur Lehre vom Gedächtnis. *Zeitschrift Psychologie,* pp. 322–447.

Naisbitt, J., & Aburdene, P. (1990). *Mega-trends 2000: Ten new directions for the 1990's.* New York: William Morrow.

Newman, E. A., & Hartline, P. H. (1982). The infrared "vision" of snakes. *Scientific American, 246,* 98–107.

Newmeyer, F. J. (1988). *Language: Psychological and biological aspects* (Vol. 3). Cambridge, England: Cambridge University Press.

Oldfield, R. (1971). The assessment and analysis of handedness: The Edinburgh inventory. *Neuropsychologia, 19,* 97–113.

Olson, E. D. (1985, July). Intelligent life in space. *Astronomy,* pp. 7–22.

Oppenheimer, R. (1956). Analogy in science. *American Psychologist, 11,* 127–135.

Osgood, C. E., & McGuigan, F. J. (1973). Psychophysiological correlates of meaning: Essences or tracers? In F. J. McGuigan & R. A. Schoonover (Eds.), *The psychophysiology of thinking.* New York: Academic Press.

Osgood, C. E., Suci, G. J., & Tannenbaum, P. H. (1957). *The measurement of meaning.* Urbana: University of Illinois Press.

Paffenbarger, R. S., Hyde, R. T., & Wing, A. L. (1986). Physical activity, all-cause mortality, and longevity of college alumni. *New England Journal of Medicine, 314,* 605–613.

Papez, J. W. (1937). A proposed mechanism of emotion. *Archives of Neurology and Psychiatry, 38*(10), 725–743.

Penfield, W. (1958). *The excitable cortex in conscious man.* Springfield, IL: Charles C Thomas.

Peters, M. (1988). Footedness: Asymmetries in foot preference and skill and neuropsychological assessment of foot movement. *Psychological Bulletin, 103,* 179–192.

Pirke, K. M., & Ploog, D. (Eds.). (1984). *The psychobiology of anorexia nervosa.* Berlin: Springer-Verlag.

Premack, A. J. (1979). *Why chimps can read.* New York: Harper & Row.

Pribram, K. H. (1971). *Languages of the brain.* Englewood Cliffs, NJ: Prentice Hall.

Raibert, M. H., & Sutherland, I. E. (1983). Machines that walk. *Scientific American, 248,* 32–41.

Raimy, V. (1950). *Training in clinical psychology.* Englewood Cliffs, NJ: Prentice Hall.

Raup, D. M. (1986). *The Nemesis affair.* New York: W. W. Norton.

Regelson, W., & Sinex, F. M. (Eds.). (1983). *Intervention in the aging process. Part A: Quantitation, epidemiology and clinical research* (Vol. 3, A modern aging research). New York: Alan R. Liss.

Rhode, W. S. (1984). Cochlear mechanics. *Annual Reviews of Physiology, 46,* 231–246.

Rinn, W. E. (1984). The neuropsychology of facial expression: A review of the neurological and psychological mechanisms for producing facial expressions. *Psychological Bulletin, 95,* 52–77.

Rosenbaum, J., & Barr, K. (1986, Spring). Systemic health benefits of aerobic dance. *Professional Nurses Quarterly,* p. 20.

Rosenblueth, A., & Wiener, N. (1950). Purposeful and non-purposeful behavior. *Philosophy of Science, 17,* 318.

Rosenblueth, A., Wiener, N., & Bigelow, J. (1943). Behavior, purpose and teleology. *Philosophy of Science, 10,* 18–24.

Rosenfeld, A. H. (1985, June). Depression: Dispelling despair. *Psychology Today,* pp. 29–34.

Salthouse, T. A. (1984). The skill of typing. *Scientific American, 250,* 95–99.

Schmitt, F. O. (Ed.). (1972). *The neurosciences: Second study program.* New York: Rockefeller University Press.

Schwartz, G. E., Fair, P. L., Mandel, M. R., Salt, P., Mieske, M., & Klerman, G. L. (1978). Facial electromyography in the assessment of improvement of depression. *Psychosomatic Medicine, 40,* 355–360.

Schwartz, G. E., Fair, P. L., Salt, P., Mandel, M. R., & Klerman, G. L. (1976). Facial muscle patterning to affective imagery in depressed and non-depressed subjects. *Science, 192,* 489–491.

Sechenov, I. M. (1863). Reflexes of the brain. In I. M. Sechenov, *Selected Works.* Moscow and Leningrad: State Publishing House for Biological and Medical Literature.

Seeley, T. D. (1982). How honeybees find a home. *Scientific American, 247,* 144–152.

Segalowitz, S. J. (1983). *Two sides of the brain.* Englewood Cliffs, NJ: Prentice Hall.

Sherrington, S. C. (1906). *The integrative action of the nervous system.* New Haven: Yale University Press.

Shettleworth, S. J. (1983). Memory in food-hoarding birds. *Scientific American, 248,* 86–94.

Skinner, B. F. (1938). *Behavior of organisms.* New York: Appleton-Century-Crofts.

Skinner, B. F. (1989). *Recent issues in the analysis of behavior.* Columbus, OH: Merrill.

Smith, O. A., & DeVito, J. L. (1984). Central neural integration for the control of autonomic responses associated with emotion. *Annual Reviews of Neuroscience, 7,* 43–65.

Smith, S. M., Brown, H. O., Toman, J. E. P., & Goodman, L. S. (1947). The lack of cerebral effects of *d*-tubocurarine. *Anesthesiology, 8,* 1–14.

Sommer, B. (1984, August). PMS in the courts: Are all women on trial? *Psychology Today,* pp. 36–38.

Squire, L. R. (1982). The neuropsychology of human memory. *Annual Review of Neuroscience, 5,* 241–273.

Squire, L. R. (1987). *Memory and brain.* New York: Oxford University Press.

Squire, L. R., & Butter, S. N. (Eds.). (1984). *Neuropsychology of memory.* New York: Guilford Press.

Squire, L. R., Shimamura, A. P., & Amaral, D. G. (1989). Memory and the hippocampus. In J. Byrnf & W. Berry (Eds.), *Neural models of plasticity.* New York: Academic Press.

Stallones, R. A. (1980, November). The rise and fall of ischemic heart disease. *Scientific American, 43*–49.

Stelmach, G. E. (Ed.). (1976). *Motor control—issues and trends.* New York: Academic Press.

Stelmach, G. E. (Ed.). (1978). *Information processing in motor control and learning.* New York: Academic Press.

Sternberg, S., Monsell, S., Knoll, R. L., & Wright, C. E. (1978). The latency and duration of rapid movement sequences: Comparison of speech and typewriting. In G. E. Stelmach (Ed.), *Information processing in motor control and learning* (pp. 118–150). New York: Academic Press.

Storer, T. I. (1943). *General zoology.* New York: McGraw-Hill.

Strupp, H. H. (1986a). Psychotherapy: Research, practice, and public policy (How to avoid dead ends). *American Psychologist, 41,* 120–130.

Strupp, H. H. (1986b). How honest was Freud? *Contemporary Psychology, 31,* 293–294.

Stuss, D. T., & Benson, D. F. (1984). Neuropsychological studies of the frontal lobes. *Psychological Bulletin, 95,* 3–28.

Sussman, H. M. (1972). What the tongue tells the brain. *Psychological Bulletin, 77,* 262–272.

Szentagothai, J. (1984). Downward causation? *Annual Review of Neurosociology, 7,* 1–11.

Taub, E. (1980). Somatosensory deafferentation research with monkeys: Implications for rehabilitation medicine. In L. P. Ince (Ed.), *Behavioral psychology in rehabilitation medicine: Clinical applications* (pp. 371–401). Baltimore: Williams and Wilkins.

Terrace, H. S. (1979). *Nim: A chimpanzee who learned sign language.* New York: Knopf.

Thach, W. T. (1978). Correlation of neural discharge pattern and force of muscular activity, joint position, and direction of intended text movement in motor cortex and cerebellum. *Journal of Neurophysiology, 41,* 654–676.

Thornton, E. M. (1983). *Freud and cocaine: The Freudian fallacy.* London: Blond & Briggs.

Torrey, E. F. (1992). *Freudian fraud.* New York: HarperCollins.

Tuke, D. H. (1884). *The influence of the mind upon the body, II* (2nd ed.). London: Churchill.

Underwager, R. C., & Wakefield, H. C. (1990). *The real world of child interrogations.* Springfield, IL: Charles C Thomas.

Vyner, H. M. (1988). *Invisible trauma: The psychological effects of invisible environmental containments.* Lexington, MA: Lexington Books.

Wagenen, W. V., & Herren, R. (1940). Surgical division of commissural pathways in the corpus callosum. *Archives of Neurology and Psychiatry, 44,* 740–759.

Wakefield, H. C., & Underwager, R. C. (1988). *Accusations of sexual child abuse.* Springfield, IL: Charles C Thomas.

Walsh, A. (1991). *The science of love: Understanding love and its effects on mind and body.* Buffalo, NY: Prometheus Books.

Washington, A. M. (1989). *Cocaine addiction: Treatment, recovery, and relapse prevention.* New York: Norton.

Webb, W. B. (1975). *Sleep: The gentle tyrant.* Englewood Cliffs, NJ: Prentice Hall.

West, D. J. (1967). *Homosexuality.* Chicago: Aldine.

West, M. A. (1980). Meditation and the EEG. *Psychological Medicine, 10,* 369–375.

Wever, E. G., & Bray, C. W. (1930). Action currents in the auditory nerve in response to acoustical stimulation. *Proceedings of the National Academy of Science, 16,* 344–350.

Whalen, R. E., & Simon, N. G. (1984). Biological motivation. *Annual Review of Psychology, 35,* 257–276.

Wiener, N. (1948). *Cybernetics.* New York: John Wiley & Sons.

Willshaw, D. J., Buneman, O. P., & Longuet-Higgens, H. C. (1969). Non-holographic associative memory. *Nature, 222,* 960–962.

Wimer, R. E., & Wimer, C. C. (1984). Animal behavior genetics: A search for the biological foundations of behavior. *Annual Review of Psychology, 36,* 172–186.

Wing, A. M. (1978). Response timing in handwriting. In G. E. Stelmach (Ed.), *Information processing in motor control and learning* (pp. 153–171). New York: Academic Press.

Wolfe, J. M. (1983). Hidden visual processes. *Scientific American, 248,* 72–85.

Woody, C. D. (1986). Understanding the cellular basis of memory and learning. *Annual Review of Psychology, 37,* 433–471.

Woodworth, R. S. (1938). *Experimental psychology.* New York: Henry Holt and Company.

Yates, A. (1991). *Compulsive exercise and the eating disorders: Toward an integrated theory of activity.* New York: Brunner/Mazel.

Zola-Morgan, S., Squire, L. R., & Amaral, D. G. (1986). Human amnesia and the medial temporal region: Enduring memory impairment following a bilateral lesion limited to field CAI of the hippocampus. *Journal of Neuroscience, 10,* 2950–2967.

Name Index

A

Adams, J. A., 199, 200, 208
Ader, R., 483
Adrian, E. D., 234
Alkon, D. L., 334
Ampere, A. M., 4
Anokhin, P., 314, 315
Anrep, G. V., 301
Arandish, G., 264
Asratyan, E. A., 331

B

Babinski, J., 285, 312
Bailey, J. M., 263
Bain, A., xi, 71, 504
Ban, T., 210
Bandler, R., xi
Bandura, A., 267
Barnum, P. T., 501
Bashore, T., 390, 392
Beach, F. A., 320
Bechterev, V. M., 72
Bekesy, G. V., 124
Bell, C., 38, 205
Benson, D. F., 363
Benussi, V., 425
Berg, I., 519
Berger, H., 155, 234
Berger, S. M., 267, 444
Berkeley, G., 61
Berkowitz, L., 256
Bernard, C., 11, 38
Bernstein, N. A., 15, 314
Bertalanffy, L. V., 22
Beurle, R. L., 344
Binet, A., 72
Bitterman, M. E., 322, 431–432
Blair, S., 395
Blass, E., 323
Bleuler, E., 464
Bogen, J., 366
Borkan, G. A., 392
Botkin, S. P., 479
Botwinick, J., 392
Bowman, J. P., 204
Braid, J., 516
Brever, J., 517
Brittain, R. W., 324
Broca, P., 242
Brown, J. W., 363
Bryden, M. P., 376
Buck, R., 286
Burnet, M., 482
Butters, N., 449

C

Cannon, W., 10, 16
Carrol, L., 320
Carter, S., 263
Cajal, S. R. Y., 39, 40, 182
Carver, R. P., 417
Cherry, C., 412
Clube, V., 553
Corballis, M. C., 360
Cousins, N., 463, 482, 500
Couvilon, P. A., 322
Cunningham, A. J., 482
Cutrow, R. J., 427

D

Darrow, C., 425
Darwin, C., 41, 284, 286, 291, 355
Dashiell, J., xi
Davidson, J., 261
Davy, H., 523
Dawson, H., 235
Delis, D., 263
Denenberg, V., 369
De Puysegur, 516
Descartes, R., 10, 36, 60
De Casper, A., 323
Deutsch, J. A., 333
Dewan, E. M., 338
Dimberg, U., 286
Divac, I., 166
Dobzhansky, T. H., 43
Donders, F. C., 432
Dottl, S., 395
Du Bois-Reymond, E., 230
Duchenne, G. B., 205
Duncan, C., 503
Dunlap, K., 203

E

Ebbinghaus, H., 325, 346
Eccles, J. C., 43, 44, 49, 51, 66, 110, 111, 179, 346
Edelman, G. M., 205, 482
Edwards, J. R., 500
Ehrlich, P., 480
Eigen, M., 45
Einstein, A., 34, 36, 561
Ekman, P., 287
Ellenberger, H. F., 518
Elliot, M. H., 431
Erasistratus, 425–426
Eron, L. D., 267
Evan, W. F., 73
Eysenck, H. J., 446, 518

Subject Index